The ~~Autobiography~~
of Goethe

Truth and poetry: from my own life

Johann Wolfgang von Goethe

Translator: John Oxenford

Alpha Editions

This edition published in 2020

ISBN : 9789354015700

Design and Setting By
Alpha Editions
email - alphaedis@gmail.com

ADVERTISEMENT.

Before the following translation was commenced, the first Ten Books had already appeared in America. It was the intention of the Publisher to reprint these without alteration, but, on comparing them with the original, it was perceived that the American version was not sufficiently faithful, and therefore the present was undertaken. The Translator, however, is bound to acknowledge, that he found many successful renderings in the work of his predecessor, and these he has engrafted without hesitation.

The title "Truth and Poetry" is adopted in common with the American translation, as the nearest rendering of *Dichtung und Wahrheit*, and preferable to "Truth and Fiction," which has sometimes been used. The poet, by the expression *Dichtung*, did not mean that he invented incidents in the Auto-Biography, but merely that they were of a poetic or romantic character; while "*Wahrheit*" implies, that they also possessed the truth of history. The "Prose and Poetry of my Life" would, perhaps, convey to the English reader the exact meaning of the Author, although not literally his words.

ERRATA.

Page 442, line 6 from bottom, *omit* "that."

„ 451, „ 4 from bottom, *for* "theatrical," *read* "theoretical."

„ 464, „ 2 from the bottom, *for* "thus a certain," *read* "thus arose a certain."

„ 490, „ 9, *for* "co-operation," *read* "corporation."

„ 494, „ 20, *for* "Dident," *read* "Diderot."

„ 495, „ 8 from bottom, *for* "caricaturing," *read* "country."

„ 502, „ 9 from bottom, *after* "solitude," *read* "whoever resigns himself to it flies all opposition, and what is more opposed to him than," &c.

„ 505, „ 3, *read* "more frequently made sad than pleasant," &c.

„ 511, 5 from bottom, *after* "household," *read* "remedy."

AUTHOR'S PREFACE.

As a preface to the present work, which, perhaps, more than
another requires one, I adduce the letter of a friend, by
which so serious an undertaking was occasioned.

" We have now, my dear friend, collected the twelve parts of
your poetical works, and on reading them through, find much
that is known, much that is unknown; while much that had
been forgotten is revived by this collection. These twelve
volumes, standing before us, in uniform appearance, we cannot
refrain from regarding as a whole; and one would like to sketch
therefrom some image of the author and his talents. But it
cannot be denied, considering the vigour with which he began
his literary career, and the length of time which has since
elapsed, that a dozen small volumes must appear incommen-
surate. Nor can one forget that, with respect to the detached
pieces, they have mostly been called forth by special occasions,
and reflect particular external objects, as well as distinct
grades of inward culture; while it is equally clear, that temporary moral and æsthetic maxims and convictions prevail
in them. As a whole, however, these productions remain
without connexion; nay, it is often difficult to believe that
they emanate from one and the same writer.

" Your friends, in the meantime, have not relinquished the
inquiry, and try, as they become more closely acquainted with
your mode of life and thought, to guess many a riddle, to solve
many a problem; indeed, with the assistance of an old liking,
and a connexion of many years' standing, they find a charm
even in the difficulties which present themselves. Yet a little
assistance here and there would not be unacceptable, and you
cannot well refuse this to our friendly entreaties.

" The first thing, then, we require, is that your poetical
works, arranged in the late edition according to some internal relations, may be presented by you in chronological

order, and that the states of life and feeling which afforded
the examples that influenced you, and the theoretical principles by which you were governed, may be imparted in
some kind of connexion. Bestow this labour for the gratifi-
cation of a limited circle, and perhaps it may give rise
to something that will be entertaining and useful to an
extensive one. The author, to the most advanced period
of his life, should not relinquish the advantage of communicating, even at a distance, with those whom affection
binds to him; and if it is not granted to every one to step
forth anew, at a certain age, with surprising and powerful
productions, yet just at that period of life when knowledge is most perfect, and consciousness most distinct, it
must be a very agreeable and re-animating task to treat
former creations as new matter, and work them up into a
kind of Last Part, which may serve once more for the edification of those who have been previously edified with and
by the artist."

This desire, so kindly expressed, immediately awakened
within me an inclination to comply with it: for, if in the
early years of life our passions lead us to follow our own
course, and, in order not to swerve from it, we impatiently
repel the demands of others, so, in our later days, it becomes
highly advantageous to us, should any sympathy excite and
determine us, cordially, to new activity. I therefore instantly
undertook the preparatory labour of separating the poems of
my twelve volumes, both great and small, and of arranging
them according to years. I strove to recall the times and
circumstances under which each had been produced. But the
task soon grew more difficult, as full explanatory notes and
illustrations were necessary to fill up the chasms between those
which had already been given to the world. For, in the first
place, all on which I had originally exercised myself were
wanting, many that had been begun and not finished were
also wanting, and of many that were finished even the external
form had completely disappeared, having since been entirely
reworked and cast into a different shape. Besides, I had also
to call to mind how I had laboured in the sciences and other
arts, and what, in such apparently foreign departments, both
individually and in conjunction with friends, I had practised
in silence, or had laid before the public.

All this I wished to introduce by degrees for the satisfaction of my well-wishers ; but my efforts and reflections always led me further on ; since while I was anxious to comply with that very considerate request, and laboured to set forth in succession my internal emotions, external influences, and the steps which, theoretically and practically, I had trod, I was carried out of my narrow private sphere into the wide world. The images of a hundred important men, who either directly or indirectly had influenced me, presented themselves to my view ; and even the prodigious movements of the great political world, which had operated most extensively upon me, as well as upon the whole mass of my contemporaries, had to be particularly considered. For this seems to be the main object of Biography, to exhibit the man in relation to the features of his time ; and to show to what extent they have opposed or favoured his progress ; what view of mankind and the world he has formed from them, and how far he himself, if an artist, poet, or author, may externally reflect them. But for this is required what is scarcely attainable, namely, that the individual should know himself and his age : himself, so far as he has remained the same under all circumstances ; his age, as that which carries along with it, determines and fashions, both the willing and the unwilling ; so that one may venture to pronounce, that any person born ten years earlier or later would have been quite a different being, both as regards his own culture and his influence on others.

In this manner, from such reflections and endeavours, from such recollections and considerations, arose the present delineation ; and from this point of view, as to its origin, will it be the best enjoyed and used, and most impartially estimated. For anything further it may be needful to say, particularly with respect to the half-poetical, half-historic mode of treatment, an opportunity will, no doubt, frequently occur in the course of the narrative.

CONTENTS.

PART THE FIRST.

	Page
FIRST BOOK	1
SECOND BOOK	32
THIRD BOOK	64
FOURTH BOOK	92
FIFTH BOOK	135

PART THE SECOND.

SIXTH BOOK	181
SEVENTH BOOK	218
EIGHTH BOOK	264
NINTH BOOK	303
TENTH BOOK	342

PART THE THIRD.

ELEVENTH BOOK	388
TWELFTH BOOK	437
THIRTEENTH BOOK	484

TRUTH AND POETRY;

FROM MY OWN LIFE.

PART THE FIRST.

'Ο μὴ δαρεὶς ἄνθρωπος οὐ παιδεύεται.

FIRST BOOK.

On the 28th of August, 1749, at mid-day, as the clock struck twelve, I came into the world, at Frankfort-on-the-Maine. My horoscope was propitious: the sun stood in the sign of the Virgin, and had culminated for the day; Jupiter and Venus looked on him with a friendly eye, and Mercury not adversely: while Saturn and Mars kept themselves indifferent; the Moon alone, just full, exerted the power of her reflection all the more, as she had then reached her planetary hour. She opposed herself, therefore, to my birth, which could not be accomplished until this hour was passed.

These good aspects, which the astrologers managed subsequently to reckon very auspicious for me, may have been the causes of my preservation; for, through the unskilfulness of the midwife, I came into the world as dead, and only after various efforts was I enabled to see the light. This event, which had put our household into sore straits, turned to the advantage of my fellow-citizens, inasmuch as my grandfather, the *Schultheiss*,* John Wolfgang Textor, took occasion from it to have an *accoucheur* established, and to introduce or revive the tuition of midwives, which may have done some good to those who were born after me.

When we desire to recall what befel us in the earliest period of youth, it often happens that we confound what we have heard from others with that which we really possess from our own direct experience. Without, therefore, instituting a very close investigation into the point, which after all could

* A chief judge or magistrate of the town.

B

lead to nothing, I am conscious that we lived in an old house,
which in fact consisted of two adjoining houses, that had
been opened into each other. A spiral stair-case led to rooms
on different levels, and the unevenness of the stories was
remedied by steps. For us children, a younger sister and
myself, the favourite resort was a spacious floor below, near
the door of which was a large wooden lattice that allowed us
direct communication with the street and open air. A bird-
cage of this sort, with which many houses were provided, was
called a Frame (*Geräms*). The women sat in it to sew and
knit; the cook picked her salad there; female neighbours
chatted with each other, and the streets consequently in the
fine season wore a southern aspect. One felt at ease while
in communication with the public. We children, too, by
means of these frames, were brought into contact with our
neighbours, of whom three brothers Von Ochsenstein, the
surviving sons of the deceased Schultheiss, living on the other
side of the way, won my love, and occupied and diverted
themselves with me in many ways.

Our family liked to tell of all sorts of waggeries to which I
was enticed by these otherwise grave and solitary men. Let
one of these pranks suffice for all. A crockery fair had just
been held, from which not only our kitchen had been supplied
for a while with articles for a long time to come, but a great
deal of small gear of the same ware had been purchased as
playthings for us children. One fine afternoon, when every
thing was quiet in the house, I whiled away the time with
my pots and dishes in the Frame, and finding that nothing
more was to be got out of them, hurled one of them into the
street. The Von Ochsensteins, who saw me so delighted at
the fine smash it made, that I clapped my hands for joy, cried
out, "Another." I was not long in flinging out a pot, and as
they made no end to their calls for more, by degrees the
whole collection, platters, pipkins, mugs and all, were dashed
upon the pavement. My neighbours continued to express
their approbation, and I was highly delighted to give them
pleasure. But my stock was exhausted, and still they shouted,
"More." I ran, therefore, straight to the kitchen, and
brought the earthenware, which produced a still livelier spectacle in breaking, and thus I kept running backwards and
forwards, fetching one plate after another as I could reach it

from where they stood in rows on the shelf. But as that did
not satisfy my audience, I devoted all the ware that I could
drag out to similar destruction. It was not till afterwards
that any one appeared to hinder and save. The mischief was
done, and in place of so much broken crockery, there was at
least a ludicrous story, in which the roguish authors took
special delight to the end of their days.

My father's mother, in whose house we properly dwelt,
lived in a large back-room directly on the ground floor, and
we were accustomed to carry on our sports even up to her
chair, and when she was ill, up to her bedside. I remember
her, as it were, a spirit,—a handsome, thin woman, always
neatly dressed in white. Mild, gentle, and kind, she has ever
remained in my memory.

The street in which our house was situated passed by the
name of the Stag-Ditch; but as neither stags nor ditches
were to be seen, we wished to have the expression explained.
They told us that our house stood on a spot that was once
outside the city, and that where the street now ran had
formerly been a ditch, in which a number of stags were kept.
These stags were preserved and fed here because the senate
every year, according to an ancient custom, feasted publicly
on a stag, which was therefore always at hand in the ditch
for such a festival, in case princes or knights interfered with
the city's right of chase outside, or the walls were encompassed or besieged by an enemy. This pleased us much, and
we wished that such a lair for tame animals could have been
seen in our times.

The back of the house, from the second story particularly,
commanded a very pleasant prospect over an almost immeasurable extent of neighbouring gardens, stretching to the very
walls of the city. But, alas! in transforming what were once
public grounds into private gardens, our house and some
others lying towards the corner of the street had been much
stinted, since the houses towards the horse-market had appropriated spacious out-houses and large gardens to themselves,
while a tolerably high wall shut us out from these adjacent
paradises.

On the second floor was a room which was called the gar-
den-room, because they had there endeavoured to supply the
want of a garden by means of a few plants placed before the

window. As I grew older, it was there that I made my
favourite, not melancholy but somewhat sentimental, retreat.
Over these gardens, beyond the city's walls and ramparts,
might be seen a beautiful and fertile plain; the same which
stretches towards Hoechst. In the summer season I commonly
learned my lessons there, and watched the thunder-storms, but
could never look my fill at the setting sun, which went down
directly opposite my windows. And when, at the same time,
I saw the neighbours wandering through their gardens taking
care of their flowers, the children playing, parties of friends
enjoying themselves, and could hear the bowls rolling and the
nine pins dropping, it early excited within me a feeling of
solitude, and a sense of vague longing resulting from it,
which, conspiring with the seriousness and awe implanted in
me by Nature, exerted its influence at an early age, and
showed itself more distinctly in after years.

The old, many cornered, and gloomy arrangement of the
house was moreover adapted to awaken dread and terror
in childish minds. Unfortunately, too, the principle of discipline that young persons should be early deprived of all
fear for the awful and invisible, and accustomed to the terrible,
still prevailed. We children, therefore, were compelled to
sleep alone, and when we found this impossible, and softly
slipped from our beds to seek the society of the servants and
maids, our father, with his dressing-gown turned inside out,
which disguised him sufficiently for the purpose, placed himself in the way, and frightened us back to our resting-places.
The evil effect of this any one may imagine. How is he who
is encompassed with a double terror to be emancipated from
fear? My mother, always cheerful and gay, and willing to
render others so, discovered a much better pedagogical expedient. She managed to gain her end by rewards. It was
the season for peaches, the plentiful enjoyment of which she
promised us every morning if we overcame our fears during
the night. In this way she succeeded, and both parties were
satisfied.

In the interior of the house my eyes were chiefly attracted
by a series of Roman Views, with which my father had ornamented an ante-room. They were engravings by some of the
accomplished predecessors of Piranesi, who well understood
perspective and architecture, and whose touches were clear

and excellent. There I saw every day, the *Piazza del Popolo*, the *Colosseum*, the Piazza of *St. Peter's* and St. Peter's Church, within and without, the castle of *St. Angelo*, and many other places. These images impressed themselves deeply upon me, and my otherwise very laconic father was often so kind as to furnish descriptions of the objects. His partiality for the Italian language, and for every thing pertaining to Italy, was very decided. A small collection of marbles and natural curiosities, which he had brought with him thence, he often showed to us; and he devoted a great part of his time to a description of his travels, written in Italian, the copying and correction of which he slowly and accurately completed, in several parcels, with his own hand. A lively old teacher of Italian, called Giovinazzi, was of service to him in this work. The old man moreover did not sing badly, and my mother every day must needs accompany him and herself upon the clavichord, and thus I speedily learned the *Solitario bosco ombroso* so as to know it by heart before I understood it.

My father was altogether of a didactic turn, and in his retirement from business liked to communicate to others what he knew or was able to do. Thus, during the first years of their marriage, he had kept my mother busily engaged in writing, playing the clavichord, and singing, by which means she had been laid under the necessity of acquiring some knowledge and a slight readiness in the Italian tongue.

Generally we passed all our leisure hours with my grandmother, in whose spacious apartment we found plenty of room for our sports. She contrived to engage us with various trifles, and to regale us with all sorts of nice morsels. But one Christmas evening, she crowned all her kind deeds, by having a puppet-show exhibited before us, and thus unfolding a new world in the old house. This unexpected drama attracted our young minds with great force; upon the Boy particularly it made a very strong impression, which continued to vibrate with a great and lasting effect.

The little stage with its speechless personages, which at the outset had only been exhibited to us, but was afterwards given over for our own use and dramatic vivification, was prized more highly by us children, as it was the last bequest of our good grandmother, whom encroaching disease first withdrew from our sight, and death next tore away from our

hearts for ever. Her departure was of still more importance
to our family, as it drew after it a complete change in our
condition.

As long as my grandmother lived, my father had refrained
from any attempt to change or renovate the house, even in the
slightest particular, though it was known that he had pretty
large plans of building, which were now immediately begun.
In Frankfort, as in many other old towns, when anybody put
up a wooden structure, he ventured, for the sake of space, to
make not only the first, but each successive story project
over the lower one, by which means narrow streets especially
were rendered somewhat dark and confined. At last a law
was passed, that every one putting up a new house from the
ground, should confine his projections to the first upper story,
and carry the others up perpendicularly. My father, that he
might not lose the projecting space in the second story, caring
little for outward architectural appearance, and anxious only
for the good and convenient arrangement of the interior,
resorted to the expedient which others had employed before
him, of propping the upper part of the house, until one part
after another had been removed from the bottom upwards,
and a new house, as it were, inserted in its place. Thus,
while comparatively none of the old structure remained, the
new one merely passed for a repair. Now as the tearing down
and building up was done gradually, my father determined
not to quit the house, that he might better direct and give
his orders—as he possessed a good knowledge of the techni-
calities of building. At the same time he would not suffer his
family to leave him. This new epoch was very surprising and
strange for the children. To see the rooms in which they
had so often been confined and pestered with wearisome tasks
and studies, the passages they had played in, the walls which
had always been kept so carefully clean, all falling before the
mason's hatchet and the carpenter's axe—and that from the
bottom upwards ; to float as it were in the air, propped up by
beams, being, at the same time, constantly confined to a
certain lesson, or definite task—all this produced a commotion in our young heads that was not easily settled. But the
young people felt the inconvenience less, because they had
somewhat more space for play than before, and had many
opportunities of swinging on beams, and playing at see-saw
with the boards.

At first my father obstinately persisted in carrying out his
plan; but when at last even the roof was partly removed, and
the rain reached our beds, in spite of the carpets that had
been taken up, converted into tarpaulin, and stretched over
as a defence, he determined, though reluctantly, that the
children should be entrusted for a time to some kind friends,
who had already offered their services, and sent to a public
school.

This transition was rather unpleasant; for when the children who had all along been kept at home in a secluded,
pure, refined, yet strict manner, were thrown among a rude
mass of young creatures, they were compelled unexpectedly to
suffer everything from the vulgar, bad, and even base, since
they lacked both weapons and skill to protect themselves.

It was properly about this period that I first became acquainted with my native city, which I strolled over with more
and more freedom, in every direction, sometimes alone, and
sometimes in the company of lively companions. To convey to
others in any degree the impression made upon me by these
grave and revered spots, I must here introduce a description
of my birth-place, as in its different parts it was gradually
unfolded to me. I loved more than anything else to promenade on the great bridge over the Maine. Its length, its
firmness, and its fine appearance, rendered it a notable structure, and it was, besides, almost the only memorial left from
ancient times of the precautions due from the civil government to its citizens. The beautiful stream above and below
bridge, attracted my eye, and when the gilt weathercock on
the bridge-cross glittered in the sunshine, I always had a
pleasant feeling. Generally I extended my walk through
Sachsenhausen, and for a *Kreutzer* was ferried comfortably
across the river. I was now again on this side of the stream,
stole along to the wine market, and admired the mechanism
of the cranes when goods were unloaded. But it was particularly entertaining to watch the arrival of the market-boats,
from which so many and such extraordinary figures were seen
to disembark. On entering the city, the Saalhof, which at
least stood on the spot where the Castle of Emperor Charlemagne and his successors was reported to have been, was
greeted every time with profound reverence. One liked to
lose oneself in the old trading town, particularly on market-

days, among the crowd collected about the church of St. Bartholomew. From the earliest times, throngs of buyers and
sellers had gathered there, and the place being thus occupied,
it was not easy in later days to bring about a more roomy and
cheerful arrangement. The booths of the so-called *Pfarreisen*
were very important places for us children, and we carried
many a *Batzen* to them in order to purchase sheets of coloured
paper stamped with gold animals. But seldom, however,
could one make one's way through the narrow, crowded, and
dirty market-place. I call to mind, also, that I always flew
past the adjoining meat-stalls, narrow and disgusting as they
were, in perfect horror. On the other hand, the Roman Hill
(*Römerberg*) was a most delightful place for walking. The
way to the New-Town, along by the new shops, was always
cheering and pleasant; yet we regretted that a street did not
lead directly towards the Church of the Holy Virgin, and that
we always had to go a round-about way by the Hasengasse,
or the Catherine Gate. But what chiefly attracted the child's
attention, were the many little towns within the town, the
fortresses within the fortress; viz., the walled monastic en-
closures, and several other precincts, remaining from earlier
times, and more or less like castles—as the Nuremberg Court,
the Compostella, the Braunfels, the ancestral house of the
family of Stallburg, and several strongholds, in later days
transformed into dwellings and warehouses. No architecture
of an elevating kind was then to be seen in Frankfort, and
every thing pointed to a period long past and unquiet, both
for town and district. Gates and towers, which defined the
bounds of the old city,—then further on again, gates, towers,
walls, bridges, ramparts, moats, with which the new city was
encompassed,—all showed, but too plainly, that a necessity
for guarding the common weal in disastrous times had in
duced these arrangements, that all the squares and streets,
even the newest, broadest, and best laid out, owed their
origin to chance and caprice and not to any regulating mind.
A certain liking for the antique was thus implanted in the
Boy, and was specially nourished and promoted by old chronicles and wood-cuts, as for instance, those of Grave relating
to the siege of Frankfort. At the same time a different taste
was developed in him for observing the conditions of mankind, in their manifold variety and naturalness, without

regard to their importance or beauty. It was, therefore, one
of our favourite walks, which we endeavoured to take now
and then in the course of a year, to follow the circuit of the
path inside the city walls. Gardens, courts, and back buildings extend to the *Zwinger*; and we saw many thousand
people amid their little domestic and secluded circumstances.
From the ornamental and show gardens of the rich, to the
orchards of the citizen, anxious about his necessities—from
thence to the factories, bleaching-grounds, and similar establishments, even to the burying-grounds—for a little world
lay within the limits of the city—we passed a varied, strange,
spectacle, which changed at every step, and with the enjoyment of which our childish curiosity was never satisfied. In
fact, the celebrated Devil-upon-two-sticks, when he lifted the
roofs of Madrid at night, scarcely did more for his friend,
than was here done for us in the bright sunshine and open air.
The keys that were to be made use of in this journey, to
gain us a passage through many a tower, stair and postern,
were in the hands of the authorities, whose subordinates we
never failed to coax into good-humour.

But a more important, and in one sense more fruitful place
for us, was the Council-House, named from the Romans. In
its lower vault-like halls we liked but too well to lose ourselves. We obtained an entrance, too, into the large and
very simple session-room of the Council. The walls as well
as the arched ceiling were white, though wainscotted to a
certain height, and the whole was without a trace of painting,
or any kind of carved work; only, high up on the middle
wall, might be read this brief inscription:

" One man's word is no man's word,
Justice needs that both be heard."

After the most ancient fashion, benches were ranged around
the wainscotting, and raised one step above the floor for the
accommodation of the members of the assembly. This readily
suggested to us why the order of rank in our senate was distributed by benches. To the left of the door, on the opposite corner, sat the *Schöffen*; in the corner itself the *Schultheiss*, who alone had a small table before him; those of the
second bench sat in the space to his left as far as the wall to
where the windows were; while along the windows ran the

third bench, occupied by the craftsmen. In the midst of the
hall stood a table for the registrar (*Protoculführer*).
Once within the *Römer*, we even mingled with the crowd
at the audiences of the burgomasters. But whatever related
to the election and coronation of the Emperors possessed a
greater charm. We managed to gain the favour of the
keepers, so as to be allowed to mount the new gay imperial
staircase, which was painted in fresco, and on other occasions
closed with a grating. The election-chamber, with its purple
hangings and admirably-fringed gold borders, filled us with
awe. The representations of animals on which little children
or genii, clothed in the imperial ornaments and laden with
the insignia of the Empire, made a curious figure, were
observed by us with great attention; and we even hoped
that we might live to see, some time or other, a coronation
with our own eyes. They had great difficulty to get us out
of the great imperial hall, when we had been once fortunate
enough to steal in; and we reckoned him our truest friend
who, while we looked at the half-lengths of all the emperors
painted around at a certain height, would tell us something
of their deeds.

We listened to many a legend of Charlemagne. But that
which was historically interesting for us began with Rudolph
of Hapsburg, who by his courage put an end to such violent
commotions. Charles the Fourth also attracted our notice.
We had already heard of the Golden Bull, and of the statutes
for the administration of criminal justice. We knew, too, that
he had not made the Frankforters suffer for their adhesion to
his noble rival, Emperor Gunther of Schwarzburg. We heard
Maximilian praised both as a friend to mankind, and to the
townsmen, his subjects, and were also told that it had been
prophesied of him he would be the last Emperor of a German
house; which unhappily came to pass, as after his death the
choice wavered only between the King of Spain, (*afterwards*)
Charles V., and the King of France, Francis I. With some
anxiety it was added, that a similar prophecy, or rather intimation, was once more in circulation; for it was obvious
that there was room left for the portrait of only one more
emperor—a circumstance which, though seemingly accidental,
filled the patriotic with concern.

Having once entered upon this circuit, we did not fail to

repair to the cathedral, and there visit the grave of that brave
Gunther, so much prized both by friend and foe. The famous
stone which formerly covered it is set up in the choir. The
door close by, leading into the conclave, remained long shut
against us, until we at last managed through the higher
authorities, to gain access to this celebrated place. But we
should have done better had we continued as before to picture
it merely in our imagination; for we found this room, which
is so remarkable in German history, where the most powerful
princes were accustomed to meet for an act so momentous, in
no respect worthily adorned, and even disfigured with beams,
poles, scaffolding, and similar lumber, which people had
wanted to put out of the way. The imagination, for that
very reason, was the more excited and the heart elevated,
when we soon after received permission to be present in the
Council-House, at the exhibition of the Golden Bull to some
distinguished strangers.

The Boy then heard, with much curiosity, what his own
family, as well as other older relations and acquaintances,
liked to tell and repeat, viz., the histories of the two last
coronations, which had followed close upon each other; for
there was no Frankforter of a certain age who would not
have regarded these two events, and their attendant circumstances, as the crowning glory of his whole life. Splendid as
had been the coronation of Charles Seventh, during which
particularly the French Ambassador had given magnificent
feasts at great cost and with distinguished taste, the results
were all the more afflicting to the good Emperor, who could
not preserve his capital Munich, and was compelled in some
degree to implore the hospitality of his imperial towns.

If the coronation of Francis First was not so strikingly
splendid as the former one, it was dignified by the presence
of the Empress Maria Theresa, whose beauty appears to have
created as much impression on the men, as the earnest and
noble form and the blue eyes of Charles Seventh on the
women. At any rate, the sexes rivalled each other in giving
to the attentive Boy a highly favourable opinion of both these
personages. All these descriptions and narratives were given
in a serene and quiet state of mind; for the peace of Aix-la-
Chapelle had, for the moment, put an end to all feuds; and
they spoke at their ease of past contests, as well as of their

former festivities—the battle of Dettingen, for instance, and
other remarkable events of by-gone years; and all that was
important or dangerous seemed, as generally happens when a
peace has been concluded, to have occurred only to afford
entertainment to prosperous and unconcerned people.

Half a year had scarcely passed away in this narrow
patriotism before the fairs began, which always produced an
incredible ferment in the heads of all children. The erection,
in so short a time, of so many booths, creating a new town
within the old one, the roll and crush, the unloading and
unpacking of wares, excited from the very first dawn of consciousness an insatiable active curiosity and a boundless
desire for childish property, which the Boy with increasing
years endeavoured to gratify, in one way or another, as far as
his little purse permitted. At the same time he obtained a
notion of what the world produces, what it wants, and what
the inhabitants of its different parts exchange with each
other.

These great epochs, which came round regularly in spring
and autumn, were announced by curious solemnities, which
seemed the more dignified because they vividly brought
before us the old time, and what had come down from it to
ourselves. On Escort-day, the whole population were on
their legs, thronging to the *Fahrgasse*, to the bridge, and
beyond *Sachsenhausen*; all the windows were occupied, though
nothing unusual took place on that day; the crowd seeming
to be there only for the sake of jostling each other, and the
spectators merely to look at one another: for the real occasion of their coming did not begin till nightfall, and was then
rather taken upon trust than seen with the eyes.

The affair was thus: in those old, unquiet times, when every
one did wrong according to his pleasure, or helped the right
as his liking led him, traders on their way to the fairs were
so wilfully beset and harassed by waylayers, both of noble and
ignoble birth, that princes and other persons of power caused
their people to be accompanied to Frankfort by an armed
escort. Now the burghers of the imperial city would yield
no rights pertaining to themselves or their district; they went
out to meet the advancing party; and thus contests often arose
as to how far the escort should advance, or whether it had a
right to enter the city at all. But, as this took place, not only

in regard to matters of trade and fairs, but also when high
personages came, in times of peace or war, and especially on
the days of election; and as the affair often came to blows
when a train which was not to be endured in the city strove
to make its way in along with its lord, many negotiations had
from time to time been resorted to, and many temporary
arrangements concluded, though always with reservations of
rights on both sides. The hope had not been relinquished of
composing once for all a quarrel that had already lasted for
centuries, inasmuch as the whole institution, on account of
which it had been so long and often so hotly contested, might
be looked upon as nearly useless, or at least as superfluous.

Meanwhile, on those days, the city cavalry in several divisions, each having a commander in front, rode forth from
different gates and found on a certain spot some troopers or
hussars of the persons entitled to an escort, who with their
leaders were well received and entertained. They stayed till
towards evening, and then rode back to the city, scarcely
visible to the expectant crowd, many a city knight not being
in a condition to manage his horse, or keep himself in the
saddle. The most important bands returned by the bridge-
gate, where the pressure was consequently the strongest. Last
of all, just as night fell, the Nuremberg post-coach arrived,
escorted in the same way, and always containing, as the
people fancied, in pursuance of custom, an old woman. Its
arrival, therefore, was a signal for all the urchins to break out
into an ear-splitting shout, though it was utterly impossible to
distinguish any one of the passengers within. The throng
that pressed after the coach through the bridge-gate was quite
incredible, and perfectly bewildering to the senses. The houses
nearest the bridge were those, therefore, most in demand
among spectators.

Another more singular ceremony, by which the people were
excited in broad daylight, was the Piper's-court (*Pfeifer-
gericht*). It commemorated those early times when important
larger trading-towns endeavoured, if not to abolish tolls altogether, at least to bring about a reduction of them, as they
increased in proportion with trade and industry. They were
allowed this privilege by the Emperor who needed their aid,
when it was in his power to grant it, but commonly only for
one year; so that it had to be annually renewed. This was

effected by means of symbolical gifts, which were presented
before the opening of St. Bartholomew's Fair to the imperial
magistrate (*Schultheiss*), who might have sometimes been the
chief toll-gatherer ; and, for the sake of a more imposing
show, the gifts were offered when he was sitting in full court
with the *Schöffen*. But when the chief magistrate afterwards
came to be no longer appointed by the Emperor, and was
elected by the city itself, he still retained these privileges ;
and thus both the immunities of the cities from toll, and the
ceremonies by which the representatives from Worms, Nuremberg, and Old Bamberg once acknowledged the ancient
favour, had come down to our times. The day before Lady-
day, an open court was proclaimed. In an enclosed space in
the great Imperial Hall, the Schöffen took their elevated seats;
a step higher, sat the *Schultheiss* in the midst of them ; while
below on the right hand, were the procurators of both parties
invested with plenipotentiary powers. The *Actuarius* begins to
read aloud the weighty judgments reserved for this day ; the
lawyers demand copies, appeal, or do whatever else seems necessary. All at once a singular sort of music announces, if we may
so speak, the advent of former centuries. It proceeds from
three pipers, one of whom plays an old *shawm*, another a *sack-
but*, and the third a *pommer*, or oboe. They wear blue mantles
trimmed with gold, having the notes made fast to their sleeves,
and their heads covered. Having thus left their inn at ten
o'clock, followed by the deputies and their attendants, and
stared at by all, natives and strangers, they enter the hall.
The law proceedings are stayed—the pipers and their train
halt before the railing—the deputy steps in and stations himself in front of the *Schultheiss*. The emblematic presents,
which were required to be precisely the same as in the old
precedents, consisted commonly of the staple wares of the
city offering them. Pepper passed, as it were, for everything
else ; and, even on this occasion, the deputy brought a handsomely turned wooden goblet filled with pepper. Upon it lay
a pair of gloves, curiously slashed, stitched, and tasseled with
silk—a token of a favour granted and received—such as the
Emperor himself made use of in certain cases. Along with
this was a white staff, which in former times was not easily
dispensable in judicial proceedings. Some small pieces of
silver money were added ; and the city of Worms brought an

old felt hat, which was always redeemed again, so that the
same one had been a witness of these ceremonies for many
years.

After the deputy had made his address, handed over his
present, and received from the *Schultheiss* assurance of continued favour, he quitted the enclosed circle, the pipers blew,
the train departed as it had come, the court pursued its business, until the second and at last the third deputy had been
introduced. For each came some time after the other; partly
that the pleasure of the public might thus be prolonged,
and partly because they were always the same antiquated
virtuosi whom Nuremberg, for itself and its co-cities, had
undertaken to maintain and produce annually at the appointed
place.

We children were particularly interested in this festival,
because we were not a little flattered to see our grandfather in
a place of so much honour; and because commonly, on the
self-same day, we used to visit him, quite modestly, in order
that we might, when my grandmother had emptied the pepper
into her spice box, lay hold of a cup or small rod, a pair of
gloves or an old *Räder Albus.* * These symbolical ceremonies,
restoring antiquity as if by magic, could not be explained to
us without leading us back into past times and informing us
of the manners, customs, and feelings of those early ancestors
who were so strangely made present to us, by pipers and
deputies seemingly risen from the dead, and by tangible gifts,
which might be possessed by ourselves.

These venerable solemnities were followed, in the fine season, by many festivals, delightful for us children, which took
place in the open air, outside of the city. On the right shore
of the Maine going down, about half an hour's walk from the
gate, there rises a sulphur-spring, neatly enclosed and surrounded by aged lindens. Not far from it stands the *Good-
People's-Court*, formerly a hospital erected for the sake of the
waters. On the commons around, the herds of cattle from the
neighbourhood were collected on a certain day of the year;
and the herdsmen, together with their sweethearts, celebrated
a rural festival, with dancing and singing, with all sorts of
pleasure and clownishness. On the other side of the city lay

---

* An old silver coin.

a similar but larger common, likewise graced with a spring
and still finer lindens. Thither, at Whitsuntide, the flocks of
sheep were driven ; and, at the same time, the poor, pale
orphan children were allowed to come out of their walls into
the open air ; for the thought had not yet occurred that these
destitute creatures, who must some time or other help themselves through the world, ought soon to be brought in contact
with it ; that instead of being kept in dreary confinement,
they should rather be accustomed to serve and to endure ; and
that there was every reason to strengthen them physically and
morally from their infancy. The nurses and maids, always
ready to take a walk, never failed to carry or conduct us to
such places, even in our first years ; so that these rural festivals belong to the earliest impressions that I can recall.

Meanwhile, our house had been finished, and that too in
tolerably short time, because everything had been judiciously
planned and prepared, and the needful money provided. We
now found ourselves all together again, and felt comfortable :
for, when a well-considered plan is once carried out, we forget
the various inconveniences of the means that were necessary
to its accomplishment. The building, for a private residence,
was roomy enough : light and cheerful throughout, with broad
staircases, agreeable parlours, and a prospect of the gardens
that could be enjoyed easily from several of the windows.
The internal completion, and what pertained to mere ornament and finish, was gradually accomplished, and served at
the same time for occupation and amusement.

The first thing brought into order was my father's collection of books, the best of which, in calf and half-calf binding, were to ornament the walls of his office and study. He
possessed the beautiful Dutch editions of the Latin classics,
which for the sake of outward uniformity he had endeavoured
to procure all in quarto ; and also many other works relating to Roman antiquities, and the more elegant jurisprudence. The most eminent Italian poets were not wanting,
and for Tasso he showed a great predilection. There were
also the best and most recent Travels ; and he took great
delight in correcting and completing Keyssler and Nemeiz
from them. Nor had he omitted to surround himself with all
needful assistants to learning, such as dictionaries of various
languages, and encyclopedias of science and art, which with

much else adapted to profit and amusement, might be consulted at will.

The other half of this collection, in neat parchment bindings, with very beautifully written titles, was placed in a
separate attic. The acquisition of new books, as well as their
binding and arrangement, he pursued with great composure
and love of order; and he was much influenced in his opinion
by the critical notices that ascribed particular merit to any
work. His collection of juridical treatises was annually increased by some volumes.

Next, the pictures, which in the old house had hung about
promiscuously, were now collected and symmetrically hung on
the walls of a cheerful room near the study, all in black
frames, set off with gilt mouldings. My father had a principle, which he often and strongly expressed, that one ought to
employ the living Masters, and to spend less upon the departed,
in the estimation of whom prejudice greatly concurred. He
had the notion that it was precisely the same with pictures
as with Rhenish wines, which, though age may impart to them
a higher value, can be produced in any coming year of just as
excellent quality as in years past. After the lapse of some
time, the new wine also becomes old, quite as valuable and
perhaps more delicious. This opinion he chiefly confirmed by
the observation that many old pictures seemed to derive their
chief value for lovers of art from the fact that they had
become darker and browner; and that the harmony of tone
in such pictures was often vaunted. My father, on the other
hand, protested that he had no fear that the new pictures
would not also turn black in time, though whether they were
likely to gain anything by this he was not so positive.

In pursuance of these principles, he employed for many
years the whole of the Frankfort artists:—the painter HIRT,
who excelled in animating oak and beech woods, and other so-
called rural scenes, with cattle; TRAUTMANN, who had
adopted Rembrandt as his model, and had attained great perfection in inclosed lights and reflections, as well as in effective
conflagrations, so that he was once ordered to paint a com-
panion-piece to a Rembrandt; SCHÜTZ, who diligently elaborated landscapes of the Rhine country, in the manner of
SACHTLEBENS; and JUNKER, who executed with great purity
flower and fruit pieces, still life, and figures quietly employed,

c

after the models of the Dutch. But now, by the new arrangement, by more convenient room, and still more by the acquaintance of a skilful artist, our love of art was again quickened and
animated. This artist was SEEKATZ, a pupil of Brinkmann,
court-painter at Darmstadt, whose talent and character will be
more minutely unfolded in the sequel.

In this way, the remaining rooms were finished, according
to their several purposes. Cleanliness and order prevailed
throughout. Above all, the large panes of plate-glass contributed towards a perfect lightness, which had been wanting in
the old house for many causes, but chiefly on account of the
panes, which were for the most part round. My father was
cheerful on account of the success of his undertaking, and if
his good humour had not been often interrupted because the
diligence and exactness of the mechanics did not come up to
his wishes, a happier life than ours could not have been conceived, since much good partly arose in the family itself, and
partly flowed from without.

But an extraordinary event deeply disturbed the Boy's peace
of mind, for the first time. On the 1st of November, 1755,
the earthquake at Lisbon took place, and spread a prodigious
alarm over the world, long accustomed to peace and quiet.
A great and magnificent capital, which was, at the same time,
a trading and mercantile city, is smitten, without warning, by
a most fearful calamity. The earth trembles and totters, the
sea roars up, ships dash together, houses fall in, and over them
churches and towers, the royal palace is in part swallowed by
the waters, the bursting land seems to vomit flames, since
smoke and fire are seen everywhere amid the ruins. Sixty
thousand persons, a moment before in ease and comfort, fall
together, and he is to be deemed most fortunate who is no
longer capable of a thought or feeling about the disaster.
The flames rage on, and with them rage a troop of despera-
does, before concealed, or set at large by the event. The
wretched survivors are exposed to pillage, massacre, and every
outrage: and thus, on all sides, Nature asserts her boundless
capriciousness.

Intimations of this event had spread over wide regions
more quickly than the authentic reports: slight shocks had been
felt in many places: in many springs, particularly those of a
mineral nature, an unusual receding of the waters had been

remarked; and so much the greater was the effect of the accounts themselves, which were rapidly circulated, at first in general terms, but finally with dreadful particulars. Hereupon, the religious were neither wanting in reflections, nor the philosophic in grounds for consolation, nor the clergy in warnings. So complicated an event arrested the attention of the world for a long time ; and, as additional and more detailed accounts of the extensive effects of this explosion came from every quarter, the minds already aroused by the misfortunes of strangers, began to be more and more anxious about themselves and their friends. Perhaps the demon of terror had never so speedily and powerfully diffused his terrors over the earth.

The Boy, who was compelled to put up with frequent repetitions of the whole matter, was not a little staggered. God, the Creator and Preserver of Heaven and Earth, whom the explanation of the first article of the Creed declared so wise and benignant, having given both the just and the unjust a prey to the same destruction, had not manifested Himself, by any means, in a fatherly character. In vain the young mind strove to resist these impressions. It was the more impossible, as the wise and scripture-learned could not themselves agree as to the light in which such a phenomenon should be regarded.

The next summer gave a closer opportunity of knowing directly that angry God, of whom the Old Testament records so much. A sudden hail-storm, accompanied by thunder and lightning, violently broke the new panes at the back of our house, which looked towards the west, damaged the new furniture, destroyed some valuable books and other things of worth, and was the more terrible to the children, as the whole household, quite beside themselves, dragged them into a dark passage, where, on their knees, with frightful groans and cries, they thought to conciliate the wrathful Deity. Meanwhile, my father, who was alone self-possessed, forced open and unhinged the window-frames, by which we saved much glass, but made a broader inlet for the rain that followed the hail, so that after we were finally quieted, we found ourselves in the rooms and on the stairs completely surrounded by floods and streams of water.

These events, startling as they were on the whole, did not greatly interrupt the course of instruction which my father

c 2

himself had undertaken to give us children. He had passed
his youth in the Cobourg Gymnasium, which stood as one of
the first among German educational institutions. He had
there laid a good foundation in languages, and other matters
reckoned part of a learned education, had subsequently applied
himself to jurisprudence at Leipzig, and had at last taken his
degree at Giessen. His dissertation, " *Electa de aditione
Hereditatis,*" which had been earnestly and carefully written,
is yet cited by jurists with approval.

It is a pious wish of all fathers to see what they have themselves failed to attain, realized in their sons, as if in this way
they could live their lives over again, and, at last, make a
proper use of their early experience. Conscious of his acquirements, with the certainty of faithful perseverance, and dis-
trusting the teachers of the day, my father undertook to
instruct his own children, allowing them to take particular
lesson from particular masters only so far as seemed absolutely
necessary. A pedagogical *dilettantism* was already beginning
to show itself everywhere. The pedantry and heaviness of
the masters appointed in the public schools had probably
given rise to this evil. Something better was sought for, but
it was forgotten how defective all instruction must be, which
is not given by persons who are teachers by profession.

My father had prospered in his own career tolerably according to his wishes : I was to follow the same course, only
more easily, and much farther. He prized my natural endowments the more, because he was himself wanting in them ;
for he had acquired everything only by means of unspeakable
diligence, pertinacity, and repetition. He often assured me,
early and late, both in jest and earnest, that with my talents
he would have deported himself very differently, and would
not have turned them to such small account.

By means of a ready apprehension, practice, and a good
memory, I very soon outgrew the instructions which my
father and the other teachers were able to give, without being
thoroughly grounded in anything. Grammar displeased me,
because I regarded it as a mere arbitrary law ; the rules
seemed ridiculous, inasmuch as they were invalidated by so
many exceptions, which had all to be learned by themselves.
And if the first Latin work had not been in rhyme, I should
have got on but badly in that ; but as it was, I hummed and

sang it to myself readily enough. In the same way we had a
Geography in memory-verses, in which the most wretched
doggerel best served to fix the recollection of that which was
to be retained; *e. g.*:

> Upper-Yssel has many a fen,
> Which makes it hateful to all men.

The forms and inflections of language I caught with ease;
and I also quickly unravelled what lay in the conception of a
thing. In rhetoric, composition, and such matters, no one
excelled me, although I was often put back for faults of grammar. Yet these were the attempts that gave my father
particular pleasure, and for which he rewarded me with many
presents of money, considerable for such a lad.

My father taught my sister Italian in the same room in
which I had to commit Cellarius to memory. As I was soon
ready with my task, and was yet obliged to sit quiet, I listened
with my book before me, and very readily caught the Italian,
which struck me as an agreeable softening of Latin.

Other precocities, with respect to memory and the power
to combine, I possessed in common with those children who
thus acquire an early reputation. For that reason my father
could scarcely wait for me to go to college. He very soon
declared, that I must study jurisprudence in Leipzig, for
which he retained a strong predilection, and I was afterwards
to visit some other university and take my degree. As for
this second one he was indifferent which I might choose,
except that he had for some reason or other a disinclination
to Göttingen, to my disappointment, since it was precisely
there that I had placed such confidence and high hopes.

He told me further, that I was to go to Wetzlar and Ratisbon as well as to Vienna, and thence towards Italy, although
he repeatedly mentioned that Paris should first be seen, because after coming out of Italy nothing else could be pleasing.

These tales of my future youthful travels, often as they
were repeated, I listened to eagerly, the more since they
always led to accounts of Italy, and at last to a description of
Naples. His otherwise serious and dry manner seemed on
these occasions to relax and quicken, and thus a passionate
wish awoke in us children to participate in the paradise he
described.

Private lessons, which now gradually multiplied, were
shared with the children of the neighbours. This learning
in common did not advance me; the teachers followed their
routine; and the rudeness, sometimes the ill-nature, of my
companions, interrupted the brief hours of study with tumult,
vexation, and disturbance. Chrestomathies, by which learning is made pleasant and varied, had not yet reached us.
Cornelius Nepos, so dry to young people, the New Testament,
which was much too easy, and which by preaching and religious instructions had been rendered even common-place,
Cellarius and Pasor could impart no kind of interest; on the
other hand, a certain rage for rhyme and versification, a
consequence of reading the prevalent German poets, took
complete possession of us. Me it had seized much earlier, as
I had found it agreeable to pass from the rhetorical to the
poetical treatment of subjects.

We boys held a Sunday assembly where each of us was to
produce original verses. And here I was struck by something
strange, which long caused me uneasiness. My poems, whatever they might be, always seemed to me the best. But I
soon remarked, that my competitors who brought forth very
lame affairs, were in the same condition, and thought no less
of themselves. Nay, what appeared yet more suspicious, a
good lad (though in such matters altogether unskilful), whom
I liked in other respects, but who had his rhymes made by
his tutor, not only regarded these as the best, but was
thoroughly persuaded they were his own, as he always maintained in our confidential intercourse. Now, as this illusion
and error was obvious to me, the question one day forced itself
upon me, whether I myself might not be in the same state,
whether those poems were not really better than mine, and
whether I might not justly appear to those boys as mad as
they to me? This disturbed me much and long; for it was
altogether impossible for me to find any external criterion of
the truth; I even ceased from producing, until at length I was
quieted by my own light temperament, and the feeling of my
own powers, and lastly by a trial of skill—started on the spur
of the moment by our teachers and parents, who had noted
our sport—in which I came off well and won general praise.

No libraries for children had at that time been established.
The old had themselves still childish notions, and found it

convenient to impart their own education to their successors.
Except the *Orbis Pictus* of Amos Comenius, no book of the
sort fell into our hands ; but the large folio Bible, with copper-
plates by Merian, was diligently gone over leaf by leaf: Gottfried's Chronicles, with plates by the same master, taught us
the most notable events of Universal History ; the *Acerra
Philologica* added thereto all sorts of fables, mythologies and
wonders ; and, as I soon became familiar with Ovid's Metamorphoses, the first books of which in particular I studied
carefully, my young brain was rapidly furnished with a mass
of images and events, of significant and wonderful shapes and
occurrences, and I never felt time hang upon my hands, as I
always occupied myself in working over, repeating, and re-
producing these acquisitions.

A more salutary moral effect than that of these rude and
hazardous antiquities, was produced by Fenelon's *Telemachus*,
with which I first became acquainted in Neukirch's translation, and which, imperfectly as it was executed, had a sweet
and beneficent influence on my mind. That *Robinson Crusoe*
was added in due time, follows in the nature of things ; and
it may be imagined that the *Island of Falsenberg* was not
wanting. Lord Anson's *Voyage round the Globe* combined
the dignity of truth with the rich fancies of fable, and while
our thoughts accompanied this excellent seaman, we were conducted over all the world, and endeavoured to follow him with
our fingers on the globe. But a still richer harvest was to
spring up before me, when I lighted on a mass of writings,
which, in their present state, it is true, cannot be called excellent, but the contents of which, in a harmless way, bring near
to us many a meritorious action of former times.

The publication, or rather the manufacture, of those books
which have at a later day become so well known and celebrated under the name *Volkschriften, Volksbücher* (popular
works or books), was carried on in Frankfort. The enor-
mous sales they met with, led to their being almost illegibly
printed from stereotypes on horrible blotting-paper. We
children were so fortunate as to find these precious remains of
the Middle Ages every day on a little table at the door of a
dealer in cheap books, and to obtain them at the cost of a
couple of *kreutzer*. The Eulenspiegel, the Four Sons of Haimon, the Emperor Octavian, the Fair Melusina, the Beautiful

Magelone, Fortunatus, with the whole race down to the Wandering Jew, were all at our service, as often as we preferred the relish of these works to the taste of sweet things. The greatest benefit of this was, that when we had read through or damaged such a sheet, it could soon be reprocured and swallowed a second time.

As a family pic-nic in summer is vexatiously disturbed by a sudden storm, which transforms a pleasant state of things into the very reverse, so the diseases of childhood fall unexpectedly on the most beautiful season of early life. And thus it happened with me. I had just purchased Fortunatus with his Purse and Wishing-hat, when I was attacked by a restlessness and fever which announced the small-pox. Inoculation was still with us considered very problematical, and although it had already been intelligibly and urgently recommended by popular writers, the German physicians hesitated to perform an operation that seemed to forestall Nature. Speculative Englishmen, therefore, had come to the Continent and inoculated, for a considerable fee, the children of such persons as were opulent and free from prejudices. Still the majority were exposed to the old disease ; the infection raged through families, killed and disfigured many children ; and few parents dared to avail themselves of a method, the probable efficacy of which had been abundantly confirmed by the result. The evil now invaded our house and attacked me with unusual severity. My whole body was sown over with spots, and my face covered, and for several days I lay blind and in great pain. They tried the only possible alleviation, and promised me heaps of gold if I would keep quiet and not increase the mischief by rubbing and scratching. I controlled myself, while, according to the prevailing prejudice, they kept me as warm as possible, and thus only rendered my suffering more acute. At last, after a woful time, there fell as it were a mask from my face. The blotches had left no visible mark upon the skin, but the features were plainly altered. I myself was satisfied merely with seeing the light of day again, and gradually putting off my spotted skin ; but others were pitiless enough to remind me often of my previous condition ; especially a very lively aunt, who had formerly regarded me with idolatry, but in after years could seldom look at me without exclaiming—" The deuce, cousin ! what a fright he's grown!" Then she would tell me circumstantially how I had once been her delight, and what attention she had excited when she carried me about; and thus I early learned that people very often subject us to a severe atonement for the pleasure which we have afforded them.

I neither escaped measles, nor chicken-pox, nor any other of the tormenting demons of childhood; and I was assured each time that it was a great piece of good luck that this malady was now past for ever. But, alas! another again threatened in the back-ground, and advanced. All these things increased my propensity to reflection; and as I had already practised myself in fortitude, in order to remove the torture of impatience, the virtues which I had heard praised in the Stoics appeared to me highly worthy of imitation, and the more so, as something similar was commended by the Christian doctrine of patience.

While on the subject of these family diseases, I will mention a brother about three years younger than myself, who was likewise attacked by that infection, and suffered not a little from it. He was of a tender nature, quiet and capricious, and we were never on the most friendly terms. Besides, he scarcely survived the years of childhood. Among several other children born afterwards, who like him did not live long, I only remember a very pretty and agreeable girl, who also soon passed away; so that, after the lapse of some years, my sister and I remained alone, and were therefore the more deeply and affectionately attached to each other.

These maladies and other unpleasant interruptions were in their consequences doubly grievous; for my father, who seemed to have laid down for himself a certain calendar of education and instruction, was resolved immediately to repair every delay, and imposed double lessons upon the young convalescent. These were not hard for me to accomplish, but were so far troublesome, that they hindered, and to a certain extent repressed, my inward development, which had taken a decided direction.

From these didactic and pedagogic oppressions, we commonly fled to my grandfather and grandmother. Their house stood in the *Friedberg*-street, and appeared to have been formerly a fortress; for, on approaching it, nothing was seen but a large gate with battlements, which were joined on either side

to the two neighbouring houses. On entering through a narrow passage, we reached at last a tolerably broad court,
surrounded by irregular buildings, which were now all united
into one dwelling. We usually hastened at once into the
garden, which extended to a considerable length and breadth
behind the buildings, and was very well kept. The walks
were mostly skirted by vine trellises ; one part of the space
was used for vegetables, and another devoted to flowers, which
from spring till autumn adorned in rich succession the borders
as well as the beds. The long wall erected towards the south
was used for some well-trained espalier peach-trees, the forbidden fruit of which ripened temptingly before us through the
summer. Yet we rather avoided this side, because we here
could not satisfy our dainty appetites ; and we turned to the
side opposite, where an interminable row of currant and goose-
berry bushes furnished our voracity with a succession of har-
vests till autumn. Not less important to us was an old, high,
wide-spreading mulberry-tree, both on account of its fruits,
and because we were told that the silk-worms fed upon its
leaves. In this peaceful region my grandfather was found
every evening, tending with genial care and with his own
hand the finer growths of fruits and flowers ; while a gardener
managed the drudgery. He was never vexed by the various
toils which were necessary to preserve and increase a fine
show of pinks. The branches of the peach-trees were carefully tied to the espaliers with his own hands, in a fan-shape,
in order to bring about a full and easy growth of the fruit.
The sorting of the bulbs of tulips, hyacinths, and plants of a
similar nature, as well as the care of their preservation, he
entrusted to none ; and I still with pleasure recall to my mind
how diligently he occupied himself in inoculating the different
varieties of roses. That he might protect himself from the
thorns, he put on a pair of those ancient leather gloves, of
which three pair were given him annually at the Piper's Court,
so that there was no dearth of the article. He wore also a
loose dressing-gown, and a folded black velvet cap upon his
head, so that he might have passed for an intermediate person
between Alcinous and Laertes.

All this work in the garden he pursued as regularly and
with as much precision as his official business : for, before he
came down, he always arranged the list of causes for the next

day, and read the legal papers. In the morning he proceeded
to the Council House, dined after his return, then nodded
in his easy chair, and so went through the same routine every
day. He conversed little, never exhibited any vehemence,
and I do not remember ever to have seen him angry. All that
surrounded him was in the fashion of the olden time. I never
perceived any alteration in his wainscotted room. His library
contained, besides law works, only the earliest books of travels,
sea voyages, and discoveries of countries. Altogether I can
call to mind no situation more adapted than his to awaken
the feeling of uninterrupted peace and eternal duration.

But the reverence which we entertained for this venerable
old man was raised to the highest degree by a conviction that
he possessed the gift of prophecy, especially in matters that
pertained to himself and his destiny. It is true he revealed
himself to no one, distinctly and minutely, except to my
grandmother; yet we were all aware that he was informed
of what was going to happen, by significant dreams. He
assured his wife, for instance, at a time when he was still a
junior Councillor, that on the first vacancy he would obtain
the place left open on the bench of the *Schöffen*; and soon
afterwards when one of those officers actually died of apoplexy,
my grandfather gave orders that his house should be quietly
got ready prepared on the day of electing and balloting, to
receive his guests and congratulators. Sure enough, the decisive gold ball was drawn in his favour. The simple dream
by which he had learned this, he confided to his wife as follows: He had seen himself in the ordinary full assembly of
Councilmen, where all went on just as usual. Suddenly, the
late *Schöff* rose from his seat, descended the steps, pressed
him in the most complimentary manner to take the vacant
place, and then departed by the door.

Something like this occurred on the death of the *Schultheiss*. They make no delay in supplying this place, as they
always have to fear that the Emperor will at some time
resume his ancient right of nominating the officer. On this
occasion, the messenger of the Court came at midnight to
summon an extraordinary session for the next morning; and
as the light in his lantern was about to expire, he asked for a
candle's end to help him on his way. " Give him a whole
one," said my grandfather to the ladies, " he takes the trouble

all on my account." This expression anticipated the result—
he was made *Schultheiss;* and what rendered the circumstance particularly remarkable was, that although his representative was the third and last to draw at the ballot, the
two silver balls first came out, leaving the golden ball at the
bottom of the bag for him.

Perfectly prosaic, simple, and without a trace of the fantastic or miraculous, were the other dreams, of which we
were informed. Moreover, I remember that once, as a boy, I
was turning over his books and memoranda, and found among
some other remarks which related to gardening, such sentences as these : " To-night N. N. came to me and said——"
the name and revelation being written in cipher; or " This
night I saw——" all the rest being again in cipher, except
the conjunctions and similar words, from which nothing could
be learned.

It is worthy of note also, that persons who showed no signs
of prophetic insight at other times, acquired, for the moment,
while in his presence, and that by means of some sensible
evidence, presentiments of diseases or deaths which were then
occurring in distant places. But no such gift has been trans-
mitted to any of his children or grandchildren, who for the
most part have been hearty people, enjoying life, and never
going beyond the Actual.

While on this subject, I remember with gratitude many
kindnesses I received from them in my youth. Thus, for
example, we were employed and entertained in many ways
when we visited the second daughter, married to the druggist
Melbert, whose house and shop stood near the market, in the
midst of the liveliest and most crowded part of the town.
There we could look down from the windows pleasantly
enough upon the hurly-burly in which we feared to lose ourselves ; and though, at first, of all the goods in the shop,
nothing had much interest for us but the liquorice, and the
little brown stamped cakes made from it, we became in time
better acquainted with the multitude of articles bought and
sold in that business. This aunt was the most vivacious of
all the family. When my mother, in her early years, took
pleasure in being neatly dressed, working at some domestic
occupation, or reading a book, the other, on the contrary, ran
about the neighbourhood to pick up neglected children, take

care of them, comb them, and carry them round, as indeed
she did me for a good while. At a time of public festivities,
such as coronations, it was impossible to keep her at home.
When a little child, she had already scrambled for the money
scattered on such occasions; and it was related of her, that
once when she had got a good many together, and was
looking at them with great delight in the palm of her hand,
it was struck by somebody, and all her well-earned booty
vanished at a blow. There was another incident of which
she was very proud. Once, while standing on a post as the
Emperor Charles VII. was passing, at a moment when all the
people were silent, she shouted a vigorous "Vivat!" into the
coach, which made him take off his hat to her, and thank
her quite graciously for her bold salutation.

Everything in her house was stirring, lively, and cheerful,
and we children owed her many a gay hour.

In a quieter situation, which was however suited to her
character, was a second aunt, married to the Pastor Stark,
incumbent of St. Catharine's Church. He lived much alone,
in accordance with his temperament and vocation, and possessed a fine library. Here I first became acquainted with
Homer, in a prose translation, which may be found in the
seventh part of Herr Von Loen's new collection of the most
remarkable travels, under the title, *Homer's Description of
the Conquest of the Kingdom of Troy*, ornamented with copper-
plates, in the theatrical French taste. These pictures perverted my imagination to such a degree, that for a long time
I could conceive the Homeric heroes only under such forms.
The incidents themselves gave me unspeakable delight; though
I found great fault with the work for affording us no account
of the capture of Troy, and breaking off so abruptly with the
death of Hector. My uncle, to whom I mentioned this
defect, referred me to Virgil, who perfectly satisfied my
demands.

It will be taken for granted, that we children had among
our other lessons, a continued and progressive instruction in
religion. But the Church-Protestantism imparted to us was,
properly speaking, nothing but a kind of dry morality:
ingenious exposition was not thought of; and the doctrine
appealed neither to the understanding nor to the heart. For
that reason, there were various secessions from the Esta-

blished Church. Separatists, Pietists, Herrnhuter (Moravians),
Quiet-in-the-Lands, and others differently named and charac-
terized sprang up, all of whom were animated by the same
purpose of approaching the Deity, especially through Christ,
more closely than seemed to them possible under the forms
of the established religion.

The Boy heard these opinions and sentiments constantly
spoken of; for the clergy as well as the laity divided themselves into *pro* and *con*. The minority were composed of
those who dissented more or less broadly, but their modes
of thinking attracted by originality, heartiness, perseverance,
and independence. All sorts of stories were told of their
virtues and of the way in which they were manifested. The
reply of a certain pious tinman was especially noted, who,
when one of his craft attempted to shame him by asking
" who is really your confessor?" answered with great cheerfulness and confidence in the goodness of his cause,—" I have
a famous one—no less than the confessor of King David."

Things of this sort naturally made an impression on the
Boy, and led him into similar states of mind. In fact, he
came to the thought that he might immediately approach the
great God of Nature, the Creator and Preserver of Heaven
and Earth, whose earlier manifestations of wrath had been
long forgotten in the beauty of the world, and the manifold
blessings in which we participate while upon it. The way he
took to accomplish this was very curious.

The Boy had chiefly kept to the first article of Belief. The
God who stands in immediate connexion with nature, and
owns and loves it as his work, seemed to him the proper God,
who might be brought into closer relationship with man, as
with everything else, and who would take care of him, as of
the motion of the stars, the days and seasons, the animals
and plants. There were texts of the Gospels which explicitly
stated this. The Boy could ascribe no form to this Being;
he therefore sought Him in His works, and would, in the good
Old Testament fashion, build Him an altar. Natural productions were set forth as images of the world, over which a
flame was to burn, signifying the aspirations of man's heart
towards his Maker. He brought out of the collection of
natural objects which he possessed, and which had been increased as chance directed, the best ores and other specimens.

But the next difficulty was, as to how they should be arranged and raised into a pile. His father possessed a beautiful red-lackered music-stand, ornamented with gilt flowers, in the form of a four-sided pyramid, with different elevations, which had been found convenient for quartets, but lately was not much in use. The Boy laid hands on this, and built up his representatives of Nature one above the other in steps, so that it all looked quite pretty and at the same time sufficiently significant. On an early sunrise his first worship of God was to be celebrated, but the young priest had not yet settled how to produce a flame which should at the same time emit an agreeable odour. At last it occurred to him to combine the two, as he possessed a few fumigating pastils, which diffused a pleasant fragrance with a glimmer, if not with a flame. Nay, this soft burning and exhalation seemed a better representation of what passes in the heart, than an open flame. The sun had already risen for a long time, but the neigbouring houses concealed the East. At last it glittered above the roofs, a burning-glass was at once taken up and applied to the pastils, which were fixed on the summit in a fine porcelain saucer. Everything succeeded according to the wish, and the devotion was perfect. The altar remained as a peculiar ornament of the room which had been assigned him in the new house. Every one regarded it only as a well-arranged collection of natural curiosities. The Boy knew better, but concealed his knowledge. He longed for a repetition of the solemnity. But unfortunately, just as the most opportune sun arose, the porcelain cup was not at hand; he placed the pastils immediately on the upper surface of the stand; they were kindled, and so great was the devotion of the priest, that he did not observe, until it was too late, the mischief his sacrifice was doing. The pastils had burned mercilessly into the red lacker and beautiful gold flowers, and as if some evil spirit had disappeared, had left their black, ineffaceable footprints. By this the young priest was thrown into the most extreme perplexity. The mischief could be covered up, it was true, with the larger pieces of his show-materials, but the spirit for new offerings was gone, and the accident might almost be considered a hint and warning of the danger there always is in wishing to approach the Deity in such a way.

SECOND BOOK.

ALL that has been hitherto recorded indicates that happy and easy condition in which nations exist during a long peace. But nowhere probably is such a beautiful time enjoyed in greater comfort than in cities living under their own laws, and large enough to include a considerable number of citizens, and so situated as to enrich them by trade and commerce. Strangers find it to their advantage to come and go, and are under a necessity of bringing profit in order to acquire profit. Even if such cities rule but a small territory, they are the better qualified to advance their internal prosperity, as their external relations expose them to no costly undertakings or alliances.

Thus, the Frankforters passed a series of prosperous years during my childhood; but scarcely, on the 28th of August, 1756, had I completed my seventh year, than that world-renowned war broke out, which was also to exert great influence upon the next seven years of my life. Frederick the Second, King of Prussia, had fallen upon Saxony, with sixty thousand men; and instead of announcing his invasion by a declaration of war, he followed it up with a manifesto, composed by himself, as it was said, which explained the causes that had moved and justified him in so monstrous a step. The world, which saw itself appealed to not merely as spectator but as judge, immediately split into two parties, and our family was an image of the great whole.

My grandfather, who, as *Schoff* of Frankfort, had carried the coronation canopy over Francis the First, and had received from the Empress a heavy gold chain with her likeness, took the Austrian side along with some of his sons-in-law and daughters. My father having been nominated to the imperial council by Charles the Seventh, and sympathising sincerely in the fate of that unhappy monarch, leaned towards Prussia, with the other and smaller half of the family. Our meetings, which had been held on Sundays for many years uninter-

ruptedly, were very soon disturbed. The misunderstandings
so common among relatives by marriage, now first found a
form in which they could be expressed. Contention, discord,
silence, and separation ensued. My grandfather, otherwise
a serene, quiet, and easy man, became impatient. The
women vainly endeavoured to smother the flames; and after
some unpleasant scenes, my father was the first to quit the
society. At home now we rejoiced undisturbed in the Prussian victories, which were commonly announced with great
glee by our vivacious aunt. Every other interest was forced
to give way to this, and we passed the rest of the year in
perpetual agitation. The occupation of Dresden, the moderation of the king at the outset, his slow but secure advances,
the victory at Lowositz, the capture of the Saxons, were so
many triumphs for our party. Everything that could be
alleged for the advantage of our opponents was denied or
depreciated; and as the members of the family on the other
side did the same, they could not meet in the streets without
disputes arising, as in *Romeo and Juliet.*

Thus I also was then a Prussian in my views, or, to speak
more correctly, a Fritzian; since what cared we for Prussia?
It was the personal character of the great king that worked
upon all hearts. I rejoiced with my father in our conquests,
readily copied the songs of triumph, and almost more willingly
the lampoons directed against the other party, poor as the
rhymes might be.

As the eldest grandson and godchild, I had dined every
Sunday since my infancy with my grandfather and grandmother, and the hours so spent had been the most delightful
of the whole week. But now I relished no morsel that I
tasted, because I was compelled to hear the most horrible
slanders of my hero. Here blew another wind, here sounded
another tone than at home. My liking and even my respect
for my grandfather and grandmother fell off. I could mention
nothing of this to my parents, but avoided the matter, both on
account of my own feelings, and because I had been warned
by my mother. In this way I was thrown back upon myself;
and as in my sixth year, after the earthquake at Lisbon, the
goodness of God had become to me in some measure suspicious,
so I began now, on account of Frederick the Second, to doubt
the justice of the public. My heart was naturally inclined to

D

reverence, and it required a great shock to stagger my faith in anything that was venerable. But alas! they had commended good manners and a becoming deportment to us, not for their own sake, but for the sake of the people. What will people say? was always the cry, and I thought that the people must be right good people, and would know how to judge of anything and everything. But my experience went just to the contrary. The greatest and most signal services were defamed and attacked; the noblest deeds, if not denied, were at least misrepresented and diminished; and this base injustice was done to the only man who was manifestly elevated above all his contemporaries, and who daily proved what he was able to do,— and that, not by the populace, but by distinguished men, as I took my grandfather and uncles to be. That parties existed, and that he himself belonged to a party, had never entered into the conceptions of the Boy. He, therefore, believed himself all the more right, and dared hold his own opinion for the better one, since he and those of like mind appreciated the beauty and other good qualities of Maria Theresa, and even did not grudge the Emperor Francis his love of jewelry and money. That Count Daun was often called an old dozer, they thought justifiable.

But now I consider the matter more closely, I trace here the germ of that disregard and even disdain of the public, which clung to me for a whole period of my life, and only in later days was brought within bounds by insight and cultivation. Suffice it to say, that the perception of the injustice of parties had even then a very unpleasant, nay, an injurious effect upon the Boy, as it accustomed him to separate himself from beloved and highly-valued persons. The quick succession of battles and events left the parties neither quiet nor rest. We ever found a malicious delight in reviving and re-sharpening those imaginary evils and capricious disputes; and thus we continued to tease each other, until the occupation of Frankfort by the French some years afterwards, brought real inconvenience into our homes.

Although to most of us the important events occurring in distant parts served only for topics of ardent controversy, there were others who perceived the seriousness of the times, and feared that the sympathy of France might open a scene of war in our own vicinity. They kept us children at home

more than before, and strove in many ways to occupy and
amuse us. With this view, the puppet-show bequeathed by
our grandmother was again brought forth, and arranged in
such a way that the spectators sat in my gable room, while
the persons managing and performing, as well as the theatre
itself as far as the proscenium, found a place in the room
adjoining. We were allowed, as a special favour, to invite
first one and then another of the neighbours' children as
spectators, and thus at the outset I gained many friends;
but the restlessness inherent in children, did not suffer them
to remain long a patient audience. They interrupted the
play, and we were compelled to seek a younger public, which
could at any rate be kept in order by the nurses and maids,
The original drama to which the puppets had been specially
adapted, we had learnt by heart, and in the beginning this was
exclusively performed. Soon growing weary of it, however,
we changed the dresses and decorations, and attempted various
other pieces, which were indeed on too grand a scale for so
narrow a stage. Although this presumption spoiled and finally
quite destroyed what we performed, such childish pleasures and
employments nevertheless exercised and advanced in many
ways my power of invention and representation, my fancy and
a certain technical skill, to a degree which in any other way
could not perhaps have been secured in so short a time, in
so confined a space, and at so little expense.

I had early learned to use compasses and ruler, because all
the instructions they gave me in geometry were forthwith
put into practice, and I occupied myself greatly with paste-
board-work. I did not stop at geometrical figures, little
boxes, and such things, but invented pretty pleasure-houses
adorned with pilasters, steps, and flat roofs. However, but
little of this was completed.

Far more persevering was I, on the other hand, in arranging,
with the help of our domestic (a tailor by trade), an armoury
for the service of our plays and tragedies, which we ourselves
performed with delight when we had outgrown the puppets.
My playfellows, too, prepared for themselves such armouries,
which they regarded as quite as fine and good as mine; but I
had made provision not for the wants of one person only, and
could furnish several of the little band with every requisite,
and thus made myself more and more indispensable to our

little circle. That such games tended to factions, quarrels,
and blows, and commonly came to a sad end in tumult and
vexation, may easily be supposed. In such cases certain of
my companions generally took part with me, while others
sided against me; though many changes of party occurred.
One single boy, whom I will call Pylades, urged by the others,
once only left my party, but could scarcely for a moment
maintain his hostile position. We were reconciled amid many
tears, and for a long time afterwards kept faithfully together.

To him, as well as other well-wishers, I could render myself
very agreeable by telling tales, which they most delighted to
hear when I was the hero of my own story. It greatly rejoiced them to know that such wonderful things could befall
one of their own playfellows: nor was it any harm that they
did not understand how I could find time and space for such
adventures, as they must have been pretty well aware of all my
comings and goings, and how I was occupied the entire day.
Not the less necessary was it for me to select the localities
of these occurrences, if not in another world, at least in another
spot; and yet all was told as having taken place only to-day
or yesterday. They rather, therefore, deceived themselves,
than were imposed upon by me. If I had not gradually
learned, in accordance with the instincts of my nature, to
work up these visions and conceits into artistic forms, such
vain-glorious beginnings could not have gone on without
producing evil consequences in the end.

Considering this impulse more closely, we may see in it
that presumption with which the poet authoritatively utters
the greatest improbabilities, and requires every one to recognise as real whatever may in any way seem to him, the
inventor, as true.

But what is here told only in general terms, and by way of
reflection, will perhaps become more apparent and interesting
by means of an example. I subjoin, therefore, one of these
tales, which, as I often had to repeat it to my comrades,
still hovers entire in my imagination and memory.

THE NEW PARIS.

A BOY'S LEGEND.

ON the night before Whit Sunday, not long since, I dreamed
that I stood before a mirror, engaged with the new summer
clothes which my dear parents had given me for the holiday.
The dress consisted, as you know, of shoes of polished leather,
with large silver buckles, fine cotton stockings, black nether
garments of serge, and a coat of green baracan with gold
buttons. The waistcoat of gold cloth was cut out of my
father's bridal waistcoat. My hair had been frizzled and powdered, and my curls stuck out from my head like little wings;
but I could not finish dressing myself, because I kept confusing
the different articles, the first always falling off as soon as I
was about to put on the next. In this dilemma, a young and
handsome man came to me, and greeted me in the friendliest
manner. "O! you are welcome!" said I, "I am very glad to
see you here." "Do you know me, then?" replied he, smiling.
"Why not?" was my no less smiling answer: "you are Mercury—I have often enough seen you represented in pictures."
"I am, indeed," replied he; "and am sent to you by the gods
on an important errand. Do you see these three apples?"—he
stretched forth his hand, and showed me three apples, which
it could hardly hold, and which were as wonderfully beautiful
as they were large, the one of a red, the other of a yellow,
the third of a green colour. One could not help thinking
they were precious stones made into the form of fruit. I
would have snatched them, but he drew back, and said, "You
must know, in the first place, that they are not for you. You
must give them to the three handsomest youths of the city, who
then, each according to his lot, will find wives to the utmost
of their wishes. Take them, and success to you!" said he, as
he departed, leaving the apples in my open hands. They
appeared to me to have become still larger. I held them up
at once against the light and found them quite transparent;
but soon they expanded upwards, and became three beautiful
little ladies, about as large as middle-sized dolls, whose clothes
were of the colours of the apples. They glided gently up my
fingers, and when I was about to catch at them, to make sure
of one at least, they had already soared high and far, and I

had to put up with the disappointment. I stood there all
amazed and petrified, holding up my hands and staring at my
fingers, as if there were still something on them to see. Suddenly I beheld, upon the very tips, a most lovely girl dancing,
smaller than those, but pretty and lively, and as she did not
fly away like the others, but remained dancing, now on one
finger-point now on another, I regarded her for a long while
with admiration. And, as she pleased me so much, I thought
in the end I could catch her, and made as I fancied a very
adroit grasp. But at the moment I felt such a blow on my
head, that I fell down stunned, and did not awake from my
stupor till it was time to dress myself and go to church.

During the service I often recalled those images to mind;
and also when I was eating dinner at my grand-father's
table. In the afternoon, I wished to visit some friends,
partly to show myself in my new dress, with my hat under
my arm and my sword by my side, and partly to return
their visits. I found no one at home, and, as I heard that
they were gone to the gardens, I resolved to follow them, and
pass the evening pleasantly. My way led towards the en-
trenchments, and I came to the spot which is rightly called
the Bad Wall; for it is never quite safe from ghosts there. I
walked slowly, and thought of my three goddesses, but especially of the little nymph; and often held up my fingers, in
hopes she might be kind enough to balance herself there
again. With such thoughts I was proceeding, when I saw in
the wall on my left hand a little gate, which I did not remember to have ever noticed before. It looked low, but its pointed
arch would have allowed the tallest man to enter. Arch and
wall were chiselled out in the handsomest way, both by mason
and sculptor: but it was the door itself which first properly
attracted my attention. The old brown wood, though slightly
ornamented, was crossed with broad bands of brass, wrought
both in relief and intaglio. The foliage on these, with the
most natural birds sitting in it, I could not sufficiently admire.
But, what seemed most remarkable, no keyhole could be seen,
no latch, no knocker; and from this I conjectured that the
door could be opened only from within. I was not in error;
for when I went nearer, in order to touch the ornaments, it
opened inwards, and there appeared a man whose dress was
somewhat long, wide, and singular. A venerable beard enve-

loped his chin, so that I was inclined to think him a Jew. But he, as if he had divined my thoughts, made the sign of the Holy Cross, by which he gave me to understand that he was a good Catholic Christian. " Young gentleman, how came you here, and what are you doing?"—he said to me, with a friendly voice and manner. " I am admiring," I replied, " the workmanship of this door; for I have never seen anything like it, except in some small pieces in the collections of amateurs." " I am glad," he answered, ' that you like such works. The door is much more beautiful inside. Come in, if you like." My heart, in some degree, failed me. The mysterious dress of the porter, the seclusion, and a something, I know not what, that seemed to be in the air, oppressed me. I paused, therefore, under the pretext of examining the outside still longer; and at the same time I cast stolen glances into the garden, for a garden it was which had opened before me. Just inside the door I saw a space. Old linden trees, standing at regular distances from each other, entirely covered it with their thickly interwoven branches, so that the most numerous parties, during the hottest of the day, might have refreshed themselves in the shade. Already I had stepped upon the threshold, and the old man contrived gradually to allure me on. Properly speaking, I did not resist ; for I had always heard that a prince or sultan in such a case must never ask whether there be danger at hand. I had my sword by my side, too ; and could I not soon have finished with the old man, in case of hostile demonstrations? I therefore entered perfectly reassured ; the keeper closed the door, which bolted so softly that I scarcely heard it. He now showed me the workmanship on the inside, which in truth was still more artistic than the outside, explained it to me, and at the same time manifested particular good-will. Being thus entirely at my ease, I let myself be guided in the shaded space by the wall, that formed a circle, where I found much to admire. Niches tastefully adorned with shells, corals, and pieces of ore, poured a profusion of water from the mouths of Tritons into marble basins. Between them were aviaries and other lattice-work, in which squirrels frisked about, guinea-pigs ran hither and thither, with as many other pretty little creatures as one could wish to see. The birds called and sang to us as we advanced ; the starlings particularly chattered the

silliest stuff. One always cried, Paris! Paris! and the other,
Narcissus! Narcissus! as plainly as a schoolboy can say them.
The old man seemed to continue looking at me earnestly while
the birds called out thus, but I feigned not to notice it, and
had in truth no time to attend to him; for I could easily perceive that we went round and round, and that this shaded
space was in fact a great circle, which inclosed another much
more important. Indeed we had actually reached the small
door again, and it seemed as though the old man would let me
out. But my eyes remained directed towards a golden railing,
which seemed to hedge round the middle of this wonderful
garden, and which I had found means enough of observing in
our walk, although the old man managed to keep me always
close to the wall, and therefore pretty far from the centre.
And now, just as he was going to the door, I said to him, with
a bow. "You have been so extremely kind to me, that I would
fain venture to make one more request before I part from you.
Might I not look more closely at that golden railing, which
appears to inclose in a very wide circle the interior of the
garden?" "Very willingly," replied he: "but in that case
you must submit to some conditions." "In what do they
consist?" I asked hastily. "You must leave here your hat
and sword, and must not let go my hand while I accompany
you." "Most willingly." I replied: and laid my hat and
sword on the nearest stone bench. Immediately he grasped
my left hand with his right, held it fast, and led me with
some force straight forwards. When we reached the railing,
my wonder changed into amazement. On a high socle of
marble stood innumerable spears and partisans, ranged beneath
each other, joined by their strangely ornamented points, and
forming a complete circle. I looked through the intervals,
and saw just behind a gently flowing piece of water, bounded
on both sides by marble, and displaying in its clear depths a
multitude of gold and silver fish, which moved about now
slowly and now swiftly, now alone and now in shoals. I would
also fain have looked beyond the canal, to see what there was
in the heart of the garden. But I found, to my great sorrow,
that the other side of the water was bordered by a similar
railing, and with so much art, that to each interval on this
side exactly fitted a spear or partisan on the other. These
and the other ornaments rendered it impossible for one to see

through, stand as one would. Besides, the old man, who still
held me fast, prevented me from moving freely. My curiosity,
meanwhile, after all that I had seen, increased more and more;
and I took heart to ask the old man whether one could not
pass over. " Why not?" returned he, " but on new conditions." When I asked him what these were, he gave me to
understand that I must put on other clothes. I was satisfied
to do so; he led me back towards the wall, into a small neat
room, on the sides of which hung many kinds of garments, all
of which seemed to approach the oriental costume. I soon
changed my dress. He confined my powdered hair under a
many coloured net, after having to my horror violently dusted
it out. Now standing before a great mirror, I found myself
quite handsome in my disguise, and pleased myself better
than in my formal Sunday clothes. I made gestures and
leaped as I had seen the dancers do at the Fair-theatre. In
the midst of this I looked in the glass, and saw by chance the
image of a niche which was behind me. On its white ground
hung three green cords, each of them twisted up in a way
which from the distance I could not clearly discern. I therefore turned round rather hastily, and asked the old man about
the niche as well as the cords. He very courteously took a
cord down, and showed it to me. It was a band of green silk
of moderate thickness; the ends of which joined by green
leather with two holes in it, gave it the appearance of an instrument for no very desirable purpose. The thing struck me
as suspicious, and I asked the old man the meaning. He
answered me very quietly and kindly, " This is for those who
abuse the confidence which is here readily shown them." He
hung the cord again in its place, and immediately desired me
to follow him; for this time he did not hold me, and so I
walked freely beside him.

My chief curiosity now was to discover where the gate and
bridge, for passing through the railing and over the canal,
might be; since as yet I had not been able to find anything of
the kind. I therefore watched the golden fence very narrowly
as we hastened towards it. But in a moment my sight failed;
lances, spears, halberds, and partisans, began unexpectedly to
rattle and quiver, and this strange movement ended in all the
points sinking towards each other, just as if two ancient hosts,
armed with pikes, were about to charge. The confusion to

the eyes, the clatter to the ears, was hardly to be borne; but
infinitely surprising was the sight when falling perfectly level,
they covered the circle of the canal, and formed the most
glorious bridge that one can imagine. For now a most variegated garden parterre met my sight. It was laid out in cur-
vilinear beds, which, looked at together, formed a labyrinth of
ornaments; all with green borders of a low woolly plant,
which I had never seen before; all with flowers, each division
of different colours, which being likewise low and close to the
ground, allowed the plan to be easily traced. This delicious
sight, which I enjoyed in the full sunshine, quite rivetted my
eyes. But I hardly knew where I was to set my foot; for the
serpentine paths were most delicately laid with blue sand, which
seemed to form upon the earth a darker sky, or a sky seen in
the water: and so I walked for a while beside my conductor,
with my eyes fixed upon the ground, until at last I perceived
that, in the middle of this round of beds and flowers, there
was a great circle of cypresses or poplar-like trees, through
which one could not see, because the lowest branches seemed
to spring out of the ground. My guide, without taking me
directly the shortest way, led me nevertheless immediately
towards that centre: and how was I astonished, when on
entering the circle of high trees, I saw before me the peristyle
of a magnificent garden-house, which seemed to have similar
prospects and entrances on the other sides! The heavenly
music which streamed from the building, transported me
still more than this model of architecture. I fancied that I
heard now a lute, now a harp, now a guitar, and now something jingling, which did not belong to any of these instruments. The door which we approached opened soon after
a light touch by the old man. But how was I amazed, when
the porteress, who came out, perfectly resembled the delicate
girl who had danced upon my fingers in the dream! She
greeted me as if we were already acquainted, and invited me
to walk in. The old man remained behind, and I went with
her through a short passage, arched and finely ornamented, to
the middle hall, the splendid dome-like ceiling of which
attracted my gaze on my entrance, and filled me with astonishment. Yet my eye could not linger long on this, being
allured down by a more charming spectacle. On a carpet,
directly under the middle of the cupola, sat three women, in

a triangle, clad in three different colours; one red, the other yellow, the third green. The seats were gilt, and the carpet was a perfect flower-bed. In their arms lay the three instruments which I had been able to distinguish from the outside; for being disturbed by my arrival, they had stopped their playing. " Welcome!" said the middle one, who sat with her face to the door, in a red dress, and with the harp. " Sit down by Alert, and listen, if you are a lover of music."

Now first I remarked that there was a rather long bench placed obliquely before them, on which lay a mandoline. The pretty girl took it up, sat down, and drew me to her side. Now also I looked at the second lady on my right. She wore the yellow dress, and had the guitar in her hand; and if the harp-player was dignified in form, grand in features, and majestic in her deportment, one might remark in the guitar-player an easy grace and cheerfulness. She was a slender blonde—while the other was adorned by dark brown hair. The variety and accordance of their music could not prevent me from remarking the third beauty, in the green dress, whose lute-playing was for me at once touching and striking. She was the one who seemed to notice me the most, and to direct her music to me; only I could not make up my mind about her; for she appeared to me now tender, now whimsical, now frank, now self-willed, according as she changed her mien and mode of playing. Sometimes she seemed to wish to move me, sometimes to teaze me; but do what she would, she got little out of me; for my little neighbour, by whom I sat elbow to elbow, had gained me entirely to herself; and while I clearly saw in those three ladies the Sylphides of my dream, and recognised the colours of the apples, I conceived that I had no cause to detain them. The pretty little maiden I would rather have captured, if I had not but too feelingly remembered the blow which she had given me in my dream. Hitherto she had remained quite quiet with her mandoline; but when her mistresses had ceased, they commanded her to perform some pleasant little piece. Scarcely had she jingled off some dancing tune, in a most exciting manner, than she sprang up; I did the same. She played and danced; I was hurried on to accompany her steps, and we executed a kind of little ballet, with which the ladies seemed satisfied; for as soon as we had done, they commanded the little girl to refresh

me with something nice till supper should come in. I had
indeed forgotten that there was anything in the world beyond
this paradise. Alert led me back immediately into the passage
by which I had entered. On one side of it she had two well-
arranged rooms. In that in which she lived, she set before me
oranges, figs, peaches, and grapes; and I enjoyed with great
gusto both the fruits of foreign lands and those of our own
not yet in season. Confectionary there was in profusion;
she filled, too, a goblet of polished crystal with foaming wine;
but I had no need to drink, as I had refreshed myself with
the fruits. "Now we will play," said she, and led me into
the other room. Here all looked like a Christmas fair; but
such costly and exquisite things were never seen in a Christmas booth. There were all kinds of dolls, dolls' clothes, and
dolls' furniture; kitchens, parlours, and shops, and single toys
innumerable. She led me round to all the glass cases, in
which these ingenious works were preserved. But she soon
closed again the first cases, and said—"That is nothing
for you, I know well enough. Here," she said, "we could
find building materials, walls and towers, houses, palaces,
churches, to put together a great city. But this does not
entertain me. We will take something else, which will be
pleasant alike to both of us." Then she brought out some
boxes, in which I saw an army of little soldiers piled one upon
the other, of which I must needs confess that I had never seen
anything so beautiful. She did not leave me time to examine
them closely in detail, but took one box under her arm, while I
seized the other.—"We will go," she said, "upon the golden
bridge. There one plays best with soldiers: the lances give
at once the direction in which the armies are to be opposed to
each other." We had now reached the golden trembling
floor; and below me I could hear the waters gurgle, and the
fishes splash, while I knelt down to range my columns. All,
as I now saw, were cavalry. She boasted that she had the
Queen of the Amazons as leader of her female host. I, on
the contrary, found Achilles and a very stately Grecian
cavalry. The armies stood facing each other, and nothing
could have been seen more beautiful. They were not flat
leaden horsemen like ours, but man and horse were round and
solid, and most finely wrought; nor could one conceive how
they kept their balance, for they stood of themselves, without
a support for their feet.

Both of us had inspected our hosts with much self-complacency, when she announced the onset. We had found ordnance
in our chests, viz., little boxes full of well-polished agate balls.
With these we were to fight against each other from a certain
distance, while, however, it was an express condition that we
should not throw with more force than was necessary to upset
the figures, as none of them were to be injured. Now the
cannonade began on both sides, and at first it succeeded to the
satisfaction of us both. But when my adversary observed
that I aimed better than she, and might in the end win the
victory, which depended on the majority of pieces remaining
upright, she came nearer, and her girlish way of throwing
had then the desired result. She prostrated a multitude of
my best troops, and the more I protested the more eagerly
did she throw. This at last vexed me, and I declared that I
would do the same. In fact, I not only went nearer, but in
my rage threw with much more violence, so that it was not
long before a pair of her little centauresses flew in pieces. In
her eagerness she did not instantly notice it, but I stood
petrified when the broken figures joined together again of
themselves : Amazon and horse became again one whole, and
also perfectly close, set up a gallop from the golden bridge
under the lime-trees, and running swiftly backwards and forwards, were lost in their career, I know not how, in the
direction of the wall. My fair opponent had hardly perceived
this, when she broke out into loud weeping and lamentation,
and exclaimed that I had caused her an irreparable loss, which
was far greater than could be expressed. But I, by this time
provoked, was glad to annoy her, and blindly flung a couple
of the remaining agate balls with force into the midst of her
army. Unhappily I hit the queen, who had hitherto, during
our regular game, been excepted. She flew in pieces, and
her nearest officers were also shivered. But they swiftly set
themselves up again, and started off like the others, galloping
very merrily about under the lime-trees, and disappearing
against the wall. My opponent scolded and abused me ; but
being now in full play, I stooped to pick up some agate balls
which rolled about upon the golden lances. It was my fierce
desire to destroy her whole army. She, on the other hand,
not idle, sprang at me, and gave me a box on the ear which
made my head ring again. Having always heard that a

hearty kiss was the proper response to a girl's box of the ear,
I took her by the ears, and kissed her repeatedly. But she
gave such a piercing cry as frightened even me; I let her go,
and it was fortunate that I did so; for in a moment I knew
not what was happening to me. The ground beneath me
began to quake and rattle; I soon remarked that the railings
again set themselves in motion; but I had no time to consider, nor could I get a footing so as to fly. I feared every
instant to be pierced, for the partisans and lances, which had
lifted themselves up, were already slitting my clothes. It is
sufficient to say that, I know not how it was, hearing and sight
failed me, and I recovered from my swoon and terror at the
foot of a lime-tree, against which the pikes in springing up
had thrown me. As I awoke, my anger awakened also, and
violently increased when I heard from the other side the gibes
and laughter of my opponent, who had probably reached the
earth somewhat more softly than I. Thereupon I sprang up,
and as I saw the little host, with its leader Achilles, scattered
around me, having been driven over with me by the rising of
the rails, I seized the hero first and threw him against a tree.
His resuscitation and flight now pleased me doubly, a malicious
pleasure combining with the prettiest sight in the world; and
I was on the point of sending all the other Greeks after him,
when suddenly hissing waters spurted at me on all sides, from
stones and walls, from ground and branches; and wherever I
turned dashed against me crossways.

My light garment was in a short time wet through; it was
already rent, and I did not hesitate to tear it entirely off my
body. I cast away my slippers, and one covering after
another. Nay, at last I found it very agreeable to let such a
shower-bath play over me in the warm day. Now, being
quite naked, I walked gravely along between these welcome
waters, where I thought to enjoy myself for some time. My
anger cooled, and I wished for nothing more than a reconciliation with my little adversary. But, in a twinkling the water
stopped, and I stood drenched upon the saturated ground.
The presence of the old man, who appeared before me unexpectedly, was by no means welcome; I could have wished, if
not to hide, at least to clothe myself. The shame, the shiver-
ing, the effort to cover myself in some degree, made me cut a
most piteous figure. The old man employed the moment in

venting the severest reproaches against me. "What hinders
me," he exclaimed, "from taking one of the green cords, and
fitting it, if not to your neck, to your back?" This threat I
took in very ill part. "Refrain," I cried, "from such words,
even from such thoughts, for otherwise you and your mistresses will be lost." "Who then are you," he asked in
defiance, "who dare speak thus?" "A favourite of the
gods," I said, "on whom it depends whether those ladies shall
find worthy husbands and pass a happy life, or be left to pine
and wither in their magic cell." The old man stepped some
paces back. "Who has revealed that to you?" he inquired,
with astonishment and concern. "Three apples," I said—
"three jewels." "And what reward do you require?" he
exclaimed. "Before all things, the little creature," I replied,
"who has brought me into this accursed state." The old man
cast himself down before me, without shrinking from the wet
and miry soil; then he arose without being wetted, took me
kindly by the hand, led me into the hall, clad me again
quickly, and I was soon once more decked out and frizzled in
my Sunday fashion as before. The porter did not speak
another word; but before he let me pass the entrance, he
stopped me, and showed me some objects on the way over the
way, while, at the same time, he pointed backwards to the
door. I understood him; he wished to imprint the objects on
my mind, that I might the more certainly find the door, which
had unexpectedly closed behind me. I now took good notice
of what was opposite to me. Above a high wall rose the
boughs of extremely old nut-trees, and partly covered the
cornice at the top. The branches reached down to a stone
tablet, the ornamented border of which I could perfectly
recognise, though I could not read the inscription. It rested
on the corbel of a niche, in which a finely-wrought fountain
poured water from cup to cup into a great basin, that formed,
as it were, a little pond, and disappeared in the earth. Fountain, inscription, nut-trees, all stood directly one above
another; I would paint it as I saw it.

Now, it may well be conceived how I passed this evening
and many following days, and how often I repeated to myself
this story, which even I could hardly believe. As soon as it
was in any degree possible, I went again to the Bad Wall, at
least to refresh my remembrance of these signs, and to look at

the precious door. But, to my great amazement, I found all changed. Nut-trees, indeed, overtopped the wall, but they did not stand immediately in contact. A tablet also was inserted in the wall, but far to the right of the trees, without ornament, and with a legible inscription. A niche with a fountain was found far to the left, but with no resemblance whatever to that which I had seen ; so that I almost believed that the second adventure was, like the first, a dream ; for of the door there is not the slightest trace. The only thing that consoles me is the observation, that these three objects seem always to change their places. For in repeated visits to the spot, I think I have noticed that the nut-trees have moved somewhat nearer together, and that the tablet and the fountain seem likewise to approach each other. Probably, when all is brought together again, the door, too, will once more be visible; and I will do my best to take up the thread of the adventure. Whether I shall be able to tell you what further happens, or whether it will be expressly forbidden me, I cannot say.

This tale, of the truth of which my playfellows vehemently strove to convince themselves, received great applause. Each of them visited alone the place described, without confiding it to me or the others, and discovered the nut-trees, the tablet, and the spring, though always at a distance from each other ; as they at last confessed to me afterwards, because it is not easy to conceal a secret at that early age. But here the contest first arose. One asserted that the objects did not stir from the spot and always maintained the same distance: a second averred that they did move, and that too away from each other : a third agreed with the latter as to the first point of their moving, though it seemed to him that the nut-tree, tablet, and fountain rather drew near together : while a fourth had something still more wonderful to announce, which was, that the nut-trees were in the middle, but that the tablet and the fountain were on sides opposite to those which I had stated. With respect to the traces of the little door they also varied. And thus they furnished me an early instance of the contradictory views men can hold and maintain in regard to matters quite simple and easily cleared up. As I obstinately refused the continuation of my tale, a repetition of the first part was often desired. I was on my guard, however, not to change the circumstances much, and by the uniformity of the narrative I converted the fable into truth in the minds of my hearers.

Yet I was averse to falsehood and dissimulation, and altogether by no means frivolous. Rather, on the contrary, the inward earnestness with which I had early begun to consider myself and the world, was seen even in my exterior, and I was frequently called to account, often in a friendly way, and often in raillery, for a certain dignity which I had assumed. For, although good and chosen friends were certainly not wanting to me, we were always a minority against those who found pleasure in assailing us with wanton rudeness, and who indeed often awoke us in no gentle fashion from that legendary and self-complacent dreaming in which we—I by inventing, and my companions by sympathising—were too readily absorbed. Thus we learned once more, that instead of sinking into effeminacy and fantastic delights, there was reason rather for hardening ourselves, in order either to bear or to counteract inevitable evils.

Among the stoical exercises which I cultivated, as earnestly as it was possible for a lad, was even the endurance of bodily pain. Our teachers often treated us very unkindly and unskilfully, with blows and cuffs, against which we hardened ourselves all the more as refractoriness was forbidden under the severest penalties. A great many of the sports of youth, moreover, depend on a rivalry in such endurances; as, for instance, when they strike each other alternately, with two fingers or the whole fist, till the limbs are numbed, or when they bear the penalty of blows, incurred in certain games, with more or less firmness; when in wrestling or scuffling they do not let themselves be perplexed by the pinches of a half-conquered opponent; or finally, when they suppress the pain inflicted, for the sake of teasing, and even treat with indifference the nips and ticklings with which young persons are so active towards each other. Thus we gain a great advantage, of which others cannot speedily deprive us.

But as I made a sort of boast of this impassiveness, the importunity of the others was increased; and, since rude barbarity knows no limits, it managed to force me beyond my bounds. Let one case suffice for several. It happened once that the teacher did not come at the usual hour for instruction.

E

As long as we children were all together, we entertained ourselves quite agreeably; but when my adherents, after waiting long enough, went away, and I remained alone with three of my enemies, these took it into their heads to torment me, to shame me, and to drive me away. Having left me an instant in the room, they came back with switches, which they had made by quickly cutting up a broom. I noted their design, and as I supposed the end of the hour near, I at once resolved not to resist them till the clock struck. They began, therefore, without remorse, to lash my legs and calves in the cruellest fashion. I did not stir, but soon felt that I had miscalculated, and that such pain greatly lengthened the minutes. My wrath grew with my endurance, and at the first stroke of the hour, I grasped the one who least expected it by the hair behind, hurled him to the earth in an instant, pressing my knee upon his back; the second, a younger and weaker one, who attacked me from behind, I drew by the head under my arm, and almost throttled him with the pressure. The last, and not the weakest, still remained; and my left hand only was left for my defence. But I seized him by the clothes, and with a dexterous twist on my part, and an over precipitate one on his, I brought him down and struck his face on the ground. They were not wanting in bites, pinches, and kicks, but I had nothing but revenge in my limbs as well as in my heart. With the advantage which I had acquired, I repeatedly knocked their heads together. At last they raised a dreadful shout of murder, and we were soon surrounded by all the inmates of the house. The switches scattered around, and my legs, which I had bared of the stockings, soon bore witness for me. They put off the punishment, and let me leave the house; but I declared that in future, on the slightest offence, I would scratch out the eyes, tear off the ears, of any one of them, if not throttle him.

This event, though, as usually happens in childish affairs, it was soon forgotten, and even laughed over, was yet the cause that these instructions in common became fewer, and at last entirely ceased. I was thus again, as formerly, kept more at home, where I found my sister Cornelia, who was only one year younger than myself, a companion always growing more agreeable.

Still, I will not leave this topic without narrating some more stories of the many vexations caused me by my playfellows; for this is the instructive part of such moral communications, that a man may learn how it has gone with others, and what he also has to expect from life; and that whatever comes to pass, he may consider that it happens to him as a man, and not as one specially fortunate or unfortunate. If such knowledge is of little use for avoiding evils, it is very serviceable so far as it qualifies us to understand our condition, and bear or even to overcome it.

Another general remark will not be out of place here, which is, that as the children of the cultivated classes grow up, a great contradiction appears. I refer to the fact, that they are urged and trained, by parents and teachers, to deport themselves moderately, intelligently, and even wisely; to give pain to no one from petulance or arrogance, and to suppress all the evil impulses which may be developed in them; but yet, on the other hand, while the young creatures are engaged in this discipline, they have to suffer from others that which in them is reprimanded and punished. In this way, the poor things are brought into a sad strait between the natural and civilised states, and after restraining themselves for a while, break out according to their characters into cunning or violence.

Force is rather to be put down by force; but a well-disposed child, inclined to love and sympathy, has little to oppose to scorn and ill-will. Though I managed pretty well to keep off the active assaults of my companions, I was by no means equal to them in sarcasm and abuse; because he who merely defends himself in such cases, is always a loser. Attacks of this sort, consequently, when they went so far as to excite anger, were repelled with physical force, or at least excited strange reflections in me, which could not be without results. Among other advantages which my ill-wishers grudged me, was the pleasure I took in the relations that accrued to the family from my grandfather's position of Schultheiss, since, as he was the first of his class, this had no small effect on those belonging to him. Once, when after the holding of the Piper's-court, I appeared to pride myself on having seen my grandfather in the midst of the council, one step higher than the rest, enthroned, as it were, under the portrait of the Emperor, one of the boys said to me in derision, that like the peacock contemplating his feet, I should cast my eyes back to my

E 2

paternal grandfather, who had been keeper of the Willow-inn,
and would never have aspired to thrones and coronets. I
replied that I was in no wise ashamed of that, as it was the
glory and honour of our native city that all its citizens might
consider each other equal, and every one derive profit and
honour from his exertions in his own way. I was sorry only
that the good man had been so long dead; for I had often
yearned to know him in person, had many times gazed upon
his likeness, nay, had visited his tomb, and had at least
derived pleasure from the inscription on the simple monument of that past existence to which I was indebted for my
own. Another ill-wisher, who was the most malicious of all,
took the first aside, and whispered something in his ear, while
they still looked at me scornfully. My gall already began
to rise, and I challenged them to speak out. "What is more,
then, if you will have it," continued the first, "this one thinks
you might go looking about a long time before you could find
your grandfather!" I now threatened them more vehemently
if they did not more clearly explain themselves. Thereupon
they brought forward an old story, which they pretended to
have overheard from their parents, that my father was the son
of some eminent man, while that good citizen had shown himself willing to take outwardly the paternal office. They had
the impudence to produce all sorts of arguments; as, for
example, that our property came exclusively from our grandmother, that the other collateral relations, who lived in Fried-
burg and other places, were all alike destitute of property,
and other reasons of the sort, which could merely derive their
weight from malice. I listened to them more composedly than
they expected, for they stood ready to fly the very moment
that I should make a gesture as if I would seize their hair.
But I replied quite calmly, and in substance, "that even this
was no great injury to me. Life was such a boon, that one
might be quite indifferent as to whom one had to thank for
it, since at least it must be derived from God, before whom
we all were equals." As they could make nothing of it, they
let the matter drop for this time; we went on playing together
as before, which among children is an approved mode of
reconciliation.

Still these spiteful words inoculated me with a sort of moral
disease, which crept on in secret. It would not have dis-

pleased me at all to have been the grandson of any person of
consideration, even if it had not been in the most lawful way.
My acuteness followed up the scent—my imagination was
excited, and my sagacity put in requisition. I began to investigate the allegation, and invented or found for it new grounds
of probability. I had heard little said of my grandfather,
except that his likeness, together with my grandmother's, had
hung in a parlour of the old house ; both of which, after the
building of the new one, had been kept in an upper chamber.
My grandmother must have been a very handsome woman, and
of the same age as her husband. I remembered, also, to have
seen in her room the miniature of a handsome gentleman in
uniform, with star and order, which, after her death, and
during the confusion of house-building, had disappeared with
many other small pieces of furniture. These, and many other
things, I put together in my childish head, and exercised that
modern poetical talent which contrives to obtain the sympathies of the whole cultivated world by a marvellous combination of the important events of human life.

But as I did not venture to trust such an affair to any one,
or even to ask the most remote questions concerning it, I was
not wanting in a secret diligence, in order to get, if possible,
somewhat nearer to the matter. I had heard it explicitly
maintained, that sons often bore a decided resemblance to
their fathers or grandfathers. Many of our friends, especially
Councillor Schneider, a friend of the family, were connected
by business with all the princes and noblemen of the neighbourhood, of whom, including both the ruling and the younger
branches, not a few had estates on the Rhine and Maine, and
in the intermediate country, and who at times honoured their
faithful agents with their portraits. These, which I had often
seen on the walls from my infancy, I now regarded with redoubled attention, seeking whether I could not detect some
resemblance to my father or even to myself, which too often
happened to lead me to any degree of certainty. For now
it was the eyes of this, now the nose of that, which seemed
to indicate some relationship. Thus these marks led me
delusively backwards and forwards ; and though in the end I
was compelled to regard the reproach as a completely empty
tale, the impression remained, and I could not from time to
time refrain from privately calling up and testing all the noble-

men whose images had remained very clear in my fancy. So true is it that whatever inwardly confirms man in his self-conceit, or flatters his secret vanity, is so highly desirable to him, that he does not ask further, whether in other respects it may turn to his honour or his disgrace.

But instead of mingling here serious and even reproachful reflections, I rather turn my look away from those beautiful times ; for who is able to speak worthily of the fulness of childhood ? We cannot behold the little creatures which flit about before us otherwise than with delight, nay, with admiration ; for they generally promise more than they perform, and it seems that nature, among the other roguish tricks that she plays us, here also especially designs to make sport of us. The first organs she bestows upon children coming into the world, are adapted to the nearest immediate condition of the creature, which, unassuming and artless, makes use of them in the readiest way for its present purposes. The child, considered in and for itself, with its equals, and in relations suited to its powers, seems so intelligent and rational, and at the same time so easy, cheerful, and clever, that one can hardly wish it further cultivation. If children grew up according to early indications, we should have nothing but geniuses ; but growth is not merely development ; the various organic systems which constitute one man, spring one from another, follow each other, change into each other, supplant each other, and even consume each other ; so that after a time scarcely a trace is to be found of many aptitudes and manifestations of ability. Even when the talents of the man have on the whole a decided direction, it will be hard for the greatest and most experienced connoisseur to declare them beforehand with confidence, although afterwards it is easy to remark what has pointed to a future.

By no means, therefore, is it my design wholly to comprise the stories of my childhood in these first books ; but I will rather afterwards resume and continue many a thread which ran through the early years unnoticed. Here, however, I must remark what an increasing influence the incidents of the war gradually exercised upon our sentiments and mode of life.

The peaceful citizen stands in a wonderful relation to the great events of the world. They already excite and disquiet him from a distance, and even if they do not touch him, he can scarcely refrain from an opinion and a sympathy. Soon he takes a side, as his character or external circumstances may determine. But when such grand fatalities, such important changes, draw nearer to him, then with many outward inconveniences remains that inward discomfort, which doubles and sharpens the evil and destroys the good which is still possible. Then he has really to suffer from friends and foes, often more from those than from these, and he knows not how to secure and preserve either his interests or his inclinations.

The year 1757, which still passed in perfectly civic tranquillity, kept us, nevertheless, in great uneasiness of mind. Perhaps no other was more fruitful of events than this. Conquests, achievements, misfortunes, restorations, followed one upon another, swallowed up and seemed to destroy each other: yet the image of Frederick, his name and glory, soon hovered again above all. The enthusiasm of his worshippers grew always stronger and more animated, the hatred of his enemies more bitter, and the diversity of opinion, which separated even families, contributed not a little to isolate citizens, already sundered in many ways and on other grounds. For in a city like Frankfort, where three religions divide the inhabitants into three unequal masses, where only a few men, even of the ruling faith, can attain to political power, there must be many wealthy and educated persons who are thrown back upon themselves, and, by means of studies and tastes, form for themselves an individual and secluded existence. It will be necessary for us to speak of such men, now and hereafter, if we are to bring before us the peculiarities of a Frankfort citizen of that time.

My father, immediately after his return from his travels, had in his own way formed the design, that to prepare himself for the service of the city, he would undertake one of the subordinate offices, and discharge its duties without emolument, if it were conferred upon him without balloting. In the consciousness of his good intentions, and according to his way of thinking and the conception which he had of himself, he believed that he deserved such a distinction, which indeed was not conformable to law or precedent. Consequently, when his suit was rejected, he fell into ill-humour and disgust, vowed that he would never accept of any place, and in order to render it impossible, procured the title of Imperial Councillor,

which the Schultheiss and elder *Schöffen* bear as a special
honour. He had thus made himself an equal of the highest,
and could not begin again at the bottom. The same impulse
induced him also to woo the eldest daughter of the Schultheiss,
so that he was excluded from the council on this side also.
He was now of that number of recluses who never form themselves into a society. They are as much isolated in respect to
each other as they are in regard to the whole, and the more
so as in this seclusion the character becomes more and more
uncouth. My father, in his travels and in the world which he
had seen, might have formed some conception of a more
elegant and liberal mode of life than was, perhaps, common
among his fellow-citizens. In this respect, however, he was
not entirely without predecessors and associates.

The name of UFFENBACH is well known. At that time
there was a Schoff von Uffenbach, who was generally respected.
He had been in Italy, had applied himself particularly to
music, sang an agreeable tenor, and having brought home a
fine collection of pieces, concerts and oratorios were performed
at his house. Now, as he sang in these himself, and held
musicians in great favour, it was not thought altogether suitable to his dignity, and his invited guests, as well as the
other people of the country, allowed themselves many a jocose
remark on the matter.

I remember, too, a BARON VON HAKEL, a rich nobleman,
who being married, but childless, occupied a charming house
in the Antonius-street, fitted up with all the appurtenances
of a dignified position in life. He also possessed good
pictures, engravings, antiques, and much else which generally
accumulates with collectors and lovers of art. From time
to time he asked the more noted personages to dinner, and was
beneficent in a careful way of his own, since he clothed the
poor in his own house, but kept back their old rags, and gave
them a weekly charity, on condition that they should present
themselves every time clean and neat in the clothes bestowed
on them. I can recall him but indistinctly, as a genial, well-
made man; but more clearly his auction, which I attended
from beginning to end, and, partly by command of my father,
partly from my own impulse, purchased many things that are
still to be found in my collections.

At an earlier date than this—so early that I scarcely set

eyes upon him—John Michael von Loen gained considerable repute in the literary world, as well as at Frankfort. Not a native of Frankfort, he settled there, and married a sister of my grandmother Textor, whose maiden-name was Lindheim. Familiar with the court and political world, and rejoicing in a renewed title of nobility, he had acquired reputation by daring to take part in the various excitements which arose in Church and State. He wrote the *Count of Rivera*, a didactic romance, the subject of which is made apparent by the second title, "or, the Honest Man at Court." This work was well received, because it insisted on morality even in courts, where prudence only is generally at home; and thus his labour brought him applause and respect. A second work, for that very reason, would be accompanied by more danger. He wrote *The Only True Religion*, a book designed to advance tolerance, especially between Lutherans and Calvinists. But here he got in a controversy with the theologians: one Dr. Benner, of Giessen, in particular, wrote against him. Von Loen rejoined: the contest grew violent and personal, and the unpleasantness which arose from it caused him to accept the office of President at Lingen, which Frederick II. offered him, supposing that he was an enlightened, unprejudiced man, and not averse to the new views that more extensively obtained in France. His former countrymen, whom he left in some displeasure, averred that he was not contented there, nay, could not be so, as a place like Lingen was not to be compared with Frankfort. My father also doubted whether the President would be happy, and asserted that the good uncle would have done better not to connect himself with the king, as it was generally hazardous to get too near him, extraordinary sovereign as he undoubtedly was; for it had been seen how disgracefully the famous Voltaire had been arrested in Frankfort, at the requisition of the Prussian Resident Freitag, though he had formerly stood so high in favour, and had been regarded as the king's teacher in French poetry. There was no want, on such occasions, of reflections and examples, to warn one against courts and princes' service, of which a native Frankforter could scarcely form a conception.

An excellent man, Dr. Orth, I will only mention by name, because here I have not so much to erect a monument to the deserving citizens of Frankfort, but rather refer to them so far forth as their renown or personal character had some influence upon me in my earliest years. Dr. Orth was a wealthy man, and was also of that number who never took part in the government, although perfectly qualified to do so by his knowledge and penetration. The antiquities of Germany, and more especially of Frankfort, have been much indebted to him; he published remarks on the so-called *Reformation of Frankfort*, a work in which the statutes of the state are collected. The historical portions of this book I diligently read in my youth.

Von Ochsenstein, the eldest of the three brothers whom I have mentioned above as our neighbours, had not been remarkable during his lifetime, in consequence of his recluse habits, but became the more remarkable after his death, by leaving behind him a direction that common working-men should carry him to the grave, early in the morning, in perfect silence, and without an attendant or follower. This was done, and the affair excited great attention in the city, where they were accustomed to the most pompous funerals. All who discharged the customary offices on such occasions, rose against the innovation. But the stout patrician found imitators in all classes, and though such ceremonies were derisively called ox-burials,* they came into fashion, to the advantage of many of the more poorly-provided families, while funeral parades were less and less in vogue. I bring forward this circumstance, because it presents one of the earlier symptoms of that tendency to humility and equality, which in the second half of the last century was manifested in so many ways, from above downwards, and broke out in such unlooked-for effects.

Nor was there any lack of antiquarian amateurs. There were cabinets of pictures, collections of engravings, while the curiosities of our own country especially were zealously sought and hoarded. The older decrees and mandates of the imperial city, of which no collection had been prepared, were carefully searched for in print and manuscript, arranged in the order of time, and preserved with reverence, as a treasure of native laws and customs. The portraits of Frankforters, which existed in great number, were also brought together, and formed a special department of the cabinets.

* **A pun upon the name of Ochsenstein.—*Trans.***

Such men my father appears generally to have taken as his
models. He was wanting in none of the qualities that pertain
to an upright and respectable citizen. Thus, after he had
built his house, he put his property of every sort into order.
An excellent collection of maps by Schenck and other
geographers at that time eminent, the aforesaid decrees and
mandates, the portraits, a chest of ancient weapons, a case of
remarkable Venetian glasses, cups and goblets, natural curiosities, works in ivory, bronzes, and a hundred other things, were
separated and displayed, and I did not fail, whenever an
auction occurred, to get some commission for the increase of
his possessions.

I must still speak of one important family, of which I had
heard strange things since my earliest years, and of some of
whose members I myself lived to see a great deal that was
wonderful—I mean the SENKENBERGS. The father, of whom
I have little to say, was an opulent man. He had three sons,
who even in their youth uniformly distinguished themselves
as oddities. Such things are not well received in a limited city,
where no one is suffered to render himself conspicuous, either
for good or evil. Nicknames and odd stories, long kept in
memory, are generally the fruit of such singularity. The
father lived at the corner of Hare-street (*Hasengasse*), which
took its name from a sign on the house, that represented one
hare at least, if not three hares. They consequently called
these three brothers only the three Hares, which nick-name
they could not shake off for a long while. But as great
endowments often announce themselves in youth in the form
of singularity and awkwardness, so was it also in this case.
The eldest of the brothers was the *Reichshofrath* (Imperial
Councillor) von Senkenberg afterwards so celebrated. The
second was admitted into the magistracy, and displayed
eminent abilities, which, however, he subsequently abused in
a pettifogging and even infamous way, if not to the injury
of his native city, certainly to that of his colleagues. The
third brother, a physician and man of great integrity, but who
practised little, and that only in high families, preserved even
in his old age a somewhat whimsical exterior. He was
always very neatly dressed, and was never seen in the street
otherwise than in shoes and stockings, with a well-powdered
curled wig, and his hat under his arm. He walked on

rapidly, but with a singular sort of stagger, so that he was sometimes on one and sometimes on the other side of the way, and formed a complete zigzag as he went. The wags said that he made this irregular step to get out of the way of the departed souls, who might follow him in a straight line, and that he imitated those who are afraid of a crocodile. But all these jests and many merry sayings were transformed at last into respect for him, when he devoted his handsome dwelling-house in Eschenheimer-street, with court, garden, and all other appurtenances, to a medical establishment, where, in addition to a hospital designed exclusively for the citizens of Frankfort, a botanic garden, an anatomical theatre, a chemical laboratory, a considerable library, and a house for the director, were instituted in a way of which no university need have been ashamed.

Another eminent man, whose efficiency in the neighbourhood and whose writings, rather than his presence, had a very important influence upon me, was CHARLES FREDERICK VON MOSER, who was perpetually referred to in our district for his activity in business. He also had a character essentially moral, which as the vices of human nature frequently gave him trouble, inclined him to the so-called pious. Thus, what Von Loen had tried to do in respect to court life, he would have done for business-life, introducing into it a more conscientious mode of proceeding. The great number of small German courts gave rise to a multitude of princes and servants, the former of whom desired unconditional obedience, while the latter, for the most part, would work or serve only according to their own convictions. Thus arose an endless conflict, and rapid changes and explosions, because the effects of an unrestricted course of proceeding become much sooner noticeable and injurious on a small scale than on a large one. Many families were in debt, and Imperial Commissions of Debts were appointed; others found themselves sooner or later on the same road; while the officers either reaped an unconscionable profit, or conscientiously made themselves disagreeable and odious. Moser wished to act as a statesman and man of business, and here his hereditary talent, cultivated to a profession, gave him a decided advantage; but he at the same time wished to act as a man and a citizen, and surrender as little as possible of his moral dignity. His *Prince and*

Servant, his *Daniel in the Lions' Den,* his *Relics,* paint throughout his own condition, in which he felt himself not indeed tortured, but always cramped. They all indicate impatience in a condition, to the bearings of which one cannot reconcile oneself, yet from which one cannot get free. With this mode of thinking and feeling, he was, indeed, often compelled to seek other employments, which, on account of his great cleverness, were never wanting. I remember him as a pleasing, active, and at the same time gentle man.

The name of KLOPSTOCK had already produced a great effect upon us, even at a distance. In the outset, people wondered how so excellent a man could be so strangely named; but they soon got accustomed to this, and thought no more of the meaning of the syllables. In my father's library I had hitherto found only the earlier poets, especially those who in his day had gradually appeared and acquired fame. All these had written in rhyme, and my father held rhyme as indispensable in poetical works. Canitz, Hagedorn, Drollinger, Gellert, Creuz, Haller, stood in a row, in handsome calf bindings, to these were added Neukirch's *Telemachus,* Koppen's *Jerusalem Delivered,* and other translations. I had from my childhood diligently read through the whole of these works, and committed portions to memory, whence I was often called upon to amuse the company. A vexatious era on the other hand opened upon my father, when through Klopstock's *Messiah,* verses, which seemed to him no verses, became an object of public admiration.* He had taken good care not to buy this book; but the friend of the family, Councillor Schneider, smuggled it in, and slipped it into the hands of my mother and her children.

On this man of business, who read but little, the *Messiah,* as soon as it appeared, made a powerful impression. Those pious feelings, so naturally expressed, and yet so beautifully elevated, that agreeable language, even if considered merely as harmonious prose, had so won the otherwise dry man of business, that he regarded the first ten cantos, of which alone we are properly speaking, as the finest Book of Devotion, and once every year in Passion week, when he managed to escape from business, read it quietly through by himself, and thus refreshed himself for the entire year. In the beginning he

---

* The *Messiah* is written in hexameter verse.—*Trans.*

thought to communicate his emotions to his old friend; but
he was much shocked when forced to perceive an incurable
dislike cherished against a book of such valuable substance,
merely because of what appeared to him an indifferent external form.   It may readily be supposed that their conversation often reverted to this topic; but both parties diverged
more and more widely from each other, there were violent
scenes, and the compliant man was at last pleased to be silent
on his favourite work, that he might not lose, at the same
time, a friend of his youth, and a good Sunday meal.

It is the most natural wish of every man to make proselytes,
and how much did our friend find himself rewarded in secret,
when he discovered in the rest of the family hearts so openly
disposed for his saint.   The copy which he used only one week
during the year, was devoted to us all the remaining time.
My mother kept it secret, and we children took possession of
it when we could, that in leisure hours, hidden in some nook,
we might learn the most striking passages by heart, and particularly might impress the most tender as well as the most
violent parts on our memory, as quickly as possible.

Porcia's dream we recited in a sort of rivalry, and divided
between us the wild dialogue of despair between Satan and
Adramelech, who have been cast into the Red Sea.   The first
part, as the strongest, had been assigned to me, and the
second, as a little more pathetic, was undertaken by my
sister.   The alternate and horrible but well-sounding curses
flowed only thus from our mouths, and we seized every
opportunity to accost each other with these infernal phrases.

One Saturday evening, in winter—my father always had
himself shaved over night, that on Sunday morning he might
dress himself for church at his ease—we sat on a footstool
behind the stove, and muttered our customary imprecations in
a tolerably low voice, while the barber was putting on the
lather.   But now Adramelech had to lay his iron hands on
Satan; my sister seized me with violence, and recited, softly
enough, but with increasing passion :—

" Give me thine aid, I intreat thee, will worship thee, if thou requirest,
Thee, thou monster abandoned, yes thee, of all criminals blackest ;
And me, I suffer the tortures of death, which is vengeful, eternal,
Once, in the times gone by, with a hot fierce hate I could hate thee,
Now I can hate thee no more ! E'en this is the sharpest of tortures."

Thus far all went on tolerably; but loudly, with a dreadful voice, she cried the following words:—

"How am I crushed!"

The good surgeon was startled, and emptied the lather-basin into my father's bosom. There was a great uproar, and a severe investigation was held, especially with respect to the mischief which might have been done if the shaving had been actually going forward. In order to relieve ourselves of all suspicions of wantonness in the affair, we confessed our Satanic characters, and the misfortune occasioned by the hexameters was so apparent, that they were again condemned and banished.

Thus children and common people are accustomed to transform the great and sublime into a sport, and even a jest; and how indeed could they otherwise abide and tolerate it?

THIRD BOOK.

At that time the general interchange of personal good wishes made the city very lively on New Year's day. Those who otherwise did not easily leave home, donned their best clothes, that for a moment they might be friendly and courteous to their friends and patrons. The festivities at my grandfather's house on this day were pleasures particularly desired by us children. At early dawn the grandchildren had already assembled there to hear the drums, oboes, clarionets, trumpets, and cornets played upon by the military, the city musicians, and whoever else might furnish his tones. The New Year's gifts, sealed and superscribed, were divided by us children among the humbler congratulators, and, as the day advanced, the number of those of higher rank increased. The relations and intimate friends appeared first, then the subordinate officials; even the gentlemen of the council did not fail to pay their respects to the *Schultheiss*, and a select number were entertained in the evening in rooms which were else scarcely opened throughout the year. The tarts, biscuits, marchpane, and sweet wine had the greatest charm for the children, and, besides, the *Schultheiss* and the two Burgomasters annually received from some institutions some article of silver, which was then bestowed upon the grandchildren and godchildren in regular gradation. In fine, this small festival was not wanting in any of those things which usually glorify the greatest.

The New Year's day of 1759 approached, as desirable and pleasant to us children as any preceding one, but full of import and foreboding to older persons. To the passage of the French troops people certainly had become accustomed, and they happened often, but they had been most frequent in the last days of the past year. According to the old usage of an imperial town, the warder of the chief tower sounded his trumpet whenever troops approached, and on this New Year's day he would not leave off, which was a sign that large bodies were in motion on several sides. They actually

marched through the city in greater masses on this day, and the
people ran to see them pass by. We had generally been used
to see them go through in small parties, but these gradually
swelled, and there was neither power nor inclination to stop
them. In short, on the 2nd of January, after a column had
come through Sachsenhausen over the bridge, through the
Fahrgasse, as far as the Police Guard House—it halted, overpowered the small company which escorted it, took possession
of the before-mentioned Guard House, marched down the
Zeile, and after a slight resistance, the main guard were also
obliged to yield. In a moment the peaceful streets were
turned into a scene of war. The troops remained and
bivouacked there until lodgings were provided for them by
regular billetting.

This unexpected, and, for many years, unheard-of burden
weighed heavily upon the comfortable citizens, and to none
could it be more cumbersome than to my father, who was
obliged to take foreign military inhabitants into his scarcely
finished house, to open for them his well-furnished reception
rooms, which were generally closed, and to abandon to the
caprices of strangers all that he had been used to arrange and
keep so carefully. Siding as he did with the Prussians, he
was now to find himself besieged in his own chambers by the
French :—it was, according to his way of thinking, the greatest
misfortune that could happen to him. Had it, however, been
possible for him to have taken the matter more easily, he
might have saved himself and us many sad hours, since he spoke
French well, and could deport himself with dignity and grace
in the daily intercourse of life. For it was the King's Lieutenant who was quartered on us, and he, although a military
person, had only to settle civil occurrences, disputes between
soldiers and citizens, and questions of debt and quarrels.
This was the Count Thorane, a native of Grasse in Provence,
not far from Antibes; a tall, thin, stern figure, with a face
much disfigured by the small pox, black fiery eyes, and a dignified, reserved demeanour. His first entrance was at once
favourable for the inmates of the house. They spoke of the
different apartments, some of which were to be given up, and
others retained by the family; and when the Count heard a
picture-room mentioned, he immediately requested permission,
although it was already night, at least to give a hasty look at

F

the pictures by candlelight. He took extreme pleasure in these things, behaved in the most obliging manner to my father, who accompanied him, and when he heard that the greater part of the artists were still living, and resided in Frankfort and its neighbourhood, he assured us that he desired nothing more than to know them as soon as possible, and to employ them.

But even this sympathy in respect to art could not change my father's feelings nor bend his character. He permitted what he could not prevent, but kept at a distance in inactivity, and the uncommon state of things around him was intolerable to him, even in the veriest trifle.

Count Thorane behaved himself meanwhile in an exemplary manner. He would not even have his maps nailed on the walls, that he might not injure the new hangings. His people were skilful, quiet, and orderly; but, in truth, as during the whole day and a part of the night there was no quiet with him, one complainant quickly following another, arrested persons being brought in and led out, and all officers and adjutants being admitted to his presence;—as, moreover, the Count kept an open table every day; it made in the moderately-sized house, arranged only for a family, and with but one open staircase running from top to bottom, a movement and a buzzing like that in a beehive, although everything was managed with moderation, gravity, and severity.

As mediator between the irritable master of the house, who became daily more of a hypochondriac self-tormentor, and his well-intentioned, but stern and precise military guest, there was a pleasant interpreter, a handsome, corpulent, lively man, who was a citizen of Frankfort, spoke French well, knew how to adapt himself to everything, and only made a jest of many little annoyances. Through him my mother had sent a representation to the Count of the situation in which she was placed, owing to her husband's state of mind. He had explained the matter so skilfully—had laid before him the new and scarcely furnished house, the natural reserve of the owner, his occupation in the education of his family—and all that could be said to the same effect, that the Count, who in his capacity took the greatest pride in the utmost justice, integrity, and honourable conduct, resolved here also to behave in an exemplary manner to those upon whom he was quartered, and, indeed, never swerved from this resolution under varying circumstances during the several years he stayed with us.

My mother possessed some knowledge of Italian, a language not altogether unknown to any of the family: she therefore resolved to learn French immediately, for which purpose the interpreter, for whose child she had stood godmother during these stormy times, and who now therefore, as a gossip,* felt a redoubled interest in our house, devoted every spare moment to his child's godmother—for he lived directly opposite—and above all, he taught her those phrases which she would be obliged to use in her personal intercourse with the Count. This succeeded admirably. The Count was flattered by the pains taken by the mistress of the house at her years, and as he had a cheerful, witty vein in his character, and he liked to exhibit a certain dry gallantry, a most friendly relation arose between them, and the allied godmother and father could obtain whatever they wanted from him.

As I said before, if it had been possible to cheer up my father, this altered state of things would have caused little inconvenience. The Count practised the severest disinterestedness: he even declined receiving gifts which pertained to his situation: the most trifling thing which could have borne the appearance of bribery, he rejected angrily, and even punished. His people were most strictly forbidden to put the proprietor of the house to the least expense. We children, on the contrary, were bountifully supplied from the dessert. To give an idea of the simplicity of those times, I must take this opportunity to mention that my mother grieved us excessively one day by throwing away the ices which had been sent us from the table, because she would not believe it possible for the stomach to bear real ice, however it might be sweetened.

Besides these dainties, which we gradually learned to enjoy and to digest with perfect ease, it was very agreeable for us children to be in some measure released from fixed hours of study and strict discipline. My father's ill-humour increased, he could not resign himself to the unavoidable. How he

---

* The obsolete word "gossip" has been revived as an equivalent for the German "Gevatter." But it should be observed that this word not only signifies godfather, but that the person whose child has another person for godfather (or godmother) is that person's Gevatter, or Gevatterin (feminine).

tormented himself, my mother, the interpreter, the councillors, and all his friends, only to rid him of the Count! In vain they represented to him that under existing circumstances the presence of such a man in the house was an actual benefit, and that the removal of the Count would be followed by a constant succession of officers or of privates. None of these arguments had any effect. To him the present seemed so intolerable, that his indignation prevented his conceiving anything worse that could follow.

In this way his activity, which he had been used chiefly to employ upon us, was crippled. The lessons he gave us were no longer required with the former exactness, and we tried to gratify our curiosity for military and other public proceedings as much as possible, not only at home, but also in the streets, which was the more easily done, as the front door, open day and night, was guarded by sentries who paid no attention to the running to and fro of restless children.

The many affairs which were settled before the tribunal of the Royal Lieutenant had quite a peculiar charm, from his making it a point to accompany his decisions with some witty, ingenious, or lively turn. What he decreed was strictly just, his manner of expressing it whimsical and piquant. He seemed to have taken the Duke of Ossuna as his model. Scarcely a day passed in which the interpreter did not tell some anecdote or other of this kind to amuse us and my mother. This lively man had made a little collection of such Selomonian decisions; but I only remember the general impression, and cannot recall to my mind any particular case.

By degrees we became better acquainted with the strange character of the Count. This man clearly understood his own peculiarities, and as there were times in which he was seized with a sort of dejection, hypochondria, or by whatever name we may call the evil demon, he withdrew into his room at such hours, which were often lengthened into days, saw no one but his valet, and in urgent cases could not even be prevailed upon to receive any one. But as soon as the Evil Spirit had left him, he appeared as before, active, mild, and cheerful. It might be inferred from the talk of his valet, Saint Jean, a small, thin man of lively good-nature, that in his earlier years he had caused a great misfortune when overcome by this temper; and that therefore, in so important a position as his,

exposed to the eyes of all the world, he had earnestly resolved
to avoid similar aberrations.

During the very first days of the Count's residence with us,
all the Frankfort artists, as Hirt, Schütz, Trautmann, Nothnagel, and Junker, were called to him. They showed their
finished pictures, and the Count bought what were for sale.
My pretty, light room in the gable-end of the attic was given
up to him, and immediately turned into a cabinet and studio,
for he designed to keep all the artists at work for a long time,
especially Seekatz of Darmstadt, whose pencil, particularly in
simple and natural representations, highly pleased him. He
therefore caused to be sent from Grasse, where his elder
brother possessed a handsome house, the dimensions of all
the rooms and cabinets ; then considered with the artists, the
divisions of the walls, and fixed accordingly upon the size or
the large oil-pictures, which were not to be set in frames, but
to be fastened upon the walls like pieces of tapestry. And
now the work went on zealously. Seekatz undertook country
scenes, and succeeded extremely well in his old people and
children, which were copied directly from nature. His young
men did not answer so well, they were almost all too thin, and
his women failed from the opposite cause. For as he had a
little, fat, good, but unpleasant-looking wife, who would let
him have no model but herself, he could produce nothing
agreeable. He was also obliged to exceed the usual size of
his figures. His trees had truth, but the foliage was over
minute. He was a pupil of Brinkmann, whose pencil in easel
pictures is not contemptible.

Schütz, the landscape painter, had perhaps the best of the
matter. He was thoroughly master of the Rhine country, and
of the sunny tone which animates it in the fine season. Nor
was he entirely unaccustomed to work on a larger scale, and
then he showed no want of execution or keeping. His
paintings were of a cheerful cast.

Trautmann *Rembrandtized* some resurrection-miracles out of
the New Testament, and alongside of them set fire to villages
and mills. One cabinet was entirely allotted to him, as I
found from the designs of the rooms. Hirt painted some
good oak and beech forests. His cattle were praiseworthy.
Junker, accustomed to the imitation of the most elaborate
Dutch, was least able to manage this tapestry-work, but he

condescended to ornament many compartments with flowers and fruits for a handsome price.

As I had known all these men from my earliest youth, and had often visited them in their studios, and as the Count also liked to have me with him, I was present at the suggestions, consultations, and orders, as well as at the deliveries of the pictures, and ventured to speak my opinion freely when sketches and designs were handed in. I had already gained among amateurs, particularly at auctions, which I attended diligently, the reputation of being able to tell at once what any historical picture represented, whether taken from Biblical or Profane History, or from Mythology; and even if I did not always hit upon the meaning of allegorical pictures, there was seldom any one present who understood it better than I. Often had I persuaded the artists to represent this or that subject, and I now joyfully made use of these advantages. I still remember writing a circumstantial essay, in which I described twelve pictures which were to exhibit the history of Joseph; some of them were executed.

After these achievements, which were certainly laudable in a boy, I will mention a little disgrace which happened to me within this circle of artists. I was well acquainted with all the pictures which had been from time to time brought into that room. My youthful curiosity left nothing unseen or unexplored. I once found a little black box behind the stove; I did not fail to investigate what might be concealed in it, and drew back the bolt without long deliberation. The picture contained was certainly of a kind not usually exposed to view, and although I tried to bolt it again immediately, I was not quick enough. The Count entered and caught me—" Who allowed you to open that box?" he asked, with all his air of a Royal Lieutenant. I had not much to say for myself, and he immediately pronounced my sentence in a very stern manner: " For eight days," said he, " you shall not enter this room." I made a bow, and walked out. Even this order I obeyed most punctually, so that the good Seekatz, who was then at work in the room, was very much annoyed, for he liked to have me about him; and, out of a little spite, I carried my obedience so far, that I left Seekatz's coffee, which I generally brought him, upon the threshold. He was then obliged to leave his work and fetch it, which he took so ill, that he almost conceived a dislike to me.

It now seems necessary to state more circumstantially and, to make intelligible how, under these circumstances, I made my way with more or less ease through the French language, which, however, I had never learned. Here, too, my natural gift was of service to me, enabling me easily to catch the sound of a language, its movement, accent, tone, and all other outward peculiarities. I knew many words from the Latin; Italian suggested still more; and by listening to servants and soldiers, sentries and visitors, I soon picked up so much that, if I could not join in conversation, I could at any rate manage single questions and answers. All this, however, was little compared to the profit I derived from the theatre. My grandfather had given me a free ticket, which I used daily, in spite of my father's reluctance, by dint of my mother's support. There I sat in the pit, before a foreign stage, and watched the more narrowly the movement and the expression, both of gesture and speech, as I understood little or nothing of what was said, and therefore could only derive entertainment from the action and the tone of voice. I understood least of comedy, because it was spoken rapidly, and related to the affairs of common life, of the phrases of which I knew nothing. Tragedy was not so often played, and the measured step, the rhythm of the Alexandrines, the generality of the expression, made it more intelligible to me in every way. It was not long before I took up Racine, which I found in my father's library, and declaimed the pieces to myself, in the theatrical style and manner, as the organ of my ear and the organ of speech, so nearly akin to that, had caught it, and this with considerable animation, although I could not perceive the connexion of a whole speech. I even learned entire passages by rote, like a trained talking-bird, which was easier to me, from having previously committed to memory passages from the Bible which are generally unintelligible to a child, and accustomed myself to reciting them in the tone of the Protestant preachers. The versified French comedy was then much in vogue; the pieces of Destouches, Marivaux, and La Chaussée, were often produced, and I still remember distinctly many characteristic figures. Of those of Molière I recollect less. What made the greatest impression upon me was the *Hypermnestra* of Lemière, which, as a new piece, was brought out with care and often repeated. The *Devin du Village, Rose et Colas, Annette et*

Lubin, made each a very pleasant impression upon me. I can even now recall the youths and maidens decorated with ribands, and their gestures. It was not long before the wish arose in me to see the interior of the theatre, for which many opportunities were offered me. For as I had not always patience to hear out the whole pieces, and often carried on all sorts of games with other children of my age in the corridors, and in the milder season even before the door, a handsome, lively boy joined us, who belonged to the theatre, and whom I had seen in many little parts, though only casually. He came to a better understanding with me than with the rest, as I could turn my French to account with him, and he the more attached himself to me because there was no boy of his age or his nation at the theatre, or anywhere in the neighbourhood. We also went together at other times, as well as during the play, and even while the representations went on he seldom left me in peace. He was a most delightful little braggart, chattered away charmingly and incessantly, and could tell so much of his adventures, quarrels, and other strange incidents, that he amused me wonderfully, and I learned from him in four weeks more of the language, and of the power of expressing myself in it, than can be imagined; so that no one knew how I had attained the foreign tongue all at once, as if by inspiration.

In the very earliest days of our acquaintance he took me with him upon the stage, and led me especially to the *foyers*, where the actors and actresses remained during the intervals of the performance, and dressed and undressed. The place was neither convenient nor agreeable, for they had squeezed the theatre into a concert-room, so that there were no separate chambers for the actors behind the stage. A tolerably large room adjoining, which had formerly served for card-parties, was now mostly used by both sexes in common, who appeared to feel as little ashamed before each other as before us children, if there was not always the strictest propriety in putting on or changing the articles of dress. I had never seen anything of the kind before, and yet from habit, after repeated visits, I soon found it quite natural.

It was not long before a very peculiar interest of my own arose. Young Derones, for so I will call the boy whose acquaintance I still kept up, was, with the exception of his boasting, a youth of good manners and very courteous demeanour. He made me acquainted with his sister, a girl who was a few years older than we were, and a very pleasant, well-grown girl, of regular form, brown complexion, black hair and eyes; her whole deportment had about it something quiet, even sad. I tried to make myself agreeable to her in every way, but I could not attract her notice. Young girls think themselves far advanced beyond younger boys, and while aspiring to young men, they assume the manner of an aunt towards the boy whose first inclination is turned towards them.—With a younger brother of his I had no acquaintance.

Often, when their mother had gone to rehearsals, or was out visiting, we met at her house to play and amuse ourselves. I never went there without presenting the fair one with a flower, a fruit, or something else, which she always received very courteously, and thanked me for most politely, but I never saw her sad look brighten, and found no trace of her having given me a further thought. At last I fancied I had discovered her secret. The boy showed me a crayon-drawing of a handsome man, behind his mother's bed, which was hung with elegant silk curtains, remarking at the same time, with a sly look, that this was not papa, but just the same as papa; and as he glorified this man, and told me many things in his circumstantial and ostentatious manner, I thought I had discovered that the daughter might belong to the father, but the other two children to the intimate friend. I thus explained to myself her melancholy look, and loved her for it all the more.

My liking for this girl assisted me in bearing the extravagances of her brother, who was not always within bounds. I had often to endure prolix accounts of his exploits, how he had already often fought, without wishing to injure the other —all for the mere sake of honour. He had always contrived to disarm his adversary, and had then forgiven him; nay, he was such a good fencer, that he was once very much perplexed by striking the sword of his opponent up into a high tree, so that it was not easy to be got again.

What much facilitated my visits to the theatre was, that my free ticket, coming from the hands of the *Schultheiss*, gave me access to any of the seats, and therefore also to those in the proscenium. This was very deep, after the French style,

and was bordered on both sides with seats, which, surrounded
by a low rail, ascended in several rows one behind another,
so that the first seats were but a little elevated above the
stage. The whole was considered a place of special honour,
and was generally used only by officers, although the nearness
of the actors destroyed, I will not say all illusion, but, in a
measure, all enjoyment. I have thus experienced and seen
with my own eyes the usage or abuse of which Voltaire so
much complains. When the house was very full, and at
the time troops were passing through the town, officers of
distinction strove for this place of honour, which was generally occupied already, some rows of benches and chairs were
placed in the proscenium on the stage itself, and nothing remained for the heroes and heroines but to reveal their secrets
in the very limited space between the uniforms and orders.
I have even seen the *Hypermnestra* performed under such
circumstances.

The curtain did not fall between the acts, and I must yet
mention a strange custom which I thought quite extraordinary, as its inconsistency with art was to me, as a good
German boy, quite unendurable. The theatre was considered
the greatest sanctuary, and any disturbance occurring there
would have been instantly resented as the highest crime
against the majesty of the public. Therefore in all comedies,
two grenadiers stood with their arms grounded, in full view,
at the two sides of the back scene, and were witnesses of all
that occurred in the bosom of the family. Since, as I said
before, the curtain did not fall between the acts, two others,
while music struck up, relieved guard, by coming from the
wings, directly in front of the first, who retired in the same
measured manner. Now, if such a practice was well fitted to
destroy all that in the theatre is called illusion, this is the
more striking, because it was done at a time when, according to Diderot's principles and examples, the most *natural
naturalness* was required upon the stage, and a perfect deception was proposed as the proper aim of theatrical art. Tragedy, however, was absolved from any such military-police
regulations, and the heroes of antiquity had the right of
guarding themselves; nevertheless, the same grenadiers stood
near enough behind the side-scenes.

I will also mention that I saw Diderot's "Father of a

Family," and " The Philosophers" of Palissot, and still perfectly remember the figure of the philosopher in the latter
piece going upon all fours, and biting into a raw head of
lettuce.

All this theatrical variety could not, however, keep us children always in the theatre. In fine weather we played in front
of it, and in the neighbourhood, and committed all manner of
absurdities, which, especially on Sundays and festivals, by no
means corresponded to our personal appearance; for I and my
comrades then appeared dressed as I described myself in the
tale, with the hat under the arm, and a little sword, the hilt of
which was ornamented with a large silk knot. One day when
we had long gone in this way, and Derones had joined us, he
took it into his head to assert to me that I had insulted him,
and must give him satisfaction. I could not, in truth, conceive what was the cause of this; but I accepted his challenge, and was going to draw my sword. However, he
assured me that in such cases it was customary to go to
secluded spots, in order to be able to settle the matter more
conveniently. We therefore went behind some barns, and
placed ourselves in the proper position. The duel took place
in a somewhat theatrical style, the blades clashed, and the
thrusts followed close upon each other; but in the heat of the
combat he remained with the point of his sword lodged in
the knot of my hilt. This was pierced through, and he
assured me that he had received the most complete satisfaction; then embraced me, also theatrically, and we went to
the next coffee-house to refresh ourselves with a glass of
almond-milk after our mental agitation, and to knit more
closely the old bond of friendship.

On this occasion I will relate another adventure which also
happened to me at the theatre, although at a later time. I
was sitting very quietly in the pit with one of my playmates,
and we looked with pleasure at a *pas seul*, which was executed
with much skill and grace by a pretty boy about our own age
—the son of a French dancing-master who was passing through
the city. After the fashion of dancers, he was dressed in a
close vest of red silk, which ending in a short hoop-petticoat,
like a runner's apron, floated above the knee. We had given
our meed of applause to this young artist with the whole
public, when—I know not how—it occurred to me to make a

moral reflection. I said to my companion, "How handsomely this boy was dressed, and how well he looked; who knows in how tattered a jacket he may sleep to-night!"—All had already risen, but the crowd prevented our moving. A woman who had sat by me, and who was now standing close beside me, chanced to be the mother of the young artist, and felt much offended by my reflection. Unfortunately, she knew German enough to understand me, and spoke it just as much as was necessary to scold. She abused me violently. Who was I, she would like to know, that had a right to doubt the family and respectability of this young man? At all events, she would be bound he was as good as I, and his talents might probably procure him a fortune, of which I could not even venture to dream. This moral lecture she read me in the crowd, and made those about me wonder what rudeness I had committed. As I could neither excuse myself nor escape from her, I was really embarrassed, and when she paused for a moment, said without thinking, "Well! why do you make such a noise about it?—to-day red, to-morrow dead."* These words seemed to strike the woman dumb. She stared at me, and moved away from me as soon as it was in any degree possible. I thought no more of my words; only, some time afterwards, they occurred to me, when the boy, instead of continuing to perform, became ill, and that very dangerously. Whether he died or not, I cannot say.

Such intimations, by an unseasonably or even improperly spoken word, were held in repute even by the ancients, and it is very remarkable that the forms of belief and of superstition have always remained the same among all people and in all times.

From the first day of the occupation of our city, there was no lack of constant diversion, especially for children and young people. Plays and balls, parades, and marches through the town, attracted our attention in all directions. The last particularly were always increasing, and the soldiers' life seemed to us very merry and agreeable.

The residence of the King's Lieutenant at our house procured us the advantage of seeing by degrees all the distinguished persons in the French army, and especially of

---

* A German proverb, "Heute roth, morgen todt."

beholding close at hand the leaders whose names had already
been made known to us by reputation. Thus we looked from
stairs and landing-places, as if from galleries, very conveniently
upon the generals who passed by. Before all I remember the
PRINCE SOUBISE as a handsome, courteous gentleman, but
most distinctly the MARECHAL DE BROGLIO, who was a
younger man, not tall, but well-built, lively, active, and
abounding in keen glances.

He often came to the King's Lieutenant, and it was soon
remarked that the conversation was on weighty matters. We
had scarcely become accustomed to having strangers quartered
upon us in the first three months, than a rumour was obscurely
circulated that the Allies were on the march, and that Duke
Ferdinand of Brunswick was coming to drive the French from
the Maine. Of these, who could not boast of any especial
success in war, no high opinion was held, and after the battle
of Rossbach it was thought they might be dispersed. The
greatest confidence was placed in Duke Ferdinand, and all
those favourable to Prussia awaited with eagerness their delivery from the yoke hitherto borne My father was in somewhat better spirits—my mother was apprehensive. She was
wise enough to see that a small present evil might easily be
exchanged for a great affliction; since it was but too plain
that the French would not advance to meet the Duke, but
would wait an attack in the neighbourhood of the city. A
defeat of the French, a flight, a defence of the city, if it were
only to cover their rear and hold the bridge, a bombardment,
a sack—all these presented themselves to the excited imagination, and gave anxiety to both parties. My mother, who
could bear everything but suspense, imparted her fears to the
Count through the interpreter. She received the answer
usual in such cases: she might be quite easy, for there was
nothing to fear, and should keep quiet and mention the matter
to no one.

Many troops passed through the city; we learned that they
halted at Bergen. The coming and going, the riding and
running constantly increased, and our house was in an uproar
day and night. At this time I often saw Marshal de Broglio,
always cheerful, always the same in look and manner, and I
was afterwards pleased to find a man whose form had made
such a good and lasting impression upon me, so honourably
mentioned in history.

Thus, after an unquiet Passion-week, the Good-Friday of
1759 arrived. A profound stillness announced the approaching storm. We children were forbidden to quit the house:
my father had no quiet, and went out. The battle began: I
ascended to the garret, where indeed I was prevented seeing
the country round, but could very well hear the thunder of
cannon and the general discharge of musketry. After some
hours we saw the first symptoms of the battle in a line of
wagons, in which the wounded, with various sad mutilations
and gestures, were slowly drawn by us, to be taken to the con-
vent of St. Mary, now transformed into a hospital. The compassion of the citizens was instantly moved. Beer, wine, bread,
and money were distributed to those who were yet able to take
them. But when, some time after, wounded and captive Germans were seen in the train, the pity knew no limits, and it
seemed as if everybody would strip himself of every moveable
that he possessed to assist his suffering countrymen.

The prisoners, however, were an evidence of a battle unfavourable to the allies. My father, whose party feelings made
him quite certain that these would come off victorious, had
the violent temerity to go forth to meet the expected victors,
without thinking that the beaten party must pass over him
in their flight. He first repaired to his garden before the
Friedberg gate, where he found everything lonely and quiet,
then he ventured to the Bornheim heath, where he soon
descried various stragglers of the army, who were scattered
and amused themselves by shooting at the boundary-stones,
so that the rebounding lead whizzed round the head of the
inquisitive wanderer. He therefore considered it more prudent to go back, and learned on enquiry what the report of
the firing might have before informed him, that all stood well
for the French, and that there was no thought of retreating.
Reaching home in an ill-humour, the sight of his wounded
and captured countrymen brought him altogether out of his
usual self-command. He also caused various donations to be
given to the passers by, but only the Germans were to have
them, which was not always possible, as fate had packed
together both friend and foe.

My mother and we children, who had already relied on
the Count's word, and had therefore passed a tolerably quiet
day, were highly rejoiced, and my mother doubly consoled, the

next day, when having consulted the oracle of her treasure-
box, by the prick of a needle, she received a very comfortable
answer, both for present and future. We wished our father
similar faith and feelings; we flattered him as much as we
could; we entreated him to take some food, from which he
had abstained all day; but he repulsed our caresses and
every enjoyment, and betook himself to his chamber. Our
joy, however, was not interrupted; the affair was decided;
the King's Lieutenant, who, against his habit, had been on
horseback to-day, at last returned home, where his presence
was more necessary than ever. We sprang to meet him,
kissed his hands, and testified our delight. This seemed
much to please him. "Well," said he more kindly than
usual, "I am glad also for your sakes, my dear children."
He immediately ordered that sweetmeats, sweet wine, and the
best of everything should be given us, and went to his room,
already surrounded by a crowd of the urgent, the demanding,
and the suppliant.

We had now a fine collation, pitied our poor father who
would not partake of it, and pressed our mother to call him
in; but she, more prudent than we, well knew how distasteful
such gifts would be to him. In the meantime she had prepared some supper, and would readily have sent a portion up
to his room, but he never tolerated such an irregularity even
in the most extreme cases; and after the sweet things were
removed, we endeavoured to persuade him to come down
into the ordinary dining-room. At last he allowed himself to
be persuaded unwillingly, and we had no notion of the mischief
which we were preparing for him and ourselves. The staircase ran through the whole house, along all the ante-rooms.
My father in coming down had to go directly past the Count's
apartment. This ante-room was so full of people, that the
Count, to get through much at once, resolved to come out,
and this happened unfortunately at the moment when my
father descended. The Count met him cheerfully, greeted
him, and remarked, "You will congratulate yourselves and
us that this dangerous affair is so happily terminated." "By
no means!" replied my father in a rage; "would that it had
driven you to the devil, even if I had gone with you." The
Count restrained himself for a moment, and then broke out
with wrath—"You shall pay for this," cried he; "you shall

find that you have not thus insulted the good cause and myself for nothing!"

My father, meanwhile, came down very calmly, seated himself near us, seemed more cheerful than before, and began to eat. We were glad of this, unconscious of the dangerous method in which he had rolled the stone from his heart. Soon afterwards my mother was called out, and we had great pleasure in chattering to our father about the sweet things the Count had given us. Our mother did not return. At last the interpreter came in. At a hint from him we were sent to bed; it was already late, and we willingly obeyed. After a night quietly slept through, we heard of the violent commotion which had shaken the house the previous evening. The King's Lieutenant had instantly ordered my father to be led to the guard-house. The subalterns well knew that he was never to be contradicted; yet they had often earned thanks by delaying the execution of his orders. The interpreter, whose presence of mind never forsook him, contrived to excite this disposition in them very strongly. The tumult, moreover, was so great, that a delay brought with it its own concealment and excuse. He had called out my mother, and put her, as it were, into the hands of the adjutants, that by prayers and representations she might gain a brief postponement of the matter. He himself hurried up to the Count, who with great self-command had immediately retired into the inner room, and would rather allow the most urgent affair to stand still, than wreak on an innocent person the ill-humour once excited in him, and give a decision derogatory to his dignity.

The address of the interpreter to the Count, the train of the whole conversation, were often enough repeated to us by the fat interpreter, who prided himself not a little on the fortunate result, so that I can still describe it from recollection.

The interpreter had ventured to open the cabinet and enter, an act which was severely prohibited. "What do you want?" shouted the Count, angrily. "Out with you!—no one but St. Jean has a right to enter here."

"Well, suppose I am St. Jean for a moment," answered the interpreter.

"It would need a powerful imagination for that! Two of him would not make one such as you. Retire!"

"Count, you have received a great gift from heaven, and to that I appeal."

"You think to flatter me! Do not fancy you will succeed."

"You have the great gift, Count, even in moments of passion—in moments of rage, of listening to the opinions of others."

"Well, well, the question now is just about opinions, to which I have listened too long. I know but too well that we are not liked here, and that these citizens look askance at us."

"Not all!"

"Very many. What! These towns will be imperial towns, will they? They saw their emperor elected and crowned, and when, being unjustly attacked, he is in danger of losing his dominions and surrendering to an usurper; when he fortunately finds faithful allies who pour out their blood and treasure in his behalf—they will not put up with the slight burden that falls to their share, towards humbling the enemy!"

"But you have long known these sentiments, and have endured them like a wise man; they are, besides, held only by a minority. A few, dazzled by the splendid qualities of the enemy, whom you yourself prize as an extraordinary man, a few only—as you are aware."

"Yes, indeed! I have known and suffered it too long! otherwise this man would not have presumed to utter such insults to my face, and at the most critical moment. Let them be as many as they please, they shall be punished in the person of this their audacious representative, and perceive what they have to expect."

"Only delay, Count."

"In certain things one cannot act too promptly."

"Only a little delay, Count."

"Neighbour, you think to mislead me into a false step; you shall not succeed."

"I would neither lead you into a false step nor restrain you from one; your resolution is just; it becomes the Frenchman and the King's Lieutenant; but consider that you are also Count Thorane!"

"He has no right to interfere here."

"But the gallant man has a right to be heard."

G

" What would he say then?"

" King's Lieutenant," he would begin, " you have so long had patience with so many gloomy, untoward, bungling men, if they were not really too bad. This man has certainly been too bad, but control yourself, King's Lieutenant, and every one will praise and extol you on that account."

" You know I can often endure your jests, but do not abuse my good-will. These men—are they then completely blinded? Suppose we had lost the battle, what would have been their fate at this moment? We fight up to the gates, we shut up the city, we halt, we defend ourselves to cover our retreat over the bridge. Think you, the enemy would have stood with his hands before him? He throws grenades, and what he has at hand, and they catch where they can. This house-holder—what would he have? Here, in these rooms, a bomb might now have burst, and another have followed it;—in these rooms, the cursed China-paper of which I have spared, in-commoding myself, by not nailing up my maps! They ought to have spent the whole day on their knees."

" How many would have done that!"

" They ought to have prayed for a blessing on us, and to have gone out to meet the generals and officers with tokens of honour and joy, and the wearied soldiers with refreshments. Instead of this, the poison of party-spirit de-stroys the fairest and happiest moments of my life, won by so many cares and efforts."

" It is party-spirit; but you will only increase it by the punishment of this man. Those who think with him will proclaim you a tyrant and a barbarian:—they will consider him a martyr, who has suffered for the good cause; and even those of the other opinion, who are now his opponents, will see in him only their fellow-citizen, will pity him, and while they confess your justice, will yet feel that you have pro-ceeded too severely."

" I have listened to you too much already,—now, away with you!"

" Hear only this. Remember this is the most unheard-of thing that could befall this man, this family. You have had no reason to be edified by the good-will of the master of the house; but the mistress has anticipated all your wishes, and the children have regarded you as their uncle. With this

single blow, you will for ever destroy the peace and happiness of this dwelling. Indeed, I may say, that a bomb falling
into the house, would not have occasioned greater desolation.
I have so often admired your self-command, Count; give me
this time opportunity to adore you. A warrior is worthy of
honour who considers himself a guest in the house of an
enemy; but here there is no enemy, only a mistaking man.
Control yourself, and you will acquire an everlasting fame."

"That would be odd," replied the Count, with a smile.

"Merely natural," continued the interpreter; "I have not
sent the wife and children to your feet, because I know you
detest such scenes; but I will depict to you this wife and
these children, how they will thank you. I will depict them
to you conversing all their lives of the battle of Bergen, and
of your magnanimity on this day, relating it to their children,
and children's children, and inspiring even strangers with
their own interest for you: an act of this kind can never
perish."

"But you do not hit my weak side yet, interpreter! About
posthumous fame I am not in the habit of thinking; that is
for others, not for me; but to do right at the moment, not to
neglect my duty, not to prejudice my honour—that is my
care. We have already had too many words; now go—and
receive the thanks of the thankless, whom I spare."

The interpreter, surprised and moved by this unexpectedly
favourable issue, could not restrain his tears, and would have
kissed the Count's hands. The Count motioned him off, and
said severely and seriously, "You know I cannot bear such
things." And with these words he went into the ante-room,
to attend to his pressing affairs, and hear the claims of so
many expectant persons. So the matter was disposed of,
and the next morning we celebrated with the remnants of the
yesterday's sweetmeats, the passing over of an evil through
the threatenings of which we had happily slept.

Whether the interpreter really spoke so wisely, or merely
so painted the scene to himself, as one is apt to do after
a good and fortunate action, I will not decide; at least he
never varied it in repeating it. Indeed, this day seemed
to him both the most anxious and the most glorious in his
life.

One little incident will show how the Count in general

rejected all false parade, never assumed a title which did not belong to him, and how witty he was in his more cheerful moods.

A man of the higher class, who was one of the abstruse, solitary Frankforters, thought he must complain of the quartering of the soldiers upon him. He came in person, and the interpreter proffered him his services, but the other supposed that he did not need them. He came before the Count with a most becoming bow, and said, "Your excellency!" The Count returned the bow, as well as the "excellency." Struck by this mark of honour, and not supposing but that the title was too humble, he stooped lower, and said, "Monseigneur." "Sir," said the Count, very seriously, "we will not go further, or else we may easily bring it to Majesty." The other gentleman was extremely confused, and had not a word to utter. The interpreter. standing at some distance, and apprised of the whole affair, was wicked enough not to move, but the Count, with much cheerfulness, continued, "Well now, for instance, sir, what is your name?" "Spangenberg," replied the other. "And mine," said the Count, "is Thorane. Spangenberg, what is your business with Thorane? Now, then, let us sit down; the affair shall at once be settled."

And thus the affair was indeed settled at once, to the great satisfaction of the person I have here named Spangenberg, and the same evening, in our family circle, the story was not only told by the waggish interpreter, but was given with all the circumstances and gestures.

After these confusions, disquietudes, and grievances, the former security and thoughtlessness soon returned, in which the young particularly live from day to day, if it be in any degree possible. My passion for the French theatre grew with every performance. I did not miss an evening, though on every occasion, when after the play I sat down with the family to supper,—often putting up with the remains,—I had to endure the constant reproaches of my father, that theatres were useless, and would lead to nothing. In these cases I adduced all and every argument which is at hand for the apologists of the stage when they fall into a difficulty like mine. Vice in prosperity and virtue in misfortune, are in the end set right by poetical justice. Those beautiful examples of misdeeds punished, *Miss Sarah Sampson*, and the *Mer-*

chant of London, were very energetically cited on my part; but, on the other hand, I often came off worst when the *Fouberies de Scapin*, and others of the sort, were in the bill, and I was forced to bear reproaches for the delight felt by the public in the deceits of intriguing servants, and the successful follies of prodigal young men. Neither party was convinced; but my father was very soon reconciled to the theatre when he saw that I advanced with incredible rapidity in the French language.

Men are so constituted that everybody would rather undertake himself what he sees done by others, whether he has aptitude for it or not. I had soon exhausted the whole range of the French stage; several pieces I had already witnessed for the third and fourth times; all had passed before my eyes and mind, from the stateliest tragedy to the most frivolous afterpiece; and as when a child I had presumed to imitate Terence, I did not fail now as a boy, on a much more inciting occasion, to copy the French forms to the best of my ability and want of ability. There were then performed some half-mythological, half-allegorical pieces in the taste of PIRON; they partook somewhat of the nature of parody, and were much liked. These representations particularly attracted me: the little gold wings of a lively Mercury, the thunderbolt of a disguised Jupiter. an amorous Danaë, or by whatever name a fair one visited by the gods might be called, if indeed it were not a shepherdess or huntress to whom they descended. And as elements of this kind, from *Ovid's Metamorphosis*, or the *Pantheon Mythicum* of Pomey, were humming in swarms about my head—I had soon put together in my imagination a little piece of the kind, of which I can only say that the scene was rural, and that there was no lack in it of king's daughters, princes, or gods. Mercury, especially, made so vivid an impression on my senses, that I could almost be sworn that I had seen him with my own eyes.

I presented my friend Derones with a very neat copy, made by myself, which he accepted with quite a special grace, and with a truly patronizing air, glanced hastily over the manuscript, pointed out a few grammatical blunders, found some speeches too long, and at last promised to examine and judge the work more attentively when he had the requisite leisure.

To my modest question, whether the piece could by any
chance be performed, he assured me that it was not altogether impossible. In the theatre, he said, a great deal went
by favour, and he would support me with all his heart: only
the affair must be kept private: for he had himself once on a
time surprised the directors with a piece of his own, and it
would certainly have been acted if it had not been too soon
detected that he was the author. I promised him all possible
silence: and already saw in my mind's eye the name of my
piece posted up in large letters on the corners of the streets
and squares.

Light-minded as my friend generally was, the opportunity
of playing the master was but too desirable. He read the
piece through with attention, and while he sat down with me
to make some trivial alterations, turned the whole thing, in
the course of the conversation, completely topsy-turvy, so
that not one stone remained on another. He struck out,
added, took away one character, substituted another,—in
short, went on with the maddest wantonness in the world, so
that my hair stood on end. My previous persuasion that he
must understand the matter, allowed him to have his way;
for he had often laid before me so much about the Three
Unities of Aristotle, the regularity of the French drama, the
probability, the harmony of the verse, and all that belongs to
these, that I was forced to regard him, not merely as informed,
but thoroughly grounded. He abused the English and scorned
the Germans: in short, he laid before me the whole drama-
turgic litany which I have so often in my life been compelled
to hear.

Like the boy in the fable, I carried my mangled offspring
home, and strove in vain to bring it to life. As, however, I
would not quite abandon it, I caused a fair copy of my first
manuscript, after a few alterations, to be made by our clerk,
which I presented to my father, and thus gained so much that
for a long time he let me eat my supper in quiet after the
play was over.

This unsuccessful attempt had made me reflective, and I
resolved now to learn at the very sources, these theories,
these laws, to which every one appealed, but which had become suspicious to me chiefly through the unpoliteness of my
arrogant master. This was not indeed difficult, but laborious.

I immediately read Corneille's *Treatise on the Three Unities*, and learned from that how people would have it, but why they desired it so was by no means clear to me; and what was worst of all, I fell at once into still greater confusion when I made myself acquainted with the disputes on the *Cid*, and read the prefaces in which Corneille and Racine are obliged to defend themselves against the critics and public. Here at least I plainly saw that no man knew what he wanted; that a piece like the *Cid*, which had produced the noblest effect, was to be condemned at the command of an all-powerful cardinal; that Racine, the idol of the French living in my day, who had now also become my idol—(for I had got intimately acquainted with him when Schöff Von Olenschlager made us children act *Britannicus*, in which the part of Nero fell to me)—that Racine, I say, even in his own day, was not able to get on with the amateurs nor critics. Through all this I became more perplexed than ever, and after having pestered myself a long time with this talking backwards and forwards, and theoretical quackery of the previous century, threw them to the dogs, and was the more resolute in casting all the rubbish away, the more I thought I observed that the authors themselves who had produced excellent things, when they began to speak about them, when they set forth the grounds of their treatment, when they desired to defend, justify, or excuse themselves, were not always able to hit the proper mark. I hastened back again, therefore, to the living present, attended the theatre far more zealously, read more scrupulously and connectedly, so that I had perseverance enough this time to work through the whole of Racine and Molière, and a great part of Corneille.

The King's Lieutenant still lived at our house. He in no respect had changed his deportment, especially towards us; but it was observable, and the interpreter made it still more evident to us, that he no longer discharged his duties with the same cheerfulness and zeal as at the outset, though always with the same rectitude and fidelity. His character and habits, which showed the Spaniard rather than the Frenchman; his caprices, which were not without their influence on his business; his unbending will under all circumstances; his susceptibility as to everything that concerned his person or reputation—all this together might perhaps sometimes bring

him into conflict with his superiors. Add to this, that he had
been wounded in a duel, which had arisen in the theatre, and
it was deemed wrong that the King's Lieutenant, himself
chief of police, should have committed a punishable offence.
As I have said, all this may have contributed to make him
live more retired, and here and there perhaps to act with less
energy.

Meanwhile, a considerable part of the pictures he had ordered had been delivered. Count Thorane passed his leisure
hours in examining them, while in the aforesaid gable-room
he had them nailed up, canvas after canvas, large and small,
side by side, and because there was want of space, even one
over another, and then taken down and rolled up. The works
were constantly inspected anew; the parts that were considered the most successful were repeatedly enjoyed; but
there was no want of wishes that this or that had been differently done.

Hence arose a new and very singular operation. As one
painter best executed figures, another middle-grounds and
distances, a third trees, a fourth flowers, it struck the Count
that these talents might perhaps be combined in the paintings, and that in this way perfect works might be produced.
A beginning was made at once, by having for instance some
beautiful cattle painted into a finished landscape. But because there was not always adequate room for all, and a few
sheep more or less was no great matter to the cattle-painter,
the largest landscape proved in the end too narrow. Now
also the painter of figures had to introduce the shepherd, and
some travellers; these deprived each other of air, as we may
say; and we marvelled that they were not all stifled, even in
the most open country. No one could anticipate what was
to come of the matter, and when it was finished it gave no
satisfaction. The painters were annoyed. They had gained
something by their first orders, but lost by these after-labours,
though the Count paid for them also very liberally. And as
the parts worked into each other in one picture by several
hands, produced no good effect after all the trouble, every
one, at last, fancied that his own work had been spoiled and
destroyed by that of the others; hence the artists were within
a hair's-breadth of falling out, and becoming irreconcilably
hostile to each other. These alterations, or rather additions,

were made in the before-mentioned studio, where I remained
quite alone with the artists; and it amused me to hunt out
from the studies, particularly of animals, this or that individual or group, and to propose it for the foreground or the
distance, in which respect they many times, either from conviction or kindness, complied with my wishes.

The partners in this affair were therefore greatly discouraged, especially Seekatz, a very hypochondriacal, retired
man, who indeed by his incomparable humour was the best
of companions among friends, but who, when he worked,
desired to work alone, abstracted and perfectly free. This
man, after solving difficult problems, and finishing them with
the greatest diligence and the warmest love, of which he was
always capable, was forced to travel repeatedly from Darmstadt to Frankfort, either to change something in his own pictures, or to touch up those of others, or even to allow, under
his superintendence, a third person to convert his pictures into
a variegated mess. His peevishness augmented, his resistance
became more decided, and a great deal of effort was necessary
on our part to guide this "gossip"—for he was one also—
according to the Count's wishes. I still remember that when
the boxes were standing ready to pack up all the pictures, in
the order in which the upholsterer at their place of destination might fix them up at once, a small but indispensable bit
of afterwork was demanded, but Seekatz could not be moved
to come over. He had, by way of conclusion, done the best
he could, having represented in paintings to be placed over
the doors, the four elements as children and boys, after life,
and having expended the greatest care, not only on the figures,
but on the accessories. These were delivered and paid for,
and he thought he was quit of the business for ever; but now
he was to come over again, that he might enlarge, by a
few touches of his pencil, some figures, the size of which was
too small. Another, he thought, could do it just as well; he
had already set about some new work; in short, he would not
come. The time for sending off the pictures was at hand;
they must also have opportunity to dry; every delay was pre-
carious; and the Count, in despair, was about to have him
fetched in military fashion. We all wished to see the pictures finally gone, and found at last no expedient than for the
gossip interpreter to seat himself in a wagon, and fetch over

the refractory subject, with his wife and child. He was kindly
received by the Count, well treated, and at last dismissed with
liberal payment.

After the pictures had been sent away, there was great
peace in the house. The gable-room in the attic was cleaned
and given up to me; and my father, when he saw the boxes
go, could not refrain from wishing to send off the Count after
them. For much as the tastes of the Count coincided with
his own, much as he must have rejoiced to see his principle of
patronizing living artists so generously followed out by a man
richer than himself, much as it may have flattered him that
his collection had been the occasion of bringing so considerable a profit to a number of brave artists in a pressing time,
he nevertheless felt such a repugnance to the foreigner who
had intruded into his house, that he could not think well
of any of his doings. One ought to employ painters, but not
degrade them to paper-stainers; one ought to be satisfied with
what they have done, according to their conviction and ability,
even if it does not thoroughly please one, and not be perpetually carping at it. In short, in spite of all the Count's
own generous endeavours, there could, once for all, be no
mutual understanding. My father only visited that room when
the Count was at table, and I can recall but one instance,
when, Seekatz having excelled himself, and the wish to see
these pictures having brought the whole house together, my
father and the Count met, and manifested a common pleasure
in these works of art, which they could not take in each other.

Scarcely, therefore, had the house been cleared of the chests
and boxes, than the plan for removing the Count, which had
formerly been begun, but was afterwards interrupted, was resumed. The endeavour was made to gain justice by representations, equity by entreaties, favour by influence, and the
quarter-masters were prevailed upon to decide thus: the
Count was to change his lodgings, and our house, in consideration of the burden borne day and night for several
years uninterruptedly, was to be exempt for the future from
billetting. But, to furnish a plausible pretext for this, we
were to take in lodgers on the first floor, which the Count
had occupied, and thus render a new quartering as it were
impossible. The Count, who after the separation from his
dear pictures felt no further peculiar interest in the house,

and hoped moreover to be soon recalled and placed else-
where, was pleased to move without opposition to another
good residence, and left us in peace and good-will. Soon
afterwards he quitted the city, and received different ap-
pointments in gradation, but, it was rumoured, not to his
own satisfaction. Meantime, he had the pleasure of seeing
the pictures which he had preserved with so much care felici-
tously arranged in his brother's chateau ; he wrote sometimes,
sent dimensions, and had different pieces executed by the
artists so often named. At last we heard nothing further
about him, except after several years we were assured that he
had died as governor of one of the French colonies in the
West Indies.

FOURTH BOOK.

Much inconvenience as the quartering of the French had occasioned us, we had become so accustomed to it, that we could not fail to miss it, nor could we children fail to feel as if the house were deserted. Moreover it was not decreed that we should again attain perfect family unity. New lodgers were already agreed upon, and after some sweeping and scouring, planing and rubbing with bees'-wax, painting and varnishing, the house was completely restored again. The chancery-director Moritz, with his family, very worthy friends of my parents, moved in. He was not a native of Frankfort, but an able jurist and man of business, and managed the legal affairs of many small princes, counts, and lords. I never saw him otherwise than cheerful and pleasant, and diligent with his law papers. His wife and children, gentle, quiet, and benevolent, did not indeed increase the sociableness of our house, for they kept to themselves; but a stillness, a peace returned, which we had not enjoyed for a long time. I now again occupied my attic room, in which the ghosts of the many pictures sometimes hovered before me, while I strove to frighten them away by labour and study.

The Counsellor of Legation Moritz, a brother of the chancellor, came from this time often to our house. He was even more a man of the world, had a handsome figure, while his manners were easy and agreeable. He also managed the affairs of different persons of rank, and on occasions of meetings of creditors and imperial commissions frequently came into contact with my father. They had a high opinion of each other, and commonly stood on the side of the creditors, though they were generally obliged to perceive, much to their vexation, that a majority of the agents on such occasions are usually gained over to the side of the debtors. The counsellor of legation readily communicated his knowledge, was a friend to the mathematics, and as these did not occur in his present course of life, he made himself a pleasure by helping me on in this branch of study. I was thus enabled to finish my architectural sketches more accurately than heretofore, and to profit more by the instruction of a drawing-master, who now also occupied us an hour every day.

This good old man was indeed only half an artist. We were obliged to draw and combine strokes, from which eyes and noses, lips and ears, nay, at last, whole faces and heads, were to arise, but of natural or artistic forms there was no thought. We were tormented a long while with this *quid pro quo* of the human figure, and when the so-called Passions of Le Brun were given us to copy, it was supposed at last that we had made great progress. But even these caricatures did not improve us. Then we went off to landscapes, foliage, and all the things which in ordinary instruction are practised without consistency or method. Finally we dropped into close imitation and neatness of strokes, without troubling ourselves about the merit or taste of the original.

In these attempts our father led the way in an exemplary manner. He had never drawn, but he was unwilling to remain behind now that his children pursued this art, and would give, even in his old age, an example how they should proceed in their youth. Several heads, therefore, of Piazzetta, from his well-known sheets in small octavo, he copied with an English lead-pencil upon the finest Dutch paper. In these he not only observed the greatest clearness of outline, but most accurately imitated the hatching of the copper-plate with a light hand—only too slightly, as in his desire to avoid hardness he brought no keeping into his sketches. Yet they were always soft and accurate. His unrelaxing and untiring assiduity went so far, that he drew the whole considerable collection number by number, while we children jumped from one head to another, and chose only those that pleased us.

About this time the long-debated project, long under consideration, for giving us lessons in music, was carried into effect; and the last impulse to it certainly deserves mention. It was settled that we should learn the harpsichord: but there was always a dispute about the choice of a master. At last I went once accidentally into the room of one of my companions, who was just taking his lesson on the harpsichord, and found the teacher a most charming man. For each

finger of the right and left hand he had a nickname, by
which he indicated in the merriest way when it was to be
used. The black and white keys were likewise symbolically
designated, and even the tones appeared under figurative
names. Such a motley company worked most pleasantly
together. Fingering and time seemed to become perfectly
easy and obvious, and while the scholar was put into the
best humour, everything else succeeded beautifully

Scarcely had I reached home, than I importuned my
parents to set about the matter in good earnest at last, and
give us this incomparable man for our master on the harpsichord. They hesitated, and made inquiries; they indeed
heard nothing bad of the teacher; but, at the same time,
nothing particularly good. Meanwhile I had informed my
sister of all the droll names; we could hardly wait for the
lesson, and succeeded in having the man engaged.

The reading of the notes began first, but as no jokes
occurred here, we comforted ourselves with the hope that
when we went to the harpsichord, and the fingers were
needed, the jocular method would commence. But neither
keys nor fingering seemed to afford opportunity for any comparisons. Dry as the notes were, with their strokes on and
between the five lines, the black and white keys were no less so;
and not a syllable was heard either of "thumbling," "point-
erling," or "goldfinger," while the countenance of the man
remained as imperturbable during his dry teaching as it had
been before during his dry jests. My sister reproached me
most bitterly for having deceived her, and actually believed
that it was all an invention of mine. But I was myself confounded and learned little, though the man at once went
regularly enough to work; for I kept always expecting that
the early jokes would make their appearance, and so consoled my sister from one day to another. They did not
reappear, however, and I should never have been able to
explain the riddle if another accident had not solved it for
me.

One of my companions came in during a lesson, and at
once all the pipes of the humorous *jet d'eau* were opened:
the "thumblings" and "pointerlings," the "pickers" and
"stealers," as he used to call the fingers, the "falings"
and "galings," meaning "f" and "g," the "fielings" and

"gielings," meaning "f" and "g" sharp,* became once more
extant, and made the most wonderful mannikins. My young
friend could not leave off laughing, and was rejoiced that
one could learn in such a merry manner. He vowed that
he would give his parents no peace until they had given him
such an excellent man for a teacher.

And thus the way to two arts was early enough opened to
me, according to the principles of a modern theory of education, merely by good luck, and without any conviction that I
should be furthered therein by a native talent. My father
maintained that everybody ought to learn drawing; for
which reason, he especially venerated the Emperor Maximilian, by whom this had been expressly commanded. He
therefore held me to it more steadily than to music, which,
on the other hand, he especially recommended to my sister,
and even out of the hours for lessons kept her fast, during
a good part of the day, at her harpsichord.

But the more I was in this way made to press on, the
more I wished to press forward of myself, and my hours
of leisure were employed in all sorts of curious occupations.
From my earliest years I felt a love for the investigation of
natural things. It is often regarded as an instinct of cruelty
that children like at last to break, tear, and devour objects
with which for a long time they have played, and which
they have handled in various manners. Yet even in this way
is manifested the curiosity, the desire of learning how such
things hang together, how they look within. I remember
that as a child, I pulled flowers to pieces to see how the leaves
were inserted into the calyx, or even plucked birds to observe
how the feathers were inserted into the wings. Children are
not to be blamed for this, when even our naturalists believe
they get their knowledge oftener by separation and division
than by union and combination,—more by killing than by
making alive.

An armed loadstone, very neatly sewed up in scarlet cloth,
was one day destined to experience the effects of this spirit of
inquiry. For the secret force of attraction which it exercised
not only on the little iron bar attached to it, but which was
of such a kind that it could gain strength and could daily

* The names of the sharp notes in German terminate in "is," and
hence "f" and "g" sharp are called "fis" and "gis."

bear a heavier weight—this mysterious virtue had so excited my admiration, that for a long time I was pleased with merely staring at its operation. But at last I thought I might arrive at some nearer revelation by tearing away the external covering. This was done, but I became no wiser in consequence, as the naked iron taught me nothing further. This also I took off, and I held in my hand the mere stone, with which I never grew weary of making experiments of various kinds on filings and needles—experiments from which my youthful mind drew no further advantage beyond that of a varied experience. I could not manage to reconstruct the whole arrangement; the parts were scattered, and I lost the wondrous phenomenon at the same time with the apparatus.

Nor was I more fortunate in putting together an electrical machine. A friend of the family, whose youth had fallen in the time when electricity occupied all minds, often told us how as a child he had desired to possess such a machine, had got together the principal requisites, and by the aid of an old spinning-wheel and some medicine bottles, had produced tolerable results. As he readily and frequently repeated the story, and imparted to us some general information on electricity, we children found the thing very plausible, and long tormented ourselves with an old spinning-wheel and some medicine bottles, without producing even the smallest result. We nevertheless adhered to our belief, and were much delighted when at the time of the fair, among other rarities, magical and legerdemain tricks, an electrical machine performed its marvels, which, like those of magnetism, were at that time already very numerous.

The want of confidence in the public method of instruction was daily increasing. People looked about for private tutors, and because single families could not afford the expense, several of them united to attain their object. Yet the children seldom agreed, the young man had not sufficient authority, and after frequently repeated vexations, there were only angry partings. It is not surprising, therefore, that other arrangements were thought of which should be more permanent as well as more advantageous.

The thought of establishing boarding-schools (*Pensionen*) had arisen from the necessity which every one felt for having the French language taught and communicated orally. My

father had brought up a young person who had been his foot-
man, valet, secretary, and in short successively all in all.
This man, whose name was Pfeil, spoke French well. After
he had married, and his patrons had to think of a situation
for him, they hit upon the plan of making him establish a
boarding-school, which extended gradually into a small academy, in which everything necessary, and at last even Greek
and Latin, were taught. The extensive connexions of Frankfort caused young French and English men to be brought to
this establishment, that they might learn German and be otherwise cultivated. Pfeil, who was a man in the prime of life,
and of the most wonderful energy and activity, superintended
the whole very laudably, and as he could never be employed
enough, and was obliged to keep music-teachers for his
scholars, he set about music on the occasion, and practised the
harpsichord with such zeal that, without having previously
touched a note, he very soon played with perfect readiness and
spirit. He seemed to have adopted my father's maxim, that
nothing can more cheer and excite young people, than when
at mature years one declares one's self again a learner, and at
an age when new accomplishments are acquired with difficulty, one endeavours, nevertheless, by zeal and perseverance,
to excel the younger, who are more favoured by nature.

By this love of harpsichord-playing Pfeil was led to the
instruments themselves, and while he hoped to obtain the
best, came into connexion with Frederici of Gera, whose instruments were celebrated far and wide. He took a number
of them on commission, and had now the joy of seeing not
only one piano, but many, set up in his residence, and of
practising and being heard upon them.

The vivacity of this man brought a great rage for music
into our house. My father remained on lasting good terms
with him up to certain points of dispute. A large piano of
Frederici was purchased also for us, which I, adhering to my
harpsichord, hardly touched, but which so much increased
the troubles of my sister, as, to do proper honour to the new
instrument, she had to spend some time every day in practice ; while my father as overseer, and Pfeil as a model and
encouraging friend, alternately took their positions at her
side.

A singular taste of my father caused much inconvenience to

us children. This was the cultivation of silk, of the advantages of which, when it should be more widely extended, he had a high opinion. Some acquaintances at Hanau, where the breeding of the worms was carried on with great care, gave him the immediate impulse. At the proper season, the eggs were sent to him from that place, and as soon as the mulberry-trees showed sufficient leaves, they had to be stripped, and the scarcely visible creatures were most diligently tended. Tables and stands, with boards, were set up in a garret chamber, to afford them more room and sustenance; for they grew rapidly, and after their last change of skin were so voracious, that it was scarcely possible to get leaves enough to feed them; nay, they had to be fed day and night, as everything depends upon there being no deficiency of nourishment when the great and wondrous change is about to take place in them. If the weather was favourable, this business might indeed be regarded as a pleasant amusement; but if the cold set in, so that the mulberry-trees suffered, it was exceedingly troublesome. Still more unpleasant was it when rain fell during the last epoch, for these creatures cannot at all endure moisture, and the wet leaves had to be carefully wiped and dried, which could not always be done quite perfectly; and for this, or perhaps some other reason also, various diseases came among the flock, by which the poor things were swept off in thousands. The corruption which ensued produced a smell really pestilential, and because the dead and diseased had to be taken away and separated from the healthy, the business was indeed extremely wearisome and repulsive, and caused many an unhappy hour to us children.

After we had one year passed the finest weeks of the spring and summer in tending the silk-worms, we were obliged to assist our father in another business, which, though simpler, was no less troublesome. The Roman views, which, bound by black rods at the top and bottom, had hung for many years on the walls of the old house, had become very yellow, through the light, dust, and smoke, and not a little unsightly through the flies. If such uncleanliness was not to be tolerated in the new house, yet, on the other hand, these pictures had gained in value to my father, in consequence of his longer absence from the places represented. For in the outset such copies only serve to refresh and vivify the impressions shortly before received.

They seem trifling in comparison, and at the best only a melancholy substitute. But as the remembrance of the original forms fades more and more, the copies imperceptibly assume their place, they become as dear to us as those once were, and what we at first contemned, now gains esteem and affection. Thus it is with all copies, and particularly with portraits. No one is easily satisfied with the counterfeit of an object still present, but how we value every *silhouette* of one who is absent or departed.

In short, with this feeling of his former extravagance, my father wished that these engravings might be restored as much as possible. It was well known that this could be done by bleaching; and the operation, always critical with large plates, was undertaken under rather unfavourable circumstances. For the large boards on which the smoked engravings were moistened and exposed to the sun, stood in the gutters before the garret windows, leaning against the roof, and were therefore liable to many accidents. The chief point was, that the paper should never thoroughly dry, but must be kept constantly moist. This was the duty of my sister and myself; and the idleness, which would have been otherwise so desirable, was excessively annoying, on account of the tedium and impatience, and the watchfulness which allowed of no distraction. The end, however, was attained, and the bookbinder who fixed each sheet upon thick paper, did his best to match and repair the margins, which had been here and there torn by our inadvertence. All the sheets together were bound in a volume, and for this time preserved.

That we children might not be wanting in every variety of life and learning, a teacher of the English language must announce himself just at this time, who pledged himself to teach English to anybody not entirely raw in languages, within four weeks; and to advance him to such a degree that, with some diligence, he could help himself further. His price was moderate, and he was indifferent as to the number of scholars at one lesson. My father instantly determined to make the attempt, and took lessons, in connexion with my sister and myself, from this expeditious master. The hours were faithfully kept; there was no want of repeating our lessons; other exercises were neglected rather than this, during the four weeks; and the teacher parted from us, and we from him, with satisfaction. As he remained longer in the town, and found many employers, he came from time to time to look after us and to help us, grateful that we had been among the first who placed confidence in him, and proud to be able to cite us as examples to the others.

My father, in consequence of this, entertained a new anxiety that English might neatly stand in the series of my other studies in languages. Now, I will confess that it became more and more burdensome for me to take my occasions for study now from this grammar or collection of examples, now from that; now from one author, now from another, and thus to divert my interest in a subject every hour. It occurred to me, therefore, that I might despatch all at once, and I invented a romance of six or seven brothers and sisters, who, separated from each other and scattered over the world, should communicate with each other alternately as to their conditions and feelings. The eldest brother gives an account in good German of all the manifold objects and incidents of his journey. The sister, in a ladylike style, with short sentences and nothing but stops, much as *Siegwart* was afterwards written, answers now him, now the other brothers, partly about domestic matters, and partly about affairs of the heart. One brother studies theology, and writes a very formal Latin, to which he often adds a Greek postscript. To another brother, holding the place of mercantile clerk at Hamburgh, the English correspondence naturally falls, while a still younger one at Marseilles has the French. For the Italian was found a musician, on his first trip into the world; while the youngest of all, a sort of pert nestling, had applied himself to Jew-German, the other languages having been cut off from him, and by means of his frightful cyphers brought the rest of them into despair, and my parents into a hearty laugh at the good notion.

I sought for matter to fill up this singular form by studying the geography of the countries in which my creations resided, and by inventing for those dry localities all sorts of human incidents, which had some affinity with the characters and employments of my heroes. Thus my exercise-books became much more voluminous, my father was better satisfied, and I was much sooner made aware of the acquirements and the sort of readiness in which I was wanting.

Now, as such things once begun have no end and no limits, so it happened in the present case; for, while I strove to attain the odd Jew-German, and to write it as well as I could read it, I soon discovered that I ought to know Hebrew, from which alone the modern corrupted dialect could be derived and handled with any certainty. I consequently explained the necessity of my learning Hebrew to my father, and earnestly besought his consent, for I had a still higher object. Everywhere I heard it said that to understand the Old as well as the New Testament, the original languages were requisite. The latter I could read quite easily, because, that there might be no want of exercise even on Sundays, the so-called Epistles and Gospels had, after church, to be recited, translated, and in some measure explained. I now designed doing the same thing with the Old Testament, the peculiarities of which had always especially interested me.

My father, who did not like to do anything by halves, determined to request the rector of our Gymnasium, one Dr. ALBRECHT, to give me private lessons weekly, until I should have acquired what was most essential in so simple a language, for he hoped that if it would not be despatched as soon as English was learned, it could at least be managed in double the time.

Rector Albrecht was one of the most original figures in the world, short, broad, but not fat, ill-shaped without being deformed,—in short, an Æsop in gown and wig. His more than seventy-years-old face was completely twisted into a sarcastic smile, while his eyes always remained large, and, though red, were always brilliant and intelligent. He lived in the old cloister of the Barefoot Friars, the seat of the Gymnasium. Even as a child, I had often visited him in company with my parents, and had, with a kind of trembling delight, glided through the long dark passages, the chapels transformed into reception-rooms, the place broken up and full of stairs and corners. Without annoying me, he questioned me familiarly whenever we met, and praised and encouraged me. One day, on the changing of the pupil's places after a public examination, he saw me standing as a mere spectator, not far from his chair, while he distributed the silver *præmia virtutis et diligentiæ*. I was probably gazing very eagerly upon the little bag out of which he drew

the medals; he nodded to me, descended a step, and handed
me one of the silver pieces. My joy was great, although
others thought that this gift bestowed upon a boy not belonging to the school was out of all order. But for this the good
old man cared but little, having always played the eccentric,
and that in a striking manner. He had a very good reputation as a schoolmaster, and understood his business, although
age no more allowed him to practise it thoroughly. But
almost more than by his own infirmities was he hindered by
greater circumstances, and, as I already knew, he was satisfied neither with the consistory, the inspectors, the clergy,
nor the teachers. To his natural temperament, which inclined
to satire, and the watching for faults and defects, he allowed
free play, both in his programs and his public speeches, and
as Lucian was almost the only writer whom he read and
esteemed, he spiced all that he said and wrote with biting
ingredients.

Fortunately for those with whom he was dissatisfied, he
never went directly to work, but only jeered at the defects
which he wanted to reprove, with hints, allusions, classic
passages, and Scripture texts. His delivery, moreover—he
always read his discourses—was unpleasant, unintelligible,
and, above all, was often interrupted by a cough, but more
frequently by a hollow paunch-convulsing laugh, with which
he was wont to announce and accompany the biting passages. This singular man I found to be mild and obliging
when I began to take lessons from him. I now went to him
daily at six o'clock in the evening, and always experienced
a secret pleasure when the outer door closed behind me, and
I had to thread the long dark cloister-passage. We sat in
his library at a table covered with oil-cloth, a much-read
Lucian never quitting his side.

In spite of all my willingness, I did not get at the matter
without difficulty, for my teacher could not suppress certain
sarcastic remarks as to the real truth about Hebrew. I concealed from him my designs upon Jew-German, and spoke of a
better understanding of the original text. He smiled at this,
and said I should be satisfied if I only learned to read. This
vexed me in secret, and I concentrated all my attention when
we came to the letters. I found an alphabet something like
the Greek, of which the forms were easy, and the names, for

the most part, not strange to me. All this I had soon comprehended and retained, and supposed we should now go to
reading. That this was done from right to left I was well
aware. But now, all at once appeared a new army of little
characters and signs, of points and strokes of all sorts, which
were in fact to represent vowels. At this I wondered the
more, as there were manifestly vowels in the larger alphabet,
and the others only appeared to be hidden under strange
appellations. It was also taught, that the Jewish nation, so
long as it flourished, actually were satisfied with the first
signs, and knew no other way to write and read. Most willingly then would I have gone on along this ancient, and, as
it seemed to me, easier path; but my old man declared rather
sternly, that we must go by the grammar as it had been
approved and composed. Reading without these points and
strokes, he said, was a very hard undertaking, and could be
accomplished only by the learned, and those who were well
practised. I must therefore make up my mind to learn these
little characters; but the matter became to me more and more
confused. Now, it seemed, some of the first and larger primitive letters had no value in their places, in order that their
little after-born kindred might not stand there in vain. Now
they indicated a gentle breathing, now a guttural more or
less rough, and now served as mere supports. But, finally,
when one fancied that one had well noted everything, some
of these personages, both great and small, were rendered
inoperative, so that the eyes always had very much, and the
lips very little to do.

As that of which I already knew the contents had now to
be stuttered in a strange gibberish, in which a certain snuffle
and gargle were not a little commended as something unattainable, I in a certain degree deviated from the matter, and
diverted myself in a childish way with the singular names of
these accumulated signs. There were "emperors," "kings,"
and "dukes," * which, as accents, governing here and there,
gave me not a little entertainment. But even these shallow
jests soon lost their charm. Nevertheless, I was indemnified,
inasmuch as by reading, translating, repeating, and commit-
ting to memory, the substance of the book came out more

* These are the technical names for classes of accents in the Hebrew
grammar.—*Trans.*

vividly, and it was this, properly, about which I desired to
be enlightened. Even before this time the contradiction between tradition and the actual and possible had appeared to
me very striking, and I had often put my private tutors to
a non-plus with the sun which stood still on Gibeon, and the
moon in the vale of Ajalon, to say nothing of other improbabilities and incongruities. Everything of this kind was
now awakened, while, in order to master the Hebrew, I occupied myself exclusively with the Old Testament, and studied
it, though no longer in Luther's translation, but in the literal
version of Sebastian Schmid, printed under the text which
my father had procured for me. Here, unfortunately, our
lessons began to be defective, so far as practice in the language was concerned. Reading, interpreting, grammar, tran-
scribing, and the repetition of words, seldom lasted a full half
hour; for I immediately began to aim at the sense of the
matter, and, though we were still engaged in the first book
of Moses, to utter several things suggested to me by the later
books. At first the good old man tried to restrain me from
such digressions, but at last they seemed to entertain him
also. It was impossible for him to suppress his characteristic
cough and chuckle, and although he carefully avoided giving
me any information that might have compromised himself, my
importunity was not relaxed; nay, as I cared more to set forth
my doubts than to learn their solution, I grew constantly more
vivacious and bold, seeming justified by his deportment. Yet
I could get nothing out of him, except that ever and anon he
would exclaim, with his peculiar shaking laugh, " Ah! mad
fellow! ah! mad boy!"

Still, my childish vivacity, which scrutinized the Bible on
all sides, may have seemed to him tolerably serious and worthy
of some assistance. He therefore referred me, after a time, to
the large English Biblical work which stood in his library,
and in which the interpretation of difficult and doubtful passages was attempted in an intelligent and judicious manner.
By the great labours of German divines the translation had
obtained advantages over the original. The different opinions
were cited, and at last a kind of reconciliation was attempted,
so that the dignity of the book, the ground of religion, and the
human understanding might in some degree co-exist. Now,
as often as towards the end of the lesson I came out with my

usual questions and doubts, so often did he point to the repository. I took the volume, he let me read, turned over his Lucian, and when I made any remarks on the book, his ordinary laugh was the only answer to my sagacity. In the long summer days he let me sit as long as I could read, many times alone; after a time he suffered me to take one volume after another home with me.

A man may turn whither he pleases, and undertake anything whatsoever, but he will always return to the path which nature has once prescribed for him. Thus it happened also with me in the present case. My trouble about the language, about the contents of the Sacred Scriptures themselves, ended at last in producing in my imagination a livelier picture of that beautiful and famous land, its environs and its vicinities, as well as of the people and events by which that little spot of earth was made glorious for thousands of years.

This small space was to see the origin and growth of the human race; thence we were to derive our first and only accounts of primitive history: and such a locality was to lie before our imagination, no less simple and comprehensible than varied and adapted to the most wonderful migrations and settlements. Here, between four designated rivers, a small delightful spot was separated from the whole habitable earth, for youthful man. Here he was to unfold his first capacities, and here at the same time was the lot to befal him, which was appointed for all his posterity, namely, that of losing peace by striving after knowledge. Paradise was trifled away; men increased and grew worse; and the Elohim, not yet accustomed to the wickedness of the new race, became impatient and utterly destroyed it. Only a few were saved from the universal deluge: and scarcely had this dreadful flood ceased, than the well known ancestral soil lay once more before the grateful eyes of the preserved.

Two rivers out of four, the Euphrates and Tigris, still flowed in their beds. The name of the first remained; the other seemed to be pointed out by its course. Minuter traces of Paradise were not to be looked for after so great a revolution. The renewed race of man went forth from hence a second time; it found occasion to sustain and employ itself in all sorts of ways, but chiefly to gather around it large herds of tame animals, and to wander with them in every direction.

This mode of life, as well as the increase of the families, soon compelled the people to disperse. They could not at once resolve to let their relatives and friends go for ever; they hit upon the thought of building a lofty tower which should show them the way back from the far distance. But this attempt, like their first endeavour, miscarried. They could not be at the same time happy and wise, numerous and united. The Elohim confounded their minds—the building remained unfinished—the men were dispersed—the world was peopled, but sundered.

But our regards, our interests, are still fastened to these regions. At last the founder of a race again goes forth from hence, and is so fortunate as to stamp a distinct character upon his descendants, and by that means to unite them for all time to come into a great nation, inseparable through all changes of place or destiny.

From the Euphrates, Abraham, not without divine guidance, wanders towards the west. The desert opposes no invincible barrier to his march. He attains the Jordan, passes over its waters, and spreads himself over the fair southern regions of Palestine. This land was already occupied, and tolerably inhabited. Mountains, not extremely high, but rocky and barren, were severed by many watered vales favourable to cultivation. Towns, villages, and solitary settlements lay scattered over the plain and on the slopes of the great valley, the waters of which are collected in Jordan. Thus inhabited, thus tilled was the land; but the world was still large enough, and the men were not so circumspect, necessitous, and active, as to usurp at once the whole adjacent country. Between their possessions were extended large spaces, in which grazing herds could freely move in every direction. In one of these spaces Abraham resides; his brother Lot is near him; but they cannot long remain in such places. The very condition of a land, the population of which is now increasing, now decreasing, and the productions of which are never kept in equilibrium with the wants, produces unexpectedly a famine, and the stranger suffers alike with the native, whose own support he has rendered difficult by his accidental presence. The two Chaldean brothers move onward to Egypt, and thus is traced out for us the theatre on which, for some thousands of years, the most important events of the world were to be enacted. From the Tigris to the Euphrates, from the Euphrates to the Nile, we see the earth peopled; and this space also is traversed by a well-known, heaven-beloved man, who has already become worthy to us, moving to and fro with his goods and cattle, and, in a short time, abundantly increasing them. The brothers return; but, taught by the distress they have endured, they determine to part. Both, indeed, tarry in Southern Canaan; but while Abraham remains at Hebron, near the wood of Mamre, Lot departs for the valley of Siddim, which, if our imagination is bold enough to give Jordan a subterranean outlet, so that in place of the present Dead Sea we should have dry ground, can and must appear like a second Paradise; a conjecture all the more probable, because the residents about there, notorious for effeminacy and wickedness, lead us to infer that they led an easy and luxurious life. Lot lives among them, but apart.

But Hebron and the wood of Mamre appear to us as the important place where the Lord speaks with Abraham, and promises him all the land as far as his eye can reach in four directions. From these quiet districts, from these shepherd tribes, who can associate with celestials, entertain them as guests, and hold many conversations with them, we are compelled to turn our glance once more towards the East, and to think of the condition of the surrounding world, which on the whole, perhaps, may have been like that of Canaan.

Families hold together: they unite, and the mode of life of the tribes is determined by the locality which they have appropriated or appropriate. On the mountains which send down their waters to the Tigris, we find warlike populations, who even thus early foreshadow those world-conquerors and world-rulers—and in a campaign, prodigious for those times, give us a prelude of future achievements. Chedor Laomer, king of Elam, has already a mighty influence over his allies. He reigns a long while: for twelve years before Abraham's arrival in Canaan, he had made all the people tributary to him as far as the Jordan. They revolted at last, and the allies equipped for war. We find them unawares upon a route by which probably Abraham also reached Canaan. The people on the left and lower side of the Jordan were subdued. Chedor Laomer directs his march southwards towards the people of the Desert, then wending north, he smites the Amalekites, and when he

has also overcome the Amorites, he reaches Canaan, falls upon
the kings of the valley of Siddim, smites and scatters them,
and marches with great spoil up the Jordan, in order to extend
his conquests as far as Lebanon.

Among the captives, despoiled and dragged along with their
property, is Lot, who shares the fate of the country in which
he lives a guest. Abraham learns this, and here at once we
behold the patriarch a warrior and hero. He gathers together
his servants, divides them into troops, attacks and falls upon
the luggage of booty, confuses the victors, who could not suspect another enemy in the rear, and brings back his brother
and his goods, with a great deal more belonging to the conquered kings. Abraham, by means of this brief contest,
acquires, as it were, the whole land. To the inhabitants he
appears as a protector, saviour, and, by his disinterestedness,
a king. Gratefully the kings of the valley receive him;—
Melchisedek, the king and priest, with blessings.

Now the prophecies of an endless posterity are renewed,
nay, they take a wider and wider scope. From the waters of
the Euphrates to the river of Egypt all the lands are promised
him; but yet there seems a difficulty with respect to his next
heirs. He is eighty years of age, and has no son. Sarai, less
trusting in the heavenly powers than he, becomes impatient;
she desires, after the oriental fashion, to have a descendant
by means of her maid. But scarcely is Hagar given up to the
master of the house, scarcely is there hope of a son, than dis-
sensions arise. The wife treats her own dependent ill enough,
and Hagar flies to seek a happier position among other tribes.
She returns, not without a higher intimation, and Ishmael is
born.

Abraham is now ninety-nine years old, and the promises of
a numerous posterity are constantly repeated, so that in the
end the pair regard them as ridiculous. And yet Sarai becomes at last pregnant and brings forth a son, to whom the
name of Isaac is given.

History, for the most part, rests upon the legitimate propa-
gation of the human race. The most important events of the
world require to be traced to the secrets of families: and thus
the marriages of the patriarchs give occasion for peculiar considerations. It is as if the Divinity, who loves to guide the
destiny of mankind, wished to prefigure here connubial events

of every kind. Abraham, so long united by childless marriage
to a beautiful woman whom many coveted, finds himself, in
his hundredth year, the husband of two women, the father of
two sons; and at this moment his domestic peace is broken.
Two women, and two sons by different mothers, cannot possibly agree. The party less favoured by law, usage, and
opinion, must yield. Abraham must sacrifice his attachment
to Hagar and Ishmael. Both are dismissed, and Hagar is
compelled now, against her will, to go upon a road which
she once took in voluntary flight, at first, it seems, to the
destruction of herself and child; but the angel of the Lord,
who had before sent her back, now rescues her again, that
Ishmael also may become a great people, and that the most
improbable of all promises may be fulfilled beyond its limits.

Two parents in advanced years, and one son of their old
age—here, at last, one might expect domestic quiet and
earthly happiness. By no means. Heaven is yet preparing
the heaviest trial for the patriarch. But of this we cannot
speak without premising several considerations.

If a natural universal religion was to arise, and a special
revealed one to be developed from it, the countries in which
our imagination has hitherto lingered, the mode of life, the
race of men, were the fittest for the purpose. At least, we do
not find in the whole world anything equally favourable and
encouraging. Even to natural religion, if we assume that it
arose earlier in the human mind, there pertains much of delicacy of sentiment; for it rests upon the conviction of an
universal providence, which conducts the order of the world
as a whole. A particular religion, revealed by Heaven to this
or that people, carries with it the belief in a special providence which the Divine Being vouchsafes to certain favoured
men, families, races, and people. This faith seems to develope
itself with difficulty from man's inward nature. It requires
tradition, usage, and the warrant of a primitive time.

Beautiful is it, therefore, that the Israelitish tradition represents the very first men who confide in this particular providence as heroes of faith, following all the commands of that
high Being on whom they acknowledge themselves dependent,
just as blindly as, undisturbed by doubts, they are unwearied
in awaiting the later fulfilments of his promises.

As a particular revealed religion rests upon the idea that

one man can be more favoured by Heaven than another, so it also arises pre-eminently from the separation of classes. The first men appeared closely allied; but their employments soon divided them. The hunter was the freest of all; from him was developed the warrior and the ruler. Those who tilled the field bound themselves to the soil, erected dwellings and barns to preserve what they had gained, and could estimate themselves pretty highly, because their condition promised durability and security. The herdsman in his position seemed to have acquired the most unbounded condition and unlimited property. The increase of herds proceeded without end, and the space which was to support them widened itself on all sides. These three classes seemed from the very first to have regarded each other with dislike and contempt; and as the herdsman was an abomination to the townsman, so did he in turn separate from the other. The hunters vanish from our sight among the hills, and re-appear only as conquerors.

The patriarchs belonged to the shepherd class. Their manner of life upon the ocean of deserts and pastures, gave breadth and freedom to their minds; the vault of heaven, under which they dwelt, with all its nightly stars, elevated their feelings; and they, more than the active, skilful huntsman, or the secure, careful, householding husbandman, had need of the immovable faith that a God walked beside them, visited them, cared for them, guided and saved them.

We are compelled to make another reflection in passing to the rest of the history. Humane, beautiful, and cheering as the religion of the patriarchs appears, yet traits of savageness and cruelty run through it, out of which man may emerge, or into which he may again be sunk.

That hatred should seek to appease itself by the blood, by the death of the conquered enemy, is natural; that men concluded a peace upon the battle-field among the ranks of the slain, may easily be conceived; that they should in like manner think to give validity to a contract by slain animals, follows from the preceding. The notion also that slain creatures could attract, propitiate, and gain over the gods, whom they always looked upon as partisans, either opponents or allies, is likewise not at all surprising. But if we confine our attention to the sacrifices, and consider the way in which they were offered in that primitive time, we find a singular, and, to our notions, altogether repugnant custom, probably derived from the usages of war, viz., that the sacrificed animals of every kind, and whatever number was devoted, had to be hewn in two halves, and laid out on two sides, so that in the space between them were those who wished to make a covenant with the Deity.

Another dreadful feature wonderfully and portentously pervades that fair world, namely, that everything consecrated or vowed must die. This also was probably an usage of war transferred to peace. The inhabitants of a city which forcibly defends itself are threatened with such a vow; it is taken by storm or otherwise. Nothing is left alive ;—men never, and often women, children, and even cattle, share a similar fate. Such sacrifices are rashly and superstitiously and with more or less distinctness promised to the gods, and those whom the votary would willingly spare, even his nearest of kin, his own children, may thus bleed, the expiatory victims of such a delusion.

In the mild and truly patriarchal character of Abraham, such a savage kind of worship could not arise ; but the Godhead,* which often, to tempt us, seems to put forth those qualities which man is inclined to assign to it, imposes a monstrous task upon him. He must offer up his son as a pledge of the new covenant, and, if he follows the usage, must not only kill and burn him, but cut him in two, and await between the smoking entrails a new promise from the benignant Deity. Abraham blindly, and without lingering, prepares to execute the command ; to Heaven the will is sufficient. Abraham's trials are now at an end, for they could not be carried further. But Sarai dies, and this gives Abraham an opportunity for taking typical possession of the land of Canaan. He requires a grave, and this is the first time he looks out for a possession in this earth. He had before this probably sought out a two-fold cave by the grove of Mamre. This he purchases with the adjacent field, and the legal form which he observes on the occasion, shows how important this possession is to him. Indeed it was more so, perhaps, than he himself supposed ; for there he, his sons and his grandsons, were to rest, and by this means, the nearest title to the whole land, as well

---

* It should be observed that in this Biblical narrative, when we have used the expressions "Deity," "Godhead," or "Divinity," Göthe generally has "die Götter," or "the Gods."—*Trans.*

as the everlasting desire of his posterity to gather themselves there, was most properly grounded.

From this time forth the manifold incidents of the family life become varied. Abraham still keeps strictly apart from the inhabitants, and though Ishmael, the son of an Egyptian woman, has married a daughter of that land, Isaac is obliged to wed a kinswoman of equal birth with himself.

Abraham despatches his servant to Mesopotamia, to the relatives whom he had left behind there. The prudent Eleazer arrives unknown, and, in order to take home the right bride, tries the readiness to serve of the girls at the well. He asks to drink himself, and Rebecca, unasked, waters his camels also. He gives her presents, he demands her in marriage, and his suit is not rejected. He conducts her to the home of his lord, and she is wedded to Isaac. In this case, too, issue has to be long expected. Rebecca is not blessed until after some years of probation, and the same discord which in Abraham's double marriage arose through two mothers, here proceeds from one. Two boys of opposite characters wrestle already in their mother's womb. They come to light, the elder lively and vigorous, the younger gentle and prudent. The former becomes the father's, the latter the mother's favourite. The strife for precedence, which begins even at birth, is ever going on. Esau is quiet and indifferent as to the birthright which fate has given him; Jacob never forgets that his brother forced him back. Watching every opportunity of gaining the desirable privilege, he buys the birthright of his brother, and defrauds him of their father's blessing. Esau is indignant, and vows his brother's death; Jacob flees to seek his fortune in the land of his forefathers.

Now, for the first time, in so noble a family appears a member who has no scruple in attaining by prudence and cunning the advantages which nature and circumstances have denied him. It has often enough been remarked and expressed, that the Sacred Scriptures by no means intend to set up any of the patriarchs and other divinely-favoured men as models of virtue. They, too, are persons of the most different characters, with many defects and failings. But there is one leading trait, in which none of these men after God's own heart can be wanting—that is, an immovable faith that God has special care of them and their families.

General, natural religion, properly speaking, requires no
faith; for the persuasion that a great producing, regulating,
and conducting Being conceals himself, as it were, behind
Nature, to make himself comprehensible to us—such a conviction forces itself upon every one. Nay, if we for a moment
let drop this thread, which conducts us through life, it may be
immediately and everywhere resumed. But it is different
with a special religion, which announces to us that this Great
Being distinctly and pre-eminently interests himself for one
individual, one family, one people, one country. This religion
is founded on faith, which must be immovable if it would not
be instantly destroyed. Every doubt of such a religion is
fatal to it. One may return to conviction, but not to faith.
Hence the endless probation, the delay in the fulfilment of so
often repeated promises, by which the capacity for faith in
those ancestors is set in the clearest light.

It is in this faith also that Jacob begins his expedition, and
if by his craft and deceit he has not gained our affections, he
wins them by his lasting and inviolable love for Rachel, whom
he himself woos on the instant, as Eleazar had courted Rebecca for his father. In him the promise of a countless people
was first to be fully unfolded; he was to see many sons around
him, but through them and their mothers was to endure manifold sorrows of heart.

Seven years he serves for his beloved, without impatience
and without wavering. His father-in-law, crafty like himself,
and disposed, like him, to consider legitimate this means to an
end, deceives him, and so repays him for what he has done to
his brother. Jacob finds in his arms a wife whom he does not
love. Laban, indeed, endeavours to appease him, by giving
him his beloved also after a short time, and this but on the condition of seven years of further service. Vexation arises out of
vexation. The wife he does not love is fruitful, the beloved
one bears no children. The latter, like Sarai, desires to become
a mother through her handmaiden; the former grudges her
even this advantage. She also presents her husband with a
maid; but the good patriarch is now the most troubled man
in the world—he has four women, children by three, and none
from her he loves. Finally she also is favoured, and Joseph
comes into the world, the late fruit of the most passionate
attachment. Jacob's fourteen years of service are over, but

I

Laban is unwilling to part with him, his chief and most trusty servant. They enter into a new compact, and portion the flocks between them. Laban retains the white ones as most numerous, Jacob has to put up with the spotted ones, as the mere refuse. But he is able here too to secure his own advantage; and as by a paltry mess (*of pottage*) he had procured the birthright, and by a disguise his father's blessing, he manages by art and sympathy to appropriate to himself the best and largest part of the herds; and on this side also he becomes the truly worthy progenitor of the people of Israel, and a model for his descendants. Laban and his household remark the result, if not the stratagem. Vexation ensues; Jacob flees with his family and goods, and partly by fortune, partly by cunning, escapes the pursuit of Laban. Rachel is now about to present him another son, but dies in the travail: Benjamin, the child of sorrow, survives her; but the aged father is to experience a still greater sorrow from the apparent loss of his son Joseph.

Perhaps some one may ask why I have so circumstantially narrated histories so universally known and so often repeated and explained. Let the inquirer be satisfied with the answer, that I could in no other way exhibit, how with my distracted life and desultory education, I concentrated my mind and feelings in quiet action on one point; that I was able in no other way to depict the peace that prevailed about me, even when all without was so wild and strange. If an ever busy imagination, of which that tale may bear witness, led me hither and thither, if the medley of fable and history, mythology and religion, threatened to bewilder me, I readily fled to those oriental regions, plunged into the first books of Moses, and there, amid the scattered shepherd-tribes, found myself at once in the greatest solitude and the greatest society.

These family scenes, before they were to lose themselves in a history of the Jewish nation, show us now, in conclusion, a form by which the hopes and fancies of the young in particular are agreeably excited: Joseph, the child of the most passionate wedded love. He seems to us tranquil and clear, and predicts to himself the advantages which are to elevate him above his family. Cast into misfortune by his brothers, he remains steadfast and upright in slavery, resists the most dangerous temptations, rescues himself by prophecy, and is elevated according to his deserts to high honours. He shows himself first serviceable and useful to a great kingdom, then to his own kindred. He is like his ancestor Abraham in repose and greatness, his grandfather Isaac in silence and devotedness. The talent for traffic inherited from his father he exercises on a large scale. It is no longer flocks which are gained for himself from a father-in-law, but people, with all their possessions, which he knows how to purchase for a king. Extremely graceful is this natural story, only it appears too short, and one feels called upon to paint it in detail.

Such a filling-up of biblical characters and events given only in outline, was no longer strange to the Germans. The personages of both the Old and New Testaments had received through Klopstock a tender and affectionate nature, highly pleasing to the Boy as well as to many of his contemporaries. Of Bodmer's efforts in this line little or nothing came to him ; but *Daniel in the Lion's Den*, by Moser, made a great impression on the young heart. In that work a right-minded man of business and courtier arrives at high honours through manifold tribulations, and the piety for which they threatened to destroy him became early and late his sword and buckler. It had long seemed to me desirable to work out the history of Joseph, but I could not get on with the form, particularly as I was conversant with no kind of versification which would have been adapted to such a work. But now I found a treatment of it in prose very suitable, and I applied all my strength to its execution. I now endeavoured to discriminate and paint the characters, and by the interpolation of incidents and episodes, to make the old simple history a new and independent work. I did not consider, what, indeed, youth cannot consider, that subject-matter was necessary to such a design, and that this could only arise by the perceptions of experience. Suffice it to say, that I represented to myself all the incidents down to the minutest details, and narrated them accurately to myself in their succession.

What greatly lightened this labour was a circumstance which threatened to render this work, and my authorship in general, exceedingly voluminous. A young man of various capacities, but who had become imbecile from over exertion and conceit, resided as a ward in my father's house, lived quietly with the family, and if allowed to go on in his usual

way, was contented and agreeable. He had with great care
written out notes of his academical course, and had acquired
a rapid legible hand. He liked to employ himself in writing
better than in anything else, and was pleased when something was given him to copy; but still more when he was
dictated to, because he then felt carried back to his happy
academical years. To my father, who was not expeditious
in writing, and whose German letters were small and tremu-
lous, nothing could be more desirable, and he was consequently accustomed, in the conduct of his own and other
business, to dictate for some hours a day to this young
man. I found it no less convenient, during the intervals, to
see all that passed through my head fixed upon paper by the
hand of another, and my natural gift of feeling and imitation
grew with the facility of catching up and preserving.

As yet I had not undertaken any work so large as that
biblical prose-epic. The times were tolerably quiet, and nothing recalled my imagination from Palestine and Egypt.
Thus my manuscripts swelled more and more every day, as
the poem, which I recited to myself, as it were, in the air,
stretched along the paper; and only a few pages from time
to time needed to be rewritten.

When the work was done—for to my own astonishment it
really came to an end—I reflected that from former years
many poems were extant, which did not even now appear to
me utterly despicable, and which, if written together in the
same size with JOSEPH, would make a very neat quarto, to
which the title "Miscellaneous Poems" might be given. I
was pleased with this, as it gave me an opportunity of quietly
imitating well-known and celebrated authors. I had composed a good number of so-called Anacreontic poems, which,
on account of the convenience of the metre and the easiness
of the subject, flowed forth readily enough. But these I
could not well take, as they were not in rhyme, and my desire
before all things was to show my father something that would
please him. So much the more, therefore, did the spiritual
odes seem suitable, which I had very zealously attempted in
imitation of the *Last Judgment* of Elias Schlegel. One of
these, written to celebrate the descent of Christ into hell,
received much applause from my parents and friends, and had
the good fortune to please myself for some years afterwards.

The so-called texts of the Sunday church-music, which were always to be had printed, I studied with diligence. They were, indeed, very weak, and I could well believe that my verses, of which I had composed many in the prescribed manner, were equally worthy of being set to music, and performed for the edification of the congregation. These and many like them I had for more than a year before copied with my own hand, because through this private exercise I was released from the copies of the writing-master. Now, all were corrected and put in order, and no great persuasion was needed to have them neatly copied by the young man who was so fond of writing. I hastened with them to the book-binder, and when very soon after I handed the nice-looking volume to my father, he encouraged me with peculiar satisfaction to furnish a similar quarto every year; which he did with the greater conviction, as I had produced the whole in my spare moments alone.

Another circumstance increased my tendency to these theological, or rather biblical studies. The senior of the ministry, JOHN PHILIP FRESENIUS, a mild man, of handsome, agreeable appearance, who was respected by his congregation and the whole city as an exemplary pastor and good preacher, but who, because he stood forth against the Herrnhuters, was not in the best odour with the peculiarly pious; while, on the other hand, he had made himself famous, and almost sacred, with the multitude, by the conversion of a free-thinking General who had been mortally wounded—this man died, and his successor, Plitt, a tall, handsome, dignified man, who brought from his *Chair* (he had been a Professor in Marburg) the gift of teaching rather than of edifying, immediately announced a sort of religious course, to which his sermons were to be devoted in a certain methodical connexion. I had already, as I was compelled to go to church, remarked the distribution of the subject, and could now and then show myself off by a pretty complete recitation of a sermon. But now as much was said in the congregation, both for and against the new senior, and many placed no great confidence in his announced didactic sermons, I undertook to write them out more carefully, and I succeeded the better from having made smaller attempts in a seat very convenient for hearing, but concealed from sight. I was extremely attentive and on the alert; the moment he said

Amen I hastened from the church and consumed a couple of
hours in rapidly dictating what I had fixed in my memory
and on paper, so that I could hand in the written sermon before dinner. My father was very proud of this success, and
the good friend of the family, who had just come in to dinner,
also shared in the joy. Indeed, this friend was very well-
disposed to me, because I had so made his *Messiah* my own,
that in my repeated visits to him to get impressions of seals
for my collection of coats-of-arms, I could recite long passages
from it till the tears stood in his eyes.

The next Sunday I prosecuted the work with equal zeal, and
as the mechanical part of it mainly interested me, I did not
reflect upon what I wrote and preserved. During the first
quarter these efforts may have continued pretty much the
same ; but as I fancied at last, in my self-conceit, that I found
no particular enlightenment as to the Bible, nor clearer insight
into dogmas, the small vanity which was thus gratified seemed
to me too dearly purchased for me to pursue the matter with
the same zeal. The sermons, once so many-leaved, grew more
and more meagre ; and before long I should have relinquished
this labour altogether, if my father, who was a fast friend to
completeness, had not, by words and promises, induced me to
persevere till the last Sunday in Trinity—though, at the conclusion, scarcely more than the text, the statement, and the
divisions were scribbled on little pieces of paper.

My father was particularly pertinacious on this point of completeness. What was once undertaken must be finished, even
if the inconvenience, tedium, vexation, nay, uselessness of the
thing begun were plainly manifested in the meantime. It
seemed as if he regarded completeness as the only end, and
perseverance as the only virtue. If in our family circle, in the
long winter evenings, we had begun to read a book aloud, we
were compelled to finish, though we were all in despair about
it, and my father himself was the first to yawn. I still remember such a winter when we had thus to work our way
through Bower's *History of the Popes*. It was a terrible time,
as little or nothing that occurs in ecclesiastical affairs can
interest children and young people. Still, with all my inat-
tention and repugnance, so much of that reading remained in
my mind that I was able, in after times, to take up many
threads of the narrative.

Amid all these heterogeneous occupations and labours, which followed each other so rapidly that one could hardly reflect whether they were permissible and useful, my father did not lose sight of the main object. He endeavoured to direct my memory and my talent for apprehending and combining to objects of jurisprudence, and therefore gave me a small book by Hopp, in the shape of a catechism, and worked up according to the form and substance of the Institutions. I soon learned questions and answers by heart, and could represent the catechist as well as the catechumen; and, as in religious instruction at that time, one of the chief exercises was to find passages in the Bible as readily as possible, so here a similar acquaintance with the *Corpus Juris* was found necessary, in which, also, I soon became completely versed. My father wished me to go on, and the little STRUVE was taken in hand; but here affairs did not proceed so rapidly. The form of the work was not so favourable for beginners, that they could help themselves on, nor was my father's method of teaching so liberal as greatly to interest me.

Not only by the warlike state in which we lived for some years, but also by civil life itself, and the perusal of history and romances, was it made clear to me that there were many cases in which the laws are silent and give no help to the individual, who must then see how to get out of the difficulty by himself. We had now reached the period when, according to the old routine, we were, besides other things, to learn to fence and ride, that we might guard our skins upon occasion, and have no pedantic appearance on horseback. As to the first, the practice was very agreeable to us; for we had already, long ago, contrived to make broad-swords out of hazel-sticks, with basket-hilts, neatly woven of willow, to protect the hands. Now we might get real steel blades, and the clash we made with them was very merry.

There were two fencing-masters in the city: an old earnest German, who went to work in a severe and solid style, and a Frenchman, who sought to gain his advantage by advancing and retreating, and by light fugitive thrusts, which he always accompanied by cries. Opinions varied as to whose manner was the best. The little company with which I was to take lessons sided with the Frenchman, and we speedily accustomed ourselves to move backwards and forwards, make passes

and recover, always breaking out into the usual exclamations.
But several of our acquaintance had gone to the German
teacher, and practised precisely the opposite. These distinct
modes of treating so important an exercise, the conviction of
each that his master was the best, really caused a dissension
among the young people, who were of about the same age,
and the fencing-schools occasioned serious battles,—for there
was almost as much fighting with words as with swords ; and
to decide the matter in the end, a trial of skill between the
two teachers was arranged, the consequences of which I need
not circumstantially describe. The German stood in his position like a wall, watched his opportunity, and contrived to
disarm his opponent over and over again with his cut and
thrust. The latter maintained that this mattered not, and
proceeded to exhaust the other's wind by his agility. He
fetched the German several lunges, too, which, however, if
they had been in earnest, would have sent himself into the
next world.

On the whole, nothing was decided or improved, except
that some went over to our countryman, of whom I was one.
But I had already acquired too much from the first master ;
and hence a considerable time elapsed before the new one
could break me of it, who was altogether less satisfied with
us renegades than with his original pupils.

As to riding, it fared still worse with me. It happened
that they sent me to the course in the autumn, so that I commenced in the cool and damp season. The pedantic treatment of this noble art was highly repugnant to me. From
first to last the whole talk was about sitting the horse, and
yet no one could say in what a proper sitting consisted,
though all depended on that ; for they went to and fro on the
horse without stirrups. Moreover, the instruction seemed
contrived only for cheating and degrading the scholars. If
one forgot to hook or loosen the curb-chain, or let his switch
fall down, or even his hat,—every delay, every misfortune,
had to be atoned for by money, and one was even laughed at
besides. This put me in the worst of humours, particularly
when I found the place of exercise itself quite intolerable.
The great nasty space, either wet or dusty, the cold, the
mouldy smell, all together was in the highest degree repugnant to me ; and since the stable-master always gave the others

the best and me the worst horses to ride, perhaps because they bribed him by breakfasts and other gifts, or even by their own cleverness; since he kept me waiting, and, as it seemed, slighted me, I spent the most disagreeable hours in an employment that ought to have been the most pleasant in the world. Nay, the impression of that time and of these circumstances has remained with me so vividly, that although I afterwards became a passionate and daring rider, and for days and weeks together scarcely got off my horse, I carefully shunned covered riding-courses, and at least passed only a few moments in them. The case often happens that when the elements of an exclusive art are taught us, this is done in a painful and revolting manner. The conviction that this is both wearisome and injurious, has given rise in later times to the educational maxim, that the young must be taught everything in an easy, cheerful, and agreeable way: from which, however, other evils and disadvantages have proceeded.

With the approach of spring, times became again more quiet with us, and if in earlier days I had endeavoured to obtain a sight of the city, its ecclesiastical, civil, public and private structures, and especially found great delight in the still prevailing antiquities, I afterwards endeavoured, by means of Lersner's *Chronicle*, and other Frankfortian books and pamphlets belonging to my father, to revive the persons of past times. This seemed to me to be well attained by great attention to the peculiarities of times and manners, and of distinguished individuals.

Among the ancient remains, that which, from my childhood, had been remarkable to me, was the skull of a state criminal, fastened up on the tower of the bridge, who, out of three or four, as the naked iron spikes showed, had, since 1616, been preserved in spite of the encroachments of time and weather. Whenever one returned from Sachsenhausen to Frankfort, one had this tower before one, and the skull was directly in view. As a boy, I liked to hear related the history of these rebels—Fettmilch and his confederates—how they had become dissatisfied with the government of the city, had risen up against it, plotted a mutiny, plundered the Jews' quarter, and excited a fearful riot, but were at last captured, and condemned to death by a deputy of the emperor. Afterwards I felt anxious to know the most minute circumstance,

and to hear what sort of people they were. When from an
old cotemporary book, ornamented with woodcuts, I learned
that while these men had indeed been condemned to death,
many councillors had at the same time been deposed, because
various kinds of disorder and very much that was unwarrant-
able was then going on; when I heard the nearer particulars
how all took place, I pitied the unfortunate persons who
might be regarded as sacrifices made for a future better constitution. For from that time was dated the regulation which
allows the noble old house of Limpurg, the Frauenstein-
house, sprung from a club, besides lawyers, tradespeople,
and artisans, to take a part in a government, which, completed by a system of ballot, complicated in the Venetian
fashion, and restricted by the civil colleges, was called to do
right, without acquiring any special privilege to do wrong.

Among the things which excited the misgivings of the Boy,
and even of the youth, was especially the state of the Jewish
quarter of the city (*Judenstadt*), properly called the Jew-
street (*Judengasse*), as it consisted of little more than a single
street, which in early times may have been hemmed in between
the walls and trenches of the town, as in a prison (*Zwinger*).
The closeness, the filth, the crowd, the accent of an unpleasant
language, altogether made a most disagreeable impression,
even if one only looked in as one passed the gate. It was
long before I ventured in alone, and I did not return there
readily, when I had once escaped the importunities of so
many men unwearied in demanding and offering to traffic.
At the same time the old legends of the cruelty of the Jews
towards Christian children, which we had seen hideously illustrated in Godfrey's *Chronicles*, hovered gloomily before my
young mind. And although they were thought better of in
modern times, the large caricature, still to be seen, to their
disgrace, on an arched wall under the bridge tower, bore
extraordinary witness against them; for it had been made,
not through private ill-will, but by public order.

However, they still remained, nevertheless, the chosen
people of God, and passed, no matter how it came about, as
a memorial of the most ancient times. Besides, they also were
men, active and obliging, and even to the tenacity with which
they clung to their peculiar customs, one could not refuse one's
respect. The girls, moreover, were pretty, and were far from

displeased when a Christian lad, meeting them on the sabbath
in the Fischerfeld, showed himself kindly and attentive. I was
consequently extremely curious to become acquainted with
their ceremonies. I did not desist until I had frequently
visited their school, had assisted at a circumcision and a wedding, and had formed a notion of the Feast of the Tabernacles.
Everywhere I was well received, pleasantly entertained, and
invited to come again; for they were persons of influence by
whom I had been either introduced or recommended.

Thus, as a young resident in a large city, I was thrown
about from one object to another, and horrible scenes were
not wanting in the midst of the municipal quiet and security.
Sometimes a more or less remote fire aroused us from our
domestic peace, sometimes the discovery of a great crime,
with its investigation and punishment, set the whole city in
an uproar for many weeks. We were forced to be witnesses of
different executions; and it is worth remembering, that I was
also once present at the burning of a book. The publication
was a French comic romance, which indeed spared the state,
but not religion and manners. There was really something
dreadful in seeing punishment inflicted on a lifeless thing.
The packages exploded in the fire, and were raked asunder by
an oven-fork, to be brought in closer contact with the flames.
It was not long before the kindled sheets were wafted about
in the air, and the crowd caught at them with eagerness. Nor
could we rest until we had hunted up a copy, while not a few
managed likewise to procure the forbidden pleasure. Nay,
if it had been done to give the author publicity, he could not
himself have made a more effectual provision.

But there were also more peaceable inducements which
took me about in every part of the city. My father had
early accustomed me to manage for him his little affairs of
business. He charged me particularly to stir up the labourers
whom he set to work, as they commonly kept him waiting
longer than was proper; because he wished everything
done accurately, and was used in the end to lower the price
for a prompt payment. In this way, I gained access to all
the workshops; and as it was natural to me to enter into the
condition of others, to feel every species of human existence,
and sympathize in it with pleasure, these commissions were
to me the occasion of many most delightful hours, and I

learned to know every one's method of proceeding, and what
joy and sorrow, what advantages and hardships, were incident
to the indispensable conditions of this or that mode of life.
I was thus brought nearer to that active class which connects
the lower and upper classes. For, if on the one side stand
those who are employed in the simple and rude products, and
on the other those who desire to enjoy something that has
been already worked up ; the manufacturer, with his skill
and hand, is the mediator through whom the other two receive
something from each other ; each is enabled to gratify his
wishes in his own way. The household economy of many
crafts. which took its form and colour from the occupation,
was likewise an object of my quiet attention ; and thus was
developed and strengthened in me the feeling of the equality,
if not of all men, yet of all human conditions,—the mere fact
of existence seeming to me the main point, and all the rest
indifferent and accidental.

As my father did not readily allow himself an expense which
would be at once consumed in a momentary enjoyment—as I can
scarcely call to mind that we ever took a walk together, and
spent anything in a place of amusement,—he was, on the other
hand, not niggardly in procuring such things as had a
good external appearance in addition to inward value. No
one could desire peace more than he, although he had not felt
the smallest inconvenience during the last days of the war.
With this feeling, he had promised my mother a gold snuff-
box, set with diamonds, which she was to receive as soon as
peace should be publicly declared. In the expectation of the
happy event, they had laboured now for some years on this
present. The box, which was tolerably large, had been executed in Hanau, for my father was on good terms with
the gold-workers there, as well as with the heads of the silk
establishments. Many designs were made for it ; the cover
was adorned by a basket of flowers, over which hovered a
dove with the olive-branch. A vacant space was left for the
jewels, which were to be set partly in the dove and partly on
the spot where the box is usually opened. The jeweller to
whom the execution and the requisite stones were entrusted
was named Lautensak, and was a brisk, skilful man, who
like many artists, seldom did what was necessary, but usually
works of caprice, which gave him pleasure. The jewels were

very soon set, in the shape in which they were to be put
upon the box, on some black wax, and looked very well; but
they would not come off to be transferred to the gold. In
the outset, my father let the matter rest; but as the hope
of peace became livelier, and finally when the stipulations—
particularly the elevation of the Archduke Joseph to the
Roman throne—seemed more precisely known, he grew more
and more impatient, and I had to go several times a week,
nay, at last, almost daily, to visit the tardy artist. By means
of my unremitted teazing and exhortation, the work went on,
though slowly enough; for as it was of that kind which can
be taken in hand or laid aside at will, there was always
something by which it was thrust out of the way, and put
aside.

The chief cause of this conduct, however, was a task which
the artist had undertaken on his own account. Everybody
knew that the Emperor Francis cherished a strong liking for
jewels, and especially for coloured stones. Lautensak had expended a considerable sum, and as it afterwards turned out
larger than his means, on such gems, out of which he had
begun to shape a nosegay, in which every stone was to be
tastefully disposed, according to its shape and colour, and the
whole form a work of art worthy to stand in the treasure-
vaults of an emperor. He had, in his desultory way, laboured
for many years upon it, and now hastened—because after the
hoped-for peace the arrival of the Emperor, for the coronation of his son, was expected in Frankfort—to complete it
and finally to put it together. My desire to become acquainted with such things he used very dexterously in order
to distract me as a bearer of threats, and to lead me away
from my intention. He strove to impart a knowledge of
these stones to me, and made me attentive to their pro-
perties and value, so that in the end I knew his whole
bouquet by heart, and quite as well as he could have demon-
strated its virtues to a customer. It is even now before me,
and I have since seen more costly, but not more graceful
specimens of show and magnificence in this sort. He possessed, moreover, a pretty collection of engravings, and other
works of art, with which he liked to amuse himself; and
I passed many hours with him, not without profit. Finally,
when the Congress of Hubertsburg was finally fixed, he did

for my sake more than was due; and the dove and flowers
actually reached my mother's hands on the festival in celebra-
tion of the peace.

I then received also many similar commissions to urge on
painters with respect to pictures which had been ordered.
My father had confirmed himself in the notion—and few men
were free from it—that a picture painted on wood was greatly
to be preferred to one that was merely put on canvas. It was
therefore his great care to possess good oak boards, of every
shape, because he well knew that just on this important point
the more careless artists trusted to the joiners. The oldest planks
were hunted up, the joiners were obliged to go accurately to
work with gluing, painting, and arranging, and they were
then kept for years in an upper room, where they could be
sufficiently dried. A precious board of this kind was intrusted
to the painter JUNKER, who was to represent on it an ornamental flower-pot, with the most important flowers drawn
after nature in his artistic and elegant manner. It was just
about the spring-time, and I did not fail to take him several
times a week the most beautiful flowers that fell in my way,
which he immediately put in, and by degrees composed the
whole out of these elements with the utmost care and fidelity.
On one occasion I had caught a mouse, which I took to him,
and which he desired to copy as a very pretty animal; nay,
really represented it, as accurately as possible, gnawing an ear
of corn at the foot of the flower-pot. Many such inoffen-
sive natural objects, such as butterflies and chafers, were
brought in and represented, so that finally, as far as imitation
and execution were concerned, a highly valuable picture was
put together.

Hence I was not a little astonished when the good man
formally declared one day, when the work was just about to
be delivered, that the picture no longer pleased him,—since,
while it had turned out quite well in its details, it was not
well composed as a whole, because it had been produced in
this gradual manner: and he had perpetrated a blunder in
the outset, in not at least devising a general plan for light and
shade, as well as for colour, according to which the single
flowers might have been arranged. He examined with me
the minutest parts of the picture, which had arisen before my
eyes during a half year, and had in many respects pleased me,

and managed to convince me perfectly, much to my regret. Even the copy of the mouse he regarded as a mistake; for many persons, he said, have a sort of horror of such animals, and they should not be introduced where the object is to excite pleasure. As it commonly happens with those who are cured of a prejudice, and imagine themselves much more knowing than they were before, I now had a real contempt for this work of art, and agreed perfectly with the artist when he caused to be prepared another tablet of the same size, on which, according to his taste, he painted a better formed vessel and a more artistically arranged nosegay, and also managed to select and distribute the little living accessories in an ornamental and agreeable way. This tablet also he painted with the greatest care, though altogether after the former copied one, or from memory, which, through a very long and assiduous practice, came to his aid. Both paintings were now ready, and we were thoroughly delighted with the last, which was certainly the more artistic and striking of the two. My father was surprised with two pictures instead of one, and to him the choice was left. He approved of our opinion, and of the reasons for it, and especially of our good-will and activity; but, after considering both pictures some days, decided in favour of the first, without saying much about the motives of his choice. The artist, in an ill-humour, took back his second well-meant picture, and could not refrain from the remark that the good oaken tablet on which the first was painted had certainly its effect on my father's decision.

Now I am again speaking of painting, I am reminded of a large establishment, where I passed much time, because both it and its managers especially attracted me. It was the great oil-cloth factory which the painter NOTHNAGEL had erected; an expert artist, but one who by his mode of thought inclined more to manufacture than to art. In a very large space of courts and gardens, all sorts of oil-cloths were made, from the coarsest that are spread with a trowel, and used for baggage-wagons and similar purposes, and the carpets impressed with figures, to the finer and the finest, on which sometimes Chinese and grotesque, sometimes natural flowers, sometimes figures, sometimes landscapes were represented by the pencils of accomplished workmen. This multiplicity, to which there was no end, amused me vastly. The occupation of so many

men, from the commonest labour to that in which a certain
artistic worth could not be denied, was to me extremely attractive. I made the acquaintance of this multitude of younger
and older men, working in several rooms one behind the other,
and occasionally lent a hand myself. The sale of these com-
modities was extraordinarily brisk. Whoever at that time
was building or furnishing a house, wished to provide for
his lifetime, and this oil-cloth carpeting was certainly quite
indestructible. Nothnagel had enough to do in managing
the whole, and sat in his office surrounded by factors and
clerks. The remainder of his time he employed in his collection
of works of art, consisting chiefly of engravings, in which, as
well as in the pictures he possessed, he traded occasionally.
At the same time he had acquired a taste for etching; he
etched a variety of plates, and prosecuted this branch of art
even into his latest years.

As his dwelling lay near the Eschenheim gate, my way
when I had visited him led me out of the city to some pieces
of ground which my father owned beyond the gates. One was
a large orchard, the soil of which was used as a meadow, and
in which my father carefully attended the transplanting of
trees, and whatever else pertained to their preservation, though
the ground itself was leased. Still more occupation was furnished by a very well-preserved vineyard beyond the Friedberg gate, where between the rows of vines, rows of asparagus
were planted and tended with great care. Scarcely a day
passed in the fine season in which my father did not go there,
and as on these occasions we might generally accompany him,
we were provided with joy and delight from the earliest productions of spring to the last of autumn. We also learned
to occupy ourselves with gardening matters, which, as they
were repeated every year, became in the end perfectly known
and familiar to us. But after the manifold fruits of summer
and autumn, the vintage at last was the most lively and the
most desirable: nay, there is no question that as wine gives
a freer character to the very places and districts where it is
grown and drunk, so also do these vintage-days, while they
close summer and at the same time open the winter, diffuse
an incredible cheerfulness. Joy and jubilation pervade a
whole district. In the daytime, huzzas and shoutings are
heard from every end and corner, and at night rockets and

fire-balls, now here, now there, announce that the people, everywhere awake and lively, would willingly make this festival last as long as possible. The subsequent labour at the wine-press, and during the fermentation in the cellar, gave us also a cheerful employment at home, and thus we ordinarily reached winter without being properly aware of it.

These rural possessions delighted us so much the more in the spring of 1763, as the 15th of February in that year was celebrated as a festival day, on account of the conclusion of the Hubertsberg peace, under the happy results of which the greater part of my life was to flow away. But before I go further, I think I am bound to mention some men who exerted an important influence on my youth.

Von Olenschlager, a member of the Frauenstein family, a Schöff, and son-in-law of the above-mentioned Dr. Orth, a handsome, comfortable, sanguine man. In his official holiday costume he could well have personated the most important French prelate. After his academical course, he had employed himself in political and state affairs, and directed even his travels to that end. He greatly esteemed me, and often conversed with me on matters which chiefly interested him. I was with him when he wrote his *Illustration of the Golden Bull;* when he managed to explain to me very clearly the worth and dignity of that document. My imagination was led back by it to those wild and unquiet times, so that I could not forbear representing what he related historically, as if it were present, by pictures of characters and circumstances, and often by mimicry. In this he took great delight, and by his applause excited me to repetition.

I had from childhood the singular habit of always learning by heart the beginnings of books, and the divisions of a work, first of the five books of Moses, and then of the *Æneid* and Ovid's *Metamorphoses.* I now did the same thing with the *Golden Bull,* and often provoked my patron to a smile, when I quite seriously and unexpectedly exclaimed, " *Omne regnum in se divisum desolabitur; nam principes ejus facti sunt socii furum.*" * The knowing man shook his head, smiling, and said doubtingly, " What times those must have been, when

* Every kingdom divided against itself shall be brought to desolation; for the princes thereof have become the associates of robbers.— *Trans.*

K

at a grand Diet, the Emperor had such words published in the face of his princes!"

There was a great charm in Von Olenschlager's society. He received little company, but was strongly inclined to intellectual amusement, and induced us young people from time to time to perform a play; for such exercises were deemed particularly useful to the young. We gave the CANUTE of Schlegel, in which the part of the king was assigned to me, Elfrida to my sister, and Ulfo to the younger son of the family. We then ventured on the BRITANNICUS,* for, besides our dramatic talents, we were to bring the language into practice. I took Nero, my sister, Agrippina, and the younger son, Britannicus. We were more praised than we deserved, and fancied that we had done it even beyond the amount of praise. Thus I stood on the best terms with this family, and have been indebted to them for many pleasures and a speedier development.

VON REINECK, of an old patrician family, able, honest, but stubborn, a meagre, swarthy man, whom I never saw smile. The misfortune befell him that his only daughter was carried off by a friend of the family. He pursued his son-in-law with the most vehement prosecution; and because the tribunals, with their formality, were neither speedy nor sharp enough to gratify his desire of vengeance, he fell out with them; and there arose quarrel on quarrel, suit on suit. He retired completely into his own house and its adjacent garden, lived in a spacious but melancholy lower-room, into which for many years no brush of a whitewasher, and perhaps scarcely the broom of a maid-servant, had found its way. Me he could readily endure, and he had especially commended to me his younger son. He many times asked his oldest friends, who knew how to humour him, his men of business and agents, to dine with him, and on these occasions never omitted inviting me. There was good eating and better drinking at his house. But a large stove, that let out the smoke from many cracks, caused the greatest pain to his guests. One of the most intimate of these once ventured to remark upon this, by asking the host whether he could put up with such an inconvenience all the winter. He answered, like a second Timon or Heautontimoroumenos: "Would to God this was the greatest evil of those which torment

* Racine's tragedy.—*Trans.*

me!" It was long before he allowed himself to be persuaded
to see his daughter and grandson. The son-in-law never again
dared to come into his presence.

On this excellent but unfortunate man my visits had a very
favourable effect ; for while he liked to converse with me, and
particularly instructed me on world and state affairs, he seemed
to feel himself relieved and cheered. The few old friends who
still gathered round him, often, therefore, made use of me
when they wished to soften his peevish humour, and persuade
him to any diversion. He now really rode out with us many
times, and again contemplated the country, on which he had
not cast an eye for so many years. He called to mind the old
landowners, and told stories of their characters and actions, in
which he showed himself always severe, but often cheerful and
witty. We now tried also to bring him again among other
men, which, however, nearly turned out badly.

About the same age, if indeed not older, was one HERR
VON MALAPERT, a rich man, who possessed a very handsome
house by the Horse-market, and derived a good income from
salt-pits. He also lived quite secluded : but in summer he
was a great deal in his garden, near the Bockenheim gate,
where he watched and tended a very fine plot of pinks.

Von Reineck was likewise an amateur of pinks ; the season
of flowering had come, and suggestions were made as to
whether these two could not visit each other. We introduced
the matter, and persisted in it, till at last Von Reineck resolved
to go out with us one Sunday afternoon. The greeting of the
two old gentlemen was very laconic, indeed, almost panto-
mimic, and they walked up and down by the long pink frames
with true diplomatic strides. The display was really extraordinarily beautiful, and the particular forms and colours of the
different flowers, the advantages of one over the other, and
their rarity, gave at last occasion to a sort of conversation
which appeared to get quite friendly : at which we others
rejoiced the more because we saw the most precious old
Rhine wine in cut decanters, fine fruits, and other good things
spread upon a table in a neighbouring bower. But these, alas!
we were not to enjoy. For Von Reineck unfortunately saw a
very fine pink with its head somewhat hanging down ; he
therefore took the stalk near the calyx very cautiously between
his fore and middle fingers, and lifted the flower so that he

K 2

could well inspect it. But even this gentle handling vexed
the owner. Von Malapert courteously, indeed, but stiffly
enough, and somewhat self-complacently, reminded him of
the *Oculis, non manibus*.* Von Reineck had already let go the
flower, but at once took fire at the words, and said in his
usual dry, earnest manner, that it was quite consistent with
an amateur to touch and examine them in such a manner.
Whereupon he repeated the act, and took the flower again
between his fingers. The friends of both parties—for Von
Malapert also had one present—were now in the greatest perplexity. They set one hare to catch another (that was our
proverbial expression, when a conversation was to be interrupted, and turned to another subject), but it would not do;
the old gentleman had become quite silent, and we feared every
moment that Von Reineck would repeat the act, when it would
be all over with us. The two friends kept their principals
apart by occupying them, now here, now there, and at last we
found it most expedient to make preparation for departure.
Thus, alas! we were forced to turn our backs on the inviting
side-board, yet unenjoyed.

HOFRATH HUISGEN, not born in Frankfort, of the reformed†
religion, and therefore incapable of public office, including the
profession of advocate, which, however, because much confidence was placed in him as an excellent jurist, he managed
to exercise quietly, both in the Frankfort and the imperial
courts, under assumed signatures, was already sixty years
old when I took writing lessons with his son, and so came
into his house. His figure was tall without being thin, and
broad without corpulency. You could not look, for the
first time, on his face, which was not only disfigured by small-
pox, but deprived of an eye, without apprehension. He always
wore on his bald head a perfectly white bell-shaped cap, tied
at the top with a ribbon. His morning-gowns, of calamanco or
damask, were always very clean. He dwelt in a very cheerful suite of rooms on the ground-floor by the *Allée*, and the
neatness of everything about him corresponded with this cheerfulness. The perfect arrangement of his papers, books, and
maps, produced a favourable impression. His son Heinrich

* Eyes, not hands.—*Trans.*

† That is to say, he was a Calvinist, as distinguished from a Lutheran.
—*Trans.*

Sebastian, afterwards known by various writings on Art, gave little promise in his youth. Good-natured but dull, not rude but blunt, and without any special liking for instruction, he rather sought to avoid the presence of his father, as he could get all he wanted from his mother. I, on the other hand, grew more and more intimate with the old man, the more I knew of him. As he attended only to important cases, he had time enough to occupy and amuse himself in another manner. I had not long frequented his house, and heard his doctrines, than I could well perceive that he stood in opposition to God and the world. One of his favourite books was *Agrippa de Vanitate Scientiarum*, which he especially commended to me, and so set my young brains in a considerable whirl for a long time. In the happiness of youth I was inclined to a sort of optimism, and had again pretty well reconciled myself with God or the Gods ; for the experience of a series of years had taught me that there was much to counterbalance evil, that one can well recover from misfortune, and may be saved from dangers without always going about breaking one's neck. I looked with tolerance, too, on what men did and pursued, and found many things worthy of praise which my old gentleman could not by any means abide. Indeed, once when he had sketched the world to me, rather from the distorted side, I observed from his appearance that he meant to close the game with an important trump-card. He shut tight his blind left eye, as he was wont to do in such cases, looked sharp out of the other, and said in a nasal voice, " Even in God I discover defects."

My Timonic mentor was also a mathematician, but his practical turn drove him to mechanics, though he did not work himself. A clock, wonderful indeed in those days, which indicated not only the days and hours, but the motions of the sun and moon, he caused to be made according to his own plan. On Sunday, about ten o'clock in the morning, he always wound it up himself, which he could do the more regularly, as he never went to church. I never saw company nor guests at his house ; and only twice in ten years do I remember to have seen him dressed and out of doors.

My various conversations with these men were not insignificant, and each of them influenced me in his own way. From every one I had as much attention as his own children, if not

more, and each strove to increase his delight in me as in a beloved son, while he aspired to mould me into his moral counterpart.   Olenschlager would have made me a courtier, Von Reineck a diplomatic man of business; both, the latter particularly,
sought to disgust me with poetry and authorship.   Huisgen
wished me to be a Timon after his fashion, but, at the same
time, an able juris-consult; a necessary profession, as he
thought, with which one could in a regular manner defend
oneself and friends against the rabble of mankind, succour the
oppressed, and above all, pay off a rogue ; though the last is
neither especially practicable nor advisable.

But if I liked to be at the side of these men to profit by their
counsels and directions, younger persons, only a little older
than myself, roused me to immediate emulation. I name here
before all others, the brothers SCHLOSSER and GRIESBACH.
But, as I came subsequently into a more intimate connexion
with these, which lasted for many years uninterruptedly, I will
only say for the present, that they were then praised as being
distinguished in languages and other studies which opened the
academical course, and held up as models, and that everybody
cherished the certain expectation that they would once do
something uncommon in church and state.

With respect to myself, I also had it in my mind to produce
something extraordinary, but in what it was to consist was not
clear.   But as we are apt to think rather upon the reward
which may be received than upon the merit which is to be
acquired, so, I do not deny, that if I thought of a desirable
piece of good fortune, it appeared to me most fascinating in
the shape of that laurel garland which is woven to adorn the
poet.

FIFTH BOOK.

EVERY bird has its decoy, and every man is led and misled in a way peculiar to himself. Nature, education, circumstances, and habit kept me apart from all that was rude; and though I often came into contact with the lower classes of people, particularly mechanics, no close connexion grew out of it. I had indeed boldness enough to undertake something uncommon and perhaps dangerous, and many times felt disposed to do so; but I was without the handle by which to grasp and hold it.

Meanwhile I was quite unexpectedly involved in an affair which brought me near to a great hazard, and at least for a long time into perplexity and distress. The good terms on which I before stood with the boy whom I have already named Pylades was maintained up to the time of my youth. We indeed saw each other less often, because our parents did not stand on the best footing with each other; but when we did meet, the old raptures of friendship broke out immediately. Once we met in the alleys which offer a very agreeable walk between the outer and inner gate of Saint Gallus. We had scarcely returned greetings, than he said to me, "I hold to the same opinion as ever about your verses. Those which you recently communicated to me, I read aloud to some pleasant companions, and not one of them will believe that you have made them." "Let it pass," I answered; "we will make them and enjoy them, and the others may think and say of them what they please."

"There comes the unbeliever now," added my friend. "We will not speak of it," I replied; "what is the use of it? one cannot convert them." "By no means," said my friend; "I cannot let the affair pass off in this way."

After a short and indifferent conversation, my young comrade, who was but too well disposed towards me, could not suffer the matter to drop, without saying to the other, with some resentment, "Here is my friend who made those pretty verses, for which you will not give him credit!" "He will certainly not be offended at that," answered the other, "for we do him an honour when we suppose that more learning is required to make such verses than one of his years can possess." I replied with something indifferent; but my friend continued, "It will not cost much labour to convince you. Give him any theme, and he will make you a poem on the spot." I assented, we were agreed, and the other asked me whether I would venture to compose a pretty love-letter in rhyme, which a modest young woman might be supposed to write to a young man, to declare her inclination. "Nothing is easier than that," I answered, "if I only had writing materials." He pulled out his pocket almanac, in which there were a great many blank leaves, and I sat down upon a bench to write. They walked about in the meanwhile, but always kept me in sight. I immediately brought the required situation before my mind, and thought how agreeable it must be if some pretty girl were really attached to me, and would reveal her sentiments to me, either in prose or verse. I therefore began my declaration with delight, and in a little while executed it in a flowing measure, between doggerel and madrigal, with the greatest possible *naïveté*, and in such a way that the sceptic was overcome with admiration, and my friend with delight. The request of the former to possess the poem I could the less refuse, as it was written in his almanac; and I willingly saw the documentary evidence of my capabilities in his hands. He departed with many assurances of admiration and respect, and wished for nothing more than that we should often meet; so we settled soon to go together into the country.

Our party actually took place, and was joined by several more young people of the same rank. They were men of the middle, or, if you please, of the lower class, who were not wanting in brains, and who moreover, as they had gone through school, were possessed of various knowledge and a certain degree of culture. In a large, rich city there are many modes of gaining a livelihood. These got on by copying for the lawyers, and by advancing the children of the lower order more than is usual in common schools. With grown-up children, who were about to be confirmed, they went through the religious courses; then, again, they assisted factors and merchants in some way, and were thus enabled to enjoy them-

selves frugally in the evenings, and particularly on Sundays
and festivals.

On the way there, while they highly extolled my love-
letter, they confessed to me that they had made a very merry
use of it, viz.—that it had been copied in a feigned hand,
and, with a few pertinent allusions, had been sent to a con-
ceited young man, who was now firmly persuaded that a lady
to whom he had paid distant court was excessively enamoured
of him, and sought an opportunity for closer acquaintance.
They at the same time told me in confidence, that he desired
nothing more now than to be able to answer her in verse ; but
that neither he nor they were skilful enough, so that they
earnestly solicited me to compose the much-desired reply.

Mystifications are and will continue to be an amusement
for idle people, whether more or less ingenious. A venial
wickedness, a self-complacent malice, is an enjoyment for
those who have neither resources in themselves nor a wholesome external activity. No age is quite exempt from such
pruriences. We had often tricked each other in our childish
years ; many sports turn upon mystification and trick. The
present jest did not seem to me to go further ; I gave my consent. They imparted to me many particulars which the letter
ought to contain, and we brought it home already finished.

A little while afterwards I was urgently invited, through
my friend, to take part in one of the evening feasts of that
society. The lover, he said, was willing to bear the expense
on this occasion, and desired expressly to thank the friend
who had shown himself so excellent a poetical secretary.

We came together late enough, the meal was most frugal, the
wine drinkable : while as for the conversation, it turned almost
entirely on jokes upon the young man, who was present, and
certainly not very bright, and who, after repeated readings of
the letter, almost believed that he had written it himself.

My natural good-nature would not allow me to take much
pleasure in such a malicious deception, and the repetition of
the same subject soon disgusted me. I should certainly have
passed a tedious evening, if an unexpected apparition had not
revived me. On our arrival the table had already been neatly
and orderly covered, and sufficient wine had been put on ;
we sat down and remained alone, without requiring further
service. As there was, however, a want of wine at last, one

of them called for the maid; but instead of the maid there
came in a girl of uncommon, and, when one saw her with all
around her, of incredible beauty. "What do you desire?"
she asked, after having cordially wished us a good evening;
"the maid is ill in bed. Can I serve you?" "The wine is
out," said one; "if you would fetch us a few bottles, it would
be very kind." "Do it, Gretchen,"* said another, "it is but
a cat's leap from here." "Why not?" she answered, and
taking a few empty bottles from the table, she hastened out.
Her form, as seen from behind, was almost more elegant.
The little cap sat so neatly upon her little head, which a
slender throat united very gracefully to her neck and shoulders. Everything about her seemed choice, and one could
survey her whole form the more at ease, as one's attention
was no more exclusively attracted and fettered by the quiet,
honest eyes and lovely mouth. I reproved my comrades for
sending the girl out alone at night, but they only laughed at
me, and I was soon consoled by her return, as the publican
lived only just across the way. "Sit down with us, in return," said one. She did so; but, alas, she did not come
near me. She drank a glass to our health, and speedily
departed, advising us not to stay very long together, and not
to be so noisy, as her mother was just going to bed. It
was not, however, her own mother, but the mother of our
hosts.

The form of that girl followed me from that moment on every
path; it was the first durable impression which a female being
had made upon me; and as I could find no pretext to see her
at home, and would not seek one, I went to church for love of
her, and had soon traced out where she sat. Thus, during
the long Protestant service, I gazed my fill at her. When
the congregation left the church I did not venture to accost
her, much less to accompany her, and was perfectly delighted
if she seemed to have remarked me and to have returned my
greeting with a nod. Yet I was not long denied the happiness
of approaching her. They had persuaded the lover, whose
poetical secretary I had been, that the letter written in his
name had been actually despatched to the lady, and had
strained to the utmost his expectations that an answer must
soon come. This, also, I was to write, and the waggish com-

* The diminutive of Margaret.—*Trans.*

pany entreated me earnestly, through Pylades, to exert all my
wit and employ all my art, in order that this piece might be
quite elegant and perfect.

In the hope of again seeing my fair one, I went immediately
to work, and thought of everything that would be in the highest degree pleasing if Gretchen were writing it to me. I
imagined I had written out everything so completely from her
form, her nature, her manner, and her mind, that I could not
refrain from wishing that it were so in reality, and lost myself
in rapture at the mere thought that something similar could
be sent from her to me. Thus I mystified myself, while I
intended to impose upon another; and much joy and much
trouble was yet to arise out of the affair. When I was once
more summoned, I had finished, promised to come, and did
not fail at the appointed hour. There was only one of the
young people at home; Gretchen sat at the window spinning;
the mother was going to and fro. The young man desired
that I should read to him aloud; I did so, and read not without emotion, as I glanced over the paper at the beautiful girl;
and when I fancied that I remarked a certain uneasiness in
her deportment, and a gentle flush on her cheeks, I uttered
better and with more animation that which I wished to hear
from herself. The cousin, who had often interrupted me with
commendations, at last entreated me to make some amend-
ments. These affected some passages which indeed were
rather suited to the condition of Gretchen than to that of the
lady, who was of a good family, wealthy, and known and
respected in the city. After the young man had designated
the desired changes, and had brought me an inkstand, but had
taken leave for a short time on account of some business,
I remained sitting on the bench against the wall, behind the
large table, and essayed the alterations that were to be made,
on the large slate, which almost covered the whole table,
using a style that always lay in the window, because upon this
slate reckonings were often made, and various memoranda
noted down, and those coming in or going out even communicated with each other.

I had for a while written different things and rubbed them
out again, when I exclaimed impatiently, "It will not do!"
"So much the better," said the dear girl, in a grave tone;
"I wished that it might not do! You should not meddle in

such matters." She arose from the distaff, and stepping towards the table, gave me a severe lecture, with a great deal of good sense and kindliness. "The thing seems an innocent jest ; it is a jest, but it is not innocent. I have already lived to see several cases, in which our young people, for the sake of such mere mischief, have brought themselves into great difficulty." "But what shall I do ?" I asked ; "the letter is written, and they rely upon me to alter it." "Trust me," she replied, "and do not alter it ; nay, take it back, put it in your pocket, go away, and try to make the matter straight through your friend. I will also put in a word ; for look you, though I am a poor girl, and dependent upon these relations, —who indeed do nothing bad, though they often, for the sake of sport or profit, undertake a good deal that is rash,—I have resisted them, and would not copy the first letter, as they requested. They transcribed it in a feigned hand, and if it is not otherwise, so may they also do with this. And you, a young man of good family, rich, independent, why will you allow yourself to be used as a tool in a business which can certainly bring no good to you, and may possibly bring much that is unpleasant ?" I was glad to hear her speaking thus continuously, for generally she introduced but few words into conversation. My liking for her grew incredibly,—I was not master of myself,—and replied, " I am not so independent as you suppose ; and of what use is wealth to me, when the most precious thing I can desire is wanting ?"

She had drawn my sketch of the poetic epistle towards her, and read it half aloud in a sweet and graceful manner. "That is very pretty," said she, stopping at a sort of *naïve* point ; "but it is a pity that it is not destined for a real purpose." "That were indeed very desirable," I cried, "and, oh ! how happy must he be, who receives from a girl he infinitely loves, such an assurance of her affection." "There is much required for that," she answered ; "and yet many things are possible." "For example," I continued, "if any one who knew, prized, honoured, and adored you, laid such a paper before you, what would you do ?" I pushed the paper nearer to her, which she had previously pushed back to me. She smiled, reflected for a moment, took the pen, and subscribed her name. I was beside myself with rapture, sprang up, and would have embraced her. "No kissing !" said she, "that is so vulgar; but let us love if we can." I had taken up the paper, and thrust it into my pocket. "No one shall ever get it," said I; "the affair is closed. You have saved me." "Now complete the salvation," she exclaimed, "and hurry off, before the others arrive, and you fall into trouble and embarrassment." I could not tear myself away from her; but she asked me in so kindly a manner, while she took my right hand in both of hers, and lovingly pressed it! The tears stood in my eyes; I thought hers looked moist. I pressed my face upon her hands and hastened away. Never in my life had I found myself in such perplexity.

The first propensities to love in an uncorrupted youth take altogether a spiritual direction. Nature seems to desire that one sex may by the senses perceive goodness and beauty in the other. And thus to me, by the sight of this girl—by my strong inclination for her—a new world of the beautiful and the excellent had arisen. I read my poetical epistle a hundred times through, gazed upon the signature, kissed it, pressed it to my heart, and rejoiced in this amiable confession. But the more my transports increased, the more did it pain me, not to be able to visit her immediately, and to see and converse with her again; for I dreaded the reproofs and importunities of her cousins. The good Pylades, who might have arranged the affair, I could not contrive to meet. The next Sunday, therefore, I set out for Niederrad, where these associates generally used to go, and actually found them there. I was, however, greatly surprised, when, instead of behaving in a cross, distant manner, they came up to me with joyful countenances. The youngest particularly was very friendly, took me by the hand, and said, "You have lately played us a sorry trick, and we were very angry with you; but your absconding and taking away the poetical epistle has suggested a good thought to us, which otherwise might never have occurred. By way of atonement, you may treat us to-day, and you shall learn at the same time the notion we have, which will certainly give you pleasure." This address put me in no little perplexity; for I had about me only money enough to regale myself and a friend; but to treat a whole company, and especially one which did not always stop at the right time, I was by no means prepared; nay, the proposal astonished me the more, as they had always insisted, in the most honourable manner, that each one should pay only his own share. They smiled at my distress, and the youngest proceeded, "Let us first take a seat in the bower, and then you shall learn more." We sat down, and he said, "When you had taken the love-letter with you, we talked the whole affair over again, and came to a conclusion that we had gratuitously misused your talent to the vexation of others and our own danger, for the sake of a mere paltry love of mischief, when we could have employed it to the advantage of all of us. See, I have here an order for a wedding-poem, as well as for a dirge. The second must be ready immediately, the other can wait a week. Now, if you make these, which is easy for you, you will treat us twice, and we shall long remain your debtors." This proposition pleased me in every respect; for I had already in my childhood looked with a certain envy on the occasional poems,* of which then several circulated every week, and at respectable marriages especially came to light by the dozen, because I thought I could make such things as well, nay, better than others. Now an opportunity was offered me to show myself, and especially to see myself in print. I did not appear disinclined. They acquainted me with the personal particulars and the position of the family; I went somewhat aside, made my plan, and produced some stanzas. However, when I returned to the company, and the wine was not spared, the poem began to halt, and I could not deliver it that evening. "There is still time till to-morrow evening," they said; "and we will confess to you that the fee which we receive for the dirge is enough to get us another pleasant evening to-morrow. Come to us; for it is but fair that Gretchen too should sup with us, as it was she properly who gave us the notion." My joy was unspeakable. On my way home I had only the remaining stanzas in my head, wrote down the whole before I went to sleep, and the next morning made a very neat fair copy. The day seemed infinitely long to me; and scarcely was it dusk, than I found myself again in the narrow little dwelling beside the dearest of girls.

The young persons with whom in this way I formed a closer and closer connexion were not properly low, but ordinary sort of people. Their activity was commendable, and

* That is to say, a poem written for a certain occasion, as a wedding, funeral, &c. The German word is "Gelegenheitsgedicht."—Trans.

I listened to them with pleasure when they spoke of the manifold ways and means by which one could gain a living; above all they loved to tell of people, now very rich, who had begun with nothing. Others to whom they referred had, as poor clerks, rendered themselves indispensable to their employers, and had finally risen to be their sons-in-law; while others had so enlarged and improved a little trade in matches and the like, that they were now prosperous merchants and tradesmen. But above all, to young men, who were active on their feet, the trade of agent and factor, and the undertaking of all sorts of commissions and charges for helpless rich men was, they said, a most profitable means of gaining a livelihood. We all heard this eagerly, and each one fancied himself somebody, when he imagined, at the moment, that there was enough in him, not only to get on in the world, but to acquire an extraordinary fortune. But no one seemed to carry on this conversation more earnestly than Pylades, who at last confessed that he had an extraordinary passion for a girl, and was actually engaged to her. The circumstances of his parents would not allow him to go to universities, but he had endeavoured to acquire a fine handwriting, a knowledge of accounts, and the modern languages, and would now do his best in hopes of attaining that domestic felicity. The cousins praised him for this, although they did not approve of a premature engagement to a girl, and they added, that while forced to acknowledge him to be a fine good fellow, they did not consider him active or enterprising enough to do anything extraordinary. While he, in vindication of himself, circumstantially set forth what he thought himself fit for, and how he was going to begin, the others were also incited, and each one began to tell what he was now able to do, doing, or carrying on, what he had already accomplished, and what he saw immediately before him. The turn at last came to me. I was to set forth my course of life and prospects, and while I was considering, Pylades said, " I make this one proviso, if we all would stand on a level, that he does not bring into the account the external advantages of his position. He should rather tell us a tale how he would proceed if at this moment he were thrown entirely upon his own resources, as we are."

Gretchen, who till this moment had kept on spinning, rose and seated herself as usual at the end of the table. We had

already emptied some bottles, and I began to relate the hypo-
thetical history of my life in the best humour. " First of all,
then, I commend myself to you," said I, " that you may continue the custom you have begun to bestow on me. If you gradually procure me the profit of all the occasional poems, and
we do not consume them in mere feasting, I shall soon come
to something. But then you must not take it ill if I dabble
also in your handicraft." Upon this I told them what I had
observed in their occupations, and for which I held myself fit
at any rate. Each one had previously rated his services in
money, and I asked them to assist me also in completing my
establishment. Gretchen had listened to all hitherto very
attentively, and that in a position which well suited her,
whether she chose to hear or to speak. With both hands she
clasped her folded arms, and rested them on the edge of the
table. Thus she could sit a long while without moving anything but her head, which was never done without occasion or
meaning. She had several times put in a word and helped us
on over this and that, when we halted in our projects, and
then was again still and quiet as usual. I kept her in my eye,
and it may readily be supposed that I had not devised and
uttered my plan without reference to her. My passion for her
gave to what I said such an air of truth and probability, that
for a moment I deceived myself, imagined myself as lonely and
helpless as my story supposed, and felt extremely happy in
the prospect of possessing her. Pylades had closed his confession with marriage, and the question arose among the rest
of us, whether our plans went as far as that. " I have not
the least doubt on that score," said I, " for properly a wife is
necessary to every one of us, in order to preserve at home and
enable us to enjoy as a whole what we rake together abroad
in such an odd way." I then made a sketch of a wife, such
as I wished, and it must have turned out strangely if she had
not been a perfect counterpart of Gretchen.

The dirge was consumed ; the epithalamium now stood beneficially at hand ; I overcame all fear and care, and contrived,
as I had many acquaintances, to conceal my actual evening
entertainments from my family. To see and to be near the
dear girl was soon an indispensable condition of my being.
The friends had grown just as accustomed to me, and we were
almost daily together, as if it could not be otherwise. Pylades

had, in the meantime, introduced his fair one into the house, and this pair passed many an evening with us. They, as bride and bridegroom, though still very much in the bud, did not conceal their tenderness; Gretchen's deportment towards me was only suited to keep me at a distance. She gave her hand to no one, not even to me; she allowed no touch; yet she many times seated herself near me, particularly when I wrote or read aloud, and then laying her arm familiarly upon my shoulder, she looked over the book or paper. If, however, I ventured on a similar freedom towards her, she withdrew, and would not soon return. This position she often repeated, and indeed all her attitudes and motions were very uniform, but always equally fitting, beautiful, and charming. But such a familiarity I never saw her practise towards anybody else.

One of the most innocent, and at the same time amusing, parties of pleasure in which I engaged with different companies of young people, was this: that we seated ourselves in the Höchst market-ship, observed the strange passengers packed away in it, and bantered and teased, now this one, now that, as pleasure or caprice prompted. At Höchst we got out at the same time as the market-boat from Mentz arrived. At a hotel there was a well-spread table, where the better sort of travellers, coming and going, ate with each other, and then proceeded, each on his way, as both ships returned. Every time, after dining, we sailed up to Frankfort, having, with a very large company, made the cheapest water-excursion that was possible. Once I had undertaken this journey with Gretchen's cousins, when a young man joined us at table in Höchst, who might be a little older than we were. They knew him, and he got himself introduced to me. He had something very pleasing in his manner, though he was not otherwise distinguished. Coming from Mentz, he now went back with us to Frankfort, and conversed with me of everything that related to the internal arrangements of the city, and the public offices and places, on which he seemed to me to be very well informed. When we separated he bade me farewell, and added, that he wished I might think well of him, as he hoped on occasion to avail himself of my recommendation. I did not know what he meant by this, but the cousins enlightened me some days after; they spoke favourably of him, and requested me to intercede with my grandfather, as a middle place was

L

just now vacant, which this friend would like to obtain. I at first excused myself, because I had never meddled in such affairs; but they went on urging me until I resolved to do it. I had already many times remarked that, in these grants of offices, which unfortunately were often regarded as matters of favour, the mediation of my grandmother or an aunt had not been without effect. I was now so advanced as to arrogate some influence to myself. For that reason, to gratify my friends, who declared themselves under every sort of obligation for such a kindness, I overcame the timidity of a grandchild, and undertook to deliver a written application that was handed in to me.

One Sunday, after dinner, as my grandfather was busy in his garden, all the more because autumn was approaching, and I tried to assist him on every side, I came forward with my request and the petition, after some hesitation. He looked at it, and asked me whether I knew the young man. I told him in general terms what was to be said, and he let the matter rest there. " If he has merit, and moreover good testimonials, I will favour him for your sake and his own." He said no more, and for a long while I heard nothing of the matter.

For some time I had observed that Gretchen span no more, but on the other hand was employed in sewing, and that, too, on very fine work, which surprised me the more, as the days were already shortening, and winter was coming on. I thought no further about it, only it troubled me that several times I had not found her at home in the morning as formerly, and could not learn, without importunity, whither she had gone. Yet I was destined one day to be surprised in a very odd manner. My sister, who was getting herself ready for a ball, asked me to fetch her some so-called Italian flowers, at a fashionable milliner's. They were made in convents, and were small and pretty; myrtles especially, dwarf-roses, and the like, came out quite beautifully and naturally. I granted her the favour, and went to the shop where I had already often been with her. Hardly had I entered and greeted the proprietress, than I saw sitting in the window a lady, who in a lace cap looked very young and pretty, and in a silk mantilla seemed very well shaped. I could easily recognize that she was an assistant, for she was occupied in fastening a ribbon and feathers upon a hat. The milliner showed me the long box with single flowers of various sorts; I looked them over, and as I made my choice glanced again towards the lady in the window; but how great was my astonishment when I perceived an incredible similarity to Gretchen, nay, was forced to be convinced at last that it was Gretchen herself. No doubt remained, when she winked with her eyes and gave me a sign that I must not betray our acquaintance. I now with my choosing and rejecting drove the milliner into despair more than even a lady could have done. I had, in fact, no choice, for I was excessively confused, and at the same time liked to linger, because it kept me near the girl, whose disguise annoyed me, though in that disguise she appeared to me more enchanting than ever. Finally, the milliner seemed to lose all patience, and with her own hands selected for me a whole bandbox full of flowers, which I was to place before my sister and let her choose for herself. Thus I was, as it were, driven out of the shop, while she sent the box first by one of her girls.

Scarcely had I reached home than my father caused me to be called, and communicated to me that it was now quite certain that the Archduke Joseph would be elected and crowned King of Rome. An event so highly important was not to be expected without preparation, nor allowed to pass with mere gaping and staring. He wished, therefore, he said, to go through with me the election- and coronation-diaries of the two last coronations, as well as through the last capitulations of election, in order to remark what new conditions might be added in the present instance. The diaries were opened, and we occupied ourselves with them the whole day till far into the night, while the pretty girl, sometimes in her old house-dress, sometimes in her new costume, ever hovered before me, backwards and forwards among the most august objects of the Holy Roman Empire. This evening it was impossible to see her, and I lay awake through a very restless night. The study of yesterday was the next day zealously resumed, and it was not till towards evening that I found it possible to visit my fair one, whom I met again in her usual house-dress. She smiled when she saw me, but I did not venture to mention anything before the others. When the whole company sat quietly together again, she began and said, "It is unfair that you do not confide to our friend what we have lately resolved upon." She then continued to relate, that after our late conversation, in which the discussion was how any one could get

on in the world, something was also said of the way in which
a woman could enhance the value of her talent and labour, and
advantageously employ her time. The cousins had consequently proposed that she should make an experiment at a
milliner's who was just then in want of an assistant. They
had, she said, arranged with the woman; she went there so
many hours a-day, and was well paid; only when there she
was obliged, for propriety's sake, to conform to a certain dress,
which, however, she left behind her every time, as it did not
at all suit her other modes of life and employment. I was
indeed set at rest by this declaration, but it did not quite please
me to know that the pretty girl was in a public shop, and at a
place where the fashionable world found a convenient resort.
But I betrayed nothing, and strove to work off my jealous
care in silence. For this the younger cousin did not allow me
a long time, as he once more came forward with a proposal for
an occasional poem, told me all the personalities, and at once
desired me to prepare myself for the invention and disposition
of the work. He had already spoken with me several times
concerning the proper treatment of such a theme, and as I was
voluble in these cases, he readily asked me to explain to him
circumstantially what is rhetorical in these things, to give him
a notion of the matter, and to make use of my own and others'
labours in this kind for examples. The young man had some
brains, though he was without a trace of a poetical vein, and now
he went so much into particulars, and wished to have such an
account of everything, that I gave utterance to the remark: "It
seems as if you wanted to encroach upon my trade and steal away
my customers!" "I will not deny it," said he, smiling, "as
I shall do you no harm by it. This will only continue to the
time when you go to the university, and till then you must
allow me still to profit something by your society." "Most
cordially," I replied, and I encouraged him to draw out a plan,
to choose a metre according to the character of his subject,
and to do whatever else might seem necessary. He went to
work in earnest, but did not succeed. I was in the end compelled to re-write so much of it, that I could more easily and
better have written it all from the beginning myself. Yet this
teaching and learning, this mutual labour, afforded us good
entertainment: Gretchen took part in it and had many a pretty
notion, so that we were all pleased, we may indeed say, happy.

During the day she worked at the milliner's: in the evenings we generally met together, and our contentment was not even disturbed when at last the commissions for occasional poems began to leave off. Still we felt hurt once, when one of them came back under protest, because it did not suit the party who ordered it. We consoled ourselves, however, as we considered it our very best work, and could therefore declare the other a bad judge. The cousin, who was determined to learn something at any rate, resorted to the expedient of inventing problems, in the solution of which we always found amusement enough, but as they brought in nothing, our little banquets had to be much more frugally managed.

That great political object, the election and coronation of a King of Rome, was pursued with more and more earnestness. The assembling of the electoral college, originally appointed to take place at Augsburg in the October of 1763, was now transferred to Frankfort, and both at the end of this year and in the beginning of the next, preparations went forward, which should usher in this important business. The beginning was made by a parade never yet seen by us. One of our chancery officials on horseback, escorted by four trumpeters likewise mounted, and surrounded by a guard of infantry, read in a loud clear voice at all the corners of the city, a prolix edict, which announced the forthcoming proceedings, and exhorted the citizens to a becoming deportment suitable to the circumstances. The council was occupied with weighty considerations, and it was not long before the Imperial Quarter-Master, despatched by the Hereditary Grand Marshal, made his appearance, in order to arrange and designate the residences of the ambassadors and their suites, according to the old custom. Our house lay in the Palatine district, and we had to provide for a new but agreeable billetting. The middle story, which Count Thorane had formerly occupied, was given up to a cavalier of the Palatinate, and as Baron von Königsthal, the Nuremberg *chargé d'affaires*, occupied the upper floor, we were still more crowded than in the time of the French. This served me as a new excuse to be out of doors, and to pass the greater part of the day in the streets, that I might see all that was open to public view.

After the preliminary alteration and arrangement of the rooms in the town-house had seemed to us worth seeing, after the arrival of the ambassadors one after another, and their first solemn ascent in a body, on the 6th of February, had taken place, we admired the coming in of the imperial commissioners, and their ascent also to the *Römer*, which was made with great pomp. The dignified person of the PRINCE of LICHTENSTEIN made a good impression; yet connoisseurs maintained that the showy liveries had already been used on another occasion, and that this election and coronation would hardly equal in brilliancy that of Charles the Seventh. We younger folks were content with what was before our eyes; all seemed to us very fine, and much of it perfectly astonishing.

The electoral congress was fixed at last for the 3rd of March. New formalities again set the city in motion, and the alternate visits of ceremony on the part of the ambassadors kept us always on our legs. We were compelled, too, to watch closely, as we were not only to gape about, but to note everything well, in order to give a proper report at home, and even to make out many little memoirs, on which my father and Herr von Königsthal had deliberated, partly for our exercise and partly for their own information. And certainly this was of peculiar advantage to me, as I was enabled very tolerably to keep a living election- and coronation-diary, as far as regarded externals.

The person who first of all made a durable impression upon me was the chief ambassador from the electorate of Mentz, BARON VON ERTHAL, afterwards Elector. Without having anything striking in his figure, he was always highly pleasing to me in his black gown trimmed with lace. The second ambassador, BARON VON GROSCHLAG, was a well-formed man of the world, easy in his exterior, but conducting himself with great decorum. He everywhere produced a very agreeable impression. PRINCE ESTERHAZY, the Bohemian envoy, was not tall, though well-formed, lively, and at the same time eminently decorous, without pride or coldness. I had a special liking for him, because he reminded me of MARSHAL DE BROGLIO. Yet the form and dignity of these excellent persons vanished, in a certain degree, before the prejudice that was entertained in favour of BARON VON PLOTHO, the Brandenburg ambassador. This man, who was distinguished by a certain parsimony, both in his own clothes and in his liveries and equipages, had been greatly renowned from the time of the seven years' war, as a diplomatic hero. At Ratisbon, when the

Notary April thought, in the presence of witnesses, to serve
him with the declaration of outlawry which had been issued
against his king, he had, with the laconic exclamation:
" What! you serve?" thrown him, or caused him to be thrown,
down stairs. We believed the first, because it pleased us best,
and we could readily believe it of the little compact man, with
his black, fiery eyes glancing here and there. All eyes were
directed towards him, particularly when he alighted. There
arose every time a sort of joyous whispering, and but little was
wanting to a regular explosion, or a shout of *Vivat! Bravo!*
So high did the king, and all who were devoted to him, body
and soul, stand in favour with the crowd, among whom, besides
the Frankforters, were Germans from all parts.

On the one hand these things gave me much pleasure; as
all that took place, no matter of what nature it might be, concealed a certain meaning, indicated some internal relation, and
such symbolic ceremonies again, for a moment, represented
as living the old Empire of Germany, almost choked to death
by so many parchments, papers, and books. But, on the other
hand, I could not suppress a secret displeasure, when I was
forced, at home, on my father's account, to transcribe the internal transactions, and at the same time to remark that here
several powers, which balanced each other, stood in opposition,
and only so far agreed, as they designed to limit the new ruler
even more than the old one; that every one valued his influence
only so far as he hoped to retain or enlarge his privileges, and
better to secure his independence. Nay, on this occasion they
were more attentive than usual, because they began to fear
Joseph the Second, his vehemence and probable plans.

With my grandfather and other members of the council,
whose families I used to visit, this was no pleasant time, they
had so much to do with meeting distinguished guests, compli-
menting, and the delivery of presents. No less had the magistrate, both in general and in particular, to defend himself, to
resist, and to protest, as every one on such occasions desires
to extort something from him, or burden him with something,
and few of those to whom he appeals support him, or lend him
their aid. In short, all that I had read in *Lersner's Chronicles*
of similar incidents on similar occasions, with admiration of
the patience and perseverance of those good old councilmen,
came once more vividly before my eyes.

Many vexations arise also from this, that the city is gradually overrun with people, both useful and needless. In vain are the courts reminded, on the part of the city, of prescriptions of the Golden Bull, now, indeed, obsolete. Not only the deputies with their attendants, but many persons of rank, and others who come from curiosity or for private objects, stand under protection, and the question as to who is to be billetted out, and who is to hire his own lodging, is not always decided at once. The tumult constantly increases, and even those who have nothing to give, or to answer for, begin to feel uncomfortable.

Even we young people, who could quietly contemplate it all, ever found something which did not quite satisfy our eyes or our imagination. The Spanish mantles, the huge feathered hats of the ambassadors, and other objects here and there, had indeed a truly antique look; but there was a great deal, on the other hand, so half-new or entirely modern, that the affair assumed throughout a motley, unsatisfactory, often tasteless appearance. We were very happy to learn, therefore, that great preparations were made on account of the journey to Frankfort of the Emperor and future King; that the proceedings of the college of electors, which were based on the last electoral capitulation, were now going forward rapidly; and that the day of election had been appointed for the 27th of March. Now there was a thought of fetching the insignia of the Empire from Nuremberg and Aix-la-Chapelle, and next we expected the entrance of the Elector of Mentz, while the disputes with his ambassadors about the quartering ever continued.

Meanwhile I pursued my clerical labours at home very actively, and perceived many little suggestions (*monita*) which came in from all sides, and were to be regarded in the new capitulation. Every rank desired to see its privileges guaranteed and its importance increased in this document. Very many such observations and desires were, however, put aside; much remained as it was, though the suggestors (*monentes*) received the most positive assurances that the neglect should in no wise enure to their prejudice.

In the meanwhile the office of Imperial Marshal was forced to undertake many dangerous affairs; the crowd of strangers increased, and it became more and more difficult to find

lodgings for them. Nor was there unanimity as to the limits
of the different precincts of the Electors. The magistracy
wished to keep from the citizens the burdens which they were
not bound to bear, and thus day and night there were hourly
grievances, redresses, contests, and misunderstandings.

The entrance of the Elector of Mentz happened on the
21st of May. Then began the cannonading, with which for a
long time we were often to be deafened. This solemnity was
important in the series of ceremonies; for all the men whom
we had hitherto seen, high as they were in rank, were still
only subordinates; but here appeared a sovereign, an independent prince, the first after the Emperor, preceded and
accompanied by a large retinue worthy of himself. Of the
pomp which marked his entrance I should have much to tell,
if I did not purpose returning to it hereafter, and on an occasion which no one could easily guess.

What I refer to is this :—the same day, LAVATER, on his
return home from Berlin, came through Frankfort, and saw the
solemnity. Now, though such worldly formalities could not
have the least value for him, this procession, with its display
and all its accessaries, might have been distinctly impressed
on his very lively imagination; for, many years afterwards,
when this eminent but singular man showed me a poetical
paraphrase of, I believe, the Revelation of St. John, I discovered the entrance of Anti-Christ copied, step by step,
figure by figure, circumstance by circumstance, from the entrance of the Elector of Mentz into Frankfort, in such a
manner, too, that even the tassels on the heads of the dun-
coloured horses were not wanting. More can be said on
this point when I reach the epoch of that strange kind of
poetry, by which it was supposed that the myths of the Old
and New Testaments were brought nearer to our view and
feelings when they were completely travestied into the modern
style, and clothed with the vestments of present life, whether
gentle or simple. How this mode of treatment gradually
obtained favour, will be likewise discussed hereafter; yet
I may here simply remark that it could not well be carried further than it was by Lavater and his emulators, one
of these having described the three holy kings riding into
Bethlehem, in such modern form, that the princes and gentlemen whom Lavater used to visit were not to be mistaken
as the persons.

We will then for the present allow the ELECTOR EMERIC
JOSEPH to enter the Compostello incognito, so to speak,
and turn to Gretchen, whom, just as the crowd was dis-
persing, I spied in the crowd, accompanied by Pylades and
his mistress, the three now seeming to be inseparable. We
had scarcely come up to each other and exchanged greetings,
than it was agreed that we should pass the evening together,
and I kept the appointment punctually. The usual company
had assembled, and each one had something to relate, to say,
or to remark—how one had been most struck by this thing
and another by that. "Your speeches," said Gretchen at
last, "perplex me even more than the events of the time
themselves. What I have seen I cannot make out; and
should very much like to know what a great deal of it means."
I replied that it was easy for me to render her this service. She had only to say what particularly interested her.
This she did, and as I was about to explain some points, it
was found that it would be better to proceed in order. I not
unskilfully compared these solemnities and functions to a
play, in which the curtain was let down at will, while the
actors played on, and was then raised again, so that the spectators could once more, to some extent, take part in the action.
As now I was very loquacious when I was allowed my
own way, I related the whole, from the beginning down to
the time present, in the best order; and to make the subject
of my discourse more apparent, did not fail to use the
pencil and the large slate. Being only slightly interrupted by
some questions and obstinate assertions of the others, I
brought my discourse to a close, to the general satisfaction,
while Gretchen, by her unbroken attention, had highly encouraged me. At last she thanked me, and envied, as she said,
all who were informed of the affairs of this world, and knew
how this and that came about and what it signified. She
wished she were a boy, and managed to acknowledge, with
much kindness, that she was indebted to me for a great deal
of instruction. "If I were a boy," said she, "we would
learn something good together at the university." The conversation continued in this strain; she definitively resolved
to take instruction in French, of the absolute necessity of
which she had become well aware in the milliner's shop. I
asked her why she no longer went there; for during the latter

times, not being able to go out much in the evening, I had often passed the shop during the day for her sake, merely to see her for a moment. She explained that she had not liked to expose herself there in these unsettled times. As soon as the city returned to its former condition she intended to go there again.

Then the discourse was on the impending day of election. I contrived to tell, at length, what was going to happen, and how, and to support my demonstrations in detail by drawings on the tablet; for I had the place of conclave, with its altars, thrones, seats, and chairs, perfectly before my mind. We separated at the proper time, and in a peculiarly comfortable frame of mind.

For, with a young couple who are in any degree harmoniously formed by nature, nothing can conduce to a more beautiful union than when the maiden is anxious to learn, and the youth inclined to teach. There arises from it a well-grounded and agreeable relation. She sees in him the creator of her spiritual existence, and he sees in her a creature that ascribes her perfection, not to nature, not to chance, nor to any one-sided inclination, but to a mutual will; and this reciprocation is so sweet, that we cannot wonder, if from the days of the old and the new* Abelard, the most violent passions, and as much happiness as unhappiness, have arisen from such an intercourse of two beings.

With the next day began great commotion in the city, on account of the visits paid and returned which now took place with the greatest ceremony. But what particularly interested me, as a citizen of Frankfort, and gave rise to a great many reflections, was the taking of the oath of security (*Sicherheitseides*) by the council, the military, and the body of citizens, not through representatives, but personally, and in mass: first, in the great hall of the Römer, by the magistracy and staff-officers; then in the great square (*Platz*), the Römerberg, by all the citizens, according to their respective ranks, gradations, or quarterings; and lastly by the rest of the military. Here one could survey at a single glance the entire commonwealth, assembled for the honourable purpose of swearing security to the head and members of the Empire, and un-

* The "*new* Abelard" is St. Preux, in the *Nouvelle Héloise* of Rousseau.—*Trans.*

broken peace during the great work now impending. The Electors of Treves and of Cologne had now also arrived in person. On the evening before the day of election all strangers are sent out of the city, the gates are closed, the Jews are confined to their quarter, and the citizen of Frankfort prides himself not a little that he alone may be a witness of so great a solemnity.

All that had hitherto taken place was tolerably modern; the highest and high personages moved about only in coaches; but now we were going to see them in the primitive manner on horseback. The concourse and rush were extraordinary. I managed to squeeze myself into the Römer, which I knew as familiarly as a mouse does the private corn-loft, till I reached the main entrance, before which the Electors and ambassadors, who had first arrived in their state-coaches, and had assembled above, were now to mount their horses. The stately, well-trained steeds were covered with richly laced housings, and ornamented in every way. The Elector Emeric Joseph, a comfortable-looking man, looked well on horseback. Of the other two I remember less, excepting that the red princes' mantles, trimmed with ermine, which we had been accustomed to see only in pictures before, seemed to us very romantic in the open air. The ambassadors of the absent temporal Electors, with their Spanish dresses of gold brocade, embroidered over with gold, and trimmed with gold lace, likewise did our eyes good; and the large feathers particularly, that waved most splendidly from the hats, which were cocked in the antique style. But what did not please me were the short modern breeches, the white silk stockings, and the fashionable shoes. We should have liked half-boots —gilded as much as they pleased—sandals, or something of the kind, that we might have seen a more consistent costume.

In deportment the Ambassador Von Plotho again distinguished himself from all the rest. He appeared lively and cheerful, and seemed to have no great respect for the whole ceremony. For when his front-man, an elderly gentleman, could not leap immediately on his horse, and he was therefore forced to wait some time in the grand entrance, he did not refrain from laughing, till his own horse was brought forward, upon which he swung himself very dexterously, and was again admired by us as a most worthy representative of Frederick the Second.

Now the curtain was for us once more let down. I had
indeed tried to force my way into the church; but that place
was more inconvenient than agreeable. The voters had withdrawn into the *sanctum*, where prolix ceremonies usurped the
place of a deliberate consideration as to the election. After
long delay, pressure, and bustle, the people at last heard the
name of Joseph the Second, who was proclaimed King of
Rome.

The thronging of strangers into the city became greater and
greater. Everybody went about in his holiday clothes, so
that at last none but dresses entirely of gold were found
worthy of note. The Emperor and King had already arrived
at *Heusenstamm*, a castle of the Counts of Schönborn, and
were there in the customary manner greeted and welcomed;
but the city celebrated this important epoch by spiritual festivals of all the religions, by high masses and sermons; and on
the temporal side by incessant firing of cannon as an accompaniment to the *Te Deums*.

If all these public solemnities, from the beginning up to
this point, had been regarded as a deliberate work of art, not
much to find fault with would have been found. All was well
prepared. The public scenes opened gradually, and went on
increasing in importance; the men grew in number, the personages in dignity, their appurtenances, as well as themselves,
in splendour; and thus it advanced with every day, till at
last even a well-prepared and firm eye became bewildered.

The entrance of the Elector of Mentz, which we have refused to describe more completely, was magnificent and imposing enough to suggest to the imagination of an eminent
man, the advent of a great prophesied World-Ruler; even we
were not a little dazzled by it. But now our expectation was
stretched to the utmost, as it was said that the Emperor and
the future King were approaching the city. At a little distance from Sachsenhausen, a tent had been erected, in which
the entire magistracy remained, to show the appropriate
honour, and to proffer the keys of the city to the chief of the
Empire. Further out, on a fair spacious plain, stood another
—a state pavilion, whither the whole body of electoral princes
and ambassadors repaired, while their retinues extended
along the whole way, that gradually, as their turns came, they
might again move towards the city, and enter properly into

the procession. By this time the Emperor reached the tent, entered it, and the princes and ambassadors, after a most respectful reception, withdrew, to facilitate the passage of the chief ruler.

We others who remained in the city to admire this pomp within the walls and streets, still more than could have been done in the open fields, were very well entertained for a while by the barricade set up by the citizens in the lanes, by the throng of people, and by the various jests and improprieties which arose, till the ringing of bells and the thunder of cannon announced to us the immediate approach of Majesty. What must have been particularly grateful to a Frankforter was, that on this occasion, in the presence of so many sovereigns and their representatives, the imperial city of Frankfort also appeared as a little sovereign ; for her equerry opened the procession ; chargers with armorial trappings, upon which the white eagle on a red field looked very fine, followed him ; then came attendants and officials, drummers and trumpeters, and deputies of the council, accompanied by the clerks of the council, in the city livery, on foot. Immediately behind these were the three companies of citizen cavalry, very well mounted—the same that we had seen from our youth, at the reception of the escort and on other public occasions. We rejoiced in our participation of the honour, and in our hundred-thousandth part of a sovereignty which now appeared in its full brilliancy. The different trains of the Hereditary Imperial Marshal, and of the envoys deputed by the six temporal Electors, marched after these step by step. None of them consisted of less than twenty attendants, and two state-carriages—some even of a greater number. The retinue of the spiritual Electors was ever on the increase,—their servants and domestic officers seemed innumerable,—the Elector of Cologne and the Elector of Treves had above twenty state-carriages, and the Elector of Mentz quite as many alone. The servants, both on horseback and on foot, were clothed most splendidly throughout: the lords in the equipages, spiritual and temporal, had not omitted to appear richly and venerably dressed, and adorned with all the badges of their orders. The train of his Imperial Majesty now, as was fit, surpassed all the rest. The riding-masters, the led horses, the equipages, the shabracks and caparisons, attracted every eye, and the sixteen six-horse gala-wagons of the Imperial Chamberlains, Privy Councillors, High Chamberlain, High Stewards, and High Equerry, closed, with great pomp, this division of the procession, which, in spite of its magnificence and extent, was still only to be the van-guard.

But now the line concentrated itself more and more, while the dignity and parade kept on increasing. For, in the midst of a chosen escort of their own domestic attendants, the most of them on foot, and a few on horseback, appeared the Electoral ambassadors as well as the Electors in person, in ascending order, each one in a magnificent state-carriage. Immediately behind the Elector of Mentz, ten imperial footmen, one and forty lackeys, and eight Heyducks,* announced their Majesties. The most magnificent state-carriage, furnished even at the back part with an entire window of plate-glass, ornamented with paintings, lacker, carved work, and gilding, covered with red embroidered velvet on the top and inside, allowed us very conveniently to behold the Emperor and King, the long-desired heads, in all their glory. The procession was led a long circuitous route, partly from necessity, that it might be able to unfold itself, and partly to render it visible to the great multitude of people. It had passed through Sachsenhausen, over the bridge, up the Fahrgasse, then down the Zeile, and turned towards the inner city through the Katharinenpforte, formerly a gate, and since the enlargement of the city, an open thoroughfare. Here it had been fortunately considered that, for a series of years, the external grandeur of the world had gone on expanding both in height and breadth. Measure had been taken, and it was found that the present imperial state-carriage could not, without striking its carved work and other outward decorations, get through this gateway, through which so many princes and emperors had gone backwards and forwards. The matter was debated, and to avoid an inconvenient circuit, it was resolved to take up the pavements, and to contrive a gentle ascent and descent. With the same view they had also removed all the projecting eaves from the shops and booths in the street, that neither crown, nor eagle, nor the genii should receive any shock or injury.

Eagerly as we directed our eyes to the high personages when this precious vessel with such precious contents approached us,

* A class of attendants dressed in Hungarian costume.—*Trans.*

we could not avoid turning our looks upon the noble horses, their harness, and its embroidery; but the strange coachmen and outriders, both sitting on the horses, particularly struck us. They looked as if they had come from some other nation, or even from another world, with their long black and yellow velvet coats, and their caps with large plumes of feathers, after the imperial court fashion. Now the crowd became so dense that it was impossible to distinguish much more. The Swiss guard on both sides of the carriage, the Hereditary Marshal holding the Saxon sword upwards in his right hand, the Field-Marshals, as leaders of the Imperial Guard, riding behind the carriage, the imperial pages in a body, and finally, the Imperial Horse-guard (*Hatschiergarde*) itself, in black velvet frocks (*Flügelröck*), with all the seams edged with gold, under which were red coats and leather-coloured camisoles, likewise richly decked with gold! One scarcely recovered oneself from sheer seeing, pointing, and showing, so that the scarcely less splendidly clad body-guards of the Electors were barely looked at, and we should perhaps have withdrawn from the windows, if we had not wished to take a view of our own magistracy, who closed the procession in their fifteen two-horse coaches, and particularly the clerk of the council, with the city keys on red velvet cushions. That our company of city grenadiers should cover the rear, seemed to us honourable enough, and we felt doubly and highly edified as Germans and as Frankforters by this great day.

We had taken our place in a house which the procession had to pass again when it returned from the cathedral. Of religious services, of music, of rites and solemnities, of addresses and answers, of propositions and readings aloud, there was so much in church, choir, and conclave, before it came to the swearing of the electoral capitulation, that we had time enough to partake of an excellent collation, and to empty several flasks to the health of our old and young ruler. The conversation, in the meanwhile, as is usual on such occasions, reverted to the time past, and there were not wanting aged persons who preferred that to the present, at least with respect to a certain human interest and impassioned sympathy which then prevailed. At the coronation of Francis the First all had not been so settled as now; peace had not yet been concluded; France and the Electors of Brandenburg and the Palatinate

were opposed to the election ; the troops of the future emperor
were stationed at Heidelberg, where he had his head-quarters,
and the insignia of the Empire coming from Aix, were almost
carried off by the inhabitants of the Palatinate.   Meanwhile
negotiations went on, and on neither side was the affair conducted in the strictest manner.   MARIA THERESA, though
then pregnant, comes in person to see the coronation of her
husband, which is at last carried into effect.   She arrived at
Aschaffenburg, and went on board a yacht in order to repair
to Frankfort.   Francis, from Heidelberg, thinks to meet his
wife, but comes too late; she has already departed. Unknown,
he throws himself into a little boat, hastens after her, reaches
her ship, and the loving pair is delighted at this surprising
meeting.   The story spreads immediately, and all the world
sympathizes with this tender pair, so richly blessed with their
children, who have been so inseparable since their union, that
once on a journey from Vienna to Florence they are forced to
keep quarantine together on the Venetian border.   Maria
Theresa is welcomed in the city with rejoicings, she enters the
Roman Emperor inn, while the great tent for the reception of
her husband is erected on the Bornheim heath.   There of the
spiritual Electors is found only Mentz, and of the ambassadors
of the temporal Electors, only Saxony, Bohemia, and Hanover.
The entrance begins, and what it may lack of completeness
and splendour is richly compensated by the presence of a beautiful lady.   She stands upon the balcony of the well-situated
house, and greets her husband with cries of *Vivat* and clapping
of hands ; the people joined, excited to the highest enthusiasm.
As the great are, after all, men, the citizen thinks them his
equals when he wishes to love them, and that he can best do
when he can picture them to himself as loving husbands, tender
parents, devoted brothers, and true friends.   At that time all
happiness had been wished and prophesied, and to-day it was
seen fulfilled in the first-born son ; to whom everybody was
well inclined on account of his handsome youthful form, and
upon whom the world set the greatest hopes, on account of
the great qualities that he showed.

   We had become quite absorbed in the past and future, when
some friends who came in recalled us to the present.   They
were of those who know the value of novelty, and therefore
hasten to announce it first.   They were even able to tell of a fine

M

humane trait in those exalted personages whom we had seen go by with the greatest pomp. It had been concerted that on the way, between Heusenstamm and the great tent, the Emperor and King should find the Landgrave of Darmstadt in the forest. This old prince, now approaching the grave, wished to see once more the master to whom he had been devoted in former times. Both might remember the day when the Landgrave brought over to Heidelberg the decree of the Electors choosing Francis as Emperor, and replied to the valuable presents he received with protestations of unalterable devotion. These eminent persons stood in a grove of firs, and the Landgrave, weak with old age, supported himself against a pine, to continue the conversation, which was not without emotion on both sides. The place was afterwards marked in an innocent way, and we young people sometimes wandered to it.

Thus several hours had passed in remembrance of the old and consideration of the new, when the procession, though curtailed and more compact, again passed before our eyes, and we were enabled to observe and mark the detail more closely, and imprint it on our minds for the future.

From that moment the city was in uninterrupted motion; for until each and every one whom it behoved, and of whom it was required, had paid their respects to the highest dignities, and exhibited themselves one by one, there was no end to the marching to and fro, and the court of each one of the high persons present could be very conveniently repeated in detail.

Now, too, the insignia of the Empire arrived. But that no ancient usage might be omitted even in this respect, they had to remain half a day till late at night in the open field, on account of a dispute about territory and escort between the Elector of Mentz and the city. The latter yielded, the people of Mentz escorted the insignia as far as the barricade, and so the affair terminated for this time.

In these days I did not come to myself. At home I had to write and copy ; everything had to be seen ; and so ended the month of March, the second half of which had been so rich in festivals for us. I had promised Gretchen a faithful and complete account of what had lately happened, and of what was to be expected on the coronation-day. This great day approached ; I thought more how I should tell it to her than of what properly was to be told ; all that came under my eyes and my pen I merely worked up rapidly for this sole and immediate use. At last I reached her residence somewhat late one evening, and was not a little proud to think how my discourse on this occasion would be much more successful than the first unprepared one. But a momentary incitement often brings us, and others through us, more joy than the most deliberate purpose can afford. I found, indeed, pretty nearly the same company, but there were some unknown persons among them. They sat down to play, all except Gretchen and her younger cousin, who remained with me at the slate. The dear girl expressed most gracefully her delight that she, though a stranger, had passed for a citizen on the election-day, and had taken part in that unique spectacle. She thanked me most warmly for having managed to take care of her, and for having been so attentive as to procure her, through Pylades, all sorts of admissions by means of billets, directions, friends, and intercessions.

She liked to hear about the jewels of the Empire. I promised her that we should, if possible, see these together. She made some jesting remarks when she learned that the garments and crown had been tried on the young king. I knew where she would gaze at the solemnities of the coronation-day, and directed her attention to everything that was impending, and particularly to what might be minutely inspected from her place of view.

Thus we forgot to think about time; it was already past midnight; and I found that I unfortunately had not the house-key with me. I could not enter the house without making the greatest disturbance. I communicated my embarrassment to her. "After all," said she, "it will be best for the company to remain together." The cousins and the strangers had already had this in mind, because it was not known where they would be lodged for the night. The matter was soon decided; Gretchen went to make some coffee, after bringing in and lighting a large brass lamp, furnished with oil and wick, because the candles threatened to burn out.

The coffee served to enliven us for several hours, but the game gradually slackened; conversation failed; the mother slept in the great chair; the strangers, weary from travelling, nodded here and there, and Pylades and his fair one sat in a corner. She had laid her head on his shoulder and had gone to

sleep, and he did not keep long awake. The younger cousin
sitting opposite to us by the slate, had crossed his arms before
him, and slept with his face resting upon them. I sat in the
window-corner, behind the table, and Gretchen by me. We
talked in a low voice; but at last sleep overcame her also, she
leaned her head on my shoulder, and sank at once into a slumber.
Thus I now sat, the only one awake, in a most singular position, in which the kind brother of death soon put me also to
rest. I went to sleep, and when I awoke it was already bright
day. Gretchen was standing before the mirror arranging her
little cap; she was more lovely than ever, and when I departed cordially pressed my hands. I crept home by a round-
about way; for, on the side towards the little *Stag-ditch*, my
father had opened a sort of little peep-hole in the wall, not
without the opposition of his neighbour. This side we avoided
when we wanted not to be observed by him in coming home.
My mother, whose mediation always came in well for us, had
endeavoured to palliate my absence in the morning at breakfast,
by the supposition that I had gone out early, and I experienced
no disagreeable effects from this innocent night.

Taken as a whole, this infinitely various world which surrounded me, produced upon me but a very simple impression.
I had no interest but to mark closely the outside of the objects,
no business but that with which I had been charged by my
father and Herr von Königsthal, by which, indeed, I perceived
the inner course of things. I had no liking but for Gretchen,
and no other view than to see and apprehend all properly, that
I might be able to repeat it with her, and explain it to her.
Often when a train was going by, I described it half aloud to
myself, to assure myself of all the particulars, and to be praised
by my fair one for this attention and accuracy; the applause
and acknowledgments of the others I regarded as a mere
appendix.

I was indeed presented to many exalted and distinguished
persons; but partly, no one had time to trouble himself about
others, and partly, older people do not know at once how they
should converse with a young man and try him. I, on my
side, was likewise not particularly skilful in adapting myself
to people. Generally I acquired their favour, but not their
approbation. Whatever occupied me was completely present
to me; but I did not ask whether it might be also suitable to

others. I was mostly too lively or too quiet, and appeared either importunate or sullen, just as persons attracted or repelled me; and thus I was considered to be indeed full of promise, but at the same time was declared eccentric.

The coronation-day dawned at last, on the 3rd of April, 1764; the weather was favourable, and everybody was in motion. I, with several of my relations and friends, had been provided with a good place in one of the upper stories of the Römer itself, where we might completely survey the whole. We betook ourselves to the spot very early in the morning, and from above, as in a bird's-eye view, contemplated the arrangements which we had inspected more closely the day before. There was the newly-erected fountain, with two large tubs on the left and right, into which the double-eagle on the post was to pour from its two beaks white wine on this side and red wine on that. There, gathered into a heap, lay the oats; here stood the large wooden hut, in which we had several days since seen the whole fat ox roasted and basted on a huge spit before a charcoal fire. All the avenues leading out from the Römer, and from other streets back to the Römer, were secured on both sides by barriers and guards. The great square was gradually filled, and the waving and pressure grew every moment stronger and more in motion, as the multitude always, if possible, endeavoured to reach the spot where some new scene arose, and something particular was announced.

All this time there reigned a tolerable stillness, and when the alarm-bells were sounded, all the people seemed struck with terror and amazement. What first attracted the attention of all who could overlook the square from above, was the train in which the lords of Aix and Nuremberg brought the crown-jewels to the cathedral. These, as palladia, had been assigned the first place in the carriage, and the deputies sat before them on the back seat with becoming reverence. Now the three Electors betake themselves to the cathedral. After the presentation of the insignia to the Elector of Mentz, the crown and sword are immediately carried to the imperial quarters. The further arrangements and manifold ceremonies occupied, in the interim, the chief persons, as well as the spectators, in the church, as we other well-informed persons could well imagine.

In the meanwhile before our eyes the ambassadors ascended

to the Römer, from which the canopy is carried by the under-officers into the imperial quarters. The Hereditary Marshal COUNT VON PAPPENHEIM instantly mounts his horse; he was a very handsome, slender gentleman, whom the Spanish costume, the rich doublet, the gold mantle, the high feathered hat, and the loose flying hair, became very well. He puts himself in motion, and, amid the sound of all the bells, the ambassadors follow him on horseback to the quarters of the Emperor in still greater magnificence than on the day of election. One would have liked to be there too, as indeed on this day it would have been altogether desirable to multiply one's-self. However, we told each other what was going on there. Now the Emperor is putting on his domestic robes, we said, a new dress, made after the old Carolingian pattern. The hereditary officers receive the insignia, and with them get on horseback. The Emperor in his robes, the Roman King in the Spanish habit, immediately mount their steeds; and while this is done, the endless procession which precedes them has already announced them.

The eye was already wearied by the multitude of richly-dressed attendants and magistrates, and by the nobility who, in stately fashion, were moving along; but when the Electoral envoys, the hereditary officers, and at last, under the richly-embroidered canopy, borne by twelve *Schöffen* and senators, the Emperor, in romantic costume, and to the left, a little behind him, in the Spanish dress, his son, slowly floated along on magnificently-adorned horses, the eye was no more sufficient for the sight. One would have liked to detain the scene, but for a moment, by a magic charm; but the glory passed on without stopping, and the space that was scarcely quitted was immediately filled again by the crowd, which poured in like billows.

But now a new pressure took place; for another approach from the market to the Römer gate had to be opened, and a road of planks to be bridged over it, on which the train returning from the cathedral was to walk.

What passed within the cathedral, the endless ceremonies which precede and accompany the anointing, the crowning, the dubbing of knighthood,—all this we were glad to hear told afterwards by those who had sacrificed much else to be present in the church.

The rest of us, in the interim, partook of a frugal repast; for in this festal day we had to be contented with cold meat. But, on the other hand, the best and oldest wine had been brought out of all the family-cellars, so that in this respect at least we celebrated the ancient festival in ancient style.

In the square, the sight most worth seeing was now the bridge, which had been finished, and covered with orange and white cloth; and we who had stared at the Emperor, first in his carriage and then on horseback, were now to admire him walking on foot. Singularly enough, the last pleased us the most; for we thought that in this way he exhibited himself both in the most natural and in the most dignified manner.

Older persons, who were present at the coronation of Francis the First, related that Maria Theresa, beautiful beyond measure, had looked on this solemnity from a balcony window of the Frauenstein house, close to the Römer. As her consort returned from the cathedral in his strange costume, and seemed to her, so to speak, like a ghost of Charlemagne, he had, as if in jest, raised both his hands, and shown her the imperial globe, the sceptre, and the curious gloves, at which she had broken out into immoderate laughter, which served for the great delight and edification of the crowd, which was thus honoured with a sight of the good and natural matrimonial understanding between the most exalted couple of Christendom. But when the Empress, to greet her consort, waved her handkerchief, and even shouted a loud *vivat* to him, the enthusiasm and exultation of the people was raised to the highest, so that there was no end to the cheers of joy.

Now, the sound of bells, and the van of the long train which gently made its way over the many-coloured bridge, announced that all was done. The attention was greater than ever, and the procession more distinct than before, particularly for us, since it now came directly up to us. We saw it, as well as the whole of the square, which was thronged with people, almost as if on a ground-plan. Only at the end the magnificence was too much crowded; for the envoys, the hereditary officers, the Emperor and King, under the canopy (*Baldachin*), the three spiritual Electors, who immediately followed, the Schöffen and senators, dressed in black, the gold embroidered canopy (*Himmel*),—all seemed only one mass, which moved by a single will, splendidly harmonious, and thus stepping from the temple amid the sound of the bells, beamed towards us as something holy.

A politico-religious ceremony possesses an infinite charm. We behold earthly majesty before our eyes, surrounded by all the symbols of its power; but while it bends before that of heaven, it brings to our minds the communion of both. For even the individual can only prove his relationship with the Deity by subjecting himself and adoring

The rejoicings, which resounded from the market-place, now spread likewise over the great square, and a boisterous *vivat* burst forth from thousands upon thousands of throats, and doubtless from as many hearts. For this grand festival was to be the pledge of a lasting peace, which indeed for many a long year actually blessed Germany.

Several days before, it had been made known by public proclamation, that neither the bridge nor the eagle over the fountain were to be exposed to the people, and were therefore not, as at other times, to be touched. This was done to prevent the mischief inevitable with such a rush of persons. But in order to sacrifice in some degree to the genius of the mob, persons expressly appointed went behind the procession, loosened the cloth from the bridge, wound it up like a flag, and threw it into the air. This gave rise to no disaster, but to a laughable mishap; for the cloth unrolled itself in the air, and, as it fell, covered a larger or smaller number of persons. Those now who took hold of the ends and drew them towards themselves, pulled all those in the middle to the ground, enveloped them and teased them till they tore or cut themselves through, and everybody, in his own way, had borne off a corner of the stuff made sacred by the footsteps of Majesty.

I did not long contemplate this rude sport, but hastened from my high position, through all sorts of little steps and passages, down to the great Römer stairs, where the distinguished and majestic mass, which had been stared at from the distance, was to ascend in its undulating course. The crowd was not great, because the entrances to the council-house were well garrisoned, and I fortunately reached at once the iron balustrades above. Now the chief personages ascended past me, while their followers remained behind in the lower arched passages, and I could observe them on the thrice broken stairs from all sides, and at last quite close.

Finally both their Majesties came up. Father and son were altogether dressed like Menaechini. The Emperor's domestic robes, of purple-coloured silk, richly adorned with pearls and stones, as well as his crown, sceptre, and imperial orb, struck the eye with good effect. For all in them was new, and the imitation of the antique was tasteful. He moved, too, quite easily in his attire, and his true-hearted, dignified face, indicated at once the emperor and the father. The young King, on the contrary, in his monstrous articles of dress, with the crown-jewels of Charlemagne, dragged himself along as if he had been in a disguise, so that he himself, looking at his father from time to time, could not refrain from laughing. The crown, which it had been necessary to line a great deal, stood out from his head like an overhanging roof. The dalmatica, the stole, well as they had been fitted and taken in by sewing, presented by no means an advantageous appearance. The sceptre and imperial orb excited some admiration; but one would, for the sake of a more princely effect, rather have seen a strong form, suited to the dress, invested and adorned with it.

Scarcely were the gates of the great hall closed behind these figures, than I hurried to my former place, which being already occupied by others, I only regained with some trouble.

It was precisely at the right time that I again took possession of my window; for the most remarkable part of all that was to be seen in public was just about to take place. All the people had turned towards the Römer, and a reiterated shout of *vivat* gave us to understand that the Emperor and King, in their vestments, were showing themselves to the populace from the balcony of the great hall. But they were not alone to serve as a spectacle, since another strange spectacle occurred before their eyes. First of all, the handsome slender Hereditary Marshal flung himself upon his steed; he had laid aside his sword; in his right hand he held a silver-handled vessel, and a tin spatula in his left. He rode within the barriers to the great heap of oats, sprang in, filled the vessel to overflow, smoothed it off, and carried it back again with great dignity. The imperial stable was now provided for. The Hereditary Chamberlain then rode likewise to the spot, and brought back a basin with ewer and towel. But more entertaining for the spectators was the Hereditary Carver, who came to fetch a

piece of the roasted ox. He also rode, with a silver dish,
through the barriers, to the large wooden kitchen, and came
forth again with his portion covered, that he might go back
to the Römer. Now it was the turn of the Hereditary Cup-
bearer, who rode to the fountain and fetched wine. Thus
now was the imperial table furnished, and every eye waited
upon the Hereditary Treasurer, who was to throw about the
money. He, too, mounted a fine steed, to the sides of whose
saddle, instead of holsters, a couple of splendid bags embroidered with the arms of the Palatinate, were suspended.
Scarcely had he put himself in motion than he plunged his
hands into these pockets, and generously scattered right and
left gold and silver coins, which on every occasion glittered
merrily in the air like metallic rain. A thousand hands
waved instantly in the air to catch the gifts ; but hardly had
the coins fallen than the crowd tumbled over each other on
the ground, and struggled violently for the pieces which
might have reached the earth. As this agitation was constantly repeated on both sides as the giver rode forwards, it
afforded the spectators a very diverting sight. It was most
lively at the close, when he threw out the bags themselves,
and everybody tried to catch this highest prize.

Their Majesties had retired from the balcony, and another
offering was to be made to the mob, who, on such occasions,
would rather steal the gifts than receive them tranquilly and
gratefully. The custom prevailed, in more rude and uncouth
times, of giving up to the people on the spot the oats, as
soon as the Hereditary Marshal had taken away his share,
the fountain and the kitchen, after the cup-bearer and the
carver had performed their offices. But this time, to guard
against all mischief, order and moderation were preserved as
far as possible. But the old malicious jokes, that when one
filled a sack with oats another cut a hole in it, with sallies of
the kind, were revived. About the roasted ox, a serious
battle on this occasion, as usual, was waged. This could
only be contested *en masse*. Two guilds, the butchers and the
wine-porters, had, according to ancient custom, again stationed
themselves so that the monstrous roast must fall to one of
the two. The butchers believed that they had the best right
to an ox which they provided entire for the kitchen ; the
wine-porters, on the other hand, laid claim because the

kitchen was built near the abode of their guild, and because
they had gained the victory the last time, the horns of the
captured steer still projecting from the latticed gable-window
of their guild and meeting-house as a sign of victory. Both
these companies had very strong and able members ; but which
of them conquered this time, I no longer remember.

But as a festival of this kind must always close with
something dangerous and frightful, it was really a terrible
moment when the wooden kitchen itself was made a prize.
The roof of it swarmed instantly with men, no one knowing
how they got there, the boards were torn loose, and pitched
down, so that one could not help supposing, particularly
at a distance, that each would kill a few of those pressing to
the spot. In a trice the hut was unroofed, and single individuals hung to the beams and rafters, in order to pull them
also out of their joinings; nay, many floated above upon
the posts which had been already sawn off below, and the
whole skeleton, moving backwards and forwards, threatened
to fall in. Sensitive persons turned their eyes away, and
everybody expected a great calamity ; but we did not hear of
any mischief, and the whole affair, though impetuous and
violent, had passed off happily.

Everybody knew now that the Emperor and King would
return from the cabinet, whither they had retired from the
balcony, and feast in the great hall of the Römer. We had
been able to admire the arrangements made for it, the day
before ; and my most anxious wish was, if possible, to look in
to-day. I repaired, therefore, by the usual path, to the great
staircase, which stands directly opposite the door of the hall.
Here I gazed at the distinguished personages who this day
acted as the servants of the head of the Empire. Forty-four
counts, all splendidly dressed, passed me, carrying the dishes
from the kitchen, so that the contrast between their dignity and
their occupation might well be bewildering to a boy. The
crowd was not great, but, considering the little space, sufficiently perceptible. The hall-door was guarded, while those
who were authorised went frequently in and out. I saw one
of the Palatine domestic officials, whom I asked whether he
could not take me in with him. He did not deliberate
long, but gave me one of the silver vessels he just then bore,—
which he could do so much the more as I was neatly clad;

and thus I reached the sanctuary. The Palatine buffet stood to the left, directly by the door, and with some steps I placed myself on the elevation of it, behind the barriers.

At the other end of the hall, immediately by the windows, raised on the steps of the throne, and under canopies, sat the Emperor and King in their robes; but the crown and sceptre lay at some distance behind them on gold cushions. The three spiritual Electors, their buffets behind them, had taken their places on single elevations; the Elector of Mentz opposite their Majesties, the Elector of Treves at the right, and the Elector of Cologne at the left. This upper part of the hall was imposing and cheerful to behold, and excited the remark that the spiritual power likes to keep as long as possible with the ruler. On the contrary, the buffets and tables of all the temporal Electors, which were, indeed, magnificently ornamented, but without occupants, made one think of the misunderstanding which had gradually arisen for centuries between them and the head of the Empire. Their ambassadors had already withdrawn to eat in a side-chamber; and if the greater part of the hall assumed a sort of spectral appearance, by so many invisible guests being so magnificently attended, a large unfurnished table in the middle was still more sad to look upon; for there also many covers stood empty, because all those who had certainly a right to sit there had, for appearance sake, kept away, that on the greatest day of honour they might not renounce any of their honour, if, indeed, they were then to be found in the city.

Neither my years nor the mass of present objects allowed me to make many reflections. I strove to see all as much as possible; and when the dessert was brought in and the ambassadors re-entered to pay their court, I sought the open air, and contrived to refresh myself with good friends in the neighbourhood, after a day's half-fasting, and to prepare for the illumination in the evening.

This brilliant night I purposed celebrating in a right hearty way; for I had agreed with Gretchen, and Pylades and his mistress, that we should meet somewhere at nightfall. The city was already resplendent at every end and corner when I met my beloved. I offered Gretchen my arm; we went from one quarter to another, and found ourselves very happy in each other's society. The cousins at first were also of our party, but were afterwards lost in the multitude of people. Before the houses of some of the ambassadors, where magnificent illuminations were exhibited (those of the Elector-Palatine were pre-eminently distinguished), it was as clear as day. Lest I should be recognised, I had disguised myself to a certain extent, and Gretchen did not find it amiss. We admired the various brilliant representations and the fairy-like structures of flame by which each ambassador strove to outshine the others. But Prince Esterhazy's arrangements surpassed all the rest. Our little company were in raptures both with the invention and the execution, and we were just about to enjoy this in detail, when the cousins again met us, and spoke to us of the glorious illumination with which the Brandenburg ambassador had adorned his quarters. We were not displeased at taking the long way from the Rossmarkt (Horse-market) to the Saalhof; but found that we had been villanously hoaxed.

The Saalhof is, towards the Maine, a regular and handsome structure, but the part in the direction of the city is exceedingly old, irregular, and unsightly. Small windows, agreeing neither in form nor size, neither in a line nor placed at equal distances, gates and doors arranged without symmetry, a ground-floor mostly turned into shops,—it forms a confused outside, which is never observed by any one. Now here this accidental, irregular, unconnected architecture had been followed, and every window, every door, every opening, was surrounded by lamps; as indeed can be done with a well-built house; but here the most wretched and ill-formed of all façades was thus quite incredibly placed in the clearest light. Did one amuse oneself with this as with the jests of the Pagliasso,* though not without scruple, since everybody must recognise something intentional in it;—just as people had before glossed over the previous external deportment of Von Plotho, so much prized in other respects, and when once inclined towards him, had admired him as a wag, who, like his king, would place himself above all ceremonies—one nevertheless gladly returned to the fairy kingdom of Esterhazy.

This eminent envoy, to honour the day, had quite passed over his own unfavourably situated quarters, and in their

* A sort of buffoon.

stead had caused the great esplanade of linden-trees in the
Horse-market to be decorated in the front with a portal illuminated with colours, and at the back with a still more magnificent prospect. The entire enclosure was marked by lamps.
Between the trees stood pyramids and spheres of light, upon
transparent pedestals; from one tree to another were stretched
glittering garlands, on which floated suspended lights. In
several places bread and sausages were distributed among the
people, and there was no want of wine.

Here now, four abreast, we walked very comfortably up
and down, and I, by Gretchen's side, fancied that I really
wandered in those happy Elysian fields where they pluck
from the trees crystal cups that immediately fill themselves
with the wine desired, and shake down fruits that change into
every dish at will. At last we also felt such a necessity, and
conducted by Pylades, we found a neat, well-arranged eating-
house. When we encountered no more guests, since everybody was going about the streets, we were all the better
pleased, and passed the greatest part of the night most happily and cheerfully, in the feeling of friendship, love, and
attachment. When I had accompanied Gretchen as far as
her door, she kissed me on the forehead. It was the first and
last time that she granted me this favour; for, alas, I was not
to see her again.

The next morning, while I was yet in bed, my mother
entered, in trouble and anxiety. It was easy to see when she
was at all distressed. "Get up," she said, "and prepare
yourself for something unpleasant. It has come out that you
frequent very bad company, and have involved yourself in
very dangerous and bad affairs. Your father is beside himself,
and we have only been able to get thus much from him, that
he will investigate the affair by means of a third party. Remain in your chamber and await what may happen. Councillor
Schneider will come to you: he has the commission both
from your father and from the authorities; for the matter is
already prosecuted, and may take a very bad turn."

I saw that they took the affair for much worse than it was;
yet I felt myself not a little disquieted, even if only the actual
state of things should be detected. My old *Messiah*-loving friend
finally entered, with the tears standing in his eyes; he took
me by the arm, and said, "I am heartily sorry to come to you

on such an affair. I could not have supposed that you could go astray so far. But what will not wicked companions and bad example do! Thus can a young inexperienced man be led step by step into crime!' "I am conscious of no crime," I replied, "and as little of having frequented bad company." "The question now is not one of defence," said he, interrupting me, "but of investigation, and on your part of an upright confession." "What do you want to know?" retorted I. He seated himself, drew out a paper, and began to question me: "Have you not recommended N. N. to your grandfather as a candidate for the * * place?" I answered, "Yes." "Where did you become acquainted with him?" "In my walks." "In what company?" I started: for I would not willingly betray my friends. "Silence will not do now," he continued, "for all is sufficiently known." "What is known then?" said I. "That this man has been introduced to you by others like him —in fact, by * * *." Here he named three persons whom I had never seen nor known: which I immediately explained to the questioner. "You pretend," he resumed, "not to know these men, and have yet had frequent meetings with them." "Not in the least," I replied: "for, as I have said, except the first, I do not know one of them, and even him I have never seen in a house." "Have you not often been in * * * street?" "Never," I replied. This was not entirely conformable to the truth. I had once accompanied Pylades to his sweetheart, who lived in that street; but we had entered by the back-door, and remained in the summer-house. I therefore supposed that I might permit myself the subterfuge, that I had not been in the street itself.

The good man put more questions, all of which I could answer with a denial: for of all that he wished to learn I knew nothing. At last he seemed to become vexed, and said, "You repay my confidence and good-will very badly: I come to save you. You cannot deny that you have composed letters for these people themselves or for their accomplices, have furnished them writings, and have thus been accessory to their evil acts: for the question is of nothing less than of forged papers, false wills, counterfeit bonds, and things of the sort. I come not only as a friend of the family, I come in the name and by order of the magistrates, who, in consideration of your connexions and youth, would spare you and some other young persons,

who, like you, have been lured into the net." It was strange
to me that among the persons he named, none of those with
whom I had been intimate were found. The circumstances
touched, without agreeing, and I could still hope to save my
young friends. But the good man grew more and more urgent.
I could not deny that I had come home late many nights, that
I had contrived to have a house-key made, that I had been
seen at public places more than once with persons of low rank
and suspicious looks, that some girls were mixed up in the
affair; in short, everything seemed to be discovered but the
names. This gave me courage to persist steadfastly in my
silence. " Do not," said my excellent friend, " let me go away
from you; the affair allows of no delay; immediately after me
another will come, who will not grant you so much scope. Do
not make the matter, which is bad enough, worse by your
obstinacy."

I represented very vividly to myself the good cousins, and
particularly Gretchen: I saw them arrested, tried, punished,
disgraced, and then it went through my soul like a flash of
lightning, that the cousins, though they always observed integrity towards me, might have engaged in such bad affairs,
at least the oldest, who never quite pleased me, who came
home later and later, and had little to tell of a cheerful sort.
Still I kept back my confession. " Personally," said I, " I am
conscious of nothing evil, and can rest satisfied on that side,
but it is not impossible that those with whom I have associated
may have been guilty of some daring or illegal act. They may
be sought, found, convicted, punished; I have hitherto nothing
to reproach myself with; and will not do any wrong to those
who have behaved well and kindly to me." He did not let
me finish, but exclaimed with some agitation, " Yes, they will
be found out. These villains met in three houses. (He named
the streets, he pointed out the houses, and, unfortunately,
among them was the one to which I used to go.) The first
nest is already broken up, and at this moment so are the two
others. In a few hours the whole will be clear. Avoid, by a
frank confession, a judicial inquiry, a confrontation, and all
other disagreeable matters." The house was known and marked.
Now I deemed silence useless; nay, considering the innocence
of our meetings, I could hope to be still more useful to them
than to myself. " Sit down," I exclaimed, fetching him back

from the door: " I will tell all, and at once lighten your heart and mine ; only one thing I ask ; henceforth let there be no doubt of my veracity."

I soon told my friend the whole progress of the affair, and was, at first, calm and collected ; but the more I brought to mind and pictured to myself the persons, objects, and events, so many innocent pleasures and charming enjoyments, and was forced to depose as before a criminal court, the more did the most painful feeling increase, so that at last I burst forth in tears and gave myself up to unrestrained passion. The family friend, who hoped that now the real secret was coming to light (for he regarded my distress as a symptom that I was on the point of confessing with repugnance something monstrous), sought to pacify me, as with him the discovery was the all-important matter. In this he only partly succeeded, but so far, however, that I could eke out my story to the end. Though satisfied of the innocence of the proceedings, he was still doubtful to some extent, and put further questions to me, which excited me afresh, and transported me with pain and rage. I asserted, finally, that I had nothing more to say, and well knew that I need fear nothing, for I was innocent, of a good family, and well reputed ; but that they might be just as guiltless without having it recognised, or being otherwise favoured. I declared at the same time, that if they were not spared like myself, that if their follies were not regarded with indulgence, and their faults pardoned, that if anything in the least harsh or unjust happened to them, I would do myself a mischief, and no one should prevent me. In this, too, my friend tried to pacify me ; but I did not trust him, and was, when he quitted me at last, in a most terrible state. I now reproached myself for having told the affair, and brought all the positions to light. I foresaw that our childish actions, our youthful inclinations and confidences, might be quite differently interpreted, and that I might perhaps involve the excellent Pylades in the matter, and render him very unhappy. All these images pressed vividly one after the other before my soul, sharpened and spurred my distress, so that I did not know what to do for sorrow. I cast myself at full length upon the floor, and moistened it with my tears.

I know not how long I might have lain, when my sister entered, was frightened at my gestures, and did all that she

N

could to raise me up. She told me that a person connected
with the magistracy had waited below with my father for the
return of the family friend, and that after they had been
closeted together for some time, both the gentlemen had departed, had talked to each other with apparent satisfaction,
and had even laughed. She believed that she had heard the
words—"It is all right; the affair is of no consequence."
"Indeed!" I broke out, "the affair is of no consequence for
me,—for us; for I have committed no crime, and if I had, they
would contrive to help me through: but the others, the others,"
I cried, "who will stand by them!"

My sister tried to comfort me by circumstantially arguing
that if those of higher rank were to be saved, a veil must also
be cast over the faults of the more lowly. All this was of no
avail. She had scarcely left than I again abandoned myself
to my grief, and ever recalled alternately the images both of
my affection and passion and of the present and possible misfortune. I repeated to myself tale after tale, saw only unhappiness following unhappiness, and did not fail in particular
to make Gretchen and myself truly wretched.

The family friend had ordered me to remain in my room,
and have nothing to do with any one but the family. This
was just what I wanted, for I found myself best alone. My
mother and sister visited me from time to time, and did not
fail to assist me vigorously with all sorts of good consolation; nay, even on the second day they came in the name of
my father, who was now better informed, to offer me a perfect
amnesty, which indeed I gratefully accepted; but the proposal
that I should go out with him and look at the insignia of the
Empire, which were now exposed to the curious, I stubbornly
rejected, and I asserted that I wanted to know nothing either
of the world or of the Roman Empire till I was informed how
that distressing affair, which for me could have no further consequences, had turned out for my poor acquaintance. They
had nothing to say on this head, and left me alone. Yet the
next day some further attempts were made to get me out of
the house and excite in me a sympathy for the public ceremonies. In vain! neither the great gala-day, nor what happened on the occasion of so many elevations of rank, nor the
public table of the Emperor and King,—in short, nothing could
move me. The Elector of the Palatinate might come and wait

on both their Majesties; these might visit the Electors; the last electoral sitting might be attended for the despatch of business in arrear, and the renewal of the electoral union;— nothing could call me forth from my passionate solitude. I let the bells ring for the rejoicings, the Emperor repair to the Capuchin church, the Electors and Emperor depart, without on that account moving one step from my chamber. The final cannonading, immoderate as it might be, did not arouse me, and as the smoke of the powder dispersed, and the sound died away, so had all this glory vanished from my soul.

I now experienced no satisfaction but in chewing the cud of my misery, and in a thousandfold imaginary multiplication of it. My whole inventive faculty, my poetry and rhetoric, had cast themselves on this diseased spot, and threatened, precisely by means of this vitality, to involve body and soul into an incurable disorder. In this melancholy condition nothing more seemed to me worth a desire, nothing worth a wish. An infinite yearning, indeed, seized me at times to know how it had gone with my poor friends and my beloved, what had been the result of a stricter scrutiny, how far they were implicated in those crimes, or had been found guiltless. This also I circumstantially painted to myself in the most various ways, and did not fail to hold them as innocent and truly unfortunate. Sometimes I longed to see myself freed from this uncertainty, and wrote vehemently threatening letters to the family friend, insisting that he should not withhold from me the further progress of the affair. Sometimes I tore them up again, from the fear of learning my unhappiness quite distinctly, and of losing the principal consolation with which hitherto I had alternately tormented and supported myself.

Thus I passed both day and night in great disquiet, in raving and lassitude, so that I felt happy at last when a bodily illness seized me with considerable violence, when they had to call in the help of a physician, and think of every way to quiet me. They supposed that they could do it generally by the sacred assurance that all who were more or less involved in the guilt had been treated with the greatest forbearance, that my nearest friends, being as good as innocent, had been dismissed with a slight reprimand, and that Gretchen had retired from the city and had returned to her own home. They lingered the most

over this last point, and I did not take it in the best part ; for
I could discover in it, not a voluntary departure, but only a
shameful banishment.   My bodily and mental condition was
not improved by this ; my distress now first really began, and
I had time enough to torment myself by picturing the strangest
romance of sad events, and an inevitably tragical catastrophe.

PART THE SECOND.

WHATEVER ONE WISHES IN YOUTH: IN AGE ONE HAS ABUNDANCE.

SIXTH BOOK.

Thus was I driven alternately to assist and to retard my
recovery, and a certain secret chagrin was now added to my
other sensations; for I plainly perceived that I was watched,
—that they were loth to hand me any sealed paper without
taking notice what effect it produced—whether I kept it
secret—whether I laid it down open, and the like. I therefore conjectured that Pylades, or one of the cousins, or even
Gretchen herself, might have attempted to write to me, either
to give or to obtain information. In addition to my sorrow,
I was now for the first time thoroughly cross, and had again
fresh opportunities to exercise my conjectures, and to mislead
myself into the strangest combinations.

It was not long before they gave me a special overseer.
Fortunately, it was a man whom I loved and valued. He
had held the place of tutor in the family of one of our friends;
and his former pupil had gone alone to the university. He
often visited me in my sad condition, and they at last found
nothing more natural than to give him a chamber next to
mine, as he was then to employ me, pacify me, and, as I
marked, keep his eye upon me. Still, as I esteemed him
from my heart, and had already confided many things to him,
though not my affection for Gretchen, I determined so much
the more to be perfectly candid and straightforward with him,
as it was intolerable to me to live in daily intercourse with
any one, and at the same time to stand on an uncertain, unpleasant footing with him. It was not long, then, before I spoke
to him about the affair, refreshed myself by the relation and
repetition of the minutest circumstances of my past happiness,
and thus gained so much, that he, like a sensible man, saw it
would be better to make me acquainted with the issue of the
story, and that too in its details and particulars, so that

I might be clear as to the whole, and that with earnestness and
zeal. I might be persuaded of the necessity of composing
myself, throwing the past behind me, and beginning a new
life. First he confided to me who the other young people of
quality were who had allowed themselves to be seduced, at
the outset, into daring hoaxes, then into sportive breaches of
police, afterwards into frolicsome impositions on others, and
other such dangerous matters. Thus actually had arisen a
little conspiracy, which unprincipled men had joined, who,
by forging papers and counterfeiting signatures, had perpetrated many criminal acts, and had still more criminal matters in preparation. The cousins, after whom I at last impatiently inquired, had been found to be quite innocent, only very
generally acquainted with those others, and not at all implicated
with them. My client, by recommending whom to my grandfather I had in fact put people on the scent, was one of the
worst, and had sued for that office chiefly that he might undertake or conceal certain villanies. After all this, I could at
last contain myself no longer, and asked what had become of
Gretchen, for whom I, once for all, confessed the strongest
attachment. My friend shook his head and smiled,—" Make
yourself easy," replied he ; " this girl has passed her examination very well, and has borne off honourable testimony to
that effect. They could discover nothing in her but what was
good and amiable, the examiners themselves were well-disposed
to her, and could not refuse her desire of removing from the
city. Even what she has confessed in respect to you, too,
my friend, does her honour ; I have read her deposition in the
secret reports myself, and seen her signature." " The signature !" exclaimed I, " which makes me so happy and so
miserable. What has she confessed, then ? What has she
subscribed ?" My friend delayed answering ; but the cheerfulness of his face showed me that he concealed nothing dangerous. " If you must know, then," replied he at last, " when
she was interrogated concerning you, and her intercourse
with you, she said quite frankly, ' I cannot deny that I have
seen him often and with pleasure ; but I have always treated
him as a child, and my affection for him was truly that of a
sister. In many cases I have given him good advice, and
instead of instigating him to any equivocal action, I have hindered him from taking part in wanton tricks, which might
have brought him into trouble.' "

My friend still went on making Gretchen speak like a
governess; but I had already for some time ceased to listen to
him; for I was terribly affronted that she had set me down
in the reports as a child, and believed myself at once cured of
all passion for her. I even hastily assured my friend that all
was now over. I also spoke no more of her, named her no
more; but I could not leave off the bad habit of thinking about
her, and of recalling her form, her air, her demeanour, though
now, in fact, all appeared to me in quite another light. I felt
it intolerable that a girl, at the most only a couple of years
older than me, should regard me as a child, while I conceived
I passed with her for a very sensible and clever youth. Her
cold and repelling manner, which had before so charmed me,
now seemed to me quite repugnant; the familiarities which
she had allowed herself to take with me, but had not
permitted me to return, were altogether odious. Yet all
would have been well enough for me, if by subscribing that
poetical love-letter, in which she had confessed a formal
attachment to me, she had not given me a right to regard her
as a sly and selfish coquette. Her masquerading it at the
milliner's, too, no longer seemed to me so innocent; and I
turned these annoying reflections over and over within myself
until I had entirely stripped her of all her amiable qualities.
My judgment was convinced, and I thought I must cast her
away; but her image!—her image gave me the lie as often
as it again hovered before me, which indeed happened often
enough.

Nevertheless, this arrow with its barbed hooks was torn
out of my heart, and the question then was, how the inward
sanative power of youth could be brought to one's aid? I
really put on the man; and the first thing instantly laid aside
was the weeping and raving, which I now regarded as childish
in the highest degree. A great stride for the better! For I
had often, half the night through, given myself up to this grief,
with the greatest violence, so that at last, from my tears and
sobbing, I came to such a point that I could scarce swallow
any more, the pleasure of eating and drinking became painful
to me, and my breast, which was so nearly concerned, seemed
to suffer. The vexation which I had constantly felt since the
discovery, made me banish every weakness. I found it frightful,
that I had sacrificed sleep, repose and health, for the sake of

a girl who was pleased to consider me a babe, and to imagine herself, with respect to me, something very much like a nurse.

These depressing reflections, as I was soon convinced, were only to be banished by activity; but of what was I to take hold? I had, indeed, much to make up for in many things, and to prepare myself, in more than one sense, for the university, which I was now to attend; but I relished and accomplished nothing. Much appeared to me familiar and trivial; for grounding myself, in several respects, I found neither strength within nor opportunity without; and I therefore suffered myself to be moved by the taste of my good room-neighbour, to a study which was altogether new and strange to me, and which for a long time offered me a wide field of information and thought. My friend began, namely, to make me acquainted with the secrets of philosophy. He had studied in Jena, under Daries, and, possessing a well-regulated mind, had acutely seized the relations of that doctrine, which he now sought to impart to me. But, unfortunately, these things would not hang together in such a fashion in my brain. I put questions, which he promised to answer afterwards; I made demands, which he promised to satisfy in future. But our most important difference was this, that I maintained a separate philosophy was not necessary, as the whole of it was already contained in religion and poetry. This he would by no means allow, but rather tried to prove to me that these must first be founded on philosophy; which I stubbornly denied, and at every step in the progress of our discussions, found arguments for my opinion. For, as in poetry a certain faith in the impossible, and as in religion a like faith in the inscrutable, must have a place, the philosophers appeared to me to be in a very false position who would demonstrate and explain both of them from their own field of vision. Besides, it was very quickly proved, from the history of philosophy, that one always sought a ground different from that of the other, and that the sceptic, in the end, pronounced them all groundless and useless.

However, this very history of philosophy, which my friend was compelled to go over with me, because I could learn nothing from dogmatical discourse, amused me very much, but only on this account, that one doctrine or opinion seemed to me as good as another, so far, at least, as I was capable of

penetrating into it. With the most ancient men and schools I
was best pleased, because poetry, religion, and philosophy were
completely combined into one ; and I only maintained that first
opinion of mine with the more animation, when the book of Job
and the Song and Proverbs of Solomon, as well as the lays of
Orpheus and Hesiod, seemed to bear valid witness in its favour.
My friend had taken the smaller work of Brucker as the foundation of his discourse ; and the further we went on, the less
I could make of it. I could not clearly see what the first
Greek philosophers would have. Socrates I esteemed as an
excellent, wise man, who in his life and death might well be
compared with Christ. His disciples, on the other hand, seemed
to me to bear a strong resemblance to the Apostles, who dis-
agreed immediately after their Master's death, when each
manifestly recognised only a limited view as the right one.
Neither the keenness of Aristotle nor the fulness of Plato produced the least fruit in me. For the Stoics, on the contrary, I
had already conceived some affection, and even procured Epic-
tetus, whom I studied with much interest. My friend unwillingly let me have my way in this one-sidedness, from which
he could not draw me ; for, in spite of his varied studies, he
did not know how to bring the leading question into a narrow
compass. He need only have said to me that in life action
is everything, and that joy and sorrow come of themselves.
However, youth should be allowed its own course ; it does
not stick to false maxims very long ; life soon tears or charms
it away again.

The season had become fine ; we often went together into
the open air, and visited the places of amusement which surrounded the city in great numbers. But it was precisely here
that matters went worse with me : for I still saw the ghosts
of the cousins everywhere, and feared, now here, now there,
to see one of them step forward. Even the most indifferent glances of men annoyed me. I had lost that unconscious
happiness of wandering about unknown and unblamed, and
of thinking of no observer, even in the greatest crowds.
Now hypochondriacal fancies began to torment me, as if I
attracted the attention of the people, as if their eyes were
turned on my demeanour, to fix it on their memories, to scan
and to find fault.

I therefore drew my friend into the woods, and while I

shunned the monotonous firs, I sought those fine leafy groves, which do not indeed spread far in the district, but are yet of sufficient compass for a poor wounded heart to hide itself. In the remotest depth of the forest I sought out a solemn spot, where the oldest oaks and beeches formed a large, noble shaded space. The ground was somewhat sloping, and made the worth of the old trunks only the more perceptible. Round this open circle closed the densest thickets, from which the mossy rocks mightily and venerably peered forth, and made a rapid fall for a copious brook.

Scarcely had I compelled my friend hither, who would rather have been in the open country by the stream, among men, than he playfully assured me that I showed myself a true German. He related to me circumstantially, out of Tacitus, how our ancestors found pleasure in the feelings which nature so provides for us, in such solitudes, with her inartificial architecture. He had not been long discoursing of this, when I exclaimed, " Oh ! why did not this precious spot lie in a deeper wilderness ! why may we not train a hedge around it, to hallow and separate from the world both it and ourselves ! Surely there is no more beautiful adoration of the Deity than that which needs no image, but which springs up in our bosom merely from the intercourse with nature !" What I then felt, is still present to me ; what I said, I know not how to recall. Thus much, however, is certain, that the undetermined, widely-expanding feelings of youth and of uncultivated nations are alone adapted to the sublime, which, if it is to be excited in us through external objects, formless, or moulded into incomprehensible forms, must surround us with a greatness to which we are not equal.

All men, more or less, feel such a disposition of the soul, and seek to satisfy this noble necessity in various ways. But as the sublime is easily produced by twilight and night, when objects are blended, it is, on the other hand, scared away by the day, which separates and sunders everything, and so must it also be destroyed by every increase of cultivation, if it be not fortunate enough to take refuge with the beautiful, and unite itself closely with it, by which both become equally undying and indestructible.

The brief moments of such enjoyments were still more shortened by my meditative friend ; but when I turned back into

the world, it was altogether in vain that I sought, among the
bright and barren objects around, again to arouse such feelings
within me ; nay, I could scarce retain even the remembrance
of them. My heart, however, was too far spoiled to be able
to compose itself ; it had loved, and the object was snatched
away from it ; it had lived, and life to it was embittered. A
friend who makes it too perceptible that he designs to form
you, excites no feeling of comfort ; while a woman who
is forming you, while she seems to spoil you, is adored
as a heavenly, joy-bringing being. But that form in which
the idea of beauty manifested itself to me, had vanished far
away ; it often visited me under the shade of my oak trees,
but I could not hold it fast, and I felt a powerful impulse to
seek something similar in the distance.

I had imperceptibly accustomed, nay, compelled my friend
and overseer to leave me alone ; for even in my sacred grove,
those undefined, gigantic feelings were not sufficient for me.
The eye was, above all others, the organ by which I seized
the world. I had, from childhood, lived among painters, and
had accustomed myself to look at objects, as they did, with
reference to art. Now I was left to myself and to solitude,
this gift, half natural, half acquired, made its appearance.
Wherever I looked, I saw a picture, and whatever struck me,
whatever gave me delight, I wished to fix, and began, in the
most awkward manner, to draw after nature.   In this I
lacked nothing less than everything : yet, though without any
technical means, I obstinately persisted in trying to imitate the
most magnificent things that offered themselves to my sight.
Thus, to be sure, I acquired a great attention to objects ; but
I only seized them as a whole, so far as they produced an
effect ; and, little as nature had meant me for a descriptive
poet, just as little would she grant me the capacity of a
draughtsman for details. Since, however, this was the only way
left me of expressing myself, I stuck to it with so much stubbornness, nay, even with melancholy, that I always continued
my labours the more zealously, the less I saw they produced.

But I will not deny that there was a certain mixture of
roguery : for I had remarked that if I chose for an irksome
study a half-shaded old trunk, to the hugely curved roots of
which clung well-lit fern, combined with twinkling maiden-
hair, my friend, who knew from experience that I should not
be disengaged in less than an hour, commonly resolved to seek,

with his books, some other pleasant little spot. Now nothing
disturbed me in prosecuting my taste, which was so much the
more active, since my paper was endeared to me by the circumstance that I had accustomed myself to see in it, not so
much what stood upon it, as what I had been thinking of at
any time and hour when I drew. Thus plants and flowers
of the commonest kind may form a charming diary for us,
because nothing that calls back the remembrance of a happy
moment can be insignificant; and even now it would be hard
for me to destroy as worthless many things of the kind that
have remained to me from different epochs, because they
transport me immediately to those times which I remember
with melancholy indeed, but not unwillingly.

But if such drawings may have had anything of interest in
themselves, they were indebted for this advantage to the
sympathy and attention of my father. He, informed by my
overseer that I had become gradually reconciled to my condition, and, in particular, had applied myself passionately to
drawing from nature, was very well satisfied—partly because
he himself set a high value on drawing and painting, partly
because gossip Seekatz had once said to him, that it was a pity
I was not destined for a painter. But here again the peculiarities of the father and son came into conflict; for it was almost
impossible for me to make use of a good, white, perfectly clean
sheet of paper; grey old leaves, even if scribbled over on one
side already, charmed me most, just as if my awkwardness had
feared the touchstone of a white ground. Nor were any of my
drawings quite finished; and how should I have executed a
whole, which indeed I saw with my eyes, but did not comprehend, and how an individual object, which I had neither skill
nor patience to follow out? The pedagogism of my father on
this point, too, was really to be admired. He kindly asked
for my attempts, and drew lines round every imperfect sketch.
He wished, by this means, to compel me to completeness and
fulness of detail. The irregular leaves he cut straight, and thus
made the beginning of a collection, in which he wished, at some
future time, to rejoice at the progress of his son. It was
therefore by no means disagreeable to him when my wild,
restless disposition sent me roving about the country; he
rather seemed pleased when I brought back a parcel of drawings on which he could exercise his patience, and in some
measure strengthen his hopes.

They no longer said that I might relapse into my former attachments and connexions; they left me by degrees perfect liberty. By accidental inducements and in accidental society I undertook many journeys to the mountain-range which, from my childhood, had stood so distant and solemn before me. Thus we visited Homburg, Kroneburg, ascended the Feldberg, from which the prospect invited us still further and further into the distance. Konigstein, too, was not left unvisited; Wiesbaden, Schwalbach, with its environs, occupied us many days; we reached the Rhine, which, from the heights, we had seen winding along far off. Mentz astonished us, but could not chain a youthful mind, which was running into the open country; we were delighted with the situation of Biberich; and, contented and happy, we resumed our journey home.

This whole tour, from which my father had promised himself many a drawing, might have been almost without fruit; for what taste, what talent, what experience does it not require to seize an extensive landscape as a picture! I was again imperceptibly drawn into a narrow compass, from which I derived some profit; for I met no ruined castle, no piece of wall which pointed to antiquity, that I did not think an object worthy of my pencil, and imitate as well as I could. Even the monument of Drusenstein, on the ramparts of Mentz, I copied at some risk, and with inconveniences which every one must experience who wishes to carry home with him some pictorial reminiscences of his travels. Unfortunately I had again taken with me nothing but the most miserable common paper, and had clumsily crowded several objects into one sheet. But my paternal teacher was not perplexed at this; he cut the sheets apart, had the parts which belonged to each other put together by the bookbinder, surrounded the single leaves with lines, and thus actually compelled me to draw the outline of different mountains up to the margin, and to fill up the foreground with some weeds and stones.

If his faithful endeavours could not increase my talent, nevertheless this mark of his love of order had upon me a secret influence, which afterwards manifested itself vigorously in more ways than one.

From such rambling excursions, undertaken partly for pleasure, partly for art, and which could be performed in a short time and often repeated, I was again drawn home, and that by

a magnet which always acted upon me strongly: this was my
sister. She, only a year younger than I, had lived my whole
conscious period of life with me, and was thus bound to me by
the closest ties. To these natural causes was added a forcible
motive, which proceeded from our domestic position ; a father
certainly affectionate and well-meaning, but grave, who, because he cherished within a very tender heart, externally, with
incredible consistency, maintained a brazen sternness, that
he might attain the end of giving his children the best education, and of building up, regulating, and preserving his well-
founded house ; a mother, on the other hand, as yet almost a
child, who first grew up to consciousness with and in her two
eldest children ; these three, as they looked at the world with
healthy eyes, capable of life, and desiring present enjoyment.
This contradiction floating in the family increased with years.
My father followed out his views unshaken and uninterrupted ;
the mother and children could not give up their feelings, their
claims, their wishes.

Under these circumstances it was natural that brother and
sister should attach themselves close to each other, and adhere
to their mother, that they might singly snatch the pleasures
forbidden as a whole. But since the hours of solitude and
toil were very long compared to the moments of recreation
and enjoyment, especially for my sister, who could never leave
the house for so long a time as I could, the necessity she felt
for entertaining herself with me was still sharpened by the
sense of longing with which she accompanied me to a distance.

And as, in our first years, playing and learning, growth and
education, had been quite common to both of us, so that we
might well have been taken for twins, so did this community,
this confidence, remain during the development of our physical
and moral powers. That interest of youth, that amazement at
the awakening of sensual impulses which clothe themselves in
mental forms, of mental necessities which clothe themselves in
sensual images, all the reflections upon these, which obscure
rather than enlighten us, as the fog covers over and does not illu-
mine the vale from which it is about to rise, the many errors and
aberrations springing therefrom,—all these the brother and
sister shared and endured hand in hand, and were the less enlightened as to their strange condition, as the nearer they
wished to approach each other, to clear up their minds, the

more forcibly did the sacred awe of their close relationship
keep them apart.

Reluctantly do I mention, in general terms, what I undertook to perform, years ago, without being able to accomplish
it. As I lost this beloved, incomprehensible being, but too
soon, I felt inducement enough to make her worth present to
me, and thus arose in me the conception of a poetic whole, in
which it might be possible to exhibit her individuality : but
for this no other form could be devised than that of the Ri-
chardsonian novels. Only by the minutest detail, by endless
particularities which bear vividly all the character of the whole,
and as they spring up from a wonderful depth give some feeling of that depth ;—only in such a manner would it have been
in some degree possible to give a representation of this remarkable personality : for the spring can be apprehended only
while it is flowing. But from this beautiful and pious design,
as from so many others, the tumult of the world drew me back,
and nothing now remains for me but to call up for a moment
that blessed spirit, as if by the aid of a magic mirror.

She was tall, well and delicately formed, and had something
naturally dignified in her demeanour, which melted away into
a pleasing mildness. The lineaments of her face, neither striking nor beautiful, indicated a character which was not and
could not be at union with itself. Her eyes were not the finest
I have ever seen, but the deepest, behind which you expected
the most ; and when they expressed any affection, any love,
their brilliancy was unequalled. And yet, properly speaking,
this expression was not tender, like that which comes from
the heart, and at the same time carries with it something of
longing and desire ; this expression came from the soul, it was
full and rich, it seemed as if it would only give, without need-
ing to receive.

But what in a manner quite peculiar disfigured her face, so
that she would often appear positively ugly, was the fashion of
those times, which not only bared the forehead, but, either
accidentally or on purpose, did everything apparently or really
to enlarge it. Now, as she had the most feminine, most neatly
arched forehead, and moreover a pair of strong black eyebrows,
and prominent eyes, these circumstances occasioned a contrast,
which, if it did not repel every stranger at the first glance, at
least did not attract him. She early felt it, and this feeling

became constantly the more painful to her, the further she advanced into the years when both sexes find an innocent pleasure in being mutually agreeable.

To nobody can his own form be repugnant; the ugliest as well as the most beautiful has a right to enjoy his own presence; and as favour beautifies, and every one regards himself in the looking-glass with favour, it may be asserted that every one must see himself with complacency, even if he would struggle against the feeling. Yet my sister had such a decided foundation of good sense, that she could not possibly be blind and silly in this respect; on the contrary, she perhaps knew more clearly than she ought, that she stood far behind her female playfellows in external beauty, without feeling consoled by the fact that she infinitely surpassed them in internal advantages.

If a lady can be recompensed for the want of beauty, then was she richly so by the unbounded confidence, the regard, and love which all her female friends bore to her; whether they were older or younger, all cherished the same sentiments. A very pleasant society had collected around her; young men were not wanting who knew how to insinuate themselves; nearly every girl found an admirer; she alone had remained without a partner. Indeed, if her exterior was in some measure repulsive, the mind that gleamed through it was also rather repelling than attractive; for the presence of any excellence throws others back upon themselves. She felt this sensibly, she did not conceal it from me, and her love was directed to me with so much the greater force. The case was singular enough. As confidants to whom one reveals a love-affair actually by genuine sympathy become lovers also, nay, grow into rivals, and at last, perchance, transfer the passion to themselves, so it was with us two: for, when my connexion with Gretchen was torn asunder, my sister consoled me the more earnestly, because she secretly felt the satisfaction of having gotten rid of a rival; and I, too, could not but feel a quiet, half-delicious pleasure, when she did me the justice to assure me that I was the only one who truly loved, understood, and esteemed her. If now, from time to time, my grief for the loss of Gretchen revived, and I suddenly began to weep, to lament, and to act in a disorderly manner, my despair for my lost one awakened in her likewise a similar despairing impatience as to the never-possessings, the failures, and miscarriages of such youthful attachments, that we both thought ourselves infinitely unhappy, and the more so as, in this singular case, the confidants dared not change themselves into lovers.

Fortunately, however, the capricious god of Love, who needlessly does so much mischief, here for once interfered beneficially, to extricate us out of all perplexity. I had much intercourse with a young Englishman who was educated in Pfeil's boarding-school. He could give a good account of his own language, I practised it with him, and thus learned much concerning his country and people. He went in and out of our house long enough without my remarking in him a liking for my sister, yet he may have been nourishing it in secret, even to passion, for at last it declared itself unexpectedly and at once. She knew him, she esteemed him, and he deserved it. She had often made the third at our English conversations, we had both tried to catch from his mouth the irregularities of the English pronunciation, and thereby accustomed ourselves not only to the peculiarities of its accent and sound, but even to what was most peculiar in the personal qualities of our teacher; so that at last it sounded strangely enough when we all seemed to speak as if out of one mouth. The pains he took to learn as much German from us in the like manner, were to no purpose, and I think I have remarked that even this little love-affair also, both in speaking and writing, was carried on in the English language. Both the young persons were very well suited to each other; he was tall and well-built, as she was, only still more slender; his face, small and compact, might really have been pretty, had it not been too much disfigured by the small-pox; his manner was calm, precise, one might often have called it dry and cold; but his heart was full of kindness and love, his soul full of generosity, and his attachments as lasting as they were decided and moderate. Now this serious pair, who had but lately formed an attachment, were quite peculiarly distinguished among the others, who, being already better acquainted with each other, of more frivolous character, and careless as to the future, roved about with levity in these connexions, which commonly pass away as the mere fruitless prelude to subsequent and more serious ties, and very seldom produce a lasting effect upon life.

The fine weather and the beautiful country did not remain
unenjoyed by so lively a company ; water excursions were frequently arranged, because these are the most sociable of all
parties of pleasure. Yet whether we were moving on water
or on land, the individual attracting powers immediately
showed themselves ; each couple kept together, and for some
men who were not engaged, of whom I was one, there remained either no conversation with the ladies at all, or only
such as no one would have chosen for a day of pleasure. A
friend who found himself in this situation, and who might
have been in want of a partner chiefly for this reason, that
with the best humour he lacked tenderness, and with much
intelligence, that delicate attention, without which connexions
of this kind are not to be thought of ;—this man, after often
humorously and wittily lamenting his condition, promised at
the next meeting to make a proposal which would benefit himself and the whole company. Nor did he fail to perform his
promise : for, when after a brilliant trip by water, and a very
pleasant walk, reclining on the grass between shady knolls, or
sitting on mossy rocks and roots of trees, we had cheerfully
and happily consumed a rural meal, and our friend saw us all
cheerful and in good spirits, he, with a waggish dignity, commanded us to sit close round him in a semicircle, before
which he stepped, and began to make an emphatic peroration
as follows :—

" Most worthy friends of both sexes, paired and unpaired!"
—It was already evident, from this address, how necessary it
was that a preacher of repentance should arise and sharpen
the conscience of the company. " One part of my noble
friends is paired, and they may find themselves quite happy ;
another unpaired, and these find themselves in the highest
degree miserable, as I can assure you from my own experience ;
and although the loving couples are here in the majority, yet
I would have them consider whether it is not a social duty to
take thought for the whole? Why do so many of us unite
together but to take a mutual interest in each other? and how
can that be done when so many little secessions are to be seen
in our circle? Far be it from me to insinuate anything against
such sweet connexions, or even to wish to disturb them ; but
' there is a time for all things!' an excellent great saying, of
which, indeed, nobody thinks when his own amusement is
sufficiently provided for.'

He then went on with constantly increasing liveliness and gaiety to compare the social virtues with the tender sentiments. "The latter," said he, "can never fail us; we always carry them about with us, and every one becomes a master in them without practice; but we must go in quest of the former, we must take some trouble about them, and though we progress in them as much as we will, we have never done learning them." Now he went into particulars. Many felt themselves hit off, and they could not help casting glances at each other; yet our friend had this privilege, that nothing he did was taken ill, and so he could proceed without interruption.

" It is not enough to discover deficiencies; indeed, it is unjust to do so, if at the same time one cannot contrive to give the means for bettering the state of affairs. I will not, therefore, my friends, something like a preacher in Passion-week, exhort you in general terms to repentance and amendment; I rather wish all amiable couples the longest and most enduring happiness, and to contribute to it myself in the surest manner, I propose to sever and abolish these most charming little segregations during our social hours. I have," he continued, "already provided for the execution of my project, if it should meet your approbation. Here is a bag in which are the names of the gentlemen; now draw, my fair ones, and be pleased to favour as your servant, for a week, him whom fate shall send you. This is binding only within our circle; as soon as that is broken up, these connexions are also abolished, and the heart may decide who shall attend you home."

A large part of the company had been delighted with this address, and the manner in which he delivered it, and seemed to approve of the notion; yet some couples looked at each other as if they thought they would not find their account in it: he therefore cried with humorous vehemence :—

"Truly! it surprises me that some one does not spring up, and, though others hesitate, extol my plan, explain its advantages, and spare me the pain of being my own encomiast. I am the oldest among you; may God forgive me for that! Already have I a bald pate, which is owing to my great meditation,"—

Here he took off his hat—

" But I would expose it to view with joy and honour if my lucubrations, which dry up my skin, and rob me of my finest

ornament, could only be in some measure beneficial to myself
and others. We are young, my friends,—that is good; we
shall grow older,—that is bad ; we take little offence at each
other,—that is right, and in accordance with the season. But
soon, my friends, the days will come when we shall have much
to be displeased at in ourselves ; then let every one see that
he makes all right with himself; but, at the same time, others
will take things ill of us, and on what account we shall not
understand ; for this we must prepare ourselves ; this shall
now be done."

He had delivered the whole speech, but especially the last
part, with the tone and gesture of a Capuchin ; for as he was
a catholic, he might have had abundant opportunity to study
the oratory of these fathers. He now appeared out of breath,
wiped his youthful bald head, which really gave him the look
of a priest, and by these drolleries put the light-hearted company in such good humour that every one was eager to hear
him longer. But instead of proceeding, he drew open the
bag, and turned to the nearest lady—" Now for a trial of it !"
exclaimed he ; " the work will do credit to the master. If in
a week's time we do not like it, we will give it up, and stick
to the old plan."

Half willingly, half on compulsion, the ladies drew their
tickets, and it was easy to see that various passions were in
play during this little affair. Fortunately it happened that
the merry-minded were separated, while the more serious remained together ; and so, too, my sister kept her Englishman,
which, on both sides, they took very kindly of the god of Love
and Luck. The new chance-couples were immediately united
by the *Antistes*, their healths were drank, and to all the more
joy was wished, as its duration was to be but short. This
was certainly the merriest moment that our company had
enjoyed for a long time. The young men to whose share no
lady had fallen, held, for this week, the office of providing
for the mind, the soul, and the body, as our orator expressed
himself, but especially, he hinted, for the soul, since both the
others already knew how to help themselves.

These masters of ceremonies, who wished at once to do
themselves credit, brought into play some very pretty new
games, prepared at some distance a supper, which we had not
reckoned on, and illuminated the yacht on our return at night,

although there was no necessity for it in the bright moonlight; but they excused themselves by saying that it was quite conformable to the new social regulation to outshine the tender glances of the heavenly moon by earthly candles. The moment we touched the shore, our Solon cried, " *Ite, missa est!*" Each one now handed out of the vessel the lady who had fallen to him by lot, and then surrendered her to her proper partner, on receiving his own in exchange.

At our next meeting this weekly regulation was established for the summer, and the lots were drawn once more. There was no question but that this pleasantry gave a new and unexpected turn to the company, and every one was stimulated to display whatever of wit and grace was in him, and to pay court to his temporary fair one in the most obliging manner, since he might depend on having a sufficient store of complaisance for one week at least.

We had scarcely settled ourselves, than, instead of thanking our orator, we reproached him for having kept to himself the best part of his speech—the conclusion. He thereupon protested that the best part of a speech was persuasion; and that he who did not aim at persuasion should make no speech; for, as to conviction, that was a ticklish business. As, however, they gave him no peace, he began a Capuchinade on the spot, more comical than ever, perhaps, for the very reason that he took it into his head to speak on the most serious subjects. For, with texts out of the Bible which had nothing to do with the business—with similes which did not fit—with allusions which illustrated nothing— he carried out the proposition, that whosoever does not know how to conceal his passions, inclinations, wishes, purposes and plans, will come to no good in the world, but will be disturbed and made a butt in every end and corner; and that especially if one would be happy in love, one must take pains to keep it a most profound secret.

This thought ran through the whole, without, properly speaking, a single word of it being said. If you would form a conception of this singular man, let it be considered that, being born with a good foundation, he had cultivated his talents, and especially his acuteness, in Jesuit schools, and had amassed an extensive knowledge of the world and of men, but only on the bad side. He was some two-and-twenty

years old, and would gladly have made me a proselyte to his
contempt for mankind ; but this would not take with me, as
I always had a great desire to be good myself, and to find
good in others. Meanwhile I was by him made attentive to
many things.

To complete the *dramatis personæ* of every merry company,
an actor is necessary, who feels pleasure when the others, to
enliven many an indifferent moment, point the arrows of their
wit at him. If he is not merely a stuffed Saracen, like those
on whom the knights used to practise their lances in mock
battles, but understands himself how to skirmish, to rally and
to challenge, how to wound lightly, and recover himself again,
and, while he seems to expose himself, to give others a thrust
home, nothing more agreeable can be found. Such a man we
possessed in our friend Horn, whose name, to begin with,
gave occasion for all sorts of jokes, and who, on account of
his small figure, was called nothing but Hörnchen (little
Horn). He was, in fact, the smallest in the company, of a
stout, but pleasing form ; a pug-nose, a mouth somewhat
pouting, little sparkling eyes, made up a swarthy countenance,
which always seemed to invite laughter. His little compact skull was thickly covered with curly black hair ; his
beard was prematurely grey, and he would have liked to let
it grow, that, as a comic mask, he might always keep the
company laughing. For the rest, he was neat and nimble,
but insisted that he had bandy legs, which everybody granted,
since he was bent on having it so, but about which many a
joke arose : for since he was in request as a very good dancer,
he reckoned it among the peculiarities of the fair sex, that
they always liked to see bandy legs on the floor. His cheerfulness was indestructible, and his presence at every meeting
indispensable. We two kept more together because he was
to follow me to the university ; and he well deserves that I
should mention him with all honour, as he adhered to me for
many years with infinite love, faithfulness, and patience.

By my ease in rhyming, and in winning from common
objects a poetical side, he had allowed himself to be seduced
into similar labours. Our little social excursions, parties of
pleasure, and the contingencies that occurred in them, we
decked out poetically, and thus by the description of an event,
a new event always arose. But as such social jests commonly

degenerate into personal ridicule, and my friend Horn, with his
burlesque representations, did not always keep within proper
bounds, many a misunderstanding arose, which, however,
could soon be softened down and effaced.

Thus, also, he tried his skill in a species of poetry which
was then very much the order of the day—the comic heroical
poem. Pope's *Rape of the Lock* had called forth many imitations; Zachariä cultivated this branch of poetry on German
soil, and it pleased every one, because the ordinary subject of
it was some awkward fellow, of whom the genii made game,
while they favoured the better one.

It is not wonderful, but yet it excites wonder, when, in
contemplating a literature, especially the German, one observes how a whole nation cannot get free from a subject
which has been once given, and happily treated in a certain
form, but will have it repeated in every manner, until, at
last, the original itself is covered up, and stifled by the
heaps of imitations.

The heroic poem of my friend was a voucher for this remark. At a great sledging party, an awkward man has
assigned to him a lady who does not like him; comically
enough there befalls him, one after another, every accident
that can happen on such an occasion, until at last, as he is
entreating for the sledge-driver's right (a kiss), he falls from
the back seat: for just then, as was natural, the genii tripped
him up. The fair one seizes the reins, and drives home alone,
where a favoured friend receives her, and triumphs over his
presumptuous rival. As to the rest, it was very prettily contrived that the four different kinds of spirits should worry him
in turn, till at the end the gnomes hoist him completely out
of the saddle. The poem, written in Alexandrines, and founded
on a true story, highly delighted our little public, and we
were convinced that it could well be compared with the
Walpurgisnight of Löven, or the *Renommist* of Zachariä.*

While, now, our social pleasures required but an evening,
and the preparations for them only a few hours, I had enough
time to read, and, as I thought, to study. To please my
father, I diligently repeated the smaller work of Hopp, and
could stand an examination in it forwards and backwards, by

* This word, which signifies something like our "bully," is specially
used to designate a fighting student.—*Trans.*

which means I made myself complete master of the chief contents of the Institutes. But a restless eagerness for knowledge urged me further; I lit upon the history of ancient literature, and from that fell into an encyclopedism, in which I read through Gessner's *Isagoge* and Morhov's *Polyhistor*, and thus gained a general notion of how many strange things might have happened in learning and life. By this persevering and rapid industry, continued day and night, I more confused than instructed myself; but I lost myself in a still greater labyrinth when I found Bayle in my father's library, and plunged deep into him.

But a leading conviction, which was continually revived within me, was that of the importance of the ancient tongues; since from amidst this literary hurly-burly, thus much continually forced itself upon me, that in them were preserved all the models of oratory, and at the same time everything else of worth that the world has ever possessed. Hebrew, together with biblical studies, had retired into the background, and Greek likewise, since my acquaintance with it did not extend beyond the New Testament. I therefore the more zealously kept to Latin, the master-pieces in which lie nearer to us, and which, besides its splendid original productions, offers us the other wealth of all ages in translations, and the works of the greatest scholars. I consequently read much in this language, with great ease, and was bold enough to believe I understood the authors, because I missed nothing of the literal sense. Indeed I was very indignant when I heard that Grotius had insolently declared, "he did not read Terence as boys do." Happy narrow-mindedness of youth!—nay, of men in general, that they can, at every moment of their existence, fancy themselves finished, and inquire after neither the true nor the false, after neither the high nor the deep, but merely after that which is suited to them.

I had thus learned Latin, like German, French, and English, merely by practice, without rules, and without conception. Whoever knows the condition of school instruction then, will not think it strange that I skipped grammar as well as rhetoric; all seemed to me to come together naturally; I retained the words, their forms and inflexions, in my ear and mind, and used the language with ease in writing and in chattering.

Michaelmas, the time when I was to go to the university, was approaching, and my mind was excited quite as much about my life as about my learning. I grew more and more clearly conscious of an aversion to my native city. By Gretchen's removal, the heart had been broken out of the boyish and youthful plant; it needed time to bud forth again from its sides, and surmount the first injury by a new growth. My ramblings through the streets had ceased; I now, like others, only went such ways as were necessary. I never went again into Gretchen's quarter of the city, not even into its vicinity; and as my old walls and towers became gradually disagreeable to me, so also was I displeased at the constitution of the city; all that hitherto seemed so worthy of honour, now appeared to me in distorted shapes. As grandson of the Schultheiss, the secret defects of such a republic had not remained unknown to me; the less so, as children feel quite a peculiar surprise, and are excited to busy researches, as soon as something which they have hitherto implicitly revered becomes in any degree suspicious to them. The fruitless indignation of upright men, in opposition to those who are to be gained and even bribed by factions, had become but too plain to me; I hated every injustice beyond measure; for children are all moral rigorists. My father, who was concerned in the affairs of the city only as a private citizen, expressed himself with very lively indignation about much that had failed. And did I not see him, after so many studies, endeavours, pains, travels, and so much varied cultivation, between his four walls, leading a solitary life, such as I could never desire for myself? All this put together, lay as a horrible load on my mind, from which I could only free myself by trying to contrive a plan of life altogether different from that which had been marked out for me. In thought, I threw away my legal studies, and devoted myself solely to the languages, to antiquities, to history, and to all that flows from them.

Indeed, at all times, the poetic imitation of what I had perceived in myself, in others, and in nature, afforded me the greatest pleasure. I did it with ever-increasing facility, because it came by instinct, and no criticism had led me astray; and if I did not feel full confidence in my productions, I could certainly regard them as defective, but not such as to be utterly rejected. Was this or that censured in them, I still retained in private my conviction that I could not but gradually improve, and that some time I might be honourably named along with Hagedorn, Gellert, and other such men. But such a distinction alone seemed to me too empty and inadequate; I wished to devote myself professionally and with zeal to those aforesaid fundamental studies, and while I thought to advance myself more rapidly in my own works by a more thorough insight into antiquity, to qualify myself for a university professorship, which seemed to me the most desirable thing for a young man who intended to cultivate himself and to contribute to the cultivation of others.

With these intentions, I always had my eye upon Göttingen. My whole confidence rested upon men like Heyne, Michaelis, and so many others; my most ardent wish was to sit at their feet, and attend to their instructions. But my father remained inflexible. However, some family friends, who were of my opinion, tried to influence him; he persisted that I must go to Leipzig. I was now resolved, contrary to his views and wishes, to choose a line of studies and of life for myself, by way of self-defence. The obstinacy of my father, who, without knowing it, opposed himself to my plans, strengthened me in my impiety, so that I made no scruple to listen to him by the hour, while he described and repeated to me the course of study and of life which I should pursue at the universities and in the world.

Since all hopes of Göttingen were cut off, I now turned my eyes towards Leipzig. There Ernesti appeared to me as a brilliant light; Morus, too, already awakened much confidence. I planned for myself in secret an opposition-course, or rather I built a castle in the air, on a tolerably solid foundation; and it seemed to me quite romantically honourable to mark out my own path of life, which appeared the less visionary, as Griesbach had already made great progress in a similar way, and was commended for it by every one. The secret joy of a prisoner, when he has unbound the fetters and rapidly filed through the bars of his gaol-window, cannot be greater than was mine as I saw day after day disappear, and October draw nigh. The inclement season and the bad roads, of which everybody had something to tell, did not frighten me. The thought of paying my entrance-fee in a strange place, and in winter, did not make me sad; suffice it to say, that I only saw my present situation was gloomy, and represented to myself the other unknown world as light and cheerful. Thus I formed my dreams, to which I gave myself up exclusively, and promised myself nothing but happiness and content in the distance.

Closely as I kept these projects a secret from every one else, I could not hide them from my sister, who, after being very much alarmed about them at first, was finally consoled when I promised to send after her, so that she could enjoy with me the brilliant station I was to obtain, and share my comfort with me.

Michaelmas, so longingly expected, came at last, when I set out with delight, in company with the bookseller Fleischer and his wife (whose maiden name was Triller, and who was going to visit her father in Wittemberg); and I left behind me the worthy city in which I had been born and bred, with indifference, as if I wished never to set foot in it again.

Thus, at certain epochs, children part from parents, servants from masters, *protégés* from their patrons; and whether it succeed or not, such an attempt to stand on one's own feet, to make one's self independent, to live for one's self, is always in accordance with the will of nature.

We had driven out through the Allerheiligen (*All Saints*) gate, and had soon left Hanau behind us, after which we reached scenes which aroused my attention by their novelty, if, at this season of the year, they offered little that was pleasing. A continual rain had completely spoiled the roads, which, generally speaking, were not then in such good order as we find them now; and our journey was thus neither pleasant nor happy. Yet I was indebted to this damp weather for the sight of a natural phenomenon which must be exceedingly rare, for I have seen nothing like it since, nor have I heard of its being observed by others. At night, namely, we were driving up a rising ground between Hanau and Gelhausen, and, although it was dark, we preferred walking to exposing ourselves to the danger and difficulty of that part of the road. All at once, in a ravine on the right-hand side of the way, I saw a sort of amphitheatre, wonderfully illuminated. In a funnel-shaped space there were innumerable little lights gleaming, ranged step-fashion over one another, and they shone so brilliantly that the eye was dazzled. But what still more

confused the sight was, that they did not keep still, but jumped
about here and there, as well downwards from above as *vice
versâ*, and in every direction. The most of them, however,
remained stationary, and beamed on. It was only with the
greatest reluctance that I suffered myself to be called away
from this spectacle, which I could have wished to examine
more closely. On interrogating the postillion, he indeed knew
nothing about such a phenomenon, but said that there was in
the neighbourhood an old stone-quarry, the excavation of which
was filled with water. Now whether this was a pandemonium
of will-o'-the-wisps, or a company of shining creatures, I
will not decide.

The roads through Thuringia were yet worse, and unfortunately, at night-fall, our coach stuck fast in the vicinity of
Auerstädt. We were far removed from all mankind, and did
everything possible to work ourselves out. I failed not to exert
myself zealously, and might thereby have overstrained the
ligaments of my chest; for soon afterwards I felt a pain, which
went off and returned, and did not leave me entirely until after
many years.

Yet on that same night, as if it had been destined for alternate good and bad luck, I was forced, after an unexpectedly
fortunate incident, to experience a teazing vexation. We met,
in Auerstädt, a genteel married couple, who had also just
arrived, having been delayed by a similar accident; a pleasing,
dignified man, in his best years, with a very handsome wife.
They politely persuaded us to sup in their company, and I felt
very happy when the excellent lady addressed a friendly word
to me. But when I was sent out to accelerate the soup which
had been ordered, not having been accustomed to the loss of
rest and the fatigues of travelling, such an unconquerable
drowsiness overtook me, that actually I fell asleep while walking, returned into the room with my hat on my head, and
without remarking that the others were saying grace, placed
myself with quiet unconsciousness behind the chair, and never
dreamed that by my conduct I had come to disturb their de-
votions in a very droll way. Madame Fleischer, who lacked
neither spirit nor wit, nor tongue, entreated the strangers,
before they had seated themselves, not to be surprised at anything they might see here; for that their young fellow-traveller
had in his nature much of the peculiarity of the Quakers, who

believe that they cannot honour God and the king better than
with covered heads. The handsome lady, who could not restrain her laughter, looked prettier than ever in consequence,
and I would have given everything in the world not to have
been the cause of a merriment which was so beautifully becoming in her countenance. I had, however, scarcely laid aside
my hat, than these persons, in accordance with their polished
manners, immediately dropped the joke, and with the best
wine from their bottle-case completely extinguished sleep,
chagrin, and the memory of all past troubles.

I arrived in Leipzig just at the time of the fair, from which I
derived particular pleasure : for here I saw before me the continuation of a state of things belonging to my native city, familiar
wares and traders:—only in other places, and in a different
order. I rambled about the market and the booths with much
interest, but my attention was particularly attracted by the
inhabitants of the Eastern countries in their strange dresses, the
Poles and Russians, and above all, the Greeks, for the sake of
whose handsome forms and dignified costume I often went to
the spot.

But this animating bustle was soon over, and now the city
itself appeared before me, with its handsome, high, and uniform houses. It made a very good impression upon me, and
it cannot be denied, that in general, but especially in the silent
moments of Sundays and holidays, it has something imposing ;
and when in the moonlight the streets were half in shadow,
half-illuminated, they often invited me to nocturnal promenades.

In the meantime, as compared with that to which I had
hitherto been accustomed, this new state of affairs was by no
means satisfactory. Leipzig calls up before the spectator no
antique time ; it is a new, recently elapsed epoch, testifying
commercial activity, comfort and wealth, which announces
itself to us in these monuments. Yet quite to my taste were
the huge-looking buildings, which, fronting two streets, and
embracing a citizen-world within their large court-yards, built
round with lofty walls, are like large castles, nay, even half-
cities. In one of these strange places I quartered myself,
namely, in the Bombshell Tavern (*Feuerkugel*), between the
Old and the New Newmarket (*Neumarkt*). A couple of pleasant
rooms looking out upon a court-yard, which, on account of the
thoroughfare, was not without animation, were occupied by the

bookseller Fleischer during the fair : and by me taken for the
rest of the time at a moderate price. As a fellow-lodger I
found a theological student, who was deeply learned in his
professional studies, a sound thinker, but poor, and suffering
much from his eyes, which caused him great anxiety for the
future. He had brought this affliction upon himself by his
inordinate reading till the latest dusk of the evening, and even
by moonlight, to save a little oil. Our old hostess showed
herself benevolent to him, always friendly to me, and careful
for us both.

I now hastened with my letters of introduction to Hofrath
Böhme, who once a pupil of Maskow, and now his successor,
was professor of history and public law. A little, thick-set,
lively man, received me kindly enough, and introduced me to
his wife. Both of them, as well as the other persons whom I
waited on, gave me the pleasantest hopes as to my future residence; but at first I let no one know of the design I entertained,
although I could scarcely wait for the favourable moment when
I should declare myself free from jurisprudence, and devoted
to the study of the classics. I cautiously waited till the
Fleischers had returned, that my purpose might not be too
prematurely betrayed to my family. But I then went, without delay, to Hofrath Böhme, to whom, before all, I thought
I must confide the matter, and with much self-importance and
boldness of speech disclosed my views to him. However, I
found by no means a good reception of my proposition. As
professor of history and public law, he had a declared hatred
for everything that savoured of the *belles lettres*. Unfortunately he did not stand on the best footing with those who
cultivated them, and Gellert in particular, in whom I had,
awkwardly enough, expressed much confidence, he could not
even endure. To send a faithful student to those men, therefore, while he deprived himself of one, and especially under
such circumstances, seemed to him altogether out of the question. He therefore gave me a severe lecture on the spot, in
which he protested that he could not permit such a step without the permission of my parents, even if he approved of it
himself, which was not the case in this instance. He then
passionately inveighed against philology and the study of languages, but still more against poetical exercises, which I had
indeed allowed to peep out in the back-ground. He finally

concluded that, if I wished to enter more closely into the study of the ancients, it could be done much better by the way of jurisprudence. He brought to my recollection many elegant jurists, such as Eberhard, Otto, and Heineccius, promised me mountains of gold from Roman antiquities and the history of law, and showed me, clear as the sun, that I should here be taking no roundabout way, even if afterwards, on more mature deliberation, and with the consent of my parents, I should determine to follow out my own plan. He begged me, in a friendly manner, to think the matter over once more, and to open my mind to him soon, as it would be necessary to come to a determination at once, on account of the impending commencement of the lectures.

It was, however, very polite of him not to press me on the spot. His arguments, and the weight with which he advanced them, had already convinced my pliant youth, and I now first saw the difficulties and doubtfulness of a matter which I had privately pictured to myself as so feasible. Frau Hofrath Bohme invited me to see her shortly afterwards. I found her alone. She was no longer young, and had very delicate health, was gentle and tender to an infinite degree, and formed a decided contrast to her husband, whose good-nature was even blustering. She spoke of the conversation her husband had lately had with me, and once more placed the subject before me, in all its bearings, in so cordial a manner, so affectionately and sensibly, that I could not help yielding : the few reservations on which I insisted were also agreed upon by the other side.

Thereupon her husband regulated my hours : for I was to hear lectures on philosophy, the history of law, the Institutes, and some other matters. I was content with this : but I carried my point so as to attend Gellert's history of literature (with Stockhausen for a text-book), and his *Practicum* besides.

The reverence and love with which Gellert was regarded by all young people was extraordinary. I had already visited him, and had been kindly received by him. Not of tall stature, elegant without being lean, soft and rather pensive eyes, a very fine forehead, a nose aquiline, but not too much so, a delicate mouth, a face of an agreeable oval,—all made his presence pleasing and desirable. It cost some trouble to reach him. His two *Famuli* appeared like priests who guard a sanctuary, the access to which is not permitted to everybody, nor at every time ; and such a precaution was very necessary : for he would have sacrificed his whole time, had he been willing to receive and satisfy all those who wished to become intimate with him.

At first I attended my lectures assiduously and faithfully : but the philosophy would not enlighten me at all. In the logic it seemed strange to me that I had so to tear asunder, isolate, and, as it were, destroy those operations of the mind which I had performed with the greatest ease from my youth upwards, and this in order to see into the right use of them. Of the thing itself, of the world, and of God, I thought I knew about as much as the professor himself, and in more places than one the affair seemed to me to come into a tremendous strait. Yet all went on in tolerable order till towards Shrovetide, when, in the neighbourhood of Professor Winkler's house on the *Thomas-place*, the most delicious fritters came hot out of the pan just at the hour of lecture, and these delayed us so long, that our note-books became disordered, and the conclusion of them, towards spring, melted away, together with the snow, and was lost.

It was soon quite as bad with the law lectures : for I already knew just as much as the professor thought good to communicate to us. My stubborn industry in writing down the lectures at first, was paralyzed by degrees, for I found it excessively tedious to pen down once more that which, partly by question, partly by answer, I had repeated with my father often enough to retain it for ever in my memory. The harm which is done when young people at school are advanced too far in many things, was afterwards manifested still more when time and attention were diverted from exercises in the languages, and a foundation in what are, properly speaking, preparatory studies, in order to be applied to what are called " Realities," which dissipate more than they cultivate, if they are not methodically and thoroughly taught.

I here mention, by the way, another evil by which students are much embarrassed. Professors, as well as other men in office, cannot all be of the same age : but when the younger ones teach, in fact, only that they may learn, and moreover, if they have talent, anticipate their age, they acquire their own cultivation altogether at the cost of their hearers, since these are not instructed in what they really need, but in that which the professor finds it necessary to elaborate for himself. Among the oldest professors, on the contrary, many are for a long time stationary; they deliver on the whole only fixed views, and, in the details, much that time has already condemned as useless and false. Between the two arises a sad conflict, in which young minds are dragged hither and thither, and which can scarcely be set right by the middle-aged professors, who, though sufficiently instructed and cultivated, always feel within themselves an active endeavour after knowledge and reflection.

Now as in this way I learned to know much more than I could digest, whereby a constantly increasing uncomfortableness was forced upon me, so also from life I experienced many disagreeable trifles, as indeed one must always pay the entrance-fee when one changes one's place and comes into a new position. The first thing that the ladies blamed in me related to my dress; for I had come from home to the university rather oddly equipped.

My father, who detested nothing so much as when something happened in vain, when any one did not know how to make use of his time, or found no opportunity for turning it to account, carried his economy of time and abilities so far, that nothing gave him greater pleasure than to kill two birds with one stone.* He had therefore never engaged a servant who could not be useful to the house in something else. Now, as he had always written everything with his own hand, and had, latterly, the convenience of dictating to the young inmate of the house, he found it most advantageous to have tailors for his domestics, who were obliged to make good use of their time, as they not only had to make their own liveries, but the clothes for my father and the children, besides doing all the mending. My father himself took pains to have the best cloths and stuffs, by getting fine wares of the foreign merchants at the fair, and laying them up in store. I still remember well that he always visited the Herrn von Löwenicht, of Aix-la-Chapelle, and from my earliest youth made me acquainted with these and other eminent merchants.

Care was also taken for the fitness of the stuff, and there was a plentiful stock of different kinds of cloth, serge, and Götting stuff, besides the requisite lining, so that, as far as the materials were concerned, we might well venture to be seen.

* Literally: " to strike two flies with one flapper."—*Trans.*

P

But the form spoiled almost everything. For if one of our home-tailors was anything of a clever hand at sewing and making up a coat which had been cut out for him in masterly fashion, he was now obliged also to cut out the dress for himself, which did not always succeed to perfection. In addition to this my father kept whatever belonged to his clothing in very good and neat order, and preserved more than used it for many years. Thus he had a predilection for certain old cuts and trimmings, by which our dress sometimes acquired a strange appearance.

In this same way had the wardrobe which I took with me to the university been furnished : it was very complete and handsome, and there was even a laced suit amongst the rest. Already accustomed to this kind of attire, I thought myself sufficiently well dressed ; but it was not long before my female friends, first by gentle raillery, then by sensible remonstrances, convinced me that I looked as if I had dropped down out of another world. Much as I felt vexed at this, I did not at first see how I could help myself. But when Herr von Masuren, the favourite poetical country squire, once entered the theatre in a similar costume, and was heartily laughed at, more by reason of his external than his internal absurdity, I took courage, and ventured at once to exchange my whole wardrobe for a new-fashioned one, suited to the place, by which, however, it shrunk considerably.

After this trial was surmounted, a new one was to make its appearance, which proved to be far more unpleasant, because it concerned a matter which one does not so easily put off and exchange.

I had been born and bred in the Upper-German dialect, and although my father always laboured after a certain purity of language, and, from our youth upwards, had made us children attentive to what may be really called the defects of that idiom, and so prepared us for a better manner of speaking, I retained nevertheless many deeper-seated peculiarities, which, because they pleased me by their *naiveté*, I was fond of making conspicuous, and thus every time I used them incurred a severe reprimand from my new fellow-townsmen. The Upper-German, and perhaps chiefly he who lives by the Rhine and Maine (for great rivers, like the sea-coast, always have something animating about them), expresses himself much in similes and allusions, and makes use of proverbial sayings with a native

common-sense aptness. In both cases he is often blunt, but
when one sees the drift of the expression, it is always appropriate; only something, to be sure, may often slip in, which
proves offensive to a more delicate ear.

Every province loves its own dialect: for it is, properly
speaking, the element in which the soul draws its breath.
But every one knows with what obstinacy the Misnian dialect
has contrived to domineer over the rest, and even, for a long
time, to exclude them. We have suffered for many years
under this pedantic tyranny, and only by reiterated struggles
have all the provinces again established themselves in their
ancient rights. What a lively young man had to endure from
this continual tutoring, may be easily inferred by any one who
reflects that modes of thought, imagination, feeling, native
character, must be sacrificed with the pronunciation which
one at last consents to alter. And this intolerable demand
was made by men and women of education, whose convictions
I could not adopt, whose injustice I believed I felt, though I
was unable to make it plain to myself. Allusions to the pithy
biblical texts were to be forbidden me, as well as the use of
the honest-hearted expressions from the Chronicles. I had to
forget that I had read the *Kaiser von Kaisersberg*, and eschew
the use of proverbs, which nevertheless, instead of much fiddle-
faddle, just hit the nail upon the head:—all this, which I had
appropriated to myself with youthful ardour, I was now to do
without; I felt myself paralyzed to the core, and scarcely
knew any more how I had to express myself on the commonest
things. I was told, besides, that one should speak as one
writes, and write as one speaks; while, to me, speaking and
writing seemed once for all two different things, each of which
might well maintain its own rights. And even in the Misnian
dialect had I to hear many things which would have made no
great figure on paper.

Every one who perceives in this the influence which men
and women of education, the learned, and other persons who
take pleasure in refined society, so decidedly exercise over a
young student, would be immediately convinced that we were
in Leipzig, even if it had not been mentioned. Each one of
the German universities has a particular character: for, as no
universal cultivation can pervade our fatherland, every place
adheres to its own fashion, and carries out, even to the last,

P 2

its own characteristic peculiarities; exactly the same thing holds good of the universities. In Jena and Halle roughness had been carried to the highest pitch : bodily strength, skill in fighting, the wildest self-help was there the order of the day ; and such a state of affairs can only be maintained and propagated by the most universal riot. The relations of the students to the inhabitants of those cities, various as they might be, nevertheless agreed in this, that the wild stranger had no regard for the citizen, and looked upon himself as a peculiar being, privileged to all sorts of freedom and insolence. In Leipzig, on the contrary, a student could scarcely be anything else than polite, as soon as he wished to stand on any footing at all with the rich, well-bred, and punctilious inhabitants.

All politeness, indeed, when it does not present itself as the flowering of a great and comprehensive mode of life, must appear restrained, stationary, and from some points of view, perhaps, absurd : and so those wild huntsmen from the Saale * thought they had a great superiority over the tame shepherds on the Pleisse.† Zachariä's *Renommist* will always be a valuable document, from which the manner of life and thought at that time rises visibly forth ; as in general his poems must be welcome to every one who wishes to form for himself a conception of the then prevailing state of social life and manners, which was indeed feeble, but amiable on account of its innocence and childlike simplicity.

All manners which result from the given relations of a common existence are indestructible, and, in my time, many things still reminded us of Zachariä's epic poem. Only one of our fellow-academicians thought himself rich and independent enough to snap his fingers at public opinion. He drank acquaintance with all the hackney-coachmen, whom he allowed to sit inside the coach as if they were gentlemen, while he drove them on the box, thought it a great joke to upset them now and then, and contrived to satisfy them for their smashed vehicles as well as for their occasional bruises: but otherwise he did no harm to any one, seeming only to make a mock of the public *en masse*. Once, on a most beautiful promenade-day, he and a comrade of his seized upon the don-

* The river on which Halle is built.—*Trans.*
† The river that flows by Leipzig.—*Trans.*

keys of the miller in St. Thomas's-square; well-dressed, and in their shoes and stockings, they rode around the city with the greatest solemnity, stared at by all the promenaders, with whom the glacis was swarming. When some sensible persons remonstrated with him on the subject, he assured them, quite unembarrassed, that he only wanted to see how the Lord Christ might have looked in a like case. Yet he found no imitators, and few companions.

For the student of any wealth and standing had every reason to show himself attentive to the mercantile class, and to be the more solicitous about the proper external forms, as the colony* exhibited a model of French manners. The professors, opulent both from their private property and from their liberal salaries, were not dependent upon their scholars, and many subjects of the state, educated at the Government schools or other gymnasia, and hoping for preferment, did not venture to throw off the traditional customs. The neighbourhood of Dresden, the attention paid to us from thence, and the true piety of the superintendent of the course of study, could not be without a moral, nay, a religious influence.

At first this kind of life was not repugnant to me; my letters of introduction had given me the *entrée* into good families, whose circle of relatives also received me well. But as I was soon forced to feel that the company had much to find fault with in me, and that after dressing myself in their fashion, I must now talk according to their tongue also, and as, moreover, I could plainly see that I was, on the other hand, but little benefited by the instruction and mental improvement I had promised myself from my academical residence, I began to be lazy, and to neglect the social duties of visiting, and other attentions, and indeed I should have sooner withdrawn from all such connexions, had not fear and esteem bound me fast to Hofrath Böhme, and confidence and affection to his wife. The husband, unfortunately, had not the happy gift of dealing with young people, of winning their confidence, and of guiding them, for the moment, as occasion might require. When I visited him I never got any good by it; his wife, on the contrary, showed a genuine interest in me. Her ill health

---

* Leipzig was so called, because a large and influential portion of its citizens were sprung from a colony of Huguenots, who settled there after the revocation of the edict of Nantes.—*American Note.*

kept her constantly at home. She invited me to spend many
an evening with her, and knew how to direct and improve me
in many little external particulars; for my manners were good,
indeed, but I was not yet master of what is properly termed
étiquette. Only one female friend spent the evenings with her;
but she was more dictatorial and pedantic, for which reason
she displeased me excessively, and, out of spite to her, I often
resumed those unmannerly habits from which the other had
already weaned me. Nevertheless she always had patience
enough with me, taught me piquet, ombre, and similar games,
the knowledge and practice of which is held indispensable in
society.

But it was in the matter of taste that Madame Böhme had
the greatest influence upon me; in a negative way truly, yet
one in which she agreed perfectly with the critics. The
Gottsched waters* had inundated the German world with a
true deluge, which threatened to rise up even over the highest
mountains. It takes a long time for such a flood to subside
again, for the mire to dry away; and as in any epoch there
are numberless aping poets, so the imitation of the flat and
watery produced a chaos, of which now scarcely a notion
remains. To find out that trash was trash was hence the
greatest sport, yea, the triumph of the critics of those days.
Whoever had only a little common sense, was superficially acquainted with the ancients, and was somewhat more familiar
with the moderns, thought himself provided with a standard
scale which he could everywhere apply. Madame Böhme
was an educated woman, who opposed the trivial, weak, and
commonplace; she was, besides, the wife of a man who lived
on bad terms with poetry in general, and would not even allow
that of which she perhaps might have somewhat approved.
She listened, indeed, for some time, with patience, when I ventured to recite to her the verse or prose of famous poets, who
already stood in good repute,—for then, as always, I knew by
heart everything that chanced in any degree to please me;
but her complaisance was not of long duration. The first
whom she outrageously abused were the poets of the Weisse
school, who were just then often quoted with great applause,
and had delighted me very particularly. If I looked more

* That is to say, the influence of Gottsched on German literature, of
which more is said in the next book.—*Trans.*

closely into the matter, I could not say she was wrong. I had
sometimes even ventured to repeat to her, though anonymously, some of my own poems; but these fared no better
than the rest of the set. And thus, in a short time, the beautiful variegated meadows at the foot of the German Parnassus,
where I was fond of luxuriating, were mercilessly mowed
down, and I was even compelled to toss about the drying hay
myself, and to ridicule that as lifeless which, a short time
before, had given me such lively joy.

Without knowing it, Professor Morus came to strengthen
her instructions. He was an uncommonly gentle and friendly
man, with whom I became acquainted at the table of Hofrath
Ludwig, and who received me very pleasantly when I begged
the privilege of visiting him. Now while making inquiries of
him concerning antiquity, I did not conceal from him what
delighted me among the moderns; when he spoke about such
things with more calmness, but, what was still worse, with
more profundity than Madame Böhme; and he thus opened
my eyes, at first to my greatest chagrin, but afterwards to my
surprise, and at last to my edification.

Besides this, there came the *Jeremiads*, with which Gellert, in his *Practicum*, was wont to warn us against poetry.
He wished only for prose essays, and always criticised these
first. Verses he treated as a sorry addition, and what was
the worst of all, even my prose found little favour in his eyes;
for, after my old fashion, I used always to lay, as the foundation,
a little romance, which I loved to work out in the epistolary
form. The subjects were impassioned, the style went beyond
ordinary prose, and the contents probably did not display
any very deep knowledge of mankind in the author; and so
I stood in very little favour with our professor, although he
carefully looked over my labours as well as those of the
others, corrected them with red ink, and here and there added
a moral remark. Many leaves of this kind, which I kept for
a long time with satisfaction, have unfortunately, in the course
of years, at last disappeared from among my papers.

If elderly persons wish to play the pedagogue properly,
they should neither prohibit nor render disagreeable to a
young man anything which gives him pleasure, of whatever
kind it may be, unless, at the same time, they have something
else to put in its place, or can contrive a substitute. Every-

body protested against my tastes and inclinations; and, on
the other hand, what they commended to me, lay either so
far from me that I could not perceive its excellencies, or stood
so near me that I thought it not a whit better than what they
inveighed against. I thus became thoroughly perplexed on
the subject, and promised myself the best results from a lecture of Ernesti's on *Cicero de Oratore*. I learned something,
indeed, from this lecture, but was not enlightened on the
subject which particularly concerned me. I required a
standard of opinion, and thought I perceived that nobody
possessed it; for no one agreed with another, even when they
brought forward examples; and where were we to get a settled judgment, when they managed to reckon up against a
man like Wieland so many faults in his amiable writings,
which so completely captivated us younger folks?

Amid this manifold distraction, this dismemberment of my
existence and my studies, it happened that I took my dinners
at Hofrath Ludwig's. He was a medical man, a botanist,
and his company, with the exception of Morus, consisted of
physicians just commencing or near the completion of their
studies. Now during these hours I heard no other conversation than about medicine or natural history, and my imagination was drawn over into quite a new field. I heard the
names of Haller, Linnæus, Buffon, mentioned with great
respect; and even if disputes often arose about mistakes into
which it was said they had fallen, all agreed in the end to
honour the acknowledged abundance of their merits. The
subjects were entertaining and important, and enchained my
attention. By degrees I became familiar with many names
and a copious terminology, which I caught up the more willingly as I was afraid to write down a rhyme, however spon-
taneously it presented itself, or to read a poem, for I was
fearful that it might please me at the time, and that perhaps
immediately afterwards, like so much else, I should be forced
to pronounce it bad.

This uncertainty of taste and judgment disquieted me
more and more every day, so that at last I fell into despair.
I had brought with me those of my youthful labours which
I thought the best, partly because I hoped to get some credit
by them, partly that I might be able to test my progress with
greater certainty; but I found myself in the miserable situation

in which one is placed when a complete change of mind is
required,—a renunciation of all that one has hitherto loved and
found good. However, after some time, and many struggles,
I conceived so great a contempt for my labours, begun and
ended, that one day I burnt up poetry and prose, plans,
sketches, and projects all together on the kitchen hearth,
and threw our good old landlady into no small fright and
anxiety by the smoke which filled the whole house.

SEVENTH BOOK.

About the condition of German literature at that time so
much has been written, and that so sufficiently, that every one
who takes any interest in it can be completely informed; the
judgments of it are now pretty well agreed; and what at present I intend to say piece-meal and disconnectedly concerning
it, relates not so much to how it was constituted in itself, as
to how it stood towards me. I will therefore first speak of
those things by which the public is particularly excited; of
those two hereditary foes of all comfortable life, and of all
cheerful, self-sufficient, living poetry :—I mean, satire and
criticism.

In quiet times every one will live after his own fashion ; the
citizen will carry on his trade or his business, and enjoy the
fruits of it afterwards ; thus will the author too willingly compose something, publish his labours, and since he thinks he has
done something good and useful, hope for praise, if not reward.
In this tranquillity the citizen is disturbed by the satirist, the
author by the critic, and peaceful society is thus put into a
disagreeable agitation.

The literary epoch in which I was born was developed out
of the preceding one by opposition. Germany, so long inundated by foreign people, interpenetrated by other nations,
directed to foreign languages in learned and diplomatic transactions, could not possibly cultivate her own. Together with
so many new ideas, innumerable strange words were obtruded
necessarily and unnecessarily upon her, and even for objects
already known, people were induced to make use of foreign
expressions and turns of language. The German, having run
wild for nearly two hundred years in an unhappy tumultuary
state, went to school to the French to learn manners, and to
the Romans in order to express himself properly. But this
was to be done in the mother-tongue, when the literal application of those idioms, and their half-Germanization, made
both the social and business style ridiculous. Besides this,

they adopted without moderation the similes of the southern languages, and employed them most extravagantly. Just so they transferred the stately deportment of the prince-like citizens of Rome to the learned German small-town officers, and were at home nowhere, least of all with themselves.

But as in this epoch works of genius had already appeared, the German sense of freedom and joy also began to stir itself. This, accompanied by a genuine earnestness, insisted that men should write purely and naturally, without the intermixture of foreign words, and as common intelligible sense dictated. By these praiseworthy endeavours, however, the doors and gates were thrown open to an extended national insipidity, nay, the dike was dug through by which the great deluge was shortly to rush in. Meanwhile, a stiff pedantry long stood its ground in all the four faculties, until at last, much later, it fled for refuge from one of them into another.

Men of parts, children of nature looking freely about them, had therefore two objects on which they could exercise themselves, against which they could labour, and, as the matter was of no great importance, give a vent to their petulance; these were: a language disfigured by foreign words, forms, and turns of speech on the one hand, and the worthlessness of such writings as had been careful to keep themselves free from those faults on the other, though it occurred to nobody, that while they were battling against one evil, the other was called on for assistance.

Liskow, a daring young man, first ventured to attack by name a shallow, silly writer, whose awkward demeanour soon gave him an opportunity to proceed still more severely. He then went further, and constantly aimed his scorn at particular persons and objects, whom he despised and sought to render despicable, nay, even persecuted them with passionate hatred. But his career was short; for he soon died, and was gradually forgotten as a restless, irregular youth. The talent and character shown in what he did, although he had accomplished little, may have seemed valuable to his countrymen: for the Germans have always shown a peculiar pious kindliness to talents of good promise, when prematurely cut off. Suffice it to say, that Liskow was very early praised and recommended to us as an excellent satirist, who could have attained a rank even above the universally-beloved Rabener. Here, indeed,

we saw ourselves no better off than before : for we could discover nothing in his writings, except that he had found the
silly, silly, which seemed to us quite a matter of course.

RABENER, well educated, grown up under good scholastic instruction, of a cheerful, and by no means passionate or malicious
disposition, took up general satire. His censure of the so-
called vices and follies springs from the clear views of a quiet
common sense, and from a fixed moral conception of what the
world ought to be. His denunciation of faults and failings is
harmless and cheerful ; and in order to excuse even the slight
boldness of his writings, it is supposed that the improving of
fools by ridicule is no fruitless undertaking.

Rabener's personal character will not easily appear again.
As an able, punctual man of business, he does his duty, and
thus gains the good opinion of his fellow-townsmen and the
confidence of his superiors ; along with which, he gives himself up, by way of recreation, to a want of esteem for all that
immediately surrounds him. Pedantic *literati*, vain youngsters,
every sort of narrowness and conceit, he banters rather than
satirizes, and even his banter expresses no contempt. Just in
the same way does he jest about his own condition, his misfortune, his life, and his death.

There is little of the æsthetic in the manner in which this
writer treats his subjects. In external forms he is indeed
varied enough, but throughout he makes too much use of direct
irony, namely, in praising the blameworthy and blaming the
praiseworthy, whereas this figure of speech should be used but
extremely seldom : for, in the long run, it becomes annoying to
clear-sighted men, perplexes the weak, while indeed it pleases
the great middle class, who, without any special expense of
mind, can fancy themselves more knowing than others. But
all that he brings before us, and however he does it, alike bears
witness to his rectitude, cheerfulness, and equanimity, so that
we always feel prepossessed in his favour. The unbounded
applause of his own times was a consequence of such moral
excellencies.

That people looked for originals to his general descriptions
and found them, was natural ; that individuals complained of
him, followed from the above : his over-long apologies that
his satire is not personal, prove the spite which has been provoked. Some of his letters crown him at once as a man and

an author. The confidential epistle in which he describes the siege of Dresden, and how he loses his house, his effects, his writings, and his wigs, without having his equanimity in the least shaken or his cheerfulness clouded, is highly valuable, although his contemporaries and fellow-citizens could not forgive him his happy turn of mind. The letter where he speaks of the decay of his strength and of his approaching death is in the highest degree worthy of respect, and Rabener deserves to be honoured as a saint by all cheerful intelligent men, who cheerfully resign themselves to earthly events.

I tear myself away from him reluctantly, yet I would make this remark: his satire refers throughout to the middle-class; he lets us see here and there that he is also well acquainted with the higher ranks, but does not hold it advisable to come in contact with them. It may be said, that he has had no successor, that no one has been found who could consider himself equal, or even similar to him.

Now for criticism! and first of all for the theoretic attempts. It is not going too far when we say that the ideal had, at that time, escaped out of the world into religion; it scarcely even made its appearance in moral philosophy; of a highest principle of art no one had a notion. They put Gottsched's *Critical Art of Poetry* into our hands; it was useful and instructive enough, for it gave us a historical information of all the kinds of poetry, as well as of rhythm and its different movements; the poetic genius was presupposed! But besides that the poet was to have acquirements and even learning, he should possess taste, and everything else of that kind. They directed us at last to Horace's *Art of Poetry*; we gazed at single golden maxims of this invaluable work, but did not know in the least what to do with it as a whole, or how we should use it.

The Swiss stepped forth as Gottsched's antagonists; they must take it into their heads to do something different, to accomplish something better: accordingly we heard that they were, in fact, superior. BREITINGER's *Critical Art of Poetry* was taken in hand. Here we reached a wider field, but, properly speaking, only a greater labyrinth, which was so much the more tiresome, as an able man, in whom we had confidence, was driving us about in it. Let a brief review justify these words.

For poetry in itself they had been able to find no funda-

mental axiom; it was too spiritual and too volatile. Painting,
an art which one could hold fast with one's eyes, and follow
step by step with the external senses, seemed more favourable
for such an end; the English and French had already theorized
about plastic art, and by a comparison drawn from this, it was
thought that poetry might be grounded. The former placed
images before the eyes, the latter before the fancy; poetical
images, therefore, were the first thing which was taken into
consideration. People began with comparisons, descriptions
followed, and only that was expressed which had always been
apparent to the external senses.

Images, then! But where should these images be got except from nature? The painter professedly imitated nature;
why not the poet also? But nature, as she lies before us,
cannot be imitated: she contains so much that is insignificant
and worthless, that one must make a selection; but what determines the choice? one must select that which is important;
but what is important?

To answer this question the Swiss may have taken a long
time to consider: for they came to a notion, which is indeed
singular, but clever, and even comical, inasmuch as they say,
the new is always the most important: and after they have
considered this for a while, they discover that the marvellous
is always newer than everything else.

They had now pretty well collected their poetical requisitions; but they had still to consider that the marvellous might
also be empty and without relation to man. But this relation,
demanded as necessary, must be a moral one, from which the
improvement of mankind should manifestly follow, and thus a
poem had reached its utmost aim when, with everything else
accomplished, it was useful besides. They now wished to test
the different kinds of poetry according to all these requisites;
those which imitated nature, besides being marvellous, and at
the same time of a moral aim and use, were to rank as the first
and highest. And after much deliberation this great pre-
eminence was at last ascribed, with the highest degree of conviction, to Æsop's fables!

Strange as such a deduction may now appear, it had the
most decided influence on the best minds. That GELLERT
and subsequently LICHTWER devoted themselves to this department, that even LESSING attempted to labour in it, that

so many others turned their talents towards it, speaks for the
confidence which this species of poetry had gained. Theory
and practice always act upon each other; one can see from
their works what is the men's opinion; and, from their opinions,
predict what they will do.

Yet we must not dismiss our Swiss theory without doing it
justice. BODMER, with all the pains he took, remained theoretically and practically a child all his life. BREITINGER was
an able, learned, sagacious man, whom when he looked rightly
about him, the essentials of a poem did not all escape; nay, it
can be shown that he may have dimly felt the deficiencies of his
system. Remarkable, for instance, is his query :—" Whether
a certain descriptive poem by König, on the *Review-camp
of Augustus the Second*, is properly a poem?" and the answer
to it displays good sense. But it may serve for his complete
justification that he, starting from a false point, on a circle
almost run out already, still struck upon the main principle, and
at the end of his book finds himself compelled to recommend
as additions, so to speak, the representation of manners, character, passions, in short, the whole inner man; to which,
indeed, poetry pre-eminently belongs.

It may well be imagined into what perplexity young minds
felt themselves thrown by such dislocated maxims, half-under-
stood laws, and shivered up dogmas. We adhered to examples,
and there, too, were no better off; foreigners as well as the
ancients stood too far from us, and from the best native poets
always peeped out a decided individuality, to the good points
of which we could not lay claim, and into the faults of which
we could not but be afraid of falling. For him who felt anything productive in himself it was a desperate condition.

When one considers closely what was wanting in the German poetry, it was a material, and that, too, a national one;
there was never a lack of talent. Here we make mention
only of GUENTHER, who may be called a poet in the full sense
of the word. A decided talent, endowed with sensuousness,
imagination, memory, the gifts of conception and representation, productive in the highest degree, ready at rhythm, ingenious, witty, and of varied information besides :—he possessed, in short, all the requisites for creating, by means of
poetry, a second life within life, even within common real life.
We admire the great facility with which, in his occasional

poems, he elevates all circumstances by the feelings, and embellishes them with suitable sentiments, images, and historical and fabulous traditions. Their roughness and wildness belong to his time, his mode of life, and especially to his character, or if one would have it so, his want of fixed character. He did not know how to curb himself, and so his life, like his poetry, melted away from him.

By his vacillating conduct, Günther had trifled away the good fortune of being appointed at the court of Augustus the Second, where, in addition to every other species of ostentation, they were also looking about for a court-poet, who could give elevation and grace to their festivities, and immortalize a transitory pomp. Von Koenig was more mannerly and more fortunate; he filled this post with dignity and applause.

In all sovereign states the material for poetry comes downwards from above, and the *Review-camp at Mühlberg* (*Das Lustlager bei Mühlberg*) was, perhaps, the first worthy object, provincial, if not national, which presented itself to a poet. Two kings saluting one another in the presence of a great host, their whole courts and military state around them, well-appointed troops, a mock-fight, *fêtes* of all kinds,—this is business enough for the outward sense, and overflowing material for delineating and descriptive poetry.

This subject had, indeed, the internal defect, that it was only pomp and show, from which no real action could result. None except the very first distinguished themselves, and even if they had done so, the poet could not render any one conspicuous lest he should offend the others. He had to consult the *Court and State Calendar*, and the delineation of the persons therefore went off pretty drily; nay, even his contemporaries very strongly reproached him with having described the horses better than the men. But should not this redound to his credit, that he showed his art just where an object for it presented itself? The main difficulty, too, seems soon to have manifested itself to him—since the poem never advanced beyond the first canto.

Amidst such studies and reflections, an unexpected event surprised me, and frustrated my laudable design of becoming acquainted with our new literature from the beginning. My countryman, JOHN GEORGE SCHLOSSER, after spending his academical years with industry and exertion, had repaired to

Frankfort-on-the-Maine, in the customary profession of an advocate; but his mind, aspiring and seeking after the universal, could not reconcile itself to this situation for many reasons. He accepted, without hesitation, an office as private secretary to the Duke Ludwig of Wurtemberg, who resided in Treptow; for the Prince was named among those great men who, in a noble and independent manner, purposed to enlighten themselves, their families, and the world, and to unite for higher aims. It was this Prince Ludwig who, to ask advice about the education of his children, had written to Rousseau, whose well-known answer began with the suspicious-looking phrase—"*Si j'avais le malheur d'être né prince.*"

Not only in the affairs of the Prince, but also in the education of his children, Schlosser was now willingly to assist in word and deed, if not to superintend them. This noble young man, who harboured the best will, and laboured after a perfect purity of morals, would have easily kept men from him by a certain dry austerity, if his fine and rare literary cultivation, his knowledge of languages, and his facility at expressing himself by writing, both in verse and prose, had not attracted every one, and made living with him more agreeable. It had been announced to me that he would pass through Leipzig, and I expected him with longing. He came and put up at a little inn or wine-house that stood in the *Bruhl* (Marsh), and the host of which was named Schönkopf. This man had a Frankfort woman for his wife, and although he entertained few persons during the rest of the year, and could lodge no guests in his little house, yet at fair-time he was visited by many Frankforters, who used to eat, and, in case of need, even take quarters there also. Thither I hastened to seek after Schlosser, when he had sent to inform me of his arrival. I scarcely remembered having seen him before, and found a young, well-formed man, with a round, compressed face, without the features losing their sharpness on that account. The form of his rounded forehead, between black eyebrows and locks, indicated earnestness, sternness, and perhaps obstinacy. He was, in a certain measure, the opposite of myself, and this very thing doubtless laid the foundation of our lasting friendship. I had the greatest respect for his talents, the more so as I very well saw that in the certainty with which he acted and produced, he was completely my superior. The respect and

Q

the confidence which I showed him confirmed his affection, and increased the indulgence he was compelled to have for my lively, impetuous, and ever-excitable disposition, in such contrast with his own. He studied the English writers diligently; Pope, if not his model, was his aim, and in opposition to that author's *Essay on Man*, he had written a poem in like form and measure, which was to give the Christian religion the triumph over the deism of the other work. From the great store of papers which he carried with him, he showed me poetical and prose compositions in all languages, which, as they challenged me to imitation, once more gave me infinite disquietude. Yet I contrived to help myself immediately by activity. I wrote German, French, English and Italian poems, addressed to him, the subject-matter of which I took from our conversations, which were always important and instructive.

Schlosser did not wish to leave Leipzig without having seen face to face the men who had a name. I willingly took him to those I knew; with those whom I had not yet visited, I in this way became honourably acquainted, since he was received with distinction as a well-informed man of education, of already established character, and well knew how to pay for the outlay of conversation. I cannot pass over our visit to GOTTSCHED, as it exemplifies the character and manners of that man. He lived very respectably in the first story of the Golden Bear, where the elder Breitkopf, on account of the great advantage which Gottsched's writings, translations, and other aids had brought to the trade, had promised him a lodging for life.

We were announced. The servant led us into a large chamber, saying his master would come immediately. Now whether we misunderstood a gesture which he made, I cannot say; it is enough, we thought he directed us into an adjoining room. We entered, and to a singular scene; for, on the instant, Gottsched, that tall, broad, gigantic man, came in at the opposite door in a morning-gown of green damask lined with red taffeta; but his monstrous head was bald and uncovered. This, however, was to be immediately provided for; the servant sprang in at a side-door with a great full-bottomed wig in his hand (the curls came down to the elbows), and handed the head-ornament to his master with gestures of terror. Gottsched, without manifesting the least vexation, raised the wig from the servant's arm with his left hand, and while he very dexterously swung it up on his head, gave the poor fellow such a box on the ear with his right paw, that the latter, as often happens in a comedy, went spinning out at the door; whereupon the respectable old grandfather invited us quite gravely to be seated, and kept up a pretty long discourse with good grace.

As long as Schlosser remained in Leipzig, I dined daily with him, and became acquainted with a very pleasant set of boarders. Some Livonians, and the son of HERMANN chief court-preacher in Dresden, afterwards burgermaster in Leipzig, and their tutors; HOFRATH PFEIL, author of the *Count von P.*, a continuation of Gellert's *Swedish Countess*; ZACHARIAE, a brother of the poet; and KREBEL, editor of geographical and genealogical manuals; all these were polite, cheerful, and friendly men. Zacharia was the most quiet; Pfeil, an elegant man, who had something almost diplomatic about him, yet without affectation, and with great good-humour; Krebel, a genuine Falstaff, tall, corpulent, fair, with prominent, merry eyes, as bright as the sky, always happy and in good spirits. These persons all treated me in the most handsome manner, partly on Schlosser's account—partly, too, on account of my own frank good-humour and obliging disposition; and it needed no great persuasion to make me partake of their table in future. In fact, I remained with them after Schlosser's departure, deserted Ludwig's table, and found myself so much the better off in this society, which was limited to a certain number, as I was very well pleased with the daughter of the family, a very neat, pretty girl, and had opportunities to exchange friendly glances with her,—a comfort which I had neither sought nor found by accident since the mischance with Gretchen. I spent the dinner-hours with my friends cheerfully and profitably. Krebel, indeed, loved me, and continued to tease me and stimulate me in moderation; Pfeil, on the contrary, showed his earnest affection for me by trying to guide and settle my judgment upon many points.

During this intercourse, I perceived through conversation, through examples, and through my own reflections, that the first step in delivering ourselves from the wishy-washy, long-winded, empty epoch, could be taken only by definiteness, precision, and brevity. In the style which had hitherto pre-

Q 2

vailed, one could not distinguish the commonplace from what
was better, since all were brought down to a level with each
other. Authors had already tried to escape from this wide-
spread disease, with more or less success. HALLER and
RAMLER were inclined to compression by nature; LESSING
and WIELAND were led to it by reflection. The former became by degrees quite epigrammatical in his poems, terse in
Minna, laconic in *Emilia Galotti*,—it was not till afterwards
that he returned to that serene *naïveté* which becomes him so
well in *Nathan*. Wieland, who had been occasionally prolix
in *Agathon*, *Don Sylvio*, and the *Comic Tales*, becomes condensed and precise to a wonderful degree, as well as exceedingly graceful, in *Musarion* and *Idris*. KLOPSTOCK, in the first
cantos of the *Messiah*, is not without diffuseness; in his *Odes*
and other minor poems he appears compressed, as also in his
tragedies. By his emulation of the ancients, especially Tacitus,
he sees himself constantly forced into narrower limits, by which
he at last becomes obscure and unpalatable. GERSTENBERG,
a fine but eccentric talent, also distinguishes himself; his
merit is appreciated, but on the whole he gives little pleasure.
GLEIM, diffuse and easy by nature, is scarcely once concise
in his war-songs. RAMLER is properly more a critic than
a poet. He begins to collect what the Germans have accomplished in lyric poetry. He now finds that scarcely one poem
fully satisfies him; he must leave out, arrange, and alter, that
the things may have some shape or other. By this means he
makes himself almost as many enemies as there are poets and
amateurs, since every one, properly speaking, recognizes himself only in his defects; and the public interests itself sooner
for a faulty individuality than for that which is produced or
amended according to a universal law of taste. Rhythm lay
yet in the cradle, and no one knew of a method to shorten its
childhood. Poetical prose came into the ascendant. GESSNER
and KLOPSTOCK excited many imitators: others, again, still
demanded an intelligible metre, and translated this prose into
rhythm. But even these gave nobody satisfaction; for they
were obliged to omit and add, and the prose original always
passed for the better of the two. But the more, with all this,
conciseness is aimed at, the more does a judgment become possible, since that which is important, being more closely compressed, allows a certain comparison at last. It happened,

also, at the same time, that many kinds of truly poetical forms
arose ; for as they tried to represent only what was necessary
in the objects they wished to imitate, they were forced to do
justice to every one of these ; and in this manner, though no
one did it consciously, the modes of representation multiplied
themselves, among which, indeed, were some which were really
caricatures, while many an attempt proved unsuccessful.

Without question, WIELAND possessed the finest natural
gifts of all. He had early cultivated himself thoroughly in
those ideal regions where youth so readily lingers ; but when,
by what is called experience, by the events of the world and
women, these were rendered distasteful to him, he threw himself on the side of the actual, and pleased himself and others
with the contest of the two worlds, where, in light skirmish-
ing between jest and earnest, his talent displayed itself most
beautifully. How many of his brilliant productions fall into the
time of my academic years ! *Musarion* had the most effect upon
me, and I can yet remember the place and the very spot where
I got sight of the first proof-sheet, which Oeser gave me.
Here it was that I believed I saw antiquity again living and
fresh. Everything that is plastic in Wieland's genius here
showed itself in its highest perfection ; and when that Phanias-
Timon, condemned to an unhappy insipidity, finally reconciles
himself to his mistress and to the world, one can well, with
him, live through the misanthropical epoch. For the rest, we
willingly conceded to these works a cheerful aversion from those
exalted sentiments, which, by reason of their easy misapplica-
tion to life, are often open to the suspicion of dreaminess.
We pardoned the author for prosecuting with ridicule what
we held as true and reverend, the more readily, as he thereby
gave us to understand that it caused him continual trouble.

How miserably criticism then received such labours may
be seen from the first volumes of the *Universal German
Library.* Of the *Comic Tales* there is honourable mention ;
but there is no trace of any insight into the character of the
kind of poetry. The reviewer, like every one at that time,
had formed his taste on examples. He never takes it into
consideration that, in a judgment of such parodistical works,
one must first of all have before one's eyes the original noble,
beautiful object, in order to see whether the parodist has really
gotten from it a weak and comical side, whether he has bor-

rowed anything from it, or, under the appearance of such an imitation, has perhaps given us an excellent invention of his own. Of all this there is not a notion, but that poems are praised and blamed by passages. The reviewer, as he himself confesses, has marked so much that pleased him, that he cannot quote it all in print. When they even meet the highly meritorious translation of Shakspeare with the exclamation: " By rights, a man like Shakspeare should not have been translated at all!" it will be understood, without further remark, how infinitely the *Universal German Library* was behindhand in matters of taste, and that young people, animated by true feeling, had to look about them for other guiding stars. The material which, in this manner, more or less determined the form, the Germans sought everywhere. They had handled few national subjects, or none at all. Schlegel's *Hermann* only showed the way. The idyllic tendency extended itself without end. The want of distinctive character with Gessner, with all his great gracefulness and childlike heartiness, made every one think that he could do something of the same kind. Just in the same manner, out of the more generally human, some snatch those poems which should have portrayed a foreign nationality, as, for instance, the Jewish pastoral poems, those on the patriarchs altogether, and whatever else related to the Old Testament. Bodmer's *Noachide* was a perfect symbol of the watery deluge that swelled high around the German Parnassus, and which abated but slowly. The leading-strings of Anacreon likewise allowed innumerable mediocre geniuses to reel about at large. The precision of Horace compelled the Germans, though but slowly, to conform to him. Comic heroic poems, mostly after the model of Pope's *Rape of the Lock*, did not serve to bring in a better time.

Yet I must here mention a delusion, which operated as seriously as it must be ridiculous when one examines it more closely. The Germans had now sufficient historical knowledge of all the kinds of poetry in which the different nations had distinguished themselves. This pigeon-hole work, which, properly speaking, totally destroys the inner conception of poetry, had been already pretty completely hammered together by Gottsched in his *Critical Art of Poetry*, and it had been shown at the same time that German poets, too, had already known how to fill up all the rubrics with excellent works. And thus it ever went on. Each year the collection was more considerable, but every year one work pushed another out of the place in which it had hitherto shone. We now possessed, if not Homers, yet Virgils and Miltons; if not a Pindar, yet a Horace; of Theocrituses there was no lack; and thus they weighed themselves by comparisons from without, whilst the mass of poetical works always increased, so that at last there could be a comparison from within.

Now, though matters of taste stood on a very uncertain footing, there could be no dispute but that, within the Protestant part of Germany and of Switzerland, what is generally called common-sense began to bestir itself briskly at that epoch. The scholastic philosophy—which always has the merit of propounding according to received axioms, in a favourite order, and under fixed rubrics, everything about which man can at all inquire,—had, by the frequent darkness and apparent uselessness of its subject-matter, by its unseasonable application of a method in itself respectable, and by its too great extension over so many subjects, made itself foreign to the mass, unpalatable, and at last dispensable. Many a one became convinced that nature had endowed him with as great a portion of good and straightforward sense as, perchance, he required to form such a clear notion of objects that he could manage them and turn them to his own profit, and that of others, without laboriously troubling himself about the most universal problems, and inquiring how the most remote things which do not particularly affect us may hang together. Men made the trial, opened their eyes, looked straight before them, observant, industrious, active, and believed that when one decides upon and acts correctly in one's own circle, one may well presume to speak of other things also, which lie at a greater distance.

In accordance with such a notion, every one was now entitled, not only to philosophize, but also by degrees to consider himself a philosopher. Philosophy, therefore, was more or less sound and practised common sense, which ventured to enter upon the universal, and to decide upon inner and outer experiences. A clear-sighted acuteness and an especial moderation, while the middle path and fairness to all opinions was held to be right, procured respect and confidence for writings and oral statements of the sort, and thus at last philosophers were found in all the faculties, nay, in all classes and trades.

In this way the theologians could not help inclining to what is called natural religion, and when the discussion was how far the light of nature may suffice to advance us in the knowledge of God and the improving and ennobling of ourselves, they commonly ventured to decide in its favour without much scruple. According to the same principle of moderation, they then granted equal rights to all positive religions, by which they all became alike indifferent and uncertain. For the rest, they let everything stand, and since the Bible is so full of matter, that, more than any other book, it offers material for reflection and opportunity for meditation on human affairs, it could still, as before, be always laid as the foundation of all sermons and other religious treatises.

But over this work, as well as over the whole body of profane writers, was impending a singular fate, which, in the lapse of time, was not to be averted. Hitherto it had been received as a matter of implicit faith, that this book of books was composed in one spirit; that it was even inspired, and, as it were, dictated by the Divine Spirit. Yet already for a long time the discrepancies of the different parts of it had been now cavilled at, now apologized for, by believers and unbelievers. English, French, and Germans had attacked the Bible with more or less violence, acuteness, audacity, and wantonness; and just as often had it been taken under the protection of earnest, sound-thinking men of each nation. As for myself, I loved and valued it: for almost to it alone did I owe my moral culture, and the events, the doctrines, the symbols, the similes, had all impressed themselves deeply upon me, and had influenced me in one way or another. These unjust, scoffing, and perverting attacks, therefore, disgusted me; but people had already gone so far as very willingly to admit, partly as a main ground for the defence of many passages, that God had accommodated himself to the modes of thought and power of comprehension in men; that even those moved by the Spirit had not on that account been able to renounce their character, their individuality, and that Amos, a cow-herd, did not wield the language of Isaiah, who is said to have been a prince.

Out of such views and convictions, especially with a constantly increasing knowledge of languages, was very naturally developed that kind of study by which it was attempted to examine more accurately the oriental localities, nationalities, natural products, and phenomena, and in this manner to make present to one's-self that ancient time. Michaelis employed the whole strength of his talents and his knowledge on this side. Descriptions of travels became a powerful help in explaining the Holy Scriptures, and later travellers, furnished with numerous questions, were made, by the answers to them, to bear witness for the prophets and apostles.

But whilst they were on all sides busied to bring the Holy Scriptures to a natural intuition, and to render peculiar modes of thought and representation in them more universally comprehensible, that by this historico-critical aspect many an objection might be removed, many offensive things effaced, and many a shallow scoffing be made ineffective, there appeared in some men just the opposite disposition, since these chose the darkest, most mysterious writings as the subject of their meditations, and wished, if not to elucidate them, yet to confirm them through internal evidence, by means of conjectures, calculations, and other ingenious and strange combinations, and so far as they contained prophecies, to prove them by the results, and thus to justify a faith in what was next to be expected.

The venerable BENGEL had procured a decided reception for his labours on the Revelations of St. John, from the fact that he was known as an intelligent, upright, God-fearing, blameless man. Deep minds are compelled to live in the past as well as in the future. The ordinary movements of the world can be of no importance to them, if they do not, in the course of ages up to the present, revere prophecies which have been revealed, and in the immediate, as well as in the most remote futurity, predictions still veiled. Hence arises a connexion that is wanting in history, which seems to give us only an accidental wavering backwards and forwards in a necessarily limited circle. Doctor CRUSIUS was one of those whom the prophetic part of Scripture suited more than any other, since it brings into action the two most opposite qualities of human nature, the affections, and the acuteness of the intellect. Many young men had devoted themselves to this doctrine, and already formed a respectable body, which attracted the more attention, as ERNESTI with his friends threatened, not to illuminate, but completely to disperse the obscurity in which these delighted. Hence arose controversies, hatred, persecution and much that was unpleasant. I attached myself to the lucid party, and sought to appropriate to myself their principles and advantages, although I ventured to forebode, that by this extremely praiseworthy, intelligent method of interpretation, the poetic contents of the writings must at last be lost along with the prophetical.

But those who devoted themselves to German literature and the *belles lettres* were more nearly concerned with the efforts of such men, who, as JERUSALEM, ZOLLIKOFER, and SPALDING, tried, by means of a good and pure style in their sermons and treatises, to gain even among persons of a certain degree of sense and taste, applause and attachment for religion, and for the moral philosophy which is so closely related to it. A pleasing manner of writing began to be everywhere necessary; and since such a manner must, above all, be comprehensible, so did writers arise, on many sides, who undertook to write about their studies and their professions clearly, perspicuously, and impressively, and as well for the adepts as for the multitude.

After the example of Tissot, a foreigner, the physicians also now began to labour zealously for the general cultivation. HALLER, UNZER, ZIMMERMAN had a very great influence, and whatever may be said against them in detail, especially the last, they produced a very great effect in their time. And mention should be made of this in history, but particularly in biography: for a man remains of consequence, not so far as he leaves something behind him, but so far as he acts and enjoys, and rouses others to action and enjoyment.

The jurists, accustomed from their youth upwards to an abstruse style, which, in all legal papers, from the petty court of the Immediate Knight up to the Imperial Diet at Ratisbon, was still maintained in all its quaintness, could not easily elevate themselves to a certain freedom, the less so as the subjects of which they had to treat were most intimately connected with the external form, and consequently also with the style. Yet the younger VON MOSER had already shown himself an independent and original writer, and PÜTTER, by the clearness of his delivery, had also brought clearness into his subject, and the style in which he was to treat it. All that proceeded from his school was distinguished by this. And even the philosophers, in order to be popular, now found themselves compelled to write clearly and intelligibly. MENDELSOHN and GARVE appeared, and excited universal interest and admiration.

With the cultivation of the German language and style in every department, the capacity for forming a judgment also increased, and we admire the reviews then published of works upon religious and moral, as well as medical subjects; while, on the contrary, we remark that the judgments of poems, and of whatever else may relate to the *belles lettres*, will be found, if not pitiful, at least very feeble. This holds good of the *Literary Epistles* (*Literaturbriefen*), and of the *Universal German Library*, as well as of the *Library of the Belles Lettres*, notable instances of which could easily be produced.

No matter in how motley a manner all this might be confused, still for every one who contemplated producing anything from himself, who would not merely take the words and phrases out of the mouths of his predecessors, there was nothing further left but, early and late, to look about him for some subject-matter which he might determine to use. Here, too, we were much led astray. People were constantly repeating a saying of KLEIST, which we had to hear often enough. He had sportively, ingeniously, and truly replied to those who took him to task on account of his frequent lonely walks: " that he was not idle at such times,—he was going to the image hunt." This simile was very suitable for a nobleman and soldier, who by it placed himself in contrast with the men of his rank, who did not neglect going out, with their guns on their shoulders, harehunting and patridge-shooting, as often as an opportunity presented itself. Hence we find in Kleist's poems many such individual images, happily seized, although not always happily elaborated, which in a kindly manner remind us of nature. But now they also recommended us, quite seriously, to go out on the image-hunt, which did not at last leave us wholly without fruit, although Apel's Garden, the kitchen-gardens the Rosenthal, Gohs, Raschwitz and Konnewitz, would be the oddest ground to beat up poetical game in. And yet I was often induced by that motive to contrive that my walk should be solitary, and, because many objects neither beautiful nor sublime met the eye of the beholder, and in the truly splendid Rosenthal, the gnats, in the best season of the year, allowed no tender thoughts to arise, so did I, by unwearied, persevering endeavour, become extremely attentive to the small life of

nature, (I would use this word after the analogy of " still
life,") and since the pretty events which one perceives within
this circle represent but little in themselves, so I accustomed
myself to see in them a significance, which inclined now towards the symbolical, now towards the allegorical side, accordingly as intuition, feeling, or reflection had the preponderance.
I will relate one incident, in place of many.

I was, after the fashion of humanity, in love with my name,
and, as young uneducated people commonly do, I wrote it
down everywhere. Once I had carved it very handsomely
and accurately on the smooth bark of a linden-tree of moderate age. The following autumn, when my affection for Annette was in its fullest bloom, I took the trouble to cut hers
above it. Towards the end of the winter, in the meantime,
like a capricious lover, I had wantonly sought many opportunities to teaze her and cause her vexation; in the spring I
chanced to visit the spot, and the sap, which was rising
strongly in the trees, had welled out through the incisions
which formed her name, and which were not yet crusted over,
and moistened with innocent vegetable tears the already
hardened traces of my own. Thus to see her here weeping
over me,—me, who had so often called up her tears by my
ill-conduct, filled me with confusion. At the remembrance of
my injustice and of her love, even the tears came into my
eyes. I hastened to implore pardon of her, doubly and trebly,
and I turned this incident into an idyl*, which I never could
read to myself without affection, or to others without emotion.

While I now, like a shepherd on the Pleisse, was absorbed
childishly enough in such tender subjects, and always chose
only such as I could easily recall into my bosom, provision
from a greater and more important side had long been made
for German poets.

The first true and really vital material of the higher order
came into German poetry through Frederick the Great and
the deeds of the Seven Years' War. All national poetry must
be shallow or become shallow which does not rest on that
which is most universally human,—upon the events of nations
and their shepherds, when both stand for one man. Kings
are to be represented in war and danger, where, by that very
means, they appear as the first, because they determine and

* This idyl is lost.—*Trans.*

share the fate of the very least, and thus become much more interesting than the gods themselves, who, when they have once determined the fates, withdraw from all participation in them. In this view of the subject, every nation, if it would be worth anything at all, must possess an epopee, to which the precise form of the epic poem is not necessary.

The war-songs started by Gleim maintain so high a rank among German poems, because they arose with and in the achievements which are their subject, and because, moreover, their felicitous form, just as if a fellow-combatant had produced them in the loftiest moments, makes us feel the most complete effectiveness.

Ramler sings the deeds of his king in a different and most noble manner. All his poems are full of matter, and occupy us with great, heart-elevating objects, and thus already maintain an indestructible value.

For the internal matter of the subject worked is the beginning and end of art. It will not, indeed, be denied that genius, that thoroughly cultivated artistical talent, can make everything out of everything by its method of treatment, and can subdue the most refractory material. But when closely examined, the result is rather a trick of art than a work of art, which should rest upon a worthy object, that the treatment of it by skill, pains, and industry, may present to us the dignity of the subject-matter only the more happily and splendidly.

The Prussians, and with them Protestant Germany, acquired thus for their literature a treasure which the opposite party lacked, and the want of which they have been able to supply by no subsequent endeavours. Upon the great idea which the Prussian writers could well entertain of their king, they first established themselves, and the more zealously as he, in whose name they did it all, wished once for all to know nothing about them. Already before this, through the French colony, afterwards through the king's predilection for the literature of that nation, and for their financial institutions, had a mass of French civilization come into Prussia, which was highly advantageous to the Germans, since by it they were challenged to contradiction and resistance; thus the very aversion of Frederick from German was a fortunate thing for the formation of its literary character. They did everything to attract the king's attention, not indeed to be honoured, but only noticed by him; yet they did it in German fashion, from an internal conviction; they did what they held to be right, and desired and wished that the king should recognize and prize this German uprightness. That did not and could not happen; for how can it be required of a king, who wishes to live and enjoy himself intellectually, that he shall lose his years in order to see what he thinks barbarous developed and rendered palatable too late? In matters of trade and manufacture, he might indeed force upon himself, but especially upon his people, very moderate substitutes instead of excellent foreign wares; but here everything comes to perfection more rapidly, and it needs not a man's life-time to bring such things to maturity.

But I must here, first of all, make honourable mention of one work, the most genuine production of the Seven Years' War, and of perfect North German nationality; it is the first theatrical production caught from the important events of life, one of specific temporary value, and one which therefore produced an incalculable effect,—*Minna von Barnhelm*. Lessing, who, in opposition to Klopstock and Gleim, was fond of casting off his personal dignity, because he was confident that he could at any moment seize it and take it up again, delighted in a dissipated life in taverns and the world, as he always needed a strong counterpoise to his powerfully labouring interior; and for this reason also he had joined the suite of General Tauentzien. One easily discovers how the above-mentioned piece was generated betwixt war and peace, hatred and affection. It was this production which happily opened the view into a higher, more significant world, from the literary and citizen world in which poetic art had hitherto moved.

The intense hatred in which the Prussians and Saxons stood towards each other during this war, could not be removed by its termination. The Saxon now first felt, with true bitterness, the wounds which the upstart Prussian had inflicted upon him. Political peace could not immediately re-establish a peace between their dispositions. But this was to be brought about symbolically by the above-mentioned drama. The grace and amiability of the Saxon ladies conquer the worth, the dignity, and the stubbornness of the

Prussians, and, in the principal as well as in the subordinate characters, a happy union of bizarre and contradictory elements is artistically represented.

If I have put my reader in some perplexity by these cursory and desultory remarks on German literature, I have succeeded in giving them a conception of that chaotic condition in which my poor brain found itself, when, in the conflict of two epochs so important for the literary fatherland, so much that was new crowded in upon me before I could come to terms with the old, so much that was old yet made me feel its right over me, when I believed I had already cause to venture on renouncing it altogether. I will at present try to impart, as well as possible, the way I entered on to extricate myself from this difficulty, if only step by step.

The period of prolixity into which my youth had fallen, I had laboured through with genuine industry, in company with so many worthy men. The numerous quarto volumes of manuscript which I left behind with my father might serve for sufficient witnesses of this; and what a mass of essays, rough draughts, and half-executed designs, had, more from despondency than conviction, gone up in smoke! Now, through conversation, through instruction in general, through so many conflicting opinions, but especially through my fellow-boarder Hofrath Pfeil, I learned to value more and more the importance of the subject-matter, and the conciseness of the treatment; without, however, being able to make it clear to myself where the former was to be sought, or how the latter was to be attained. For, what with the great narrowness of my situation,—what with the indifference of my companions, the reserve of the professors, the exclusiveness of the educated inhabitants, and what with the perfect insignificance of the natural objects, I was compelled to seek for everything within myself. If I now desired a true basis in feeling or reflection for my poems, I was forced to grasp into my own bosom; if I required for my poetic representation an immediate intuition of an object or an event, I could not step outside the circle which was fitted to teach me and inspire me with an interest. In this view I wrote at first certain little poems, in the form of songs or in a freer measure; they are founded on reflection, treat of the past, and for the most part take an epigrammatic turn.

And thus began that tendency from which I could not deviate my whole life through ; namely, the tendency to turn into an image, into a poem, everything that delighted or troubled me, or otherwise occupied me, and to come to some certain understanding with myself upon it, that I might both rectify my conceptions of external things, and set my mind at rest about them. The faculty of doing this was necessary to no one more than to me, for my natural disposition whirled me constantly from one extreme to the other. All, therefore, that has been confessed by me, consists of fragments of a great confession, and this little book is an attempt which I have ventured on to render it complete.

My early affection for Gretchen I had now transferred to one Annette (*Aennchen*), of whom I can say nothing more than that she was young, handsome, sprightly, loving, and so agreeable that she well deserved to be set up for a time in the shrine of the heart as a little saint, that she might receive all that reverence which it often causes more pleasure to bestow than to receive. I saw her daily without hindrance ; she helped to prepare the meals which I enjoyed, she brought, in the evening at least, the wine which I drank, and indeed our select club of noon-day boarders was a warranty that the little house, which was visited by few guests except during the fair, well merited its good reputation. Opportunity and inclination were found for various kinds of amusement. But as she neither could nor dared go much out of the house, the pastime was somewhat limited. We sang the songs of Zacharia, played the *Duke Michael* of Krüger, in which a knotted handkerchief had to take the place of the nightingale ; and so, for a while, it went on quite tolerably. But since such connexions, the more innocent they are, afford the less variety in the long run,—so was I seized with that wicked distemper which seduces us to derive amusement from the torment of a beloved one, and to domineer over a girl's devotedness with wanton and tyrannical caprice. My ill-humour at the failure of my poetical attempts, at the apparent impossibility of coming to a clear understanding about them, and at everything else that might pinch me here and there, I thought I might vent on her, because she truly loved me with all her heart, and did whatever she could to please me. By unfounded and absurd fits of jealousy, I destroyed our most

delightful days both for myself and her. She endured it for
a time with incredible patience, which I was cruel enough
to try to the uttermost. But to my shame and despair I was
at last forced to remark that her heart was alienated from me,
and that I might now have good ground for the madness in
which I had indulged without necessity and without cause.
There were also terrible scenes between us, in which I gained
nothing: and I then first felt that I had truly loved her, and
could not bear to lose her. My passion grew, and assumed
all the forms of which it is capable under such circumstances;
nay, at last I even took up the *rôle* which the girl had hitherto
played. I sought everything possible in order to be agreeable
to her, even to procure her pleasure by means of others: for
I could not renounce the hope of winning her again. But it
was too late! I had lost her really, and the frenzy with which
I revenged my fault upon myself, by assaulting in various
frantic ways my physical nature, in order to inflict some hurt
on my moral nature, contributed very much to the bodily
maladies under which I lost some of the best years of my life;
indeed I should perchance have been completely ruined by
this loss, had not my poetic talent here shown itself particularly helpful with its healing power.

Already, at many intervals before, I had clearly enough
perceived my ill-conduct. I really pitied the poor child,
when I saw her so thoroughly wounded by me, without
necessity. I pictured to myself so often and so circumstantially, her condition and my own, and, as a contrast, the contented state of another couple in our company, that at last I
could not forbear treating this situation dramatically, as a
painful and instructive penance. Hence arose the oldest of
my extant dramatic labours, the little piece entitled, *Die
Laune des Verliebten* (*The Lover's Caprice*); in the simple
nature of which one may at the same time perceive the
impetus of a boiling passion.

But before this, a deep, significant, impulsive world had
already interested me. Through my adventure with Gretchen
and its consequences, I had early looked into the strange
labyrinths by which civil society is undermined. Religion, morals, law, rank, connexions, custom, all rule only
the surface of city existence. The streets, bordered by
splendid houses, are kept neat, and every one behaves him-

R

self there properly enough; but indoors, it often seems only so much the more disordered; and a smooth exterior, like a thin coat of mortar, plasters over many a rotten wall that tumbles together overnight, and produces an effect the more frightful, as it comes into the midst of a condition of repose. How many families, far and near, had I not already seen, either overwhelmed in ruin or kept miserably hanging on the brink of it, by means of bankruptcies, divorces, seduced daughters, murders, house-robberies, poisonings; and young as I was, I had often, in such cases, lent a hand for help and preservation. For as my frankness awakened confidence, as my secrecy was proved, as my activity feared no sacrifice, and loved best to exert itself in the most dangerous affairs, I had often enough found opportunity to mediate, to hush up, to divert the lightning-flash, with every other assistance of the kind; in the course of which, as well in my own person as through others, I could not fail to come to the knowledge of many afflicting and humiliating facts. To relieve myself I designed several plays, and wrote the arguments* of most of them. But since the intrigues were always obliged to be painful, and almost all these pieces threatened a tragical conclusion, I let them drop one after another. *Die Mitschuldigen* (*The Accomplices*) is the only one that was finished, the cheerful and burlesque tone of which upon the gloomy family-ground appears as if accompanied by somewhat of apprehension, so that on the whole it is painful in representation, although it pleases in detached passages. The illegal deeds, harshly expressed, wound the æsthetic and moral feeling, and the piece could therefore find no favour on the German stage, although the imitations of it, which steered clear of those rocks, were received with applause.

Both the above-mentioned pieces were however written from a more elevated point of view, without my having been aware of it. They direct us to a considerate forbearance in casting moral imputations, and in somewhat harsh and coarse touches sportively express that most Christian maxim: *Let him who is without sin among you, cast the first stone.*

Through this earnestness, which cast a gloom over my first

* "*Exposition*," in a dramatic sense, properly means a statement of the events which take place before the action of the play commences.— *Trans.*

pieces. I committed the fault of neglecting very favourable
materials which lay quite decidedly in my natural disposition.
In the midst of these serious, and for a young man, fearful
experiences, was developed in me a reckless humour, which
feels itself superior to the moment, and not only fears no
danger, but rather wantonly courts it. The ground of this lay
in the exuberance of spirits in which the vigorous time of
life so much delights, and which, if it manifests itself in a
frolicsome way, causes much pleasure, both at the moment and
in remembrance. These things are so usual that in the
vocabulary of our young university friends they are called
Suites, and on account of the close similarity of signification,
to say "play *suites*," means just the same as to "play
pranks."*

Such humorous acts of daring, brought on the theatre
with wit and sense, are of the greatest effect. They are
distinguished from intrigue, inasmuch as they are momentary,
and that their aim, whenever they are to have one, must not
be remote. Beaumarchais has seized their full value, and the
effects of his *Figaro* spring pre-eminently from this. If now
such good-humoured roguish and half-knavish pranks are
practised with personal risk for noble ends, the situations
which arise from them are æsthetically and morally considered of the greatest value for the theatre; as for instance
the opera of the *Water-Carrier* treats perhaps the happiest
subject which we have ever yet seen upon the stage.

To enliven the endless tedium of daily life, I played off
numberless tricks of the sort, partly without any aim at all,
partly in the service of my friends whom I liked to please.
For myself, I could not say that I had once acted in this
designedly, nor did I ever happen to consider a feat of the
kind as a subject for art. Had I, however, seized upon and
elaborated such materials, which were so close at hand, my
earliest labours would have been more cheerful and available.
Some incidents of this kind occur indeed later, but isolated
and without design. For since the heart always lies nearer
to us than the head, and gives us trouble when the latter
knows well how to help itself, so the affairs of the heart had

* The real meaning of the passage is that the idiom "Possen reissen,"
is used also with the university word "Suite," so that one can say "Suiten
reissen."—*Trans.*

R 2

always appeared to me as the most important. I was never weary of reflecting upon the transient nature of attachments, the mutability of human character, moral sensuality, and all the heights and depths, the combination of which in our nature may be considered as the riddle of human life. Here, too, I sought to get rid of that which troubled me, in a song, an epigram, in some kind of rhyme, which, since they referred to the most private feelings and the most peculiar circumstances, could scarcely interest any one but myself.

In the meanwhile, my external position had very much changed after the lapse of a short time. Madame Böhme, after a long and melancholy illness, had at last died; she had latterly ceased to admit me to her presence. Her husband could not be particularly satisfied with me; I seemed to him not sufficiently industrious, and too frivolous. He especially took it very ill of me, when it was told him that, at the lectures on German Public Law, instead of taking proper notes, I had been drawing on the margin of my note-book the personages presented to our notice in them, such as the President of the Chamber, the Moderators and Assessors, in strange wigs; and by this drollery had disturbed my attentive neighbours and set them laughing. After the loss of his wife he lived still more retired than before, and at last I shunned him in order to avoid his reproaches. But it was peculiarly unfortunate that Gellert would not use the power which he might have exercised over us. Indeed he had not time to play the father-confessor, and to inquire after the character and faults of everybody; he therefore took the matter very much in the lump, and thought to curb us by means of the church forms. For this reason, commonly, when he once admitted us to his presence, he used to lower his little head, and, in his weeping, winning voice, to ask us whether we went regularly to church, who was our confessor, and whether we took the holy communion? If now we came off badly at this examination we were dismissed with lamentations; we were more vexed than edified, yet could not help loving the man heartily.

On this occasion, I cannot forbear recalling somewhat of my earlier youth, in order to make it obvious that the great affairs of the ecclesiastical religion must be carried on with order and coherence, if they are to prove as fruitful as is expected. The Protestant service has too little fulness and consistency to be able to hold the congregation together; hence, it easily happens that members secede from it, and either form little congregations of their own, or, without ecclesiastical connexion, quietly carry on their citizen-life side by side. Thus for a considerable time complaints were made that the church-goers were diminishing from year to year, and, just in the same ratio, the persons who partook of the Lord's Supper. With respect to both, but especially the latter, the cause lies close at hand; but who dares to speak it out? We will make the attempt.

In moral and religious, as well as in physical and civil matters, man does not like to do anything on the spur of the moment; he needs a sequence from which results habit; what he is to love and to perform, he cannot represent to himself as single or isolated, and if he is to repeat anything willingly, it must not have become strange to him. If the Protestant worship lacks fulness in general, so let it be investigated in detail, and it will be found that the Protestant has too few sacraments, nay, indeed he has only one in which he is himself an actor,—the Lord's Supper: for baptism he sees only when it is performed on others, and is not greatly edified by it. The sacraments are the highest part of religion, the symbols to our senses of an extraordinary divine favour and grace. In the Lord's Supper earthly lips are to receive a divine Being embodied, and partake of an heavenly under the form of an earthly nourishment. This sense is just the same in all Christian churches; whether the Sacrament is taken with more or less submission to the mystery, with more or less accommodation as to that which is intelligible; it always remains a great holy thing, which in reality takes the place of the possible or the impossible, the place of that which man can neither attain nor do without. But such a sacrament should not stand alone; no Christian can partake of it with the true joy for which it is given, if the symbolical or sacramental sense is not fostered within him. He must be accustomed to regard the inner religion of the heart and that of the external church as perfectly one, as the great universal sacrament, which again divides itself into so many others, and communicates to these parts its holiness, indestructibleness, and eternity.

Here a youthful pair give their hands to one another, not for a passing salutation or for the dance; the priest pronounces his blessing upon them, and the bond is indissoluble. It is not long before this wedded pair bring a likeness to the threshold of the altar; it is purified with holy water, and so incorporated into the church, that it cannot forfeit this benefit but through the most monstrous apostacy. The child in the course of life practises himself in earthly things of his own accord, in heavenly things he must be instructed. Does it prove on examination that this has been fully done, he is now received into the bosom of the church as an actual citizen, as a true and voluntary professor, not without outward tokens of the weightiness of this act. Now is he first decidedly a Christian, now for the first time he knows his advantages, and also his duties. But, in the meanwhile, much that is strange has happened to him as a man; through instruction and affliction he has come to know how critical appears the state of his inner self, and there will constantly be a question of doctrines and of transgressions; but punishment shall no longer take place. For here, in the infinite confusion in which he must entangle himself, amid the conflict of natural and religious claims, an admirable expedient is given him, in confiding his deeds and misdeeds, his infirmities and doubts, to a worthy man, appointed expressly for that purpose, who knows how to calm, to warn, to strengthen him, to chasten him likewise by symbolical punishments, and at last by a complete washing away of his guilt, to render him happy and to give him back, pure and cleansed, the tablet of his manhood. Thus prepared, and purely calmed to rest by several sacramental acts, which, on closer examination, branch forth again into minuter sacramental traits, he kneels down to receive the host; and that the mystery of this high act may be still enhanced, he sees the chalice only in the distance; it is no common eating and drinking that satisfies, it is a heavenly feast, which makes him thirst after heavenly drink.

Yet let not the youth believe that this is all he has to do; let not even the man believe it. In earthly relations we are at last accustomed to depend on ourselves, and, even there, knowledge, understanding, and character, will not always suffice; in heavenly things, on the contrary, we have never finished learning. The higher feeling within us, which often finds itself not even truly at home, is, besides, oppressed by so much from without, that our own power hardly administers all that is necessary for counsel, consolation, and help. But, to this end, that remedy is instituted for our whole life, and an intelligent, pious man is continually waiting to show the right way to the wanderers, and to relieve the distressed.

And what has been so well tried through the whole life, is now to show forth all its healing power with tenfold activity at the gate of Death. According to a trustful custom, inculcated from youth upwards, the dying man receives with fervour those symbolical, significant assurances, and there, where every earthly warranty fails, he is assured, by a heavenly one, of a blessed existence for all eternity. He feels himself perfectly convinced that neither a hostile element nor a malignant spirit can hinder him from clothing himself with a glorified body, so that, in immediate relation with the Godhead, he may partake of the boundless happiness which flows forth from Him.

Then in conclusion, that the whole may be made holy, the feet also are anointed and blessed. They are to feel, even in the event of possible recovery, a repugnance to touching this earthly, hard, impenetrable soil. A wonderful nimbleness is to be imparted to them, by which they spurn from under them the clod of earth which hitherto attracted them. And so, through a brilliant circle of equally holy acts, the beauty of which we have only briefly hinted at, the cradle and the grave, however far asunder they may chance to be, are bound in one continuous circle.

But all these spiritual wonders spring not, like other fruits, from the natural soil, where they can neither be sown, nor planted, nor cherished. We must supplicate for them from another region, a thing which cannot be done by all persons, nor at all times. Here we meet the highest of these symbols, derived from pious tradition. We are told that one man can be more favoured, blessed, and sanctified from above than another. But that this may not appear as a natural gift, this great boon, bound up with a heavy duty, must be communicated to others by one authorized person to another: and the greatest good that a man can attain, without his having to obtain it by his own wrestling or grasping, must be preserved and perpetuated on earth by spiritual heirship. In the very

ordination of the priest, is comprehended all that is necessary
for the effectual solemnizing of those holy acts, by which the
multitude receive grace, without any other activity being
needful on their part, than that of faith and implicit confidence. And thus the priest steps forth in the line of his
predecessors and successors, in the circle of those anointed
with him, representing the highest source of blessings, so
much the more gloriously, as it is not he, the priest, whom
we reverence, but his office ; it is not his nod to which we
bow the knee, but the blessing which he imparts, and which
seems the more holy, and to come the more immediately from
heaven, because the earthly instrument cannot at all weaken
or invalidate it by its own sinful, nay, wicked nature.

How is this truly spiritual connexion shattered to pieces in
Protestantism, by part of the above-mentioned symbols being
declared apocryphal, and only a few canonical ;—and how,
by their indifference to one of these, will they prepare us for
the high dignity of the others ?

In my time I had been confided to the religious instruction
of a good old infirm clergyman, who had been confessor of
the family for many years. The *Catechism*, a *Paraphrase* of
it, and the *Scheme of Salvation*, I had at my fingers' ends, I
lacked not one of the strongly proving biblical texts, but from
all this I reaped no fruit ; for as they assured me that the
honest old man arranged his chief examination according to
an old set form, I lost all pleasure and inclination for the
business, spent the last week in all sorts of diversions, laid in
my hat the loose leaves borrowed from an older friend, who
had gotten them from the clergyman, and unfeelingly and
senselessly read aloud all that I should have known how to
utter with feeling and conviction.

But I found my good-will and my aspirations in this important matter still more paralyzed by a dry, spiritless routine,
when I was now to approach the confessional. I was indeed
conscious to myself of many failings, but of no great faults ;
and that very consciousness diminished them, since it directed
me to the moral strength which lay within me, and which,
with resolution and perseverance, was at last to become
master over the old Adam. We were taught that we were
much better than the catholics for this very reason : that we
were not obliged to acknowledge anything in particular in the

confessional, nay, that this would not be at all proper, even if we wished to do it. This last did not seem right to me; for I had the strangest religious doubts, which I would readily have had cleared up on such an occasion. Now as this was not to be done, I composed a confession for myself, which, while it well expressed my state of mind, was to confess to an intelligent man, in general terms, that which I was forbidden to tell him in detail. But when I entered the old choir of the Barefoot Friars, when I approached the strange latticed closets in which the reverend gentlemen used to be found for that purpose, when the sexton opened the door for me, when I now saw myself shut up in the narrow place face to face with my spiritual grandsire, and he bade me welcome with his weak nasal voice, all the light of my mind and heart was extinguished at once, the well-conned confession-speech would not cross my lips; I opened, in my embarrassment, the book which I had in hand, and read from it the first short form I saw, which was so general, that anybody might have spoken it with quite a safe conscience. I received absolution, and withdrew neither warm nor cold; went the next day with my parents to the Table of the Lord, and, for a few days, behaved myself as was becoming after so holy an act.

In the sequel, however, there came over me that evil, which from the fact of our religion being complicated by various dogmas, and founded on texts of scripture which admit of several interpretations, attacks scrupulous men in such a manner, that it brings on a hypochondriacal condition, and raises this to its highest point, to fixed ideas. I have known several men who, though their manner of thinking and living was perfectly rational, could not free themselves from thinking about the sin against the Holy Ghost, and from the fear that they had committed it. A similar trouble threatened me on the subject of the communion, for the text that one who unworthily partakes of the Sacrament *eateth and drinketh damnation to himself*, had, very early, already made a monstrous impression upon me. Every fearful thing that I had read in the histories of the middle ages, of the judgments of God, of those most strange ordeals, by red-hot iron, flaming fire, swelling water, and even what the Bible tells us of the draught which agrees well with the innocent, but puffs up and bursts the guilty,—all this pictured itself to my imagination; and formed itself into the most frightful combinations, since false vows, hypocrisy, perjury, blasphemy, all seemed to weigh down the unworthy person at this most holy act, which was so much the more horrible, as no one could dare to pronounce himself worthy, and the forgiveness of sins, by which everything was to be at last done away, was found limited by so many conditions, that one could not with certainty dare appropriate it to oneself.

This gloomy scruple troubled me to such a degree, and the expedient which they would represent to me as sufficient, seemed so bald and feeble, that it gave the bugbear only a more fearful aspect, and, as soon as I had reached Leipzig, I tried to free myself altogether from my connexion with the church. How oppressive then must have been to me the exhortations of Gellert, whom, considering the generally laconic style with which he was obliged to repel our obtrusiveness, I was unwilling to trouble with such singular questions, and the less so as in my more cheerful hours I was myself ashamed of them; and at last left completely behind me this strange anguish of conscience, together with church and altar.

Gellert, in accordance with his pious feelings, had composed for himself a course of ethics, which from time to time he publicly read, and thus in an honourable manner acquitted himself of his duty to the public. Gellert's writings had already, for a long time, been the foundation of German moral culture, and every one anxiously wished to see that work printed; but as this was not to be done till after the good man's death, people thought themselves very fortunate to hear him deliver it himself in his lifetime. The philosophical auditorium* was at such times crowded, and the beautiful soul, the pure will, and the interest of the noble man in our welfare, his exhortations, warnings, and entreaties, uttered in a somewhat hollow and sorrowful tone, made indeed an impression for the moment, but this did not last long, the less so, as there were many scoffers, who contrived to make us suspicious of this tender, and, as they thought, enervating manner. I remember a Frenchman travelling through the town, who inquired after the maxims and opinions of the man who attracted such an immense concourse. When we

* The lecture-room. The word is also used in university language to denote a professor's audience.

had given him the necessary information, he shook his head and said, smiling, *Laissez le faire, il nous forme des dupes.*

And thus also did good society, which cannot easily endure anything estimable in its neighbourhood, know how to spoil on occasion the moral influence which Gellert might have had upon us. Now it was taken ill of him that he instructed the Danes of distinction and wealth, who were particularly recommended to him, better than the other students, and had a marked solicitude for them; now he was charged with selfishness and nepotism for causing a table d'hôte to be established for these young men at his brother's house. This brother, a tall, good-looking, blunt, unceremonious and somewhat rude man, had, it was said, been a fencing-master, and notwithstanding the too great lenity of his brother, the noble boarders were often treated harshly and roughly; hence the people thought they must again take the part of these young folks, and pulled about the good reputation of the excellent Gellert to such a degree, that, in order not to be mistaken about him, we became indifferent towards him, and visited him no more; yet we always saluted him in our best manner when he came riding along on his tame grey horse. This horse the Elector had sent him, to oblige him to take an exercise so necessary for his health;—a distinction which was not easily forgiven him.

And thus, by degrees, the epoch approached when all authority was to vanish from before me, and I was to become suspicious, nay, to despair, even of the greatest and best individuals whom I had known or imagined.

Frederick the Second still stood at the head of all the distinguished men of the century, in my thoughts, and it must therefore have appeared very surprising to me, that I could praise him as little before the inhabitants of Leipzig as formerly in my grandfather's house. They had felt the hand of war heavily, it is true, and therefore they were not to blame for not thinking the best of him who had begun and continued it. They therefore were willing to let him pass as a distinguished, but by no means as a great man. "There was no art," they said, "in performing something with great means; and if one spares neither lands, nor money, nor blood, one may well accomplish one's purpose at last. Frederick had shown himself great in none of his plans, and in nothing that he had, properly speaking, undertaken. So long as it depended on himself, he had only gone on making blunders, and what was extraordinary in him, had only come to light when he was compelled to make these blunders good again. It was purely from this that he had obtained his great reputation, since every man wishes for himself that same talent of making good, in a clever way, the blunders which he frequently commits. If one goes through the Seven Years' War, step by step, it will be found that the king quite uselessly sacrificed his fine army, and that it was his own fault that this ruinous feud had been protracted to so great a length. A truly great man and general would have got the better of his enemies much sooner." In support of these opinions they could cite infinite details, which I did not know how to deny; and I felt the unbounded reverence which I had devoted to this remarkable prince, from my youth upwards, gradually cooling away.

As the inhabitants of Leipzig had now destroyed for me the pleasant feeling of revering a great man, so did a new friend whom I gained at the time very much diminish the respect which I entertained for my present fellow-citizens. This friend was one of the strangest fellows in the world. He was named Behrisch, and was tutor to the young Count Lindenau. Even his exterior was singular enough. Lean and well-built, far advanced in the thirties, a very large nose, and altogether marked features; he wore from morning till night a scratch which might well have been called a peruke, but dressed himself very neatly, and never went out but with his sword by his side, and his hat under his arm. He was one of those men who have quite a peculiar gift of killing time, or rather, who know how to make something out of nothing, in order to pass time away. Everything that he did must be done with slowness, and a certain deportment which might have been called affected, if Behrisch had not even by nature had something affected in his manner. He resembled an old Frenchman, and also spoke and wrote French very well and easily. His greatest delight was to busy himself seriously about drolleries, and to follow up without end any silly notion. Thus he was constantly dressed in grey, and as the different parts of his attire were of different stuffs, and also of different shades, he could reflect for whole days as to how he should procure one grey more for his body, and was happy when he had succeeded

in this, and could put to shame us who had doubted it, or
had pronounced it impossible. He then gave us long severe
lectures, about our lack of inventive power, and our want of
faith in his talents.

For the rest, he had studied well, was particularly versed in
the modern languages and their literature, and wrote an
excellent hand. He was very well disposed to me, and I,
having been always accustomed and inclined to the society of
older persons, soon attached myself to him. My intercourse,
too, served him for a special amusement, since he took pleasure in taming my restlessness and impatience, with which,
on the other hand, I gave him enough to do. In the art of
poetry he had what is called taste, a certain general opinion
about the good and bad, the mediocre and tolerable; but his
judgment was rather censorious, and he destroyed even the
little faith in contemporary writers which I cherished within
me, by unfeeling remarks, which he knew how to advance
with wit and humour, about the writings and poems of this
man and that. He received my own affairs with indulgence,
and let me have my way, but only on the condition that I
should have nothing printed. He promised me, on the other
hand, that he himself would copy those pieces which he
thought good, and would present me with them in a handsome volume. This undertaking now afforded an opportunity
for the greatest possible waste of time. For before he could
find the right paper, before he could make up his mind as to
the size, before he had settled the breadth of the margin, and
the form of handwriting, before the crow-quills were provided and cut into pens, and Indian ink was rubbed, whole
weeks passed, without the least bit having been done. With
just as much ado he always set about his writing, and really,
by degrees, put together a most charming manuscript. The
title of the poems was in German text, the verses themselves
in a perpendicular Saxon hand, and at the end of every poem
was an analogous vignette, which he had either selected somewhere or other, or had invented himself, and in which he
contrived to imitate very neatly the hatching of the wood-cuts
and tail-pieces which are used for such purposes. To show
me these things as he went on, to celebrate beforehand in a
comico-pathetical manner my good fortune in seeing myself
immortalized in such exquisite handwriting, and that in a

style which no printing-press could attain, gave another occasion for passing the most agreeable hours. In the meantime, his intercourse was always secretly instructive, by reason of his liberal acquirements, and, as he knew how to subdue my restless impetuous disposition, was also quite wholesome for me in a moral sense. He had, too, quite a peculiar abhorrence of roughness, and his jests were always quaint, without ever falling into the coarse or the trivial. He indulged himself in a distorted aversion from his countrymen, and described with ludicrous touches even what they were able to undertake. He was particularly inexhaustible in a comical representation of individual persons, as he found something to find fault with in the exterior of every one. Thus, when we lay together at the window, he could occupy himself for hours criticising the passers-by, and when he had censured them long enough, in showing exactly and circumstantially how they ought to have dressed themselves, ought to have walked, and ought to have behaved to look like orderly people. Such attempts, for the most part, ended in something improper and absurd, so that we did not so much laugh at how the man looked, but at how, perchance, he might have looked, had he been mad enough to caricature himself. In all such matters, Behrisch went quite unmercifully to work, without being in the slightest degree malicious. On the other hand, we knew how to teaze him, on our side, by assuring him that, to judge from his exterior, he must be taken, if not for a French dancing-master, at least for the academical teacher of the language. This reproval was usually the signal for dissertations an hour long, in which he used to set forth the difference, wide as the heavens, which there was between him and an old Frenchman. At the same time he commonly imputed to us all sorts of awkward attempts, that we might possibly have made for the alteration and modification of his wardrobe.

The direction of my poetizing, which I only carried on the more zealously as the transcript went on becoming more beautiful and more careful, now inclined altogether to the natural and the true; and if the subjects could not always be important, I nevertheless always endeavoured to express them clearly and pointedly, the more so as my friend often gave me to understand, what a great thing it was to write down a verse on

Dutch paper, with the crow-quill and Indian ink; what time, talent, and exertion it required, which ought not to be squandered on anything empty and superfluous. At the same time, he commonly used to open a finished parcel and circumstantially to explain what ought not to stand in this or that place, or congratulate us that it actually did not stand there. He then spoke, with great contempt, of the art of printing, mimicked the compositor, ridiculed his gestures and his hurried picking out of letters here and there, and derived from this manœuvre all the calamities of literature. On the other hand, he extolled the grace and the noble posture of a writer, and immediately sat down himself to exhibit it to us, while he rated us at the same time for not demeaning ourselves at the writing-table precisely after his example and model. He now returned to the contrast with the compositor, turned a begun letter upside down, and showed how unseemly it would be to write anything from the bottom to the top, or from the right to the left, with other things of like kind with which whole volumes might have been filled.

With such harmless fooleries we lavished away our precious time, while it could have occurred to none of us, that anything would chance to proceed out of our circle, which would awaken a general sensation and bring us into not the best repute.

Gellert may have taken little pleasure in his *Practicum*, and if, perhaps, he took pleasure in giving some directions as to prose and poetical style, he did it most privately only to a few, among whom we could not number ourselves. Professor Clodius thought to fill the gap which thus arose in the public instruction. He had gained some renown in literature, criticism, and poetry, and as a young, lively, obliging man, found many friends both in the university and in the city. Gellert himself referred us to the lectures now commenced by him, and, as far as the principal matter was concerned, we remarked little difference. He, too, only criticised details, corrected likewise with red ink, and one found oneself in company with mere blunders, without a prospect as to where the right was to be sought. I had brought to him some of my little labours, which he did not treat harshly. But just at this time they wrote to me from home, that I must without fail furnish a poem for my uncle's wedding. I felt myself far from that light and frivolous period in which a similar thing would have given me pleasure, and since I could get nothing out of the actual circumstance itself, I determined to trick out my work in the best manner, with extraneous ornament. I therefore convened all Olympus to consult about the marriage of a Frankfort lawyer; and seriously enough, to be sure, as well became the festival of such an honourable man. Venus and Themis had quarrelled for his sake; but a roguish prank which Amor played the latter, gained the suit for the former, and the gods decided in favour of the marriage.

My work by no means displeased me. I received from home a handsome letter in its praise, took the trouble to have another fair copy, and hoped to extort some applause from my professor also. But here I had missed my aim. He took the matter severely, and as he did not notice the tone of parody, which nevertheless lay in the notion, he declared the great expenditure of divine means for such an insignificant human end, in the highest degree reprehensible; inveighed against the use and abuse of such mythological figures, as a false habit originating in pedantic times; found the expression now too high, now too low, and in divers particulars had indeed not spared the red ink, though he asserted that he had yet done too little.

Such pieces were read out and criticised anonymously, it is true; but we used to watch each other, and it remained no secret that this unfortunate assembly of the gods was my work. Yet since his critique, when I took his point of view, seemed to be perfectly just, and those divinities more nearly inspected were in fact only hollow shadow-forms; I cursed all Olympus, flung the whole mythic Pantheon away, and from that time Amor and Luna have been the only divinities which at all appear in my little poems.

Among the persons whom Behrisch had chosen as the butts of his wit, Clodius stood just at the head; nor was it hard to find a comical side in him. As a little, rather stout, thick-set figure, he was violent in his motions, somewhat impetuous in his utterances, and restless in his demeanour. In all this he differed from his fellow-citizens, who, nevertheless, willingly put up with him on account of his good qualities and the fine promise which he gave.

He was usually commissioned with the poems which had

become necessary on festal occasions. In the so-called *Ode*, he followed the manner used by Ramler, whom, however, it alone suited. But Clodius, as an imitator, had especially marked the foreign words by means of which the poems of Ramler come forth with a majestic pomp, which, because it is conformable to the greatness of his subject and the rest of his poetic treatment, produces a very good effect on the ear, feelings, and imagination. In Clodius, on the contrary, these expressions had a heterogeneous air, since his poetry was in other respects not calculated to elevate the mind in any manner.

Now we had often been obliged to see such poems printed and highly lauded in our presence, and we found it highly offensive, that he who had sequestered the heathen gods from us, now wished to hammer together another ladder to Parnassus out of Greek and Roman word-rungs. These oft-recurring expressions stamped themselves firmly on our memory, and in a merry hour, when we were eating some most excellent cakes in the Kitchen-gardens (*Kohlgärten*), it all at once struck me to put together these words of might and power, in a poem on the cake-baker Hendel. No sooner thought than done! And let it stand here, too, as it was written on the wall of the house with a lead-pencil.

> " O Hendel, dessen Ruhm vom *Süd* zum *Norden* reicht,
> Vernimm den *Päan* der zu deinen Ohren steigt
> Du bäckst was *Gallien* und *Britten* emsig suchen,
> Mit *schopfrischen Genie, originelle* Kuchen.
> Des Kaffee's *Ocean*, der sich vor dir ergiesst,
> Ist süsser als der Saft der vom *Hymettus* fliesst.
> Dein Haus ein *Monument*, wie wir den Künsten lohnen
> Umhangen mit *Trophän*, erzählt den *Nationen :*
> Auch ohne *Diadem* fand Hendel hier sein Glück
> Und raubte dem *Cothurn* gar manch Achtgroschenstück.
> Glanzt deine *Urn* dereinst in majestäts'chen *Pompe*,
> Dann weint der *Patriot* un deinem *Katacombe.*
> Doch leb ! dein *Torus* sey von edler Brut ein *Nest,*
> Steh'hoch wie der *Olymp*, wie der *Parnassus* fest !
> Kein *Phalanx* Griechenland mit Römischen *Ballisten*
> Vermög *Germanien* und Hendel zu verwüsten.
> Dein *Wohl* is unser *Stolz,* dein *Leiden* unser *Schmerz*
> Und Hendel's *Tempel ist der Musensöhne Herz.**"

* The humour of the above consists, not in the thoughts, but in the particular words employed. These have no remarkable effect in English,

S

This poem stood a long time among many others which disfigured the walls of that room, without being noticed, and we, who had sufficiently amused ourselves with it, forgot it altogether amongst other things. A long time afterwards, Clodius came out with his *Medon*, whose wisdom, magnanimity and virtue we found infinitely ridiculous, much as the first representation of the piece was applauded. That evening, when we met together in the wine-house, I made a prologue in doggerel verse, in which Harlequin steps out with two great sacks, places them on each side of the *proscenium*, and after various preliminary jokes, tells the spectators in confidence, that in the two sacks moral æsthetic dust is to be found, which the actors will very frequently throw into their eyes. One, to wit, was filled with good deeds, that cost nothing, and the other with splendidly expressed opinions, that had no meaning behind them. He reluctantly withdrew, and sometimes came back, earnestly exhorted the spectators to attend to his warning and shut their eyes, reminded them that he had always been their friend, and meant well with them, with many more things of the kind. This prologue was acted in the room, on the spot, by friend Horn, but the jest remained quite among ourselves, not even a copy had been taken, and the paper was soon lost. However, Horn, who had per-

as to us the words of Latin origin are often as familiar as those which have Teutonic roots, and these form the chief peculiarity of the style. We have therefore given the poem in the original language, with the peculiar words (as indicated by Göthe) in italics, and subjoin a literal translation. It will be observed that we have said that the peculiarity consists *chiefly*, not *solely*, in the use of the foreign words, for there are two or three instances of unquestionably German words, which are italicised on account of their high-sounding pomp.

"Oh Hendel, whose fame extends from *south* to *north*, hear the *Pæan* which ascends to thine ears. Thou bakest that which *Gauls* and *Britons* industriously seek, (thou bakest) with *creative genius original* cakes. The *ocean* of coffee which pours itself out before thee, is sweeter than the juice which flows from *Hymettus*. Thy house, a *monument*, how we reward the arts, hung round with *trophies*, tells the *nations:* 'Even without a *diadem*, Hendel formed his fortune here, and robbed the *Cothurnus* of many an eight-groschen-piece.' When thine *urn* shines hereafter in majestic *pomp*, then will the *patriot* weep at thy *catacomb*. But live! let thy bed (*torus*) be the *nest* of a noble brood, stand high as *Olympus*, and firm as *Parnassus*. May no *phalanx* of Greece with Roman *ballistæ* be able to destroy *Germania* and Hendel. Thy *weal* is our *pride*, thy *suffering* our pain, and Hendel's *temple* is the *heart* of the *sons of the Muses*."—*Trans.*

formed the Harlequin very prettily, took it into his head to
enlarge my poem to Hendel by several verses, and then to
make it refer to *Medon*. He read it aloud to us, and we
could not take any pleasure in it, for we did not find the
additions even ingenious, while the first poem, being written
for quite a different purpose, seemed to us disfigured. Our
friend, out of humour at our indifference, or rather censure, may have shown it to others, who found it new and
amusing. Copies were now made of it, to which the reputation of Clodius's *Medon* gave at once a rapid publicity. Universal disapproval was the consequence, and the originators
(it was soon found out that the poem had proceeded from our
clique) were severely censured; for nothing of the sort had
been seen since Cronegk's and Rost's attacks upon Gottsched.
We had besides already secluded ourselves, and now found
ourselves quite in the case of the owl with respect to the
other birds. In Dresden, too, they did not like the affair, and
it had for us serious, if not unpleasant consequences. For
some time, already, Count Lindenau had not been quite
satisfied with his son's tutor. For, although the young man
was by no means neglected, and Behrisch kept himself either
in the chamber of the young Count, or at least close to it, when
the instructors gave their daily lessons, regularly frequented the
lectures with him, never went out in the day-time without
him, and accompanied him in all his walks; yet the rest of
us were always to be found in Apel's house, and joined them
whenever they went on a pleasure ramble: this already
excited some attention. Behrisch, too, accustomed himself
to our society, and at last, towards nine o'clock in the evenings, generally transferred his pupil into the hands of the
valet de chambre, and went in quest of us to the wine-house,
whither, however, he never used to come but in shoes and
stockings, with his sword by his side, and commonly his hat
under his arm. The jokes and fooleries, which he generally
started, went on *ad infinitum*. Thus, for instance, one of our
friends had a habit of going away precisely at ten, because he
had a connexion with a pretty girl, with whom he could converse only at that hour. We did not like to lose him; and
one evening, when we sat very happily together, Behrisch
secretly determined that he would not let him off this time.
At the stroke of ten, the other arose and took leave. Behrisch

called after him and begged him to wait a moment, as he
was just going with him. He now began, in the most
amusing manner, first to look after his sword, which stood
just before his eyes, and in buckling it on behaved awkwardly, so that he could never accomplish it. He did this,
too, so naturally, that no one took offence at it. But when, to
vary the theme, he at last went further, so that the sword
came now on the right side, now between his legs, an universal laughter arose, in which the man in a hurry, who was
likewise a merry fellow, chimed in, and let Behrisch have his
own way till the happy hour was past, when, for the first
time, there followed general pleasure and agreeable conversation till deep into the night.

Unfortunately Behrisch, and we through him, had a certain
other propensity for some girls who were better than their
reputation; by which our own reputation could not be improved. We had often been seen in their garden, and we
directed our walks thither, even when the young Count was
with us. All this may have been treasured up, and at last
communicated to his father; enough, he sought, in a gentle-
manly manner, to get rid of the tutor, to whom the event
proved fortunate. His good exterior, his knowledge and
talents, his integrity, which no one could call in question, had
won him the affection and esteem of distinguished persons, on
whose recommendation he was appointed tutor to the hereditary prince of Dessau; and at the court of a prince, excellent
in every respect, found a solid happiness.

The loss of a friend like Behrisch was of the greatest consequence to me. He had spoiled, while he cultivated me, and
his presence was necessary, if the pains he had thought good
to spend upon me were in any degree to bring forth fruit for
society. He knew how to engage me in all kinds of pretty and
agreeable things, in whatever was just appropriate, and to
bring out my social talents. But as I had gained no self-
dependence in such things, so when I was alone again, I immediately relapsed into my confused and crabbed disposition,
which always increased, the more discontented I was with
those about me, since I fancied that they were not contented
with me. With the most arbitrary caprice, I took offence at
what I might have reckoned as an advantage to me; thus
alienated many with whom I had hitherto stood on a tolerable

footing ; and, on account of the many disagreeable consequences which I had drawn on myself and others, whether by
doing or leaving undone, by doing too much or too little,
was obliged to hear the remark from my well-wishers, that
I lacked experience. The same thing was told me by every
person of sound sense who saw my productions, especially
when these referred to the external world. I observed this
as well as I could, but found in it little that was edifying,
and was still forced to add enough of my own to make it only
tolerable. I had often pressed my friend Behrisch, too, that he
would make plain to me what experience might be? But,
because he was full of nonsense, he put me off with fair
words from one day to another, and at last, after great preparations, disclosed to me, that true experience was properly
when one experiences how an experienced man must experience in experiencing his experience. Now when we scolded
him outrageously, and called him to account for this, he
assured us that a great mystery lay hidden behind these
words, which we could not comprehend until we had experienced . . . and so on without end ;—for it cost him
nothing to talk on in that way by the quarter of an hour :—
since the experience would always become more experienced,
and at last come to true experience. When we were falling
into despair at such fooleries, he protested that he had learned
this way of making himself intelligible and impressive from
the latest and greatest authors, who had made us observe
how one can rest a restful rest, and how silence, in being
silent, can constantly become more silent.

By chance an officer, who came among us on furlough, was
praised in good company as a remarkable sound-minded and
experienced man, who had fought through the Seven Years'
War, and had gained universal confidence. It was not difficult for me to approach him, and we often went walking with
each other. The idea of experience had almost become fixed
in my brain, and the craving to make it clear to me passionate. Open-hearted as I was, I disclosed to him the
uneasiness in which I found myself. He smiled, and was
kind enough to tell me, as an answer to my question, something of his own life, and generally of the world immediately
about us ; from which, indeed, little better was to be gathered
than that experience convinces us that our best thoughts,

wishes and designs are unattainable, and that he who fosters
such vagaries and advances them with eagerness, is especially
held to be an inexperienced man.

Yet, as he was a gallant, good fellow, he assured me that
he had himself not quite given up these vagaries, and felt
himself tolerably well off with the little faith, love, and hope
which remained. He then felt obliged to tell me a great
deal about war, about the sort of life in the field, about skir-
mishes and battles, especially so far as he had taken part in
them; when these vast events, by being considered in relation
to a single individual, gained a very odd aspect. I then led
him on to an open narration of the late situation of the court,
which seemed to me quite like a tale. I heard of the
bodily strength of Augustus the Second, of his many children and his vast expenses, then of his successor's love of
art and of making collections, of Count Brühl and his boundless love of magnificence, which in detail appeared almost
absurd, of his numerous banquets and gorgeous amusements,
which were all cut off by Frederick's invasion of Saxony.
The royal castles now lay in ruins, Brühl's splendours were
annihilated, and, of the whole, a glorious land, much injured,
alone remained.

When he saw me astonished at that mad enjoyment of
fortune, and then grieved by the calamity that followed, and
informed me that one expects from an experienced man
exactly this, that he shall be astonished at neither the one
nor the other, nor take too lively an interest in them, I felt
a great desire still to remain awhile in the same inexperience
as hitherto: in which desire he strengthened me, and very
urgently entreated me, for the present at least, always to
cling to agreeable experiences, and to try to avoid those that
were disagreeable as much as possible, if they should intrude
themselves upon me. But once, when the discussion was
again about experience in general, and I related to him those
ludicrous phrases of my friend Behrisch, he shook his head,
smiling, and said, "There, one sees how it is with words
which are only once uttered! These sound so comical, nay,
so silly, that it would seem almost impossible to put a rational
meaning into them; and yet, perhaps, the attempt might be
made."

And when I pressed him, he replied in his intelligent,

cheerful manner, " If you will allow me, while commenting on and completing your friend, to go on after his fashion, I think he meant to say, that experience is nothing else than that one experiences what one does not wish to experience; which is what it amounts to for the most part, at least in this world."

EIGHTH BOOK.

ANOTHER man, although infinitely different from Behrisch in every respect, might yet be compared with him in a certain sense; I mean OESER, who was also one of those men who dream away their lives in a comfortable state of being busy. His friends themselves secretly acknowledged that, with very fine natural powers, he had not spent his younger years in sufficient activity; for which reason, he never went so far as to practise his art with perfect technicality. Yet a certain diligence appeared to be reserved for his old age, and, during the many years which I knew him, he never lacked invention or laboriousness. From the very first moment he had much attracted me : even his residence, strange and portentous, was highly charming to me. In the old castle Pleissenburg, at the right-hand corner, one ascended a repaired, cheerful, winding staircase. The saloons of the Academy of Design, of which he was director, were found to the left, and were light and roomy ; but he himself could only be reached through a narrow, dark passage, at the end of which one first sought the entrance into his apartments, having just passed between the whole suite of them and an extensive granary. The first apartment was adorned with pictures from the later Italian school, by masters whose grace he used highly to commend. As I, with some noblemen, had taken private lessons of him, we were permitted to draw here, and we often penetrated into his adjoining private cabinet, which contained at the same time his few books, collections of art and natural curiosities, and whatever else might have most interested him. Everything was arranged with taste, simply, and in such a manner that the little space held a great deal. The furniture, presses, and portfolios were elegant, without affectation or superfluity. Thus also the first thing which he recommended to us, and to which he always recurred, was simplicity in everything that art and manual labour united are called upon to produce. As a sworn foe of the scroll-and-shell style, and of the whole taste for quaintness, he showed us in copper-plates and drawings old patterns of the sort, contrasted with better decorations and simpler forms of furniture, as well as with other appurtenances of a room; and, because everything about him corresponded with these maxims, his words and instructions made a good and lasting impression on us. Besides this, he had an opportunity to let us see his opinions in practice, since he stood in good consideration both with private and with official persons, and was asked for advice when there were new buildings and alterations. He seemed in general to be more fond of preparing anything on occasion, for a certain end and use, than of undertaking and completing things which exist for themselves and require a greater perfection; he was therefore always ready and at hand when the publishers needed larger and smaller copper-plates for any work; thus the vignettes to Winckelmann's first writings were etched by him. But he often made only very sketchy drawings, to which Geyser knew very well how to adapt himself. His figures had throughout something general, not to say ideal. His women were pleasing and agreeable, his children *naïve* enough; only he could not succeed with the men, who, in his spirited but always cloudy and at the same time foreshortening manner, had for the most part the look of *Lazzaroni*. Since he designed his composition less with regard to form than to light, shade, and masses, the general effect was good; as indeed all that he did and produced was attended by a peculiar grace. As he at the same time neither could nor would control a deep-rooted propensity to the significant and the allegorical—to that which excites a secondary thought, so his works always furnished something to reflect upon, and were complete through a conception, even where they could not be so from art and execution. This bias, which is always dangerous, frequently led him to the very bounds of good taste, if not beyond them. He often sought to attain his views by the oddest notions, and by whimsical jests; nay, his best works always have a touch of humour. If the public were not always satisfied with such things, he revenged himself by a new and even stranger drollery. Thus he afterwards exhibited in the ante-room of the great concert-hall, an ideal female figure, in his own style, who was raising a pair of snuffers to a taper, and he was extraordinarily delighted when he was able to cause a dispute on the question: whether this

singular muse meant to snuff the light or to extinguish it? when
he roguishly allowed all sorts of bantering by-thoughts to peep
forth.

But the building of the new theatre, in my time, made the
greatest noise; in which his curtain, when it was still quite
new, had certainly an uncommonly charming effect. Oeser
had taken the Muses out of the clouds, upon which they
usually hover on such occasions, and set them upon the earth.
The statues of Sophocles and Aristophanes, around whom
all the modern dramatic writers were assembled, adorned a
vestibule to the Temple of Fame. Here, too, the goddesses
of the arts were likewise present, and all was dignified and
beautiful. But now comes the oddity! Through the open
centre was seen the portal of the distant temple, and a man
in a light jerkin was passing between the two above-mentioned groups, and without troubling himself about them,
directly up to the temple; he was seen from behind, and was
not particularly distinguished. Now this man was to represent Shakspeare, who, without predecessors or followers, without concerning himself about models, went to meet immortality
in his own way. This work was executed on the great floor
over the new theatre. We often assembled round him there,
and in that place I read aloud to him the proof-sheets of
Musarion.

As to myself, I by no means advanced in the practice of the
art. His instructions worked upon our mind and our taste;
but his own drawing was too undefined to guide me, who had
only glimmered along by the objects of art and of nature, to a
severe and decided practice. Of the faces and bodies he gave
us rather the aspect than the forms, rather the postures than
the proportions. He gave us the conceptions of the figures,
and desired that we should impress them vividly upon our
minds. That might have been beautifully and properly done, if
he had not had mere beginners before him. If, on this account,
a pre-eminent talent for instruction may be well denied him,
it must, on the other hand, be acknowledged that he was very
discreet and politic, and that a happy adroitness of mind qualified him very peculiarly for a teacher in a higher sense. The
deficiencies under which each one laboured he clearly saw;
but he disdained to reprove them directly, and rather hinted
his praise and censure indirectly and very laconically. One

was now compelled to think over the matter, and soon came
to a far deeper insight. Thus, for instance, I had very carefully executed, after a pattern, a nosegay on blue paper, with
white and black crayon, and partly with the stump, partly by
hatching it up, had tried to give effect to the little picture.
After I had been long labouring in this way, he once came
behind me and said: " More paper!" upon which he immediately withdrew. My neighbour and I puzzled our heads as
to what this could mean: for my bouquet, on a large half-sheet,
had plenty of space around it. After we had reflected a long
while, we thought, at last, that we had hit his meaning, when
we remarked that, by working together the black and the
white, I had quite covered up the blue ground, had destroyed
the middle tint, and, in fact, with great industry, had produced a disagreeable drawing. As to the rest, he did not fail
to instruct us in perspective, and in light and shade, sufficiently
indeed, but always so that we had to exert and torment ourselves to find the application of the principles communicated.
Probably his view with regard to us who did not intend to
become artists, was only to form the judgment and taste, and
to make us acquainted with the requisites of a work of art,
without precisely requiring that we should produce one. Since,
moreover, patient industry was not my talent, for nothing gave
me pleasure except what came to me at once, so by degrees I
became discouraged, if not lazy, and as knowledge is more
comfortable than doing, I was quite content to follow wherever
he chose, after his own fashion, to lead us.

At this time the *Lives of the Painters*, by D'Argenville, was
translated into German; I obtained it quite fresh, and studied
it assiduously enough. This seemed to please Oeser, and he
procured us an opportunity of seeing many a portfolio out of
the great Leipzig collections, and thus introduced us to the
history of the art. But even these exercises produced in me
an effect different from that which he probably had in mind.
The manifold subjects which I saw treated by artists awakened
the poetic talent in me, and as one easily makes an en-
graving for a poem, so did I now make poems to the engravings and drawings, by contriving to present to myself the
personages introduced in them, in their previous and subsequent condition, and sometimes to compose a little song which
might have suited them; and thus accustomed myself to con-

sider the arts in connexion with each other. Even the mistakes
which I made, so that my poems were often descriptive, were
useful to me in the sequel, when I came to more reflection, by
making me attentive to the differences between the arts.   Of
such little things many were in the collection which Behrisch
had arranged ; but there is nothing left of them now.

The atmosphere of art and taste in which Oeser lived, and
into which one was drawn, provided one visited him frequently, was the more and more worthy and delightful, because
he was fond of remembering departed or absent persons, with
whom he had been, or still continued to be, on good terms ;
for if he had once given any one his esteem, he remained unalterable in his conduct towards him, and always showed
himself equally friendly.

After we had heard CAYLUS pre-eminently extolled among
the French, he made us also acquainted with Germans of
activity in this department.   Thus we learned that Professor
CHRIST, as an amateur, a collector, a connoisseur, a fellow-
labourer, had done good service for art ; and had applied his
learning to its true improvement.   HEINECKE, on the contrary, could not be honourably mentioned, partly because he
devoted himself too assiduously to the ever-childish beginnings
of German art, which Oeser little valued, partly because he
had once treated Winckelmann shabbily, which could never
be forgiven him.   Our attention, however, was strongly drawn
to the labours of LIPPERT, since our instructor knew how to
set forth his merits sufficiently.   " For," he said, " although
single statues and larger groups of sculpture remain the foundation and the summit of all knowledge of art, yet either as
originals or as casts they are seldom to be seen ; on the contrary, by Lippert, a little world of gems is made known, in
which the more comprehensible merit of the ancients, their
happy invention, judicious composition, tasteful treatment, are
made more striking and intelligible, while, from the great
number of them, comparison is much more possible."   While
now we were busying ourselves with these as much as was
allowed, WINCKELMANN's lofty life of art in Italy was pointed
out, and we took his first writings in hand with devotion: for
Oeser had a passionate reverence for him, which he was able
easily to instil into us.   The problematical part of those little
treatises, which are, besides, confused even from their irony,

and from their referring to opinions and events altogether peculiar, we were, indeed, unable to decipher ; but as Oeser had great influence over us, and incessantly gave them out to us as the gospel of the beautiful, and still more of the tasteful and the pleasing, we found out the general sense, and fancied that with such interpretations we should go on the more securely, as we regarded it no small happiness to draw from the same fountain from which Winckelmann had allayed his earliest thirst.

No greater good fortune can befall a city, than when several educated men, like-minded in what is good and right, live together in it. Leipzig had this advantage, and enjoyed it the more peacefully, as so many differences of judgment had not yet manifested themselves. Huber, a print collector, and a well-experienced connoisseur, had furthermore the gratefully acknowledged merit of having determined to make the worth of German literature known to the French ; Kreuchauf, an amateur with a practised eye, who, as the friend of the whole society of art, might regard all collections as his own ; Wink-ler, who much loved to share with others the intelligent delight which he cherished for his treasures; many more who were added to the list, all lived and laboured with one feeling, and often as I was permitted to be present when they examined works of art, I do not remember that a dispute ever arose : the school from which the artist had proceeded, the time in which he lived, the peculiar talent which nature had bestowed on him, and the degree of excellence to which he had brought it in his performances, were always fairly considered. There was no prejudice for spiritual or terrestrial subjects, for landscape or for city views, for animate or inanimate ; the question was always about the accordance with art.

Now although from their situation, mode of thought, abilities, and opportunities, these amateurs and collectors inclined more to the Dutch school, yet, while the eye was practised on the endless merits of the north-western artist, a look of reverential longing was always turned towards the south-east.

And so the university, where I neglected the ends both of my family and myself, was to ground me in that in which I afterwards found the greatest satisfaction of my life ; the impression of those localities, too, in which I received such important incitements, has always remained to me most dear and precious. The old Pleissenburg, the rooms of the Academy, but, above all, the abode of Oeser, and no less the collections of Winkler and Richter, I have always vividly present before me.

But a young man who, while older persons are conversing with each other on subjects already familiar to them, is instructed only incidentally, and for whom the most difficult part of the business, that of rightly arranging all, yet remains, must find himself in a very painful situation. I therefore, as well as others, looked about with longing for some new light, which was indeed to come to us from a man to whom we owed so much already.

The mind can be highly delighted in two ways, by perception and conception. But the former demands a worthy object, which is not always at hand, and a proportionate culture, which one does not immediately attain. Conception, on the other hand, requires only susceptibility; it brings its subject-matter with it, and is itself the instrument of culture. Hence that beam of light was most welcome to us which that most excellent thinker brought down to us through dark clouds. One must be a young man to render present to oneself the effect which Lessing's *Laocoon* produced upon us, by transporting us out of the region of scanty perceptions into the open fields of thought. The so long misunderstood *ut pictura poesis* was at once laid aside, the difference between plastic and speaking art* was made clear, the summits of the two now appeared sundered, however near their bases might border on each other. The plastic artist was to keep himself within the bounds of the beautiful, if the artist of language, who cannot dispense with the significant in any kind, is permitted to ramble abroad beyond them. The former labours for the outer sense, which is satisfied only by the beautiful; the latter for the imagination, which may even reconcile itself to the ugly. All the consequences of this splendid thought were illumined to us as by a lightning flash; all the criticism which had hitherto guided and judged was thrown away like a worn-out coat; we considered ourselves freed from all evil, and fancied we might venture to look down with some compassion upon the other-

* " Bildende und Redende Kunst." The expression " speaking art " is used to produce a corresponding antithesis, though " *belles lettres* " would be the ordinary rendering.—*Trans.*

wise so splendid sixteenth century, when, in German sculptures and poems, they knew how to represent life only under the form of a fool hung with bells, death under the misformed shape of a rattling skeleton, and the necessary and accidental evils of the world under the image of the caricatured devil.

We were the most enchanted with the beauty of that thought, that the ancients had recognised death as the brother of sleep, and had represented them similar even to confusion, as becomes Menæchmi. Here we could first do high honour to the triumph of the beautiful, and banish the ugly of every kind into the low sphere of the ridiculous in the kingdom of art, since it could not be utterly driven out of the world.

The splendour of such leading and fundamental conceptions appears only to the mind upon which they exercise their infinite activity—appears only to the age in which, after being longed for, they come forth at the right moment. Then do those to whom such nourishment is offered, fondly occupy whole periods of their lives with it, and rejoice in an over-abundant growth; while men are not wanting, meanwhile, who resist such an effect on the spot, nor others who afterwards haggle and cavil at its high meaning.

But as conception and perception mutually require each other, I could not long work up these new thoughts, without an infinite desire arising within me to see important works of art, once and away, in great number. I therefore determined to visit Dresden without delay. I was not in want of the necessary cash; but there were other difficulties to overcome, which I needlessly increased still farther, through my whimsical disposition; for I kept my purpose a secret from every one, because I wished to contemplate the treasures of art there quite after my own way, and, as I thought, to allow no one to perplex me. Besides this, so simple a matter became more complicated by still another eccentricity.

We have weaknesses, both by birth and by education, and it may be questioned which of the two gives us the most trouble. Willingly as I made myself familiar with all sorts of conditions, and many as had been my inducements to do so, an excessive aversion from all inns had nevertheless been instilled into me by my father. This feeling had rooted itself firmly in him on his travels through Italy, France, and Germany. Although he seldom spoke in images, and only called them to

his aid when he was very cheerful, yet he used often to repeat
that he always fancied he saw a great cobweb spun across the
gate of an inn, so ingeniously that the insects could indeed fly
in, but that even the privileged wasps could not fly out again
unplucked. It seemed to him something horrible, that one
should be obliged to pay immoderately for renouncing one's
habits and all that was dear to one in life, and living after the
manner of publicans and waiters. He praised the hospitality
of the olden time, and reluctantly as he otherwise endured
even anything unusual in the house, he yet practised hospitality,
especially towards artists and virtuosi; thus gossip Seekatz
always had his quarters with us, and Abel, the last musician
who handled the *viol di gamba* with success and applause, was
well received and entertained. With such youthful impressions, which nothing had as yet rubbed off, how could I have
resolved to set foot in an inn in a strange city? Nothing
would have been easier than to find quarters with good
friends. Hofrath Krebel, Assessor Hermann, and others had
often spoken to me about it already; but even to these my
trip was to remain a secret, and I hit upon a most singular
notion. My next-room neighbour, the industrious theologian,
whose eyes unfortunately constantly grew weaker and weaker,
had a relation in Dresden, a shoemaker, with whom from
time to time he corresponded. For a long while already this
man had been highly remarkable to me on account of his expressions, and the arrival of one of his letters was always
celebrated by us as a holiday. The mode in which he replied
to the complaints of his cousin, who feared blindness, was
quite peculiar; for he did not trouble himself about grounds
of consolation, which are always hard to find; but the
cheerful way in which he looked upon his own narrow, poor,
toilsome life, the merriment which he drew even from evils
and inconveniences, the indestructible conviction that life is
in itself and on its own account a blessing, communicated itself
to him who read the letter, and, for the moment at least, transposed him into a like mood. Enthusiastic as I was, I had often
sent my compliments to this man, extolled his happy natural
gift, and expressed the wish to become acquainted with him.
All this being premised, nothing seemed to me more natural
than to seek him out, to converse with him, nay, to lodge
with him, and to learn to know him intimately. My good

candidate, after some opposition, gave me a letter, written
with difficulty, to carry with me, and, full of longing, I went
to Dresden in the yellow coach, with my matriculation in my
pocket.

I looked for my shoemaker, and soon found him in the
suburb (*Vorstadt*). He received me in a friendly manner,
sitting upon his stool, and said smiling, after he had read the
letter, " I see from this, young Sir, that you are a whimsical
Christian." " How so, master?" replied I. " No offence
meant by '*whimsical*,' " he continued ; " one calls every one so
who is not consistent with himself ; and I call you a whimsical
Christian because you acknowledge yourself a follower of our
Lord in one thing, but not in another." On my requesting
him to enlighten me, he said further : " It seems that your
view is to announce glad tidings to the poor and lowly ; that
is good, and this imitation of the Lord is praiseworthy ; but
you should reflect besides, that he rather sat down to table
with prosperous rich folks, where there was good fare, and
that he himself did not despise the sweet scent of the oint-
ment, of which you will find the opposite in my house."

This pleasant beginning put me at once in good-humour,
and we rallied each other for some time. His wife stood
doubting how she should board and lodge such a guest. On
this point, too, he had notions which referred not only
to the Bible, but also to *Gottfried's Chronicle*, and when we
were agreed that I was to stay, I gave my purse, such as it
was, into the charge of my hostess, and requested her to furnish herself from it, if anything should be necessary. When
he would have declined it, and somewhat waggishly gave me
to understand that he was not so burnt out as he might
appear, I disarmed him by saying, " Even if it were only
to change water into wine, such a well-tried domestic re-
source would not be out of place, since there are no more
miracles now-a-days." The hostess seemed to find my conduct less and less strange ; we had soon accommodated ourselves to each other, and spent a very merry evening. He
remained always the same, because all flowed from one source.
His peculiarity was an apt common-sense, which rested upon
a cheerful disposition, and took delight in uniform habitual
activity. That he should labour incessantly was his first and
most necessary care ; that he regarded everything else as

T

secondary,—this kept up his comfortable state of mind; and
I must reckon him before many others in the class of those
who are called practical unconscious philosophers.*

The hour when the gallery was to open, after being expected
with impatience, appeared. I entered into this sanctuary,
and my astonishment surpassed every conception which I had
formed. This saloon, returning into itself, in which splendour
and neatness reigned, together with the deepest stillness,
the dazzling frames, all nearer to the time in which they had
been gilded, the floor polished with bees'-wax, the spaces
more trodden by spectators than used by copyists, imparted
a feeling of solemnity, unique of its kind, which so much the
more resembled the sensation with which one treads a church,
as the adornments of so many a temple, the objects of so much
adoration, seemed here again set up only for the sacred purposes of art. I readily put up with the cursory description
of my conductor; only I requested that I might be allowed
to remain in the outer gallery. Here, to my comfort, I found
myself really at home. I had already seen the works of several artists, others I knew from engravings, others by name.
I did not conceal this, and I thus inspired my conductor with
some confidence; nay, the rapture which I expressed at pieces
where the pencil had gained the victory over nature, delighted
him; for such were the things which principally attracted
me, where the comparison with known nature must necessarily enhance the value of art.

When I again entered my shoemaker's house to dinner, I
scarcely believed my eyes: for I fancied I saw before me a
picture by Ostade, so perfect that one could only hang it up
in the gallery. The position of the objects, the light, the
shadow, the brownish tint of the whole, the magical keeping,
everything that one admires in those pictures, I here saw in
reality. It was the first time that I perceived, in so high a
degree, the faculty which I afterwards exercised with more
consciousness, namely, that of seeing nature with the eyes of
this or that artist, to whose works I had devoted a particular
attention. This faculty has afforded me much enjoyment,

* " Pratische Philosophen, bewusstlose Weltweisen." It is impossible
to give two substantives, as in the original, since this is effected by using
first the word of Greek, then the word of German origin, whereas we
have but one.—*Trans.*

but has also increased the desire zealously to abandon myself, from time to time, to the exercise of a talent which nature seemed to have denied me.

I visited the gallery at all permitted hours, and continued to express too loudly my ecstacy at many precious works. I thus frustrated my laudable purpose of remaining unknown and unnoticed; and whereas only one of the under-keepers had hitherto had intercourse with me, the gallery-inspector, Counsellor Riedel, now also took notice of me, and made me attentive to many things which seemed chiefly to lie within my sphere. I found this excellent man just as active and obliging then, as when I afterwards saw him during many years, and as he shows himself to this day. His image has, for me, interwoven itself so closely with those treasures of art, that I can never regard the two apart; the remembrance of him has even accompanied me to Italy, where, in many large and rich collections, his presence would have been very desirable.

Since, even with strangers and unknown persons, one cannot gaze on such works silently and without mutual sympathy, nay, since the first sight of them is rather adapted, in the highest degree, to open hearts towards each other, I fell there into conversation with a young man who seemed to be residing at Dresden, and to belong to some embassy. He invited me to come in the evening to an inn where a lively company met, and where, by each one's paying a moderate reckoning, one could pass some very pleasant hours.

I repaired thither, but did not find the company; and the waiter somewhat surprised me when he delivered the compliments of the gentleman who made the appointment with me, by which the latter sent an excuse for coming somewhat later, with the addition that I must not take offence at anything that might occur: also, that I should have nothing to pay beyond my own score. I knew not what to make of these words; my father's cobwebs came into my head, and I composed myself to await whatever might befall. The company assembled, my acquaintance introduced me, and I could not be attentive long, without discovering that they were aiming at the mystification of a young man, who showed himself a novice by an obstreperous, assuming deportment: I therefore kept very much on my guard, so that they might not

find delight in selecting me as his fellow. At table this
intention became more apparent to everybody, except to
himself. They drank deeper and deeper, and when a *vivat*
in honour of sweethearts was started, every one solemnly
swore that there should never be another out of those glasses;
they flung them behind them; and this was the signal for
far greater follies. At last I withdrew, very quietly, and the
waiter, while demanding quite a moderate reckoning, requested me to come again, as they did not go on so wildly
every evening. I was far from my lodgings, and it was near
midnight when I reached them. I found the doors unlocked,
everybody was in bed, and one lamp illuminated the narrow
domestic household, where my eye, more and more practised,
immediately perceived the finest picture by Schalken, from
which I could not tear myself away, so that it banished from
me all sleep.

The few days of my residence in Dresden were solely devoted to the picture-gallery. The antiquities still stood in
the pavilion of the great garden, but I declined seeing them,
as well as all the other precious things which Dresden contained; being but too full of the conviction that, even in and
about the collection of paintings much must yet remain hidden from me. Thus I took the excellence of the Italian masters more on trust and in faith, than by pretending to any
insight into them. What I could not look upon as nature,
put in the place of nature, and compare with a known object,
was without effect upon me. It is the material impression
which makes the beginning even to every more elevated
amateurship.

With my shoemaker I lived on very good terms. He was
witty and varied enough, and we often outvied each other in
merry conceits; nevertheless, a man who thinks himself happy,
and desires others to do the same, makes us discontented;
indeed, the repetition of such sentiments produces weariness.
I found myself well occupied, entertained, excited, but
by no means happy; and the shoes from his last would not
fit me. We parted, however, as the best friends; and even
my hostess, on my departure, was not dissatisfied with me.

Shortly before my departure, something else very pleasant was to happen. By the mediation of that young man,
who wished to restore himself to some credit with me, I was

introduced to the Director Von Hagedorn, who with great
kindness showed me his collection, and was highly delighted
with the enthusiasm of the young lover of art. He himself,
as becomes a connoisseur, was quite peculiarly in love with
the pictures which he possessed, and therefore seldom found
in others an interest such as he wished. It gave him particular satisfaction that I was beyond measure pleased with a
picture by Schwanefeld, and that I was not tired of praising
and extolling it in every single part; for landscapes, which
again reminded me of the beautiful clear sky under which I
had grown up—of the vegetable luxuriance of those spots—
and of whatever other favours a warmer climate offers to man,
were just the things that most affected me in the imitation,
while they awakened in me a longing remembrance.

These precious experiences, preparing both mind and sense
for true art, were nevertheless interrupted and damped by one
of the most melancholy sights, by the destroyed and desolate
condition of so many of the streets of Dresden through which
I took my way. The Mohrenstrasse in ruins, and the Church
(*Kreuzkirche*) of the Cross, with its shattered tower, impressed
themselves deeply upon me, and still stand like a gloomy spot
in my imagination. From the cupola of the Lady Church
(*Frankirche*) I saw these pitiable ruins scattered about amid
the beautiful order of the city. Here the clerk commended
to me the art of the architect, who had already fitted up
church and cupola for so undesirable an event, and had built
them bomb-proof. The good sacristan then pointed out to me
the ruins on all sides, and said doubtfully and laconically,
" *The enemy hath done this !* "

Now then, at last, though unwillingly, I returned back to
Leipzig, and found my friends, who were not used to such
digressions in me, in great astonishment, busied with all sorts
of conjectures as to what might be the import of my mysterious
journey. When upon this I told them my story quite in
order, they declared it was only a made-up tale, and saga-
ciously tried to get at the bottom of the riddle which I had
been waggish enough to conceal under my shoemaker-
lodgings.

But could they have looked into my heart, they would have
discovered no waggery there; for the truth of that old proverb, " He that increaseth knowledge increaseth sorrow," had

struck me with all its force; and the more I struggled to
arrange and appropriate to myself what I had seen, the less
I succeeded. I had at last to content myself with a silent
after-operation. Ordinary life carried me away again, and I
at last felt myself quite comfortable when a friendly intercourse, improvement in branches of knowledge which were
suitable for me, and a certain practice of the hand, engaged
me in a manner less important, but more in accordance with
my strength.

Very pleasant and wholesome for me was the connexion
which I formed with the Breitkopf family. BERNHARD
CHRISTOPH BREITKOPF, the proper founder of the family,
who had come to Leipzig as a poor journeyman printer, was
yet living, and occupied the Golden Bear, a respectable house
in the new Newmarket, with Gottsched as an inmate. The
son, Johann Gottlob Immanuel, had already been long married, and was the father of many children. They thought
they could not spend a part of their considerable wealth better
than in putting up, opposite the first house, a large new one,
the Silver Bear, which they built higher and more extensive
than the original house itself. Just at the time of the building I became acquainted with the family. The eldest son
might have been some years older than I was, a well-formed
young man, devoted to music, and practised to play skilfully
on both the piano and the violin. The second, a true, good soul,
likewise musical, enlivened the concerts which were often got
up, no less than his elder brother. They were both kindly disposed towards me, as well as their parents and sisters. I lent
them a helping-hand during the building up and the finishing,
the furnishing and the moving in, and thus formed a conception of much that belongs to such an affair: I also had an
opportunity of seeing Oeser's instructions put in practice. In
the new house, which I had thus seen erected, I was often a
visitor. We had many pursuits in common, and the eldest
son set some of my songs to music, which, when printed, bore
his name, but not mine, and have been little known. I have
selected the best, and inserted them among my other little
poems. The father had invented or perfected musical type.
He permitted me the use of a fine library, which related
principally to the origin and progress of printing, and thus I
gained some knowledge in that department. I found there,

moreover, good copper-plates, which exhibited antiquity, and
advanced on this side also my studies, which were still further
promoted by the circumstance that a considerable collection
of sulphurs had fallen into disorder in moving. I set them
right again as well as I could, and in doing so was compelled
to search Lippert and other authorities. A physician, Doctor
Reichel, likewise an inmate of the house, I consulted from
time to time when I felt, if not sick, yet unwell, and thus we
led together a quiet, pleasant life.

I was now to enter into another sort of connexion in this
house : for the copper-plate engraver, Stock, had moved into
the attic. He was a native of Nuremberg, a very industrious
man, and, in his labours, precise and methodical. He also,
like Geyser, engraved, after Oeser's designs, larger and
smaller plates, which came more and more into vogue for
novels and poems. He etched very neatly, so that his work
came out of the aquafortis almost finished, and but little
touching-up remained to be done with the graver, which he
handled very well. He made an exact calculation how long
a plate would occupy him, and nothing could call him off
from his work if he had not completed the daily task he had
set himself. Thus he sat at a broad work-table, by the great
gable-window, in a very neat and orderly chamber, where his
wife and two daughters afforded him a domestic society. Of
these last, one is happily married, and the other is an excellent artist : they have continued my friends all my life long.
I now divided my time between the upper and lower stories,
and attached myself much to the man, who, together with his
persevering industry, possessed an excellent humour, and was
good-nature itself.

The technical neatness of this branch of art charmed me,
and I associated myself with him to execute something of the
kind. My predilection was again directed towards landscape,
which, while it amused me in my solitary walks, seemed in
itself more attainable and more comprehensible for works of
art than the human figure, which discouraged me. Under his
directions, therefore, I etched, after Thiele and others,
various landscapes, which, although executed by an unprac-
tised hand, produced some effect, and were well received.
The grounding (varnishing) of the plates, the putting in the
high lights, the etching, and at last the biting with aquafortis,

gave me variety of occupation, and I soon got so far that I
could assist my master in many things. I did not lack the
attention necessary for the biting, and I seldom failed in anything; but I had not care enough in guarding against the
deleterious vapours which are generated on such occasions,
and these may have contributed to the maladies which afterwards troubled me for a long time. Amidst such labours,
that everything might be tried, I often made wood-cuts also.
I prepared various little printing-blocks after French patterns,
and many of them were found fit for use.

Let me here make mention of some other men who resided
in Leipzig, or tarried there for a short time. WEISSE, the
custom-house collector of the district, in his best years, cheerful, friendly, and obliging, was loved and esteemed by us.
We would not, indeed, allow his theatrical pieces to be models
throughout, but we suffered ourselves to be carried away by
them, and his operas, set to music by Hiller in an easy style,
gave us much pleasure. SCHIEBLER, of Hamburgh, pursued
the same track; and his *Lisuard and Dariolette* was likewise
favoured by us. ESCHENBURG, a handsome young man, but
little older than we were, distinguished himself advantageously
among the students. ZACHARIE was pleased to spend some
weeks with us, and being introduced by his brother, dined
every day with us at the same table. We rightly deemed it
an honour to gratify our guest in return, by a few extra
dishes, a richer dessert, and choicer wine; for, as a tall, well-
formed, comfortable man, he did not conceal his love of good
eating. LESSING came at a time when we had I know not
what in our heads: it was our good pleasure to go nowhere
on his account, nay, even to avoid the places to which he
came, probably because we thought ourselves too good to
stand at a distance, and could make no pretension to obtain a
closer intimacy with him. This momentary absurdity, which,
however, is nothing rare in presuming and freakish youth,
proved, indeed, its own punishment in the sequel: for I have
never set eyes on that eminent man, who was most highly
esteemed by me.

Notwithstanding all our efforts relative to art and antiquity, we each of us always had WINCKELMANN before our
eyes, whose ability was acknowledged in his fatherland with
enthusiasm. We read his writings diligently, and tried to

make ourselves acquainted with the circumstances under which he had written the first of them. We found in them many views which seemed to have originated with Oeser, even jests and whims after his fashion, and we did not rest until we had formed some general conception of the occasion on which these remarkable and sometimes so enigmatical writings had arisen, though we were not very accurate; for youth likes better to be excited than instructed, and it was not the last time that I was to be indebted to Sibylline leaves for an important step in cultivation.

It was then a fine period in literature, when eminent men were yet treated with respect, although the disputes of Klotz and Lessing's controversies, already indicated that this epoch would soon close. Winckelmann enjoyed an universal, unassailed reverence, and it is known how sensitive he was with regard to anything public which did not seem commensurate with his deeply felt dignity. All the periodical publications joined in his praise, the better class of tourists came back from him instructed and enraptured, and the new views which he gave extended themselves over science and life. The Prince of Dessau had raised himself up to a similar degree of respect. Young, well and nobly minded, he had on his travels and at other times shown himself truly desirable. Winckelmann was in the highest degree delighted with him, and, whenever he mentioned him, loaded him with the handsomest epithets. The laying out of a park, then unique, the taste for architecture, which Von Erdmannsdorf supported by his activity, everything spoke in favour of a prince, who, while he was a shining example for the rest, gave promise of a golden age for his servants and subjects. We young people now learned with rejoicings that Winckelmann would return back from Italy, visit his princely friend, call on Oeser by the way, and so come within our sphere of vision. We made no pretensions to speaking with him, but we hoped to see him; and as at that time of life one willingly changes every occasion into a party of pleasure, we had already agreed upon a journey to Dessau, where, in a beautiful spot, made glorious by art, in a land well governed, and at the same time externally adorned, we thought to lie in wait now here, now there, in order to see with our own eyes these men so highly exalted above us walking about. Oeser himself was quite elated if he only thought of it, and the news of Winckelmann's death fell down into the midst

of us like a thunderbolt from a clear sky. I still remember
the place where I first heard it: it was in the court of the
Pleissenburg, not far from the little gate through which one
used to go up to Oeser's residence. One of my fellow-pupils
met me and told me that Oeser was not to be seen, with the
reason why. This monstrous event * produced a monstrous
effect: there was an universal mourning and lamentation, and
Winckelmann's untimely death sharpened the attention paid to
the value of his life. Perhaps, indeed, the effect of his activity,
if he had continued it to a more advanced age, would probably
not have been so great as it now necessarily became, when, like
many other extraordinary men, he was distinguished by fate
through a strange and calamitous end.

Now, while I was infinitely lamenting the death of Winckelmann, I did not think that I should soon find myself in the
case of being apprehensive about my own life: since, during
all these events, my bodily condition had not taken the most
favourable turn. I had already brought with me from home a
certain touch of hypochondria, which, in this new sedentary
and lounging life, was rather strengthened than diminished.
The pain in the breast, which I had felt from time to time
ever since the accident at Auerstädt, and which after a fall
from horseback had perceptibly increased, made me dejected.
By an unfortunate diet, I destroyed my powers of digestion;
the heavy Merseburg beer clouded my brain; the coffee, which
gave me a peculiarly melancholy tone, especially when taken
with milk after dinner, paralysed my bowels, and seemed completely to suspend their functions, so that I experienced great
uneasiness on this account, yet without being able to embrace
a resolution for a more rational mode of life. My natural disposition, supported by the sufficient strength of youth, fluctuated between the extremes of unrestrained gaiety and melancholy discomfort. Besides this, the epoch of the cold water
bath, which was unconditionally recommended, had then begun.
One was to sleep on a hard bed, only slightly covered, by which
all the usual perspiration was suppressed. These and other
follies, in consequence of some misunderstood suggestions of
Rousseau, would, it was promised, bring us nearer to nature,
and deliver us from the corruption of morals. Now, all the
above, without discrimination, applied with injudicious alternation, were felt by many most injuriously, and I irritated my

* Winckelmann was assassinated.—*Trans.*

happy organization to such a degree, that the particular systems contained within it necessarily broke out at last into a conspiracy and revolution, in order to save the whole.

One night I awoke with a violent hæmorrhage, and had just strength and presence of mind enough to waken my next room neighbour. Dr. Reichel was called in, who assisted me in the most friendly manner, and thus for many days I wavered betwixt life and death; and even the joy of a subsequent improvement was embittered by the circumstance that, during that eruption, a tumour had formed on the left side of the neck, which, after the danger was past, they now first found time to notice. Recovery is, however, always pleasing and delightful, even though it takes place slowly and painfully; and since nature had helped herself with me, I appeared now to have become another man; for I had gained a greater cheerfulness of mind than I had known for a long time, and I was rejoiced to feel my inner self at liberty, although externally a wearisome affliction threatened me.

But what particularly set me up at this time was, to see how many eminent men had, undeservedly, given me their affection. Undeservedly, I say: for there was not one among them to whom I had not been troublesome through contradictory humours, not one whom I had not more than once wounded by morbid absurdity, nay, whom I had not stubbornly avoided for a long time, from a feeling of my own injustice. All this was forgotten; they treated me in the most affectionate manner, and sought, partly in my chamber, partly as soon as I could leave it, to amuse and divert me. They drove out with me, entertained me at their country-houses, and I seemed soon to recover.

Among these friends I name first of all Doctor HERMANN, then senator, afterwards burgomaster of Leipzig. He was among those boarders with whom I had become acquainted through Schlosser, the one with whom an always equable and enduring connexion was maintained. One might well reckon him the most industrious of his academical fellow-citizens. He attended his lectures with the greatest regularity, and his private industry remained always the same. Step by step, without the slightest deviation, I saw him attain his Doctor's degree, and then raise himself to the assessorship, without anything of all this appearing arduous to him, or his having in the least hurried or been too late with anything. The gentleness

of his character attracted me, his instructive conversation held
me fast; indeed I really believe that I took delight in his
methodical industry especially for this reason, because I
thought, by acknowledgments and high esteem, to appropriate
to myself at least a part of a merit of which I could by no
means boast.

He was just as regular in the exercise of his talents and the
enjoyment of his pleasures as in his business. He played the
harpsichord with great skill, drew from nature with feeling,
and stimulated me to do the same; when, in his manner, on
grey paper and with black and white chalk, I used to copy
many a willow-plot on the Pleisse, and many a lovely nook of
those still waters, and at the same time longingly to indulge
in my fancies. He knew how to meet my sometimes comical
disposition with merry jests, and I remember many pleasant
hours which we spent together when he invited me, with mock
solemnity, to a *tête-à-tête* supper, where, with some dignity,
by the light of waxen candles, we ate what they call a council-
hare, which had run into his kitchen as a perquisite of his
place, and with many jokes in the manner of Behrisch, were
pleased to season the meat and heighten the spirit of the wine.
That this excellent man, who is still constantly labouring in
his respectable office, rendered me the most faithful assistance
during a disease, of which there was indeed a foreboding, but
which had not been foreseen in its full extent, that he bestowed
every leisure hour upon me, and by remembrances of former
happy times, contrived to brighten the gloomy moment, I still
acknowledge with the sincerest thanks, and rejoice that after
so long a time I can give them publicly.

Besides this worthy friend, GROENING of Bremen particularly interested himself in me. I had made his acquaintance
only a short time before, and first discovered his good feeling
towards me during my misfortune; I felt the value of this
favour the more warmly, as no one is apt to seek a closer connexion with invalids. He spared nothing to give me pleasure,
to draw me away from musing on my situation, to hold up to
my view and promise me recovery and a wholesome activity in
the nearest future. How often have I been delighted, in the
progress of life, to hear how this excellent man has in the
weightiest affairs shown himself useful, and indeed a blessing
to his native city.

Here, too, it was that friend HORN uninterruptedly brought

into action his love and attention. The whole Breitkopf household, the Stock family, and many others, treated me like a near
relative ; and thus, through the good-will of so many friendly
persons, the feeling of my situation was soothed in the tenderest
manner.

I must here, however, make particular mention of a man,
with whom I first became acquainted at this time, and whose
instructive conversation so far blinded me to the miserable
state in which I was, that I actually forgot it. This was Langer, afterwards librarian at Wolfenbüttel. Eminently learned
and instructed, he was delighted at my voracious hunger after
knowledge, which, with the irritability of sickness, now broke
out into a perfect fever. He tried to calm me by perspicuous
summaries, and I have been very much indebted to his acquaintance, short as it was, since he understood how to guide me in
various ways, and made me attentive whither I had to direct
myself at the present moment. I found myself the more
obliged to this important man, as my intercourse exposed him
to some danger : for when, after Behrisch, he got the situation
of tutor to the young Count Lindenau, the father made it an
express condition with the new Mentor that he should have
no intercourse with me. Curious to become acquainted with
such a dangerous subject, he contrived to see me frequently
by assignation. I soon gained his affection, and he, more prudent than Behrisch, called for me by night, we went walking
together, conversed on interesting things, and at last I accompanied him to the very door of his mistress ; for even this externally severe, earnest, scientific man had not kept free from
the toils of a very amiable lady.

German literature, and with it my own poetical undertakings, had already for some time become strange to me, and as
is usually the result in such an auto-didactic circular course. I
turned back towards the beloved ancients who still constantly,
like distant blue mountains, distinct in their outlines and
masses, but indiscernible in their parts and internal relations,
bounded the horizon of my intellectual wishes. I made an
exchange with Langer, in which I at last played the part of
Glaucus and Diomedes; I gave up to him whole baskets of
German poets and critics, and received in return a number of
Greek authors, the reading of whom was to give me recreation,
even during the most tedious convalescence.

The confidence which new friends repose in each other usually developes itself by degrees. Common occupation and tastes are the first things in which a mutual harmony shows itself; then the mutual communication generally extends over past and present passions, especially over love affairs; but it is a lower depth which opens itself, if the connexion is to be perfected; the religious sentiments, the affairs of the heart which relate to the imperishable, are the things which both establish the foundation and adorn the summit of a friendship.

The Christian religion was wavering between its own historically positive base and a pure deism, which, grounded on morality, was in its turn to lay the foundation of ethics. The diversity of characters and modes of thought here showed itself in infinite gradations, especially when a leading difference was brought into play by the question arising as to how great a share the reason, and how great a share the feelings could and should bear a part in such convictions. The most lively and ingenious men showed themselves, in this instance, like butterflies, who, quite regardless of their caterpillar state, throw away the chrysalis veil in which they have grown up to their organic perfection. Others, more honestly and modestly minded, might be compared to the flowers, which, although they unfold themselves to the most beautiful bloom, yet do not tear themselves from the root, from the mother stalk, nay, rather through this family connexion first bring the desired fruit to maturity. Of this latter class was Langer; for, although a learned man, and eminently versed in books, he would yet give the Bible a peculiar pre-eminence over the other writings which have come down to us, and regard it as a document from which alone we could prove our moral and spiritual pedigree. He belonged to those who cannot conceive an immediate connexion with the great God of the universe; a mediation, therefore, was necessary for him, an analogy to which he thought he could find everywhere, in earthly and heavenly things. His discourse, which was pleasing and consistent, easily found a hearing with a young man who, separated from worldly things by an annoying illness, found it highly desirable to turn the activity of his mind towards the heavenly. Grounded as I was in the Bible, all that was wanted was merely the faith to explain as divine that which I had hitherto esteemed in human fashion,—a belief, the easier for me, since I had made my first acquaintance

with that book as a divine one. To a sufferer, to one who felt
himself delicate, nay, weak, the gospel was therefore welcome,
and even though Langer, with all his faith, was at the same
time a very sensible man, and firmly maintained that one
should not let the feelings prevail, should not let oneself be led
astray into mysticism, I could not have managed to occupy
myself with the New Testament without feeling and enthusiasm.

In such conversations we spent much time, and he grew
so fond of me as an honest and well-prepared proselyte, that
he did not scruple to sacrifice to me many of the hours destined
for his fair one, and even to run the risk of being betrayed and
looked upon unfavourably by his patron, like Behrisch. I returned his affection in the most grateful manner: and if what
he did for me would have been of value at any time, I could
not but regard it, in my present condition, as worthy of the
highest honour.

But as when the concert of our souls is most spiritually
attuned, the rude shrieking tones of the world usually break in
most violently and boisterously, and the contrast which has
gone on exercising a secret control affects us so much the more
sensibly when it comes forward all at once ; thus was I not to
be dismissed from the peripatetic school of my Langer without
having first witnessed an event, strange at least for Leipzig,
namely, a tumult which the students excited, and that on the
following pretence. Some young people had quarrelled with
the city soldiers, and the affair had not gone off without violence. Many of the students combined together to revenge
the injuries inflicted. The soldiers resisted stubbornly, and
the advantage was not on the side of the very discontented
academical citizens. It was now said that respectable persons
had commended and rewarded the conquerors for their valiant
resistance, and by this, the youthful feeling of honour and revenge was mightily excited. It was publicly said that on the
next evening windows would be broken in, and some friends
who brought me word that this was actually taking place, were
obliged to carry me there, for youth and the multitude are
always attracted by danger and tumult. There really began
a strange spectacle. The otherwise open street was lined on
one side with men who, quite quiet, without noise or movement, were waiting to see what would happen. About a dozen
young fellows were walking singly up and down the empty

side-walk, with the greatest apparent composure, but as soon
as they came opposite the marked house, they threw stones at
the windows as they passed by, and this repeatedly as they returned backwards and forwards, as long as the panes would
rattle.   Just as quietly as this was done, all at last dispersed,
and the affair had no further consequences.

With such a ringing echo of university exploits, I left Leipzig in the September of 1768, in a comfortable hired coach,
and in the company of some respectable persons of my acquaintance.   In the neighbourhood of Auerstädt I thought of that
previous accident; but I could not forebode that which many
years afterwards would threaten me from thence with still
greater danger; just as little as in Gotha, where we had the
castle shown to us. I could think in the great hall adorned with
stucco figures, that so much favour and affection would befall
me on that very spot.

The nearer I approached my native city, the more I recalled
to myself doubtingly the circumstances, prospects, and hopes
with which I had left home, and it was a very disheartening
feeling that I now returned, as it were, like one shipwrecked.
Yet since I had not very much with which to reproach myself,
I contrived to compose myself tolerably well; however, the
welcome was not without emotion.   The great vivacity of my
nature, excited and heightened by sickness, caused an impassioned scene.   I might have looked worse than I myself knew,
since for a long time I had not consulted a looking-glass; and
who does not become used to himself?   Enough, they silently
resolved to communicate many things to me only by degrees,
and before all things to let me have some repose both bodily
and mental.

My sister immediately associated herself with me, and as
previously, from her letters, so I could now more in detail
and accurately understand the circumstances and situation of
the family.   My father had, after my departure, concentrated
all his didactic taste upon my sister, and in a house completely
shut up, rendered secure by peace, and even cleared of lodgers,
he had cut off from her almost every means of looking about
and recreating herself abroad.   She had by turns to pursue
and work at French, Italian, and English, besides which he
compelled her to practise a great part of the day on the harpsichord.   Her writing also could not be neglected, and I had

already remarked that he had directed her correspondence with
me, and had let his doctrines come to me through her pen.
My sister was and still continued to be an undefinable being,
the most singular mixture of strength and weakness, of stubbornness and pliability, which qualities operated now united,
now isolated by will and inclination. Thus she had, in a manner which seemed to me fearful, turned the hardness of her
character against her father, whom she did not forgive for having hindered or embittered to her so many innocent joys for
these three years, and of his good and excellent qualities she
would not acknowledge even one. She did all that he commanded and arranged, but in the most unamiable manner in
the world. She did it in the established routine, but nothing
more and nothing less. From love or a desire to please she
accommodated herself to nothing, so that this was one of the
first things about which my mother complained in a private
conversation with me. But since love was as essential to my
sister as to any human being, she turned her affection wholly
on me. Her care in nursing and entertaining me absorbed all
her time; her female companions, who were swayed by her
without her intending it, had likewise to contrive all sorts of
things to be pleasing and consolatory to me. She was inventive in cheering me up, and even developed some germs of
comical humour which I had never known in her, and which
became her very well. There soon arose between us a coterie-
language, by which we could converse before all people without
their understanding us, and she often used this gibberish with
great pertness in the presence of our parents.

My father was personally in tolerable comfort. He was in
good health, spent a great part of the day in the instruction of
my sister, wrote at the description of his travels, and was longer
in tuning his lute than in playing on it. He concealed at the
same time, as well as he could, his vexation at finding instead
of a stout active son, who ought now to take his degree and
run through the prescribed course of life, an invalid who seemed
to suffer still more in soul than in body. He did not conceal
his wish that they would be expeditious with my cure; but
one was forced to be specially on one's guard in his presence
against hypochondriacal expressions, because he could then become passionate and bitter.

My mother, by nature very lively and cheerful, spent under

U

these circumstances very tedious days. Her little housekeeping was soon provided for. The mind of the good lady, internally never unoccupied, wished to find an interest in something,
and that which was nearest at hand was religion, which she
embraced the more fondly as her most eminent female friends
were cultivated and hearty worshippers of God. At the head
of these stood Fräulein von Klettenberg. She is the same
person from whose conversations and letters arose the " Con-
fessions of a Beautiful Soul," which are found inserted in
" Wilhelm Meister." She was slenderly formed, of the middle
size : a hearty natural demeanour had been made still more
pleasing by the manners of the world and the court. Her very
neat attire reminded of the dress of the Hernhutt ladies.
Her serenity and peace of mind never left her. She looked
upon her sickness as a necessary element of her transient
earthly existence ; she suffered with the greatest patience, and,
in painless intervals, was lively and talkative. Her favourite,
nay, indeed, perhaps her only conversation, was on the moral
experiences which a man who observes himself can form in
himself ; to which was added the religious views which, in a
very graceful manner, nay, with genius, came under her consideration as natural and supernatural. It scarcely needs more
to recall back to the friends of such representations, that complete delineation composed from the very depths of her soul.
Owing to the very peculiar course which she had taken from her
youth upwards, the distinguished rank in which she had been
born and educated, and the liveliness and originality of her
mind, she did not agree very well with the other ladies who had
set out on the same road to salvation. Frau Griesbach, the chief
of them, seemed too severe, too dry, too learned ; she knew,
thought, comprehended more than the others, who contented
themselves with the development of their feelings, and she was
therefore burdensome to them, because every one neither could
nor would carry with her so great an apparatus on the road to
bliss. But for this reason the most of them were indeed somewhat monotonous, since they confined themselves to a certain
terminology which might well have been compared to that of
the later sentimentalists. Fräulein von Klettenberg led her
way between both extremes, and seemed, with some self-complacency, to see her own reflection in the image of Count Zin-
zendorf, whose opinions and actions bore witness to a higher

birth and more distinguished rank. Now she found in me what
she needed, a lively young creature, striving after an unknown
happiness, who, although he could not think himself an extraordinary sinner, yet found himself in no comfortable condition,
and was perfectly healthy neither in body nor soul. She was
delighted with what nature had given me, as well as with
much which I had gained for myself. And if she conceded to
me many advantages, this was by no means humiliating to her:
for, in the first place, she never thought of emulating one of
the male sex, and secondly, she believed that in regard to religious culture she was very much in advance of me. My disquiet, my impatience, my striving, my seeking, investigating,
musing, and wavering, she interpreted in her own way, and
did not conceal from me her conviction, but assured me in plain
terms that all this proceeded from my having no reconciled God.
Now I had believed from my youth upwards that I stood on
very good terms with my God, nay, I even fancied to myself,
according to various experiences, that He might even be in
arrears to me ; and I was daring enough to think that I had
something to forgive Him. This presumption was grounded on
my infinite good-will, to which, as it seemed to me, He should
have given better assistance. It may be imagined how often
I and my female friend fell into disputes on this subject, which,
however, always terminated in the friendliest way, and often,
like my conversations with the old rector, with the remark :
" that I was a foolish fellow, for whom many allowances must
be made."

I was much troubled with the tumour in my neck, as the
physician and surgeon wished first to disperse this excrescence,
afterwards, as they said, to draw it to a head, and at last
thought good to open it; so for a long time I had to suffer
more from inconvenience than pain, although towards the end
of the cure, the continual touching with lunar caustic and other
corrosive substances could not but give me very disagreeable
prospects for every fresh day. The physician and surgeon
both belonged to the Pious Separatists, although both were of
highly different natural characters. The surgeon, a slender,
well-built man, of easy and skilful hand, was unfortunately
somewhat hectic, but endured his condition with truly Christian patience, and did not suffer his disease to perplex him in
his profession. The physician was an inexplicable, sly-look-

ing, friendly-speaking, and, moreover, abstruse man, who had
gained himself quite a peculiar confidence in the pious circle.
Active and attentive, he was consoling to the sick; but, more
than by all this, he extended his practice by the gift of showing in the background some mysterious medicines prepared by
himself, of which no one could speak, since, with us, the physicians were strictly prohibited from making up their own prescriptions. With certain powders, which may have been some
kind of digestive, he was not so reserved; but that powerful
salt, which could only be applied in the greatest danger, was
only mentioned among believers, although no one had yet seen
it or traced its effects.   To excite and strengthen our faith in
the possibility of such an universal remedy, the physician,
wherever he found any susceptibility, had recommended certain chemico-alchemical books to his patients, and given them
to understand that by one's own study of them, one could well
attain this treasure for oneself; which was the more necessary, as the mode of its preparation, both for physical and
especially for moral reasons, could not be well communicated;
nay, that in order to comprehend, produce and use this great
work, one must know the secrets of nature in connexion, since it
was not a particular but an universal remedy, and could indeed
be produced under different forms and shapes.   My friend had
listened to these enticing words. The health of the body was too
nearly allied to the health of the soul; and could a greater
benefit, a greater mercy be shown towards others, than by appro-
priating to oneself a remedy by which so many sufferings could
be assuaged, so many a danger averted? She had already secretly
studied Welling's *Opus mago-cabalisticum*, for which, however,
as the author himself immediately darkens and removes the
light he imparts, she was looking about for a friend who, in this
alternation of glare and gloom, might bear her company.   It
needed small incitement to inoculate me also with this disease.
I procured the work, which, like all writings of this kind,
could trace its pedigree in a direct line up to the Neo-Platonic
school.   My chief labour in this book was most accurately to
notice the dark hints by which the author refers from one passage to another, and thus promises to reveal what he conceals;
and to mark down on the margin the number of the page where
such passages as should explain each other were to be found.
But even thus the book still remained dark and unintelligible

enough; except that one at last studied oneself into a certain terminology, and, by using it according to one's own fancy, believed that one was at any rate saying, if not understanding, something. The before-mentioned work makes very honourable mention of its predecessors, and we were incited to investigate those original sources themselves. We turned to the works of Theophrastus, Paracelsus and Basilius Valentinus; as well as to those of Helmont, Starkey, and others whose doctrines and directions, resting more or less on nature and imagination, we endeavoured to see into and follow out. I was particularly pleased with the *Aurea Catena Homeri*, in which nature, though perhaps in fantastical fashion, is represented in a beautiful combination; and thus sometimes by ourselves, sometimes together, we employed much time on these singularities, and spent the evenings of a long winter, during which I was compelled to keep my chamber, very agreeably, since we three, my mother being included, were more delighted with these secrets than we could have been at their elucidation.

In the meantime a very severe trial was preparing for me; for a disturbed, and one might even say, for certain moments, destroyed digestion, excited such symptoms that, in great tribulation, I thought I should lose my life, and none of the remedies applied would produce any further effect. In this last extremity, my distressed mother constrained the embarrassed physician with the greatest vehemence to come out with his universal medicine; after a long refusal, he hastened home at the dead of night, and returned with a little glass of crystallized dry salt, which was dissolved in water, and swallowed by the patient. It had a decidedly alkaline taste. The salt was scarcely taken than my situation appeared relieved, and from that moment the disease took a turn which, by degrees, led to my recovery. I cannot say how far this strengthened and enhanced our faith in our physician, and our industry to make ourselves partakers of such a treasure.

My friend, who, without parents or brothers and sisters, lived in a large, well-situated house, had already before this begun to purchase herself a little air-furnace, alembics and retorts of moderate size; and, in accordance with the hints of Welling, and the significant signs of our physician and master, operated principally on iron, in which the most healing powers were said to be concealed, if one only knew how to open it.

And as the volatile salt which must be produced made a great figure in all the writings with which we were acquainted, so, for these operations, alkalies also were required, which, while they flowed away into the air, were to unite with these super-terrestrial things, and at last produce *per se*, a mysterious and excellent neutral salt.

Scarcely was I in some measure recovered, and, favoured by the change in the season, able once more to occupy my old gable-chamber, than I also began to provide myself with a little apparatus. A small air-furnace with a sand-bath was prepared, and I very soon learned to change the glass alembics, with a piece of burning match-cord, into vessels in which the different mixtures were to be evaporated. Now were the strange ingredients of the macrocosm and microcosm handled in an odd, mysterious manner, and before all I attempted to produce neutral salts in an unheard-of way. But what busied me most, for a long time, was the so-called *Liquor Silicum* (flint-juice), which is made by melting down pure quartz-flint with a proper proportion of alkali, whence results a transparent glass, which melts away on exposure to the air, and exhibits a beautiful clear fluidity. Whoever has once prepared this himself, and seen it with his own eyes, will not blame those who believe in a maiden earth, and in the possibility of producing further effects upon it by means of it. I had acquired a peculiar dexterity in preparing this *Liquor Silicum*; the fine white flints which are found in the Maine furnished a perfect material for it; and I was not wanting in the other requisites, nor in diligence. But I became weary at last, because I could not but remark that the flinty substance was by no means so closely combined with the salt as I had philosophically imagined; for it very easily separated itself again, and this most beautiful mineral fluidity, which, to my greatest astonishment, had sometimes appeared in the form of an animal jelly, always deposited a powder, which I was forced to pronounce the finest flint dust, but which gave not the least sign of anything productive in its nature, from which one could have hoped to see this maiden earth pass into the maternal state.

Strange and unconnected as these operations were, I yet learned many things from them. I paid strict attention to all the crystallizations that might occur, and became acquainted with the external forms of many natural things, and inasmuch as I well knew that in modern times chemical subjects were treated more methodically, I wished to get a general conception of them, although, as a half-adept, I had very little respect for the apothecaries and all those who operated with common fire. However, the chemical *Compendium* of Boerhaave attracted me powerfully, and led me on to read several of his writings, in which (since, moreover, my tedious illness had inclined me towards medical subjects,) I found an inducement to study also the *Aphorisms* of this excellent man, which I was glad to stamp upon my mind and in my memory.

Another employment, somewhat more human, and by far more useful for my cultivation at the moment, was reading through the letters which I had written home from Leipzig. Nothing reveals more with respect to ourselves, than when we again see before us that which has proceeded from us years before, so that we can now consider ourselves as an object of contemplation. Only, in truth, I was then too young, and the epoch which was represented by those papers was still too near. As in our younger years we do not in general easily cast off a certain self-complacent conceit, this especially shows itself in despising what we have been but a little time before; for while, indeed, we perceive, as we advance from step to step, that those things which we regard as good and excellent in ourselves and others do not stand their ground, we think we can best extricate ourselves from this dilemma by ourselves throwing away what we cannot preserve. So it was with me also. For as in Leipzig I had gradually learned to set little value on my childish labours, so now my academical course seemed to me likewise of small account, and I did not understand that for this very reason it must be of great value to me, as it elevated me to a higher degree of observation and insight. My father had carefully collected and sewed together my letters to him, as well as those to my sister; nay, he had even corrected them with attention, and improved the mistakes both in writing and in grammar.

What first struck me in these letters was their exterior; I was shocked at an incredible carelessness in the handwriting, which extended from October, 1765, to the middle of the following January. But, in the middle of March, there appeared

all at once a quite compressed, orderly hand, such as I used
formerly to employ in writing for a prize. My astonishment
at this resolved itself into gratitude towards the good Gellert,
who, as I now well remembered, whenever we handed in our
essays to him, represented to us, in his hearty tone of voice,
that it was our sacred duty to practise our hand as much,
nay, more than our style. He repeated this as often as any
scrawled, careless writing came into his sight; on which occasion he often said that he would much like to make a good
hand of his pupils the principal end in his instructions; the
more so as he had often remarked that a good hand led the
way to a good style.

I could further notice that the French and English passages
in my letters, although not free from blunders, were nevertheless written with facility and freedom. These languages
I had likewise continued to practise in my correspondence
with George Schlosser, who was still at Treptow, and I had
remained in constant communication with him, by which I
was instructed in many secular affairs (for things did not
always turn out with him quite as he had hoped), and acquired
an ever increasing confidence in his earnest, noble way of
thinking.

Another consideration which could not escape me in reading through these letters, was that my good father, with the
best intentions, had done me a special mischief, and had led
me into that odd way of life into which I had fallen at last.
He had, namely, repeatedly warned me against card-playing;
but Fran Hofrath Böhme, as long as she lived, contrived to
persuade me, after her own fashion, by declaring that my
father's warnings were only against the abuse. Now as I
likewise saw the advantages of it in society, I easily suffered
myself to be led by her. I had indeed the sense of play, but
not the spirit of play; I learned all games easily and rapidly,
but I could never keep up the proper attention for a whole
evening. Therefore, when I began very well, I invariably
failed at the end, and made myself and others lose; through
which I went off, always out of humour, either to the supper-
table or out of the company. Scarcely was Madame Böhme
dead, who, moreover, had no longer kept me in practice
during her tedious illness, than my father's doctrine gained
force; I at first excused myself from the card-tables, and as

they now did not know what else to do with me, I became
even more of a burden to myself than to others, and declined
the invitations, which then became more rare, and at last
ceased altogether. Play, which is much to be recommended
to young people, especially to those who have a practical
sense, and wish to look about in the world for themselves,
could never, indeed, become a passion with me; for I never
got further, though I might play as long as I would. Had
any one given me a general view of the subject, and made me
observe how here certain signs and more or less of chance
form a kind of material on which judgment and activity
can exercise themselves—had any one made me see several
games at once, I might sooner have become reconciled. With
all this, at the time of which I am now speaking, I had come
to the conviction, from the above considerations, that one
should not avoid social games, but should rather strive after a
certain dexterity in them. Time is infinitely long, and each
day is a vessel into which a great deal may be poured, if one
will actually fill it up.

Thus variously was I occupied in my solitude; the more
so, as the departed spirits of the different tastes to which
I had from time to time devoted myself, had an opportunity
to reappear. I thus went again to drawing; and as I always
wished to labour directly from nature, or rather from reality,
I made a picture of my chamber, with its furniture, and the
persons who were in it; and when this no more amused me,
I represented all sorts of town-tales, which were told at the
time, and in which interest was taken. All this was not
without character and a certain taste, but unfortunately the
figures lacked proportion and the proper vigour, besides which
the execution was extremely misty. My father, who continued
to take pleasure in these things, wished to have them more
distinct; everything must be finished and properly completed.
He therefore had them mounted and surrounded with ruled
lines; nay, the painter Morgenstern, his domestic artist—the
same who afterwards made himself known, and indeed famous,
by his church-views—had to insert the perspective lines of the
rooms and chambers, which then, indeed, stood in pretty harsh
contrast with those cloudy-looking figures. In this manner
he thought constantly to compel me to greater accuracy, and,
to please him, I drew various objects of still life, in which,

since the originals stood as patterns before me, I could work with
more distinctness and precision. At last I took it into my head
to etch once more. I had composed a tolerably interesting
landscape, and felt myself very happy when I could look out
for the old receipts given me by Stock, and could, at my work,
call to mind those pleasant times. I soon bit the plate and
had a proof taken. Unluckily the composition was without
light and shade, and I now tormented myself to bring in
both; but as it was not quite clear to me what was really
the essential point, I could not finish. Up to this time I
had been quite well, after my own fashion; but now a
disease attacked me which had never troubled me before.
My throat, namely, had become completely sore, and particularly what is called the *uvula* very much inflamed; I could only
swallow with great pain, and the physicians did not know what
to make of it. They tormented me with gargles and hair-
pencils, but could not free me from my misery. At last it
struck me that I had not been careful enough in the biting
of my plates, and that by often and passionately repeating it,
I had contracted this disease, and had always revived and increased it. To the physicians this cause was plausible and very
soon certain on my leaving my etching and biting, and that so
much the more readily as the attempt had by no means turned
out well, and I had more reason to conceal than to exhibit my
labours; for which I consoled myself the more easily, as I
very soon saw myself free from the troublesome disease.
Upon this I could not refrain from the reflection that my similar occupations at Leipzig might have greatly contributed to
those diseases from which I had suffered so much. It is, indeed, a tedious, and withal a melancholy business to take too
much care of ourselves, and of what injures and benefits us;
but there is no question but that with the wonderful idiosyn-
crasy of human nature on the one side, and the infinite variety
in the mode of life and pleasure on the other, it is a wonder that
the human race has not worn itself out long ago. Human nature
appears to possess a peculiar kind of toughness and many-
sidedness, since it subdues everything which approaches it, or
which it takes into itself, and if it cannot assimilate, at least
makes it indifferent. In case of any great excess, indeed, it
must yield to the elements in spite of all resistance, as the
many endemic diseases and the effects of brandy convince

us. Could we, without being morbidly anxious, keep watch over ourselves as to what operates favourably or unfavourably upon us in our complicated civil and social life, and would we leave off what is actually pleasant to us as an enjoyment, for the sake of the evil consequences, we should thus know how to remove with ease many an inconvenience which, with a constitution otherwise sound, often troubles us more than even a disease. Unfortunately, it is in dietetics as in morals; we cannot see into a fault till we have got rid of it: by which nothing is gained, for the next fault is not like the preceding one, and therefore cannot be recognised under the same form.

In reading through those letters which had been written from Leipzig to my sister, this remark, among others, could not escape me,—that from the very beginning of my academical course, I had esteemed myself very clever and wise, since, as soon as I had learned anything, I put myself in the place of the professor, and so became didactic on the spot. I was amused to see how I had immediately applied to my sister whatever Gellert had imparted or advised in his lectures, without seeing that both in life and in books, a thing may be proper for a young man without being suitable for a young lady; and we both together made merry over these mimicries. The poems also which I had composed in Leipzig were already too poor for me; and they seemed to me cold, dry, and in respect to that which was meant to express the state of the human heart or mind, too superficial. This induced me, now that I was to leave my father's house once more, and go to a second university, again to decree a great high *auto da fé* against my labours. Several commenced plays, some of which had reached the third or the fourth act, while others had only the plot fully made out, together with many other poems, letters, and papers, were given over to the fire, and scarcely anything was spared except the manuscript by Behrisch, *Die Laune des Verliebten* and *Die Mitschuldigen*, which last I constantly went on improving with peculiar affection, and, as the piece was already complete, I again worked over the plot, to make it more bustling and intelligible. Lessing, in the first two acts of his *Minna*, had set up an unattainable model of the way in which a drama should be developed, and nothing was to me of greater concern than to enter thoroughly into his mind and his views.

The recital of whatever moved, excited, and occupied me
at this time, is already circumstantial enough; but I must
nevertheless again recur to that interest with which super-
sensuous things had inspired me, of which I, once for all, so
far as might be possible, undertook to form some notion.

I experienced a great influence from an important work
that fell into my hands; it was Arnold's *History of the Church
and of Heretics*. This man is not merely a reflective histo-
rian, but at the same time pious and feeling. His sentiments
chimed in very well with mine, and what particularly delighted me in his work was, that I received a more favourable
notion of many heretics, who had been hitherto represented to
me as mad or impious. The spirit of contradiction and the love
of paradoxes stick fast in us all. I diligently studied the different opinions, and as I had often enough heard it said that
every man has his own religion at last, so nothing seemed
more natural to me than that I should form mine too, and this
I did with much satisfaction. The Neo-Platonism lay at the
foundation; the hermetical, the mystical, the cabalistic, also
contributed their share, and thus I built for myself a world
that looked strange enough.

I could well represent to myself a Godhead which has gone
on producing itself from all eternity; but as production cannot be conceived without multiplicity, so it must of necessity have immediately appeared to itself as a Second, which we
recognise under the name of the Son; now these two must
continue the act of producing, and again appear to themselves
in a Third, which was just as substantial, living, and eternal as
the Whole. With these, however, the circle of the Godhead was
complete, and it would not have been possible for them to produce another perfectly equal to them. But since, however, the
work of production always proceeded, they created a fourth,
which already fostered in himself a contradiction, inasmuch as
it was, like them, unlimited, and yet at the same time was to
be contained in them and bounded by them. Now this was
Lucifer, to whom the whole power of creation was committed
from this time, and from whom all other beings were to proceed. He immediately displayed his infinite activity by creating the whole body of angels; all, again, after his own likeness,
unlimited, but contained in him and bounded by him. Surrounded by such a glory, he forgot his higher origin, and

believed that he could find himself in himself, and from this first ingratitude sprang all that does not seem to us in accordance with the will and purposes of the Godhead. Now the more he concentrated himself within himself, the more painful must it have become to him, as well as to all the spirits whose sweet uprising to their origin he had embittered. And so that happened which is intimated to us under the form of the Fall of the Angels. One part of them concentrated itself with Lucifer, the other turned itself again to its origin. From this concentration of the whole creation, for it had proceeded out of Lucifer, and was forced to follow him, sprang all that we perceive under the form of matter, which we figure to ourselves as heavy, solid, and dark, but which, since it is descended, if not even immediately, yet by filiation, from the Divine Being, is just as unlimited, powerful, and eternal as its sire and grandsire. Since now the whole mischief, if we may call it so, merely arose through the one-sided direction of Lucifer, the better half was indeed wanting to this creation; for it possessed all that is gained by concentration, while it lacked all that can be effected by expansion alone; and so the whole creation could have destroyed itself by everlasting concentration, could have annihilated itself with its father Lucifer, and have lost all its claims to an equal eternity with the Godhead. This condition the Elohim contemplated for a time, and they had their choice, to wait for those Æons, in which the field would again have become clear, and space would be left them for a new creation; or, if they would, to seize upon that which existed already, and supply the want, according to their own eternity. Now they chose the latter, and by their mere will supplied in an instant the whole want which the consequence of Lucifer's undertaking drew after it. They gave to the Eternal Being the faculty of expanding itself, of moving itself towards them; the peculiar pulse of life was again restored, and Lucifer himself could not avoid its effects. This is the epoch when that appeared which we know as light, and when that began which we are accustomed to designate by the word creation. Greatly now as this multiplied itself by progressive degrees, through the continually working vital power of the Elohim, still a being was wanting who might be able to restore the original connexion with the Godhead: and thus man was produced, who in all things was to be similar, yea, equal to

the Godhead ; but thereby, in effect, found himself once more
in the situation of Lucifer, that of being at once unlimited and
bounded ; and, since this contradiction was to manifest itself in
him through all the categories of existence, and a perfect consciousness, as well as a decided will, was to accompany his
various conditions, it was to be foreseen that he must be at
the same time the most perfect and the most imperfect, the
most happy and the most unhappy creature.   It was not long
before he, too, completely played the part of Lucifer.   True
ingratitude is the separation from the benefactor, and thus
that fall was manifest for the second time, although the whole
creation is nothing and was nothing but a falling from and
returning to the original.

One easily sees how the Redemption is not only decreed
from eternity, but is considered as eternally necessary, nay,
that it must ever renew itself through the whole time of generation* and existence.   In this view of the subject, nothing is
more natural than for the Divinity himself to take the form of
man, which had already prepared itself as a veil, and to share
his fate for a short time, in order, by this assimilation, to
enhance his joys and alleviate his sorrows.   The history of all
religions and philosophies teaches us that this great truth, indispensable for man, has been handed down by different nations,
in different times, in various ways, and even in strange fables
and images, in accordance with their limited knowledge;
enough, if it only be acknowledged that we find ourselves in
a condition which, even if it seems to drag us down and oppress
us, yet gives us opportunity, nay, even makes it our duty, to
raise ourselves up, and to fulfil the purposes of the Godhead
in this manner, that while we are compelled on the one hand
to concentrate ourselves (*uns zu verselbsten*), we, on the other
hand, do not omit to expand ourselves (*uns zu entselbstigen*) in
regular pulsation.†

* " Das Werden," the state of becoming, as distinguished from that of
being.   The word, which is most useful to the Germans, can never be rendered properly in English.—*Trans.*

† If we could make use of some such verbs as " inself " and " unself,"
we should more accurately render this passage.—*Trans.*

NINTH BOOK.

'THE heart is often affected, moreover, to the advantage of different, but especially of social and refined virtues, and the more tender sentiments are excited and unfolded in it. Many touches, in particular, will impress themselves, which give the young reader an insight into the more hidden corner of the human heart and its passions—a knowledge which is more worth than all Latin and Greek, and of which Ovid was a very excellent master. But yet it is not on this account that the classic poets, and therefore Ovid, are placed in the hands of youth. We have from the kind Creator a variety of mental powers, to which we must not neglect giving their proper culture in our earliest years, and which cannot be cultivated either by logic or metaphysics, Latin or Greek. We have an imagination, before which, since it should not seize upon the very first conceptions that chance to present themselves, we ought to place the fittest and most beautiful images, and thus accustom and practise the mind to recognise and love the beautiful everywhere, and in nature itself, under its determined, true, and also in its finer features. A great quantity of conceptions and general knowledge is necessary to us, as well for the sciences as for daily life, which can be learned out of no compendium. Our feelings, affections, and passions should be advantageously developed and purified."

This important passage, which is found in the *Universal German Library*, was not the only one of its kind. Similar principles and similar views manifested themselves in many directions. They made upon us lively youths a very great impression, which had the more decided effect, as it was strengthened besides by Wieland's example; for the works of his second brilliant period clearly showed that he had formed himself according to such maxims. And what more could we desire? Philosophy, with its abstruse questions, was set aside—the classic languages, the acquisition of which is accompanied by so much drudgery, one saw thrust into the

background—the compendiums, about the sufficiency of which
Hamlet had already whispered a doubtful word into the ear
came more and more into suspicion. We were directed to
the contemplation of an active life, which we were so fond of
leading, and to the knowledge of the passions which we partly
felt, partly anticipated, in our own bosoms, and which, if
though they had been rebuked formerly, now appeared to us as
something important and dignified, because they were to be the
chief object of our studies, and the knowledge of them was extolled as the most excellent means of cultivating our mental
powers. Besides this, such a mode of thought was quite in
accordance with my own conviction, nay, with my poetical
mode of treatment. I therefore, without opposition, after I
had thwarted so many good designs, and seen so many fair
hopes vanish, reconciled myself to my father's intention of
sending me to Strasburg, where I was promised a cheerful
gay life, while I should prosecute my studies, and at last take
my degree.

In spring I felt my health, but still more my youthful
spirits, again restored, and once more longed to be out of my
father's house, though with reasons far different from those on
the first time. The pretty chambers and spots where I had
suffered so much had become disagreeable to me, and with
my father himself there could be no pleasant relation. I
could not quite pardon him for having manifested more impatience than was reasonable at the relapse of my disease, and
at my tedious recovery ; nay, for having, instead of comfort-
ing me by forbearance, frequently expressed himself in a cruel
manner, about that which lay in no man's hand, as if it depended only on the will. And he, too, was in various ways
hurt and offended by me.

For young people bring back from the university general
ideas, which, indeed, is quite right and good ; but because
they fancy themselves very wise in this, they apply them as
a standard to the objects that occur, which must then, for the
most part, lose by the comparison. Thus I had gained a general
notion of architecture, and of the arrangement and decoration
of houses, and imprudently, in conversation, had applied this
to our own house. My father had designed the whole arrangement of it, and carried through the building with great perseverance, and, considering that it was to be exclusively a

residence for himself and his family, nothing could be objected
to it, in this taste, also, very many of the houses in Frankfort were built. An open staircase ran up through the house,
and touched upon large ante-rooms, which might very well
have been chambers themselves, as, indeed, we always passed
the fine season in them. But this pleasant, cheerful existence
for a single family—this communication from above to below
—became the greatest inconvenience as soon as several parties
occupied the house, as we had but too well experienced on
the occasion of the French quartering. For that painful
scene with the king's lieutenant would not have happened,
nay, my father would even have felt all those disagreeable
matters less, if, after the Leipzig fashion, our staircase had
run close along the side of the house, and a separate door had
been given to each story. This style of building I once
praised highly for its advantages, and showed my father the
possibility of altering his staircase also; whereupon he fell
into an incredible passion, which was the more violent as, a
short time before, I had found fault with some scrolled looking-glass frames, and rejected certain Chinese hangings. A
scene ensued, which, indeed, was again hushed up and
smothered, but it hastened my journey to the beautiful Alsace,
which I accomplished in the newly-contrived comfortable
diligence, without delay, and in a short time.

I alighted at the Ghost (*Geist*) tavern, and hastened at
once to satisfy my most earnest desire and to approach the
minster, which had long since been pointed out to me by
fellow-travellers, and had been before my eyes for a great
distance. When I first perceived this Colossus through the
narrow lanes, and then stood too near before it, in the truly
confined little square, it made upon me an impression quite of
its own kind, which I, being unable to analyse it on the spot,
carried with me only indistinctly for this time, as I hastily
ascended the building, so as not to neglect the beautiful moment of a high and cheerful sun, which was to disclose to me
at once the broad, rich land.

And now, from the platform, I saw before me the beautiful
region in which I should for a long time live and reside: the
handsome city, the wide-spreading meadows around it, thickly
set and interwoven with magnificent trees, that striking
richness of vegetation which follows in the windings of the

x

Rhine, marks its banks, islands, and aits. Nor is the level ground, stretching down from the south, and watered by the Iller, less adorned with varied green. Even westward, towards the mountains, there are many low grounds which afford quite as charming a view of wood and meadow-growth, just as the northern and more hilly part is intersected by innumerable little brooks, which promote a rapid vegetation everywhere. If one imagines, between these luxuriant outstretched meads, between these joyously scattered groves, all land adapted for tillage, excellently prepared, verdant, and ripening, and the best and richest spots marked by hamlets and farm-houses, and this great and immeasurable plain, prepared for man, like a new paradise, bounded far and near by mountains partly cultivated, partly overgrown with woods; one will then conceive the rapture with which I blessed my fate, that it had destined me, for some time, so beautiful a dwelling-place.

Such a fresh glance into a new land in which we are to abide for a time, has still the peculiarity, both pleasant and foreboding, that the whole lies before us like an unwritten tablet. As yet no sorrows and joys which relate to ourselves are recorded upon it; this cheerful, varied, animated plain is still mute for us; the eye is only fixed on the objects so far as they are intrinsically important, and neither affection nor passion have especially to render prominent this or that spot. But a presentiment of the future already disquiets the young heart, and an unsatisfied craving secretly demands that which is to come and may come, and which, at all events, whether for good or ill, will imperceptibly assume the character of the spot in which we find ourselves.

Descended from the height, I still tarried awhile before the face of the venerable pile; but what I could not quite clearly make out, either the first or the following time, was that I regarded this miracle as a monster, which must have terrified me, if it had not, at the same time, appeared to me comprehensible by its regularity, and even pleasing in its finish. Yet I by no means busied myself with meditating on this contradiction, but suffered a monument so astonishing quietly to work upon me by its presence.

I took small, but well-situated and pleasant lodgings, on the summer side of the Fish-market, a fine long street, where

the everlasting motion came to the assistance of every unoccupied moment. I then delivered my letters of introduction,
and found among my patrons a merchant who, with his family,
was devoted to those pious opinions sufficiently known to me,
although, as far as regarded external worship, he had not
separated from the Church. He was a man of intelligence
withal, and by no means hypocritical in his actions. The
company of boarders which was recommended to me, and,
indeed, I to it, was very agreeable and entertaining. A couple
of old maids had long kept up this boarding-house with regularity and good success; there might have been about ten
persons, older and younger. Of these latter, one named
MEYER, a native of Lindau, is most vividly present to me.
From his form and face he might have been considered one of
the handsomest of men, if, at the same time, he had not had
something of the sloven in his whole appearance. In like
manner his splendid natural talents were deformed by an incredible levity, and his excellent temper by an unbounded
dissoluteness. He had an open, joyous face, more round than
oval; the organs of the senses, the eyes, nose, mouth, and
ears, could be called rich; they showed a decided fulness,
without being too large. The mouth was particularly charming, from the curling lips, and his whole physiognomy had the
peculiar expression of a rake, from the circumstance that his
eyebrows met across his nose, which, in a handsome face,
always produces a pleasant expression of sensuality. By his
jovialness, sincerity, and good-nature, he made himself beloved by all. His memory was incredible; attention at the
lectures cost him nothing; he retained all that he heard, and
was intellectual enough to take some interest in everything,
and this the more easily, as he was studying medicine. All
impressions remained lively with him, and his waggery in
repeating the lectures and mimicking the professors often
went so far, that when he had heard three different lectures
in one morning, he would, at the dinner-table, interchange
the professors with each other, paragraphwise, and often even
more abruptly, which parti-coloured lecture frequently entertained us, but often, too, became troublesome.

The rest were more or less polite, steady, serious people.
A pensioned knight of the order of St. Louis was one of
these; but the majority were students, all really good and

well-disposed, only they were not allowed to go beyond their
usual allowance of wine. That this should not be easily done
was the care of our president, one Doctor SALZMANN. Already
in the sixties and unmarried, he had attended this dinner-
table for many years, and maintained its good order and
respectability. He possessed a handsome property, kept himself close and neat in his exterior, even belonging to those
who always go in shoes and stockings, and with their hat
under their arm. To put on the hat, was with him an extraordinary action. He commonly carried an umbrella, wisely
reflecting that the finest summer-days often bring thunder-
storms and passing showers over the country.

With this man I talked over my design of continuing to
study jurisprudence at Strasburg, so as to be able to take my
degree as soon as possible. Since he was exactly informed of
everything, I asked him about the lectures I should have to
hear, and what he generally thought of the matter. To this
he replied, that it was not in Strasburg as in the German universities, where they try to educate jurists in the large and
learned sense of the term. Here, in conformity with the
relation towards France, all was really directed to the practical,
and managed in accordance with the opinions of the French,
who readily stop at what is given. They tried to impart
to every one certain general principles and preliminary knowledge, they compressed as much as possible, and communicated only what was most necessary. Hereupon he made
me acquainted with a man, in whom, as a *Repetent,** great confidence was entertained; which he very soon managed to gain
from me also. By way of introduction, I began to speak with
him on subjects of jurisprudence, and he wondered not a
little at my swaggering: for during my residence at Leipzig,
I had gained more of an insight into the requisites for the
law than I have hitherto taken occasion to state in my narrative, though all I had acquired could only be reckoned as a

* A Repetent is one of a class of persons to be found in the German
universities, and who assist students in their studies. They are somewhat analogous to the English Tutors, but not precisely; for the latter
render their aid *before* the recitation, while the Repetent *repeats* with the
student, in private, the lectures he has previously heard from the professor. Hence his name, which might be rendered *Repeater,* had we any
corresponding class of men in England or America, which would justify
an English word.—*American Note.*

general encyclopedical survey, and not as proper definite knowledge. University life, even if in the course of it we may not have to boast of our own proper industry, nevertheless affords endless advantages in every kind of cultivation, because we are always surrounded by men who either possess or are seeking science, so that, even if unconsciously, we are constantly drawing some nourishment from such an atmosphere.

My repetent, after he had had patience with my rambling discourse for some time, gave me at last to understand that I must first of all keep my immediate object in view, which was, to be examined, to take my degree, and then, perchance, to commence practice. "In order to stand the first," said he, "the subject is by no means investigated at large. It is inquired how and when a law arose, and what gave the internal or external occasion for it; there is no inquiry as to how it has been altered by time and custom, or how far it has perhaps been perverted by false interpretation or the perverted usage of the courts. It is in such investigations that learned men quite peculiarly spend their lives: but we inquire after that which exists at present, this we stamp firmly on our memory, that it may always be ready when we wish to employ it for the use and defence of our clients. Thus we qualify our young people for their future life, and the rest follows in proportion to their talents and activity." Hereupon he handed me his pamphlets, which were written in question and answer, and in which I could have stood a pretty good examination at once, for Hopp's smaller law-catechism was yet perfectly in my memory; the rest I supplied with some diligence, and, against my will, qualified myself in the easiest manner as a candidate.

But since in this way all my own activity in the study was cut off,—for I had no sense for anything positive, but wished to have everything explained historically, if not intelligibly—I found for my powers a wider field, which I employed in the most singular manner by devoting myself to a matter of interest which was accidently presented to me from without.

Most of my fellow-boarders were medical students. These, as is well known, are the only students who zealously converse about their science and profession even out of the hours of study. This lies in the nature of the case. The objects of their endeavours are the most obvious to the senses, and at the same

time the highest, the most simple and the most complicated.
Medicine employs the whole man, for it occupies itself with the
whole man. All that the young man learns refers directly to an
important, dangerous indeed, but yet in many respects lucrative
practice. He therefore devotes himself passionately to whatever is to be known and to be done, partly because it is interesting in itself, partly because it opens to him the joyous
prospect of independence and wealth.

At table then I heard nothing but medical conversations, just
as formerly in the boarding-house of Hofrath Ludwig. In our
walks and in our pleasure-parties likewise not much else was
talked about ; for my fellow-boarders, like good fellows, had
also become my companions at other times, and they were
always joined on all sides by persons of like minds and like
studies. The medical faculty in general shone above the others,
with respect both to the celebrity of the professors and the
number of the students, and I was the more easily borne along
by the stream, as I had just so much knowlege of all these
things that my desire for science could soon be increased and
inflamed. At the commencement of the second half-year,
therefore, I attended a course on chemistry by Spielmann, another on anatomy by Lobstein, and proposed to be right industrious, because by my singular preliminary or rather extra
knowledge, I had already gained some respect and confidence
in our society.

Yet this dissipation and dismemberment of my studies was
not enough, they were to be once more seriously disturbed ;
for a remarkable political event set everything in motion, and
procured us a tolerable succession of holidays. Marie An-
toinette, Archduchess of Austria and Queen of France, was to
pass through Strasburg on her road to Paris. The solemnities
by which the people are made to take notice that there is greatness in the world, were busily and abundantly prepared, and
especially remarkable to me was the building which stood on
an island in the Rhine between the two bridges, erected for
her reception and for surrendering her into the hands of her
husband's ambassadors. It was but slightly elevated above the
ground, had in the centre a grand saloon, on each side smaller
ones ; then followed other chambers, which extended somewhat backwards. Enough, had it been more durably built, it
might have answered very well as a pleasure-house for persons

of rank. But that which particularly interested me, and
for which I did not grudge many a *busel* (a little silver coin
then current) in order to procure a repeated entrance from the
porter, was the embroidered tapestry with which they had
lined the whole interior. Here, for the first time, I saw a
specimen of those tapestries worked after Raffaelle's cartoons,
and this sight was for me of very decided influence, as I became acquainted with the true and the perfect on a large scale,
though only in copies. I went and came, and came and went,
and could not satiate myself with looking; nay, a vain endeavour troubled me, because I would willingly have comprehended what interested me in so extraordinary a manner. I
found these side-chambers highly delightful and refreshing,
but the chief saloon so much the more shocking. This had
been hung with many larger, more brilliant and richer hangings, which were surrounded with crowded ornaments, worked
after pictures by the modern French.

Now I might perhaps have reconciled myself to this style
also, as my feelings, like my judgment, did not readily reject
anything entirely; but the subject was excessively revolting
to me. These pictures contained the history of Jason, Medea,
and Creusa, and therefore an example of the most unhappy
marriage. To the left of the throne was seen the bride struggling with the most horrible death, surrounded by persons full
of sympathizing woe; to the right was the father, horrified at
the murdered babes before his feet; whilst the Fury, in her
dragon-car, drove along into the air. And that the horrible
and atrocious should not lack something absurd, the white tail
of that magic ball flourished out on the right-hand from behind the red velvet of the gold-embroidered back of the throne,
while the fire-spitting beast himself, and the Jason who was
fighting with him, were completely covered by the sumptuous
drapery.

Here all the maxims which I had made my own in Oeser's
school were stirring within my bosom. It was without proper
selection and judgment, to begin with, that Christ and the
apostles were brought into the side-halls of a nuptial building,
and doubtless the size of the chambers had guided the royal
tapestry-keeper. This, however, I willingly forgave, because
it had turned out so much to my advantage; but a blunder like
that in the grand saloon put me altogether out of my self-posses-

sion, and with animation and vehemence I called on my comrades to witness such a crime against taste and feeling.
"What!" cried I, without regarding the bystanders, "is it
permitted so thoughtlessly to place before the eyes of a young
queen, at her first setting foot in her dominions, the representation of the most horrible marriage that perhaps was ever
consummated! Is there then among the French architects,
decorators, upholsterers, not a single man who understands
that pictures represent something, that pictures work upon
the mind and feelings, that they make impressions, that they
excite forebodings! It is just the same as if they had sent the
most ghastly spectre to meet this beauteous and pleasure-lov-
ing lady at the very frontiers!" I know not what I said besides;
enough, my comrades tried to quiet me and to remove me out
of the house, that there might be no offence. They then
assured me that it was not everybody's concern to look for
significance in pictures; that to themselves, at least, nothing
of the sort would have occurred, while the whole population of
Strasburg and the vicinity which was to throng thither, would
no more take such crotchets into their heads than the queen
herself and her court.

I yet remember well the beauteous and lofty mien, as cheerful as it was imposing, of this youthful lady. Perfectly visible
to us all in her glass carriage, she seemed to be jesting with
her female attendants, in familiar conversation, about the
throng that poured forth to meet her train. In the evening
we roamed through the streets to look at the various illuminated buildings, but especially the glowing spire of the minster,
with which, both near and in the distance, we could not sufficiently feast our eyes.

The queen pursued her way; the country people dispersed,
and the city was soon quiet as ever. Before the queen's
arrival, the very rational regulation had been made, that no
deformed persons, no cripples nor disgusting invalids, should
show themselves on her route. People joked about this, and
I made a little French poem in which I compared the advent
of Christ, who seemed to wander upon the world particularly
on account of the sick and the lame, with the arrival of the
queen, who scared these unfortunates away. My friends let
it pass; a Frenchman, on the contrary, who lived with us,
criticised the language and metre very unmercifully, although,

as it seemed, with too much foundation, and I do not remember that I ever made a French poem afterwards.

Scarcely had the news of the queen's happy arrival rung from the capital, than it was followed by the horrible intelligence that, owing to an oversight of the police during the festal fireworks, an infinite number of persons, with horses and carriages, had been destroyed in a street obstructed by building materials, and that the city, in the midst of the nuptial solemnities, had been plunged into mourning and sorrow. They attempted to conceal the extent of the misfortune, both from the young royal pair and from the world, by burying the dead in secret, so that many families were convinced only by the ceaseless absence of their members that they, too, had been swept off by this awful event. That, on this occasion, those ghastly figures in the grand saloon again came vividly before my mind, I need scarcely mention; for every one knows how powerful certain moral impressions are, when they embody themselves, as it were, in those of the senses.

This occurrence was, however, destined moreover to place my friends in anxiety and trouble by means of a prank in which I indulged. Among us young people who had been at Leipzig, there had been maintained ever afterwards a certain itch for imposing on and in some way mystifying one another. With this wanton love of mischief I wrote to a friend in Frankfort (he was the one who had amplified my poem on the cake-baker Hendel, applied it to *Medon*, and caused its general circulation), a letter dated from Versailles, in which I informed him of my happy arrival there, my participation in the solemnities, and other things of the kind, but at the same time enjoined the strictest secrecy. I must here remark that, from the time of that trick which had caused us so much annoyance, our little Leipzig society had accustomed itself to persecute him from time to time with mystifications, and this especially as he was the drollest man in the world, and was never more amiable than when he was discovering the cheat into which he had deliberately been led. Shortly after I had written this letter, I went on a little journey and remained absent about a fortnight. Meanwhile the news of that disaster had reached Frankfort; my friend believed me in Paris, and his affection led him to apprehend that I might have been involved in the calamity. He inquired of my parents and other persons to

whom I was accustomed to write, whether any letters had arrived, and as it was just at the time when my journey kept me
from sending any, they were altogether wanting. He went
about in the greatest uneasiness, and at last told the matter in
confidence to our nearest friends, who were now in equal
anxiety. Fortunately this conjecture did not reach my parents
until a letter had arrived, announcing my return to Strasburg.
My young friends were satisfied to learn that I was alive, but remained firmly convinced that I had been at Paris in the interim.
The affectionate intelligence of the solicitude they had felt on
my account affected me so much that I vowed to leave off such
tricks for ever, but, unfortunately, I have often since allowed
myself to be guilty of something similar. Real life frequently
loses its brilliancy to such a degree, that one is many a time
forced to polish it up again with the varnish of fiction.

This mighty stream of courtly magnificence had now flowed
by, and had left in me no other longing than after those
tapestries of Raffaelle, which I would willingly have gazed at,
revered, nay, adored, every day and every hour. Fortunately,
my passionate endeavours succeeded in interesting several persons of consequence in them, so that they were taken down
and packed up as late as possible. We now gave ourselves
up again to our quiet, easy routine of the university and society,
and in the latter the Actuary Salzmann, president of our table,
continued to be the general pedagogue. His intelligence,
complaisance, and dignity, which he always contrived to maintain amid all the jests, and often even in the little extravagances
which he allowed us, made him beloved and respected by the
whole company, and I could mention but few instances where
he showed his serious displeasure, or interposed with authority
in little quarrels and disputes. Yet among them all I was the
one who most attached myself to him, and he was not less
inclined to converse with me, as he found me more variously
accomplished than the others, and not so one-sided in judgment. I also followed his directions in external matters, so
that he could, without hesitation, publicly acknowledge me as
his companion and comrade: for although he only filled an
office which seems to be of little influence, he administered it
in a manner which redounded to his highest honour. He was
actuary to the Court of Wards (*Pupillen-Collegium*), and there,
indeed, like the perpetual secretary of an university, he had;

properly speaking, the management of affairs in his own hands. Now as he had conducted this business with the greatest exactness for many years, there was no family, from the first to the last, which did not owe him its gratitude; as indeed scarcely any one in the whole administration of government can earn more blessings or more curses than one who takes charge of the orphans, or, on the contrary, squanders or suffers to be squandered their property and goods.

The Strasburgers are passionate walkers, and they have a good right to be so. Let one turn one's steps as one will, one finds pleasure-grounds, partly natural, partly adorned by art in ancient and modern times, all of them visited and enjoyed by a cheerful, merry little people. But what made the sight of a great number of pedestrians still more agreeable here than in other places, was the various costume of the fair sex. The middle class of city girls yet retained the hair twisted up and secured by a large pin; as well as a certain close style of dress, in which anything like a train would have been unbecoming; and the pleasant part of it was, that this costume did not differ violently according to the rank of the wearer; for there were still some families of opulence and distinction, who would not permit their daughters to deviate from this costume. The rest followed the French fashion, and this party made some proselytes every year. Salzmann had many acquaintances and an entrance everywhere; a very pleasant circumstance for his companion, especially in summer, for good company and refreshment were found in all the public gardens far and near, and more than one invitation for this or that pleasant day was received. On one such occasion I found an opportunity to recommend myself very rapidly to a family which I was visiting for only the second time. We were invited, and arrived at the appointed hour. The company was not large; some played and some walked as usual. Afterwards, when they were to go to supper, I saw our hostess and her sister speaking to each other with animation, and as if in a peculiar embarrassment. I accosted them and said : " I have indeed no right, ladies, to force myself into your secrets; but perhaps I may be able to give you good council, or even to serve you." Upon this they disclosed to me their painful dilemma : namely, that they had invited twelve persons to table, and that just at that moment a relation had returned from a journey, who now, as the thirteenth, would be a fatal *memento mori*, if not for himself, yet certainly for some of the guests. "The case is very easily mended," replied I; "permit me to take my leave, and stipulate for indemnification." As they were persons of consequence and good-breeding, they would by no means allow this, but sent about in the neighbourhood to find a fourteenth. I suffered them to do so, yet when I saw the servant coming in at the garden-gate without having effected his errand, I stole away and spent my evening pleasantly under the old linden-trees of the Wanzenau. That this self-denial was richly repaid me was a very natural consequence.

A certain kind of general society is not to be thought of without card-playing. Salzmann renewed the good instructions of Madame Böhme, and I was the more docile as I had really seen that by this little sacrifice, if it be one, one may procure oneself much pleasure, and even a greater freedom in society than one would otherwise enjoy. The old piquet, which had gone to sleep, was again looked out; I learned whist; I made myself, according to the directions of my Mentor, a card-purse, which was to remain untouched under all circumstances; and I now found opportunity to spend most of my evenings with my friend in the best circles, where, for the most part, they wished me well, and pardoned many a little irregularity, to which, nevertheless, my friend, though kindly enough, used to call my attention.

But that I might experience symbolically how much one, even in externals, has to adapt oneself to society, and direct oneself according to it, I was compelled to something which seemed to me the most disagreeable thing in the world. I had really very fine hair, but my Strasburg hair-dresser at once assured me that it was cut much too short behind, and that it would be impossible to make a *frizure* of it in which I could show myself, since nothing but a few short curls in front were decreed lawful, and all the rest, from the crown, must be tied up in a queue or a hair-bag. Nothing was left but to put up with false hair till the natural growth was again restored according to the demands of the time. He promised me that nobody should ever remark this innocent cheat (against which I objected at first very earnestly), if I could resolve upon it immediately. He kept his word, and I was always looked upon as the young man who had the best and the best-dressed head of hair. But as I was obliged to remain thus propped up and powdered from early in the morning, and at the same time to take care not to betray my false ornament by heating myself or by violent motions, this restraint in fact contributed much to my behaving for a time more quietly and politely, and accustomed me to going with my hat under my arm, and consequently in shoes and stockings also; however I did not venture to neglect wearing understockings of fine leather, as a defence against the Rhine gnats, which, on the fine summer evenings, generally spread themselves over the meadows and gardens. If now, under these circumstances, a violent bodily motion was denied me, our social conversations certainly became more and more animated and impassioned; indeed they were the most interesting in which I had hitherto ever borne part.

With my way of feeling and thinking, it cost me nothing to let every one pass for what he was, nay, for that which he wished to pass for, and thus the frankness of a fresh youthful heart, which manifested itself almost for the first time in its full bloom, made me many friends and adherents. Our company of boarders increased to about twenty persons, and as Salzmann kept up his accustomed order, everything continued in its old routine; nay, the conversation was almost more decorous, as every one had to be on his guard before several. Among the new comers, was a man who particularly interested me; his name was JUNG, the same who afterwards became known under the name of STILLING. In spite of an antiquated dress, his form had something delicate about it, with a certain sturdiness. A bag-wig did not disfigure his significant and pleasing countenance. His voice was mild, without being soft and weak; it became even melodious and powerful as soon as his ardour was roused, which was very easily done. On learning to know him better, one found in him a sound common-sense, which rested on feeling, and therefore took its tone from the affections and passions, and from this very feeling sprang an enthusiasm for the good, the true, and the just, in the greatest possible purity. For the course of this man's life had been very simple, and yet crowded with events and with manifold activity. The element of his energy was an indestructible faith in God, and in an assistance flowing immediately from him, which evidently manifested itself in an uninterrupted providence, and in an

unfailing deliverance out of all troubles and from every evil.
Jung had made many such experiences in his life, and they
had often been repeated of late in Strasburg, so that, with
the greatest cheerfulness, he led a life frugal indeed, but free
from care; and devoted himself most earnestly to his studies,
although he could not reckon upon any certain subsistence from
one quarter to another. In his youth, when on a fair way to
become a charcoal burner, he took up the trade of a tailor, and
after he had instructed himself, at the same time, in higher
matters, his knowledge-loving mind drove him to the occupation of schoolmaster. This attempt failed, and he returned
to his trade, from which, however, since every one felt for
him confidence and affection, he was repeatedly called away,
again to take a place as private tutor. But for his most internal and peculiar training he had to thank that wide-spread
class of men who sought out their salvation on their own re-
sponsibilty, and who, while they strove to edify themselves by
reading the Scriptures and good books, and by mutual exhortation and confession, thereby attained a degree of cultivation
which must excite surprise. For while the interest which always
accompanied them and which maintained them in fellowship,
rested on the simplest foundation of morality, well-wishing
and well-doing, the deviations which could take place with
men of such limited circumstances were of little importance,
and hence their consciences, for the most part, remained clear,
and their minds commonly cheerful; so there arose no artificial, but a truly natural culture, which yet had this advantage
over others, that it was suitable to all ages and ranks, and
was generally social by its nature. For this reason, too, these
persons were, in their own circle, truly eloquent, and capable
of expressing themselves appropriately and pleasingly on all the
tenderest and best concerns of the heart. Now the good Jung
was in this very case. Among a few persons, who, if not
exactly like-minded with himself, did not declare themselves
averse from his mode of thought, he was found not only talkative but eloquent; in particular, he related the history of
his life in the most delightful manner, and knew how to
make all the circumstances plainly and vividly present to his
listeners. I persuaded him to write them down, and he
promised he would do so. But because in his way of expressing himself he was like a somnambulist, whom one dare

not call, lest he should fall from his elevation, or like a gentle
stream, to which one dare oppose nothing, lest it should foam,
so was he often forced to feel uncomfortable in a more numerous company. His faith tolerated no doubt, and his conviction no jest. And if in friendly communication he was inexhaustible, everything came to a standstill with him when he
suffered contradiction. I usually helped him through on such
occasions, for which he repaid me with honest affection.
Since his mode of thought was nothing strange to me, but on
the contrary I had already become accurately acquainted with
it in my very best friends of both sexes, and since, moreover,
it generally interested me with its naturalness and *naïveté*, he
found himself on the very best terms with me. The bent of his
mind was pleasing to me, and his wondrous faith in miracles,
which was so useful to him, I left unmolested. Salzmann
likewise behaved towards him with forbearance,—I say with
forbearance, for Salzmann, in conformity with his character,
his natural disposition, his age and circumstances, could not
but stand and continue on the side of the rational, or rather
the common-sense Christians, whose religion properly rested
on the rectitude of their characters, and a manly independence, and who therefore did not like to meddle or have anything to do with feelings which might easily have led them
into gloom, or with mysticism, which might easily have led
them into the dark. This class, too, was respectable and
numerous; all men of honour and capacity understood each
other, and were of the like persuasion, as well as of the
same mode of life.

LERSE, likewise our fellow-boarder, also belonged to this
number; a perfectly upright young man, and, with limited
gifts of fortune, frugal and exact. His manner of life and
housekeeping was the closest I ever knew among students.
He dressed himself the neatest of us all, and yet always appeared in the same clothes; but he managed his wardrobe
with the greatest care, kept everything about him clean, and
required all things in ordinary life to go according to his
example. He never happened to lean anywhere, or to prop
his elbow on the table; he never forgot to mark his table-
napkin, and it always went ill with the maid when the chairs
were not found perfectly clean. With all this, he had nothing
stiff in his exterior. He spoke cordially, with precise and

dry liveliness, in which a light ironical joke was very be-coming. In figure, he was well-built, slender, and of fair height, his face was pock-pitted and homely, his little blue eyes cheerful and penetrating. As he had cause to tutor us in so many respects, we let him be our fencing-master besides; for he drew a very fine rapier, and it seemed to give him sport to play off upon us, on this occasion, all the pedantry of this profession. Moreover, we really profited by him, and had to thank him for many sociable hours, which he induced us to spend in good exercise and practice.

By all these peculiarities, Lerse completely qualified himself for the office of arbitrator and umpire in all the small and great quarrels which happened, though but rarely, in our circle, and which Salzmann could not hush up in his fatherly way. Without the external forms, which do so much mischief in universities, we represented a society bound together by circumstances and good-feeling, which others might occasion-ally touch, but into which they could not intrude. Now, in his judgment of internal piques, Lerse always showed the greatest impartiality, and when the affair could no longer be settled by words and explanations, he knew how to con-duct the desired satisfaction, in an honourable way, to a harmless issue. In this no man was more clever than he; indeed, he often used to say, that since heaven had destined him for a hero neither in war nor in love, he would be con-tent, both in romances and fighting, with the part of second. Since he remained the same throughout, and might be re-garded as a true model of a good and steady disposition, the conception of him stamped itself as deeply as amiably upon me; and when I wrote *Götz von Berlichingen*, I felt myself induced to set up a memorial of our friendship, and to give the gallant fellow, who knew how to subordinate himself in so dignified a manner, the name of Franz Lerse.

While now, by his constant humorous dryness, he con-tinued always to remind us of what one owed to oneself and to others, and how one ought to behave in order to live at peace with men as long as possible, and thus gain a certain position towards them, I had to fight, both inwardly and out-wardly, with quite different circumstances and adversaries, being at strife with myself, with the objects around me, and even with the elements. I found myself in a state of health which furthered me sufficiently in all that I would and should undertake ; only there was a certain irritability left behind, which did not always let me be in equilibrium. A loud sound was disagreeable to me, diseased objects awakened in me loathing and horror. But I was especially troubled by a giddiness which came over me every time that I looked down from a height. All these infirmities I tried to remedy, and, indeed, as I wished to lose no time, in a somewhat violent way. In the evening, when they beat the tattoo, I went near the multitude of drums, the powerful rolling and beating of which might have made one's heart burst in one s bosom. All alone I ascended the highest pinnacle of the minster spire, and sat in what is called the neck, under the nob or crown, for a quarter of an hour, before I would venture to step out again into the open air, where, standing upon a platform scarce an ell square, without any particular holding, one sees the boundless prospect before, while the nearest objects and ornaments conceal the church, and everything upon and above which one stands. It is exactly as if one saw oneself carried up into the air in a balloon. Such troublesome and painful sensations I repeated until the impression became quite indifferent to me, and I have since then derived great advantage from this training, in mountain travels and geological studies, and on great buildings, where I have vied with the carpenters in running over the bare beams and the cornices of the edifice, and even in Rome, where one must run similar risks to obtain a nearer view of important works of art. Anatomy, also, was of double value to me, as it taught me to tolerate the most repulsive sights, while I satisfied my thirst for knowledge. And thus I attended, also, the clinical course of the elder Doctor Ehrmann, as well as the lectures of his son on obstetrics, with the double view of becoming acquainted with all conditions, and of freeing myself from all apprehension as to repulsive things. And I have actually succeeded so far, that nothing of this kind could ever put me out of my self-possession. But I sought to steel myself not only against these impressions on the senses, but also against the infections of the imagination. The awful and shuddering impressions of the darkness in churchyards, solitary places, churches and chapels by night, and whatever may be connected with them, I contrived to render likewise indifferent ; and in this, also, I went so far that day and night, and every

locality, were quite the same to me; so that even when, in
later times, a desire came over me once more to feel in such
scenes the pleasing shudder of youth, I could scarcely force
this, in any degree, by the strangest and most fearful images
which I called up.

In my efforts to free myself from the pressure of the too-
gloomy and powerful, which continued to rule within me,
and seemed to me sometimes as strength, sometimes as weakness, I was thoroughly assisted by that open, social, stirring
manner of life, which attracted me more and more, to which
I accustomed myself, and which I at last learned to enjoy
with perfect freedom. It is not difficult to remark in the
world, that man feels himself most freely and most perfectly
rid of his own failings, when he represents to himself the
faults of others, and expatiates upon them with complacent
censoriousness. It is a tolerably pleasant sensation even to
set ourselves above our equals by disapprobation and misre-
presentation, for which reason good society, whether it consists of few or many, is most delighted with it. But nothing
equals the comfortable self-complacency, when we erect
ourselves into judges of our superiors, and of those who are
set over us,—of princes and statesmen, when we find public
institutions unfit and injudicious, only consider the possible
and actual obstacles, and recognise neither the greatness of
the invention, nor the co-operation which is to be expected
from time and circumstances in every undertaking.

Whoever remembers the condition of the French kingdom,
and is accurately and circumstantially acquainted with it from
later writings, will easily figure to himself how, at that time,
in the Alsatian semi-France, people used to talk about the king
and his ministers, about the court and court-favourites.
These were new subjects for my love of instructing myself,
and very welcome ones to my pertness and youthful conceit.
I observed everything accurately, noted it down industriously,
and I now see, from the little that is left, that such accounts,
although only put together on the moment, out of fables and
uncertain general rumours, always have a certain value in
after-times, because they serve to confront and compare the
secret made known at last with what was then already discovered and public, and the judgments of contemporaries,
true or false, with the convictions of posterity.

Striking, and daily before the eyes of us street-loungers, was the project for beautifying the city ; the execution of which, according to draughts and plans, began in the strangest fashion to pass from sketches and plans into reality. Intendant Gayot had undertaken to new-model the angular and uneven lanes of Strasburg, and to lay the foundations of a respectable, handsome city, regulated by line and level. Upon this, Blondel, a Parisian architect, drew a plan, by which an hundred and forty householders gained in room, eighty lost, and the rest remained in their former condition. This plan, which was accepted, but was not to be put into execution at once, was now to approach completion in the course of time, and, meanwhile, the city oddly enough wavered between form and formlessness. If, for instance, a crooked side of a street was to be straightened, the first man who felt disposed to build moved forward to the appointed line ; perhaps, too, his next neighbour ; but perhaps, also, the third or fourth resident from him, by which projections the most awkward recesses were left, like front court-yards, before the houses in the background. They would not use force, yet without compulsion they would never have got on ; on which account no man, when his house was once condemned, ventured to improve or replace anything that related to the street. All these strange accidental inconveniences gave to us rambling idlers the most welcome opportunity of practising our ridicule, of making proposals, in the manner of Behrisch, for accelerating the completion, and of constantly doubting the possibility of it, although many a newly-erected handsome building should have brought us to other thoughts. How far that project was advanced by the length of time, I cannot say.

Another subject on which the Protestant Strasburgers liked to converse was the expulsion of the Jesuits. These fathers, as soon as the city had fallen to the share of the French, had made their appearance and sought a *domicilium*. But they soon extended themselves and built a magnificent college, which bordered so closely on the minster that the back of the church covered a third part of its front. It was to be a complete quadrangle, and have a garden in the middle ; three sides of it were finished. It is of stone, and solid, like all the buildings of these fathers. That the Protestants were pushed hard, if not oppressed by them, lay in the plan of the society, which made it a duty to restore the old religion in its whole compass. Their fall, therefore, awakened the greatest satisfaction in the opposite party, and people saw, not without pleasure, how they sold their wines, carried away their books, and the building was assigned to another, perhaps less active order. How glad are men when they get rid of an opponent, or only of a guardian ; and the herd does not reflect that where there is no dog, it is exposed to wolves.

Now, since every city must have its tragedy, at which children and children's children shudder, so in Strasburg frequent mention was made of the unfortunate Prætor Klingling, who, after he had mounted the highest step of earthly felicity, ruled city and country with almost absolute power, and enjoyed all that wealth, rank, and influence could afford, had at last lost the favour of the court, and was dragged up to answer for all in which he had been indulged hitherto ; nay, was even thrown into prison, where, more than seventy years old, he died an ambiguous death.

This and other tales, that knight of St. Louis, our fellow-boarder, knew how to tell with passion and animation, for which reason I was fond of accompanying him in his walks, unlike the others, who avoided such invitations, and left me alone with him. As with new acquaintances I generally suffered myself to go on for a long time without thinking much about them or the effect which they were exercising upon me, so I only remarked gradually that his stories and opinions rather unsettled and confused, than instructed and enlightened me. I never knew what to make of him, although the riddle might easily have been solved. He belonged to the many to whom life offers no results, and who therefore, from first to last, exert themselves on individual objects. Unfortunately he had, with this, a decided desire, nay, even passion for meditating, without having any capacity for thinking ; and in such men a particular notion easily fixes itself fast, which may be regarded as a mental disease. To such a fixed view he always came back again, and was thus in the long-run excessively tiresome. He used bitterly to complain of the decline of his memory, especially with regard to the latest events, and maintained by a logic of his own, that all virtue springs from a good memory, and all vice, on the

contrary, from forgetfulness. This doctrine he contrived to
carry out with much acuteness ; as, indeed, everything can be
maintained when one permits oneself to use words altogether
vaguely, and to employ and apply them in a sense now wider,
now narrower, now closer, now more remote.

At first it was amusing to hear him; nay, his persuasive-
ness even astonished us. We fancied we were standing before
a rhetorical sophist, who for jest and practice knew how to give
a fair appearance to the strangest things. Unfortunately this
first impression blunted itself but too soon ; for at the end of
every discourse, manage the thing as I would, the man came
back again to the same theme. He was not to be held fast
to older events, although they interested him,—although he
had them present to his mind with their minutest circumstances. Indeed he was often, by a small circumstance,
snatched out of the middle of a wild historical narrative, and
thrust into his detestable favourite thought.

One of our afternoon walks was particularly unfortunate in
this respect ; the account of it may stand here instead of
similar cases, which might weary, if not vex the reader.

On the way through the city we were met by an old female
mendicant, who by her beggings and importunities disturbed
him in his story. " Pack yourself off, old witch!" said he,
and walked by. She shouted after him the well-known
retort, only somewhat changed, since she saw well that the
unfriendly man was old himself.—" If you did not wish to be
old, you should have had yourself hanged in your youth !"
He turned round violently, and I feared a scene. " Hanged !"
cried he, " have myself hanged ! No, that could not have
been : I was too honest a fellow for that ; but hang myself—
hang up my own self—that is true—that I should have done ;
I should have turned a charge of powder against myself, that
I might not live to see that I am not even worth that any
more." The woman stood as if petrified ; but he continued,
" You have said a great truth, witch-mother! and as they have
neither drowned nor burned you yet, you shall be paid for
your proverb." He handed her a *büsel*, a coin not usually
given to a beggar.

We had crossed over the first Rhine-bridge, and were going
to the inn where we meant to stop, and I was trying to lead
him back to our previous conversation, when, unexpectedly,

a very pretty girl met us on the pleasant foot-path, remained
standing before us, bowed prettily and cried : " Eh, eh!
captain, where are you going?" and whatever else is usually
said on such an occasion. " Mademoiselle," replied he, somewhat embarrassed, " I know not ——" " How?" said she,
with graceful astonishment, " do you forget your friends so
soon?" The word " forget" fretted him ; he shook his head
and replied, peevishly enough, " Truly, mademoiselle, I did
not know ——!" She now retorted with some humour, yet
very temperately : " Take care, captain, I may mistake you
another time!" And so she hurried past, taking huge strides,
without looking round. At once my fellow-traveller struck
his forehead with both his fists : " O what an ass I am!" exclaimed he, " what an old ass I am! Now, you see whether I
am right or not." And then, in a very violent manner, he
went on with his usual sayings and opinions, in which this case
still more confirmed him. I cannot and would not repeat what
a philippic discourse he held against himself. At last he turned
to me and said : " I call you to witness! You remember that
small-ware woman at the corner, who is neither young nor
pretty ? I salute her every time we pass, and often exchange
a couple of friendly words with her ; and yet it is thirty years
ago since she was gracious to me. But now I swear it is not
four weeks since this young lady showed herself more complai-
sant to me than was reasonable, and yet I will not recognise
her, but insult her in return for her favours! Do I not always
say that ingratitude is the greatest of vices, and no man would
be ungrateful if he were not forgetful!"

We went into the inn, and nothing but the tippling, swarming crowd in the ante-rooms stopped the invectives which he
rattled off against himself and his contemporaries. He was
silent, and I hoped pacified, when we stepped into an upper
chamber, where we found a young man pacing up and down
alone, whom the captain saluted by name. I was pleased to
become acquainted with him : for the old fellow had said
much good of him to me, and had told me that this young man,
being employed in the war-bureau, had often disinterestedly
done him very good service when the pensions were stopped.
I was glad that the conversation took a general turn, and while
we were carrying it on we drank a bottle of wine. But here,
unluckily, another infirmity which my knight had in common

with obstinate men, developed itself. For as, on the whole, he could not get rid of that fixed notion, so did he stick fast to a disagreeable impression of the moment, and suffer his feelings to run on without moderation. His last vexation about himself had not yet died away, and now was added something new, although of quite a different kind. He had not long cast his eyes here and there before he noticed on the table a double portion of coffee and two cups, and might besides, being a man of gallantry, have traced some other indication that the young man had not been so solitary all the time. And scarcely had the conjecture arisen in his mind, and ripened into a probability, that the pretty girl had been paying a visit here, than the most outrageous jealousy added itself to that first vexation, so as completely to perplex him.

Now before I could suspect anything, for I had hitherto been conversing quite harmlessly with the young man, the captain, in an unpleasant tone, which I well knew, began to be satirical about the pair of cups, and about this and that. The young man, surprised, tried to turn it off pleasantly and sensibly, as is the custom among men of good-breeding; but the old fellow continued to be unmercifully rude, so that there was nothing left for the other to do but to seize his hat and cane, and at his departure to leave behind him a pretty unequivocal challenge. The fury of the captain now burst out the more vehemently, as he had in the interim drunk another bottle of wine almost by himself. He struck the table with his fist, and cried more than once: "I strike him dead!" It was not, however, meant quite so badly as it sounded, for he often used this phrase when any one opposed or otherwise displeased him. Just as unexpectedly the business grew worse on our return: for I had the want of foresight to represent to him his ingratitude towards the young man, and to remind him how strongly he had praised to me the ready obligingness of this official person. No! such rage of a man against himself I never saw again: it was the most passionate conclusion to that beginning to which the pretty girl had given occasion. Here I saw sorrow and repentance carried into caricature, as all passion supplies the place of genius, and is really full of genius. He then went over all the incidents of our afternoon ramble again, employed them rhetorically for his own self-reproach, brought up the old witch at last before him once more, and perplexed himself

328 TRUTH AND POETRY; FROM MY OWN LIFE.

to such a degree, that I could not help fearing he would throw himself into the Rhine. Could I have been sure of fishing him out again quickly, like Mentor his Telemachus, he might have made the leap, and I should have brought him home cooled down for this occasion.

I immediately confided the affair to Lerse, and we went the next morning to the young man, whom my friend in his dry way set laughing. We agreed to bring about an accidental meeting, where a reconciliation should take place of itself. The drollest thing about it was, that this time the captain too had slept off his rudeness, and found himself ready to apologize to the young man, to whom petty quarrels were of some consequence. All was arranged in one morning, and, as the affair had not been kept quite secret, I did not escape the jokes of my friends, who might have foretold me, from their own experience, how troublesome the friendship of the captain could become upon occasion.

But now, while I am thinking what should be imparted next, there comes again into my thoughts, by a strange play of memory, that reverend minster-building, to which in those days I devoted particular attention, and which, in general, constantly presents itself to the eye both in the city and in the country.

The more I considered the *façade*, the more was that first impression strengthened and developed, that here the sublime has entered into alliance with the pleasing. If the vast, when it appears as a mass before us, is not to terrify; if it is not to confuse, when we seek to investigate its details, it must enter into an unnatural, apparently impossible connexion, it must associate to itself the pleasing. But now, since it will be impossible for us to speak of the impression of the minster except by considering both these incompatible qualities as united, so do we already see, from this, in what high value we must hold this ancient monument, and we begin in earnest to describe how such contradictory elements could peaceably interpenetrate and unite themselves.

First of all, without thinking of the towers, we devote our considerations to the *façade* alone, which powerfully strikes the eye as an upright, oblong parallelogram. If we approach it at twilight, in the moonshine, on a starlight night, when the parts appear more or less indistinct and at last disappear, we see only a colos-

nal wall, the height of which bears an advantageous proportion
to the breadth. If we gaze on it by day, and by the power of the
mind abstract from the details, we recognise the front of a
building which not only incloses the space within, but also
covers much in its vicinity. The openings of this monstrous
surface point to internal necessities, and according to these we
can at once divide it into nine compartments. The great
middle door, which opens into the nave of the church, first
meets the eye. On both sides of it lie two smaller ones, belonging to the cross-ways. Over the chief door our glance falls
upon the wheel-shaped window, which is to spread an awe-
inspiring light within the church and its vaulted arches. At
its sides appear two large, perpendicular, oblong openings,
which form a striking contrast with the middle one, and indicate that they belong to the base of the rising towers. In the
third story are three openings in a row, which are designed for
belfries and other church necessities. Above them one sees
the whole horizontally closed by the balustrade of the gallery,
instead of a cornice. These nine spaces described, are supported, enclosed, and separated into three great perpendicular
divisions by four pillars rising up from the ground.

Now as one cannot deny to the whole mass a fine proportion
of height to breadth, so also in the details it maintains a somewhat uniform lightness by means of these pillars and the narrow compartments between them.

But if we keep to our abstraction, and imagine to ourselves
this immense wall without ornaments, with firm buttresses,
with the necessary openings in it, but only so far as necessity
requires them, we even then must allow that these chief divisions are in good proportion: thus the whole will appear solemn
and noble indeed, but always heavily unpleasant, and, being
without ornament, unartistical. For a work of art, the whole
of which is conceived in great, simple, harmonious parts, makes
indeed a noble and dignified impression, but the peculiar enjoyment which the pleasing produces can only find place in
the consonance of all developed details.

And it is precisely here that the building which we are examining satisfies us in the highest degree: for we see all the
ornaments fully suited to every part which they adorn: they
are subordinate to it, they seem to have grown out of it. Such
a manifoldness always gives great pleasure, since it flows of its

own accord from the suitable, and therefore at the same time
awakens the feeling of unity. It is only in such cases that the
execution is prized as the summit of art.

By such means, now, was a solid piece of masonry, an impenetrable wall, which had moreover to announce itself as the
base of two heaven-high towers, made to appear to the eye as
if resting on itself, consisting in itself, but at the same time
light and adorned, and, though pierced through in a thousand
places, to give the idea of indestructible firmness.

This riddle is solved in the happiest manner. The openings
in the wall, its solid parts, the pillars, everything has its peculiar character, which proceeds from its particular destination;
this communicates itself by degrees to the subdivisions; hence
everything is adorned in proportionate taste, the great as well
as the small is in the right place, and can be easily comprehended, and thus the pleasing presents itself in the vast. I
would refer only to the doors sinking in perspective into the
thickness of the wall, and adorned without end in their columns
and pointed arches: to the window with its rose springing out
of the round form, to the outline of its frame-work, as well as
to the slender reedlike pillars of the perpendicular compartments. Let one represent to himself the pillars retreating
step by step, accompanied by little, slender, light-pillared,
pointed structures, likewise striving upwards, and furnished
with canopies to shelter the images of the saints, and how at
last every rib, every boss, seems like a flower-head and row of
leaves, or some other natural object transformed into stone.
One may compare, if not the building itself, yet representations
of the whole and of its parts, for the purpose of reviewing and
giving life to what I have said. It may seem exaggerated to
many, for I myself, though transported into love for this work
at first sight, required a long time to make myself intimately
acquainted with its value.

Having grown up among those who found fault with Gothic
architecture, I cherished my aversion from the abundantly
overloaded, complicated ornaments which, by their capriciousness, made a religious, gloomy character highly adverse. I
strengthened myself in this repugnance, since I had only met
with spiritless works of this kind, in which one could perceive
neither good proportions nor a pure consistency. But here I
thought I saw a new revelation of it, since what was objec-

tionable by no means appeared, but the contrary opinion rather forced itself upon my mind.

But the longer I looked and considered, I all the while thought I discovered yet greater merits beyond that which I have already mentioned. The right proportion of the larger divisions, the ornamental, as judicious as rich, even to the minutest, were found out : but now I recognised the connexion of these manifold ornaments amongst each other, the transition from one leading part to another, the enclosing of details, homogeneous indeed, but yet greatly varying in form, from the saint to the monster, from the leaf to the dental. The more I investigated, the more I was astonished : the more I amused and wearied myself with measuring and drawing, so much the more did my attachment increase, so that I spent much time, partly in studying what actually existed, partly in restoring, in my mind and on paper, what was wanting and unfinished, especially in the towers.

Since now I found that this building had been based on old German ground, and grown thus far in genuine German times, and that the name of the master, on his modest grave-stone, was likewise of native sound and origin, I ventured, being incited by the worth of this work of art, to change the hitherto decried appellation of "Gothic architecture," and to claim it for our nation as "German architecture ;" nor did I fail to bring my patriotic views to light, first orally, and afterwards in a little treatise, dedicated to D. M. Erwini a Steinbach.

If my biographical narrative should come down to the epoch when the said sheet appeared in print, which Herder afterwards inserted in his pamphlet : *Von Deutscher Art und Kunst*, (*Of German Manner and Art*,) much more will be said on this weighty subject. But before I turn myself away from it this time, I will take the opportunity to vindicate the motto prefixed to the present volume, with those who may have entertained some doubt about it. I know indeed very well, that in opposition to this honest, hopeful old German saying : " Whatever one wishes in youth, one has abundance in old age !" many would quote contrary experience, and many trifling comments might be made : but much also is to be said in its favour, and I will explain my own thoughts on the matter.

Our wishes are presentiments of the capabilities which lie

within us, and harbingers of that which we shall be in a condition to perform. Whatever we are able and would like to do,
presents itself to our imagination, as without us and in the
future ; we feel a longing after that which we already possess
in secret. Thus a passionate anticipating grasp changes the
truly possible into a dreamed reality. Now if such a bias lies
decidedly in our nature, then, with every step of our development will a part of the first wish be fulfilled—under favourable
circumstances in the direct way, under unfavourable in the
circuitous way, from which we always come back again to the
other. Thus we see men by perseverance attain to earthly
wealth ; they surround themselves with riches, splendour, and
external honour. Others strive yet more certainly after intellectual advantages, acquire for themselves a clear survey of
things, a peacefulness of mind, and a certainty for the present
and the future.

But now there is a third direction, which is compounded of
both, and the issue of which must be the most surely successful. When, namely, the youth of a man falls into a pregnant
time, when production overweighs destruction, and a presentiment is early awakened within him as to what such an
epoch demands and promises, he will then, being forced by
outward inducements into an active interest, take hold now
here, now there, and the wish to be active on many sides will
be lively within him. But so many accidental hindrances are
associated with human limitation, that here a thing, once
begun, remains unfinished, there that which is already grasped
falls out of the hand, and one wish after another is dissipated.
But had these wishes sprung out of a pure heart, and in conformity with the necessities of the times, one might composedly
let them lie and fall right and left, and be assured that these
must not only be found out and picked up again, but that also
many kindred things, which one has never touched and never
even thought of, will come to light. If now, during our own
lifetime, we see that performed by others, to which we ourselves felt an earlier call, but had been obliged to give it up,
with much besides ; then the beautiful feeling enters the mind,
that only mankind together is the true man, and that the individual can only be joyous and happy when he has the courage
to feel himself in the whole.

This contemplation is here in the right place ; for when I

reflect on the affection which drew me to these antique edifices, when I reckon up the time which I devoted to the Strasburg minster alone, the attention with which I afterwards examined the cathedral at Cologne, and that at Freyburg, and more and more felt the value of these buildings, I could even blame myself for having afterwards lost sight of them altogether, nay, for having left them completely in the background, being attracted by a more developed art. But when I now, in the latest times, see attention again turned to those objects, when I see affection and even passion for them appearing and flourishing, when I see able young persons seized with this passion, recklessly devoting powers, time, care, and property, to these memorials of a past world, then am I reminded with pleasure that what I formerly would and wished had a value. With satisfaction I see that they not only know how to prize what was done by our forefathers, but that from existing unfinished beginnings they try to represent, in pictures at least, the original design, so as thus to make us acquainted with the thought, which is ever the beginning and end of all undertakings; and that they strive with considerate zeal to clear up and vivify what seems to be a confused past. Here I especially applaud the gallant Sulpiz Boisserée, who is indefatigably employed in a magnificent series of copper-plates to exhibit the cathedral of Cologne as the model of those vast conceptions, the spirit of which, like that of Babel, strove up to heaven, and which were so out of proportion to earthly means, that they were necessarily stopped fast in their execution. If we have been hitherto astonished that such buildings proceeded only so far, we shall learn with the greatest wonder what was really designed to be done.

May the literary-artistical undertakings of this kind be duly patronized by all who have power, wealth, and influence, that the great and gigantic views of our forefathers may be presented to our contemplation, and that we may be able to form a conception of what they dared to desire. The insight resulting from this will not remain fruitless, and the judgment will, for once at least, be in a condition to exercise itself on these works with justice. Nay, this will be done most thoroughly, if our active young friend, besides the monograph devoted to the cathedral of Cologne, follows out in detail the history of our mediæval architecture. When whatever is to be known

about the practical exercise of this art is further brought to
light, when the art is represented in all its fundamental features
by a comparison with the Graeco-Roman and the oriental
Egyptian, little can remain to be done in this department.
And I, when the results of such patriotic labours lie before
the world, as they are now known in friendly private communications, shall be able, with true content, to repeat that motto
in its best sense : " Whatever one wishes in youth, in old age
one has abundance."

But if, in operations like these, which belong to centuries,
one can trust oneself to time, and wait for opportunity, there
are, on the contrary, other things which in youth must be
enjoyed at once, fresh, like ripe fruits. Let me be permitted,
with this sudden turn, to mention dancing, of which the ear
is reminded, as the eye is of the minster, every day and every
hour in Strasburg and all Alsace. From early youth my father
himself had given my sister and me instruction in dancing,
a task which must have comported strangely enough with so
stern a man ; but he did not suffer his composure to be put
out by it ; he drilled us in the positions and steps in a manner
the most precise, and when he had brought us far enough to
dance a minuet, he played for us something easily intelligible
in three-four time, on a *flute-douce*, and we moved to it as
well as we could. On the French theatre, likewise, I had
seen from my youth upwards, if not ballets, yet *pas seuls* and
pas de deux, and had noticed in them various strange motions
of the feet, and all sorts of springs. When now we had enough
of the minuet, I begged my father for other dancing music,
of which our music-books, in their jigs and murkies,* offered
us a rich supply ; and I immediately found out, of myself,
the steps and other motions for them, the time being quite
suitable to my limbs, and, as it were, born with them. This
pleased my father to a certain degree ; indeed, he often, by
way of joke for himself and us, let the " monkies " dance in
this way. After my misfortune with Gretchen, and during
the whole of my residence in Leipzig, I did not make my
appearance again on the floor ; on the contrary, I still remember that when, at a ball, they forced me into a minuet, both
measure and motion seemed to have abandoned my limbs, and

* A " murki " is defined as an old species of short composition for the
harpsichord, with a lively murmuring accompaniment in the bass.—*Trans.*

I could no more remember either the steps or the figures, so that I should have been put to disgrace and shame if the greater part of the spectators had not maintained that my awkward behaviour was pure obstinacy, assumed with the view of depriving the ladies of all desire to invite me and draw me into their circle against my will.

During my residence in Frankfort, I was quite cut off from such pleasures; but in Strasburg, with other enjoyments of life, there soon arose in my limbs the faculty of keeping time. On Sundays and week-days, one sauntered by no pleasure-ground without finding there a joyous crowd assembled for the dance, and for the most part revolving in the circle. Moreover, there were private balls in the country-houses, and people were already talking of the brilliant masquerades of the coming winter. Here, indeed, I should have been out of my place, and useless to the company; when a friend, who waltzed very well, advised me to practise myself first in parties of a lower rank, so that afterwards I might be worth something in the highest. He took me to a dancing-master, who was well known for his skill; this man promised me that, when I had in some degree repeated the first elements, and made myself master of them, he would then lead me further. He was one of the dry, ready French characters, and received me in a friendly manner. I paid him a month in advance, and received twelve tickets, for which he agreed to give me certain hours' instruction. The man was strict and precise, but not pedantic; and as I already had some previous practice, I soon gave him satisfaction and received his commendation.

One circumstance, however, greatly facilitated the instruction of this teacher; he had two daughters, both pretty, and both yet under twenty. Having been instructed in this art from their youth upwards, they showed themselves very skilful, and might have been able, as partners, soon to help even the most clumsy scholars into some cultivation. They were both very polite, spoke nothing but French, and I, on my part, did my best, that I might not appear awkward or ridiculous before them. I had the good fortune that they likewise praised me, and were always willing to dance a minuet to their father's little violin, and, what indeed was more difficult for them, to initiate me, by degrees, into waltzing and whirling. Their father did not seem to have many customers, and they led a lonely life. For this reason they often asked me to remain with them after my hour, and to chat away the time a little; which I the more willingly did, as the younger one pleased me well, and generally they both altogether behaved very becomingly. I often read aloud something from a novel, and they did the same. The elder, who was as handsome, perhaps even handsomer, than the second, but who did not correspond with my taste so well as the latter, always conducted herself towards me more obligingly, and more kindly in every respect. She was always at hand during the hour, and often protracted it; hence I sometimes thought myself bound to offer back a couple of tickets to her father, which, however, he did not accept. The younger one, on the contrary, although she did nothing unfriendly towards me, was yet rather reserved, and waited till she was called by her father before she relieved the elder.

The cause of this became manifest to me one evening. For when, after the dance was done, I was about to go into the sitting-room with the elder, she held me back and said, " Let us remain here a little longer; for I will confess to you that my sister has with her a woman who tells fortunes from cards, and who is to reveal to her how matters stand with an absent lover, on whom her whole heart hangs, and upon whom she has placed all her hope. Mine is free," she continued, " and I must accustom myself to see it despised." I thereupon said sundry pretty things to her, replying that she could at once convince herself on that point by consulting the wise woman likewise; that I would do so myself, for I had long wished to learn something of the kind, but lacked faith. She blamed me for this, and assured me that nothing in the world was surer than the responses of this oracle, only it must be consulted, not out of sport and mischief, but solely in real affairs. However, I at last compelled her to go with me into that room, as soon as she had ascertained that the consultation was over. We found her sister in a very cheerful humour, and even towards me she was kinder than usual, sportive, and almost witty; for since she seemed to be secure of an absent friend, she may have thought it no treachery to be a little gracious with a present friend of her sister's, which she thought me to be. The old woman was now flattered, and

good payment was promised her, if she would tell the truth
to the elder sister and to me. With the usual preparations
and ceremonies she began her business, in order to tell the
fair one's fortune first. She carefully considered the situation
of the cards, but seemed to hesitate, and would not speak out
what she had to say. "I see now," said the younger, who
was already better acquainted with the interpretation of such
a magic tablet, "you hesitate, and do not wish to disclose
anything disagreeable to my sister; but that is a cursed card!"
The elder one turned pale, but composed herself, and said,
"Only speak out; it will not cost one's head!" The old
woman, after a deep sigh, showed her that she was in love,
that she was not beloved, that another person stood in the
way, and other things of like import. We saw the good
girl's embarrassment. The old woman thought somewhat to
improve the affair by giving hopes of letters and money.
"Letters," said the lovely child, "I do not expect, and money
I do not desire. If it is true, as you say, that I love, I deserve a heart that loves me in return." "Let us see if it
will not be better," replied the old woman, as she shuffled the
cards and laid them out a second time; but before the eyes of
all of us, it had only become still worse. The fair one stood
not only more lonely, but surrounded with many sorrows; her
lover had moved somewhat farther, and the intervening figures
nearer. The old woman wished to try it the third time, in
hopes of a better prospect; but the beautiful girl could restrain
herself no longer, she broke out into uncontrollable weeping,
her lovely bosom heaved violently, she turned round, and
rushed out of the room. I knew not what I should do. Inclination kept me with the one present; compassion drove me
to the other; my situation was painful enough. "Comfort
Lucinda," said the younger; "go after her." I hesitated;
how could I comfort her without at least assuring her of some
sort of affection, and could I do that at such a moment in
a cool, moderate manner? "Let us go together," said I to
Emilia. "I know not whether my presence will do her good,"
replied she. Yet we went, but found the door bolted. Lucinda made no answer; we might knock, shout, entreat, as
we would. "We must let her have her own way," said
Emilia; "she will not have it otherwise now!" And, indeed, when I called to my mind her manner from our very

z

first acquaintance, she always had something violent and unequal about her, and chiefly showed her affection for me by
not behaving to me with rudeness. What should I do?
I paid the old woman richly for the mischief she had caused,
and was about to go, when Emilia said, " I stipulate that the
cards shall now be cut for you too." The old woman was
ready. " Do not let me be present," cried I, and hastened
down stairs.

The next day I had not courage to go there. The third
day, early in the morning, Emilia sent me word by a boy who
had already brought me many a message from the sisters, and
had carried back flowers and fruits to them in return, that I
should not fail that day. I came at the usual hour, and
found the father alone, who, in many respects, improved my
paces and steps, my goings and comings, my bearing and
behaviour, and, moreover, seemed to be satisfied with me.
The younger daughter came in towards the end of the hour,
and danced with me a very graceful minuet, in which her
movements were extraordinarily pleasing, and her father declared that he had rarely seen a prettier and more nimble
pair upon his floor. After the lesson, I went as usual into
the sitting-room ; the father left us alone ; I missed Lucinda.
" She is in bed," said Emilia, " and I am glad of it : do not
be concerned about it. Her mental illness is first alleviated
when she fancies herself bodily sick ; she does not like to die,
and therefore she then does what we wish. We have certain
family medicines which she takes, and reposes ; and thus, by
degrees, the swelling waves subside. She is, indeed, too good
and amiable in such an imaginary sickness, and as she is in
reality very well, and is only attacked by passion, she imagines various kinds of romantic deaths, with which she
frightens herself in a pleasant manner, like children when we
tell them ghost-stories. Thus, yesterday evening, she announced to me with great vehemence, that this time she should
certainly die, and that only when she was really near death,
they should bring again before her the ungrateful false friend,
who had at first acted so handsomely to her, and now treated
her so ill ; she would reproach him bitterly, and then give up
the ghost." " I know not that I am guilty," exclaimed I, " of
having expressed any sort of affection for her. I know somebody who can best bear me witness in this respect." Emilia

smiled and rejoined, " I understand you; and if we are not
discreet and determined, we shall all find ourselves in a bad
plight together. What will you say if I entreat you not to
continue your lessons? You have, I believe, four tickets
yet of the last month, and my father has already declared
that he finds it inexcusable to take your money any longer,
unless you wish to devote yourself to the art of dancing in a
more serious manner: what is required by a young man of
the world you possess already." " And do you, Emilia, give
me this advice, to avoid your house?" replied I. " Yes, I
do," said she, " but not of myself. Only listen. When you
hastened away, the day before yesterday, I had the cards cut
for you, and the same response was repeated thrice, and each
time more emphatically. You were surrounded by everything
good and pleasing, by friends and great lords, and there was
no lack of money. The ladies kept themselves at some distance. My poor sister in particular stood always the farthest
off; one other advanced constantly nearer to you, but never
came up to your side, for a third person, of the male sex,
always came between. I will confess to you that I thought that
I myself was meant by the second lady, and after this confession you will best comprehend my well-meant counsel. To
an absent friend I have promised my heart and my hand, and,
until now, I loved him above all: yet it might be possible for
your presence to become more important to me than hitherto,
and what kind of a situation would you have between two
sisters, one of whom you had made unhappy by your affection, and the other by your coldness, and all this ado about
nothing and only for a short time? For if we had not known
already who you are and what are your expectations, the
cards would have placed it before my eyes in the clearest
manner. Fare you well!" said she, and gave me her hand.
I hesitated. " Now," said she, leading me towards the door,
" that it may really be the last time that we shall speak to
each other, take what I would otherwise have denied you."
She fell upon my neck, and kissed me most tenderly. I
embraced her, and pressed her to my bosom.

At this moment the side-door flew open, and her sister, in
a light but becoming night-dress, sprang out and cried, " You
shall not be the only one to take leave of him!" Emilia
let me go, and Lucinda seized me, clasped herself fast to my

heart, pressed her black locks upon my cheeks, and remained
in this position for some time. And thus I found myself in
the dilemma between two sisters which Emilia had prophesied to me a moment before. Lucinda let me loose, and
looked earnestly into my face. I would have taken her hand
and said something friendly to her, but she turned herself
away, walked with violent steps up and down the room for
some time, and then threw herself into a corner of the sofa.
Emilia went to her, but was immediately repulsed, and here
began a scene which is yet painful to me in the recollection,
and which, although really it had nothing theatrical about it,
but was quite suitable to a lively young Frenchwoman, could
only be properly repeated in the theatre by a good and
feeling actress.

Lucinda overwhelmed her sister with a thousand reproaches.
"This is not the first heart," she cried, "that was inclining
itself to me, and that you have turned away. Was it not just so
with him who is absent, and who at last betrothed himself to
you under my very eyes? I was compelled to look on; I endured it; but I know how many thousand tears it has cost me.
This one, too, you have now taken away from me, without
letting the other go; and how many do you not manage to
keep at once? I am frank and good-natured, and every one
thinks he knows me soon, and may neglect me. You are
secret and quiet, and people think wonders of what may be
concealed behind you. Yet there is nothing behind but a
cold, selfish heart that can sacrifice everything to itself; this
nobody learns so easily, because it lies deeply hidden in your
breast; and just as little do they know of my warm, true
heart, which I carry about with me as open as my face."

Emilia was silent, and had sat down by her sister, who became
constantly more and more excited in her discourse, and let certain private matters slip out, which it was not exactly proper for
me to know. Emilia, on the other hand, who was trying to
pacify her sister, made me a sign from behind that I should
withdraw; but as jealousy and suspicion see with a thousand
eyes, Lucinda seemed to have noticed this also. She sprang
up and advanced to me, but not with vehemence. She stood
before me, and seemed to be thinking of something. Then she
said, "I know that I have lost you; I make no further pretensions to you. But neither shall you have him, sister!"

With these words she grasped me very singularly by the head, thrusting both her hands into my locks, pressing my face to hers, and kissed me repeatedly on the mouth. "Now," cried she, "fear my curse! Woe upon woe, for ever and ever, to her who kisses these lips for the first time after me! Dare to have anything more to do with him! I know heaven hears me this time. And you, Sir, hasten now, hasten away as fast as you can!"

I flew down the stairs, with the firm determination never to enter the house again.

TENTH BOOK.

THE German poets, since they, as members of a corporation, no longer stood as one man, did not enjoy the smallest advantages in the citizen-world. They had neither support, standing, nor respectability, except in so far as their other position was favourable to them, and therefore it was a matter of mere chance whether talent was born to honour or to disgrace. A poor son of earth, with a consciousness of mind and faculties, was forced to crawl along painfully through life, and, from the pressure of momentary necessities, to squander the gifts which perchance he had received from the Muses. Occasional poems, the first and most genuine of all kinds of poetry, had become despicable to such a degree, that the nation even now cannot attain a conception of their high value; and a poet, if he did not strike altogether into Günther's path, appeared in the world in the most melancholy state of subserviency, as a jester and parasite, so that both on the theatre and on the stage of life he represented a character which any one and every one could abuse at pleasure.

If, on the contrary, the Muse associated herself with men of respectability, these received thereby a lustre which was reflected back to the donor. Noblemen well versed in life, like Hagedorn, dignified citizens, like Brockes, distinguished men of science, like Haller, appeared among the first in the nation, to be equal with the most eminent and the most prized. Those persons, too, were specially honoured, who, together with this pleasing talent, distinguished themselves as active, faithful men of business. In this way Uz, Rabener, and Weisse enjoyed a respect of quite a peculiar kind; people had here to value, when combined, those most heterogeneous qualities which are seldom found united.

But now the time was to come when poetic genius should become aware of itself, should create for itself its own relations, and understand how to lay the foundation of an independent dignity. Everything necessary to found such an epoch was combined in KLOPSTOCK. Considered both from the sensual and moral side, he was a pure young man. Seriously and thoroughly educated, he places, from his youth upwards, a great value upon himself and upon whatever he does, and while considerately measuring out beforehand the steps of his life, turns, with a presentiment of the whole strength of his internal nature, towards the loftiest and most grateful theme. The *Messiah*, a name which betokens infinite attributes, was to be glorified afresh by him. The Redeemer was to be the hero whom the poet thought to accompany through earthly lowliness and sorrows to the highest heavenly triumphs. Everything Godlike, angelic, and human that lay in the young soul was here called into requisition. Brought up by the Bible and nourished by its strength, he now lives with patriarchs, prophets, and forerunners, as if they were present; yet all these are only evoked from ages to draw a bright halo round the One whose humiliation they behold with astonishment, and in whose exaltation they are gloriously to bear a part. For at last, after gloomy and horrible hours, the everlasting Judge will uncloud his face, again acknowledge his Son and fellow-God, who, on the other hand, will again lead to Him alienated men, nay, even a fallen spirit. The living heavens shout with a thousand angel voices round the throne, and a radiance of love gushes out over the universe, which shortly before had fastened its looks upon a fearful place of sacrifice. The heavenly peace which Klopstock felt in the conception and execution of this poem, communicates itself even now to every one who reads the first ten cantos, without allowing certain requisitions to be brought forward, which an advancing cultivation does not willingly abandon.

The dignity of the subject elevated in the poet the feeling of his own personality. That he himself would enter hereafter into those choirs, that the God-Man would distinguish him, nay, give him face to face the reward for his labours, which even here every feeling, pious heart had fondly paid in many a pure tear—these were such innocent, childlike thoughts and hopes, as only a well-constituted mind can conceive and cherish. Thus Klopstock gained the perfect right to regard himself as a consecrated person, and thus in his actions he studied the most scrupulous purity. Even in his old age it troubled him exceedingly that he had given his earliest love

to a lady who, by marrying another, left him in uncertainty
whether she had really loved him or been worthy of him. The
sentiments which bound him to Meta, their hearty, tranquil
affection, their short sacred married life, the aversion of the
surviving husband from a second union, all is of that kind which
may well be remembered hereafter in the circle of the blessed.

This honourable conduct towards himself was still further
enhanced by his being favourably received for a long time in
well-minded Denmark, in the house of a great, and, humanly
speaking, excellent statesman. Here, in a higher circle, which
was exclusive indeed, but, at the same time, devoted to external
manners and attention towards the world, his tendency became
still more decided. A composed demeanour, a measured
speech, and a laconism even when he spoke openly and
decidedly, gave him, through his whole life, a certain diplomatic ministerial consequence, which seemed to be at variance
with his tender natural feelings, although both sprang from
one source. Of all this, his first works give a clear transcript
and type, and they thus could not but gain an incredible influence. That, however, he personally assisted others who were
struggling in life and poetry, has scarcely been mentioned, as
one of his most decided characteristics.

But just such a furtherance of young people in literary
action and pursuit, a hopeful pleasure in bringing forward
men not favoured by fortune, and making the way easy to
them, has rendered illustrious one German, who, in respect to
the dignity which he gave himself, may be named as the second,
but, in regard to his living influence, as the first. It will
escape no one that GLEIM is here meant. In possession of an
obscure, indeed, but lucrative office, residing in a pleasantly
situated spot, not too large, and enlivened by military, civic,
and literary activity, whence proceeded the revenues of a great
and wealthy institution, not without a part of them remaining
behind for the advantage of the place, he felt within himself
also a lively productive impulse, which, however, with all its
strength, was not quite enough for him, and therefore he
gave himself up to another, perhaps stronger impulse, namely,
that of making others produce something. Both these activities
were intertwined incessantly during his whole long life. He
could as easily have lived without taking breath, as without
writing poetry and making presents, and by helping needy

talents of all kinds through earlier or later embarrassments,
contributing to the honour of literature, he gained so many
friends, debtors, and dependents, that they willingly allowed his
diffuse verses to pass, since they could give him nothing in
return for his rich benefits but endurance of his poetry.

Now, the high idea which these two men might well form
of their own worth, and by which others were induced also
to think themselves somebody, has produced very great and
beautiful results, both in public and private. But this consciousness, honourable as it is, called a peculiar evil down for
themselves, for those around them, and for their time. If,
judging from their intellectual effects, both these men may
without hesitation be called great, with respect to the world
they remained but small, and considered in comparison with
a more stirring life, their external position was nought. The
day is long, and so is the night : one cannot be always writing poetry, or doing, or giving : their time could not be filled
up like that of people of the world, and men of rank and
wealth : they therefore set too high a value on their particular limited situations, attached an importance to their
daily affairs which they should only have allowed themselves
amongst each other, and took more than reasonable delight in
their own jokes, which, though they made the moment agreeable, could be of no consequence in the end. They received
praise and honour from others, as they deserved ; they gave it
back, with measure indeed, but always too profusely ; and
because they felt that their friendship was worth much, they
were pleased to express it repeatedly, and in this spared neither
paper nor ink. Thus arose those correspondences, at the deficiency of which in solid contents the modern world wonders, nor
can it be blamed, when it hardly sees the possibility of eminent
men delighting themselves in such an interchange of nothing,
or when it expresses the wish that such leaves might have
remained unprinted. But we may suffer these few volumes
always to stand along with so many others upon our book-
shelves, if we have learned from them the fact that even the
most eminent man lives only by the day, and enjoys but a
sorry entertainment, when he throws himself too much back
upon himself, and neglects to grasp into the fulness of the
external world, where alone he can find nourishment for his
growth, and at the same time a standard for its measurement.

The activity of these men was in its finest bloom, when we young folks began also to bestir ourselves in our own circle, and with my younger friends, if not with older persons too, I was pretty much in the way of falling into this sort of mutual flattery, forbearance, raising and supporting. In my immediate sphere, whatever I produced could always be reckoned good. Ladies, friends, and patrons will not consider bad that which is undertaken and written out of affection for them. From such obligations at last arises the expression of an empty satisfaction with each other, in the phrases of which a character is easily lost, if it is not from time to time steeled to higher excellence.

And thus I had the happiness to say that, by means of an unexpected acquaintance, all the self-complacency, love of the looking-glass, vanity, pride, and haughtiness that might have been resting or working within me, were exposed to a very severe trial, which was unique in its kind, by no means in accordance with the time, and therefore so much the more searching and more sorely felt.

For the most important event, one that was to have the weightiest consequences for me, was my acquaintance with HERDER, and the nearer connexion with him which sprung from it. He accompanied the travels of the Prince of Holstein-Eutin, who was in a melancholy state of mind, and had come with him to Strasburg. Our society, as soon as it knew of his arrival, was seized with a great longing to approach him, and this good fortune happened to me first, quite unexpectedly and by chance. I had gone to the Ghost tavern to inquire after some distinguished stranger or other. Just at the bottom of the staircase I found a man who was on the point of ascending, and whom I might have taken for a clergyman. His powdered hair was put up in a queue, his black clothes likewise distinguished him, but still more a long black silk mantle, the skirts of which he had gathered up and stuck into his pocket. This somewhat striking, but yet, on the whole, polite and pleasing figure, of which I had already been told, left me not the least doubt that he was the celebrated newcomer, and my address was to convince him at once that I knew him. He asked my name, which could be of no consequence to him; but my frankness seemed to please him, since he returned it with great friendliness, and as we mounted the

stairs, showed himself ready immediately for animated communication. I have forgotten whom we visited then ; it is
sufficient to say, that at parting I begged permission to wait
on him at his own residence, which he granted me kindly
enough. I did not neglect to avail myself repeatedly of this
favour, and was more and more attracted by him. He had
somewhat of softness in his manner, which was very suitable
and becoming, without being exactly easy. A round face, an
imposing forehead, a somewhat puggish nose, a mouth somewhat prominent, but highly characteristic, pleasing, and amiable ; a pair of coal-black eyes under black eye-brows, which
did not fail of their effect, although one of them used to be red
and inflamed. By various questions he tried to make himself
acquainted with me and my situation, and his power of attraction operated on me with growing strength. I was, generally
speaking, of a very confiding disposition, and with him especially I had no secrets. It was not long, however, before the
repelling pulse of his nature began to appear, and placed me
in no small uneasiness. I related to him many things of my
youthful occupations and taste, and among others, of a collection of seals, which I had principally gotten together through
the assistance of our family friend, who had an extensive correspondence. I had arranged them according to the *State
Calendar*, and by this means had become well acquainted with
the whole of the potentates, the greater and lesser mightinesses
and powers, even down to the nobility under them. These
heraldic insignia had often, and in particular at the ceremonies
of the coronation, been of use to my memory. I spoke of these
things with some complacency ; but he was of another opinion,
and not only stripped the subject of all interest, but also contrived to make it ridiculous and nearly disgusting.

From this his spirit of contradiction I had much to endure ;
for he had resolved, partly because he wished to separate from
the prince, partly on account of a complaint in his eye, to remain in Strasburg. This complaint is one of the most inconvenient and unpleasant, and the more troublesome since it can
be cured only by a painful, highly irritating and uncertain
operation. The tear-bag is closed below, so that the moisture
contained in it cannot flow off to the nose, and so much the
less as the adjacent bone is deficient in the aperture by which
this secretion should naturally take place. The bottom of the

tear-bag must therefore be cut open, and the bone bored through, when a horse-hair is drawn through the lachrymal point, then down through the opened bag, and the new canal thus put into connexion with it, and this hair is moved backwards and forwards every day, in order to restore the communication between the two parts ;—all which cannot be done or attained, if an incision is not first made externally in that place.

Herder was now separated from the prince, was moved into lodgings of his own, and resolved to have himself operated upon by Lobstein.   Here those exercises by which I had sought to blunt my sensibility did me good service ; I was able to be present at the operation, and to be serviceable and helpful in many ways to so worthy a man.   I found here every reason to admire his great firmness and endurance : for neither during the numerous surgical operations, nor at the oft-repeated painful dressings, did he show himself in any degree irritable, and of all of us he seemed to be the one who suffered least. But in the intervals, indeed, we had to endure the changes of his temper in many ways.   I say *we*, for besides myself, a pleasant Russian, named PEGLOW, was mostly with him. This man had been an early acquaintance of Herder's in Riga, and though no longer a youth, was trying to perfect himself in surgery under Lobstein's guidance.   Herder could be charmingly prepossessing and brilliant, but he could just as easily turn an ill-humoured side foremost.   All men, indeed, have this attraction and repulsion, according to their nature, some more, some less, some in longer, some in shorter pulsations ; few can really control their peculiarities in this respect, many in appearance.   As for Herder, the preponderance of his contradictory, bitter, biting humour was certainly derived from his disease and the sufferings arising from it.   This case often occurs in life : one does not sufficiently take into consideration the moral effect of sickly conditions, and one therefore judges many characters very unjustly, because it is assumed that all men are healthy, and required of them that they shall conduct themselves accordingly.

During the whole time of this cure I visited Herder morning and evening ; I even remained whole days with him, and in a short time accustomed myself so much the more to his chiding and fault-finding, as I daily learned to appreciate his beautiful and great qualities, his extensive knowledge, and his profound views. The influence of this good-natured blusterer was great and important. He was five years older than myself, which in younger days makes a great difference to begin with; and as I acknowledged him for what he was, and tried to value that which he had already produced, he necessarily gained a great superiority over me. But the situation was not comfortable; for older persons, with whom I had associated hitherto, had sought to form me with indulgence, perhaps had even spoiled me by their lenity; but from Herder, behave as one might, one could never expect approval. As now, on the one side, my great affection and reverence for him, and on the other, the discontent which he excited in me, were continually at strife with each other, there arose within me an inward struggle, the first of its kind which I had experienced in my life. Since his conversations were at all times important, whether he asked, answered, or communicated his opinions in any other manner, he could not but advance me daily, nay hourly, to new views. At Leipzig, I had accustomed myself to a narrow and circumscribed existence, and my general knowledge of German literature could not be extended by my situation in Frankfort; nay, those mystico-religio-chemical occupations had led me into obscure regions, and what had been passing for some years back in the wide literary world, had for the most part remained unknown to me. Now I was at once made acquainted by Herder with all the new aspiration, and all the tendencies which it seemed to be taking. He had already made himself sufficiently known, and by his *Fragments*, his *Kritische Wälder* (*Critical Woods*), and other works, had immediately placed himself by the side of the most eminent men who had for a long time drawn towards them the eyes of their country. What an agitation there must have been in such a mind— what a fermentation there must have been in such a nature— can neither be conceived nor described. But great was certainly the concealed effort, as will be easily admitted, when one reflects for how many years afterwards and how much he has done and produced.

We had not lived together long in this manner when he confided to me that he meant to be a competitor for the prize which was offered, at Berlin, for the best treatise on the origin of language. His work was already nearly completed, and, as he wrote a very neat hand, he could soon communicate to me, in parts, a legible manuscript. I had never reflected on such subjects, for I was yet too deeply involved in the midst of things to have thought about their beginning and end. The question, too, seemed to me in some measure an idle one; for if God had created man as man, language was just as innate in him as walking erect; he must have just as well perceived that he could sing with his throat, and modify the tones in various ways with tongue, palate, and lips, as he must have remarked that he could walk and take hold of things. If man was of divine origin, so was also language itself; and if man, considered in the circle of nature, was a natural being, language was likewise natural. These two things, like soul and body, I could never separate. Silberschlag, with a realism crude yet somewhat fantastically devised, had declared himself for the divine origin, that is, that God had played the schoolmaster to the first men. Herder's treatise went to show that man as man could and must have attained to language by his own powers. I read the treatise with much pleasure, and it was of special aid in strengthening my mind; only I did not stand high enough either in knowledge or thought to form a solid judgment upon it. I therefore gave the author my applause, adding only a few remarks which flowed from my way of viewing the subject. But one was received just like the other; there was scolding and blaming, whether one agreed with him conditionally or unconditionally. The fat surgeon had less patience than I; he humorously declined the communication of this prize-essay, and affirmed that he was not prepared to meditate on such abstract topics. He urged us in preference to a game of ombre, which we commonly played together in the evening.

During so troublesome and painful a cure, Herder lost nothing of his vivacity; but it became less and less amiable. He could not write a note to ask for anything, that would not be spiced with some scoff or other. Once, for instance, he wrote to me thus :—

" If those letters of Brutus thou hast in thy Cicero's letters,
  Thou, whom consolers of schools, deck'd out in magnificent bindings,
  Soothe from their well plan'd shelves—yet more by the outside than
      inside,
  Thou, who from gods art descended, or Goths, or from origin filthy,*
  Göthe, send them to me."

It was not polite, indeed, that he should allow himself this
jest on my name; for a man's name is not like a mantle,
which merely hangs about him, and which, perchance, may
be safely twitched and pulled; but is a perfectly fitting garment, which has grown over and over him like his very skin,
at which one cannot rake and scrape without wounding the
man himself.

The first reproach, on the contrary, was better founded.
I had brought with me to Strasburg the authors I had obtained, by exchange, from Langer, with various fine editions
from my father's collection besides, and had set them up on a
neat book-case, with the best intentions of using them. But
how should my time, which I split up into an hundred
different activities, suffice for that? Herder, who was most
attentive to books, since he had need of them every moment,
perceived my fine collection at his first visit, but soon saw,
too, that I made no use of them. He, therefore, as the
greatest enemy to all false appearances and ostentation, was
accustomed, on occasion, to rally me upon the subject.

Another sarcastic poem occurs to me, which he sent me
one evening, when I had been telling him a great deal about
the Dresden gallery. I had, indeed, not penetrated into the
higher meaning of the Italian school; but Dominico Feti, an
excellent artist, although a humorist, and therefore not of
the first rank, had interested me much. Scripture subjects
had to be painted. He confined himself to the New Testament parables, and was fond of representing them with much
originality, taste, and good-humour. He brought them altogether into every-day life, and the spirited and *naïve* details
of his compositions, recommended by a free pencil, had made
a vivid impression upon me. At this, my childish enthusiasm
for art, Herder sneered in the following fashion :—

* The German word is " Koth," and the whole object of the line is to
introduce a play on the words " Göthe," " Götter," " Gothen," and
" Koth."— *Trans.*

> " From sympathy,
> The master I like best of all
> Dominico Feti they call.
> A parable from Scripture he is able
> Neatly to turn into a crazy fable.
> From sympathy :—thou crazy parable ! "

I could mention many jokes of the kind, more or less clear or abstruse, cheerful or bitter. They did not vex me, but made me feel uncomfortable. Yet since I knew how to value highly everything that contributed to my own cultivation, and as I had often given up former opinions and inclinations, I soon accommodated myself, and only sought, as far as it was possible for me from my point of view, to distinguish just blame from unjust invectives. And thus no day passed over that had not been, in the most fruitful manner, instructive to me.

I was made acquainted by him with poetry from quite a different side, in another light than heretofore, and one, too, which suited me well. The poetic art of the Hebrews, which he treated ingeniously after his predecessor Lowth—popular poetry, the traditions of which in Alsace he urged us to search after; and the oldest records existing as poetry—all bore witness that poetry in general was a gift to the world and to nations, and not the private inheritance of a few refined, cultivated men. I swallowed all this, and the more eager I was in receiving, the more liberal was he in giving, so that we spent the most interesting hours together. The other natural studies which I had begun, I endeavoured to continue, and as one always has time enough, if one will apply it well, so amongst them all I succeeded in doing twice or thrice as much as usual. As to the fulness of those few weeks during which we lived together, I can well say that all which Herder has gradually produced since, was then announced in the germ, and that I thereby fell into the fortunate condition that I could completely attach to something higher, and expand all that I had hitherto thought, learned, and made my own. Had Herder been methodical, I should have found the most precious guide for giving a durable tendency to my cultivation; but he was more inclined to examine and stimulate, than to lead and conduct. Thus he at first made me acquainted with Hamann's writings, upon which he set a very great value.

But instead of instructing me as to these, and making the bias and drift of his extraordinary mind intelligible to me, it generally only served him for amusement when I behaved strangely enough, in trying to get at the meaning of such sibylline leaves. However, I could well feel that something in Hamann's writings appealed to me; and to this I gave myself up, without knowing whence it came or whither it was leading me.

After the cure had lasted longer than was reasonable, Lobstein had begun to hesitate, and to repeat himself in his treatment, so that the affair would not come to an end; and Peglow, too, had confided to me in private that a favourable issue was hardly to be expected; the whole position became gloomy: Herder became impatient and out of temper, he could not succeed in continuing his activity as heretofore, and was obliged to restrain himself the more, as they began to lay the blame of the surgical failure upon his too great mental exertion, and his uninterrupted, animated, nay, merry intercourse with us. It is sufficient to say, that after so much trouble and suffering, the artificial tear-channel would not form itself, and the communication intended would not take place. It was necessary to let the wound heal over in order that the disease should not become worse. If, now, during the operation, one could but admire Herder's firmness under such pains, his melancholy and even fierce resignation to the idea that he must bear such a blot about him all his life, had about it something truly sublime, by which he gained for ever the reverence of those who saw and loved him. This disease, which disfigured so expressive a countenance, must have been so much the more afflicting to him, as he had become acquainted with an excellent lady in Darmstadt, and had gained her affections. It may have been for this cause principally that he submitted to the cure, in order, on his return, to appear more free, more cheerful, and more handsome in the eyes of his half-betrothed, and to unite himself more certainly and indissolubly with her. However, he hastened away from Strasburg as soon as possible, and since his stay had hitherto been as expensive as it was unpleasant, I borrowed a sum of money for him, which he promised to refund by an appointed day. The time passed without the arrival of the money. My creditor, indeed, did not dun me; but I was for several weeks

in embarrassment. At last the letter and the money came,
and even here he did not act unlike himself; for, instead of
thanks or an apology, his letter contained nothing but satirical
things in doggerel verse, which would have puzzled, if not
alienated, another; but it did not move me at all, for I had
conceived so great and powerful an idea of his worth that it
absorbed everything of an opposite nature which could have
injured it.

One should never speak, publicly at least, of one's own
faults, or those of others, if one does not hope to effect some
useful purpose by it; on this account I will here insert certain remarks which force themselves upon me.

Gratitude and ingratitude belong to those events which
appear every moment in the moral world, and about which
men can never agree among themselves. I usually distinguish
between non-thankfulness, ingratitude, and aversion from
gratitude. The first is innate with men, nay, created with
them: for it arises from a happy volatile forgetfulness of the
repulsive as well as of the delightful, by which alone the continuation of life is possible. Man needs such an infinite
quantity of previous and concurrent assistances for a tolerable
existence, that if he would always pay to the sun and the
earth, to God and nature, to ancestors and parents, to friends
and companions, the thanks due to them, he would have
neither time nor feeling left to receive and enjoy new benefits.
But if the natural man suffers this volatility to get the control
in and over him, a cold indifference gains more and more the
ascendancy, and one at last regards one's benefactor as a
stranger, to whose injury, perhaps, anything may be undertaken, provided it be advantageous to ourselves. This alone
can properly be called ingratitude, which results from the
rudeness into which the uncultivated nature must necessarily
lose itself at last. Aversion from gratitude, however, the
rewarding of a benefit by ill-natured and sullen conduct, is
very rare, and occurs only in eminent men, such as, with great
natural gifts, and a presentiment of them, being born in a
lower rank of society or in a helpless condition, must, from
their youth upwards, force themselves along, step by step, and
receive, at every point, aids and supports, which are often
embittered and repulsive to them through the coarseness of
their benefactors, since that which they receive is earthly,

while that which, on the other hand, they give, is of a higher
kind, so that what is, strictly speaking, a compensation, is
out of the question. Lessing, with the fine knowledge of
earthly things which fell to his share in the best years of his
life, has in one place bluntly, but cheerfully expressed himself.
Herder, on the contrary, constantly embittered his finest days,
both for himself and others, because he knew not how to
moderate, by strength of mind in later years, that ill-humour
which had necessarily seized him in youth.

One may well make this demand of oneself: for, to a man's
capability of cultivation, comes, with friendly aid, the light of
nature, which is always active in enlightening him about
his condition; and generally, in many moral points of culture,
one should not construe the failings too severely, nor look
about after the most serious and remote means of correcting
them; for certain faults may be easily and even playfully
removed. Thus, for instance, by mere habit, we can excite
gratitude in ourselves, keep it alive, and even make it necessary to us.

In a biographical attempt, it is proper to speak of oneself.
I am, by nature, as little grateful as any man, and on forget-
ting the benefit received, the violent feeling of a momentary
disagreement could very easily beguile me into ingratitude.

To obviate this, I accustomed myself, in the first place,
with everything that I possessed, to call to mind with pleasure
how I came by it, from whom I received it, whether it was
by way of present, exchange, or purchase, or in any other
manner. I have accustomed myself, in showing my collections, to mention the persons by whose means I obtained each
article, nay, even to do justice to the occasion, to the accident,
to the remotest cause and coincidence, by which things which
are dear and of value to me have become mine. That which
surrounds us thus receives a life; we see in it a spiritual combination, full of love, reminding us of its origin; and, by thus
making past circumstances present to us, our momentary
existence is elevated and enriched, the originators of the gifts
rise repeatedly before the imagination, we connect with their
image a pleasing remembrance, ingratitude becomes impossible, and a return, on occasion, becomes easy and desirable.
At the same time, we are led to the consideration of that
which is not a possession palpable to the senses, and we love

to recapitulate to whom our higher endowments are to be ascribed, and whence they take their date.

Before I turn my attention from that connexion with Herder, which was so important and so rich in consequences for me, I find yet something more to adduce. Nothing was more natural than that I should by degrees become more and more reserved towards Herder, in communicating those things which had hitherto contributed to my culture, but especially such as still seriously occupied my attention at the moment. He had destroyed my enjoyment of so much that I had loved before, and had especially blamed me in the strongest manner for the pleasure I took in *Ovid's Metamorphoses*. I might defend my favourite as I would, I might say that, for a youthful fancy, nothing could be more delightful than to linger in those cheerful and glorious regions with gods and demi-gods, and to be a witness of their deeds and passions; I might circumstantially quote that previously mentioned opinion of a sober-minded man, and corroborate it by my own experience; all this, according to Herder, went for nothing; there was no immediate truth, properly so called, to be found in these poems; here was neither Greece nor Italy, neither a primitive world nor a cultivated one, everything was rather an imitation of what had already existed, and a mannerised representation, such as could be expected only from an over-cultivated man. And if at last I would maintain, that whatever an eminent individual produces is also nature, and that always, in all nations, ancient and modern, the poet alone has been the maker; this was not allowed to pass, and I had to endure much on this account, nay, I was almost disgusted with my Ovid by it; for there is no affection, no habit so strong, that it can hold out in the long run against the animadversions of eminent men in whom one places confidence. Something always cleaves to us, and if one cannot love unconditionally, love is already in a critical condition.

I most carefully concealed from him my interest in certain subjects which had rooted themselves within me, and were, by little and little, moulding themselves into poetic form. These were *Götz von Berlichingen* and *Faust*. The biography of the former had seized my inmost heart. The figure of a rude, well-meaning self-helper, in a wild anarchical time, awakened my deepest sympathy. The significant puppet-

show fable of the latter resounded and vibrated many-toned
within me. I had also wandered about in all sorts of science,
and had early enough been led to see its vanity. I had, moreover, tried all sorts of ways in real life, and had always returned
more unsatisfied and troubled. Now these things, as well as
many others, I carried about with me, and delighted myself
with them during my solitary hours, but without writing anything down. But most of all, I concealed from Herder my
mystico-cabalistical chemistry, and everything relating to it,
although, at the same time, I was still very fond of secretly
busying myself in working it out more consistently than it
had been communicated to me. Of my poetical labours, I
believe I laid before him *Die Mitschuldigen*, but I do not
recollect that on this account I received either correction
or encouragement on his part. Yet, with all this, he remained
what he was; whatever proceeded from him had an important,
if not a cheering effect, and even his handwriting exercised a
magic power over me. I do not remember having ever torn
up or thrown away one of his letters, or even a mere envelope
from his hand; yet, with my various changes of place and
time, not one document of those strange, foreboding, and
happy days is left.

That Herder's power of attraction operated upon others as
well as upon me, I should scarcely mention, had I not to remark that it extended itself particularly to JUNG, commonly
called STILLING. The true, honest striving of this man could
not but deeply interest everybody who had any feeling, and
his susceptibility must have charmed into candour every one
who was in a condition to impart anything. Even Herder
behaved towards him with more forbearance than towards the
rest of us: for his counter-action always seemed to stand in
relation with the action exerted upon him. Jung's narrowness
was accompanied by so much good-will, his urgency with so
much softness and earnestness, that a man of intelligence could
certainly not be severe against him, and a benevolent man
could not scoff at him, or turn him into ridicule. Jung was
also exhilarated to such a degree by Herder, that he felt himself strengthened and advanced in all he did; even his affection for me seemed to lose ground in the same ratio; yet we
always remained good companions, made allowances for each
other from first to last, and mutually rendered the most friendly
services.

Let us now, however, withdraw ourselves from the sick chamber of friendship, and from the general considerations which refer rather to disorder than to health of mind : let us betake ourselves into the open air, to the lofty and broad gallery of the minster, as if the time were still present, when we young fellows often appointed an evening meeting to greet the departing sun with brimming goblets. Here all conversation was lost in the contemplation of the country : here sharpness of eye-sight was put to the proof, and every one strove to perceive, nay, plainly to distinguish, the most distant objects. Good telescopes were employed to assist us, and one friend after another exactly pointed out the spot which had become the most dear and precious to him; and I also did not lack such a little spot, which, although it did not come out with importance in the landscape, nevertheless more than all the rest attracted me with an amiable magic. On these occasions the imagination was excited by relating our adventures, and several little jaunts were concerted, nay, often undertaken on the spur of the moment, of which I will circumstantially relate only one instead of a number, since in many respects it was of consequence to me.

With two worthy friends and fellow-boarders, Engelbach and Weyland, both natives of Lower Alsace, I repaired on horseback to Zabern, where, in the fine weather, the friendly little place smiled pleasantly upon us. The sight of the bishop's castle awakened our admiration ; the extent, height, and splendour of a new set of stables bore witness to the other comforts of the owner. The gorgeousness of the staircase surprised us, the chambers and saloons we trode with reverence, only the person of the cardinal, a little wreck of a man, whom we saw at table, made a contrast. The view of the garden is splendid, and a canal, three quarters of a league long, which leads straight up to the middle of the castle, gives a high idea of the taste and resources of the former possessors. We rambled up and down there, and enjoyed many parts of this beautifully situated whole, which lies on the outskirts of the magnificent plain of Alsace, at the foot of the Vosges.

After we had enjoyed ourselves at this clerical outpost of a royal power, and had made ourselves comfortable in its region, we arrived early next morning at a public work, which most nobly opens the entrance into a mighty kingdom. Illumined

by the beams of the rising sun, the famous Zabern-stairs, a
work of incredible labour, rose before us.   A road, built ser-
pentine-wise over the most fearful crags, and wide enough for
three wagons abreast, leads up hill so gently, that the ascent
is scarcely perceptible.   The hardness and smoothness of the
way, the flat-topped elevations on both sides for the foot-pas-
sengers, the stone channels to lead off the mountain-water, all
are executed as neatly as artistically and durably, so that they
afford a satisfactory view.   Thus one gradually arrives at
Pfalzburg, a modern fortification.   It lies upon a moderate
hill; the works are elegantly built on blackish rocks, and of
the same kind of stone, and the joinings being pointed out
with white mortar, show exactly the size of the square stones,
and give a striking proof of neat workmanship.   We found
the place itself, as is proper for a fortress, regular, built of
stone, and the church in good taste.   When we wandered
through the streets—it was nine o'clock on Sunday morning—we heard music: they were already waltzing in the
tavern to their hearts' content, and as the inhabitants did not
suffer themselves to be disturbed in their pleasures by the
great scarcity, nay, by the threatened famine, so also our
youthful cheerfulness was not at all troubled when the baker
on the road refused us some bread, and directed us to the
tavern, where perhaps we might procure provisions at the
usual place.

We now very willingly rode down the Zabern-stairs again
to gaze at this architectural wonder a second time, and to enjoy once more the refreshing prospect over Alsace.   We soon
reached Buchsweiler, where friend Weyland had prepared for
us a good reception.   To a fresh youthful mind the condition
of a small town is well suited: family connexions are closer
and more perceptible; domestic life, which, with moderate
activity, moves hither and thither between light official duties,
town business, agriculture and gardening, invites us to a
friendly participation; sociableness is necessary, and the
stranger finds himself very pleasantly situated in the limited
circles, if the disputes of the inhabitants, which in such places
are more palpable, do not everywhere come in contact with
him.   This little town was the chief place of the county of
Hanau-Lichtenberg, belonging to the Landgrave of Darmstadt, under French sovereignty.   A regency and board of

officers established here made the place an important centre-
point of a very beautiful and desirable principality. We
easily forgot the unequal streets and the irregular architecture
of the place when we went out to look at the old castle and
the gardens, which are excellently laid out on a hill. Numerous little pleasure-woods, a preserve for tame and wild phea-
sants, and the relics of many similar arrangements, showed
how pleasant this little residence must formerly have been.

Yet all these views were surpassed by the prospect which
met the eye, when, from the neighbouring Baschberg, one
looked over the perfectly paradisiacal region. This height,
wholly heaped together out of different kinds of shells, attracted
my attention for the first time to such documents of antiquity;
I had never before seen them together in so great a mass.
Yet the curious eye soon turned itself exclusively to the landscape. You stand on the last landward* mountain-point ;
towards the north lies a fruitful plain, interspersed with little
forests, and bounded by a stern row of mountains that stretches
itself westward towards Zaber, where the episcopal palace and
the abbey of St. John, lying a league beyond it, may be plainly
recognised. Thence the eye follows the more and more vanish-
ing chain of the Vosges towards the south. If you turn to the
north-east you see the castle of Lichtenberg upon a rock, and
towards the south-east the eye has the boundless plain of Alsace
to scrutinize, which, afar off, withdraws itself from the sight
in the more and more misty landscape, until at last the Suabian
mountains melt away like shadows into the horizon.

Already in my limited wanderings through the world, I had
remarked how important it is in travelling to inquire after the
course of the waters, and even to ask with respect to the
smallest brook, whither in reality it runs. One thus acquires
a general survey of every stream-region, in which one happens
to be, a conception of the heights and depths which bear relation to each other, and by these leading lines, which assist the
contemplation as well as the memory, extricates oneself in the
surest manner from the geological and political labyrinth.
With these observations, I took a solemn farewell of my beloved Alsace, as the next morning we meant to turn our steps
towards Lorraine.

* That is, towards *Germany* ; Germany is *the Land* by pre-eminence.
—*American Note.*

The evening passed away in familiar conversation, in which we tried to cheer ourselves up under a joyless present, by remembrances of a better past. Here, as in the whole of this small country, the name of the last Count Reinhard von Hanau was blessed above all others; his great understanding and aptitude had appeared in all his actions, and many a beautiful memorial of his existence yet remained. Such men have the advantage of being double benefactors: once to the present, which they make happy, and then to the future, the feeling of which and courage they nourish and sustain.

Now as we turned ourselves north-westward into the mountains, passed by Lützelstein, an old mountain tower, in a very hilly country, and descended into the region of the Saar and the Moselle, the heavens began to lower, as if they would render yet more sensible to us the condition of the more rugged western country. The valley of the Saar, where we first found Bockenheim, a small place, and saw opposite to it Neusaarwerden, which is well-built, with a pleasure-castle, is bordered on both sides by mountains which might be called melancholy, if at their foot an endless succession of meadows and fields, called the Huhnau, did not extend as far as Saaralbe, and beyond it, further than the eye can reach. Great buildings, belonging to the former stables of the Duke of Lorraine, here attract the eye; they are at present used as a dairy, for which purpose, indeed, they are very well situated. We passed through Saargemund to Saarbrück, and this little residence was a bright point in a land so rocky and woody. The town, small and hilly, but well adorned by the last prince, makes at once a pleasing impression, as the houses are all painted a greyish white, and the different elevation of them affords a variegated view. In the middle of a beautiful square, surrounded with handsome buildings, stands the Lutheran church, on a small scale, but in proportion with the whole. The front of the castle lies on the same level with the town; the back, on the contrary, on the declivity of a steep rock. This has not only been worked out terrace-fashion, to afford easy access to the valley, but an oblong garden-plot has also been obtained below, by turning off the stream on one side, and cutting away the rock on the other, after which this whole space was first filled up with earth and planted. The time of this undertaking fell in the epoch when they used to consult the architects about laying out gardens,

just as at present they call in the aid of the landscape-painter's
eye. The whole arrangement of the castle, the costly and the
agreeable, the rich and the ornamental, betokened a life-enjoy-
ing owner, such as the deceased prince had been ; the present
sovereign was not at home. President von Günderode received
us in the most obliging manner, and entertained us for three
days better than we had a right to expect. I made use of the
various acquaintance which we formed to instruct myself in
many respects. The life of the former prince, rich in pleasure,
gave material enough for conversation, as well as the various expedients which he hit upon to make use of the advantages supplied by the nature of his land. Here I was now
properly initiated into the interest for mountain countries,
and the love for those economical and technical investigations
which have busied me a great part of my life, was first awakened
within me. We heard of the rich coal-pits at Dutweil, of the iron
and alum works, and even of a burning mountain, and we prepared ourselves to see these wonders close.

We now rode through woody mountains, which must seem
wild and dreary to him who comes out of a magnificent fertile
land, and which can attract us only by the internal contents
of its bosom. We were made acquainted with one simple,
and one complicated piece of machinery, within a short distance of each other : namely, a scythe-smithy and a wire-
drawing factory. If one is pleased at the first because it
supplies the place of common hands, one cannot sufficiently
admire the other, for it works in a higher organic sense, from
which understanding and consciousness are scarcely to be
separated. In the alum-works we made accurate inquiries
after the production and purifying of this so necessary material, and when we saw great heaps of a white greasy, loose,
earthy matter, and asked the use of it, the labourers answered,
smiling, that it was the scum thrown up in boiling the alum,
and that Herr Stauf had it collected, as he hoped perchance
to turn it to some profit. "Is Herr Stauf alive yet?" exclaimed my companion in surprise. They answered in the
affirmative, and assured us that according to the plan of our
journey we should not pass far from his lonely dwelling.

Our road now led up along the channels by which the alum-
water is conducted down, and the principal horizontal works
(*stollen*), which they call the "*landgrube*," and from which the

famous Dutweil coals are procured. These, when they are
dry, have the blue colour of darkly tarnished steel, and the
most beautiful succession of rainbow tints plays over the surface with every movement. The deep abysses of the coal-pits,
however, attracted us so much the less as their contents lay
richly poured out around us. We now reached the open mine, in
which the roasted alum-scales are steeped in ley, and soon
after, a strange occurrence surprised us, although we had been
prepared. We entered into a chasm and found ourselves in
the region of the Burning Mountain. A strong smell of sulphur surrounded us; one side of the cavity was almost red-
hot, covered with reddish stone burnt white; thick fumes
arose from the crevices, and we felt the heat of the ground
through our strong boot-soles. An event so accidental, for it
is not known how this place became ignited, affords a great
advantage for the manufacture of alum, since the alum-scales
of which the surface of the mountain consists, lie there perfectly roasted, and may be steeped in a short time and very
well. The whole chasm had arisen by the calcined scales
being gradually removed and used up. We clambered up out
of this depth, and were on the top of the mountain. A pleasant beech-grove encircled the spot, which followed up to the
chasm and extended itself on both sides of it. Many trees
stood already dried up, some were withering near others,
which, as yet quite fresh, felt no forebodings of that fierce heat
which was approaching and threatening their roots also.

Upon this space different openings were steaming, others
had already done smoking, and this fire had thus smouldered
for ten years already through old broken-up pits and horizontal
shafts, with which the mountain is undermined. It may, too,
have penetrated to the clefts through new coal-beds: for, some
hundred paces farther into the wood, they had contemplated
following up manifest indications of an abundance of coal; but
they had not excavated far before a strong smoke burst out
against the labourers and dispersed them. The opening was
filled up again, yet we found the place still smoking as we
went on our way past it to the residence of our hermitlike
chemist. This lies amid mountains and woods; the vallies
there take very various and pleasing windings, the soil round
about is black and of the coal kind, and strata of it frequently
come in sight. A coal philosopher—*philosophus per ignem*, as

364 TRUTH AND POETRY; FROM MY OWN LIFE.

they said formerly—could scarcely have settled himself more
suitably.

We came before a small house, not inconvenient for a
dwelling, and found Herr Stauf, who immediately recognised
my friend, and received him with lamentations about the new
government. Indeed we could see from what he said, that
the alum-works, as well as many other well-meant establishments, on account of external and perhaps internal circumstances also, did not pay their expenses; with much else of
the sort. He belonged to the chemists of that time, who,
with a hearty feeling for all that could be done with the
products of nature, took delight in abstruse investigations of
trifles and secondary matters, and with their insufficient knowledge were not dexterous enough to do that from which properly economical and mercantile profit is to be derived. Thus
the use which he promised himself from that scum lay very
far in the distance; thus he had nothing to show but a cake
of sal-ammoniac, with which the Burning Mountain had
supplied him.

Ready and glad to communicate his complaints to a human
ear, the lean, decrepit little man, with a shoe on one foot and
a slipper on the other, and with stockings hanging down and
repeatedly pulled up in vain, dragged himself up the mountain
to where the resin-house stands, which he himself had erected,
and now, with great grief, sees falling to ruins. Here was
found a connected row of furnaces, where coal was to be
cleansed of sulphur, and made fit for use in iron-works; but
at the same time they wished also to turn the oil and resin to
account; nay, they would not even lose the soot; and thus
all failed together, on account of the many ends in view.
During the life-time of the former prince, the business had
been carried on in the spirit of an amateur, and in hope;
now they asked for the immediate use, which was not to be
shown.

After we left our adept to his solitude, we hastened—for it
was now late—to the glass-house in Friedrichsthal, where we
became acquainted, on our way, with one of the most important and most wonderful operations of human ingenuity.

Nevertheless, some pleasant adventures, and a surprising firework at night-fall, not far from Neukirch, interested us young
fellows almost more than these important experiences. For as

a few nights before, on the banks of the Saar, shining clouds of glow-worms hovered around us, betwixt rock and thicket, so now the spark-spitting forges played their sprightly firework towards us. We passed, in the depth of night, the smelting-houses situated in the bottom of the valley, and were delighted with the strange half-gloom of these dens of plank, which are but dimly lighted by a little opening in the glowing furnace. The noise of the water, and of the bellows driven by it, the fearful whizzing and shrieking of the blast of air which, raging into the smelted ore, stuns the ears and confuses the senses, drove us away, at last, to turn into Neukirch, which is built up against the mountain.

But, notwithstanding all the variety and fatigue of the day, I could find no rest here. I left my friend to a happy sleep, and sought the hunting-seat, which lay still farther up. It looks out far over mountain and wood, the outlines of which were only to be recognised against the clear night-sky, but the sides and depths of which were impenetrable to my sight. This well-preserved building stood as empty as it was lonely; no castellan, no huntsman was to be found. I sat before the great glass doors upon the steps which run around the whole terrace. Here, surrounded by mountains, over a forest-grown, dark soil, which seemed yet darker in contrast with the clear horizon of a summer night, with the glowing starry vault above me, I sat for a long time by myself on the deserted spot, and thought I never had felt such a solitude. How sweetly, then, was I surprised by the distant sound of a couple of French horns, which at once, like the fragrance of balsam, enlivened the peaceful atmosphere. Then there awakened within me the image of a lovely being, which had retired into the background before the motley objects of these travelling days, but which now unveiled itself more and more, and drove me from the spot back to my quarters, where I made preparations to set off with the earliest.

The return was not used like the journey out. Thus we hurried through Zwey-brücken (Deux-Ponts), which, as a beautiful and notable residence, might well have deserved our attention. We cast a glance upon the great, simple castle, on the extensive esplanades, regularly planted with linden-trees, and very well adapted for the training of race-horses, and on the large stables, and the citizens' houses which the prince had built to be raffled for. All this, as well as the costume

and manners of the inhabitants, especially of the matrons and
maids, had reference to a distant connexion, and made plainly
visible the relation with Paris, from which, for a long time,
nothing transrhenane had been able to withdraw itself. We
visited also the ducal wine-cellars, situated before the city,
which are extensive, and furnished with large, well-made tuns.
We went on further, and at last found the country like that
in the neighbourhood of Saarbrück. Between wild and savage
mountains are a few villages; one here gets rid of the habit
of looking about for corn. We mounted up, by the side of
the Hornbach, to Bitsch, which lies on the important spot
where the waters divide, and fall, a part into the Saar, a part
into the Rhine. These last were soon to attract us towards
them. Yet we could not refuse our attention to the little city
of Bitsch, which very picturesquely winds around the mountain, nor to the fortress, which lies above. This is partly
built on rocks, and partly hewn out of them. The subterra-
neous chambers are particularly worthy of remark; here is
not only space sufficient for the abode of a number of men
and cattle, but one even lights upon large vaults for the dril-
ling of troops, a mill, a chapel, and whatever else could be
required under-ground, provided the surface were in a state
of disturbance.

We now followed the down-rushing brooks through Bären-
thal. The thick forests on both the heights remain unused
by the hand of man. Here trunks of trees lie rotting on
each other by thousands, and young scions sprout up without
number from their half-mouldered progenitors. Here, in conversation with some companions on foot, the name Von
Dieterich again struck our ears, which we had often heard
honourably mentioned already in these woody regions. The
activity and cleverness of this man, his wealth, and the use
and applications of it, all seemed in proportion. He could
with justice take delight in the acquisitions which he increased,
and enjoy the profits he secured. The more I saw of the
world, the more pleasure I took, not only in the universally
famous names, but in those also, especially, which were mentioned in particular regions with reverence and love: and thus
I easily learned here, by a few questions, that Von Dieterich,
earlier than others, had known how to make successful use
of the mountain treasures, iron, coal, and wood, and had
worked his way to an ever-growing opulence.

Niederbrunn, where we now arrived, was a new proof of this. He had purchased this little place from the Count of Leiningen and other part-owners, to erect important iron-works in the place.

Here in these baths, already founded by the Romans, floated around me the spirit of antiquity, venerable relics of which, in fragments of bas-reliefs and inscriptions, capitals and shafts, shone out strangely towards me, from farm-houses, amidst household lumber and furniture.

As we were ascending the adjacent Wasenburg also, I paid my respects to a well-preserved inscription, which discharged a thankful vow to Mercury, and is situated upon the great mass of rock which forms the base of the hill on one side. The fortress itself lies on the last mountain, looking from Bitsch towards Germany. It is the ruin of a German castle built upon Roman remains. From the tower the whole of Alsace was once more surveyed, and the conspicuous minster-spire pointed out the situation of Strasburg. First of all, however, the great forest of Hagenau extended itself, and the towers of this town peered plainly from behind. I was attracted thither. We rode through Reichshof, where Von Dieterich built an imposing castle, and after we had contemplated from the hills near Niedermoder the pleasing course of the little river Moder, by the forest of Hagenau, I left my friend on a ridiculous coal-mine visitation, which, at Dutweil, might have been a somewhat more serious business, and I then rode through Hagenau, on the direct road—already indicated by my affection—to my beloved Sesenheim.

For all these views into a wild, mountain region, and then, again, into a cheerful, fruitful, joyous land, could not rivet my mind's eye, which was directed to an amiable, attractive object. This time, also, the hither way seemed to me more charming than its opposite, as it brought me again into the neighbourhood of a lady to whom I was heartily devoted, and who deserved as much respect as love. But before I lead my friends to her rural abode, let me be permitted to mention a circumstance which contributed very much to enliven and enhance my affection, and the satisfaction which it afforded me.

How far I must have been behindhand in modern literature, may be gathered from the mode of life which I led at Frank-

fort, and from the studies to which I had devoted myself;
nor could my residence in Strasburg have furthered me in
this respect. Now Herder came, and together with his great
knowledge brought many other aids, and the later publications
besides. Among these he announced to us the *Vicar of
Wakefield* as an excellent work, with the German translation
of which he would make us acquainted by reading it aloud to
us himself.

His method of reading was quite peculiar; whoever has
heard him preach will be able to form a notion of it. He
delivered everything, this romance included, in a serious and
simple style, perfectly removed from all dramatically imitative
representation; he even avoided that variety which is not only
permitted, but even required, in an epical delivery—a slight
change of tone when different persons speak, by which what
every one says is brought into relief, and the actor is distinguished from the narrator. Without being monotonous,
Herder let everything go on in the same tone, just as if
nothing was present before him, but all was merely historical;
as if the shadows of this poetic creation did not act livingly
before him, but only glided gently by. Yet this manner of
delivery from his mouth had an infinite charm; for, as he felt
all most deeply, and knew how to estimate the variety of such
a work, so the whole merit of a production appeared purely
and the more clearly, as one was not disturbed by details
sharply spoken out, nor interrupted in the feeling which the
whole was meant to produce.

A Protestant country clergyman is, perhaps, the most beautiful subject for a modern idyl: he appears, like Melchizedek,
as priest and king in one person. To the most innocent situation which can be imagined on earth, to that of a husbandman, he is, for the most part, united by similarity of occupation, as well as by equality in family relationships; he is a
father, a master of a family, an agriculturist, and thus perfectly a member of the community. On this pure, beautiful,
earthly foundation, rests his higher calling: to him is it given
to guide men through life, to take care of their spiritual education, to bless them at all the leading epochs of their existence, to instruct, to strengthen, to console them, and, if consolation is not sufficient for the present, to call up and guaran-
tee the hope of a happier future. Imagine such a man, with

pure human sentiments, strong enough not to deviate from them under any circumstances, and by this already elevated above the multitude, of whom one cannot expect purity and firmness; give him the learning necessary for his office, as well as a cheerful, equable activity, which is even passionate, as it neglects no moment to do good,—and you will have him well endowed. But at the same time add the necessary limitation, so that he must not only pause in a small circle, but may also perchance pass over to a smaller; grant him good-nature, placability, resolution, and everything else praiseworthy that springs from a decided character, and over all this a cheerful spirit of compliance, and a smiling toleration of his own failings and those of others,—then you will have put together pretty well the image of our excellent Wakefield.

The delineation of this character on his course of life through joys and sorrows, the ever-increasing interest of the story, by the combination of the entirely natural with the strange and the singular, make this novel one of the best which has ever been written; besides this, it has the great advantage that it is quite moral, nay, in a pure sense, Christian—represents the reward of a good will and perseverance in the right, strengthens an unconditional confidence in God, and attests the final triumph of good over evil; and all this without a trace of cant or pedantry. The author was preserved from both of these by an elevation of mind that shows itself throughout in the form of irony, by which this little work must appear to us as wise as it is amiable. The author, Dr. Goldsmith, has without question great insight into the moral world, into its strength and its infirmities; but at the same time he can thankfully acknowledge that he is an Englishman, and reckon highly the advantages which his country and his nation afford him. The family, with the delineation of which he occupies himself, stands upon one of the last steps of citizen comfort, and yet comes in contact with the highest; its narrow circle, which becomes still more contracted, touches upon the great world through the natural and civil course of things; this little skiff floats on the agitated waves of English life, and in weal or woe it has to expect injury or help from the vast fleet which sails around it.

I may suppose that my readers know this work, and have

2 B

it in memory; whoever hears it named for the first time here,
as well as he who is induced to read it again, will thank me.
For the former, I would merely make the cursory remark,
that the vicar's wife is of that good, busy sort, who allows
herself and her own to want for nothing, but who is also somewhat vain of herself and her own. There are two daughters,—
Olivia, handsome and more devoted to the external, and
Sophia, charming and more given to the internal; nor will I
omit to mention an industrious son, Moses, who is somewhat
blunt and emulous of his father.

If Herder could be accused of any fault in his reading aloud,
it was impatience: he did not wait until the hearer had heard
and comprehended a certain part of the progress, so as to be
able to feel and think correctly about it; hurrying on, he
would see their effect at once, and yet he was displeased even
with this when it manifested itself. He blamed the excess of
feeling which overflowed from me more and more at every
step. I felt like a man, like a young man; everything was
living, true, and present before me. He, considering only
the intrinsic contents and form, saw clearly, indeed, that I was
overpowered by the subject-matter, and this he would not
allow. Then Peglow's reflections, which were not of the most
refined, were still worse received; but he was especially angry
at our want of keenness in not seeing beforehand the contrasts
of which the author often makes use, and in suffering ourselves
to be moved and carried away by them without remarking the
oft-returning artifice. He would not pardon us for not seeing
at once, or at least suspecting at the very beginning, where
Burchell is on the point of discovering himself by passing over
in his narration from the third to the first person, that he himself is the lord of whom he is speaking; and when, finally, we
rejoiced like children at the discovery and the transformation
of the poor, needy wanderer, into a rich, powerful lord, he
immediately recalled the passage, which, according to the
author's plan, we had overlooked, and read us a powerful
lecture on our stupidity. It will be seen from this that he regarded the work merely as a production of art, and required
the same of us, who were yet wandering in that state where it
is very allowable to let works of art affect us like productions
of nature.

I did not suffer myself to be at all perplexed by Herder's

invectives; for young people have the happiness or unhappiness, that, when once anything has produced an effect on them, this effect must be wrought out within themselves; from which much good, as well as much mischief, arises. The above work had left with me a great impression, for which I could not account, but properly speaking, I felt myself in harmony with that ironical tone of mind which elevates itself above every object, above fortune and misfortune, good and evil, death and life, and thus attains to the possession of a truly poetical world. I could not, indeed, become conscious of this until later: it was enough that it gave me much to do at the moment; but I could by no means have expected to be so soon transposed from this fictitious world into a similar real one.

My fellow-boarder, Weyland, who enlivened his quiet, laborious life by visiting from time to time his friends and relations in the country (for he was a native of Alsace), did me many services on my little excursions, by introducing me to different localities and families, sometimes in person, sometimes by recommendations. He had often spoken to me about a country clergyman who lived near Drusenheim, six leagues from Strasburg, in possession of a good benefice, with an intelligent wife and a pair of amiable daughters. The hospitality and agreeableness of this family were always highly extolled. It scarcely needed so much to draw thither a young knight who had already accustomed himself to spend all his leisure days and hours on horseback and in the open air. We decided therefore upon this trip, and my friend had to promise that on introducing me he would say neither good nor ill of me, but would treat me with general indifference, and would allow me to make my appearance clad, if not meanly, yet somewhat poorly and negligently. He consented to this, and promised himself some sport from it.

It is a pardonable whim in men of consequence, to place their exterior advantages in concealment now and then, so as to allow their own internal human nature to operate with the greater purity. For this reason the incognito of princes, and the adventures resulting therefrom, are always highly pleasing: these appear disguised divinities, who can reckon at double its value all the good offices shown to them as individuals, and are in such a position that they can either make light of the disagreeable or avoid it. That Jupiter should be

2 B 2

well pleased in his incognito with Philemon and Baucis, and
Henry the Fourth with his peasants after a hunting party, is
quite conformable to nature, and we like it well; but that a
young man without importance or name, should take it into
his head to derive some pleasure from an incognito, might be
construed by many as an unpardonable piece of arrogance.
Yet since the question here is not of such views and actions,
so far as they are praiseworthy or blameable, but so far as they
can manifest themselves and actually occur, we will on this
occasion, for the sake of our own amusement, pardon the
youngster his self-conceit; and the more so, as I must here
allege, that from youth upwards, a love for disguising myself
had been excited in me even by my stern father.

This time, too, partly by some cast-off clothes of my own,
partly by some borrowed garments and by the manner of
combing my hair, I had, if not disfigured myself, yet at least
decked myself out so oddly, that my friend could not help
laughing on the way, especially as I knew how to imitate perfectly the bearing and gestures of such figures when they sit
on horseback, and which are called " Latin riders." The fine
road, the most splendid weather, and the neighbourhood of
the Rhine, put us in the best humour. At Drusenheim we
stopped a moment, he to make himself spruce, and I to re-
hearse my part, out of which I was afraid I should now and
then fall. The country here has the characteristics of all the
open, level Alsace. We rode on a pleasant foot-path over
the meadows, soon reached Sesenheim, left our horses at the
tavern, and walked leisurely towards the parsonage. " Do not be
put out," said Weyland, showing me the house from a distance,
" because it looks like an old miserable farm-house, it is so
much the younger inside." We stepped into the court-yard;
the whole pleased me well : for it had exactly that which is
called picturesque, and which had so magically interested me
in Dutch art. The effect which time produces on all human
work was strongly perceptible. House, barn, and stable were
just at that point of dilapidation where, indecisive and doubtful between preserving and rebuilding, one often neglects the
one without being able to accomplish the other.

As in the village, so in the court-yard, all was quiet and
deserted. We found the father, a little man, wrapped up
within himself, but friendly notwithstanding, quite alone, for

the family were in the fields.   He bade us welcome, and offered
us some refreshment, which we declined.   My friend hurried
away to look after the ladies, and I remained alone with our
host.   " You are perhaps surprised," said he, " to find me so
miserably quartered in a wealthy village, and with a lucrative
benefice ; but," he continued, " this proceeds from irresolu-
tion.   Long since it has been promised me by the parish, and
even by those in higher places, that the house shall be rebuilt ;
many plans have been already drawn, examined and altered,
none of them altogether rejected, and none carried into execution.   This has lasted so many years, that I scarcely know how
to command my impatience."   I made him an answer such as
I thought likely to cherish his hopes, and to encourage him to
pursue the affair more vigorously.   Upon this he proceeded to
describe familiarly the personages on whom such matters depended, and although he was no great delineator of character,
I could nevertheless easily comprehend how the whole business must have been delayed.   The confidential tone of the
man was something peculiar ; he talked to me as if he had
known me for ten years, while there was nothing in his look
from which I could have suspected that he was directing any
attention to me.   At last my friend came in with the mother.
She seemed to look at me with quite different eyes.   Her
countenance was regular, and the expression of it intelligent ;
she must have been beautiful in her youth.   Her figure was
tall and spare, but not more so than became her years, and
when seen from behind, she had yet quite a youthful and pleasing appearance.   The elder daughter then came bouncing in
briskly ; she inquired after Frederica, just as both the others
had also done.   The father assured them that he had not seen
her since all three had gone out together.   The daughter again
went out at the door to look for her sister ; the mother brought
us some refreshment, and Weyland, with the old couple, continued the conversation, which referred to nothing but known
persons and circumstances ; as, indeed, it is usually the case
when acquaintances meet after some length of time, that they
make inquiries, and mutually give each other information
about the members of a large circle.   I listened, and now
learned how much I had to promise myself from this circle.

The elder daughter again came hastily back into the room,
uneasy at not having found her sister.   They were anxious

374   TRUTH AND POETRY; FROM MY OWN LIFE.

about her, and blamed her for this or that bad habit; only the
father said, very composedly, " Let her alone; she has already
come back!" At this instant she really entered the door; and
then truly a most charming star arose in this rural heaven.
Both daughters still wore nothing but German, as they used
to call it, and this almost obsolete national costume became
Frederica particularly well. A short, white, full skirt, with a
furbelow, not so long but that the neatest little feet were
visible up to the ankle; a tight white bodice and a black
taffeta apron,—thus she stood on the boundary between
country girl and city girl. Slender and light, she tripped along
as if she had nothing to carry, and her neck seemed almost
too delicate for the large fair braids on her elegant little head.
From cheerful blue eyes she looked very plainly round, and
her pretty turned-up nose peered as freely into the air as if
there could be no care in the world; her straw hat hung on
her arm, and thus, at the first glance, I had the delight of seeing her, and acknowledging her at once in all her grace and
loveliness.

I now began to act my character with moderation, half
ashamed to play a joke on such good people, whom I had time
enough to observe : for the girls continued the previous conversation, and that with passion and some display of temper.
All the neighbours and connexions were again brought forward, and there seemed, to my imagination, such a swarm of
uncles and aunts, relations, cousins, comers, goers, gossips and
guests, that I thought myself lodged in the liveliest world pos
sible. All the members of the family had spoken some words
with me, the mother looked at me every time she came in or
went out, but Frederica first entered into conversation with
me, and as I took up and glanced through some music that
was lying around, she asked me if I played also? When I
answered in the affirmative, she requested me to perform
something : but the father would not allow this, for he maintained that it was proper to serve the guest first with some
piece of music or a song.

She played several things with some readiness, in the style
which one usually hears in the country, and on a harpsichord,
too, that the schoolmaster should have tuned long since, if he
had only had time. She was now to sing a song also, a certain tender-melancholy affair; but she did not succeed in it.

She rose up and said, smiling, or rather with that touch of serene joy which ever reposed on her countenance, " If I sing badly, I cannot lay the blame on the harpsichord or the schoolmaster; but let us go out of doors; then you shall hear my Alsatian and Swiss songs; they sound much better."

During supper, a notion which had already struck me, occupied me to such a degree, that I became meditative and silent, although the liveliness of the elder sister, and the gracefulness of the younger, shook me often enough out of my contemplations. My astonishment at finding myself so actually in the Wakefield family was beyond all expression. The father, indeed, could not be compared with that excellent man; but where will you find his like? On the other hand, all the dignity which is peculiar to that husband, here appeared in the wife. One could not see her without at the same time reverencing and fearing her. In her were remarked the fruits of a good education; her demeanour was quiet, easy, cheerful, and inviting.

If the elder daughter had not the celebrated beauty of Olivia, yet she was well-made, lively, and rather impetuous; she everywhere showed herself active, and lent a helping hand to her mother in all things. To put Frederica in the place of Primrose's Sophia was not difficult; for little is said of the latter, it is only taken for granted that she is amiable; and this girl was amiable indeed. Now as the same occupation and the same situation, wherever they may occur, produce similar, if not the same effects, so here too many things were talked about, many things happened, which had already taken place in the Wakefield family. But when at last a younger son, long announced and impatiently expected by the father, at last sprang into the room, and boldly sat himself down by us, taking but little notice of the guests, I could scarcely help exclaiming, " Moses, are you here too!"

The conversation at table extended my insight into this country and family circle, since the discourse was about various droll incidents which had happened now here, now there. Frederica, who sat by me, thence took occasion to describe to me different localities which it was worth while to visit. As one little story always calls forth another, I was able to mingle so much the better in the conversation, and to relate similar incidents, and as, besides this, a good country wine was by no

means spared, I stood in danger of slipping out of my character, for which reason my more prudent friend took advantage
of the beautiful moonlight, and proposed a walk, which was
approved at once. He gave his arm to the elder, I to the
younger, and thus we went through the wide field, paying more
attention to the heavens above us than to the earth, which lost
itself in extension around us. There was, however, nothing
of moonshine in Frederica's discourse; by the clearness with
which she spoke she turned night into day, and there was nothing in it which would have indicated or excited any feeling,
except that her expressions related more than hitherto to me,
since she represented to me her own situation, as well as the
neighbourhood and her acquaintances, just as far as I should
be acquainted with them; for she hoped, she added, I would
make no exception, and would visit them again, as all strangers
had willingly done who had once stopped with them.

It was very pleasant to me to listen silently to the description which she gave of the little world in which she moved,
and of the persons whom she particularly valued. She thereby
imparted to me a clear, and, at the same time, such an amiable
idea of her situation, that it had a very strange effect on me;
for I felt at once a deep regret that I had not lived with her
sooner, and at the same time a truly painful envious feeling
towards all who had hitherto had the good fortune to surround
her. I at once watched closely, as if I had a right to do so,
all her descriptions of men, whether they appeared under the
names of neighbours, cousins, or gossips, and my conjectures
inclined now this way, now that; but how could I have discovered anything in my complete ignorance of all the circumstances? She at last became more and more talkative, and I
more and more silent. It was so pleasant to listen to her,
and as I heard only her voice, while the form of her countenance, as well as the rest of the world, floated dimly in the
twilight, it seemed to me as if I could see into her heart,
which I could not but find very pure, since it unbosomed
itself to me in such unembarrassed loquacity.

When my companion retired with me into the guest-cham-
ber, which was prepared for us, he at once, with self-complacency, broke out into pleasant jesting, and took great
credit to himself for having surprised me so much with the
similarity to the Primrose family. I chimed in with him by

showing myself thankful. "Truly," cried he, "the story is quite complete. This family may very well be compared to that, and the gentleman in disguise here may assume the honour of passing for Mr. Burchell ; moreover, since scoundrels are not so necessary in common life as in novels, I will for this time undertake the *rôle* of the nephew, and behave myself better than he did." However, I immediately changed this conversation, pleasant as it might be to me, and asked him, before all things, on his conscience, if he had not really betrayed me ? He answered me, " No !" and I could believe him. They had rather inquired, said he, after the merry table-companion who boarded at the same house with him in Strasburg, and of whom they had been told all sorts of preposterous stuff. I now went to other questions : Had she ever been in love ? Was she now in love ? Was she engaged ? He replied to all in the negative. " In truth," replied I, " such a cheerfulness by nature is inconceivable to me. Had she loved and lost, and again recovered herself, or had she been betrothed,—in both these cases I could account for it."

Thus we chatted together far into the night, and I was awake again at the dawn. My desire to see her once more seemed unconquerable ; but while I dressed myself, I was horrified at the accursed wardrobe I had so wantonly selected. The further I advanced in putting on my clothes, the meaner I seemed in my own eyes ; for everything had been calculated for just this effect. My hair I might perchance have set to rights ; but when at last I forced myself into the borrowed, worn-out grey coat, and the short sleeves gave me the most absurd appearance, I fell the more decidedly into despair, as I could see myself only piecemeal, in a little looking-glass since one part always looked more ridiculous than the other.

During this toilette my friend awoke, and with the satisfaction of a good conscience, and in the feeling of pleasurable hope for the day, looked out at me from the quilted silk coverlet. I had for a long time already envied him his fine clothes, as they hung over the chair, and had he been of my size, I would have carried them off before his eyes, changed my dress outside, and hurrying into the garden, left my cursed husk for him ; he would have had good-humour enough to put himself into my clothes, and the tale would have found a merry ending early in the morning. But that was not now to be thought

of, no more was any other feasible accommodation. To appear
again before Frederica in the figure in which my friend could
give me out as a laborious and accomplished but poor student
of theology,—before Frederica, who the evening before had
spoken so friendly to my disguised self.—that was altogether
impossible. There I stood, vexed and thoughtful, and summoned all my power of invention ; but it deserted me ! But
now when he, comfortably stretched out, after fixing his eyes
upon me for a while, all at once burst out into a loud laugh,
and exclaimed, " No ! it is true, you do look most cursedly ! "
I replied impetuously, " And I know what I will do. Good
bye, and make my excuses ! " " Are you mad ? " cried he,
spinging out of bed and trying to detain me. But I was
already out of the door, down the stairs, out of the house and
yard, off to the tavern ; in an instant my horse was saddled,
and I hurried away in mad vexation, galloping towards Drusenheim, then through that place, and still further on.

As I now thought myself in safety, I rode more slowly,
and now first felt how infinitely against my will I was going
away. But I resigned myself to my fate, made present to my
mind the promenade of yesterday evening with the greatest
calmness, and cherished the secret hope of seeing her soon
again. But this quiet feeling soon changed itself again into
impatience, and I now determined to ride rapidly into the
city, change my dress, take a good, fresh horse, since then, as
my passion made me believe, I could at all events return before
dinner, or, as was more probable, to the dessert, or towards
evening, and beg my forgiveness.

I was just about to put spurs to my horse to execute this
plan, when another, and, as seemed to me, a very happy thought,
passed through my mind. In the tavern at Drusenheim, the
day before, I had noticed a son of the landlord very nicely
dressed, who, early this morning, being busied about his rural
arrangements, had saluted me from his court-yard. He was
of my figure, and had for the moment reminded me of myself.
No sooner thought than done ! My horse was hardly turned
round, when I found myself in Drusenheim ; I brought him
into the stable, and in a few words made the fellow my proposal, namely, that he should lend me his clothes, as I had
something merry on foot at Sesenheim. I had no need to talk
long ; he agreed to the proposition with joy, and praised me

for wishing to make some sport for the *Mamsells*; they were,
he said, such capital people, especially Mamselle Riekchen,*
and the parents, too, liked to see everything go on merrily and
pleasantly. He considered me attentively, and as from my
appearance he might have taken me for a poor starveling,
he said, "If you wish to insinuate yourself, this is the right
way." In the meanwhile we had already proceeded far in
our toilette, and properly speaking he should not have trusted
me with his holiday clothes on the strength of mine; but he
was honest-hearted, and, moreover, had my horse in his stable.
I soon stood there smart enough, gave myself a consequential
air, and my friend seemed to regard his counterpart with
complacency. "Topp,† Mr. Brother!" said he, giving me
his hand, which I grasped heartily, "don't come too near
my girl; she might make a mistake!"

My hair, which had now its full growth again, I could part
at top, much like his, and as I looked at him repeatedly, I
found it comical moderately to imitate his thicker eyebrows
with a burnt cork, and bring mine nearer together in the
middle, so that with my enigmatical intentions, I might make
myself an external riddle likewise. "Now have you not,"
said I, as he handed me his be-ribboned hat, "something or
other to be done at the parsonage, that I might announce
myself there in a natural manner?" "Good!" replied he,
"but then you must wait two hours yet. There is a woman
confined at our house: I will offer to take the cake to the
parson's wife,‡ and you may carry it over. Pride must pay
its penalty, and so must a joke." I resolved to wait, but
these two hours were infinitely long, and I was dying of impatience when the third hour passed before the cake came out
of the oven. At last I got it quite hot, and hastened away
with my credentials in the most beautiful sunshine, accompanied for a distance by my counterpart, who promised to
come after me in the evening and bring me my clothes. This,
however, I briskly declined, and stipulated that I should
deliver up to him his own.

I had not skipped far with my present, which I carried in a

* Abbreviation for Frederica.—*Trans.*
† The exclamation used on striking a bargain. It is, we believe,
employed by some trades in England.—*Trans.*
‡ The general custom of the country villages in Protestant Germany
on such interesting occasions.—*American Note.*

neat tied-up napkin, when, in the distance, I saw my friend
coming towards me with the two ladies. My heart was uneasy,
which was certainly unsuitable under this jacket. I stood
still, took breath, and tried to consider how I should begin;
and now I first remarked that the nature of the ground was
very much in my favour; for they were walking on the other
side of the brook, which, together with the strips of meadow
through which it ran, kept the two footpaths pretty far apart.
When they were just opposite to me, Frederica, who had
already perceived me long before, cried, " George, what are you
bringing there ? "   I was clever enough to cover my face with
my hat, which I took off, while I held up the loaded napkin
high in the air.   " A christening cake!" cried she at that;
" how is your sister ? "   " Well, * said I, for I tried to talk
in a strange dialect, if not exactly in the Alsatian.   " Carry it
to the house!" said the elder, " and if you do not find my
mother, give it to the maid; but wait for us, we shall soon be
back,—do you hear?"   I hastened along my path in the
joyous feeling of the best hope that, as the beginning was so
lucky, all would go off well, and I had soon reached the parsonage.   I found nobody either in the house or in the kitchen;
I did not wish to disturb the old gentleman, whom I might
suppose busy in the study; I therefore sat down on the bench
before the door, with the cake beside me, and pressed my hat
upon my face.

I cannot easily recall a pleasanter sensation. To sit again
on this threshold, over which, a short time before, I had blun-
dered out in despair; to have seen her already again, to have
already heard again her dear voice, so soon after my chagrin
had pictured to me a long separation, every moment to
be expecting herself and a discovery, at which my heart
throbbed, and yet, in this ambiguous case, a discovery without shame; for at the very beginning it was a merrier prank
than any of those they had laughed at so much yesterday.
Love and necessity are the best masters; they both acted
together here, and their pupil was not unworthy of them.

But the maid came stepping out of the barn.   " Now! did
the cakes turn out well?" cried she to me; " how is your
sister?"   " All right," said I, and pointed to the cake without
looking up.   She took up the napkin and muttered, " Now,

* In the original his answer is " Guet," for " Gut."—*Trans.*

what's the matter with you to-day again? Has Barbchen *
been looking again at somebody else? Don't let us suffer for
that! You will make a happy couple if you carry on so!"
As she spoke pretty loud, the pastor came to the window and
asked what was the matter. She showed him to me; I stood up
and turned myself towards him; but still kept the hat over my
face. When he had spoken somewhat friendly to me, and had
asked me to remain, I went towards the garden, and was just
going in, when the pastor's wife, who was entering the court-
yard gate, called to me. As the sun shone right in my face,
I one more availed myself of the advantage which my hat
afforded me, and greeted her by scraping a leg; but she went
into the house after she had bidden me not to go away without
eating something. I now walked up and down in the garden;
everything had hitherto had the best success, yet I breathed
hard when I reflected that the young people now would soon
return. But the mother unexpectedly stepped up to me,
and was just going to ask me a question, when she looked me
in the face, so that I could not conceal myself any longer, and
the words stuck in her throat. " I am looking for George,"
said she, after a pause, " and whom do I find? Is it you,
young sir? How many forms have you, then?" " In earnest
only one," replied I; " in sport as many as you like."
" Which sport I will not spoil," smiled she; " go out behind
the garden into the meadow until it strikes twelve, then come
back, and I shall already have contrived the joke." I did so;
but when I was beyond the hedges of the village gardens,
and was going along the meadows, towards me some country
people came by the footpath, and put me in some embarrassment. I therefore turned aside into a little wood,
which crowned an elevation quite near, in order to conceal
myself there till the appointed time. Yet how strangely did
I feel when I entered it; for there appeared before me a neat
place, with benches, from every one of which was a pretty
view of the country. Here was the village and the steeple,
here Drusenheim, and behind it the woody islands of the
Rhine; in the opposite direction was the Vosgian mountain
range, and at last the minster of Strasburg. These different
heaven-bright pictures were set in bushy frames, so that one
could see nothing more joyous and pleasing. I sat down

* Diminutive of Barbara.—*Trans.*

upon one of the benches, and noticed on the largest tree an
oblong little board with the inscription, " Frederica's Repose."
It never occurred to me that I might have come to disturb
this repose ; for a budding passion has this beauty about it,
that, as it is unconscious of its origin, neither can it have
any thought of an end, nor, while it feels itself glad and
cheerful, have any presentiment that it may also create
mischief.

I had scarcely had time to look about me and was losing
myself in sweet reveries, when I heard somebody coming ; it
was Frederica herself. " George, what are you doing here?"
she cried from a distance. " Not George!" cried I, running
towards her, " but one who craves forgiveness of you a thousand times." She looked at me with astonishment, but soon
collected herself, and said, after fetching her breath more
deeply, " You abominable man, how you frighten me!"
" The first disguise has led me into the second," exclaimed I ;
" the former would have been unpardonable if I had only
known in any degree to whom I was going ; but this one you
will certainly forgive, for it is the shape of persons whom you
treat so kindly." Her pale cheeks had coloured up with the
most beautiful rose-red. " You shall not be worse off than
George, at any rate! But let us sit down! I confess the
fright has gone into my limbs." I sat down beside her,
exceedingly agitated. " We know everything already, up to
this morning, from your friend," said she, " now do you tell
me the rest." I did not let her say that twice, but described
to her my horror at my yesterday's figure, and my rushing
out of the house, so comically, that she laughed heartily and
graciously; then I went on to what followed, with all modesty,
indeed, yet passionately enough, so that it might have passed
for a declaration of love in historical form. At last I solem-
nized my pleasure at finding her again, by a kiss upon her
hand, which she suffered to remain in mine. If she had taken
upon herself the expense of the conversation during yesterday
evening's moonlight walk, I now, on my part, richly repaid
the debt. The pleasure of seeing her again, and being able
to say to her everything that I had yesterday kept back, was
so great that, in my eloquence, I did not remark how meditative and silent she was. Once more she deeply fetched her
breath, and over and over again I begged her forgiveness for

the fright which I had caused her. How long we may have sat I know not; but at once we heard some one call. It was the voice of her sister. "That will be a pretty story," said the dear girl, restored to her perfect cheerfulness; "she is coming hither on my side," she added, bending so as half to conceal me; "turn yourself away, so that you may not be recognised at once." The sister entered the place, but not alone; Weyland was with her, and both, when they saw us, stood still, as if petrified.

If we should all at once see a flame burst out violently from a quiet roof, or should meet a monster whose deformity was at the same time revolting and fearful, we should not be struck with such a fierce horror as that which seizes us when, unexpectedly, we see with our own eyes what we have believed morally impossible. "What is this?" cried the elder, with the rapidity of one who is frightened; "what is this? you with George, hand-in-hand! How am I to understand this?" "Dear sister," replied Frederica, very doubtfully, "the poor fellow,—he is begging something of me; he has something to beg of you, too, but you must forgive him beforehand." "I do not understand—I do not comprehend—" said her sister, shaking her head and looking at Weyland, who, in his quiet way, stood by in perfect tranquillity, and contemplated the scene without any kind of expression. Frederica arose and drew me after her. "No hesitating!" cried she; "pardon begged and granted!" "Now do!" said I, stepping pretty near the elder; "I have need of pardon!" She drew back, gave a loud shriek, and was covered with blushes; she then threw herself down on the grass, laughed immoderately, and seemed as if she would never have done. Weyland smiled as if pleased, and cried, "You are a rare youth!" Then he shook my hand in his. He was not usually liberal with his caresses, but his shake of the hand had something hearty and enlivening about it; yet he was sparing of this also.

After somewhat recovering and collecting ourselves, we set out on our return to the village. On the way I learned how this singular meeting had been occasioned. Frederica had at last parted from the promenaders to rest herself in her little nook for a moment before dinner, and when the other two came back to the house, the mother had sent them to call Frederica with as great haste as possible, because dinner was ready.

The elder sister manifested the most extravagant delight, and
when she learned that the mother had already discovered the
secret, she exclaimed, " Now we have still to deceive my
father, my brother, the servant-man and the maid." When we
were at the garden-hedge, Frederica insisted upon going first
into the house with my friend. The maid was busy in the
kitchen-garden, and Olivia (so let the elder sister be named
here) called out to her, " Stop; I have something to tell you!"
She left me standing by the hedge, and went to the maid. I
saw that they were speaking very earnestly. Olivia represented to her that George had quarrelled with Barbara, and
seemed desirous of marrying her. The lass was not displeased
at this ; I was now called, and was to confirm what had been
said. The pretty, stout girl cast down her eyes, and remained
so until I stood quite near before her. But when, all at once,
she perceived the strange face, she too gave a loud scream and
ran away. Olivia bade me run after her and hold her fast. so
that she should not get into the house and make a noise ; while
she herself wished to go and see how it was with her father.
On the way Olivia met the servant-boy, who was in love with
the maid ; I had in the mean time hurried after the maid, and
held her fast. " Only think ! what good luck !" cried Olivia ;
" it's all over with Barbara, and George marries Liese." " That
I have thought for a long while," said the good fellow, and
remained standing in an ill-humour.

I had given the maid to understand that all we had to do
was to deceive the father. We went up to the lad, who turned
away and tried to withdraw ; but Liese brought him back, and
he, too, when he was undeceived, made the most extraordinary
gestures. We went together to the house. The table was
covered, and the father was already in the room. Olivia, who
kept me behind her, stepped to the threshold and said,
" Father, have you any objection to George dining with us to-
day? but you must let him keep his hat on." " With all my
heart!" said the old man, " but why such an unusual thing?
Has he hurt himself?" She led me forward as I stood with
my hat on. " No!" said she, leading me into the room, " but
he has a bird-cage under it, and the birds might fly out and
make a deuce of a fuss ; for there are nothing but wild ones."
The father was pleased with the joke, without precisely knowing what it meant. At this instant she took off my hat, made

a scrape, and required me to do the same. The old man looked at me and recognised me, but was not put out of his priestly self-possession. "Aye, aye, Mr. Candidate!" exclaimed he, raising a threatening finger at me; "you have changed saddles very quickly, and in the night I have lost an assistant, who yesterday promised me so faithfully that he would often mount my pulpit on week-days." He then laughed heartily, bade me welcome, and we sat down to table. Moses came in much later; for, as the youngest spoiled child, he had accustomed himself not to hear the dinner-bell. Besides, he took very little notice of the company, scarcely even when he contradicted them. In order to be more sure of him, they had placed me, not between the sisters, but at the end of the table, where George often used to sit. As he came in at the door behind me, he slapped me smartly on the shoulder, and said, "Good dinner to you, George!" "Many thanks, squire!" replied I. The strange voice and the strange face startled him. "What say you?" cried Olivia; "does he not look very like his brother?" "Yes, from behind," replied Moses, who managed to recover his composure immediately, "like all folks." He did not look at me again, and merely busied himself with zealously devouring the dishes, to make up for lost time. Then, too, he thought proper to rise on occasion and find something to do in the yard and the garden. At the dessert the real George came in, and made the whole scene still more lively. They began to banter him for his jealousy, and would not praise him for getting rid of a rival in me; but he was modest and clever enough, and, in a half-confused manner, mixed up himself, his sweetheart, his counterpart, and the *Mamsells* with each other, to such a degree, that at last nobody could tell about whom he was talking, and they were but too glad to let him consume in peace a glass of wine and a bit of his own cake.

At table there was some talk about going to walk; which, however, did not suit me very well in my peasant's clothes. But the ladies, early on that day already, when they learned who had run away in such a desperate hurry, had remembered that a fine hunting-coat (*Pekesche*) of a cousin of theirs, in which, when there, he used to go sporting, was hanging in the clothes-press. I, however, declined it, externally with all sorts of jokes, but internally with a feeling of vanity, not wishing,

2 c

as the cousin, to disturb the good impression I had made as
the peasant. The father had gone to take his afternoon-nap;
the mother, as always, was busy about her housewifery. But
my friend proposed that I should tell them some story, to which
I immediately agreed. We went into a spacious arbour, and I
gave them a tale which I have since written out under the title
of *The New Melusina*.* It bears about the same relation to
The New Paris as the youth bears to the boy, and I would
insert it here, were I not afraid of injuring, by odd plays of
fancy, the rural reality and simplicity which here agreeably
surround us. Enough: I succeeded in gaining the reward of
the inventors and narrators of such productions, namely, in
awakening curiosity, in fixing the attention, in provoking over-
hasty solutions of impenetrable riddles, in deceiving expectations, in confusing by the more wonderful which came into the
place of the wonderful, in arousing sympathy and fear, in
causing anxiety, in moving, and at last, by the change of what
was apparently earnest into an ingenious and cheerful jest, in
satisfying the mind, and in leaving the imagination materials
for new images, and the understanding materials for further
reflection.

Should any one hereafter read this tale in print, and doubt
whether it could have produced such an effect, let him remember that, properly speaking, man is only called upon to act in
the present. Writing is an abuse of language, reading silently
to oneself is a pitiful substitute for speech. Man effects all he
can upon man by his personality, youth is most powerful upon
youth, and hence also arise the purest influences. It is these
which enliven the world, and allow it neither morally nor physically to perish. I had inherited from my father a certain
didactic loquacity; from my mother the faculty of representing, clearly and forcibly, everything that the imagination can
produce or grasp, of giving a freshness to known stories, of
inventing and relating others, nay, of inventing in the course
of narration. By my paternal endowment I was for the most
part annoying to the company; for who likes to listen to the
opinions and sentiments of another, especially a youth, whose
judgment, from defective experience, always seems insufficient?
My mother, on the contrary, had thoroughly qualified me for
social conversation. The emptiest tale has in itself a high

* This is introduced in *Wilhelm Meister's Wanderjahre.—Trans.*

charm for the imagination, and the smallest quantity of solid matter is thankfully received by the understanding.

By such recitals, which cost me nothing, I made myself beloved by children, excited and delighted youth, and drew upon myself the attention of older persons. But in society, such as it commonly is, I was soon obliged to stop these exercises, and I have thereby lost but too much of the enjoyment of life and of free mental advancement. Nevertheless both these parental gifts accompanied me throughout my whole life, united with a third, namely, the necessity of expressing myself figuratively and by comparisons. In consideration of these peculiarities, which the acute and ingenious Doctor Gall discovered in me according to his theory, he assured me that I was, properly speaking, born for a popular orator. At this disclosure I was not a little alarmed; for if it had been here well founded, everything that I undertook would have proved a failure, from the fact that with my nation there was nothing to harangue about.

PART THE THIRD.

CARE IS TAKEN THAT TREES DO NOT GROW INTO THE SKY.

ELEVENTH BOOK.

AFTER I had, in that bower of Sesenheim, finished my tale, in which the ordinary and the impossible were so agreeably alternated, I perceived that my hearers, who had already shown peculiar sympathy, were now enchanted in the highest degree by my singular narrative. They pressed me urgently to write down the tale, that they might often repeat it by reading it among themselves, and to others. I promised this the more willingly, as I thus hoped to gain a pretext for repeating my visit, and for an opportunity of forming a closer connexion. The party separated for a moment, and all were inclined to feel that after a day spent in so lively a manner, the evening might fall rather flat. From this anxiety I was freed by my friend, who asked permission to take leave at once, in the name of us both, because, as an industrious academical citizen, regular in his studies, he wished to pass the night at Drusenheim, and to be early in the morning at Strasburg.

We both reached our night-quarters in silence; I, because I felt a grapple on my heart, which drew me back; he, because he had something else on his mind, which he told me as soon as we had arrived. "It is strange," he began, "that you should just hit upon this tale. Did not you remark that it made quite a peculiar impression?" "Nay," answered I, "how could I help observing that the elder one laughed more than was consistent at certain passages, that the younger one shook her head, that all of you looked significantly at each other, and that you yourself were nearly put out of countenance. I do not deny that I almost felt embarrassed myself, for it struck me that it was perhaps improper to tell the dear girls a parcel of stuff, of which they had better been

ignorant, and to give them such a bad opinion of the male sex
as they must naturally have formed from the character of the
hero." " You have not hit it at all," said he, " and, indeed,
how should you? These dear girls are not so unacquainted
with such matters as you imagine, for the great society around
them gives occasion for many reflections; and there happens
to be, on the other side of the Rhine, exactly such a married
pair as you describe, allowing a little for fancy and exaggeration; the husband just as tall, sturdy, and heavy,—the wife
so pretty and dainty, that he could easily hold her in his
hand. Their mutual position in other respects, their history
altogether, so exactly accords with your tale, that the girls
seriously asked me whether you knew the persons, and described them in jest. I assured them that you did not, and
you will do well to let the tale remain unwritten. With the
assistance of delays and pretexts, we may soon find an excuse."

I was much astonished, for I had thought of no couple on
this or the other side of the Rhine; nay, I could not have
stated how I came by the notion. In thought I liked to sport
with such pleasantries, without any particular reference, and
I believed that if I narrated them, it would be the same with
others.

When I returned to my occupations in the city, I felt them
more than usually wearisome, for a man born to activity
forms plans too extensive for his capacity, and overburdens
himself with labour. This goes on very well till some physical or moral impediment comes in the way, and clearly shows
the disproportion of the powers to the undertaking.

I pursued jurisprudence with as much diligence as was
required to take my degree with some credit. Medicine
charmed me, because it showed nature, if it did not unfold it
on every side; and to this I was attached by intercourse and
habit. To society I was obliged to devote some time and
attention; for in many families much had turned out both
honourably and agreeably. All this might have been carried
on, had not that which Herder had inculcated pressed upon
me with an infinite weight. He had torn down the curtain
which concealed from me the poverty of German literature;
he had ruthlessly destroyed so many of my prejudices; in the
sky of my fatherland there were few stars of importance left,
when he had treated all the rest as so many transient candle-

snuffs; nay, my own hopes and fancies respecting myself he
had so spoiled, that I began to doubt my own capabilities.
At the same time, however, he dragged me on to the noble
broad way which he himself was inclined to tread, drew my
attention to his favourite authors, at the head of whom stood
Swift and Hamann, and shook me up with more force than he
had bound me down. To this manifold confusion was now added
an incipient passion, which, while it threatened to absorb me,
might indeed draw me from other relations, but could scarcely
elevate me above them. Then came besides, a corporeal
malady, which made me feel after dinner as if my throat was
closed up, and of which I did not easily get rid, till afterwards,
when I abstained from a certain red wine, which I generally
and very willingly drank in the boarding-house. This intolerable inconvenience had quitted me at Sesenheim, so that
I felt double pleasure in being there, but when I came back
to my town-diet it returned, to my great annoyance. All this
made me thoughtful and morose; and my outward appearance
probably corresponded with my inward feelings.

Being in a worse humour than ever, because the malady
was violent after dinner, I attended the clinical lecture. The
great care and cheerfulness with which our respected instructor
led us from bed to bed, the minute observation of important
symptoms, the judgment of the cause of complaint in general, the
fine Hippocratic mode of proceeding, by which, without theory,
and out of an individual experience, the forms of knowledge
revealed themselves, the addresses with which he usually
crowned his lectures—all this attracted me towards him, and
made a strange department, into which I only looked as
through a crevice, so much the more agreeable and fascinating.
My disgust at the invalids gradually decreased, as I learned to
change their various states into distinct conceptions, by which
recovery and the restoration of the human form and nature
appeared possible. He probably had his eye particularly upon
me, as a singular young man, and pardoned the strange
anomaly which took me to his lectures. On this occasion he
did not conclude his lecture, as usual, with a doctrine which
might have reference to an illness that had been observed,
but said cheerfully, "Gentlemen, there are some holidays
before us; make use of them to enliven your spirits. Studies
must not only be pursued with seriousness and diligence, but

also with cheerfulness and freedom of mind. Give movement to your bodies, and traverse the beautiful country on horse and foot. He who is at home will take delight in that to which he has been accustomed, while for the stranger there will be new impressions, and pleasant reminiscences in future."

There were only two of us to whom this admonition could be directed. May the recipe have been as obvious to the other as it was to me! I thought I heard a voice from heaven, and made all the haste I could to order a horse and dress myself out neatly. I sent for Weyland, but he was not to be found. This did not delay my resolution, but the preparations unfortunately went on slowly, and I could not depart so soon as I had hoped. Fast as I rode, I was overtaken by the night. The way was not to be mistaken, and the moon shed her light on my impassioned project. The night was windy and awful, and I dashed on, that I might not have to wait till morning before I could see her.

It was already late when I put up my horse at Sesenheim. The landlord, in answer to my question, whether there was still light in the parsonage, assured me that the ladies had only just gone home; he thought he had heard they were still expecting a stranger. This did not please me, as I wished to have been the only one. I hastened, that, late as I was, I might at least appear the first. I found the two sisters sitting at the door. They did not seem much astonished, but I was, when Frederica whispered into Olivia's ear, loud enough for me to hear, " Did I not say so? Here he is!" They conducted me into a room, where I found a little collation set out. The mother greeted me as an old acquaintance; and the elder sister, when she saw me in the light, broke out into loud laughter, for she had little command over herself.

After this first and somewhat odd reception, the conversation became at once free and cheerful, and a circumstance, which had remained concealed from me this evening, I learned on the following day. Frederica had predicted that I should come; and who does not feel some satisfaction at the fulfilment of a foreboding, even if it be a mournful one? All presentiments, when confirmed by the event, give man a higher opinion of himself, whether it be that he thinks himself in possession of so fine a susceptibility as to feel a relation in the distance, or acute enough to perceive necessary but still uncertain associations. Even Olivia's laugh remained no secret; she confessed that it seemed very comical to see me dressed and decked out on this occasion. Frederica, on the other hand, found it advantageous not to explain such a phenomenon as vanity, but rather to discover in it a wish to please her.

Early in the morning Frederica asked me to take a walk. Her mother and sister were occupied in preparing everything for the reception of several guests. By the side of this beloved girl I enjoyed the noble Sunday morning in the country, as the inestimable Hebel has depicted it. She described to me the party which was expected, and asked me to remain by her, that all the pleasure might, if possible, be common to us both, and be enjoyed in a certain order. "Generally," she said, "people amuse themselves alone. Sport and play is very lightly tasted, so that at last nothing is left but cards for one part, and the excitement of dancing for the other."

We therefore sketched our plan as to what should be done after dinner, taught each other some new social games, and were united and happy, when the bell summoned us to church, where, by her side, I found a somewhat dry sermon of her father's not too long.

The presence of the beloved one always shortens time; but this hour passed amid peculiar reflections. I repeated to myself the good qualities which she had just unfolded so freely before me—her circumspect cheerfulness, her *naïveté* combined with self-consciousness, her hilarity with foresight—qualities which seem incompatible, but which nevertheless were found together in her, and gave a pleasing character to her outward appearance. But now I had to make more serious reflections upon myself, which were somewhat prejudicial to a free state of cheerfulness.

Since that impassioned girl had cursed and sanctified my lips (for every consecration involves both), I had, superstitiously enough, taken care not to kiss any girl, because I feared that I might injure her in some unheard-of spiritual manner. I therefore subdued every desire, by which a youth feels impelled to win from a charming girl this favour, which says much or little. But even in the most decorous company a heavy trial awaited me. Those little games, as they are called, which are more or less ingenious, and by which a joyous young circle is collected and combined, depend in a great measure upon forfeits, in the calling in of which kisses have no small value. I had resolved, once for all, not to kiss, and as every want or impediment stimulates us to an activity to which we should otherwise not feel inclined, I exerted all the talent and humour I possessed to help myself through, and thus to win rather than lose, before the company, and for the company. When a verse was desired for the redemption of a forfeit, the demand was usually directed to me. Now I was always prepared, and on such occasions contrived to bring out something in praise of the hostess, or of some lady who had conducted herself most agreeably towards me. If it happened that a kiss was imposed upon me at all events, I endeavoured to escape by some turn, which was considered satisfactory; and as I had time to reflect on the matter beforehand, I was never in want of various elegant excuses, although those made on the spur of the moment were always most successful.

When we reached home, the guests, who had arrived from several quarters, were buzzing merrily one with another, until Frederica collected them together, and invited and conducted them to a walk to that charming spot. There they found an abundant collation, and wished to fill up with social games the period before dinner. Here, by agreement with Frederica, though she did not know my secret, I contrived to get up and go through games without forfeits, and redemptions of forfeits without kissing.

My skill and readiness were so much the more necessary, as the company, which was otherwise quite strange to me, seemed to have suspected some connexion between me and the dear girl, and roguishly took the greatest pains to force upon me that which I secretly endeavoured to avoid. For in such circles, if people perceive a growing inclination between two young persons, they try to make them confused, or to bring them closer together, just as afterwards, when once a passion has been declared, they take trouble on purpose to part them again. Thus, to the man of society, it is totally indifferent whether he confers a benefit or an injury, provided only he is amused.

This morning I could observe, with more attention, the whole character of Frederica, so that for the whole time she

always remained to me the same. The friendly greetings of
the peasants, which were especially addressed to her, gave
me to understand that she was beneficent to them, and created
in them an agreeable feeling. The elder sister remained at
home with her mother. Nothing that demanded bodily exertion was required of Frederica; but she was spared, they said,
on account of her chest.

There are women who especially please us in a room, others
who look better in the open air. Frederica belonged to the
latter. Her whole nature, her form never appeared more
charming than when she moved along an elevated footpath;
the grace of her deportment seemed to vie with the flowery
earth, and the indestructible cheerfulness of her countenance
with the blue sky. This refreshing atmosphere which surrounded her she carried home, and it might soon be perceived that she understood how to reconcile difficulties, and
to obliterate with ease the impression made by little unpleasant contingencies.

The purest joy which we can feel with respect to a beloved
person is to find that she pleases others. Frederica's conduct in
society was beneficent to all. In walks, she floated about, an
animating spirit, and knew how to supply the gaps which
might arise here and there. The lightness of her movements
we have already commended, and she was most graceful when
she ran. As the deer seems just to fulfil its destination
when it lightly flies over the sprouting corn, so did her peculiar nature seem most plainly to express itself when she ran
with light steps over mead and furrow, to fetch something
which had been forgotten, to seek something which had been
lost, to summon a distant couple, or to order something necessary. On these occasions she was never out of breath, and
always kept her equilibrium. Hence the great anxiety of her
parents with respect to her chest must to many have appeared
excessive.

The father, who often accompanied us through meadows and
fields, was not always provided with a suitable companion
On this account I joined him, and he did not fail to touch once
more upon his favourite theme, and circumstantially to tell me
about the proposed building of the parsonage. He particularly regretted that he could not again get the carefully
finished sketches, so as to meditate upon them, and to con-

ider this or that improvement. I observed, that the loss
might be easily supplied, and offered to prepare a ground-
plan, upon which, after all, everything chiefly depended.
With this he was highly pleased, and settled that we should
have the assistance of the schoolmaster, to stir up whom he at
once hurried off, that the yard and foot-measure might be
ready early on the morrow.

When he had gone, Frederica said, " You are right to
humour my dear father on his weak side, and not, like others,
who get weary of this subject, to avoid him, or to break it off.
I must, indeed, confess to you that the rest of us do not desire
this building; it would be too expensive for the congregation
and for us also. A new house, new furniture! Our guests
would not feel more comfortable with us, now they are once
accustomed to the old building. Here we can treat them
liberally; there we should find ourselves straightened in a
wider sphere. Thus the matter stands; but do not you fail
to be agreeable. I thank you for it, from my heart."

Another lady who joined us asked about some novels,—
whether Frederica had read them. She answered in the negative, for she had read but little altogether. She had grown
up in a cheerful, decorous enjoyment of life, and was cultivated accordingly. I had the *Vicar of Wakefield* on the tip
of my tongue, but did not venture to propose it, the similarity
of the situations being too striking and too important. " I am
very fond of reading novels," she said; " one finds in them
such nice people, whom one would like to resemble."

The measurement of the house took place the following day.
It was a somewhat slow proceeding, as I was as little accustomed to such arts as the schoolmaster. At last a tolerable
project came to my aid. The good father told me his views,
and was not displeased when I asked permission to prepare
the plan more conveniently in the town. Frederica dismissed
me with joy; she was convinced of my affection, and I of
hers; and the six leagues no longer appeared a distance. It
was so easy to travel to Drusenheim in the diligence, and by
this vehicle, as well as by messengers, ordinary and extraordinary, to keep up a connexion, George being entrusted with
the despatches.

When I had arrived in the town, I occupied myself in the
earliest hours (for there was no notion of a long sleep) with

the plan, which I drew as neatly as possible. In the meanwhile I had sent Frederica some books, accompanied by a few kind words. I received an answer at once, and was charmed with her light, pretty, hearty hand. Contents and style were natural, good, amiable, as if they came from within ; and thus the pleasing impression she had made upon me was ever kept up and renewed. I but too readily recalled to myself the endowments of her beautiful nature, and nurtured the hope that I should see her soon, and for a longer time.

There was now no more any need of an address from our good instructor. He had, by those words, spoken at the right time, so completely cured me, that I had no particular inclination to see him and his patients again. The correspondence with Frederica became more animated. She invited me to a festival, to which also some friends from the other side of the Rhine would come. I was to make arrangements for a longer time. This I did, by packing a stout portmanteau upon the diligence, and in a few hours I was in her presence. I found a large merry party, took the father aside, and handed him the plan, at which he testified great delight. I talked over with him what I had thought while completing it. He was quite beside himself with joy, and especially praised the neatness of the drawing. This I had practised from my youth upwards, and had on this occasion taken especial pains, with the finest paper. But this pleasure was very soon marred for our good host, when, against my counsel, and in the joy of his heart, he laid the sketch before the company. Far from uttering the desired sympathy, some thought nothing at all of this precious work ; others, who thought they knew something of the matter, made it still worse, blaming the sketch as not artistical, and, when the old man looked off for a moment, handled the clean sheets as if they were only so many rough draughts, while one, with the hard strokes of a lead-pencil, marked his plans of improvement on the fine paper, in such a manner, that a restoration of the primitive purity was not to be thought of.

I was scarcely able to console the extremely irritated man, whose pleasures had been so outrageously destroyed, much as I assured him that I myself looked upon them only as sketches, which we would talk over, and on which we would construct new drawings. In spite of all this he went off in a very ill-

humour, and Frederica thanked me for my attention to her
father, as well as for my patience during the unmannerly
conduct of the other guests.

But I could feel no pain nor ill-humour in her presence.
The party consisted of young and tolerably noisy friends, whom,
nevertheless, an old gentleman tried to outdo, proposing even
odder stuff than they practised. Already, at breakfast, the
wine had not been spared. At a very well-furnished dinner-
table there was no want of any enjoyment, and the feast was
relished the more by everybody, after the violent bodily exercise during the somewhat warm weather, and if the official
gentleman went a little too far in the good things, the young
people were not left much behind him.

I was happy beyond all bounds at the side of Frederica;—
talkative, merry, ingenious, forward, and yet kept in moderation by feeling, esteem, and attachment. She, in a similar
position, was open, cheerful, sympathizing, and communicative.
We all appeared to live for the company, and yet lived only
for each other.

After the meal they sought the shade, social games were
begun, and the turn came to forfeits. On redeeming the forfeits, everything of every kind was carried to excess; the
gestures which were commanded, the acts which were to be
done, the problems which were to be solved, all showed a mad
joy which knew no limits. I myself heightened these wild
jokes by many a comical choice, and Frederica shone by many
a droll thought; she appeared to me more charming than ever,
all hypochondriacal superstitious fancies had vanished, and
when the opportunity offered of heartily kissing one whom I
loved so tenderly, I did not miss it, still less did I deny myself
a repetition of this pleasure.

The hope of the party for music was at last satisfied; it was
heard, and all hastened to the dance. *Allemandes*, waltzing
and turning, were beginning, middle and end. All had given
up to this national dance; even I did honour enough to my
private dancing-mistress, and Frederica, who danced as she
walked, sprang, and ran, was delighted to find in me a very
expert partner. We generally kept together, but were soon
obliged to leave off, and she was advised on all sides not to go
on any further in this wild manner. We consoled ourselves
by a solitary walk, hand in hand, and when we had reached

that quiet spot, by the warmest embrace and the most faithful assurance that we loved each other heartily.

Older persons, who had risen with us from the game, took us with them. At supper people did not return to their sober senses. Dancing went on far into the night, and there was as little want of healths and other incitements to drinking as at noon.

I had scarcely for a few hours slept very profoundly, when I was awakened by a heat and tumult in my blood. It is at such times and in such situations that care and repentance usually attack man, who is stretched out defenceless. My imagination at once presented to me the liveliest forms; I saw Lucinda, how, after the most ardent kiss, she passionately receded from me, and, with glowing cheek and sparkling eyes, uttered that curse, by which she intended to menace her sister only, but by which she also unconsciously menaced innocent persons, who were unknown to her. I saw Frederica standing opposite to her, paralysed at the sight, pale, and feeling the consequences of the curse, of which she knew nothing. I found myself between them, as little able to ward off the spiritual effects of the adventure, as to avoid the evil-boding kiss. The delicate health of Frederica seemed to hasten the threatened calamity, and now her love to me wore a most unhappy aspect, and I wished myself further.

But something still more painful to me, which lay in the background, I will not conceal. A certain conceit kept that superstition alive in me;—my lips, whether consecrated or cursed, appeared to me more important than usual, and with no little complacency was I aware of my self-denying conduct, in renouncing many an innocent pleasure, partly to preserve my magical advantage, partly to avoid injuring a harmless being by giving it up.

But now all was lost and irrevocable : I had returned into a mere common position, and I thought that I had harmed, irretrievably injured, the dearest of beings. Thus, far from my being freed from the curse, it was flung back from my lips into my own heart.

All this together raged in my blood, already excited by love and passion, wine and dancing, confused my thoughts and tortured my feelings, so that, especially as contrasted with the joys of the day before, I felt myself in a state of despair which seemed unbounded. Fortunately daylight peered in upon me through a chink in the shutter, and the sun stepping forth and vanquishing all the powers of night, set me again upon my feet; I was soon in the open air, and refreshed, if not restored.

Superstition, like many other fancies, very easily loses in power, when, instead of flattering our vanity, it stands in its way, and would fain produce an evil hour to this delicate being. We then see well enough that we can get rid of it when we choose; we renounce it the more easily, as all of which we deprive ourselves turns to our own advantage. The sight of Frederica, the feeling of her love, the cheerfulness of everything around me—all reproved me, that in the midst of the happiest days I could harbour such dismal night-birds in my bosom. The confiding conduct of the dear girl, which became more and more intimate, made me thoroughly rejoiced, and I felt truly happy, when, at parting, she openly gave a kiss to me, as well as the other friends and relations.

In the city many occupations and dissipations awaited me, from the midst of which I collected myself for the sake of my beloved, by means of a correspondence, which we regularly established. Even in her letters she always remained the same; whether she related anything new, or alluded to well-known occurrences, lightly described or cursorily reflected, it was always as if, even with her pen, she appeared going, coming, running, bounding with a step as light as it was sure. I also liked very much to write to her, for the act of rendering present her good qualities increased my affection even during absence, so that this intercourse was little inferior to a personal one, nay, afterwards became pleasanter and dearer to me.

For that superstition had been forced to give way altogether. It was indeed based upon the impressions of earlier years, but the spirit of the day, the liveliness of youth, the intercourse with cold sensible men, all was unfavourable to it, so that it would not have been easy to find among all who surrounded me a single person to whom a confession of my whims would not have been perfectly ridiculous. But the worst of it was, that the fancy, while it fled, left behind it a real contemplation of that state in which young people are placed, whose early affections can promise themselves no lasting result. So little was I assisted in getting free from error, that understanding and reflection used me still worse in this instance. My passion increased the more I learned to know the virtue of the excellent girl, and the time approached when I was to lose, perhaps for ever, so much that was dear and good.

We had quietly and pleasantly passed a long time together, when friend Weyland had the waggery to bring with him to Sesenheim the *Vicar of Wakefield*, and when they were talking of reading aloud, to hand it over to me unexpectedly, as if nothing further was to be said. I managed to collect myself, and read with as much cheerfulness and freedom as I could. Even the faces of my hearers at once brightened, and it did not seem unpleasant to them to be again forced to a comparison. If they had found comical counterparts to Raymond and Melusina, they here saw themselves in a glass which by no means gave a distorted likeness. They did not openly confess, but they did not deny, that they were moving among persons akin both by mind and feeling.

All men of a good disposition feel, with increasing cultivation, that they have a double part to play in the world,—a real one and an ideal one, and in this feeling is the ground of everything noble to be sought. The real part which has been assigned to us we experience but too plainly; with respect to the second, we seldom come to a clear understanding about it. Man may seek his higher destination on earth or in heaven, in the present or in the future, he yet remains on this account exposed to an eternal wavering, to an influence from without which ever disturbs him, until he once for all makes a resolution to declare that that is right which is suitable to himself.

Among the most venial attempts to acquire something higher, to place oneself on an equality with something higher, may be classed the youthful impulse to compare oneself with the characters in novels. This is highly innocent, and whatever may be urged against it, the very reverse of mischievous. It amuses at times when we should necessarily die of *ennui*, or grasp at the recreation of passion.

How often is repeated the litany about the mischief of novels —and yet what misfortune is it if a pretty girl or a handsome young man put themselves in the place of a person who fares better or worse than themselves? Is the citizen life worth so much? or do the necessities of the day so completely absorb the man, that he must refuse every beautiful demand which is made upon him?

The historico-poetical Christian names which have intruded into the German church in the place of the sacred names, not unfrequently to the annoyance of the officiating clergyman, are without doubt to be regarded as small ramifications of the romantico-poetical pictures. This very impulse to honour one's child by a well-sounding name—even if the name has nothing further behind it—is praiseworthy, and this connexion of an imaginary world with the real one diffuses an agreeable lustre over the whole life of the person. A beautiful child, whom with satisfaction we call " Bertha," we should think we offended if we were to call it " Urselblandine." With a cultivated man, not to say a lover, such a name would certainly falter on the lips. The cold world, which judges only from one side, is not to be blamed if it sets down as ridiculous and objectionable all that comes forward as imaginary, but the thinking connoisseur of mankind must know how to estimate it according to its worth.

For the instruction of the lovers on the lovely bank of the Rhine, this comparison, to which a wag had compelled them, produced the most agreeable results. We do not think of ourselves when we look in a mirror, but we feel ourselves, and allow ourselves to pass. Thus is it also with those moral imitations, in which we recognise our manners and inclinations, our habits and peculiarities, as in a *silhouette*, and strive to grasp it and embrace it with brotherly affection.

The habit of being together became more and more confirmed, and nothing else was known but that I belonged to this circle. The affair was allowed to take its course without the question being directly asked as to what was to be the result. And what parents are there who do not find themselves compelled to let daughters and sons continue for a while in such a wavering condition, until accidentally something is confirmed for life, better than it could have been produced by a long arranged plan.

It was thought that perfect confidence could be placed both in Frederica's sentiments and in my rectitude, of which, on account of my forbearance even from innocent caresses, a favourable opinion had been entertained. We were left unobserved, as was generally the custom, there and then, and it depended on ourselves to go over the country, with a larger or smaller party, and to visit the friends in the neighbourhood.

2 D

On both sides of the Rhine, in Hagenau, Fort-Louis, Philipps-
burg, the Ortenau, I found dispersed those persons whom I
had seen united at Sesenheim, every one by himself, a friendly,
hospitable host, throwing open kitchen and cellar just as willingly as gardens and vineyards, nay, the whole spot. The
islands on the Rhine were often a goal to our water-expedi-
tions. There, without pity, we put the cool inhabitants of the
clear Rhine into the kettle, on the spit, into the boiling fat,
and would here perhaps, more than was reasonable, have
settled ourselves in the snug fishermen's huts, if the abominable Rhine-gnats (*Rhein-schnaken*) had not, after some hours,
driven us away. At this intolerable interruption of one of our
most charming parties of pleasure, when everything else was
prosperous, when the affection of the lovers seemed to increase
with the good success of the enterprise, and we had nevertheless come home too soon, unsuitably and inopportunely, I
actually, in the presence of the good reverend father, broke
out into blasphemous expressions, and assured him that these
gnats alone were sufficient to remove from me the thought that
a good and wise Deity had created the world. The pious old
gentleman, by way of reply, solemnly called me to order, and
explained to me that these gnats and other vermin had not
arisen until after the fall of our first parents, or that if there
were any of them in Paradise, they had only pleasantly hummed
there, and had not stung. I certainly felt myself calmed at
once, for an angry man may easily be appeased if we can succeed in making him smile; but I nevertheless asserted that
there was no need of the angel with the burning sword to drive
the guilty pair out of the garden; my host, I said, must rather
allow me to think that this was effected by means of great
gnats on the Tigris and the Euphrates. And thus I again
made him laugh; for the old man understood a joke, or at any
rate let one pass.

However, the enjoyment of the day-time and season in this
noble country was more serious and more elevating to the heart.
One had only to resign oneself to the present, to enjoy the clearness of the pure sky, the brilliancy of the rich earth, the mild
evenings, the warm nights, by the side of a beloved one, or in
her vicinity. For months together we were favoured with pure
ethereal mornings, when the sky displayed itself in all its magnificence, having watered the earth with superfluous dew; and

that this spectacle might not become too simple, clouds after
clouds piled themselves over the distant mountains, now in this
spot, now in that. They stood for days, nay, for weeks, without obscuring the pure sky, and even the transient storms refreshed the country, and gave lustre to the green, which again
glistened in the sunshine before it could become dry. The
double rainbow, the two-coloured borders of a dark grey and
nearly black streak in the sky, were nobler, more highly coloured,
more decided, but also more transient, than I had ever observed.

In the midst of these objects the desire of poetising, which
I had not felt for a long time, again came forward. For Frederica I composed many songs to well-known melodies. They
would have made a pretty little book ; a few of them still remain, and will easily be found among my others.

Since on account of my strange studies and other circumstances I was often compelled to return to the town, there
arose for our affection a new life, which preserved us from all
that unpleasantness which usually attaches itself as an annoying consequence to such little love-affairs. Though far from
me, she yet laboured for me, and thought of some new amusement against I should return ; though far from her, I employed
myself for her, that by some new gift or new notion I myself
might be again new to her. Painted ribbons had then just
come into fashion. I painted at once for her a few pieces, and
sent them on with a little poem, as on this occasion I was
forced to stop away longer than I had anticipated. That I
might fulfil and even go beyond my promise to the father of a
new and elaborated plan, I persuaded a young adept in architecture to work instead of myself. He took as much pleasure
in the task as he had kindness for me, and was still further
animated by the hope of a good reception in so agreeable a
family. He finished the ground-plan, sketch, and section of
the house ; court-yard and garden were not forgotten, and a
detailed but very moderate estimate was added, to show the
possibility of carrying out an extensive project.

These testimonials of our friendly endeavours obtained
for us the kindest reception ; and since the good father saw
that we had the best will to serve him, he came forward with
one wish more ; it was the wish to see his pretty but one-
coloured chair adorned with flowers and other ornaments. We
showed ourselves accommodating. Colours, pencils, and other

requisites were fetched from the tradesmen and apothecaries of the nearest towns. But that we might not be wanting in a *Wakefield* mistake, we did not remark, until all had been most industriously and variously painted, that we had taken a false varnish which would not dry ; neither sunshine nor draught, neither fair nor wet weather were of any avail. In the meanwhile we were obliged to make use of an old lumber-room, and nothing was left us but to rub out the ornaments with more assiduity than we had painted them. The unpleasantness of this work was still increased when the girls intreated us, for heaven's sake, to proceed slowly and cautiously, for the sake of sparing the ground ; which, however, after this operation, was not again to be restored to its former brilliancy.

By such little disagreeable contigencies, which happened at intervals, we were, however, just as little interrupted in our cheerful life as Dr. Primrose and his amiable family ; for many an unexpected pleasure befell both ourselves and our friends and neighbours. Weddings and christenings, the erection of a building, an inheritance, a prize in the lottery, were reciprocally announced and enjoyed. We shared all joy together, like a common property, and wished to heighten it by mind and love. It was not the first nor the last time that I found myself in families and social circles at the very moment of their highest bloom, and if I may flatter myself that I contributed something towards the lustre of such epochs, I must, on the other hand, be reproached with the fact, that on this very account such times passed the more quickly and vanished the sooner.

But now our love was to undergo a singular trial. I will call it a trial (*Prüfung*), although this is not the right word. The country family with which I was intimate was related to some families in the city of good note and respectability, and comfortably off as to circumstances. The young towns-people were often at Sesenheim. The older persons, the mothers and aunts, being less moveable, heard so much of the life there, of the increasing charms of the daughters, and even of my influence, that they first wished to become acquainted with me, and after I had often visited them, and had been well received by them, desired also to see us once altogether, especially as they thought they owed the Sesenheim folks a friendly reception in return.

There was much discussion on all sides. The mother could
scarcely leave her household affairs, Olivia had a horror of the
town, for which she was not fitted, and Frederica had no inclination for it; and thus the affair was put off, until it was at
last brought to a decision by the fact, that it happened to be
impossible for me to come into the country; for it was better
to see each other in the city, and under some restraint, than
not to see each other at all. And thus I now found my fair
friends, whom I had been only accustomed to see in a rural
scene, and whose image had only appeared to me hitherto
before a background of waving boughs, flowing brooks, nodding
field-flowers, and a horizon open for miles: I now saw them,
I say, for the first time, in town-rooms, which were indeed spacious, but yet narrow, if we take into consideration the carpets,
glasses, clocks, and porcelain figures.

The relation to that which one loves is so decided, that the
surrounding objects have little to do with it, but nevertheless the heart desires that these shall be the suitable, natural,
and usual objects. With my lively feeling for everything present, I could not at once adapt myself to the contradiction of
the moment. The respectable and calmly noble demeanour of
the mother was perfectly adapted to the circle; she was not
different from the other ladies: Olivia, on the other hand,
showed herself as impatient as a fish out of water. As she had
formerly called to me in the gardens, or beckoned me aside
in the fields, if she had anything particular to say to me, she
also did the same here, when she drew me into the recess of
a window. This she did awkwardly and with embarrassment,
because she felt that it was not becoming, and did it notwithstanding. She had the most unimportant things in the world
to say to me—nothing but what I knew already; for instance,
that she wished herself by the Rhine, over the Rhine, or even
in Turkey. Frederica, on the contrary, was highly remarkable
in this situation. Properly speaking, she also did not suit it,
but it bore witness to her character, that, instead of finding
herself adapted to this condition, she unconsciously moulded
the condition according to herself. She acted here as she had
acted with the society in the country. She knew how to animate every moment. Without creating any disturbance, she
put all in motion, and exactly by this pacified society, which
really is only disturbed by *ennui*. She thus completely fulfilled

the desire of her town aunts, who wished for once, on their sofas, to be witnesses of those rural games and amusements. If this was done to satisfaction, so also were the wardrobe, the ornaments, and whatever besides distinguished the town nieces, who were dressed in the French fashion, considered and admired without envy. With me also Frederica had no difficulty, since she treated me the same as ever. She seemed to give me no other preference but that of communicating her desires and wishes to me rather than to another, and thus recognising me as her servant.

To this service she confidently laid claim on one of the following days, when she privately told me that the ladies wished to hear me read. The daughters of the house had spoken much on this subject, for at Sesenheim I had read what and when I was desired. I was ready at once, but craved quiet and attention for several hours. This was conceded, and one evening I read through the whole of *Hamlet* without interruption, entering into the sense of the piece as well as I was able, and expressing myself with liveliness and passion, as is possible in youth. I earned great applause. Frederica drew her breath deeply from time to time, and a transient red had passed over her cheeks. These two symptoms of a tender heart internally moved, while cheerfulness and calmness were externally apparent, were not unknown to me, and were indeed the only reward which I had striven to obtain. She joyfully collected the thanks of the party for having caused me to read, and in her graceful manner did not deny herself the little pride at having shone in me and through me.

This town visit was not to have lasted long : but the departure was delayed. Frederica did her part for the social amusement, and I was not wanting, but the abundant sources which yield so much in the country now dried up in their turn, and the situation was the more painful, as the elder sister gradually lost all self-control. The two sisters were the only persons in the society who dressed themselves in the German fashion. Frederica had never thought of herself in any other way, and believed herself so right everywhere, that she made no comparisons with any one else ; but Olivia found it quite insupportable to move about in a society of genteel appearance attired so like a maid-servant. In the country she scarcely remarked the town costume of others, and did not desire it, but in the

town she could not endure the country style. All this, together
with the different lot of town ladies, and the thousand trifles of
a series of circumstances totally opposed to her own notions,
so worked for some days in her impassioned bosom, that I was
forced to apply all my flattering attention to appease her,
according to the wish of Frederica. I feared an impassioned
scene. I looked forward to the moment when she would throw
herself at my feet, and implore me by all that was sacred to
rescue her from this situation. She was good to a heavenly
degree if she could conduct herself in her own way, but such
a restraint at once made her uncomfortable, and could at last
drive her even to despair. I now sought to hasten that which
was desired by the mother and Olivia, and not repugnant to
Frederica. I did not refrain from praising her as a contrast
to her sister; I told her what pleasure it gave me to find her
unaltered, and, even under the present circumstances, just as
free as the bird among the branches. She was courteous enough
to reply that I was there, and that she wished to go neither in
nor out when I was with her.

At last I saw them take their departure, and it seemed as
though a stone fell from my heart; for my own feelings had
shared the condition of Frederica and Olivia: I was not passionately tormented like the former, but I felt by no means as
comfortable as the latter.

Since I had properly gone to Strasburg to take my degree,
it may be rightly reckoned among the irregularities of my life,
that I treated this material business as a mere collateral affair.
All anxiety as to my examination I had put aside in a very
easy fashion, but I had now to think of the *disputation*,* for on
my departure from Frankfort I had promised my father, and
resolved within myself to write one. It is the fault of those
who can do many things, nay, much, that they trust everything
to themselves, and youth must indeed be in this position, if
anything is to be made of it. A survey of the science of jurisprudence and all its framework I had pretty well acquired,
single subjects of law sufficiently interested me, and as I had
the good Leyser for my model, I thought I should get tolerably
through with my own little common-sense. Great movements
were showing themselves in jurisprudence; judgments were to
be more according to equity, all rights by usage were daily

* A polemic dissertation written on taking an university degree.—*Trans.*

seen to be compromised, and in the criminal department especially a great change was impending. As for myself, I felt well enough that I lacked an infinite deal to fill up the legal commonplace which I had proposed. The proper knowledge was wanting, and no inner tendency urged me to such subjects. Neither was there any impulse from without, nay, quite another faculty* had completely carried me away. In general, if I was to take any interest in a thing, it was necessary for me to gain something from it, to perceive in it something that appeared fertile to me, and gave me prospects. Thus I had once more noted down some materials, had afterwards made collections, had taken my books of extracts in hand, had considered the point which I wished to maintain, the scheme according to which I wished to arrange the single elements; but I was sharp enough soon to perceive that I could not get on, and that to treat a special matter, a special and long pursuing industry was requisite, nay, that such a special task cannot be successfully accomplished unless, upon the whole, one is at any rate an old hand, if not a master.

The friends to whom I communicated my embarrassment deemed me ridiculous, because one can dispute upon *theses* as well, nay, even better, than upon a treatise, and in Strasburg this was not uncommon. I allowed myself to be very well inclined to such an expedient, but my father, to whom I wrote on the subject, desired a regular work, which, as he thought, I could very well prepare, if I only chose so to do and allowed myself proper time. I was now compelled to throw myself upon some general topic, and to choose something which I should have at my fingers' ends. Ecclesiastical history was almost better known to me than the history of the world, and that conflict in which the church—the publicly recognised worship of God—finds itself, and always will find itself, in two different directions, had always highly interested me. For now it lies in an eternal conflict with the state, over which it will exalt itself; now with the individuals, all of whom it will gather to itself. The state, on its side, will not yield the superior authority to the church, and the individuals oppose its restraints. The state desires everything for public, universal ends; the individual for ends belonging to the home, heart, and feelings. From my childhood upwards I had been a witness

* Medicine.—*Trans.*

of such movements, when the clergy now offended their authorities, now their congregations. I had therefore established it
as a principle in my young mind, that the state—the legislator
—had the right to determine a worship, according to which
the clergy should teach and conduct themselves, and the laity,
on the other hand, should direct themselves publicly and externally : while there should be no question about any one's
thoughts, feelings, or notions. Thus I perceived that I had at
once got rid of all collisions. I therefore chose for my *disputation*
the first half of this theme, namely, that the legislator was not
only authorised, but bound to establish a certain worship, from
which neither the clergy nor the laity might free themselves. I
carried out this theme partly historically, partly argumenta-
tively, showing that all public religions had been introduced by
leaders of armies, kings, and powerful men ; that this had even
been the case with Christianity. The example of Protestantism lay quite close at hand. I went to work at this task with
so much the more boldness, as I really only wrote it to satisfy
my father, and desired and hoped nothing more ardently than
that it might not pass the censorship. I had imbibed from
Behrisch an unconquerable dislike to see anything of mine in
print, and my intercourse with Herder had discovered to me
but too plainly my own insufficiency, nay, a certain mistrust
in myself had through this means been perfectly matured. As
I drew this work almost entirely out of myself, and wrote and
spoke Latin with fluency, the time which I expended on the
treatise passed very agreeably. The matter had at least some
foundation, the style, naturally speaking, was not bad, the
whole was pretty well rounded off. As soon as I had finished
it, I went through it with a good Latin scholar, who, although
he could not, on the whole, improve my style, yet easily removed all striking defects, so that something was produced
that was fit to be shown. A fair copy was at once sent to my
father, who disapproved of one thing, namely, that none of the
subjects previously taken in hand had been worked out, but
nevertheless, as a thorough Protestant, he was well pleased
with the boldness of the plan. My singularities were tolerated, my exertions were praised, and he promised himself an
important effect from the publication of the work.

I now handed over my papers to the faculty, who fortunately
behaved in a manner as prudent as it was polite. The dean,

a lively, clever man, began with many laudations of my work, then went on to what was doubtful, which he contrived gradually to change into something dangerous, and concluded by saying that it might not be advisable to publish this work as an academical dissertation. The *aspirant* had shown himself to the faculty as a thinking young man, of whom they might hope the best: they would willingly, not to delay the affair, allow me to dispute on *theses*. I could afterwards publish my treatise, either in its present condition or more elaborated, in Latin, or in another language. This would everywhere be easy to me as a private man and a Protestant, and I should have the pleasure of an applause more pure and more general. I scarcely concealed from the good man what a stone his discourse rolled from my heart; at every new argument which he advanced, that he might not trouble me nor make me angry by his refusal, my mind grew more and more easy, and so did his own at last, when, quite unexpectedly, I offered no resistance to his reasons, but, on the contrary, found them extremely obvious, and promised to conduct myself according to his counsel and guidance. I therefore sat down again with my *repetent*. *Theses* were chosen and printed, and the disputation, with the opposition of my fellow-boarders, went off with great merriment, and even with facility, for my old habit of turning over the *Corpus Juris* was very serviceable to me, and I could pass for a well instructed man. A good feast, according to custom, concluded the solemnity.

My father, however, was very dissatisfied that the little work had not been regularly printed as a *disputation*, because he had hoped that I should gain honour by it on my entrance into Frankfort. He therefore wished to publish it specially, but I represented to him that the subject, which was only sketched, could be more completely carried out at some future time. He put up the manuscript carefully for this purpose, and many years afterwards I saw it among his papers.

I took my degree on the 6th August, 1771; and on the following day Schöpflin died, in the 75th year of his age. Even without closer contact, he had had an important influence upon me: for eminent contemporaries may be compared to the greater stars, towards which, so long as they merely stand above the horizon, our eye is turned, and feels strengthened and cultivated, if it is only allowed to take such perfections into itself. Bountiful nature had given Schöpflin an advantageous exterior, a slender form, kindly eyes, a ready mouth, and a thoroughly agreeable presence. Neither had she been sparing in gifts of mind to her favourite; and his good fortune was the result of innate and carefully-cultivated merits, without any troublesome exertion. He was one of those happy men, who are inclined to unite the past and the present, and understand how to connect historical knowledge with the interests of life. Born in the Baden territory, educated at Basle and Strasburg, he quite properly belonged to the paradisiacal valley of the Rhine, as an extensive and well-situated fatherland. His mind being directed to historical and antiquarian objects, he readily seized upon them with a felicitous power of representation, and retained them by the most convenient memory. Desirous as he was both of learning and of teaching, he pursued a course of study and of life which equally advanced. He soon emerges and rises above the rest, without any kind of interruption; diffuses himself with ease through the literary and citizen-world, for historical knowledge passes everywhere, and affability attaches itself everywhere. He travels through Germany, Holland, France, Italy; he comes in contact with all the learned men of his time; he amuses princes, and it is only when, by his lively loquacity, the hours of the table or of audience are lengthened, that he is tedious to the people at court. On the other hand, he acquires the confidence of the statesmen, works out for them the most profound legal questions, and thus finds everywhere a field for his talent. In many places they attempt to retain him, but he remains faithful to Strasburg and the French court. His immoveable German honesty is recognised even there, he is even protected against the powerful Praetor Klingling, who is secretly his enemy. Sociable and talkative by nature, he extends his intercourse with the world, as well as his knowledge and occupations; and we should hardly be able to understand whence he got all his time, did we not know that a dislike to women accompanied him through his whole life; and that thus he gained many days and hours which are happily thrown away by those who are well-disposed towards the ladies.

For the rest, he belongs, as an author, to the ordinary sort of character, and, as an orator, to the multitude. His

programme, his speeches, and addresses are devoted to the particular day—to the approaching solemnity; nay, his great
work, *Alsatia Illustrata*, belongs to life, as he recalls the past,
freshens up faded forms, reanimates the hewn and the formed
stone, and brings obliterated broken inscriptions for a second
time before the eyes and mind of his reader. In such a manner, his activity fills all Alsatia and the neighbouring country;
in Baden and the Palatinate he preserves to an extreme old
age an uninterrupted influence; at Mannheim he founds the
Academy of Sciences, and remains president of it till his
death.

I never approached this eminent man, excepting on one
night, when we gave him a torch-serenade. Our pitch-torches
more filled with smoke than lighted the court-yard of the
old chapter-house, which was over-arched by linden-trees.
When the noise of the music had ended, he came forward
and stepped into the midst of us; and here also was in his
right place. The slender, well-grown, cheerful old man stood
with his light, free manners, venerably before us, and held us
worthy the honour of a well-considered address, which he delivered to us in an amiable paternal manner, without a trace
of restraint or pedantry, so that we really thought ourselves
something for the moment; for, indeed, he treated us like the
kings and princes whom he had been so often called upon to
address in public. We testified our satisfaction aloud, trumpets and drums repeatedly sounded, and the dear, hopeful
academical *plebs* then found its way home with hearty satisfaction.

His scholars and companions in study, Koch and Oberlin,
were men in close connexion with me. My taste for antiquarian remains was passionate. They often let me into the
museum, which contained, in many ways, the vouchers to his
great work on Alsace. Even this work I had not known intimately until after that journey, when I had found antiquities
on the spot, and now being perfectly advanced, I could, on
longer or shorter expeditions, render present to myself the
valley of the Rhine as a Roman possession, and finish colouring
many a dream of times past.

Scarcely had I made some progress in this, than Oberlin
directed me to the monuments of the middle ages, and made
me acquainted with the ruins and remains, the seals and docu-

ments, which those times have left behind them; nay, sought
to inspire me with an inclination for what we called the
Maine-singers and heroic poets. To this good man, as well
as to Herr Koch, I have been greatly indebted; and if things
had gone according to their wish, I should have had to
thank them for the happiness of my life. The matter stood
thus:—

Schöpflin, who for his whole lifetime had moved in the
higher sphere of political law, and well knew the great influence which such and kindred studies are likely to procure
for a sound head, in courts and cabinets, felt an insuperable,
nay, unjust aversion from the situation of a civilian, and had
inspired his scholars with the like sentiments. The above-
mentioned two men, friends of Salzmann, had taken notice of
me in a most friendly manner. My impassioned grasping at
external objects, the manner in which I continued to bring
forward their advantages, and to communicate to them a particular interest, they prized higher than I did myself. My
slight, and I may say, my scanty occupation with the civil
law, had not remained unobserved by them: they were well
enough acquainted with me to know how easily I was to be
influenced: I had made no secret of my liking for an academical life, and they therefore thought to gain me over to history, political law, and rhetoric, at first for a time, but afterwards more decidedly. The prospect of the German Chancery
at Versailles, the precedent of Schöpflin, whose merits, indeed, seemed to me unattainable, were to incite to emulation,
if not to imitation; and perhaps a similar talent was thus to
be cultivated, which might be both profitable to him who
could boast of it, and useful to others who might choose to
employ it on their own account. These, my patrons, and
Salzmann with them, set a great value on my memory and my
capacity for apprehending the sense of languages, and chiefly
by these sought to further their views and plans.

I now intend to describe, at length, how all this came to
nothing, and how it happened that I again passed over from
the French to the German side. Let me be allowed, as
hitherto, some general reflections, by way of transition.

There are few biographies which can represent a pure, quiet,
steady progress of the individual. Our life, as well as all in
which we are contained, is, in an incomprehensible manner,

composed of freedom and necessity. Our will is a prediction of what we shall do, under all circumstances. But these circumstances lay hold on us in their own fashion. The *what* lies in us, the *how* seldom depends on us, after the *wherefore* we dare not ask, and on this account we are rightly referred to the *quia*.

The French tongue I had liked from my youth upwards; I had learned to know the language through a bustling life, and a bustling life through the language. It had become my own, like a second mother-tongue, without grammar and instruction—by mere intercourse and practice. I now wished to use it with still greater fluency, and again gave Strasburg the preference, as an university residence, to other high schools : but, alas ! it was just there that I had to experience the very reverse of my hopes, and to be turned rather from than to this language and these manners.

The French, who generally aim at good behaviour, are indulgent towards foreigners who begin to speak their language ; they will not laugh any one out of countenance at a fault, or blame him in direct terms. However, since they cannot endure sins committed against their language, they have a manner of repeating, and, as it were, courteously confirming what has been said with another turn, at the same time making use of the expression which should properly have been employed ; thus leading the intelligent and the attentive to what is right and proper.

Now although, if one is in earnest—if one has self-denial enough to profess oneself a pupil, one gains a great deal, and is much advanced by this plan, one nevertheless always feels in some degree humiliated ; and, since one talks for the sake of the subject-matter also, often too much interrupted, or even distracted, so that one impatiently lets the conversation drop. This happened with me more than with others, as I always thought that I had to say something interesting, and, on the other hand, to hear something important, and did not wish to be always brought back merely to the expression,—a case which often occurred with me, as my French was just as motley as that of any other foreigner. I had observed the accent and idiom of footmen, valets, guards, young and old actors, theatrical lovers, peasants, and heroes ; and this Babylonish idiom was rendered still more confused by another odd

ingredient, as I liked to hear the French reformed clergy, and
visited their churches the more willingly, as a Sunday walk to
Bockenheim was on this account not only permitted but ordered. But even this was not enough ; for as in my youthful
years, I had always been chiefly directed to the German of the
century, I soon included the French also of that noble epoch
among the objects of my inclination. Montaigne, Amyot,
Rabelais, Marot, were my friends, and excited in me sympathy
and delight. Now all these different elements moved in my
discourse chaotically one with another, so that for the hearer
the meaning was lost in the oddity of the expression ; nay,
an educated Frenchman could no more courteously correct
me, but had to censure me and tutor me in plain terms. It
therefore happened with me here once more as it had happened in Leipzig, only that on this occasion I could not appeal
to the right of my native place to speak idiomatically, as well
as other provinces ; but being on a foreign ground and soil,
was forced to adapt myself to traditional laws.

Perhaps we might even have resigned ourselves to this, if
an evil genius had not whispered into our ears that all endeavours by a foreigner to speak French would remain unsuccessful ; for a practised ear can perfectly well detect a German, Italian, or Englishman under a French mask. One is
tolerated, but never received into the bosom of the only
language-holy church.

Only a few exceptions were granted. They named to us a
Herr von Grimm ; but even Schöpflin, it seemed, did not
reach the summit. They allowed that he had early seen the
necessity of expressing himself in French to perfection ; they
approved of his inclination to converse with every one, and
especially to entertain the great and persons of rank ; they
praised him, that living in the place where he was, he had
made the language of the country his own, and had endeavoured as much as possible to render himself a Frenchman of
society and orator. But what does he gain by the denial of
his mother-tongue, and his endeavours after a foreign one?
He cannot make it right with anybody. In society they are
pleased to deem him vain ; as if any one would or could converse with others without some feeling for self and self-complacency! Then the refined connoisseurs of the world and of
language assert that there is in him more of dissertation and

dialogue than of conversation, properly so called. The former was generally recognised as the original and fundamental sin of the Germans, the latter as the cardinal virtue of the French. As a public orator he fares no better. If he prints a well-elaborated address to the king or the princes, the Jesuits, who are ill-disposed to him as a Protestant, lay wait for him, and show that his terms of expression are *not French.*

Instead of consoling ourselves with this, and bearing as green wood that which had been laid upon the dry, we were annoyed at such pedantic injustice. We fall into despair, and, by this striking example, are the more convinced that it is a vain endeavour to try to satisfy the French by the matter itself, as they are too closely bound to the external conditions under which everything is to appear. We therefore embrace the opposite resolution of getting rid of the French language altogether, and of directing ourselves more than ever, with might and earnestness, to our own mother-tongue.

And for this we found opportunity and sympathy in actual life. Alsace had not been connected with France so long that an affectionate adherence to the old constitution, manners, language, and costume did not still exist with old and young. If the conquered party loses half his existence by compulsion, he looks upon it as disgraceful voluntarily to part with the other half. He therefore holds fast to all that can recall to him the good old time, and foster in him the hope that a better epoch will return. Very many inhabitants of Strasburg formed little circles, separate, indeed, but nevertheless united in spirit, which were always increased and recruited by the numerous subjects of German princes who held considerable lands under French sovereignty, since fathers and sons, either for the sake of study or business, resided for a longer or shorter time at Strasburg.

At our table nothing but German was spoken. Salzmann expressed himself in French with much fluency and elegance; but, with respect to his endeavours and acts, was a perfect German. Lerse might have been set up as a pattern of a German youth. Meyer, of Lindau, liked to get on with good German too well to shine in good French; and if, among the rest, many were inclined to the Gallic speech and manners, they yet, while they were with us, allowed the general tone to prevail with them.

From the language we turned to political affairs. We had not, indeed, much to say in praise of our own imperial constitution. We granted that it consisted of mere legal contradictions; but exalted ourselves so much the more above the present French constitution, which lost itself in mere lawless abuses, while the government only showed its energy in the wrong place, and was forced to admit that a complete change in affairs was already publicly prophesied with black forebodings.

If, on the other hand, we looked towards the north, we were shone upon by Frederic, the polar-star, who seemed to turn about himself Germany, Europe, nay, the whole world. His preponderance in everything was most strongly manifested when the Prussian exercise and even the Prussian stick was introduced into the French army. As for the rest, we forgave him his predilection for a foreign language, since we felt satisfaction that his French poets, philosophers, and *littérateurs* continued to annoy him, and often declared that he was to be considered and treated only as an intruder.

But what, more than all, forcibly alienated us from the French, was the unpolite opinion, repeatedly maintained, that the Germans in general, as well as the king, who was striving after French cultivation, were deficient in taste. With respect to this kind of talk, which followed every judgment like a burden, we endeavoured to solace ourselves with contempt; but we could so much the less come to a clear understanding about it, as we were assured that Menage had already said, that the French writers possessed everything but taste ; and had also learned from the then living Paris, that all the authors were wanting in taste, and that Voltaire himself could not escape this severest of reproaches. Having been before and often directed to nature, we would allow of nothing but truth and uprightness of feeling, and the quick, blunt expression of it.

> " Friendship, love, and brotherhood,
> Of themselves are understood,"

was the watchword and cry of battle, by which the members of our little academical horde used to know and enliven each other. This maxim lay at the foundation of all our social banquets, on the occasions of which we did not fail to pay

2 E

many an evening visit to Cousin Michel,* in his well-known *Germanhood.*

If, in what has hitherto been described, only external contingent causes and personal peculiarities are found, the French literature had in itself certain qualities which were rather repulsive than attractive to an aspiring youth. It was advanced in years and genteel; and by neither of these qualities can youth, which looks about for enjoyment of life and for freedom, be delighted.

Since the sixteenth century, the course of French literature had never been seen to be completely interrupted; nay, the internal and religious disturbances, as well as the external wars, had accelerated its progress; but, as we heard generally maintained, it was a hundred years ago that it had existed in its full bloom. Through favourable circumstances, they said, an abundant harvest had at once ripened, and had been happily gathered in, so that the great talents of the eighteenth century had to be moderately contented with mere gleanings.

In the meanwhile, however, much had become antiquated: first of all comedy, which had to be freshened up to adapt itself, less perfectly, indeed, but still with new interest, to actual life and manners. Of the tragedies, many had vanished from the stage, and Voltaire did not let slip the important opportunity which offered of editing Corneille's works, that he might show how defective his predecessor had been, whom, according to the general voice, he had not equalled.

And even this very Voltaire, the wonder of his time, had grown old, like the literature, which, for nearly a century, he had animated and governed. By his side still existed and vegetated many *littérateurs,* in a more or less active and happy old age, who one by one disappeared. The influence of society upon authors increased more and more; for the best society, consisting of persons of birth, rank, and property, chose for one of their chief recreations literature, which thus became quite social and genteel. Persons of rank and *littérateurs* mutually cultivated and necessarily perverted each other; for the genteel has always something excluding in its nature; and excluding also was the French criticism, being negative, detracting, and fault-finding. The higher class made use

* " Michel" is exactly to the Germans what " John Bull" is to the English.—*Trans.*

of such judgments against the authors; the authors, with
somewhat less decorum, proceeded in the same manner
against each other, nay, against their patrons. If the public
was not to be awed, they endeavoured to take it by surprise,
or gain it by humility; and thus—apart from the movements
which shook church and state to their inmost core—there
arose such a literary ferment, that Voltaire himself stood in
need of his full activity, and his whole preponderance, to keep
himself above the torrent of general disesteem. Already he
was openly called an old capricious child; his endeavours,
carried on indefatigably, were regarded as the vain efforts of
a decrepid age; certain principles, on which he had stood
during his whole life, and to the spread of which he had devoted his days, were no more held in esteem and honour;
nay, his Deity, by acknowledging whom he continued to
declare himself free from atheism, was not conceded him;
and thus he himself, the grandsire and patriarch, was forced,
like his youngest competitor, to watch the present moment,
to catch at new power—to do his friends too much good, and
his enemies too much harm; and under the appearance of a
passionate striving for the love of truth, to act deceitfully and
falsely. Was it worth the trouble to have led such a great
active life, if it was to end in greater dependence than it had
begun? How insupportable such a position was, did not
escape his high mind, his delicate sensibility. He often
relieved himself by leaps and thrusts, gave the reins to his
humour, and carried a few of his sword-cuts too far,—at
which friends and enemies, for the most part, showed themselves indignant; for every one thought he could play the
superior to him, though no one could equal him. A public
which only hears the judgment of old men, becomes over-wise
too soon; and nothing is more unsatisfactory than a mature
judgment adopted by an immature mind.

To us youths, before whom, with our German love of truth
and nature, honesty towards both ourselves and others hovered
as the best guide both in life and learning, the factious dishonesty of Voltaire and the perversion of so many worthy
subjects became more and more annoying, and we daily
strengthened ourselves in our aversion from him. He could
never have done with degrading religion and the sacred books,

for the sake of injuring priestcraft,* as they called it, and had
thus produced in me many an unpleasant sensation. But
when I now learned that, to weaken the tradition of a deluge,
he had denied all petrified shells, and only admitted them as
lusus naturæ, he entirely lost my confidence ; for my own eyes
had, on the Baschberg, plainly enough shown me that I stood
on the bottom of an old dried-up sea, among the *exuviæ* of its
original inhabitants. These mountains had certainly been
once covered with waves, whether before or during the deluge
did not concern me ; it was enough that the valley of the
Rhine had been a monstrous lake, a bay extending beyond
the reach of the eyesight ; out of this I was not to be talked.
I thought much more of advancing in the knowledge of lands
and mountains, let what would be the result.

French literature, then, had grown old and genteel in itself,
and through Voltaire. Let us devote some further consideration to this remarkable man.

From his youth upwards, Voltaire's wishes and endeavours
had been directed to an active and social life, to politics, to
gain on a large scale, to a connexion with the heads of the
earth, and a profitable use of this connexion, that he himself
might be one of the heads of the earth also. No one has
easily made himself so dependent, for the sake of being independent. He even succeeded in subjugating minds ; the nation became his own. In vain did his opponents unfold their
moderate talents, and their monstrous hate ; nothing succeeded in injuring him. The court he could never reconcile
to himself, but by way of compensation, foreign kings were
his tributaries : Katharine and Frederic the Great, Gustavus
of Sweden, Christian of Denmark, Peniotowsky of Poland,
Henry of Prussia, Charles of Brunswick, acknowledged themselves his vassals ; even popes thought they must coax him
by some acts of indulgence. That Joseph the Second had
kept aloof from him did not at all redound to the honour
of this prince, for it would have done no harm to him and his
undertakings, if, with such a fine intellect and with such

* " Um den so genannten Pfaffen zu schaden." As we have not the
word for a priest, which exactly expresses the contempt involved in
" Pfaffe," the word " priestcraft " has been introduced.—*Trans.*

noble views, he had been somewhat more practically clever,* and a better appreciator of the mind.

What I have here stated in a compressed form, and in some connexion, sounded at that time as a cry of the moment, as a perpetual discord, unconnected and uninstructive, in our ears. Nothing was heard but the praise of those who had gone before. Something good and new was required : but the newest was never liked. Scarcely had a patriot exhibited on the long inanimate stage national, French, heart-inspiring subjects,— scarcely had the *Siege of Calais* gained enthusiastic applause, than the piece, together with all its national comrades, was considered empty, and in every sense objectionable. The delineations of manners by Destouches, which had so often delighted me when a boy, were called weak ; the name of this honest man had passed away ; and how many authors could I not point out, for the sake of whom I had to endure the reproach that I judged like a provincial, if I showed any sympathy for such men and their works, in opposition to any one who was carried along by the newest literary torrent.

Thus, to our other German comrades we became more and more annoying. According to our view,—according to the peculiarity of our own nature, we had to retain the impressions of objects, to consume them but slowly, and if it was to be so, to let them go as late as possible. We were convinced that by faithful observation, by continued occupation, something might be gained from all things, and that by persevering zeal we must at last arrive at a point where the ground of the judgment may be expressed at the same time with the judgment itself. Neither did we fail to perceive that the great and noble French world offered us many an advantage and much profit : for Rousseau had really touched our sympathies. But if we considered his life and his fate, he was nevertheless compelled to find the great reward for all he did in this—that he could live unacknowledged and forgotten at Paris.

If we heard the encyclopedists mentioned, or opened a volume of their monstrous work, we felt as if we were going between the innumerable moving spools and looms in a great factory, where, what with the mere creaking and rattling—

* " Practically clever " is put as a kind of equivalent for the difficult word " geistreich."— *Trans.*

what with all the mechanism, embarrassing both eyes and
noses—what with the mere incomprehensibility of an arrangement, the parts of which work into each other in the most
manifold way—what with the contemplation of all that is
necessary to prepare a piece of cloth, we feel disgusted with
the very coat which we wear upon our backs.

Diderot was sufficiently akin to us, as, indeed, in everything, for which the French blame him, he is a true German.
But even his point of view was too high, his circle of vision
was too extended for us to range ourselves with him, and
place ourselves at his side. Nevertheless, his children of
nature, whom he continued to bring forward and dignify with
great rhetorical art, pleased us very much; his brave poachers
and smugglers enchanted us; and this rabble afterwards
throve but too well upon the German Parnassus. It was he
also, who, like Rousseau, diffused a disgust of social life—a
quiet introduction to those monstrous changes of the world,
in which everything permanent appeared to sink.

However, we ought now to put aside these considerations,
and to remark what influence these two men have had upon
art. Even here they pointed—even from here they urged us
towards nature.

The highest problem of any art is to produce by appearance
the illusion of a higher reality. But it is a false endeavour
to realize the appearance until at last only something commonly real remains.

As an ideal locality, the stage, by the application of the laws
of perspective to *coulisses* ranged one behind the other, had
attained the greatest advantage; and this very gain they now
wished wantonly to abandon, by shutting up the sides of the
theatre, and forming real room-walls. With such an arrangement of the stage, the piece itself, the actors' mode of playing,
in a word, everything was to coincide; and thus an entirely
new theatre was to arise.

The French actors had, in comedy, attained the summit of
the true in art. Their residence at Paris, their observations
of the externals of the court, the connexion of the actors and
actresses with the highest classes, by means of love affairs—
all contributed to transplant to the stage the greatest real-
ness and seemliness of social life; and on this point the
friends of nature found but little to blame. However they

thought they made a great advance, if they chose for their
pieces earnest and tragical subjects, in which the citizen-life
should not be wanting, used pure verse for the higher mode
of expression, and thus banished unnatural verse, together with
unnatural declamation and gesticulation.

It is extremely remarkable, and has not been generally
noticed, that at this time, even the old, severe, rhythmical,
artistical tragedy was threatened with a revolution, which
could only be averted by great talents and the power of
tradition.

In opposition to the actor Le Kain, who played his heroes
with especial theatrical decorum, with deliberation, elevation,
and force, and kept himself aloof from the natural and ordinary, came forward a man named Aufresne, who declared war
against everything unnatural, and in his tragic acting sought
to express the highest truth. This mode might not have
accorded with that of the other Parisian actors. He stood
alone, while they kept together, and adhering to his views
obstinately enough, he chose to leave Paris rather than alter
them, and came through Strasburg. There we saw him play
the part of Augustus in *Cinna*, that of Mithridates, and
others of the sort, with the truest and most natural dignity.
He appeared as a tall, handsome man, more slender than
strong, not, properly speaking, with an imposing, but nevertheless with a noble, pleasing demeanour. His acting was
well-considered and quiet, without being cold, and forcible
enough where force was required. He was a very well-
practised actor, and one of the few who know how to turn
the artificial completely into nature, and nature completely
into the artificial. It is really those few whose misunderstood good qualities always originate the doctrine of false
"naturalness."

And thus will I also make mention of a work, which is
indeed small, but which made an epoch in a remarkable manner,—I mean Rousseau's *Pygmalion*. A great deal could be
said upon it; for this strange production floats between nature
and art, with the full endeavour of resolving the latter into
the former. We see an artist who has produced what is
most perfect, and yet does not find any satisfaction in having,
according to art, represented his idea externally to himself,
and given to it a higher life; no, it must also be drawn down

to him into the earthly life. He will destroy the highest thing that mind and deed have produced, by the commonest act of sensuality.

All this and much else, right and foolish, true and half-true, operating upon us as it did, still more perplexed our notions ; we were driven astray through many by-ways and roundabout ways, and thus on many sides was prepared that German literary revolution, of which we were witnesses, and to which, consciously or unconsciously, willingly or unwillingly, we unceasingly contributed.

We had neither impulse nor tendency to be illumined and advanced in a philosophical manner; on religious subjects we thought we had sufficiently enlightened ourselves, and therefore the violent contest of the French philosophers with the priesthood was tolerably indifferent to us. Prohibited books condemned to the flames, which then made a great noise, produced no effect upon us. I mention as an instance, to serve for all, the *Système de la Nature*, which we took in hand out of curiosity. We did not understand how such a book could be dangerous. It appeared to us so dark, so Cimmerian, so deathlike, that we found it a trouble to endure its presence, and shuddered at it as at a spectre. The author fancies he gives his book a peculiar recommendation, when he declares in his preface, that as a decrepid old man, just sinking into the grave, he wishes to announce the truth to his cotemporaries and to posterity.

We laughed him out; for we thought we had observed that by old people nothing in the world that is loveable and good is in fact appreciated. "Old churches have dark windows; to know how cherries and berries taste, we must ask children and sparrows." These were our gibes and maxims; and thus that book, as the very quintessence of senility, appeared to us as unsavoury, nay, absurd. "All was to be of necessity," so said the book, "and therefore there was no God." But could there not be a God by necessity too? asked we. We indeed confessed, at the same time, that we could not withdraw ourselves from the necessities of day and night, the seasons, the influence of climate, physical and animal condition; but nevertheless we felt within us something that appeared like perfect freedom of will, and again something which sought to counterbalance this freedom.

The hope of becoming more and more rational, of making ourselves more and more independent of external things, nay, of ourselves, we could not give up. The word freedom sounds so beautiful, that we cannot do without it, even though it designates an error.

None of us had read the book through: for we found ourselves deceived in the expectations with which we had opened it. A system of nature was announced; and therefore we hoped to learn really something of nature—our idol. Physics and chemistry, descriptions of heaven and earth, natural history and anatomy, with much else, had now for years, and up to the last day, constantly directed us to the great adorned world; and we would willingly have heard both particulars and generals about suns and stars, planets and moons, mountains, valleys, rivers and seas, with all that live and move in them. That in the course of this, much must occur which would appear to the common man as injurious, to the clergy as dangerous, and to the state as inadmissible, we had no doubt; and we hoped that the little book had not unworthily stood the fiery ordeal. But how hollow and empty did we feel in this melancholy, atheistical half-night, in which earth vanished with all its images, heaven with all its stars. There was to be a matter in motion from all eternity, and by this motion, right and left and in every direction, without anything further, it was to produce the infinite phenomena of existence. Even all this we should have allowed to pass, if the author, out of his moved matter, had really built up the world before our eyes. But he seemed to know as little about nature as we did; for, having set up some general ideas, he quits them at once, for the sake of changing that which appears as higher than nature, or as a higher nature within nature, into material, heavy nature, which is moved, indeed, but without direction or form—and thus he fancies he has gained a great deal.

If, after all, this book did us any mischief, it was this,—that we took a hearty dislike to all philosophy, and especially metaphysics, and remained in that dislike: while, on the other hand, we threw ourselves into living knowledge, experience, action, and poetising, with all the more liveliness and passion.

Thus, on the very borders of France, we had at once got

rid and clear of everything French about us. The French way
of life we found too defined and genteel, their poetry cold,
their criticism annihilating, their philosophy abstruse, and yet
insufficient, so that we were on the point of resigning ourselves to rude nature, at least by way of experiment, if another
influence had not for a long time prepared us for higher and
freer views of the world, and intellectual enjoyments as true
as they were poetical, and swayed us, first moderately and secretly, but afterwards with more and more openness and force.

I need scarcely say that Shakspeare is intended; and having
once said this, no more need be added. Shakspeare has been
acknowledged by the Germans, more by them than by other
nations, perhaps even more than by his own. We have richly
bestowed on him all that justice, fairness, and forbearance
which we refuse to ourselves. Eminent men have occupied
themselves in showing his talents in the most favourable light;
and I have always readily subscribed to what has been said
to his honour, in his favour, or even by way of excuse for
him. The influence of this extraordinary mind upon me
has been already shown; an attempt has been made with
respect to his works, which has received approbation; and
therefore this general statement may suffice for the present,
until I am in a position to communicate to such friends as like
to hear me, a gleaning of reflections on his great deserts, such
as I was tempted to insert in this very place.

At present I will only show more clearly the manner in
which I became acquainted with him. It happened pretty
soon at Leipzig, through Dodd's *Beauties of Shakspeare.*
Whatever may be said against such collections, which give
authors in a fragmentary form, they nevertheless produce
many good effects. We are not always so collected and so
ready that we can take in a whole work according to its
merits. Do we not, in a book, mark passages which have an
immediate reference to ourselves? Young people especially,
who are wanting in a thorough cultivation, are laudably
excited by brilliant passages; and thus I myself remember,
as one of the most beautiful epochs of my life, that which is
characterised by the above-mentioned work. Those noble
peculiarities, those great sayings, those happy descriptions,
those humorous traits—all struck me singly and powerfully.

Wieland's translation now made its appearance. It was

devoured, communicated and recommended to friends and acquaintances. We Germans had the advantage that many important works of foreign nations were first brought over to us in an easy and cheerful fashion. Shakspeare, translated in prose, first by Wieland, afterwards by Eschenburg, was able, as a kind of reading universally intelligible, and suitable to any reader, to diffuse itself speedily, and to produce a great effect. I revere the rhythm as well as the rhyme, by which poetry first becomes poetry; but that which is really, deeply, and fundamentally effective—that which is really permanent and furthering, is that which remains of the poet when he is translated into prose. Then remains the pure, perfect substance, of which, when absent, a dazzling exterior often contrives to make a false show, and which, when present, such an exterior contrives to conceal. I therefore consider prose translations more advantageous than poetical, for the beginning of youthful culture; for it may be remarked that boys, to whom everything must serve as a jest, delight themselves with the sound of words and the fall of syllables, and by a sort of parodistical wantonness, destroy the deep contents of the noblest work. Hence I would have it considered whether a prose translation of Homer should not be next undertaken, though this, indeed, must be worthy of the degree at which German literature stands at present. I leave this, and what has been already said, to the consideration of our worthy pedagogues, to whom an extensive experience on this matter is most at command. I will only, in favour of my proposition, mention Luther's translation of the Bible; for the circumstance that this excellent man handed down a work, composed in the most different styles, and gave us its poetical, historical, commanding didactic tone in our mother-tongue, as if all were cast in one mould, has done more to advance religion than if he had attempted to imitate, in detail, the peculiarities of the original. In vain has been the subsequent endeavour to make Job, the Psalms, and the other lyrical books, capable of affording enjoyment in their poetical form. For the multitude, upon whom the effect is to be produced, a plain translation always remains the best. Those critical translations which vie with the original, really only seem to amuse the learned among themselves.

And thus in our Strasburg society did Shakspeare, trans-

lated and in the original, by fragments and as a whole, by passages and by extracts, influence us in such a manner, that as there
are Bible-firm (*Bibelfest*) men, so did we gradually make ourselves firm in Shakspeare, imitated in our conversations those
virtues and defects of his time with which he had made us
so well acquainted, took the greatest delight in his "quibbles,"*
and by translating them, nay, with original recklessness, sought
to emulate him. To this, the fact that I had seized upon him
above all, with great enthusiasm, did not a little contribute.
A happy confession that something higher waved over me was
infectious for my friends, who all resigned themselves to this
mode of thought. We did not deny the possibility of knowing
such merits more closely, of comprehending them, of judging
them with penetration, but this we reserved for later epochs.
At present we only wished to sympathize gladly, and to imitate
with spirit, and while we had so much enjoyment, we did not
wish to inquire and haggle about the man who afforded it, but
unconditionally to revere him.

If any one would learn immediately what was thought,
talked about, and discussed in this lively society, let him read
Herder's essay on Shakspeare, in the part of his works upon the
German manner and art (*Ueber Deutsche Art und Kunst*), and
also Lenz's remarks on the theatre (*Anmerkungen übers Theater*),
to which a translation of *Love's Labour Lost* was added.†
Herder penetrates into the deepest interior of Shakspeare's
nature, and exhibits it nobly; Lenz conducts himself more
like an Iconoclast against the traditions of the theatre, and will
have everything everywhere treated in Shakspeare's manner.
Since I have had occasion to mention this clever and eccentric
man here, it is the place to say something about him by way
of experiment. I did not become acquainted with him till
towards the end of my residence at Strasburg. We saw each
other seldom, his company was not mine, but we sought an
opportunity of meeting, and willingly communicated with each
other, because, as cotemporary youths, we harboured similar
views. He had a small but neat figure, a charming little
head, to the elegant form of which his delicate but somewhat

* This English word is used in the original.—*Trans.*

† A complete edition of Lenz's works was published by Tieck in 1828.
In that will be found the essay and play in question, to the last of which
he gives the name *Amor vincit omnia.*—*Trans.*

fiat features perfectly corresponded ; blue eyes, blond hair, in short, a person such as I have from time to time met among northern youths ; a soft and as it were cautious step, a pleasant but not quite flowing speech, and a conduct which, fluctuating between reserve and shyness, well became a young man. Small poems, especially his own, he read very well aloud. For his turn of mind I only know the English word "whimsical," which, as the dictionary shows, comprises very many singularities under one notion. No one, perhaps, was more capable than he to feel and imitate the extravagances and excrescences of Shakspeare's genius. To this the translation above mentioned bears witness. He treated his author with great freedom, was not in the least close and faithful, but he knew how to put on the armour, or rather the motley jacket, of his predecessor so very well, to adapt himself with such humour to his gestures, that he was certain to obtain applause from those who were interested in such matters.

The absurdities of the clown especially constituted our whole happiness, and we praised Lenz as a favoured man, when he succeeded in rendering as follows the epitaph on the deer shot by the princess :—

> " Die schöne Princessin schoss und traf
> Eines jungen Hirschleins Leben ;
> Es fiel dahin in schweren Schlaf
> Und wird ein Bratlein geben.
> Der Jagdhund boll ! Ein L zu Hirsch
> So wird es denn ein Hirschel ;
> Doch setzt ein römisch L zu Hirsch
> So macht es funtzig Hirschel.
> Ich mache hundert Hirsche draus
> Schreib Hirschell mit zwei LLen." *

---

* The lines in Shakspeare, which the above are intended to imitate, are the following :—

" The praiseful princess pierc'd and prick'd a pretty pleasing pricket ;
Some say a sore ; but not a sore till now made sore with shooting.
The dogs did yell : put L to sore, then sorel jumps from thicket
Or pricket, sore, or else sorel ; the people fall a-hooting.
If sore be sore, then L to sore makes fifty sores, O sore L !
Of one sore I an hundred make, by adding but one more L."

Lenz's words, which cannot be rendered intelligibly into English, furnish an instance of Göthe's meaning, when he commends Lenz as happily catching the spirit of the original, without the slightest pretence to accuracy.— *Trans.*

The tendency towards the absurd, which displays itself free
and unfettered in youth, but afterwards recedes more into the
background, without being on that account utterly lost, was
in full bloom among us, and we sought even by original jests
to celebrate our great master. We were very proud when we
could lay before the company something of the kind, which
was in any degree approved, as, for instance, the following on
a riding-master, who had been hurt on a wild horse.

> " A rider in this house you'll find,
> A master too is he,
> The two into a nosegay bind,
> 'Twill riding-master be.
> If master of the ride, I wis,
> Full well he bears the name,
> But if the ride the master is,
> On him and his be shame." *

About such things serious discussions were held as to
whether they were worthy of the clown or not, whether they
flowed from the genuine pure fool's spring, and whether sense
and understanding had at all mingled in an unfitting and inadmissible manner. Altogether our singular views were diffused
with the greater ardour, and more persons were in a position
to sympathize with them, as Lessing, in whom great confidence
was placed, had, properly speaking, given the first signal in
his *Dramaturgie.*

In a society so attuned and excited I managed to take many
a pleasant excursion into Upper Alsace, whence, however, on
this very account, I brought back no particular instruction.
The number of little verses which flowed from us on that occasion, and which might serve to adorn a lively description of a
journey, are lost. In the cross-way of Molsheim Abbey we
admired the painted windows; in the fertile spot between Col-

* The above doggrel is pretty faithful, but it is as well to give the
original.

> " Ein Ritter wohnt in diesem Haus;
> Ein Meister auch daneben;
> Macht man davon einen Blumenstrauss
> So wird's einen Rittmeister geben.
> Ist er nun Meister von dem Ritt
> Führt er mit Recht den Namen;
> Doch nimmt der Ritt den Meister mit,
> Weh ihm und seinem Samen."—*Trans.*

mar and Schlettstadt resounded some comic hymns to Ceres, the consumption of so many fruits being circumstantially set forth and extolled, and the important question as to the free or restricted trade in them being very merrily taken up. At Ensisheim we saw the monstrous aerolite hanging up in the church, and in accordance with the scepticism of the time, ridiculed the credulity of man, never suspecting that such air-born beings, if they were not to fall into our corn-fields, were at any rate to be preserved in our cabinets.

Of a pilgrimage to the Ottilienberg, accomplished with an hundred, nay, a thousand of the faithful, I still love to think. Here, where the foundation-wall of a Roman castle still remained, a count's beautiful daughter, of a pious disposition, was said to have dwelt among ruins and stony crevices. Near the chapel where the wanderers edify themselves, her well is shown, and much that is beautiful is narrated. The image which I formed of her, and her name, made a deep impression upon me. I carried both about with me for a long time, until at last I endowed with them one of my later, but not less beloved daughters,* who was so favourably received by pure and pious hearts.

On this eminence also is repeated to the eye the majestic Alsace, always the same, and always new. Just as in an amphitheatre, let one take one's place where one will, one surveys the whole people, but sees one's neighbours the plainest, so it is here with bushes, rocks, hills, woods, fields, meadows, and districts near and in the distance. They wished to show us even Basle in the horizon : that we saw it, I will not swear, but the remote blue of the Swiss mountains even here exercised its rights over us, by summoning us to itself, and since we could not follow the impulse, by leaving a painful feeling.

To such distractions and cheerful recreations I abandoned myself the more readily, and even with a degree of intoxication, because my passionate connexion with Frederica now began to trouble me. Such a youthful affection cherished at random, may be compared to a bomb-shell thrown at night, which rises with a soft brilliant light, mingles with the stars, nay, for a moment, seems to pause among them, then, in descending, describes the same path in the reverse direction, and

* By this *daughter* he means "Ottilie" in the *Elective Affinities.*— *Trans.*

at last brings destruction to the place where it has terminated
its course. Frederica always remained equal to herself; she
seemed not to think, nor to wish to think, that the connexion
would so soon terminate. Olivia, on the contrary, who indeed
also missed me with regret, but nevertheless did not lose so
much as the other, had more foresight, or was more open. She
often spoke to me about my probable departure, and sought to
console herself both on her own and her sister's account. A
girl who renounces a man to whom she has not denied her
affections, is far from being in that painful situation in which
a youth finds himself who has gone so far in his declarations
to a lady. He always plays a pitiful part, since a certain
survey of his situation is expected of him as a growing man,
and a decided levity does not suit him. The reasons of a
girl who draws back always seem sufficient, those of a man
—never.

But how should a flattering passion allow us to foresee
whither it may lead us? For even when we have quite sensibly renounced it, we cannot get rid of it; we take pleasure
in the charming habit, even if this is to be in an altered
manner. Thus it was with me. Although the presence of
Frederica pained me, I knew of nothing more pleasant than to
think of her while absent, and to converse with her. I went
to see her less frequently, but our correspondence became so
much the more animated. She knew how to bring before me
her situation with cheerfulness, her feelings with grace, and I
called her merits to mind with fervour and with passion. Alsace
made me free, and my whole affection first truly bloomed by
this communication in the distance. At such moments I could
quite blind myself as to the future ; and was sufficiently distracted by the progress of time and of pressing business. I
had hitherto made it possible to do the most various things by
always taking a lively interest in what was present and belonged to the immediate moment ; but towards the end all
became too much crowded together, as is always the case when
one is to free oneself from a place.

One more event, which happened in an interval, took from
me the last days. I found myself in a respectable society at
a country-house, whence there was a noble view of the front
of the minster, and the tower which rises over it. " It is a
pity," said some one, " that the whole was not finished, and

that we have only one tower." "It is just as unpleasant to me," answered I, "to see this one tower not quite completed, for the four volutes leave off much too bluntly; there should have been upon them four light spires, with a higher one in the middle where the clumsy cross is standing."

When I had expressed this strong opinion with my accustomed animation, a little lively man addressed me, and asked, "Who told you so?" "The tower itself," I replied; "I have observed it so long and so attentively, and have shown it so much affection, that it at last resolved to make me this open confession." "It has not misinformed you," answered he; "I am the best judge of that; for I am the person officially placed over the public edifices. We still have among our archives the original sketches, which say the same thing, and which I can show to you." On account of my speedy departure I pressed him to show me this kindness as speedily as possible. He let me see the precious rolls; I soon, with the help of oiled paper, drew the spires, which were wanting in the building as executed, and regretted that I had not been sooner informed of this treasure. But this was always to be the case with me, that by looking at things and considering them, I should first attain a conception, which perhaps would not have been so striking and so fruitful, if it had been given ready made.

Amid all this pressure and confusion I could not fail to see Frederica once more. Those were painful days, the memory of which has not remained with me. When I reached her my hand from my horse, the tears stood in her eyes, and I felt very uneasy. I now rode along the footpath towards Drusenheim, and here one of the most singular forebodings took possession of me. I saw, not with the eyes of the body, but with those of the mind, my own figure coming towards me, on horseback, and on the same road, attired in a dress which I had never worn;—it was pike-grey (*hecht-grau*) with somewhat of gold. As soon as I shook myself out of this dream, the figure had entirely disappeared. It is strange, however, that eight years afterwards, I found myself on the very road, to pay one more visit to Frederica, in the dress of which I had dreamed, and which I wore, not from choice, but by accident. However it may be with matters of this kind generally, this strange illusion in some measure calmed me at the moment of parting.

The pain of quitting for ever the noble Alsace, with all that I
had gained in it, was softened, and having at last escaped the
excitement of a farewell, I found myself on a peaceful and
quiet journey, pretty well recovered.

Arrived at Mannheim, I hastened with great eagerness to
see the hall of antiquities, of which a great boast was made.
Even at Leipzig, on the occasion of Winckelmann's and
Lessing's writings, I had heard much said of those important works of art, but so much the less had I seen them, for
except Laocoon, the father, and the Faun with the crotola,
there were no casts in the academy, and whatever Oeser
chose to say to us on the subject of those works, was enigmatical enough. How can a conception of the end of art be given
to beginners?

Director Verschaffel's reception was kind. I was conducted
to the saloon by one of his associates, who, after he had opened
it for me, left me to my own inclinations and reflections.
Here I now stood, open to the most wonderful impressions, in
a spacious, four-cornered, and, with its extraordinary height,
almost cubical saloon, in a space well lighted from above
by the windows under the cornice; with the noblest statues
of antiquity, not only ranged along the walls, but also set up
one with another over the whole area;—a forest of statues,
through which one was forced to wind; a great ideal popular
assembly, through which one was forced to press. All these
noble figures could, by opening and closing the curtains, be
placed in the most advantageous light, and besides this, they
were moveable on their pedestals, and could be turned about
at pleasure.

After I had for a time sustained the first impression of this
irresistible mass, I turned to those figures which attracted me
the most, and who can deny that the Apollo Belvidere, with
his well-proportioned colossal stature, his slender build, his
free movement, his conquering glance, carried off the victory
over our feelings in preference to all the others? I then turned
to Laocoon, whom I here saw for the first time in connexion
with his sons. I brought to mind as well as possible the discussions and contests which had been held concerning him,
and tried to get a point of view of my own; but I was now
drawn this way, now that. The dying gladiator long held me
fast, but the group of Castor and Pollux, that precious though

problematical relic, I had especially to thank for my happiest moments. I did not know how impossible it was at once to account to oneself for a sight affording enjoyment. I forced myself to reflect, and little as I succeeded in attaining any sort of clearness, I felt that every individual figure from this great assembled mass was comprehensible, that every object was natural and significant in itself.

Nevertheless my chief attention was directed to Laocoon, and I decided for myself the famous question, why he did not shriek, by declaring to myself that he could not shriek. All the actions and movements of the three figures proceeded, according to my view, from the first conception of the group. The whole position—as forcible as artistical—of the chief body was composed with reference to two impulses—the struggle against the snakes, and the flight from the momentary bite. To soften this pain, the abdomen must be drawn in, and shrieking rendered impossible. Thus I also decided that the younger son was not bitten, and in other respects sought to elicit the artistical merits of this group. I wrote a letter on the subject to Oeser, who, however, did not show any special esteem for my interpretation, but only replied to my good will with general terms of encouragement. I was, however, fortunate enough to retain that thought, and to allow it to repose in me for several years, until it was at last annexed to the whole body of my experiences and convictions, in which sense I afterwards gave it in editing my *Propylaa*.

After a zealous contemplation of so many sublime plastic works, I was not to want a foretaste of antique architecture. I found the cast of a capital of the Rotunda, and do not deny that at the sight of those acanthus-leaves, as huge as they were elegant, my faith in the northern architecture began somewhat to waver.

This early sight, although so great and so effective throughout my whole life, was nevertheless attended with but small results in the time immediately following. How willingly would I have begun a book, instead of ending one, with describing it : for no sooner was the door of the noble saloon closed behind me, than I wished to recover myself again, nay, I rather sought to remove those forms as cumbersome from my memory ; and it was only by a long circuitous route that I was

2 F 2

brought back into this sphere. However, the quiet fruitfulness
is quite inestimable of those impressions, which are received
with enjoyment, and without dissecting judgment. Youth is
capable of this highest happiness, if it will not be critical,
but allows the excellent and the good to act upon it without
investigation and division.

TWELFTH BOOK.

THE wanderer had now at last reached home,—more healthy and cheerful than on the first occasion,—but still in his whole being there appeared something over-strained, which did not fully indicate mental health. At the very first I put my mother into the position, that, between my father's sincere spirit of order and my own various eccentricities, she was forced to occupy herself with bringing passing events into a certain medium. At Mayence, a harp-playing boy had so well pleased me, that, as the fair was close at hand, I invited him to Frankfort, and promised to give him lodging and to encourage him. In this occurrence appeared once more that peculiarity which has cost me so much in my lifetime,— namely, that I liked to see younger people gather round me and attach themselves to me, by which, indeed, I am at last encumbered with their fate. One unpleasant experience after another could not reclaim me from this innate impulse, which even at present, and in spite of the clearest conviction, threatens from time to time to lead me astray. My mother, clearer than myself, plainly foresaw how strange it would appear to my father, if a musical fair-vagabond went from such a respectable house to taverns and drinking-houses to earn his bread. Hence she provided him with board and lodging in the neighbourhood. I recommended him to my friends; and thus the lad did not fare badly. After several years I saw him again, when he had grown taller and more clumsy, without having advanced much in his art. The good lady, well contented with this first attempt at squaring and hushing up, did not think that this art would immediately become completely necessary to her. My father, leading a contented life amid his old tastes and occupations, was comfortable, like one who, in spite of all hindrances and delays, carries out his plans. I had now gained my degree, and the first step to the further graduating course of citizen-life was taken. My *Disputation* had obtained his applause; a further examination of it, and many a preparation for a future edition,

gave him occupation. During my residence in Alsace, I had
written many little poems, essays, notes on travel, and several
loose sheets. He found amusement in bringing these under
heads, in arranging them, and in devising their completion; and
was delighted with the expectation that my hitherto insuperable
dislike to see any of these things printed would soon cease.
My sister had collected around her a circle of intelligent and
amiable women. Without being domineering, she domineered
over all, as her good understanding could overlook much, and
her good-will could often accommodate matters; moreover, she
was in the position of playing the confidant, rather than the
rival. Of my older friends and companions, I found in Horn
the unalterably true friend and cheerful associate. I also
became intimate with Riese, who did not fail to practise and
try my acuteness by opposing, with a persevering contradiction, doubt and negation to a dogmatic enthusiasm into which
I too readily fell. Others, by degrees, entered into this circle,
whom I shall afterwards mention; but among the persons who
rendered my new residence in my native city pleasant and
profitable, the brothers Schlosser certainly stood at the head.
The elder, Heronymus, a profound and elegant jurist, enjoyed
universal confidence as counsellor. His favourite abode was
amongst his books and papers, in rooms where the greatest
order prevailed; there I have never found him otherwise than
cheerful and sympathising. In a larger society also he showed
himself agreeable and entertaining, for his mind, by extensive
reading, was adorned with all the beauty of antiquity. He
did not, on occasion, disdain to increase the social pleasures
by agreeable Latin poems; and I still possess several sportive
distiches which he wrote under some portraits drawn by me
of strange and generally known Frankfort caricatures. Often
I consulted with him as to the course of life and business I
was now commencing; and if an hundredfold inclinations
and passions had not torn me from this path, he would have
been my surest guide.

Nearer to me, in point of age, was his brother George, who
had again returned from Treptow, from the service of the Duke
Eugene of Würtemberg. While he had advanced in knowledge of the world and in practical talent, he had not remained behindhand in a survey of German and foreign literature. He liked, as before, to write in all languages; but did

not further excite me in this respect, as I devoted myself
exclusively to German, and only cultivated other languages
so far as to enable me, in some measure, to read the best
authors in the original. His honesty showed itself the same
as ever: nay, his acquaintance with the world may have occasioned him to adhere with more severity and even obstinacy
to his well-meaning views.

Through these two friends, I very soon became acquainted
with Merk, to whom I had not been unfavourably announced
by Herder, from Strasburg. This strange man, who had the
greatest influence on my life, was a native of Darmstadt. Of
his early education I can say but little. After finishing his
studies, he conducted a young man to Switzerland, where he
remained for some time, and came back married. When I
made his acquaintance, he was military paymaster at Darmstadt. Born with mind and understanding, he had acquired
much elegant knowledge, especially in modern literature, and
had paid attention to all times and places in the history of
the world and of man. He had the talent of judging with
certainty and acuteness. He was prized as a thorough,
decisive man of business, and a ready accountant. With
ease he gained an entrance everywhere, as a very pleasant companion for those to whom he had not rendered himself formidable by sarcasms. His figure was long and lean;
a sharp prominent nose was remarkable; light blue, perhaps
grey eyes, gave something tiger-like to his glance, which wandered attentively here and there. Lavater's *Physiognomy*
has preserved his profile for us. In his character there was a
wonderful contradiction. By nature a good, noble, upright
man, he had embittered himself against the world, and allowed this morbid whim to sway him to such a degree, that
he felt an irresistible inclination to be wilfully a rogue, or even
a villain. Sensible, quiet, kind at one moment, it might
strike him in the next—just as a snail puts out his horns—to
do something which might hurt, wound, or even injure
another. Yet as one readily associates with something dangerous when one believes oneself safe from it, I felt so much
the greater inclination to live with him, and to enjoy his good
qualities, since a confident feeling allowed me to suspect that
he would not turn his bad side towards me. While now, by
this morally restless mind,—by this necessity of treating men

in a malignant and spiteful way, he on one side destroyed
social life, another disquiet, which also he very carefully
fostered within himself, opposed his internal comfort; namely,
he felt a certain *dilettantish* impulse to production, in which
he indulged the more readily, as he expressed himself easily
and happily in prose and verse, and might well venture to
play a part among the *beaux esprits* of the time. I myself
still possess poetical epistles, full of uncommon boldness,
force, and Swift-like gall, which are highly remarkable from
their original views of persons and things, but are at the
same time written with such wounding power, that I could
not publish them, even at present, but must either destroy
them or preserve them for posterity as striking documents of
the secret discord in our literature. However, the fact that
in all his labours he went to work negatively and destruc-
tively, was unpleasant to himself, and he often declared that
he envied me that innocent love of setting forth a subject
which arose from the pleasure I took both in the original and
the imitation.

For the rest, his literary *dilettantism* would have been
rather useful than injurious to him, if he had not felt an irresistible impulse to enter also into the technical and mercantile department. For when he once began to curse his faculties, and was beside himself that he could not, with sufficient
genius, satisfy his claims to a practical talent, he gave up now
plastic art, now poetry, and thought of mercantile and manu-
facturing undertakings, which were to bring in money while
they afforded him amusement.

In Darmstadt there was besides a society of very cultivated
men. Privy Councillor von Hess, Minister of the Landgrave,
Professor Petersen, Rector Wenk, and others, were the natu-
ralized persons whose worth attracted by turns many neighbours from other parts, and many travellers through the city.
The wife of the privy councillor and her sister, Demoiselle
Flachsland, were ladies of uncommon merit and talents; the
latter, who was betrothed to Herder, being doubly interesting
from her own qualities and her attachment to so excellent a
man.

How much I was animated and advanced by this circle is
not to be expressed. They readily heard me read aloud my
completed or begun works; they encouraged me, when I

openly and circumstantially told what I was then planning, and blamed me when on every new occasion I laid aside what I had already commenced. *Faust* had already advanced; *Götz von Berlichingen* was gradually building itself up in my mind; the study of the fifteenth and sixteenth centuries occupied me; and the minster had left in me a very serious impression, which could well stand as a background to such poetical inventions.

What I had thought and imagined with respect to that style of architecture, I wrote in a connected form. The first point on which I insisted was, that it should be called German, and not Gothic; that it should be considered not foreign, but native. The second point was, that it could not be compared with the architecture of the Greeks and Romans, because it sprang from quite another principle. If these, living under a more favourable sky, allowed their roof to rest upon columns, a wall, broken through, arose of its own accord. We, however, who must always protect ourselves against the weather, and everywhere surround ourselves with walls, have to revere the genius who discovered the means of endowing massive walls with variety, of apparently breaking them through, and of thus occupying the eye in a worthy and pleasing manner on the broad surface. The same principle applied to the steeples, which are not, like cupolas, to form a heaven within, but to strive towards heaven without, and to announce to the countries far around the existence of the sanctuary which lies at their base. The interior of these venerable piles I only ventured to touch by poetical contemplation and a pious tone.

If I had been pleased to write down these views, the value of which I will not deny, clearly and distinctly, in an intelligible style, the paper " On German Architecture, D. M. Erwini a Steinbach," would then, when I published it, have produced more effect, and would sooner have drawn the attention of the native friends of art. But, misled by the example of Herder and Hamann, I obscured these very simple thoughts and observations by a dusty cloud of words and phrases, and both for myself and others, darkened the light which had arisen within me. However, the paper was well received, and reprinted in Herder's work on German manner and art.

If now, partly from inclination, partly with poetical and

other views, I very readily occupied myself with the antiquities of my country, and sought to render them present to my
mind. I was from time to time distracted from this subject by
biblical studies and religious sympathies, since Luther's life
and deeds, which shine forth so magnificently in the sixteenth
century, always necessarily brought me back to the Holy
Scriptures, and to the observation of religious feelings and
opinions. To look upon the Bible as a work of compilation,
which had gradually arisen, and had been elaborated at different times, was flattering to my little self-conceit, since this
view was then by no means predominant.—much less was it
received in the circle in which I lived. With respect to the
chief sense, I adhered to Luther's expression; in matters of
detail, I went to Schmidt's literal translation, and sought to
use my little Hebrew as well as possible. That there are
contradictions in the Bible, no one will now deny. These
they sought to reconcile by laying down the plainest passage as
a foundation, and endeavouring to assimilate to that those that
were contradictory and less clear. I, on the contrary, wished
to find out, by examination, what passage best expressed the
sense of the matter. To this I adhered, and rejected the rest
as interpolated.

For a fundamental opinion had already confirmed itself in
me, without my being able to say whether it had been imparted to me, or had been excited in me, or had arisen from
my own reflection. It was this,—that in anything which is
handed down to us, especially in writing, the real point is the
ground, the interior, the sense, the tendency of the work;
that here lies the original, the divine, the effective, the intact,
the indestructible; and that no time, no external operation or
condition, can in any degree affect this internal primeval
nature, at least no more than the sickness of the body affects
a well-cultivated soul. Thus, according to my view, the language, the dialect, the peculiarity, the style, and finally the
writing, were to be regarded as the body of every work of
mind; that this body, although nearly enough akin to the internal, was yet exposed to deterioration and corruption; as,
indeed, altogether no tradition can be given quite pure,
according to its nature; nor, indeed, if one were given
pure, could it be perfectly intelligible at every following
period,—the former on account of the insufficiency of the

organs through which the tradition is made,—the latter on
account of the difference of time and place,—but especially
the diversity of human capacities and modes of thought; for
which reason the interpreters themselves never agree.

Hence it is everybody's affair to seek out for what is internal
and peculiar in a book which particularly interests us,
and at the same time, above all things, to weigh in what relation
it stands to our own inner nature, and how far, by that
vitality, our own is excited and rendered fruitful. On the
contrary, everything external that is ineffective with respect
to ourselves, or is subject to a doubt, is to be consigned over
to criticism, which, even if it should be able to dislocate
and dismember the whole, would never succeed in depriving
us of the only ground to which we hold fast, nor even in
perplexing us for a moment with respect to our once formed
confidence.

This conviction, sprung from faith and right, which in all
cases that we recognise as the most important, is applicable
and strengthening, lies at the foundation of the moral as well
as the literary edifice of my life, and is to be regarded as a well-
invested and richly productive capital, although in particular
cases we may be seduced into making an erroneous application.
By this notion, the Bible first became really accessible to me.
I had, as is the case in the religious instruction of Protestants,
run through it several times, nay, had made myself acquainted
with it, by way of leaps from beginning to end and back again.
The blunt naturalness of the Old Testament, and the tender
naïveté of the New, had attracted me in particular instances;
as a whole, indeed, it never properly appealed to me: but the
diverse characters of the different books no more perplexed
me: I knew how to represent to myself their significance
faithfully and in proper order, and had too much feeling for
the book to be ever able to do without it. By this very side
of feeling I was protected against all scoffing, because I saw
its dishonesty at once. I not only detested it, but could even
fall in a rage about it; and I still perfectly remember that in
my childishly fanatical zeal I should have completely throttled
Voltaire, on account of his Saul, if I had only got hold of
him. On the other hand, every kind of honest investigation
pleased me greatly; the revelations as to the locality and
costume of the East, which diffused more and more light, I

received with joy, and continued to exercise all my acuteness
on such valuable traditions.

It is known that at an earlier period I sought to initiate
myself into the situation of the world, as described to us by
the first book of Moses. As I now thought to proceed step-
wise, and in proper order, I seized, after a long interruption,
on the second book. But what a difference! Just as the
fulness of childhood had vanished from my life, so did I find
the second book separated from the first by a monstrous chasm.
The utter forgetfulness of a bygone time is already expressed
in the few important words, "Now there arose a new king
over Egypt, which knew not Joseph." But the people also,
innumerable as the stars of heaven, had almost forgotten the
ancestor to whom, under the starry heaven, Jehovah had
made the very promise which was now fulfilled. I worked
through the five books with unspeakable trouble and insufficient means and powers, and in doing this fell upon the
strangest notions. I thought I had discovered that it was
not our ten commandments which stood upon the tables,
that the Israelites did not wander through the desert for
forty years, but only for a short time; and thus I fancied
that I could give entirely new revelations as to the character
of Moses.

Even the New Testament was not safe from my inquiries;
with my passion for dissection, I did not spare it, but with
love and affection I chimed in with that wholesome word,
"The evangelists may contradict each other, provided only
the gospel does not contradict itself." In this region also I
thought I should make all sorts of discoveries. That gift of
tongues imparted at Pentecost with lustre and clearness, I
interpreted for myself in a somewhat abstruse manner, not
adapted to procure many adherents.

Into one of the chief Lutheran doctrines, which has been
still more sharpened by the Hernhuters,—namely, that of
regarding the sinful principle as predominant in man,—I endeavoured to accommodate myself, but without remarkable
success. Nevertheless I had made the terminology of this
doctrine tolerably my own, and made use of it in a letter,
which, in the character of country pastor, I was pleased to
send to a brother in office. However, the chief theme in
the paper was that watchword of the time, called "Tolera-

lion," which prevailed among the better order of brains and minds.

Such things, which were produced by degrees, I had printed at my own cost in the following year, to try myself with the public.—made presents of them, or sent them to Eichenberg's shop, in order to get rid of them as fast as possible, without deriving any profit myself. Here and there a review mentions them, now favourably, now unfavourably,—but they soon passed away. My father kept them carefully in his archives, otherwise I should not have possessed a copy of them. I shall add these, as well as some things of the kind which I have found, to the new edition of my works.

Since I had really been seduced into the sybilline style of such papers, as well as into the edition of them by Hamann, this seems to me a proper place to make mention of this worthy and influential man, who was then as great a mystery to us as he has always remained to his native country. His *Socratic Memorabilia* was more especially liked by those persons who could not adapt themselves to the dazzling spirit of the time. It was suspected that he was a profound, well-grounded man, who, accurately acquainted with the public world and with literature, allowed of something mysterious and unfathomable, and expressed himself on this subject in a manner quite his own. By those who then ruled the literature of the day, he was indeed considered an abstruse mystic, but an aspiring youth suffered themselves to be attracted by him. Even the " Quiet-in-the-lands," as they were called—half in jest, half in earnest—those pious souls, who, without professing themselves members of any society, formed an invisible church, turned their attention to him; while to my friend Fräulein von Klettenberg, and no less to her friend Moser, the "Magus from the North" was a welcome apparition. People put themselves the more in connexion with him, when they had learned that he was tormented by narrow domestic circumstances, but nevertheless understood how to maintain this beautiful and lofty mode of thought. With the great influence of President von Moser, it would have been easy to provide a tolerable and convenient existence for such a frugal man. The matter was set on foot, nay, so good an understanding and mutual approval was attained, that Hamann undertook the long journey from Königsberg to Darmstadt. But as the president happened to be absent, that odd man, no one knows

on what account, returned at once, though a friendly correspondence was kept up. I still possess two letters from the
Königsberger to his patron, which bear testimony to the
wondrous greatness and sincerity of their author.

But so good an understanding was not to last long. These
pious men had thought the other one pious in their own
fashion; they had treated him with reverence as the "Magus
of the North," and thought that he would continue to exhibit
himself with a reverend demeanour. But already in the
Clouds, an after-piece of *Socratic Memorabilia*, he had given
some offence; and when he now published the *Crusades of a
Philologist*, on the title-page of which was to be seen not only
the goat-profile of a horned Pan, but also on one of the first
pages, a large cock, cut in wood, and setting time to some
young cockerels, who stood before him with notes in their
claws, made an exceedingly ridiculous appearance, by which
certain church-music, of which the author did not approve,
was to be made a laughing-stock,—there arose among well-
minded and sensitive people a dissatisfaction, which was
exhibited to the author, who, not being edified by it,
shunned a closer connexion. Our attention to this man
was, however, always kept alive by Herder, who, remaining in correspondence with us and his bride, communicated to us at once all that proceeded from that extraordinary
man. To these belonged his critiques and notices, inserted
in the *Königsberg Zeitung*, all of which bore a very singular
character. I possess an almost complete collection of his
works, and a very important essay on Herder's prize paper
concerning the origin of language, in which, in the most
peculiar manner, he throws flashes of light upon this specimen
of Herder.

I do not give up the hope of superintending myself, or at
least furthering, an edition of Hamann's works; and then,
when these documents are again before the public, it will be
time to speak more closely of the author, his nature and character. In the meanwhile, however, I will here adduce something concerning him, especially as eminent men are still
living who felt a great regard for him, and whose assent or
correction will be very welcome to me. The principle to
which all Hamann's expressions may be referred is this: "All
that man undertakes to perform, whether by deed, by word,
or otherwise, must proceed from all his powers united; every-

thing isolated is worthless." A noble maxim, but hard to
follow. To life and art it may indeed be applied, and in
every communication by words, that is not exactly poetic,
there is, on the contrary, a grand difficulty ; for a word must
sever itself, isolate itself, to say or signify anything. Man,
while he speaks, must, for the moment, become one-sided;
there is no communication, no instruction, without severing.
Now since Hamann, once for all, opposed this separation, and
because he felt, imagined, and thought in unity, chose to
speak in unity likewise, and to require the same of others, he
came into opposition with his own style, and with all that
others produced. To produce the impossible, he therefore
grasps at every element ; the deepest and most mystical contemplations in which nature and mind meet each other—
illuminating flashes of the understanding, which beam forth
from such a contact—significant images, which float in these
regions—forcible aphorisms from sacred and profane writers
—with whatever else of a humorous kind could be added—
all this forms the wondrous aggregate of his style and his communications. If, now, one cannot associate oneself with him
in his depths—cannot wander with him on his heights—cannot master the forms which float before him—cannot, from
an infinitely extended literature, exactly find out the sense of
a passage which is only hinted at—we find that the more we
study him, the more dim and dark it becomes ; and this darkness always increases with years, because his allusions were
directed to certain definite peculiarities which prevailed, for
the moment, in life and in literature. In my collection there
are some of his printed sheets, where he has cited with his
own hand, in the margin, the passages to which his hints
refer. If one opens them, there is again a sort of equivocal
double light, which appears to us highly agreeable ; only one
must completely renounce what is ordinarily called understanding. Such leaves merit to be called sybilline, for this
reason, that one cannot consider them in and for themselves,
but must wait for an opportunity to seek refuge with their
oracles. Every time that one opens them one fancies one has
found something new, because the sense which abides in every
passage touches and excites us in a curious manner.

Personally I never saw him ; nor did I hold any immediate
communication with him by means of letters. It seems to

me that he was extremely clear in the relations of life and
friendship, and that he had a correct feeling for the positions
of persons among each other, and with reference to himself.
All the letters which I saw by him were excellent, and much
plainer than his works, because here the reference to time,
circumstances, and personal affairs, was more clearly prominent. I thought, however, that I could discern this much generally, that he, feeling the superiority of his mental gifts, in
the most *naive* manner, always considered himself somewhat
wiser and more shrewd than his correspondents, whom he
treated rather ironically than heartily. If this held good only
of single cases, it applied to the majority, as far as my own
observation went, and was the cause that I never felt a desire
to approach him.

On the other hand, a kindly literary communication between Herder and us was maintained with great vivacity,
though it was a pity that he could not keep himself quiet. But
Herder never left off his teazing and scolding; and much was
not required to irritate Merk, who also contrived to excite me
to impatience. Because now Herder, among all authors and
men, seems to respect Swift the most, he was among us
called the " Dean," and this gave further occasion to all sorts
of perplexities and annoyances.

Nevertheless we were highly pleased when we learned that
he was to have an appointment at Bückeburg, which would
bring him double honour, for his new patron had the highest
fame as a clear-headed and brave, though eccentric man.
Thomas Abt had been known and celebrated in this service;
his country still mourned his death, and was pleased with the
monument which his patron had erected for him. Now Herder, in the place of the untimely deceased, was to fulfil all
those hopes which his predecessor had so worthily excited.

The epoch in which this happened gave a double brilliancy
and value to such an appointment; for several German princes
already followed the example of the Count of Lippe, inasmuch as they took into their service not merely learned men,
and men of business, properly so called, but also persons of
mind and promise. Thus, it was said, Klopstock had been
invited by the Margrave Charles of Baden, not for real business, but that by his presence he might impart a grace and
be useful to the higher society. As now the regard felt for

this excellent prince, who paid attention to all that was useful and beautiful, increased in consequence, so also was the veneration for Klopstock not a little heightened. Everything that emanated from him was held dear and valuable; and we carefully wrote down his odes and elegies as we could get them. We were therefore highly delighted when the great Landgravine Caroline of Hesse-Darmstadt made a collection of them, and we obtained possession of one of the few copies, which enabled us to complete our own manuscript collection. Hence those first readings have long been most in favour with us; nay, we have often refreshed and delighted ourselves with poems which the author afterwards rejected. So true it is, that the life which presses forth out of a "fine soul" works with the greater freedom the less it appears to be drawn by criticism into the department of art.

Klopstock, by his character and conduct, had managed to attain regard and dignity, both for himself and for other men of talent; now they were also, it possible, to be indebted to him for the security and improvement of their domestic condition. For the book-trade, in the previous period, had more to do with important scientific books, belonging to the different faculties—with stock-works, for which a moderate remuneration was paid. But the production of poetical works was looked upon as something sacred; and in this case the acceptance or increase of any remuneration would have been regarded almost as simony. Authors and publishers stood in the strangest reciprocal position. Both appeared, accordingly as it was taken, as patrons and clients. The authors, who, irrespectively of their talent, were generally respected and revered by the public as highly moral men, had a mental rank, and felt themselves rewarded by the success of their labours; the publishers were well satisfied with the second place, and enjoyed a considerable profit. But now opulence again set the rich bookseller above the poor poet, and thus everything stood in the most beautiful equilibrium. Magnanimity and gratitude were not unfrequent on either side. Breitkopf and Gottsched lived, all their lives, as inmates of the same house. Stinginess and meanness, especially that of piracy, were not yet in vogue.

Nevertheless a general commotion had arisen among the German authors. They compared their own very moderate, if not poor condition, with the wealth of the eminent booksellers ; they considered how great was the fame of a Gellert, of a Rabener, and in what narrow domestic circumstances an universally esteemed German poet must struggle on, if he did not render life easy by some other calling. Even the mediocre and lesser minds felt a strong desire to see their situation improved,—to make themselves free of the publishers.

Now Klopstock came forward and offered his " Republic of Letters" (*Gelehrte Republik*) for subscription. Although the latter cantos of the *Messiah*, partly on account of their subject, partly on account of the treatment, could not produce the same effect as the earlier ones, which, themselves pure and innocent, came into a pure and innocent time, the same respect was always maintained for the poet, who, by the publication of his odes, had drawn to himself the hearts, minds, and feelings of many persons. Many well-thinking men, among whom were several of great influence, offered to secure payment beforehand. This was fixed at a *Louis d'or*, the object being, it was said, not so much to pay for the book, as on this occasion to reward the author for his services to his country. Now every one pressed forward ; even youths and young girls, who had not much to expend, opened their saving-boxes ; men and women, the higher and the middle classes, contributed to this holy offering ; and perhaps a thousand subscribers, all paying in advance, were collected. Expectation was raised to the highest pitch, and confidence was as great as possible.

After this, the work, on its appearance, was compelled to experience the strangest result in the world : it was, indeed, of important value, but by no means universally interesting. Klopstock's thoughts on poetry and literature were set forth in the form of an old German Druidical republic ; his maxims on the true and false were expressed in pithy laconic aphorisms, in which, however, much that was instructive was sacrificed to the singularity of form. For authors and *littérateurs*, the book was and is invaluable : but it was only in this circle that it could be useful and effective. He who had thought himself followed the thinker ; he who knew how to seek and prize what was genuine, found himself instructed by the profound, honest man ; but the amateur, the general reader, was not enlightened,—to him the book remained sealed ; and yet

it had been placed in all hands; and while every one expected a perfectly serviceable work, most of them obtained
one from which they could not get the smallest taste. The
astonishment was general, but the esteem for the man was
so great, that no grumbling, scarcely a murmur, arose. The
young and beautiful part of the world got over their loss, and
now freely gave away the copies they had so dearly purchased. I received several from kind female friends, but none
of them have remained with me.

This undertaking, which was successful to the author, but
a failure to the public, had the ill consequence, that there
was now no further thought about subscriptions and prepay-
ments; nevertheless the wish had been too generally diffused
for the attempt not to be renewed. The Dessau publishing-
house now offered to do this on a large scale. Learned men
and publishers were here, by a close compact, to enjoy, both
in a certain proportion, the hoped-for advantage. The necessity, so long painfully felt, again awakened a great confidence;
but this could not last long; and after a brief endeavour the
parties separated, with a loss on both sides.

However, a speedy communication among the friends of literature was already introduced. The *Musenalmanache** united
all the young poets with each other; the journals united the
poet with other authors. My own pleasure in production
was boundless: to what I had produced I remained indifferent; only when, in social circles, I made it present to myself
and others, my affection for it was renewed. Moreover, many
persons took an interest in both my larger and smaller works,
because I urgently pressed every one who felt in any degree
inclined and adapted to production, to produce something independently, after his own fashion, and was, in turn, challenged by all to new poetising and writing. These mutual
impulses, which were carried even to an extreme, gave every
one a happy influence in his own fashion; and from this
whirling and working, this living and letting-live, this taking
and giving, which was carried on by so many youths, from
their own free hearts, without any theatrical guiding-star,
according to the innate character of each, and without any
special design, arose that famed, extolled, and decried epoch
in literature, when a mass of young genial men, with all that

* Annual publications devoted to poetry only.—*Trans.*

2 G 2

audacity and assumption which is peculiar to their own period
of youth, produced, by the application of their powers, much
that was good, and by the abuse of these, much ill-feeling
and mischief; and it is, indeed, the action and reaction which
proceeded from this source, that form the chief theme of this
volume.

In what can young people take the highest interest,
how are they to excite interest among those of their own
age, if they are not animated by love, and if affairs of the
heart, of whatever kind they may be, are not living within
them? I had in secret to complain of a love I had lost; this
made me mild and tolerant, and more agreeable to society
than in those brilliant times when nothing reminded me of a
want or a fault, and I went storming along completely without
restraint.

Frederica's answer to a written adieu rent my heart. It
was the same hand, the same tone of thought, the same feeling, which had formed itself for me and by me. I now, for
the first time, felt the loss which she suffered, and saw no
means to supply it, or even to alleviate it. She was completely
present to me; I always felt that she was wanting to me;
and, what was worst of all, I could not forgive myself for my
own misfortune. Gretchen had been taken away from me;
Annette had left me; now, for the first time, I was guilty.
I had wounded the most beautiful heart to its very depths;
and the period of a gloomy repentance, with the absence of a
refreshing love, to which I had grown accustomed, was most
agonising, nay, insupportable. But man will live; and hence
I took an honest interest in others; I sought to disentangle
their embarrassments, and to unite what was about to part,
that they might not have the same lot as myself. They were
hence accustomed to call me the "confidant," and on account
of wandering about the district, the "wanderer." In producing that calm for my mind, which I felt under the open
sky, in the valleys, on the heights, in the fields and in the
woods, the situation of Frankfort was serviceable, as it lay in
the middle between Darmstadt and Hamburg, two pleasant
places, which are on good terms with each other, through
the relationship of both courts. I accustomed myself to live
on the road, and, like a messenger, to wander about between
the mountains and the flat country. Often I went alone, or

in company, through my native city, as if it did not at all concern me, dined at one of the great inns in the High-street, and after dinner went further on my way. More than ever was I directed to the open world and to free nature. On my way I sang to myself strange hymns and dithyrambics, of which one entitled "The Wanderer's Storm-song" (*Wanderer's Sturmlied*) still remains. This half-nonsense I sang aloud, in an impassioned manner, when I found myself in a terrific storm, which I was obliged to meet.

My heart was untouched and unoccupied; I conscientiously avoided all closer connexion with ladies, and thus it remained concealed from me, that, inattentive and unconscious as I was, an amiable spirit was secretly hovering round me. It was not until many years afterwards, nay, until after her death, that I learned of her secret heavenly love, in a manner that necessarily overwhelmed me. But I was innocent, and could purely and honestly pity an innocent being; nay, I could do this the more, as the discovery occurred at an epoch when, completely without passion, I had the happiness of living for myself and my own intellectual inclinations.

At the time when I was pained by my grief at Frederica's situation, I again, after my old fashion, sought aid from poetry. I again continued the poetical confession which I had commenced, that by this self-tormenting penance I might be worthy of an internal absolution. The two Marias in *Götz von Berlichingen* and *Clavigo*, and the two bad characters who play the part of their lovers, may have been the results of such penitent reflections.

But as in youth one soon overcomes mental wounds and diseases, because a healthy system of organic life can rise up for a sick one, and allow it time to grow healthy again, corporeal exercises, on many a favourable opportunity, came forward with very advantageous effect; and I was excited in many ways to man myself afresh, and to seek new pleasures of life and enjoyments. Riding gradually took the place of those sauntering, melancholy, toilsome, and at the same time tedious and aimless rambles on foot; one reached one's end more quickly, merrily, and commodiously. The young people again introduced fencing, but in particular, on the setting-in of winter, a new world was revealed to us, since I at once determined to skate,—an exercise which I had never attempted,—and, in a short time, by practice, reflection, and perseverance, brought it as far as was necessary to enjoy with others a gay, animated course on the ice, without wishing to distinguish myself.

For this new joyous activity we were also indebted to Klopstock,—to his enthusiasm for this happy species of motion, which private accounts confirmed, while his odes gave an undeniable evidence of it. I still exactly remember that on a cheerful frosty morning I sprang out of bed, and uttered aloud these passages :—

> " Already, glad with feeling of health,
> Far down along the shore, I have whiten'd
> The covering crystal.
>
> " How does the winter's advancing day
> Softly illumine the lake !   The night has cast
> The glittering frost, like stars, upon it.'

My hesitating and wavering resolution was fixed at once, and I flew straight to the place where so old a beginner might with some degree of propriety make his first trial. And, indeed, this manifestation of our strength well deserved to be commended by Klopstock, for it is an exercise which brings us into contact with the freshest childhood, summons the youth to the full enjoyment of his suppleness, and is fitted to keep off a stagnant old age. We were immoderately addicted to this pleasure. To pass thus a splendid Sunday on the ice did not satisfy us, we continued our movement late into the night. For as other exertions fatigue the body, so does this give it a constantly new power. The full moon rising from the clouds, over the wide nocturnal meadows, which were frozen into fields of ice ; the night-breeze, which rustled towards us on our course ; the solemn thunder of the ice, which sunk as the water decreased ; the strange echo of our own movements, rendered the scenes of Ossian just present to our minds. Now this friend, now that, uttered an ode of Klopstock's, in a declamatory recitative ; and if we found ourselves together at dawn, the unfeigned praise of the author of our joys broke forth :—

> " And should he not be immortal,
> Who found for us health and joys
> Which the horse, though bold in his course, never gave,
> And which even the ball is without !"

Such gratitude is earned by a man who knows how to honour and worthily to extend an earthly act by spiritual incitement.

And thus, as children of talent, whose mental gifts have, at an early period, been cultivated to an extraordinary degree, return, if they can, to the simplest sports of youth, did we, too, often forget our calling to more serious things. Nevertheless this very motion, so often carried on in solitude—this agreeable soaring in undetermined space—again excited many of my internal wants, which had, for a time, lain dormant; and I have been indebted to such hours for a more speedy elaboration of older plans.

The darker ages of German history had always occupied my desire for knowledge and my imagination. The thought of dramatizing *Gotz von Berlichingen*, with all the circumstances of his time, was one which I much liked and valued. I industriously read the chief authors; to Datt's work, *De Pace Publica*, I devoted all my attention; I had sedulously studied it through, and rendered those singular details as visible to me as possible. These endeavours, which were directed to moral and poetical ends, I could also use in another direction, and I was now to visit Wetzlar. I had sufficient historical preparation; for the Imperial Chamber had arisen in consequence of the public tranquillity, and its history could serve as an important clue through the confused events of Germany. Indeed, the constitution of the courts and armies gives the most accurate insight into the constitution of every empire. Even the finances, the influence of which are considered so important, come much less under consideration: for if the whole is deficient, it is only necessary to take from the individual what he has laboriously scraped together, and thus the state is always sufficiently rich.

What occurred to me at Wetzlar is of no great importance, but it may inspire a greater interest, if the reader will not disdain a cursory history of the Imperial Chamber, in order to render present to his mind the unfavourable moment at which I arrived there.

The lords of the earth are such, principally because they can assemble around them, in war, the bravest and most resolute, and in peace, the wisest and most just. Even to the state of a German emperor belonged a court of this kind, which always accompanied him in his expeditions through the empire. But neither this precaution, nor the Suabian law, which prevailed in the south of Germany, nor the Saxon law, which prevailed in the north,—neither the judges appointed to maintain them, nor the decisions of the peers of the contending parties,—neither the umpires recognised by agreement, nor friendly compacts instituted by the clergy, —nothing, in short, could quiet that excited chivalric spirit of feuds which had been roused, fostered, and made a custom among the Germans, by internal discord, by foreign campaigns, by the crusades especially, and even by judicial usages. To the emperor, as well as to the powerful estates, these squabbles were extremely annoying, while, through them, the less powerful became troublesome to each other, and if they combined, to the great also. All outward strength was paralysed, while internal order was destroyed; and besides this, a great part of the country was still encumbered with the *Vehmgericht*, of the horrors of which a notion may be formed, if we think that it degenerated into a secret police, which, at last, even fell into the hands of private persons.

Many attempts to steer against these evils had been made in vain, until, at last, the estates urgently proposed a court formed from among themselves. This proposal, well-meant as it might have been, nevertheless indicated an extension of the privileges of the estates, and a limitation of the imperial power. Under Frederic III. the matter is delayed; his son Maximilian, being pressed from without, complies. He appoints the chief judge, the estates send the assistants. There were to be four-and-twenty of them; but, at first, twelve are thought sufficient.

An universal fault, of which men are guilty in their undertakings, was the first and perpetual fundamental defect of the Imperial Chamber: insufficient means were applied to a great end. The number of the assessors was too small. How was the difficult and extensive problem to be solved by them? But who could urge an efficient arrangement? The emperor could not favour an institution which seemed to work more against him than for him; far more reason had he to complete the formation of his own court—his own council. If, on the other hand, we regard the interest of the estates, all that they could properly have to do with was the stoppage of bloodshed. Whether the wound was healed, did not so much concern them; and now there was to be, besides, a new expense. It may not have been quite plainly seen that by this

institution every prince increased his retinue, for a decided
end indeed,—but who readily gives money for what is necessary? Every one would be satisfied, if he could have what
is useful "for God's sake."

At first the assistants were to live on fees; then followed a
moderate grant from the estates; both were scanty. But to
meet the great and striking exigency, willing, clever, and
industrious men were found, and the court was established.
Whether it was perceived that the question here was concerning only the alleviation and not the cure of the evil,
or whether, as in similar cases, the flattering hope was entertained that much was to be done with little, is not to be decided. It is enough that the court served rather as a pretext
to punish the originators of mischief, than completely to prevent wrong. But it has scarcely met, than a power grows out
of itself; it feels the eminence on which it is placed; it recognises its own great political importance. It now endeavours, by a striking activity, to acquire for itself a more
decided respect; they briskly got through what can and must
be rapidly dispatched, what can be decided at the moment, or
what can otherwise be easily judged; and thus, throughout
the empire, they appear effective and dignified. On the
other hand, matters of weightier import, the law-suits, properly so called, remained behindhand, and this was no misfortune. The only concern of the state is, that possession
shall be certain and secure; whether it is also legal, is of
less consequence. Hence, from the monstrous and ever-
swelling number of delayed suits, no mischief arose to the
empire. Against people who employed force, provision was
already made, and with such matters could be settled; but
those, on the other hand, who legally disputed about possession, lived, enjoyed, or starved, as they could; they died, were
ruined, or made it up; but all this was the good or evil of
individual families,—the empire was gradually tranquillised.
For the Imperial Chamber was endowed with a legal club-law
against the disobedient; had it been able to publish the ban,
this would have been more effective.

But now, what with the sometimes increased, sometimes
diminished number of assessors, what with the many interruptions, what with the removal of the court from one place
to another, these arrears, these records necessarily increased

to an infinite extent. Now, in the distress of war, a part of the archives was sent for safety from Spire to Aschaffenburg, a part to Worms, the third fell into the hands of the French, who thought they had gained the state-archives, but would afterwards have been glad to get rid of such a chaos of paper, if any one would but have furnished the carriages.

During the negotiations for the peace of Westphalia, the chosen men, who were assembled, plainly saw what sort of a lever was required to move from its place a load like that of Sisyphus. Fifty assessors were now to be appointed, but the number was never made up: the half of it was again made to suffice, because the expense appeared too great; but if the parties interested had all seen their advantage in the matter, the whole might well have been afforded. To pay five-and-twenty assessors about one hundred thousand florins (*gulden*) were required, and how easily could double that amount have been raised in Germany? The proposition to endow the Imperial Chamber with confiscated church property could not pass, for how could the two religious parties agree to such a sacrifice? The Catholics were not willing to lose any more, and the Protestants wished to employ what they had gained, each for his own private ends. The division of the empire into two religious parties had here, in several respects, the worst influence. The interest which the estates took in this their court diminished more and more; the more powerful wished to free themselves from the confederation; licenses exempting their possessor from being prosecuted before any higher tribunal were sought with more and more eagerness; the greater kept back with their payments, while the lesser, who, moreover, believed themselves wronged in the estimates, delayed as long as they could.

How difficult was it, therefore, to raise the supplies necessary for payment. Hence arose a new occupation, a new loss of time for the chamber; previously the so-called annual "visitations" had taken care of this matter. Princes in person, or their councillors, went only for months or weeks to the place of the court, examined the state of the treasury, investigated the arrears, and undertook to get them in. At the same time, if anything was about to create an impediment in the course of law or the court, or any abuse to creep in, they were authorized to provide a remedy. The faults of the institution they

were to discover and remove, but it was not till afterwards
that the investigation and punishment of the personal crimes
of its members became a part of their duty. But because
parties engaged in litigation always like to extend their hopes
a moment longer, and on this account always seek and appeal to
higher authorities, so did these "visitators" become a court
of revision, from which, at first in determined manifest cases,
persons hoped to find restitution, but at last in all cases, delay
and perpetuation of the controversy, to which the appeal to
the Imperial diet, and the endeavour of the two religious
parties, if not to outweigh each other, at any rate to preserve
an equilibrium, contributed their part.

But if one considers what this court might have been without such obstacles, without such disturbing and destructive
conditions, one cannot imagine it remarkable and important
enough. Had it been supplied at the beginning with a sufficient number of persons, had a sufficient support been secured
to them, the monstrous influence which this body might have
attained, considering the aptness of the Germans, would have
been immeasurable. The honourable title of "Amphictyons,"
which was only bestowed on them oratorically, they would
actually have deserved, nay, they might have elevated themselves into an intermediate power, while revered by the head
and the members.

But far removed from such great effects, the court, excepting for a short time under Charles V., and before the Thirty
Years' war, dragged itself miserably along. One often cannot
understand how men could be found for such a thankless and
melancholy employment. But what a man does every day he
puts up with, if he has any talent for it, even if he does not
exactly see that anything will come of it. The German especially is of this persevering turn of mind, and thus for three
hundred years the worthiest men have employed themselves on
these labours and objects. A characteristic gallery of such
figures would even now excite interest and inspire courage.

For it is just in such anarchical times that the able man
takes the strongest position, and he who desires what is good
finds himself right in his place. Thus, for instance, the *Direc-
torium* of Fürstenberg was still held in blessed memory, and
with the death of this excellent man begins the epoch of many
pernicious abuses.

But all these defects, whether later or earlier, arose from
one only original source, the small number of persons. It was
decreed that the assistants were to act in a fixed order, and
according to a determined series. Every one could know when
the turn would come to him, and which of the cases belonging
to him it would affect; he could work up to this point,—he
could prepare himself. But now the innumerable arrears had
heaped themselves up, and they were forced to resolve to select
the more important cases, and to deal with them out of order.
But with a pressure of important affairs, the decision as to
which matter has the more weight, is difficult, and selection
leaves room for favour. Now, another critical case occurred.
The *Referent* tormented both himself and the court with a
difficult involved affair, and at last no one was found willing
to take up the judgment. The parties had come to an agreement, had separated, had died, had changed their minds.
Hence they resolved to take in hand only the cases of which
they were reminded. They wished to be convinced of the
continued obstinacy of the parties, and hence was given an
introduction to the greatest defects, for he who commends his
affairs, must commend them to somebody, and to whom can
one commend them better, than to him who has them already
in his hands? To keep this one regularly secret was impossible; for how could he remain concealed with so many
subordinates, all acquainted with the matter? If acceleration
is requested, favour may well be requested likewise, for the very
fact that people urge their cause, shows that they consider it
just. This will perhaps not be done in a direct manner, certainly it will be first done through subordinates; these must
be gained over, and thus an introduction is given to all sorts
of intrigues and briberies.

The Emperor Joseph, following his own impulse, and in imitation of Frederic, first directed his attention to arms and the
administration of justice. He cast his eyes upon the Imperial
Chamber; traditional wrongs, introduced abuses had not remained unknown to him. Even here something was to be
stirred up, shaken, and done. Without inquiring whether it
was his imperial right, without foreseeing the possibility of a
happy result, he proposed a revival of the " visitation," and
hastened its opening. For one hundred and sixty years no
regular " visitation" had taken place; a monstrous chaos of

papers lay swelled up and increased every year, since the
seventeen assessors were not even able to despatch the current
business. Twenty thousand processes were heaped up; sixty
could be settled every year, and double that number was
brought forward. Besides, it was not a small number of revi-
sions that awaited the "visitators,"—they were estimated at
fifty thousand. Many other abuses, in addition to this, hindered the course of justice; but the most critical matter of all
was the personal delinquency of some assessors, which appeared
in the background.

When I was about to go to Wetzlar, the "visitation" had
been already for some years in operation, the parties accused
had been suspended from office, the investigation had been
carried a long way; and because the masters and commissioners of German political law could not let pass this opportunity of exhibiting their sagacity and devoting it to the
common weal, several profound, well-designed works appeared,
from which every one, who possessed only some preparatory
knowledge, could derive solid instruction. When on this occasion they went back into the constitution of the empire and
the books written upon it, it was striking to me how the monstrous condition of this thoroughly diseased body, which was
kept alive by a miracle alone, was the very thing that most
suited the learned. For the venerable German industry,
which was more directed to the collection and development of
details than to results, found here an inexhaustible impulse to
new employment, and whether the empire was opposed to the
Emperor, the lesser to the greater estates, or the Catholics to
the Protestants, there was necessarily always, according to the
diversity of interest, a diversity of opinion, and always an
occasion for new contests and controversies.

Since I had rendered all these older and newer circumstances
as present to my mind as possible, it was impossible for me to
promise myself much pleasure from my abode at Wetzlar.
The prospect of finding in a city, which was indeed well situated, but small and ill-built, a double world; first the domestic,
old traditional world, then a foreign new one, authorized to
scrutinize the other with severity,—a judging and a judged
tribunal; many an inhabitant in fear and anxiety, lest he
might also be drawn into the impending investigation; persons
of consideration, long held in respect, convicted of the most

scandalous misdeeds, and marked out for disgraceful punishment:—all this together made the most dismal picture, and
could not lure me to go deeper into a business, which, involved
in itself, seemed so much perplexed by wrong.

That, excepting the German civil and public law, I should
find nothing remarkable in the scientific way, that I should
be without all poetical communication, I thought I could foresee, when, after some delay, the desire of altering my situation
more than impulse to knowledge led me to this spot. But
how surprised I was, when, instead of a crabbed society, a third
academical life sprang towards me. At a large *table d'hôte* I
found a number of young lively people, nearly all subordinates
to the commission; they gave me a friendly reception, and the
very first day it remained no secret to me that they had cheered
their noon-meetings by a romantic fiction. With much wit
and cheerfulness they represented a table of knights. At the
top sat the grand-master, by his side the chancellor, then the
most important officers of the state; now followed the knights,
according to their seniority. Strangers, on the other hand, who
visited, were forced to be content with the lowest places, and
to these the conversation was almost unintelligible, because the
language of the society, in addition to the chivalric expressions, was enriched with many allusions. To every one a name
with an epithet was assigned. Me they called "Götz von Berlichingen the honest." The former I earned by the attention to the gallant German patriarch, the latter by my upright
affection and devotion for the eminent men with whom I became acquainted. To the Count von Kielmannsegg I was much
indebted during this residence. He was the most serious of all,
highly clever, and to be relied on. There was Von Goué, a
man hard to be deciphered and described, a blunt, kind,
quietly reserved Hanoverian figure. He was not wanting in
talent of various kinds. It was conjectured concerning him
that he was a natural son; he loved, besides, a certain mysterious deportment, and concealed his most peculiar wishes and
plans under various eccentricities, as indeed he was, properly
speaking, the very soul of the odd confederation of knights,
without having striven to attain the post of grand-master.
On the contrary, when, just at this time, the head of the
knighthood departed, he caused another to be elected, and
through him exercised his influence. Thus he managed so to

direct several little trifles, that they appeared of importance, and could be carried out in mythical forms. But with all this no serious purpose could be remarked in him,—he was only concerned to get rid of the tedium which he and his colleagues, during their protracted occupation, necessarily felt, and to fill up the empty space, if only with cobwebs. For the rest, this mythical caricature was carried on with great external serious- ness, and no one found it ridiculous if a certain mill was treated as a castle, and the miller as lord of the fortress, if the " Four Sons of Haimon " was declared a canonical book, and on the occasion of ceremonies, extracts from it were read with veneration. The dubbing of knights took place with traditional symbols, borrowed from several orders of knighthood. A chief motive for jest was the fact, that what was manifest was treated as a secret ; the affair was carried on publicly, and yet nothing was to be said about it. The list of the whole body of knights was printed with as much importance as a calendar of the Imperial diet, and if families ventured to scoff at this, and to declare the whole matter absurd and ridiculous, they were punished by an intrigue being carried on until a solemn husband or near relation was induced to join the company and to be dubbed a knight ; for then there was a splendid burst of malicious joy at the annoyance of the connexions.

Into this chivalric state of existence another strange order had insinuated itself, which was to be philosophical and mys- tical, and had no name of its own. The first degree was called the " Transition," the second the " Transition's transition," the third the " Transition's transition to the transition," and the fourth the " Transition's transition to the transition's transition." To interpret the high sense of this series of degrees was now the duty of the initiated, and this was done according to the standard of a little printed book, in which these strange words were explained, or rather amplified, in a manner still more strange. Occupation with these things was the most desirable pastime. The folly of Behrisch and the perversity of Lenz seemed here to have united themselves ; I only repeat that not a trace of purpose was to be found behind these veils.

Although I very readily took part in such fooleries, had first brought into order the extracts from " The Four Sons of Hai-

mon," made proposals how they should be read on feasts and
solemn occasions, and even understood how to deliver them
myself with great emphasis, I had, nevertheless, grown weary of
such things before, and therefore as I missed my Frankfort and
Darmstadt circles, I was highly pleased to have found Gotter,
who attached himself to me with honest affection, and to whom
I showed in return a hearty good-will. His turn of mind was
delicate, clear, and cheerful, his talents were practised and
well regulated, he aimed at French elegance, and was pleased
with that part of English literature which is occupied with
moral and agreeable subjects. We passed together many
pleasant hours, in which we communicated to each other our
knowledge, plans, and inclinations. He excited me to many
little works, especially as, being in connexion with the people
of Göttingen, he desired some of my poems for Boie's
Almanach.

I thus came into contact with those, who, young and full of
talent, held themselves together, and afterwards effected so
much and in such various ways. The two Counts Stolberg,
Bürger, Voss, Hölty, and others were assembled in faith and
spirit around Klopstock, whose influence extended in every
direction. In such a poetical circle, which more and more
extended itself, was developed at the same time with such
manifold poetical merits, another turn of mind, to which I can
give no exactly proper name. It might be called the need of
independence, which always arises in time of peace, and exactly when, properly speaking, one is not dependent. In war
we bear the rude force as well as we can, we feel ourselves
physically and economically, but not morally, wounded; the
constraint shames no one, and it is no disgraceful service to
serve the time; we accustom ourselves to suffer from foes and
friends; we have wishes, but no particular views. In peace,
on the contrary, man's love of freedom becomes more and
more prominent, and the more free one is, the more free one
wishes to be. We will not tolerate anything over us; we will
not be restrained, no one shall be restrained; and this tender,
nay, morbid feeling, appears in noble souls under the form of
justice. This spirit and feeling then showed itself everywhere,
and just because few were oppressed, it was wished to free
even these from temporary oppression, and thus a certain
moral feud, a mixture of individuals with the government,

which, with laudable beginnings, led to inevitably unfortunate results.

Voltaire, by the protection which he had bestowed on the family of Calas, had excited great attention and made himself respected. In Germany the attempt of Lavater against the *Landvogt* (sheriff of the province) had been almost more striking and important. The æsthetical feeling, united with youthful courage, strove forward, and as, shortly before, persons had studied to obtain offices, they now began to act as overlookers of those in office; and the time was near when the dramatist and novelist loved best to seek their villains among ministers and official persons. Hence arose a world, half real, half imaginary, of action and reaction, in which we afterwards lived to see the most violent informations and instigations, which the writers of periodical publications and journals allowed themselves under the garb of justice, and went to work the more irresistibly, as they made the public believe that it was itself the true tribunal—a foolish notion, as no public has an executive power, and in dismembered Germany public opinion neither benefited nor injured any one.

Among us young people there was indeed nothing to be traced, which could have been culpable, but a certain similar notion, composed of poetry, morality, and a noble striving, and which was harmless but yet fruitless, had taken possession of us.

By his *Hermann's-Schacht,** and the dedication of it to Joseph the Second, Klopstock had produced a wonderful excitement. The Germans who freed themselves from Roman oppression were nobly and powerfully represented, and this picture was well suited to awaken the self-feeling of a nation. But because in peace patriotism really consists only in this, that every one sweeps his own door, minds his own business, and learns his own lesson, that it may go well with his house, —so did the feeling for fatherland, excited by Klopstock, find no object on which it could exercise itself. Frederic had saved the honour of one part of the Germans against an united world, and every member of the nation, by applause and reverence of this great prince, was allowed to share in his victory; but what was to come of this excited, warlike spirit of defi-

* The fight of Hermann, the "Arminius" of Tacitus, against the Romans.—*Trans.*

2 H

ance? At first it was merely a poetical form, and the songs
of the bards, afterwards so often blamed, and even found ridiculous, were accumulated through this impulse,—this incitement. There were no external enemies to fight; so people
made tyrants for themselves, and for this purpose princes and
their servants were obliged to bestow their figures, first only
in general outline, but gradually with particulars. Here it
was that poetry attached itself with vehemence to that inter-
ference with the administration of justice, which is blamed
above; and it is remarkable to see poems of that time written
in a spirit by which everything of a higher order, whether
monarchical or aristocratic, is abolished.

For my own part, I continued to make poetry the expression
of my own whims and feelings. Little poems like the "Wanderer" belong to this time; they were inserted in the *Göttingen Musenalmanach*. But from whatever of the above-mentioned mania had worked itself into me, I shortly endeavoured
to free myself in *Götz von Berlichingen*, since I described how
in disordered times this brave, well-thinking man resolves to
take the place of the law and the executive power, but is in
despair when, to the supreme authority, which he recognises
and reveres, he appears in an equivocal light, and even
rebellious.

By Klopstock's odes, it was not so much the Northern
mythology as the nomenclature of the divinities, that had
been introduced into German poetry; and although I gladly
made use of everything else that was offered me, I could not
bring myself to use this, for the following causes: I had long
become acquainted with the fables of the Edda, from the
preface to Mallet's *Danish History*, and had at once made myself
master of them. They belonged to those tales which, when
asked by a company, I most willingly related. Herder put
Resenius into my hands, and made me better acquainted with
the heroic *sagas*. But all these things, worthy as I held
them, I could not bring within the circle of my own poetic
faculty. Nobly as they excited my imagination, they nevertheless entirely withdrew themselves from the sensuous perception, while the mythology of the Greeks, changed by the
greatest artists in the world into visible, easily imagined
forms, still existed before our own eyes in abundance. Gods
in general I did not allow often to appear, because, at all

events, they had their abode out of nature, which I understood
how to imitate. What now could have induced to substitute Woden for Jupiter, and Thor for Mars, and instead
of the Southern, accurately described figures, to introduce
forms of mist, nay, mere verbal sounds, into my poems?
On the one side, they were related to the equally formless
heroes of Ossian, only they were ruder and more gigantic;
on the other, I brought them into contact with the cheerful
tale; for the humoristic vein which runs through the whole
Northern mythus, was to me highly pleasing and remarkable.
It appeared to me the only one which jests with itself
throughout,—wondrous giants, magicians, and monsters opposed to an odd dynasty of gods, and only occupied in leading
astray and deriding the highest persons during their government, while they threaten them, besides, with disgraceful and
inevitable destruction.

I felt a similar if not an equal interest for the Indian fables,
which I at first learned to know from Dapper's *Travels*, and
likewise added with great pleasure to my store of tales. In
subsequent repetitions I succeeded especially with the Altar
of Ram; and notwithstanding the great number of persons
in this tale, the ape Hannemann remained the favorite of my
public. But even these unformed and over-formed monsters
could not satisfy me in a true poetic sense; they lay too far
from the truth, towards which my mind unceasingly strove.

But against all these goblins, so repulsive to art, my sense
for the beautiful was to be protected by the noblest power.
Always fortunate is that epoch in a literature when the great
works of the past again rise up as if thawed, and come into
notice, because they then produce a perfectly fresh effect.
Even the Homeric light rose again quite new to us, and indeed quite in the spirit of the time, which highly favoured
such an appearance; for the constant reference to nature had
at last the effect, that we learned to regard even the works of
the ancients from this side. What several travellers had done
for explanation of the Holy Scriptures, others had done for
Homer. By Guys the matter was introduced; Wood gave
it an impulse. A Gottingen review of the original work,
which was at first very rare, made us acquainted with the
design, and taught us how far it had been carried out. We
now no longer saw in those poems a strained and inflated

2 H 2

heroism, but the reflected truth of a primeval present, and sought to bring this as closely to us as possible. At the same time we could not give our assent, when it was maintained that in order rightly to understand the Homeric natures, one must make oneself acquainted with the wild races and their manners, as described by the travellers in new worlds; for it cannot be denied that both Europeans and Asiatics are represented in the Homeric poems as at a higher grade of culture, —perhaps higher than the time of the Trojan war could have enjoyed. But that maxim was nevertheless in harmony with the prevailing confession of nature, and so far we let it pass.

With all these occupations, which were related to the knowledge of mankind in the higher sense, as well as most nearly and dearly to poetry, I was nevertheless forced every day to experience that I was residing in Wetzlar. The conversation on the situation of the business of the " Visitation," and its ever-increasing obstacles, the discovery of new offences, was heard every hour. Here was the holy Roman Empire once more assembled, not for mere outward forms, but for an occupation which penetrated to the very depths. But even here that half-empty banqueting-hall on the coronation-day occurred to me, where the bidden guests remained without, because they were too proud. Here, indeed, they had come, but even worse symptoms were to be seen. The want of coherence in the whole, the mutual opposition of the parts, were continually apparent; and it remained no secret that princes had confidentially communicated to each other this notion, that they must see whether, on this occasion, something could not be gained from the supreme authority.

What a bad impression the petty detail of all the anecdotes of neglects and delays, of injustices and corruptions, must make upon a young man who desired what was good, and with this view cultivated his mind, every honest person will feel. Under such circumstances, where was a reverence for the law and the judge to arise? Even if the greatest confidence had been placed in the effects of the " Visitation,"—if it could have been believed that it would fully accomplish its high purpose,—there was still no remedy to be found here for a joyous, inwardly-striving youth. The formalities of the proceeding all tended towards delay; if any one desired to do anything, and to be of any importance, he was obliged

to serve the party in the wrong—always the accused—and
to be skilled in the fencing-art of twisting and evading.

Since, amid this distraction, I could not succeed in any
æsthetic labours, I again and again lost myself in æsthetic
speculations, as indeed all theorising indicates a defect or
stagnation of productive power. Before with Merk, now
with Gotter, I endeavoured to find out the maxims according
to which one might go to work in production. But neither
with me nor with them would it succeed. Merk was a sceptic
and eclectic; Gotter adhered to such examples as pleased
him the most. The Sulzer theory was published more for
the amateur than the artist. In this sphere moral effects are
required above all things; and here at once arises a dissension
between the class that produces and that which uses; for
a good work of art can, and will indeed, have moral consequences; but to require moral ends of the artist, is to destroy
his profession.

What the ancients had said on these important subjects I
had read industriously for some years, by skips, at least, if not
in regular order. Aristotle, Cicero, Quintilian, Longinus—none
were unconsidered; but this did not help me in the least, for all
these men presupposed an experience which I lacked. They
led me into a world infinitely rich in works of art; they unfolded the merits of excellent poets and orators, of most of
whom the names alone are left us, and convinced me but too
well that a great abundance of objects must lie before us
ere we can think upon them; that one must first accomplish something oneself, nay, fail in something, to learn to
know one's own capacities, and those of others. My acquaintance with so much that was good in those old times, was
only according to school and book, and by no means vital,
since, even with the most celebrated orators, it was striking
that they had altogether formed themselves in life, and that
one could never speak of the peculiarities of their character
as artists, without at the same time mentioning the personal
peculiarities of their disposition. With the poets this seemed
less to be the case; and thus the result of all my thoughts
and endeavours was the old resolution to investigate inner
and outer nature, and to allow her to rule herself in loving
imitation.

For these operations, which rested in me neither day nor

night, lay before me two great, nay, monstrous materials, the wealth of which I had only to prize, in order to produce something of importance. There was the older epoch, into which falls the life of Götz von Berlichingen, and the modern one, the unhappy bloom of which is depicted in *Werther*. Of the historical preparation to that first work I have already spoken; the ethical occasions of the second shall now be introduced.

The resolution to preserve my internal nature according to its peculiarities, and to let external nature influence me according to its qualities, impelled me to the strange element in which *Werther* is designed and written. I sought to free myself internally from all that was foreign to me, to regard the external with love, and to allow all beings, from man downwards, as low as they were comprehensible, to act upon me, each after its own kind. Thus arose a wonderful affinity with the single objects of nature, and a hearty concord, a harmony with the whole, so that every change, whether of place and region, or of the times of the day and year, or whatever else could happen, affected me in the deepest manner. The glance of the painter associated itself to that of the poet, the beautiful rural landscape, animated by the pleasant river, increased my love of solitude, and favoured my silent observations as they extended on all sides.

But since I had left the family circle in Sesenheim, and again my family circle at Frankfort and Darmstadt, a vacuum had remained in my bosom which I was not able to fill up; I therefore found myself in a situation where the inclinations, if they appear in any degree veiled, gradually steal upon us, and can render abortive all our good resolutions.

And now, when the author has attained this step of his undertaking, he for the first time feels light-hearted in his labour, since from henceforward this book first becomes what it properly ought to be. It has not been announced as an independent work; it is much more designed to fill up the gaps of an author's life, to complete much that is fragmentary, and to preserve the memory of lost and forgotten ventures. But what is already done neither should nor can be repeated, and the poet would now vainly call upon those darkened powers of the soul, vainly ask of them to render present again those charming circumstances, which rendered the abode in Lahnthal so agreeable to him. Fortunately the genius had already pro-

vided for that, and had impelled him, in the vigorous period
of youth, to hold fast, describe, and with sufficient boldness
and at the favourable hour publicly to exhibit that which had
immediately gone by. That the little book *Werther* is here
meant, requires no further indication, but something is to be
gradually revealed, both of the persons introduced in it and
the views which it exhibits.

Among the young men, who, attached to the embassy, had
to prepare themselves for their future career of office, was one
whom we were accustomed to call only the " Bridegroom."
He distinguished himself by a calm, agreeable deportment,
clearness of views, definiteness both in speaking and in acting.
His cheerful activity, his persevering industry so much recommended him to his superiors, that an appointment at an early
period was promised him. Being justified by this, he ventured
to betroth himself to a lady, who fully corresponded to his tone
of mind and his wishes. After the death of her mother, she
had shown herself extremely active as the head of a numerous
young family, and had alone sustained her father in his widow-
hood, so that a future husband might hope the same for himself and his posterity, and expect a decided domestic felicity.
Every one confessed, without having these selfish ends immediately in view, that she was a desirable lady. She belonged to
those who, if they do not inspire ardent passion, are nevertheless formed to create a general feeling of pleasure. A figure
lightly built and neatly formed, a pure healthy temperament,
with a glad activity of life resulting from it, an unembarrassed
management of the necessities of the day—all these were given
her together. I always felt happy in the contemplation of such
qualities, and I readily associated myself to those who possessed
them; and if I did not always find opportunity to render them
real service, I rather shared with them than with others the
enjoyment of those innocent pleasures which youth can always
find at hand, and seize without any great cost or effort.
Moreover, since it is now settled that ladies decorate themselves only for each other, and are unwearied among each other
to heighten the effect of their adornments, those were always
the most agreeable to me, who, with simple purity, give their
friend, their bridegroom, the silent assurance that all is really
done for him alone, and that a whole life could be so carried
on without much circumstance and outlay.

Such persons are not too much occupied with themselves;
they have time to consider the external world, and patience
enough to direct themselves according to it, and to adapt
themselves to it; they become shrewd and sensible without
exertion, and require but few books for their cultivation.
Such was the bride.* The bridegroom, with his thoroughly
upright and confiding turn of mind, soon made many whom
he esteemed acquainted with her; and as he had to pass the
greatest part of his day in a zealous attention to business,
was pleased when his betrothed, after the domestic toils were
ended, amused herself otherwise, and took social recreation in
walks and rural parties with friends of both sexes. Charlotte
—for so we shall call her—was unpretending in two senses;
first, by her nature, which was rather directed to a general
kindly feeling than to particular inclinations; and then she
had set her mind upon a man who, being worthy of her, declared himself ready to attach his fate to hers for life. The
most cheerful atmosphere seemed to surround her; nay, if it
be a pleasing sight to see parents bestow an uninterrupted care
upon their children, there is something still more beautiful
when brothers and sisters do the same for each other. In the
former case we think we can perceive more of natural impulse
and social tradition; in the latter, more of choice and of a
free exercise of feeling.

The new comer, perfectly free from all ties, and careless in
the presence of a girl who, already engaged to another, could
not interpret the most obliging services as acts of courtship,
and could take the more pleasure in them accordingly, quietly
went his way, but was soon so drawn in and rivetted, that
he no longer knew himself. Indolent and dreamy, because
nothing present satisfied him, he found what he had lacked
in a female friend, who, while she lived for the whole year,
seemed only to live for the moment. She liked him much as
her companion; he soon could not bear her absence, as she
formed for him the connecting link with the every-day world;
and during extensive household occupations, they were inseparable companions in the fields and in the meadows, in the
vegetable-ground and in the garden. If business permitted,
the bridegroom was also of the party: they had all three ac-

* Persons betrothed are in German called "bride" and "bridegroom."—*Trans.*

customed themselves to each other without intention, and did
not know how they had become so mutually indispensable.
During the splendid summer they lived through a real German idyl, to which the fertile land gave the form and a pure
affection the poetry. Wandering through ripe corn-fields,
they took delight in the dewy morning; the song of the lark,
the cry of the quail, were pleasant tones; sultry hours followed, monstrous storms came on,—they grew more and more
attached to each other, and by this continuous love many a
little domestic annoyance was easily extinguished. And thus
one ordinary day followed another, and all seemed to be holidays,—the whole calendar should have been printed red. He
will understand me who recollects what was predicted by the
happily unhappy friend of the " New Heloise:" " And sitting
at the feet of his beloved, he will break hemp, and he will
wish to break hemp to-day, to-morrow, and the day after,
nay, for his whole life."

I can say but little, though just as much as may be necessary, respecting a young man, whose name was afterwards
but too often mentioned. This was Jerusalem, the son of the
freely and tenderly thinking theologian. He also had an appointment with an embassy; his form was pleasing, of a
middle height, and well built; his face was rather round than
long; his features were soft and calm, and he had the other
appurtenances of a handsome blond youth, with blue eyes,
rather attractive than speaking. His dress was that introduced in Lower Germany in imitation of the English,—a blue
frock, waistcoat and breeches of yellow leather, and boots
with brown tops. The author never visited him, nor saw him
at his own residence, but often met him among his friends.
The expressions of this young man were moderate but kindly.
He took interest in productions of the most different kinds,
and especially loved those designs and sketches in which the
the tranquil character of solitary spots is caught. On such
occasions he showed Gesner's etchings, and encouraged the
amateurs to study them. In all that mummery and knighthood he took no part, but lived for himself and his own sentiments. It was said he had a decided passion for the wife of
one of his friends. In public they were never seen together.
In general very little could be said of him, except that he
occupied himself with English literature. As the son of an

opulent man, he had no occasion either painfully to devote
himself to business, or to make pressing applications for an
early appointment.

Those etchings by Gesner increased the pleasure and interest in rural objects, and a little poem, which we passionately
received into our circle, allowed us from henceforward to think
of nothing else.   Goldsmith's *Deserted Village* necessarily delighted every one at that grade of cultivation, in that sphere of
thought.   Not as living and active, but as a departed, vanished
existence was described, all that one so readily looked upon,
that one loved, prized, sought passionately in the present, to
take part in it with the cheerfulness of youth.   Highdays and
holidays in the country, church consecrations and fairs, the
solemn assemblage of the elders under the village linden-tree,
supplanted in its turn by the lively delight of youth in
dancing, while the more educated classes show their sympathy.   How seemly did these pleasures appear, moderated as
they were by an excellent country pastor, who understood
how to smooth down and remove all that went too far,—that
gave occasion to quarrel and dispute.   Here again we found
an honest Wakefield, in his well-known circle, yet no longer
in his living bodily form, but as a shadow recalled by the soft
mournful tones of the elegiac poet.   The very thought of this
picture is one of the happiest possible, when once the design
is formed to evoke once more an innocent past with a graceful
melancholy.   And in this kindly endeavour, how well has the
Englishman succeeded in every sense of the word !   I shared
the enthusiasm for this charming poem with Gotter, who was
more felicitous than myself with the translation undertaken by
us both ; for I had too painfully tried to imitate in our language the delicate significance of the original, and thus had
well agreed with single passages, but not with the whole.

If now, as they say, the greatest happiness rests on a sense
of longing (*sehnsucht*), and if the genuine longing can only
be directed to something unattainable, everything had fallen
together to render the youth whom we now accompany on
his wanderings the happiest of mortals.   An affection for
one betrothed to another, the effort to acquire the master-
pieces of foreign literature for our own, the endeavour to imitate natural objects, not only with words, but also with style
and pencil, without any proper technical knowledge,—each of

these particulars would singly have sufficed to melt the heart
and oppress the bosom. But, that the sweetly suffering youth
might be torn out of this state, and that new circumstances
might be prepared for new disquiet, the following events
occurred :—

Höpfner, professor of law, was at Giessen. He was acknowledged and highly esteemed by Merk and Schlosser as
clever in his office, and as a thinking and excellent man.
I had long ago desired his acquaintance, and now, when these
two friends thought to pay him a visit, to negotiate about
some literary matters, it was agreed that I should likewise go
to Giessen on this opportunity. Because, however—as generally happens with the wilfulness of glad and peaceful times
—we could not easily do anything in the direct way, but,
like genuine children, sought to get a jest even out of what
was necessary. I was now, as an unknown person, to appear
in a strange form, and once more satisfy my desire to appear
disguised. One cheerful morning, before sunrise, I went
from Wetzlar along the Lahne, up the charming valley;
such ramblings again constituted my greatest felicity. I
invented, connected, elaborated, and was quietly happy and
cheerful with myself: I set right what the ever-contradic-
tory world had clumsily and confusedly forced upon me.
Arrived at the end of my journey, I looked out for Höpfner's
residence, and knocked at his study. When he had cried
out, "Come in!" I modestly appeared before him as a
student who was going home from the universities, and
wished on his way to become acquainted with the most
worthy men. For his questions as to my more intimate
circumstances, I was prepared; I made up a plausible, prosaic tale, with which he seemed satisfied, and as I gave myself
out for a jurist, I did not come off badly; for I well knew
his merits in this department, and also that he was occupied
with natural law. Conversation, however, sometimes came
to a stand, and it seemed as if he were looking for a *Stammbuch*,* or for me to take my leave. Nevertheless, I managed
to delay my departure, as I expected with certainty the
arrival of Schlosser, whose punctuality was well known to

* A "stammbuch" is a sort of album for autographs and short con-
tributions.— *Trans.*

me. He came in reality, and after a side glance, took little notice of me. Hopfner, however, drew me into conversation, and showed himself throughout as a humane and kindly man. I at last took my leave, and hastened to the inn, where I exchanged a few hurried words with Merk, and awaited further proceedings.

The friends had resolved to ask Hopfner to dinner, and also that Philipp Henrich Schmidt who had played a part, though a very subordinate one, in German literature. For him the affair was really designed, and he was to be punished in a mirthful manner. When the guests had assembled in the dining-room, I asked, through the waiter, whether the gentlemen would allow me to dine with them. Schlosser, whom a certain earnestness well became, opposed this proposition, because they did not wish their conversation interrupted by a third party. But, on the pressing demand of the waiter and the advocacy of Hopfner, who assured the other that I was a very tolerable person, I was admitted, and at the commencement of the meal behaved as if modest and abashed. Schlosser and Merk put no restraint upon themselves, and went on about many subjects as freely as if no stranger were present. I now showed myself somewhat bolder, and did not allow myself to be disturbed when Schlosser threw out at me much that was in earnest, and Merk something sarcastic; but I directed against Schmidt all my darts, which fell sharply and surely on the uncovered places which I well knew.

I had been moderate over my pint of table-wine, but the gentlemen ordered better wine to be brought, and did not fail to give me some. After many affairs of the day had been talked over, conversation went into general matters, and the question was discussed, which will be repeated as long as there are authors in the world,—the question, namely, whether literature was rising or declining, progressing or retrograding? This question, about which old and young, those commencing and those retiring, seldom agree, was discussed with cheerfulness, though without any exact design of coming decidedly to terms about it. At last I took up the discourse, and said, "The different literatures, as it seems to me, have seasons, which alternating with each other, as in nature, bring forth certain phenomena, and assert themselves in due order. Hence I do not believe that any epoch of a literature can be

praised or blamed on the whole; especially it displeases me
when certain talents, which are brought out by their time, are
raised and vaunted so highly, while others are censured and
depreciated. The throat of the nightingale is excited by the
spring, but at the same time also that of the cuckoo. The
butterflies, which are so agreeable to the eye, and the gnats,
which are so painful to the feelings, are called into being by
the same heat of the sun. If this were duly considered, we
should not hear the same complaints renewed every ten years,
and the vain trouble which is taken to root out this or that
offensive thing, would not so often be wasted." The party
looked at me, wondering whence I had got so much wisdom
and tolerance. I, however, continued quite calmly to compare
literary phenomena with natural productions, and (I know
not how) came to the *mollusca*, of which I contrived to set
forth all sorts of strange things. I said that there were
creatures to whom a sort of body, nay, a certain figure, could
not be denied; but that, since they had no bones, one never
knew how to set about rightly with them, and they were
nothing better than living slime; nevertheless, the sea must
have such inhabitants. Since I carried the simile beyond
its due limits to designate Schmidt, who was present, and
that class of characterless *litterateurs*, I was reminded that
a simile carried too far at last becomes nothing. " Well,
then, I will return to the earth," I replied, "and speak of
the ivy. As these creatures have no bones, so this has
no trunk; but wherever it attaches itself, it likes to play
the chief part. It belongs to old walls, in which there is
nothing more to destroy; but from new buildings it is properly removed. It sucks up the goodness of the trees; and
is most insupportable to me when it clambers up a post, and
assures me that this is a living trunk, because it has covered
it with leaves."

Notwithstanding I was again reproached with the obscurity
and inapplicability of my similes, I became more and more
warm against all parasitical creatures, and as far as my knowledge of nature then extended, managed the affair pretty well.
I at last sang a *vivat* to all independent men, a *pereat* to those
who forced themselves upon them, seized Hopfner's hand
after dinner, shook it violently, declared him to be the best
man in the world, and finally embraced both him and the

others right heartily. My excellent new friend thought he was really dreaming, until Schlosser and Merk at last solved the riddle ; and the discovered joke diffused a general hilarity, which was shared by Schmidt himself, who was appeased by an acknowledgment of his real merits, and the interest we took in his tastes.

This ingenious introduction could not do otherwise than animate and favour the literary congress, which was indeed, chiefly kept in view. Merk, active now in æsthetics, now in literature, now in commerce, had stimulated the well-thinking, well-informed Schlosser, whose knowledge extended to so many branches, to edit the Frankfort *Gelehrte Anzeige* (*Learned Advertiser*) for that year. They had associated to themselves Höpfner, and other university-men in Giessen, a meritorious schoolman, Rector Wenk in Darmstadt, and many other good men. Every one of them possessed enough historical and theoretical knowledge in his department, and the feeling of the times allowed these men to work in one spirit. The human and cosmopolitan is encouraged ; really good men justly celebrated are protected against obtrusion of every kind ; their defence is undertaken against enemies, and especially against scholars, who use what has been taught them to the detriment of their instructors. Nearly the most interesting articles are the critiques on other periodical publications, the *Berlin Library* (*Bibliothek*), the *German Mercury*, where the cleverness in so many departments, the judgment as well the fairness of the papers, is rightly admired.

As for myself, they saw well enough that I was deficient in everything that belongs to a critic, properly so called. My historical knowledge was unconnected, the histories of the world, science, and literature had only attracted me by epochs, the objects themselves only partially and in masses. My capacity of giving life to things, and rendering them present to me out of their real connexion, put me in the position that I could be perfectly at home in a certain century or in a department of science, without being in any degree instructed as to what preceded or what followed. Thus a certain theoretico-practical sense had been awakened in me, by which I could give account of things, rather as they should be than as they were, without any proper philosophical connexion, but by way of leaps. To this was added a very easy power of apprehension, and a friendly reception of the opinions of others, if they did not stand in direct opposition to my own convictions.

That literary union was also favoured by an animated correspondence, and by frequent personal communication, which was possible from the vicinity of the places. He who had first read a book was to give an account of it; often another reviewer of the same book was found; the affair was talked over, connected with kindred subjects, and if at last a certain result had been obtained, one of them took the office of editing. Thus many reviews are as clever as they are spirited, as pleasant as they are satisfactory. I often had the task of introducing the matter; my friends also permitted me to jest in their works, and to appear independently with objects to which I felt myself equal, and in which I especially took interest. In vain should I endeavour, either by description or reflection, to recall the proper spirit and sense of those days, if the two years of the above-mentioned periodical did not furnish me with the most decisive documents. Extracts from passages, in which I again recognise myself, may appear in future in their proper place, together with similar essays.

During this lively interchange of knowledge, opinions, and convictions, I very soon became better acquainted with Höpfner, and became very fond of him. As soon as we were alone I spoke with him about subjects connected with his department, which was to be my department also; and found a very naturally connected explanation and instruction. I was not then as yet plainly conscious that I could learn something from books and conversation, but not from continuous professional lectures. A book allowed me to pause at a passage, and even to look back, which is impossible with oral delivery and a teacher. Often at the beginning of the lecture, some thought in which I indulged laid hold of me, and thus I lost what followed, and altogether got out of the connexion. Thus it had happened to me with respect to the lectures on jurisprudence; and on this account I could take many opportunities of talking with Höpfner, who entered very readily into my doubts and scruples, and filled up many gaps, so that the wish arose in me to remain with him at Giessen, and derive instruction from him, without removing myself too far from Wetzlar inclinations. Against this wish of mine my two friends had laboured, first unconsciously, but afterwards consciously; for both were in a hurry, not only to leave the place themselves, but had also an interest to remove me from the spot.

Schlosser disclosed to me that he had formed, first a friendly, then a closer connexion with my sister, and that he was looking about for an early appointment that he might be united to her. This explanation surprised me to some degree, although I ought to have found it out long ago in my sister's letters; but we easily pass over that which may hurt the good opinion which we entertain of ourselves, and I now remarked for the first time that I was really jealous of my sister; a feeling which I concealed from myself the less, as, since my return from Strasburg, our connexion had been much more intimate. How much time had we not expended in communicating each little affair of the heart, love-matters, and other matters, which had occurred in the interval. In the field of imagination, too, had there not been revealed to me a new world, into which I sought to conduct her also? My own little productions, and a far-extended world-poetry, was gradually to be made known to her. Thus I made for her *impromptu* translations of those passages of Homer, in which she could take the greatest interest. Clarke's literal translation I read into German, as well as I could; my version generally found its way into metrical turns and terminations, and the liveliness with which I had apprehended the images, the force with which I expressed them, removed all the obstacles of a cramped order of words; what I gave with mind, she followed with mind also. We passed many hours of the day in this fashion; while, if her company met, the Wolf Fenris and the Ape Hannemann were unanimously called for, and how often have I not been obliged to repeat circumstantially how Thor and his comrades were deluded by the magical giants! Hence from these fictions such a pleasant impression has remained with me, that they belong to the most valuable things which my imagination can recall. Into the connexion with the Darmstadt people I had drawn my sister also, and now my wanderings and occasional absence necessarily bound us closer together, as I discoursed with her by letter respecting every thing that occurred to me, communicated to her every little poem, if even only a note of admiration, and let her first see all the letters which I received, and all the answers which I wrote. All these lively impulses had been stopped since my departure from Frankfort, my residence at Wetzlar was not fertile enough for such a correspondence, and, moreover, my attachment to Charlotte may have infringed upon my attentions to my sister; enough, she felt herself alone, perhaps neglected, and therefore the more readily gave a hearing to the honest wooing of an honourable man, who, serious and reserved, estimable and worthy of confidence, had passionately bestowed on her his affections, with which he was otherwise very niggardly. I was now forced to resign myself and grant my friend his happiness, though I did not fail in secret to say confidently to myself, that if the brother had not been absent, it would not have gone so well with the friend.

My friend and probable brother-in-law was now very anxious that I should return home, because, by my mediation, a freer intercourse was possible, of which the feelings of this man, so unexpectedly attached by a tender passion, seemed to stand extremely in need. Therefore, on his speedy departure, he elicited from me the promise that I would immediately follow him.

Of Merk, whose time was free, I hoped that he would delay his sojourn in Giessen, that I might be able to pass some hours of the day with my good Höpfner, while my friend employed his time on the Frankfort *Gelehrte Anzeige;* but he was not to be moved, and as my brother-in-law was driven from the university by love, he was driven by hate. For as there are innate antipathies—just as certain men cannot endure cats, while this or that is repugnant to the soul of others,—so was Merk a deadly enemy to all the academical citizens (the students), who indeed at that time, at Giessen, took delight in the greatest rudeness. For me they were well enough; I could have used them as masks for one of my carnival plays, but with him the sight of them by day, and their noise by night, destroyed every sort of good humour. He had spent the best days of his youth in French Switzerland, and had afterwards enjoyed the pleasant intercourse of people of the court, world, and business, and of cultivated *littérateurs;* several military persons, in whom a desire for mental culture had been awakened, sought his society, and thus he had passed his life in a very cultivated circle. That the rudeness of the students vexed him, was therefore not to be wondered at, but his aversion from them

2 I

was really more passionate than became a sound man, although
he often made me laugh by his witty descriptions of their monstrous appearance and behaviour. Hopfner's invitations and
my persuasions were of no avail ; I was obliged to depart with
him as soon as possible for Wetzlar.

I could scarcely wait any time, till I had introduced him to
Charlotte, but his presence in this circle did me no good ; for
as Mephistopheles, let him go when he will, hardly brings a
blessing with him, so did he, by his indifference towards that
beloved person, cause me no joy, even if he did not make me
waver. This I might have foreseen, if I had recollected that
it was exactly those slender, delicate persons, who diffuse a
lively cheerfulness around them, without making further pretensions, who did not remarkably please him. He very quickly
preferred the Juno-form of one of her friends, and since he
lacked time to form a close connexion, he bitterly blamed me
for not exerting myself to gain this magnificent figure, especially as she was free and without any tie. He thought that
I did not understand my own advantage, and that he here—
very unwillingly—perceived my especial taste for wasting my
time.

If it is dangerous to make a friend acquainted with the perfections of one's beloved, because he also may find her charming and desirable ; no less is the reverse danger, that he may
perplex us by his dissent. This, indeed, was not the case here,
for I had too deeply impressed upon myself the picture of her
amiability for it to be so easily obliterated ; but his presence
and his persuasions nevertheless hastened my resolution to
leave the place. He represented to me a journey on the
Rhine, which he was going to take with his wife and son, in
the most glowing colours, and excited in me the desire to see,
at last, with my own eyes those objects of which I had often
heard with envy. Now, when he had departed, I separated
myself from Charlotte with a purer conscience indeed than
from Frederica, but still not without pain. This connexion
also had by habit and indulgence grown more passionate than
was right on my side, while, on the other hand, she and her
bridegroom kept themselves with cheerfulness in a measure,
which could not be more beautiful and amiable, and the security which resulted just from this caused me to forget every

danger. I could not, however, conceal from myself that this
adventure must come to a speedy end ; for the union of the
young man with the amiable girl depended on a promotion
which was immediately to be expected, and as man, if he is in
any degree resolute, even dares to make a virtue of necessity,
so did I embrace the determination voluntarily to depart before
I was driven away by anything insupportable.

THIRTEENTH BOOK.

It was agreed with Merk, that in the fine season we should
meet at Coblentz at Frau von Laroche's. I sent to Frankfort
my baggage and whatever I might want on my way down the
Lahn by an opportunity which offered, and now wandered
down that beautiful river, so lovely in its windings, so various in its shores, free as to my resolution, but oppressed as to
my feelings—in a condition, when the presence of silently-
living nature is so beneficial to us. My eye, accustomed to
discern those beauties of a landscape that suited the painter,
and were above him, rioted in the contemplation of near and
distant objects, of bushy rocks, of sunny heights, of damp
valleys, of enthroned castles, and of the blue range of mountains inviting us from the distance.

I wandered on the right bank of the river, which at some
depth and distance below me, and partly concealed by a rich
bush of willows, glided along in the sunlight. Then again
arose in me the old wish, worthily to imitate such objects.
By chance I had a handsome pocket-knife in my left hand, and
at the moment, from the depth of my soul, arose, as it were,
an absolute command, according to which, without delay, I
was to fling this knife into the river. If I saw it fall, my
wish to become an artist would be fulfilled, but if the sinking
of the knife was concealed by the overhanging bush of willows,
I was to abandon the wish and the endeavour. This whim
had no sooner arisen in me than it was executed. For, without regarding the usefulness of the knife, which comprised
many instruments in itself, I cast it with the left hand, as I
held it, violently towards the river. But here I had to experience that deceptive ambiguity of oracles, of which, in antiquity, such bitter complaints were made. The sinking of the
knife into the water was concealed from me by the extreme
twigs of the willows, but the water, which rose from the fall,
sprang up like a strong fountain, and was perfectly visible. I
did not interpret this phenomenon in my favour, and the

doubt which it excited in me was afterwards the cause that I pursued these exercises more interruptedly and more negligently, and gave occasion for the import of the oracle to fulfil itself. For the moment at least the external world was spoiled for me, I abandoned myself to my imaginations and feelings, and left the well-situated castles and districts of Weilburg, Limburg, Diez, and Nassau one by one behind me, generally walking alone, but often for a short time associating myself with another.

After thus pleasantly wandering for some days, I arrived at Ems, where I several times enjoyed the soft bath, and then went down the river in a boat. Then the old Rhine opened itself upon me, the beautiful situation of Oberlahnstein delighted me, but noble and majestic above all appeared to me the castle Ehrenbreitstein, which stood perfectly armed in its power and strength. In most lovely contrast lay at its feet the well-built little place called Thal, where I could easily find my way to the residence of Privy Councillor von Laroche. Announced by Merk, I was very kindly received by this noble family, and soon considered as a member of it. My literary and sentimental tendencies bound me to the mother, a cheerful feeling for the world bound me to the father, and my youth bound me to the daughters.

The house, quite at the end of the valley, and little elevated above the river, had a free prospect down the stream. The rooms were high and spacious, and the walls, like a gallery, were hung with pictures, placed close together. Every window on every side formed a frame to a natural picture, which came out very vividly by the light of a mild sun. I thought I had never seen such cheerful mornings and such splendid evenings.

I was not long the only guest in the house. As a member of the congress which was held here, partly with an artistic view, partly as a matter of feeling, Leuchselring, who came up from Dusseldorf, was likewise appointed. This man, possessing a fine knowledge of modern literature, had, on different travels, but especially during a residence in Switzerland, made many acquaintances, and as he was pleasant and insinuating, had gained much favour. He carried with him several boxes, which contained the confidential correspondence with many friends; for there was altogether such a general openness among people, that one could not speak or write to a single individual, without considering it directed to many. One explored one's own heart and that of others, and with the indifference of the government towards such a communication, the great rapidity of the Taxisch* post, the security of the seal, and the reasonableness of the postage, this moral and literary intercourse soon spread itself around.

Such correspondences, especially with important persons, were carefully collected, and extracts from them were often read at friendly meetings. Thus, as political discourses had little interest, one became pretty well acquainted with the extent of the moral world.

Leuchsedring's boxes contained many treasures in this sense. The letters of one Julie Bondeli were very much esteemed; she was famed as a lady of sense and merit, and a friend of Rousseau. Whoever had stood in any relation to this extraordinary man, took part in the glory which emanated from him, and in his name a silent community had been disseminated far and wide.

I liked to be present at these readings, as I was thus transported into an unknown world, and learned to know the real truth of many an event that had just passed. All indeed was not valuable, and Herr von Laroche, a cheerful man of the world and of business, who, although a Catholic, had already in his writings made free with the monks and priesthood, thought that he here saw a fraternity, where many a worthless individual supported himself by a connexion with persons of importance, by which, in the end, he, but not they, were admired. Generally this excellent man withdrew from the company when the boxes were opened. Even if he did listen to some letters now and then, a waggish remark was to be expected. Among other things, he once said that by this correspondence he was still more convinced of what he had always believed, namely, that ladies might spare their sealing-wax, as they need only fasten their letters with pins, and might be assured that they would reach their address unopened. In the

* The post, managed by the princes of Thurn and Taxis, in different parts of Germany. An ancestor of this house first directed the post system in Tyrol, in 1450, and Alexander Ferdinand von Thurn received, in 1744, the office of Imperial Postmaster-General, as a fief of the empire.—*Trans.*

same way he was accustomed to jest with everything that lay out of the sphere of life and activity, and in this followed the disposition of his lord and master, Count Stadion, minister to the Elector of Mayence, who certainly was not fitted to counterbalance the worldliness and coldness of the boy by a reverence for everything like mysterious foreboding.

An anecdote respecting the great practical sense of the count may here find a place. When he took a liking to the orphan Laroche, and chose him for a pupil, he at once required from the boy the services of a secretary. He gave him letters to answer, despatches to prepare, which he was then obliged to copy fair, oftener to write in cipher, to seal, and to direct. This lasted for many years. When the boy had grown up into a youth, and really did that which he had hitherto only supposed he was doing, the count took him to a large writing-table, in which all his letters and packets lay unbroken, having been preserved as exercises of the former time.

Another exercise which the count required of his pupil, will not find such universal applause. Laroche had been obliged to practise himself in imitating, as accurately as possible, the handwriting of his lord and master, that he might thus relieve him from the trouble of writing himself. Not only in business, but also in love affairs, the young man had to take the place of his preceptor. The count was passionately attached to a lady of rank and talent. If he stopped in her society till late at night, his secretary was, in the meanwhile, sitting at home, and hammering out the most ardent love-letters; the count chose one of these, and sent it that very night to his beloved, who was thus necessarily convinced of the inextinguishable fire of her passionate adorer. Such early experiences were scarcely fitted to give the youth the most exalted notion of written communications about love.

An irreconcilable hatred of the priesthood had established itself in this man, who served two spiritual electors, and had probably sprung from the contemplation of the rude, tasteless, mind-destroying foolery which the monks in Germany were accustomed to carry on in many parts, and thus hindered and destroyed every sort of cultivation. His letters on Monasticism caused great attention; they were received with great applause by all Protestants and many Catholics.

If Herr Von Laroche opposed everything that can be

called sensibility, and even decidedly avoided the very appearance of it, he nevertheless did not conceal a tender paternal affection for his eldest daughter, who, indeed, was nothing
else but amiable. She was rather short than tall of stature,
and delicately built, her figure was free and graceful, her eyes
very black, while nothing could be conceived purer and more
blooming than her complexion. She also loved her father, and
inclined to his sentiments. Being an active man of business,
most of his time was consumed in works belonging to his calling; and as the guests who stopped at his house were really
attracted by his wife and not by him, society afforded him but
little pleasure. At table he was cheerful and entertaining, and
at least endeavoured to keep his board free from the spice of
sensibility.

Whoever knows the views and mode of thought of Frau von
Laroche—and by a long life and many writings, she has
become honourably known to every German,—may perhaps
suspect that a domestic incongruity must have arisen here.
Nothing of the kind. She was the most wonderful woman;
and I know no other to compare to her. Slenderly and delicately built, rather tall than short, she had, even to her more
advanced years, managed to preserve a certain elegance both
of form and of conduct, which pleasantly fluctuated between
the conduct of a noble lady and that of one of the citizen class.
Her dress had been the same for several years. A neat little
cap with wings very well became her small head and delicate
face, and her brown or grey clothing gave repose and dignity
to her presence. She spoke well, and always knew how to
give importance to what she said by an expression of feeling.
Her conduct was perfectly the same towards every body. But
with all this the greatest peculiarity of her character is not yet
expressed; it is difficult to designate it. She seemed to take
interest in everything, but really nothing acted upon her. She
was gentle towards every one, and could endure everything
without suffering: the jests of her husband, the tenderness of
her friends, the sweetness of her children—to all this she replied
in the same manner, and thus she always remained herself, without being affected in the world by good and evil, or in literature
by excellence and weakness. To this disposition she owes that
independence which she maintains even to an advanced age,
through many sad, nay, sorrowful events. But not to be un-

just, I must state that her sons, then children of dazzling beauty, often elicited from her an expression different from that which served her for daily use.

Thus I lived for a time in a wonderfully pleasant society, until Merk came with his family. Here arose at once new affinities; for while the two ladies approached each other, Merk had come into closer contact with Herr von Laroche as a connoisseur of the world and of business, as a well-informed and travelled man. The boy associated himself with the boys, and the daughters, of whom the eldest soon particularly attracted me, fell to my share. It is a very pleasant sensation when a new passion begins to stir in us, before the old one is quite extinct. Thus, when the sun is setting, one often likes to see the moon rise on the opposite side, and one takes delight in the double lustre of the two heavenly luminaries.

There was now no lack of rich entertainment either in or out of the house. We wandered about the spot, and ascended Ehrenbreitstein on this side of the river, and the Carthause on the other. The city, the Moselle-bridge, the ferry which took us over the Rhine, all gave us the most varied delight. The new castle was not yet built; we were taken to the place where it was to stand, and allowed to see the preparatory sketches.

Nevertheless, amid those cheerful circumstances was internally developed that element of unsociableness which, both in cultivated and uncultivated circles, ordinarily shows its malign effects. Merk, at once cold and restless, had not long listened to that correspondence before he uttered aloud many waggish notions concerning the things which were the subjects of discourse, as well as the persons and their circumstances, while he revealed to me in secret the oddest things, which really were concealed under them. Political secrets were never touched on, nor indeed anything that could have had a definite connexion; he only made me attentive to persons who, without remarkable talents, contrive, by a certain tact, to obtain personal influence, and, by an acquaintance with many, try to make something out of themselves; and from this time forwards I had opportunity to observe several men of the sort. Since such persons usually change their place, and, as travellers come, now here, now there, they have the advantage of novelty, which should neither be envied nor

spoiled; for this is a mere customary matter, which every traveller has often experienced to his benefit, and every resident
to his detriment.

Be that as it may, it is enough that from that time forward
we cherished an uneasy, nay, envious attention to people of
the sort, who went about on their own account, cast anchor in
every city, and sought to gain an influence at least in some
families. I have represented a tender and soft specimen of
this co-operation in " Pater Brey," another of more aptness and
bluntness in a carnival play to be hereafter published, which
bears the title, *Satyros, or the deified Wood-devil.* This I have
done, if not with fairness, at least with good humour.

However, the strange elements of our little society still
worked quite tolerably one upon another; we were partly
united by our own manner and style of breeding, and partly
restrained by the peculiar conduct of our hostess, who, being
but lightly touched by that which passed around her, always
resigned herself to certain ideal notions, and while she understood how to utter them in a friendly and benevolent way,
contrived to soften everything sharp that might arise in the
company, and to smooth down all that was uneven.

Merk had sounded a retreat just at the right time, so that
the party separated on the best of terms. I went with him and
his in a yacht, which was returning up the Rhine towards
Mayence; and although this vessel went very slowly of itself,
we nevertheless besought the captain not to hurry himself.
Thus we enjoyed at leisure the infinitely various objects, which,
in the most splendid weather, seem to increase in beauty every
hour, and both in greatness and agreeableness ever to change
anew; and I only wish that, while I utter the names, Rhein-
fels and St. Goar, Bacharach, Bingen, Elfeld, and Biberich,
every one of my readers may be able to recall these spots to
memory.

We had sketched industriously, and had thus at least gained
a deeper impression of the thousandfold changes of those
splendid shores. At the same time, by being so much longer
together, by a familiar communication on so many sorts of
things, our connexion became so much the more intimate, that
Merk gained a great influence over me, and I, as a good companion, became indispensable to him for a comfortable existence. My eye, sharpened by nature, again turned to the con-

templation of art, for which the beautiful Frankfort collections
afforded me the best opportunity, both in paintings and engravings, and I have been much indebted to the kindness of
MM. Etling and Ehrenreich, but especially to the excellent
Nothnagel. To see nature in art became with me a passion,
which, in its highest moments, must have appeared to others,
passionate amateurs as they might be, almost like madness;
and how could such an inclination be better fostered than by
a constant observation of the excellent works of the Nether-
landers? That I might make myself practically acquainted
with these things, Nothnagel gave me a cabinet, where I found
every thing that was requisite for oil painting, and painted after
nature some simple subjects of still life, upon one of which, a
tortoise-shell knife-handle, inlaid with silver, so astonished my
master, who had first visited me an hour before, that he maintained one of his subordinate artists must have been with me
during the time.

Had I patiently gone on practising myself on such objects
catching their light and the peculiarities of their surface, I
might have formed a sort of practical skill, and made a way
for something higher. I was, however, prevented by the fault
of all dilettantes—that of beginning with what is most difficult,
and ever wishing to perform the impossible, and I soon involved myself in greater undertakings, in which I stuck fast,
both because they were beyond my technical capabilities, and
because I could not always maintain pure and operative that
loving attention and patient industry, by which even the
beginner accomplishes something.

At the same time, I was once more carried into a higher
sphere, by finding an opportunity of purchasing some fine plaster
casts of antique heads. The Italians, who visit the fairs, often
brought with them good specimens of the kind, and sold them
cheap, after they had taken moulds of them. In this manner
I set up for myself a little museum, as I gradually brought
together the heads of the Laocoön, his sons, and Niobe's
daughters. I also bought miniature copies of the most important works of antiquity from the estate of a deceased friend of
art, and thus sought once more to revive, as much as possible,
the great impression which I had received at Mannheim.

While I now sought to cultivate, foster, and maintain all the
talent, taste, or other inclination that might live in me, I

applied a good part of the day, according to my father's wish,
in the duties of an advocate, for the practice of which I chanced
to find the best opportunity. After the death of my grandfather, my uncle Textor had come into the council, and consigned to me the little offices to which I was equal; while the
brothers Schlosser did the same. I made myself acquainted
with the documents; my father also read them with much pleasure, as by means of his son, he again saw himself in an activity
of which he had been long deprived. We talked the matters
over, and with great facility ; I then made the necessary statements. We had at hand an excellent copyist, on whom one
could rely for all legal formalities; and this occupation was the
more agreeable to me as it brought me closer to my father,
who, being perfectly satisfied with my conduct in this respect,
readily looked with an eye of indulgence on all my other pursuits, in the ardent expectation that I should now soon gather
in a harvest of fame as an author.

Because now, in every epoch, all things are connected together, since the ruling views and opinions are ramified in the
most various manner, so in the science of law those maxims
were gradually pursued, according to which religion and morals
were treated. Among the attorneys, as the younger people,
and then among the judges, as the elder, a spirit of humanity
was diffused, and all vied with each other in being as humane
as possible, even in legal affairs. Prisons were improved,
crimes excused, punishments lightened, legitimations rendered
easy, separations and *mésalliances* encouraged, and one of our
eminent lawyers gained for himself the highest fame, when
he contrived, by hard fighting, to gain for the son of an exe-
cutioner an entrance into the college of surgeons. In vain
did guilds and corporations oppose ; one dam after another
was broken through. The toleration of the religious parties
towards each other was not merely taught, but practised, and
the civil constitution was threatened with a still greater influence, when the effort was made to recommend to that good-
humoured age, with understanding, acuteness, and power,
toleration toward the Jews. Those new subjects for legal
treatment, which lay without the law and tradition, and only
laid claim to a fair examination, to a kindly sympathy, required
at the same time a more natural and animated style. Here
for us, the youngest, was opened a cheerful field, in which we

bustled about with delight, and I still recollect that an imperial councillor's agent, in a case of the sort, sent me a very polite letter of commendation. The French *plaidoyés* served us for patterns and for stimulants.

We were thus on the way to become better orators than jurists, a fact to which George Schlosser once called my attention, blaming me while doing so. I told him that I had read to my clients a controversial paper written with much energy in their favour, at which they had shown the greatest satisfaction. Upon this he replied to me, " In this case you have shown yourself more an author than an advocate. We must never ask how such a writing may please the client, but how it may please the judge."

As the occupations to which one devotes one's day are never so serious and pressing that one cannot find time enough in the evening to go to the play, thus was it also with me, who, in the want of a really good stage, did not cease thinking of the German theatre, in order to discover how one might cooperate upon it with any degree of activity. Its condition in the second half of the last century is sufficiently known, and every one who wishes to be instructed about it finds assistance at hand everywhere. On this account I only intend to insert here a few general remarks.

The success of the stage rested more upon the personality of the actors than upon the value of the pieces. This was especially the case with pieces half or wholly extemporized, when everything depended on the humour and talent of the comic actors. The matter of such pieces must be taken out of the commonest life, in conformity with the people before whom they are acted. From this immediate application arises the greatest applause, which these plays have always gained. They were always at home in South Germany, where they are retained to the present day; and the change of persons alone renders it necessary to give, from time to time, some change to the character of the comic masks. However, the German theatre, in conformity with the serious character of the nation, soon took a turn towards the moral, which was still more accelerated by an external cause. For the question arose, among strict Christians, whether the theatre belonged to those sinful things which are to be shunned, at all events, or to those indifferent things which can be good to the good and bad to the bad. Some zealots denied the latter, and held fast the opinion that no clergyman should ever enter the theatre. Now the opposite opinion could not be maintained with energy, unless the theatre was declared to be not only harmless, but even useful. To be useful, it must be moral; and in this direction it developed itself in North Germany the more as, by a sort of half-taste, the comic character* was banished, and although intelligent persons took his part, was forced to retire, having already gone from the coarseness of the German *hanswurst* (jack-pudding) into the neatness and delicacy of the Italian and French harlequins. Even Scapin and Crispin gradually vanished; the latter I saw played for the last time by Koch, in his old age.

Richardson's novels had already made the citizen-world attentive to a more delicate morality. The severe and inevitable consequences of a feminine *faux pas* were analysed in a frightful manner in *Clarissa*. Lessing's *Miss Sara Sampson* treated the same theme. The French dramas had the same end, but proceeded more moderately, and contrived to please by some accommodation at the end. Diderot's *Père de Famille*, the *Honourable Criminal*, the *Vinegar Dealer*, the *Philosopher without knowing it*, *Eugenie*, and other works of the sort, suited that honest feeling of citizen and family which began more and more to prevail. With us, the *Grateful Son*, the *Deserter from Parental Love*, and all of their kin, went the same way. The *Minister*, *Clementini*, and other pieces by Gehler, the *German Father of a Family*, by Gemming, all brought agreeably to view the worth of the middle and even of the lower class, and delighted the great public. Eckhoff, by his noble personality, which gave to the actor's profession a dignity in which it had hitherto been deficient, elevated to an uncommon degree the leading characters in such pieces, since, as an honest man, the expression of honesty succeeded with him to perfection.

While now the German theatre was completely inclining to effeminacy, Schröder arose as an author and actor, and on the occasion of the connexion between Hamburg and England, adapted some English comedies. The material of these he

* " Die lustige person." That is to say, the permanent buffoon, like "Kasperle" in the German puppet shows, or "Sganarelle" in Moliere's broad comedies.—*Trans.*

could only use in the most general way, since the originals are for the most part formless, and if they begin well and according to a certain plan, they wander from the mark at last. The sole concern of their authors seems to be the introduction of the oddest scenes; and whoever is accustomed to a sustained work of art, at last unwillingly finds himself driven into the boundless. Besides this, a wild, immoral, vulgarly dissolute tone so decidedly pervades the whole, to an intolerable degree, that it must have been difficult to deprive the plan and the characters of all their bad manners. They are a coarse and at the same time dangerous food, which can only be enjoyed and digested by a large and half-corrupted populace at a certain time. Schröder did more for these things than is usually known; he thoroughly altered them, assimilated them to the German mind, and softened them as much as possible. But still a bitter kernel always remains in them, because the joke often depends on the ill-usage of persons, whether they deserve it or not. In these performances, which were also widely spread upon our stage, lay a secret counterpoise to that too delicate morality; and the action of both kinds of drama against each other fortunately prevented the monotony into which people would otherwise have fallen.

The German, kind and magnanimous by nature, likes to see no one ill-treated. But as no man, however well he thinks, is secure that something may not be put upon him against his inclination, and as, moreover, comedy in general, if it is to please, always presupposes or awakens something of malice in the spectator, so, by a natural path, did people come to a conduct which hitherto had been deemed unnatural; this consisted in lowering the higher classes, and more or less attacking them. Satire, whether in prose or verse, had always avoided touching the court and nobility. Rabener refrained from all jokes in that direction, and remained in a lower circle. Zacharia occupies himself much with caricaturing noblemen, comically sets forth their tastes and peculiarities; but this is done without contempt. Thummel's *Wilhelmine*, an ingenious little composition, as pleasant as it is bold, gained great applause, perhaps because the author, himself a nobleman and courtier, treated his own class unsparingly. But the boldest step was taken by Lessing, in his *Emilia Galotti*, where the passions and intrigues of the higher classes are

delineated in a bitter and cutting manner. All these things
perfectly corresponded to the excited spirit of the time; and
men of less mind and talent thought they might do the same,
or even more; as indeed Grossmann, in six unsavoury dishes,
served up to the malicious public all the tidbits of his vulgar
kitchen. An honest man, Hofrath Reinhardt, was the major-
domo at this unpleasant board, to the comfort and edification
of all the guests. From this time forward the theatrical villains
were always chosen from the higher ranks; and a person
must be a gentleman of the bedchamber, or at least a private
secretary, to be worthy of such a distinction. But for the
most godless examples, the highest offices and places in the
court and civil list were chosen, in which high society, even
the justiciaries, found their place as villains of the first water.

But as I must fear already that I have been carried beyond
the time which is now the subject in hand, I return back to
myself, to mention the impulse which I felt to occupy myself
in my leisure hours with the theatrical plans which I had once
devised.

By my lasting interest in Shakspeare's works, I had so
expanded my mind, that the narrow compass of the stage and
the short time allotted to a representation, seemed to me by
no means sufficient to bring forward something important.
The life of the gallant Götz von Berlichingen, written by
himself, impelled me into the historic mode of treatment; and
my imagination so much extended itself, that my dramatic
form also went beyond all theatrical bounds, and sought more
and more to approach the living events. I had, as I proceeded,
talked circumstantially on this subject with my sister, who
was interested, heart and soul, in such things, and renewed
this conversation so often, without going to any work, that she
at last, growing impatient, and at the same time wishing me
well, urgently entreated me not to be always casting my words
into the air, but, once for all, to set down upon paper that
which must have been so present to my mind. Determined
by this impulse, I began one morning to write, without
having made any previous sketch or plan. I wrote the first
scenes, and in the evening they were read aloud to Cornelia.
She gave them much applause, but only conditionally, since
she doubted that I should go on so; nay, she even expressed
a decided unbelief in my perseverance. This only incited me

the more ; I wrote on the next day, and also the third. Hope
increased with the daily communications, and from step to
step everything gained more life, while the matter, moreover,
had become thoroughly my own. Thus I kept, without interruption, to my work, which I pursued straight on, looking
neither backwards nor forwards,—neither to the right nor to
the left ; and in about six weeks I had the pleasure to see the
manuscript stitched. I communicated it to Merk, who spoke
sensibly and kindly about it. I sent it to Herder, who, on
the contrary, expressed himself unkindly and severely, and
did not fail, in some lampoons written for the occasion, to
give me nicknames on account of it. I did not allow myself
to be perplexed by this, but took a clear view of my object.
The die was now cast, and the only question was how to play
the game best. I plainly saw that even here no one would
advise me ; and, as after some time I could regard my work
as if it had proceeded from another hand, I indeed perceived
that in my attempt to renounce unity of time and place, I had
also infringed upon that higher unity which is so much the
more required. Since, without plan or sketch, I had merely
abandoned myself to my imagination and to an internal impulse, I had not deviated much at the beginning, and the first
acts could fairly pass for what they were intended to be. In
the following acts, however, and especially towards the end,
I was unconsciously carried along by a wonderful passion.
While trying to describe Adelheid as amiable, I had fallen
in love with her myself,—my pen was involuntarily devoted
to her alone,—the interest in her fate gained the preponderance ; and as, apart from this consideration, Götz, towards
the end, is without activity, and afterwards only returns to an
unlucky participation in the *Bauernkrieg*,* nothing was more
natural than that a charming woman should supplant him in
the mind of the author, who, casting off the fetters of art,
thought to try himself in a new field. This defect, or rather
this culpable superfluity, I soon perceived, since the nature of
my poetry always impelled me to unity. I now, instead of the
biography of Götz and German antiquities, kept my own work
in mind, and sought to give it more and more historical and
national substance, and to cancel that which was fabulous or
merely proceeded from passion. In this I indeed sacrificed
much, as the inclination of the man had to yield to the con-

* The peasant-war, answering to the *Jaquerie* in France.—*Trans.*

2 K

viction of the artist. Thus, for instance, I had pleased myself
highly by making Adelheid enter into a terrific nocturnal
gipsy-scene, and perform wonders by her beautiful presence.
A nearer examination banished her; and the love-affair between Franz and his noble, gracious lady, which was very
circumstantially carried on in the fourth and fifth acts, was
much condensed, and could only be suffered to appear in its
chief points.

Therefore, without altering anything in the first manuscript, which I still actually possess in its original shape, I
determined to rewrite the whole, and did this with such activity, that in a few weeks an entirely new-made piece lay
before me. I went to work upon this all the quicker, the
less my intention was ever to have the second poem printed,
as I looked upon this likewise as a mere preparatory exercise,
which in future I should again lay at the foundation of a
new treatment, to be accomplished with greater industry and
deliberation.

When I began to lay before Merk many proposals as to the
way in which I should set about this task, he laughed at me,
and asked what was the meaning of this perpetual writing
and rewriting? The thing, he said, by this means, becomes
only different, and seldom better; one must see what effect
one thing produces, and then again try something new. " Be
in time at the hedge, if you would dry your linen."* he exclaimed, in the words of the proverb; hesitation and delay
only make uncertain men. On the other hand, I replied to
him that it would be unpleasant to me to offer to a bookseller
a work on which I had bestowed so much affection, and perhaps to receive a refusal as an answer; for how would they
judge of a young, nameless, and also audacious author? As
my dread of the press gradually vanished, I had wished to see
printed my comedy *Die Mitschuldigen*, upon which I set some
value, but I found no publisher inclined in my favour.

Here the technically mercantile taste of my friend was at
once excited. By means of the *Frankfort Zeitung* (Gazette),
he had already formed a connexion with learned men and
booksellers, and therefore he thought that we ought to publish
at our own expense this singular and certainly striking work,
and that we should derive a larger profit from it. Like many
others, he used often to reckon up for the booksellers their

* *Anglicé:* Make hay when the sun shines.—*Trans.*

profit, which with many works was certainly great, especially
if one left out of the account how much was lost by other
writings and commercial affairs.   Enough, it was settled that
I should procure the paper, and that he should take care of
the printing.   Thus we went heartily to work, and I was not
displeased gradually to see my wild dramatic sketch in clean
proof-sheets ; it looked really neater than I myself expected.
We completed the work, and it was sent off in many parcels.
Before long a great commotion arose everywhere ; the attention which it created became universal.   But because, with
our limited means, the copies could not be sent quick enough
to all parts, a pirated edition suddenly made its appearance.
As, moreover, there could be no immediate return, especially
in ready money, for the copies sent out, so was I, as a young
man in a family whose treasury could not be in an abundant
condition, at the very time when much attention, nay, much
applause was bestowed upon me, extremely perplexed as to how
I should pay for the paper by means of which I had made the
world acquainted with my talent.   On the other hand, Merk,
who knew better how to help himself, entertained the best
hopes that all would soon come right again; but I never
perceived that to be the case.

Through the little pamphlets which I had published anonymously, I had, at my own expense, learned to know the critics
and the public ; and I was thus pretty well prepared for praise
and blame, especially as for many years I had constantly followed up the subject, and had observed how those authors
were treated, to whom I had devoted particular attention.

Here even in my uncertainty, I could plainly remark how
much that was groundless, one-sided, and arbitrary, was recklessly uttered.   Now the same thing befel me, and if I had
not had some basis of my own, how much would the contradictions of cultivated men have perplexed me!   Thus, for
instance, there was in the *German Mercury* a diffuse, well-
meant criticism, composed by some man of limited mind.
Where he found fault, I could not agree with him,—still less
when he stated how the affair could have been done otherwise.   It was therefore highly gratifying to me, when immediately afterwards I found a pleasant explanation by Wieland,
who in general opposed the critic, and took my part against
him.   However, the former review was printed likewise ; I saw
an example of the dull state of mind among well-informed

and cultivated men.   How, then, would it look with the great
public !

The pleasure of talking over such things with Merk, and
thus gaining light upon them, was of short duration, for the
intelligent Landgravine of Hesse-Darmstadt took him with
her train on her journey to Petersburg.   The detailed letters
which he wrote to me gave me a further insight into the
world, which I could the more make my own as the descriptions were made by a well-known and friendly hand.   But
nevertheless I remained very solitary for a long time, and just
at this important epoch was deprived of his enlightening
sympathy, of which I then stood in so much need.

Just as one embraces the determination to become a soldier,
and go to the wars, and courageously resolves to bear danger
and difficulties, as well as to endure wounds and pains, and
even death, but at the same time never calls to mind the particular cases in which those generally anticipated evils may
surprise us in an extremely unpleasant manner.—so it is with
every one who ventures into the world, especially an author :
and so it was with me.   As the great part of mankind is more
excited by a subject than by the treatment of it, so it was to
the subject that the sympathy of young men for my pieces was
generally owing.   They thought they could see in them a
banner, under the guidance of which all that is wild and un-
polished in youth might find a vent ; and those of the very best
brains, who had previously harboured a similar crotchet, were
thus carried away.   I still possess a letter—I know not to
whom—from the excellent and, in many respects, unique
Bürger, which may serve as an important voucher of the effect
and excitement which was then produced by that phenomenon.
On the other side, some men blamed me for painting the club-
law in too favourable colours, and even attributed to me the
intention of bringing those disorderly times back again.   Others
took me for a profoundly learned man, and wished me to publish a new edition, with notes, of the original narrative of the
good Götz :—a task to which I felt by no means adapted,
although I allowed my name to be put on the title to the new
impression.   Because I had understood how to gather the
flowers of a great existence, they took me for a careful gardener.   However, this learning and profound knowledge of
mine were much doubted by others.   A respectable man of
business quite unexpectedly pays me a visit.   I find myself

highly honoured by this, especially as he opens his discourse
with the praise of my *Götz von Berlichingen*, and my good
insight into German history, but I am nevertheless astonished
when I remark that he has really come for the sole purpose of informing me that Götz von Berlichingen was no brother-in-law
to Franz von Sichingen, and that therefore by this poetical
matrimonial alliance I have committed a great historical error.
I sought to excuse myself by the fact, that Götz himself calls
him so, but was met by the reply, that this is a form of expression which only denotes a nearer and more friendly connexion, just as in modern times we call postilions " brothers-
in-law,"* without being bound to them by any family tie.
I thanked him as well as I could for this information, and only
regretted that the evil was now not to be remedied. This was
regretted by him also, while he exhorted me in the kindest
manner to a further study of the German history and constitution, and offered me his library, of which I afterwards made
a good use.

A droll event of the sort which occurred to me was the visit
of a bookseller, who, with cheerful openness, requested a dozen
of such pieces, and promised to pay well for them. That we
made ourselves very merry about this may be imagined ; and
yet, in fact, he was not so very far wrong, for I was already
greatly occupied in moving backwards and forwards from this
turning-point in German history, and in working up the chief
events in a similar spirit—a laudable design, which, like many
others, was frustrated by the rushing flight of time.

That play, however, had not solely occupied the author, but
while it was devised, written, rewritten, printed, and circulated,
other images and plans were moving in his mind. Those
which could be treated dramatically had the advantage of being
oftenest thought over and brought near to execution ; but at the
same time was developed a transition to another form, which
is not usually classed with those of the drama, but yet has a
great affinity with them. This transition was chiefly brought
about by a peculiarity of the author, which fashioned soliloquy
into dialogue.

Accustomed to pass his time most pleasantly in society, he
changed even solitary thought into social converse, and this in
the following manner :—He had the habit, when he was alone,

* It is a German peculiarity to apply the word " Schwager " (brother-
in-law) to a postilion.—*Trans.*

of calling before his mind any person of his acquaintance. This person he entreated to sit down, walked up and down by him, remained standing before him, and discoursed with him on the subject he had in his mind. To this the person answered as occasion required, or by the ordinary gestures signified his assent or dissent ;—in which every man has something peculiar to himself. The speaker then continued to carry out further that which seemed to please the guest, or to condition and define more closely that of which he disapproved ; and, finally, was polite enough to give up his notion. The oddest part of the affair was, that he never selected persons of his intimate acquaintance, but those whom he saw but seldom, nay, several who lived at a distance in the world, and with whom he had had a transient connexion. They were, however, chiefly persons who, more of a receptive than communicative nature, are ready with a pure feeling to take interest in the things which fall within their sphere, though he often summoned contradicting spirits to these dialectic exercises. Persons of both sexes, of every age and rank accommodated themselves to these discussions, and showed themselves obliging and agreeable, since he only conversed on subjects which were clear to them, and which they liked. Nevertheless, it would have appeared extremely strange to many of them, could they have learned how often they were summoned to these ideal conversations, since many of them would scarcely have come to a real one.

How nearly such a mental dialogue is akin to a written correspondence, is clear enough ; only in the latter one sees returned the confidence one has bestowed, while in the former, one creates for oneself a confidence which is new, ever-changing, and unreturned. When, therefore, he had to describe that disgust which men, without being driven by necessity, feel for life, the author necessarily hit at once upon the plan of giving his sentiments in letters ; for all gloominess is a birth, a pupil of solitude—and what is more opposed to it than a cheerful society ? The enjoyment in life felt by others is to him a painful reproach ; and thus, by that which should charm him out of himself, he is directed back to his inmost soul. If he at all expresses himself on this matter, it will be by letters ; for no one feels immediately opposed to a written effusion, whether it be joyful or gloomy, while an answer containing opposite reasons gives the lonely one an opportunity to confirm himself in his whims,—an occasion to grow still more obdurate. The letters of Werther, which are written in this spirit, have so various a charm, precisely because their different contents were first talked over with several individuals in such ideal dialogues, while it was afterwards in the composition itself that they appeared to be directed to one friend and sympathizer. To say more on the treatment of a little book which has formed the subject of so much discussion, would be hardly advisable, but, with respect to the contents, something may yet be added.

That disgust at life has its physical and its moral causes; the former we will leave to the investigation of the physician, the latter to that of the moralist, and in a matter so often elaborated, only consider the chief point, where the phenomenon most plainly expresses itself. All comfort in life is based upon a regular recurrence of external things. The change of day and night—of the seasons, of flowers and fruits, and whatever else meets us from epoch to epoch, so that we can and should enjoy it—these are the proper springs of earthly life. The more open we are to these enjoyments, the happier do we feel ourselves; but if the changes in these phenomena roll up and down before us without our taking interest in them, if we are insensible to such beautiful offers, then comes on the greatest evil, the heaviest disease—we regard life as a disgusting burden. It is said of an Englishman, that he hanged himself that he might no longer dress and undress himself every day. I knew a worthy gardener, the superintendent of the laying out of a large park, who once cried out with vexation, "Shall I always see these clouds moving from east to west?" The story is told of one of our most excellent men, that he saw with vexation the returning green of spring, and wished that, by way of change, it might once appear red. These are properly the symptoms of a weariness of life, which does not unfrequently result in suicide, and which, in thinking men, absorbed in themselves, was more frequent than can be imagined.

Nothing occasions this weariness more than the return of love. The first love, it is rightly said, is the only one, for in the second, and by the second, the highest sense of love is already lost. The conception of the eternal and infinite, which elevates and supports it, is destroyed, and it appears transient like everything else that recurs. The separation of the sensual from the moral, which, in the complicated, cultivated world sunders the feelings of love and desire, produces here also an exaggeration which can lead to no good.

Moreover, a young man soon perceives in others, if not in himself, that moral epochs change as well as the seasons of the year. The graciousness of the great, the favour of the strong, the encouragement of the active, the attachment of the multitude, the love of individuals—all this changes up and down, and we can no more hold it fast than the sun, moon, and stars. And yet these things are not mere natural events; they escape us either by our own or by another's fault; but change they do, and we are never sure of them.

But that which most pains a sensitive youth is the unceasing return of our faults; for how late do we learn to see that while we cultivate our virtues, we rear our faults at the same time. The former depend upon the latter as upon their root, and the latter send forth secret ramifications as strong and as various as those which the former send forth in open light. Because now we generally practise our virtues with will and consciousness, but are unconsciously surprised by our faults, the former seldom procure us any pleasure, while the latter constantly bring trouble and pain. Here lies the most difficult point in self-knowledge, that which makes it almost impossible. If we conceive, in addition to all this, a young, boiling blood, an imagination easily to be paralyzed by single objects, and, moreover, the uncertain movements of the day, we shall not find unnatural an impatient striving to free oneself from such a strait.

However, such gloomy contemplations, which lead him who has resigned himself to them into the infinite, could not have developed themselves so decidedly in the minds of the German youths, had not an outward occasion excited and furthered them in this dismal business. This was caused by English literature, especially the poetical part, the great beauties of which are accompanied by an earnest melancholy, which it communicates to every one who occupies himself with it. The intellectual Briton, from his youth upwards, sees himself surrounded by a significant world, which stimulates all his powers; he perceives, sooner or later, that he must collect all his understanding to come to terms with it. How many of their poets have in their youth led a loose and riotous life, and soon found themselves justified in complaining of the vanity of earthly things? How many of them have tried their fortune in worldly occupations, have taken parts, principal or subordinate, in parliament, at court, in the ministry, in situations with the

embassy, shown their active co-operation in the internal
troubles and changes of state and government, and if not in
themselves, at any rate in their friends and patrons, frequently
made sad and pleasant experiences! How many have been
banished, imprisoned, or injured with respect to property!

Even the circumstance of being the spectator of such great
events calls man to seriousness; and whither can seriousness
lead farther than to a contemplation of the transient nature and
worthlessness of all earthly things? The German also is serious, and thus English poetry was extremely suitable to him,
and, because it proceeded from a higher state of things, even imposing. One finds in it throughout a great, apt understanding,
well practised in the world, a deep, tender heart, an excellent
will, an impassioned action,—the very noblest qualities which
can be praised in an intellectual and cultivated man; but all this
put together still makes no poet. True poetry announces itself
thus, that, as a worldly gospel, it can by internal cheerfulness
and external comfort free us from the earthly burdens which
press upon us. Like an air-balloon, it lifts us, together with
the ballast which is attached to us, into higher regions, and
lets the confused labyrinths of the earth lie developed before us
as in a bird's-eye view. The most lively, as well as the most
serious works, have the same aim of moderating both pleasure
and pain by a felicitous intellectual form. Let us only in this
spirit consider the majority of the English poems, chiefly
morally didactic, and on the average they will only show us a
gloomy weariness of life. Not only Young's *Night Thoughts*,
where this theme is pre-eminently worked out, but even the
other contemplative poems stray, before one is aware of it, into
this dismal region, where the understanding is presented with
a problem which it cannot solve, since even religion, much as it
can always construct for itself, leaves it in the lurch. Whole
volumes might be compiled, which could serve as a commen-
tary to this frightful text—

> " Then old age and experience, hand in hand,
> Lead him to death, and make him understand,
> After a search so painful and so long,
> That all his life he has been in the wrong."

What further makes the English poets accomplished misan-
thropes, and diffuses over their writings the unpleasant feeling
of repugnance against everything, is the fact that the whole of
them, on account of the various divisions of their common-

wealth, must devote themselves for the best part, if not for the whole of their lives, to one party or another. Because now a writer of the sort cannot praise and extol those of the party to which he belongs, nor the cause to which he adheres, since, if he did, he would only excite envy and hostility, he exercises his talent in speaking as badly as possible of those on the opposite side, and in sharpening, nay, poisoning the satirical weapons as much as he can. When this is done by both parties, the world which lies between is destroyed and wholly annihilated, so that in a great mass of sensibly active people, one can discover, to use the mildest terms, nothing but folly and madness. Even their tender poems are occupied with mournful subjects. Here a deserted girl is dying, there a faithful lover is drowned, or is devoured by a shark before, by his hurried swimming, he reaches his beloved ; and if a poet like Gray lies down in a churchyard, and again begins those well-known melodies, he too may gather round him a number of friends to melancholy. Milton's *Allegro* must scare away gloom in vehement verses, before he can attain a very moderate pleasure ; and even the cheerful Goldsmith loses himself in elegiac feelings, when his *Deserted Village*, as charmingly as sadly, exhibits to us a lost Paradise which his *Traveller* seeks over the whole earth.

I do not doubt that lively works, cheerful poems, can be brought forward and opposed to what I have said, but the greatest number, and the best of them, certainly belong to the older epoch; and the newer works, which may be set down in the class, are likewise of a satirical tendency, are bitter, and treat women especially with contempt.

Enough : those serious poems, undermining human nature, which, in general terms, have been mentioned above, were the favourites which we sought out before all others, one seeking, according to his disposition, the lighter elegiac melancholy, another the heavy oppressive despair, which gives up everything. Strangely enough, our father and instructor, Shakspeare, who so well knew how to diffuse a pure cheerfulness, strengthened our feeling of dissatisfaction. Hamlet and his soliloquies were spectres which haunted all the young minds. The chief passages every one knew by heart and loved to recite, and every body fancied he had a right to be just as melancholy as the Prince of Denmark, though he had seen no ghost, and had no royal father to avenge.

But that to all this melancholy a perfectly suitable locality might not be wanting. Ossian had charmed us even to the *Ultima Thule*, where on a gray, boundless heath, wandering among prominent moss-covered grave-stones, we saw the grass around us moved by an awful wind, and a heavily clouded sky above us. It was not till moonlight that the Caledonian night became day: departed heroes, faded maidens, floated around us, until at last we really thought we saw the spirit of Loda in his fearful form.

In such an element, with such surrounding influences, with tastes and studies of this kind, tortured by unsatisfied passions, by no means excited from without to important actions, with the sole prospect that we must adhere to a dull, spiritless, citizen life, we became—in gloomy wantonness—attached to the thought, that we could at all events quit life at pleasure, if it no longer suited us, and thus miserably enough helped ourselves through the disgusts and weariness of the days. This feeling was so general, that *Werther* produced its great effect precisely because it struck a chord everywhere, and openly and intelligibly exhibited the internal nature of a morbid youthful delusion. How accurately the English were acquainted with this sort of wretchedness is shown by the few significant lines, written before the appearance of *Werther*—

> " To griefs congenial prone,
> More wounds than nature gave he knew,
> While misery's form his fancy drew
> In dark ideal hues and horrors not its own."

Suicide is an event of human nature which, whatever may be said and done with respect to it, demands the sympathy of every man, and in every epoch must be discussed anew. Montesquieu grants his heroes and great men the right of killing themselves as they think fit, since he says that it must be free to every one to close the fifth act of his tragedy as he pleases. But here the discourse is not of those persons who have led an active and important life, who have sacrificed their days for a great empire, or for the cause of freedom, and whom one cannot blame if they think to follow in another world the idea which inspires them, as soon as it has vanished from the earth. We have here to do with those whose life is embittered by a want of action, in the midst of the most peaceful circumstances in the world, through exaggerated demands upon themselves. Since I myself was in this predicament, and best knew the

pain I suffered in it, and the exertion it cost me to free myself,
I will not conceal the reflections which I made, with much
deliberation, on the various kinds of death which one might
choose.

There is something so unnatural in a man tearing himself
away from himself, not only injuring, but destroying himself,
that he mostly seizes upon mechanical means to carry his
design into execution. When Ajax falls upon his sword, it
is the weight of his body which does him the last service.
When the warrior binds his shield-bearer not to let him fall
into the hands of the enemy, it is still an external force which
he secures, only a moral instead of a physical one. Women
seek in water a cooling for their despair, and the extremely
mechanical means of fire-arms ensure a rapid act with the
very least exertion. Hanging, one does not like to mention,
because it is an ignoble death. In England one may first find
it, because there, from youth upwards, one sees so many
hanged, without the punishment being precisely dishonourable.
By poison, by opening the veins, the only intention is to depart
slowly from life; and that most refined, rapid, and painless
death by an adder, was worthy of a queen, who had passed
her life in pleasure and brilliancy. But all these are external
aids, enemies with which man forms an alliance against
himself.

When now I considered all these means, and looked about
further in history, I found among all those who killed themselves no one who did this deed with such greatness and
freedom of mind, as the Emperor Otho. He, having the
worst of it as a general, but being by no means reduced to
extremities, resolves to quit the world for the benefit of the
empire, which, in some measure, already belongs to him, and
for the sake of sparing so many thousands. He has a cheerful
supper with his friends, and the next morning it is found that
he has plunged a sharp dagger into his heart. This deed
alone seemed to me worthy of imitation; and I was convinced
that whoever could not act in this like Otho, had no right to
go voluntarily out of the world. By these convictions, I freed
myself not so much from the danger as from the whim of suicide, which in those splendid times of peace, and with an
indolent youth, had managed to creep in. Among a considerable collection of weapons, I possessed a handsome, well
polished dagger. This I laid every night by my bed, and

before I extinguished the candle, I tried whether I could
succeed in plunging the sharp point a couple of inches deep
into my heart. Since I never could succeed in this, I at last
laughed myself out of the notion, threw off all hypochondriacal
fancies, and resolved to live. But to be able to do this with
cheerfulness, I was obliged to solve a poetical problem, by
which all that I had felt, thought, and fancied upon this important point, should be reduced to words. For this purpose
I collected the elements which had been at work in me for a
few years; I rendered present to my mind the cases which had
most afflicted and tormented me; but nothing would come to
a definite form; I lacked an event, a fable, in which they could
be overlooked.

All at once I heard the news of Jerusalem's death, and immediately after the general report, the most accurate and
circumstantial description of the occurrence, and at this
moment the plan of *Werther* was formed, and the whole shot
together from all sides, and became a solid mass, just as water
in a vessel, which stands upon the point of freezing, is converted into hard ice by the most gentle shake. To hold fast
this singular prize, to render present to myself, and to carry
out in all its parts a work of such important and various contents was the more material to me, as I had again fallen into a
painful situation, which left me even less hope than those
which had preceded it, and foreboded only sadness, if not
vexation.

It is always a misfortune to step into new relations to which
one has not been inured; we are often against our will lured
into a false sympathy, the incompleteness* of such positions
troubles us, and yet we see no means either of completing
them or of removing them.

Frau von Laroche had married her eldest daughter at
Frankfort, and often came to visit her, but could not reconcile
herself to the position which she herself had chosen. Instead
of feeling comfortable, or endeavouring to make any alteration,
she indulged in lamentations, so that one was really forced to
think that her daughter was unhappy; although, as she wanted
nothing, and her husband denied her nothing, one could not
well see in what her unhappiness properly consisted. In the
meanwhile I was well received in the house, and came into

* "*Halbheit*," "Halfness"—if there were such a word—would be the
proper expression.—*Trans.*

contact with the whole circle, which consisted of persons who
had partly contributed to the marriage, partly wished for it a
happy result. The Dean of St. Leonhard Dumeix conceived
a confidence, nay, a friendship for me. He was the first
Catholic clergyman with whom I had come into close contact,
and who, because he was a clear-sighted man, gave me beautiful and sufficient explanations of the faith, usages, and external and internal relations of the oldest church. The figure of
a well-formed though not young lady, named Serviéres, I still
accurately remember. I likewise came into contact with the
Alosino-Schweizer, and other families, forming a connexion
with the sons, which long continued in the most friendly
manner, and all at once found myself domesticated in a strange
circle, in the occupations, pleasures, and even religious exercises of which I was induced, nay, compelled to take part.
My former relation to the young wife, which was, properly
speaking, only that of a brother to a sister, was continued
after marriage ; my age was suitable to her own ; I was the
only one in the whole circle in whom she heard an echo of
those intellectual tones to which she had been accustomed
from her youth. We lived on together in a childish confidence, and although there was nothing impassioned in our
intercourse, it was tormenting enough, because she also could
not reconcile herself to her new circumstances, and although
blessed with the goods of fortune, had to act as the mother of
several step-children, being moreover transplanted from the
cheerful vale of Ehrenbreitstein and a joyous state of youth
into a gloomily-situated mercantile house. Amid so many
new family connexions was I hemmed in, without any real
participation or co-operation. If they were satisfied with
each other, all seemed to go on as a matter of course ; but
most of the parties concerned turned to me in cases of vexation, which by my lively sympathy I generally rendered worse
rather than better. In a short time this situation became
quite insupportable to me; all the disgust at life which usually
springs from such half-connexions, seemed to burden me with
double and three fold weight, and a new strong resolution was
necessary to free myself from it.

Jerusalem's death, which was occasioned by his unhappy
attachment to the wife of his friend, shook me out of the
dream, and, because I not only visibly contemplated that
which had occurred to him and me, but something similar

which befel me at the moment, also stirred me to passionate emotion. I could not do otherwise than breathe into that production, which I had just undertaken, all that warmth which leaves no distinction between the poetical and the actual. I had completely isolated myself, nay, prohibited the visits of my friends, and internally also I put everything aside that did not immediately belong to the subject. On the other hand, I embraced everything that had any relation to my design, and repeated to myself my nearest life, of the contents of which I had as yet made no practical use. Under such circumstances, after such long and so many preparations in secret, I wrote *Werther* in four weeks without any scheme of the whole, or treatment of any part, being previously put on paper.

The manuscript, which was now finished, lay before me as a rough draught, with few corrections and alterations. It was stitched at once, for the binding is to a written work of about the same use as the frame is to a picture; one can much better see whether there is really anything in it. Since I had written thus much, almost unconsciously, like a somnambulist, I was myself astonished, now I went through it, that I might alter and improve it in some respects. But in the expectation that after some time, when I had seen it at a certain distance, much would occur to me that would turn to the advantage of the work, I gave it to my younger friends to read, upon whom it produced an effect so much the greater, as, contrary to my usual custom, I had told no one of it, nor discovered my design beforehand. Yet here again it was the subject-matter which really produced the effect, and in this respect they were in a frame of mind precisely the reverse of my own; for by this composition, more than by any other, I had freed myself from that stormy element, upon which, through my own fault and that of others, through a mode of life both accidental and chosen, through design and thoughtless precipitation, through obstinacy and pliability, I had been driven about in the most violent manner. I felt, as if after a general confession, once more happy and free, and justified in beginning a new life. The old household had been of excellent service to me on this occasion. But while I felt myself eased and enlightened by having turned reality into poetry, my friends were led astray by my work, for they thought that poetry ought to be turned into reality, that such a moral was to be imitated, and that at

any rate one ought to shoot oneself. What had first happened here among a few, afterwards took place among the
larger public, and this little book, which had been so beneficial
to me, was decried as extremely injurious.

But all the evils and misfortunes which it may have produced were nearly prevented by an accident, since even after
its production it ran the risk of being destroyed. The matter
stood thus :—Merk had lately returned from Petersburg; I
had spoken to him but little, because he was always occupied,
and only told him, in the most general terms, of that *Werther*
which lay next my heart. He once called upon me, and as
he did not seem very talkative, I asked him to listen to me.
He seated himself on the sofa, and I began to read the tale,
letter by letter. After I had gone on thus for a while, without
gaining from him any sign of admiration, I adopted a more
pathetic strain,—but what were my feelings, when at a pause
which I made, he struck me down in the most frightful manner, with "Good! that's very pretty," and withdrew without
adding anything more. I was quite beside myself, for, as I
took great pleasure in my works, but at first passed no judgment on them, I here firmly believed that I had made a mistake in subject, tone, and style—all of which were doubtful—
and had produced something quite inadmissible. Had a fire
been at hand, I should at once have thrown in the work; but
I again plucked up courage, and passed many painful days,
until he at last assured me in confidence, that at that moment
he had been in the most frightful situation in which a man
can be placed. On this account, he said, he had neither
seen nor heard anything, and did not even know what the
manuscript was about. In the meanwhile the matter had
been set right, as far as was possible, and Merk, in the times
of his energy, was just the man to accommodate himself to
anything monstrous : his humour returned, only it had grown
still more bitter than before. He blamed my design of rewriting *Werther*, with the same expressions which he had
used on a former occasion, and desired to see it printed just
as it was. A fair copy was made, which did not remain long
in my hands, for on the very day on which my sister was married to George Schlosser, a letter from Weygand, of Leipzig,
chanced to arrive, in which he asked me for a manuscript;
such a coincidence I looked upon as a favourable omen. I
sent off *Werther*, and was very well satisfied, when the remu-

neration I received for it was not entirely swallowed up by
the debts which I had been forced to contract on account of
Götz von Berlichingen.

The effect of this little book was great, nay immense, and
chiefly because it exactly hit the temper of the times. For as
it requires but a little match to blow up an immense mine, so
the explosion which followed my publication was mighty,
from the circumstance that the youthful world had already
undermined itself; and the shock was great, because all extravagant demands, unsatisfied passions, and imaginary wrongs,
were suddenly brought to an eruption. It cannot be expected
of the public that it should receive an intellectual work intellectually. In fact, it was only the subject, the material part,
that was considered, as I had already found to be the case
among my own friends; while at the same time arose that old
prejudice, associated with the dignity of a printed book,—
that it ought to have a moral aim. But a true picture of life
has none. It neither approves nor censures, but developes
sentiments and actions in their consequences, and thereby
enlightens and instructs.

Of the reviews I took little notice. I had completely
washed my hands of the matter, and the good folks might
now try what they could make of it. Yet my friends did not
fail to collect these things, and as they were already initiated
into my views, to make merry with them. The *Joys of
Young Werther,* with which Nicolai came forth, gave us occasion for many a jest. This otherwise excellent, meritorious,
and well-informed man, had already begun to depreciate and
oppose everything that did not accord with his own way of
thinking, which, as he was of a very narrow mind, he held to
be the only correct way. Against me, too, he must needs try
his strength, and his pamphlet was soon in our hands. The
very delicate vignette, by Chodowiecki, gave me much delight;
as at that time I admired this artist extravagantly. The
jumbling medley itself was cut out of that rough household stuff, which the human understanding, in its homely
limits, takes especial pains to make sufficiently coarse.
Without perceiving that there was nothing here to qualify,
that Werther's youthful bloom, from the very first, appears
gnawed by the deadly worm, Nicolai allows my treatment to
pass current up to the two hundred and fourteenth page, and
then, when the desolate mortal is preparing for the fatal step,

the acute psychological physician contrives to palm upon his
patient a pistol, loaded with chickens' blood, from which a
filthy spectacle, but happily no mischief, arises. Charlotte
becomes the wife of Werther, and the whole affair ends to the
satisfaction of everybody.

So much I can recall to memory, for the book never came
before my eyes again. I had cut out the vignette, and placed it
among my most favourite engravings. I then, by way of quiet,
innocent revenge, composed a little burlesque poem, "Nicolai at
the grave of Werther;" which, however, cannot be communicated. On this occasion, too, the pleasure of giving everything
a dramatic shape, was again predominant. I wrote a prose
dialogue between Charlotte and Werther, which was tolerably
comical; Werther bitterly complains that his deliverance by
chickens' blood has turned out so badly. His life is saved, it is
true, but he has shot his eyes out. He is now in despair at
being her husband, without being able to see her; for the
complete view of her person would to him be much dearer
than all those pretty details of which he could assure himself
by the touch. Charlotte, as may be imagined, has no great
catch in a blind husband, and thus occasion is given to abuse
Nicolai pretty roundly, for interfering unasked in other people's affairs. The whole was written in a good-natured spirit,
and painted, with prophetic forebodings, that unhappy, con-
ceited humour of Nicolai's, which led him to meddle with
things beyond his compass, which gave great annoyance both
to himself and others, and by which, eventually, in spite of his
undoubted merits, he entirely destroyed his literary reputation. The original of this *jeu d'esprit* was never copied,
and has been lost sight of for years. I had a special predilection for the little production. The pure, ardent attachment of the two young persons, was rather heightened than
diminished by the comico-tragic situation into which they were
thus transposed. The greatest tenderness prevailed throughout; and even my adversary was not treated illnaturedly, but
only humorously. I did not, however, let the book itself
speak quite so politely; in imitation of an old rhyme it
expressed itself thus :—

> " By that conceited man—by *him*
> I'm dangerous declar'd,
> The heavy man, who cannot swim,
> Is by the water scar'd,

That Berlin pack, priest-ridden lot—
Their ban I do not heed,
And those who understand me not
Should better learn to read."

Being prepared for all that might be alleged against *Werther*, I found those attacks, numerous as they were, by no means annoying; but I had no anticipation of the intolerable torment provided for me by sympathizers and well-wishers. These, instead of saying anything civil to me about my book just as it was, wished to know, one and all, what was really true in it; at which I grew very angry, and often expressed myself with great discourtesy. To answer this question, I should have been obliged to pull to pieces and destroy the form of a work on which I had so long pondered, with the view of giving a poetical unity to its many elements; and in this operation, if the essential parts were not destroyed, they would, at least, have been scattered and dispersed. However, upon a closer consideration of the matter, I could not take the public inquisitiveness in ill part. Jerusalem's fate had excited great attention. An educated, amiable, blameless young man, the son of one of the first theologians and authors, healthy and opulent, had at once, without any known cause, destroyed himself. Every one asked how this was possible, and when they heard of an unfortunate love affair, the whole youth were excited, and as soon as it transpired that some little annoyances had occurred to him in the higher circles, the middle classes also became excited; indeed every one was anxious to learn further particulars. Now *Werther* appeared an exact delineation, as it was thought, of the life and character of that young man. The locality and person tallied, and the narrative was so very natural, that they considered themselves fully informed and satisfied. But, on the other hand, on closer examination, there was so much that did not fit, that there arose, for those who sought the truth, an unmanageable business, because a critical investigation must necessarily produce a hundred doubts. The real groundwork of the affair was, however, not to be fathomed, for all that I had interwoven of my own life and suffering could not be deciphered, because, as an unobserved young man, I had secretly, though not silently, pursued my course.

While engaged in my work, I was fully aware how highly that artist was favoured who had an opportunity of composing a Venus from the study of a variety of beauties. Accordingly

I took leave to model my Charlotte according to the shape and
qualities of several pretty girls, although the chief characteristics were taken from the one I loved best. The inquisitive public could therefore discover similarities in various
ladies; and even to the ladies themselves it was not quite indifferent to be taken for the right one. But these several Char-
lottes caused me infinite trouble, because every one who only
looked at me seemed determined to know where the proper one
really resided. I endeavoured to save myself, like Nathan*
with the three rings, by an expedient, which, though it might
suit higher beings, would not satisfy either the believing or the
reading public. I hoped after a time to be freed from such
tormenting inquiries, but they pursued me through my whole
life. I sought, on my travels, to escape them, by assuming an
incognito, but even this remedy was, to my disappointment,
unavailing, and thus the author of the little work, had he even
done anything wrong and mischievous, was sufficiently, I may
say disproportionately, punished by such unavoidable importunities.

Subjected to this kind of infliction, I was taught but too
unequivocally, that authors and their public are separated by
an immense gulf, of which, happily. neither of them have any
conception. The uselessness, therefore, of all prefaces I had
long ago seen; for the more pains a writer takes to render his
views clear, the more occasion he gives for embarrassment.
Besides, an author may preface as elaborately as he will, the
public will always go on making precisely those demands
which he has endeavoured to avoid. With a kindred peculiarity of readers, which (particularly with those who print
their judgments) seems remarkably comical, I was likewise
soon acquainted. They live, for instance, in the delusion that
an author, in producing anything, becomes their debtor; and
he always falls short of what they wished and expected of
him, although before they had seen our work, they had not
the least notion that anything of the kind existed, or was even
possible. Independent of all this, it was now the greatest
fortune, or misfortune, that every one wished to make the
acquaintance of this strange young author, who had stepped
forward so unexpectedly and so boldly. They desired to see
him, to speak to him, and, even at a distance, to hear some-

* "Nathan the wise," in Lessing's play, founded on Boccacio's tale of
the rings.—*Trans.*

thing from him; thus he had to undergo a very considerable crowd, sometimes pleasant, sometimes disagreeable, but always distracting. For enough works already begun lay before him, nay, and would have given him abundance of work for some years, if he could have kept to them with his old fervour; but he was drawn forth from the quiet, the twilight, the obscurity, which alone can favour pure creation, into the noise of daylight, where one is lost in others, where one is led astray, alike by sympathy and by coldness, by praise and by blame, because outward contact never accords with the epoch of our inner culture, and therefore, as it cannot further us, must necessarily injure us.

Yet more than by all the distractions of the day, the author was kept from the elaboration and completion of greater works by the taste then prevalent in this society for *dramatizing* everything of importance which occurred in actual life. What that technical expression (for such it was in our inventive society) really meant, shall here be explained. Excited by intellectual meetings on days of hilarity, we were accustomed, in short extemporary performances, to communicate, in fragments, all the materials we had collected towards the formation of larger compositions. One single simple incident, a pleasantly *naïve* or even silly word, a blunder, a paradox, a clever remark, personal singularities or habits, nay, a peculiar expression, and whatever else would occur in a gay and bustling life—took the form of a dialogue, a catechism, a passing scene, or a drama,— often in prose, but oftener in verse.

By this practice, carried on with genial passion, the really poetic mode of thought was established. We allowed objects, events, persons, to stand for themselves in all their bearings, our only endeavour being to comprehend them clearly, and exhibit them vividly. Every expression of approbation or disapprobation was to pass in living forms before the eyes of the spectator. These productions might be called animated epigrams, which, though without edges or points, were richly furnished with marked and striking features. The *Jahrmarktsfest* (Fair-festival) is an epigram of this kind, or rather a collection of such epigrams. All the characters there introduced are meant for actual living members of that society, or for persons at least connected and in some degree known to it; but the meaning of the riddle remained concealed to the greater part; all laughed, and few knew that their own marked peculiarities served as the jest. The prologue to *Barth's Newest Revelations* may be looked upon as a document of another kind; the smallest pieces are among the miscellaneous poems, a great many have been destroyed or lost, and some that still exist do not admit of being published. Those which appeared in print only increased the excitement of the public, and curiosity about the author; those which were handed about in manuscript entertained the immediate circle, which was continually increasing. Doctor Barth, then at Giessen, paid me a visit, apparently courteous and confiding; he laughed over the prologue, and wished to be placed on a friendly footing. But we young people still continued to omit no opportunity at social festivals, of sporting, in a malicious vein, at the peculiarities which we had remarked in others, and successfully exhibited.

If now it was by no means displeasing to the young author to be stared at as a literary meteor, he nevertheless sought, with glad modesty, to testify his esteem for the most deserving men of his country, among whom, before all others, the admirable Justus Moser claims especial mention. The little essays on political subjects by this incomparable man, had been printed some years before in the *Osnaburg Intelligenzblätter*, and made known to me through Herder, who overlooked nothing of worth that appeared in his time, especially if in print. Möser's daughter, Frau von Voigt, was occupied in collecting these scattered papers. We had scarcely patience to wait for their publication, and I placed myself in communication with her, to assure her, with sincere interest, that the essays, which, both in matter and form, had been addressed only to a limited circle, would be useful and beneficial everywhere. She and her father received these assurances from a stranger, not altogether unknown, in the kindest manner, since an anxiety which they had felt, was thus preliminarily removed.

What is in the highest degree remarkable and commendable in these little essays, all of which being composed in one spirit, form together a perfect whole, is the very intimate knowledge they display of the whole civil state of man. We see a system resting upon the past, and still in vigorous existence. On the one hand there is a firm adherence to tradition, on the other, movement and change which cannot be prevented. Here alarm is felt at a useful novelty, there pleasure in what is new, although it be useless, or even injurious. With what freedom from prejudice the author explains the relative position of different ranks, and the connexion in which cities, towns, and villages mutually stand! We learn their prerogatives, together with the legal grounds of them; we are told where the main capital of the state is invested, and what interest it yields. We see property and its advantages on the one hand, on the other, taxes and disadvantages of various kinds; and then the numerous branches of industry; and in all this past and present times are contrasted.

Osnaburg, as a member of the Hanseatic League, we are told, had in the earlier periods an extensive and active commerce. According to the circumstances of those times, it had a remarkable and fine situation; it could receive the produce of the country, and was not too far removed from the sea to transport it in its own ships. But now, in later times, it lies deep in the interior, and is gradually removed and shut out from the sea trade. How this has occurred, is explained in all its bearings. The conflict between England and the coasts, and of the havens with the interior, is mentioned; here are set forth the great advantages of those who live on the sea-side, and deliberate plans are proposed for enabling the inhabitants of the interior to obtain similar advantages. We then learn a great deal about trades and handicrafts, and how these have been outstripped by manufactures, and undermined by shop-keeping; decline is pointed out as the result of various causes, and this result, in its turn, as the cause of a further decline, in an endless circle, which it is difficult to unravel; yet it is so clearly set forth by the vigilant citizen, that one fancies one can see the way to escape from it. The author throughout displays the clearest insight into the most minute circumstances. His proposals, his counsel—nothing is drawn from the air, and yet they are often impracticable; on which account he calls his collection "patriotic fancies," although everything in it is based on the actual and the possible.

But as everything in public life is influenced by domestic condition, this especially engages his attention. As objects both of his serious and sportive reflections, we find the changes in manners and customs, dress, diet, domestic life, and education. It would be necessary to indicate everything which exists in the civil and social world, to exhaust the list of subjects which he discusses. And his treatment of them is admirable. A thorough man of business discourses with the people in weekly papers, respecting whatever a wise and beneficent government undertakes or carries out, that he may bring it to their comprehension in its true light. This is by no means done in a learned manner, but in those varied forms which may be called poetic, and which, in the best sense of the word, must certainly be considered rhetorical. He is always elevated above his subject, and understands how to give a cheerful view of the most serious subjects; now half-concealed behind this or that mask, now speaking in his own person, always complete and exhausting his subject,—at the same time always in good humour; more or less ironical, thoroughly to the purpose, honest, well-meaning, sometimes rough and vehement;—and all this so well regulated, that the spirit, understanding, facility, skill, taste, and character of the author cannot but be admired. In the choice of subjects of general utility, deep insight, enlarged views, happy treatment, profound yet cheerful humour, I know no one to whom I can compare him but Franklin.

Such a man had an imposing effect upon us, and greatly influenced a youthful generation, which demanded something sound, and stood ready to appreciate it. We thought we could adapt ourselves to the form of his exposition; but who could hope to make himself master of so rich an entertainment, and to handle the most unmanageable subjects with so much ease?

But this is our purest and sweetest illusion—one which we cannot resign, however much pain it may cause us through life—that we would, where possible, appropriate to ourselves, nay, even reproduce and exhibit as our own, that which we prize and honour in others.

END OF THE THIRTEENTH BOOK.

LONDON: HARRISON AND CO., PRINTERS, ST. MARTIN'S LANE.

CPSIA information can be obtained
at www.ICGtesting.com
Printed in the USA
BVHW080027030222
627630BV00005B/678

9 789354 015700